If you're wondering why you should buy this new edition of *International Relations Theory*, here are ten good reasons!

1. Chapter 1, "Thinking About IR Theory," shows you the field's expansion beyond realism and liberalism.

2. Chapter 2, "Realism: The State and Balance of Power," updates you on the most recent developments in neorealism.

3. Chapter 3, "Liberalism: Interdependence and Global Governance," includes in-depth coverage of global governance.

4. Chapter 4, "Economic Structuralism: Global Capitalism and Postcolonialism," covers both world-system theory and postcolonialism.

5. Chapter 5, "The English School: International Society and Grotian Rationalism," is a new chapter that helps you understand the influence of scholars like Hugo Grotius and Immanuel Kant.

6. Chapter 6, "Constructivist Understandings," is another new chapter that examines the constructivist perspective, one of the most important theoretical developments in the field.

7. Chapter 7, "Positivism, Critical Theory and Postmodern Understandings," provides a new discussion of the critiques of scientific positivism.

8. Chapter 8, "Feminist Understandings in IR Theory," emphasizes gender as an alternative lens in IR.

9. Chapter 9, "Normative IR Theory: Ethics and Morality," discusses moral and ethical issues that confront policymakers.

10. Each chapter includes an updated bibliography to help you keep current with developments in the field and conduct further independent study.

PEARSON

FOURTH EDITION

International Relations Theory

Paul R. Viotti
University of Denver

Mark V. Kauppi
Georgetown University

Longman
New York San Francisco Boston
London Toronto Sydney Tokyo Singapore Madrid
Mexico City Munich Paris Cape Town Hong Kong Montreal

To Linda and Kathleen

Acquisitions Editor: Vikram Mukhija
Editorial Assistant: Toni Magyar
Marketing Manager: Lindsey Prudhomme
Production Manager: Stacey Kulig
Project Coordination, Text Design, and Electronic Page Makeup: S4Carlisle Publishing Services
Cover Designer/Manager: John Callahan
Cover Image: Clipart ETC., © 2003 by the University of South Florida
Senior Manufacturing Buyer: Roy Pickering
Printer and Binder: R.R. Donnelley and Sons
Cover Printer: R.R. Donnelley and Sons

Library of Congress Cataloging-in-Publication Data

Library of Congress Control Number: 2009014076
    Viotti, Paul R.
    International relations theory
Paul R. Viotti, Mark V. Kauppi. — 4th ed.
        p. cm.
    Includes bibliographical references and index.
    ISBN-13: 978-0-13-189261-3
    ISBN-10: 0-13-189261-4
    1. International relations.   I. Kauppi, Mark V.   II. Title.
    JZ1305.V56 2009
    327.101—dc22   2009014076

1 2 3 4 5 6 7 8 9 10—DOH—12 11 10 09

Longman
is an imprint of

PEARSON

www.pearsonhighered.com

ISBN-13: 978-0-13-189261-3
ISBN-10:   0-13-189261-4

BRIEF CONTENTS

DETAILED CONTENTS

PREFACE

The idea for *International Relations Theory* resulted from a conversation between the authors in 1982 as they strolled through the grounds of *Schloss Solitud,* located just outside Stuttgart, Germany. The topic of discussion was the perennial problem of presenting in a relatively coherent manner a significant portion of the vast literature that comprises the field of international relations theory. After several years of classroom experimentation and numerous other conversations, the result was the first edition of this textbook, published in 1987 with subsequent editions in 1993 and 1999. The fact that we have published this fourth edition a decade after the third is in no small measure due to continuing feedback in North America, Europe, East Asia, and elsewhere from former students, colleagues, and reviewers that we ought to readdress IR theory and take account of changes in the world and major developments within the field over the past two decades.

International relations theorists try to make the world and human interactions within it more intelligible. They try to unpack the complexities that surround our subjective and inter-subjective understandings of global politics. And they disagree substantially in these efforts. It is a field so torn by controversies that the casual observer may wonder if these IR theorists are writing about the same world. At times, IR theorists sound collectively like a cacophony of voices, discordant and anything but harmonious. On the other hand, we reflect that this out-of-tune sound is also a mark of a field in ferment, decidedly not moribund and potentially very productive of theories and understandings that may improve our grasp of how the world works.

Quite apart from changes in the world, theorists have observed the end of the Cold War, increasing globalization, the prevalence of state and non-state conflict, and global economic crises. Driving our ten-year time-out between editions was the need to reflect on and assess both the impact of these substantial developments as well as the increase diversity in thought within the images and interpretive understandings we identify.

FEATURES

This volume (1) discusses and illustrates what is meant by *theory* and why the theorizing enterprise is important; (2) analyzes and assesses the underlying assumptions and orientations that influence scholarly work in the international relations field—images that we label *realism, liberalism, economic structuralism,* and the *English School* and interpretive understandings of IR found in *social constructivism, critical theory, postmodernism,* and *feminism;* (3) provides an overview of *normative theory*—what *ought* to be done, how actors *should* conduct themselves; (4) provides in the chapters and readings representative samples of theoretical works; (5) introduces the reader to key concepts used in the IR field (some indicated in boldface type)—hence an extensive glossary substantially expanded in this edition; and (6) encourages the reader to scrutinize critically both historical and contemporary conceptual and theoretical works in the IR field.

Indeed, if we are better equipped to analyze everyday events from a conceptual or theoretical perspective, to ask the right questions, to recognize underlying assumptions in written works or public pronouncements by academics, government officials, journalists and other commentators, this would transcend any supposed achievement made simply by memorizing which author is associated with what theory.

NEW TO THIS EDITION

We have expanded coverage substantially of all the diverse perspectives now prevalent in the IR field. Rather than provide yet another unstructured laundry list of "isms" to confuse the reader new to the field, we try in this edition to cut through the complexity by identifying in addition to *normative theory* two specific categories of thought that we label *images* and *interpretive understandings,* which we define in Chapter One.

When dealing with the four images and four interpretive understandings we have identified, we hasten to underscore that these are not airtight, mutually exclusive categories of thought. Perhaps, as in earlier editions, they are best understood more as pure or ideal types— general ways of thinking about IR that can serve as benchmarks that delineate major currents in the IR field. Indeed, the work of particular scholars (and the scholars themselves) oftentimes blends or crosses from one image or interpretive understanding to another. Nevertheless, we hope these categories of thought we present here help us organize and thus make better sense of what remains a deeply divided field of inquiry.

■ Images

Images that attempt a comprehensive, overarching view of the field are the subject matter in Part One with separate chapters on (1) *realism* (with new developments in structural or neorealism) in Chapter Two, (2) *liberalism* (adding global governance found in rational or neoliberal institutionalism) in Chapter Three, (3) *economic structuralism* (with postcolonialism added to earlier discussions of world-system theory and dependency) in Chapter Four, and (4) new as an image in this edition the *English School* (with discussion of the Grotian roots of international society and prospects for a Kantian world society) in Chapter Five.

■ Interpretive Understandings

The other "isms" that now dominate the field do not pretend to provide so overarching, comprehensive a view of international relations or world politics as these four images do. Instead, their focus is on the interpretive or subjective and intersubjective understandings we and others as human beings hold about the world in which we are immersed. Although we dealt with the subject matter earlier, these chapters are not found in previous editions: (1) *social constructivists* in Chapter Six, (2) *critical theorists* and *postmodernists* in Chapter Seven who pose a substantial challenge to positivists wedded to scientific modes of inquiry, and (3) *feminists* in Chapter Eight. In Chapter Seven we also examine how the first three of the four interpretive understandings (constructivism, critical theory, and postmodernism) owe so much to the work of Max Weber on *Verstehen* or interpretive understanding and, more broadly, to phenomenology— a philosophical inquiry into human consciousness or the workings of the mind that affect our interpretations of the phenomena we observe. For its part, feminism, and its focus on gender as an interpretive lens, has a longer, also very rich history influenced by, but separate for the most part from, these philosophical or phenomenological currents. Nevertheless, we group these four modes of thinking into one broad category in Part Two precisely because each is sensitive to the importance of interpretation, the subjective and intersubjective dimensions in and among human beings, the actions they take, and interactions among them toward which our theorizing turns.

Normative Considerations

The final part of this volume takes up in Chapter Nine the philosophical underpinnings of the IR field found in political theory. Normative theory connects moral or ethical obligation to the challenges that confront policymakers. Conceptual understandings and values in political theory also underlie both the images and interpretive understandings we identify. On images, we see values or norms in the exercise of power and the search for order in realism, the multilateral or institutional remedies for global problems in liberalism, the exploitative class or interstate relations in economic structuralism, and the search for "Grotian" rules and "Kantian" norms in international or world society in the English School.

Political theory also informs the interpretive understandings scholars take to IR whether (1) they identify international norms as ideational structures as social constructivists are prone to do, (2) frame the critique offered by critical theorists looking for underlying power or other motives in ideologies masquerading as if they were scientifically grounded theories, (3) point us to the value-laden meanings in the concepts and theoretical claims IR scholars make when we deconstruct their work as postmodernists do, or (4) find, as feminists are prone to identify, the gender-related values present not only in everyday life, but also in IR theories that frequently purport to be value neutral.

Though deeply divided, when viewed as a whole, the IR field is intellectually very vibrant. Journals and recently published books have been filled with important new theoretical work as well as challenges to already established understandings and responses from their defenders. Given understandable constraints on the length of this volume, it is impossible to cover every topic as extensively as we might like, much less reprint every article suggested by colleagues, students, and reviewers. Nevertheless, we hope that this book remains a useful starting point and reference in helping readers not only to understand current trends in a still very dynamic field, but also to gain an appreciation for the extent to which current theoretical work and debates rest so heavily upon the rich conceptual foundation of earlier years and across the millennia.

SUPPLEMENTS

Longman offers several resources to qualified adopters of *International Relations Theory* and their students that will facilitate teaching and learning from this book.

For Instructors

MyPoliSciKit Video Case Studies for International Relations and Comparative Politics. Featuring video from major news sources and providing reporting and insight on recent world affairs, this DVD series helps instructors integrate current events into their courses by letting them use the clips as lecture launchers or discussion starters.

◼ For Students

Longman Atlas of World Issues (0-321-22465-5). Introduced and selected by Robert J. Art of Brandeis University and excerpted from the Penguin Atlas Series, the *Longman Atlas of World Issues* is designed to help students understand the geography and major issues facing the world today, such as terrorism, debt, and HIV/AIDS. These thematic, full-color maps examine forces shaping politics today at a global level. Explanatory information accompanies each map to help students better grasp the concepts being shown and how they affect our world today. Available at no additional charge when packaged with this book.

The Penguin Dictionary of International Relations (0-140-51397-3). This indispensable reference by Graham Evans and Jeffrey Newnham includes hundreds of cross-referenced entries on the enduring and emerging theories, concepts, and events that are shaping the academic discipline of international relations and today's world politics. Available at a discount when packaged with this book.

Research and Writing in International Relations (0-321-27766-X). Written by Laura Roselle and Sharon Spray of Elon University, this brief and affordable guide provides the basic step-by-step process and essential resources that are needed to write political science papers that go beyond simple description and into more systematic and sophisticated inquiry. This text focuses on the key areas in which students need the most help: finding a topic, developing a question, reviewing literature, designing research, analyzing findings, and last, actually writing the paper. Available at a discount when packaged with this book.

ACKNOWLEDGMENTS

We gratefully acknowledge the review and critique of earlier drafts of the manuscript for this edition by Carina Solmirano, University of Denver, who also combed the literature extensively to find representative titles we have included in the lists of Suggested Readings that append each chapter. Paul R. Viotti, Jr., University of California Santa Cruz, contributed to our discussion of interpretive understandings and recommended readings. As always, we thank Emily Kauppi for her willingness to contribute her valuable time and skills to improve the quality of the final manuscript. Reviewers who went through the manuscript line by line and offered most helpful suggestions include Andrew Cortell, Lewis and Clark College; Zaryab Iqbal, Penn State University; and Celine Jaquemin, St. Mary's University. Finally, we are grateful for substantial discussions with our editors for this edition—Vikram Mukhija, Toni Magyar, and Elizabeth Daniel. We also appreciate early inputs from Jack Donnelly, University of Denver, and Joyce Kaufman, Whittier College.

Paul R. Viotti, *University of Denver Graduate School of International Relations*
Mark V. Kauppi, *Georgetown University*

CHAPTER 1

Thinking About IR Theory

Why do wars occur? Is nationalism the primary cause? Or ideology? Or the lack of world government? Or misperception? Or are people innately aggressive? How can stability (if not peace) be achieved? Why is there such tremendous social and economic inequality among the different regions of the world? These are the sorts of questions that have preoccupied scholars and statesmen at various times over the millennia, whether the political entity in question was an ancient city-state or a modern nation-state, a centralized empire or a decentralized feudal system, a socialist or a liberal democratic society. Nor are these questions the private preserve of intellectuals, diplomatic practitioners, and assorted political pundits and commentators. At one time or another, most citizens reflect on one or more of these important queries.

THE IR FIELD IN AN AGE OF GLOBALIZATION

International relations (IR) as a field of inquiry addresses such questions. Despite the adjective *international,* the field is concerned with much more than relations between or among states. Other actors, such as international organizations, multinational corporations, environmental organizations, and terrorist groups, are all part of what could more correctly be termed *world* or *global politics.* Studies have also focused on factors internal to a state, such as its institutions, bureaucratic governmental coalitions, interest groups, decision-making processes, as well as the ideological and perceptual predispositions of individual leaders.

Beyond actors, the study of international relations also includes, for example, balance of power politics among states, the influence of economic structures at the global level, and international law, norms, and ethics. Such topics maintain their resonance in the current era which has been popularly characterized as one of **globalization.** This shrinkage of distance on a world scale is a result of an intensification of connections across borders in not only economic but also social, political, cultural, and environmental realms as well. While globalization began in earnest at the end of the nineteenth century only to be reversed during the thirty years after World War I (1914–1918), it has once again increased in recent decades. As aspects of globalization are not always necessarily beneficial (consider, for example, the spread of weapons technology, environmental degradation, labor exploitation, and financial crises no longer largely confined by national borders), it is not surprising that scholars of international relations have recently attempted to understand better its dynamics and manifestations.

Given the tremendous diversity and complexity of *what* is studied, it is not too surprising that there is a multiplicity of views concerning *how* one studies international relations. The possible avenues go well beyond the realms of history and political science. They include economics, psychology, social psychology, sociology, and anthropology in the behavioral sciences as well as philosophy and law. All this—the need to be familiar with or draw from multiple disciplines—may seem rather intimidating not just to the student, but also to those well established in the IR field.

Different perspectives on international relations naturally generate debates. Beginning in the period between the two world wars and continuing after World War II into the 1950s, **realists** and **idealists** argued over the nature of international politics and the possibility of peaceful change. In the 1960s the so-called second great debate between **traditionalists** and **behavioralists** dealt with the question of appropriate **methodology.** Traditionalists emphasized the relative utility of history, law, philosophy, and other traditional, non-quantitative modes of inquiry to understanding government and other governmental or political institutions. Behavioralists argued in favor of social science conceptualization, quantification of variables when possible, formal hypothesis testing, and causal model building in the study of political processes or patterns of behavior.

The earlier debates have been overtaken by new challenges to the dominance in the social sciences of scientific methods borrowed from the natural sciences. Following the German scholar Max Weber (1864–1920), we probe what Weber meant by the term *Verstehen*—the interpretive understandings that also underlie much of the theoretical work in the IR field. Approaches drawing on history and Marxist insights also have been the subject of much discussion in certain journals in the field, contributing as well to the growing literature on postcolonialism. Such work continues to raise the issue of not just what is studied, but how it is studied. Before one attempts to define *theory,* it is important to consider three pre-theoretical or "how" issues that directly influence the approach one takes to international relations.

EPISTEMOLOGY, METHODOLOGY, AND ONTOLOGY

Often unacknowledged by theorists are the issues of **epistemology** and **ontology.** If one is to be theoretically self-conscious, one needs to engage in some reflection on these matters. *Epistemology* involves the ways and means by which we come to know something (or at least what we think we know) about the world. For example, a popular epistemology is **empiricism**—the view that the only grounds for making truth claims is through direct observation of the world using our senses. Alternative epistemologies to empiricism exist as reflected in constructivism, critical theory, postmodernist, and feminist approaches to IR theory (all of which are discussed in subsequent chapters).

Positivism, which depending on the scholar has been variously categorized an epistemology, methodology, or combination of the two, dominates IR theorizing and is reflected in the images chapters of this book. Positivism consists of four underlying implicit assumptions or beliefs:

1. the unity of the natural and social sciences—we can study society as we study the natural world;
2. we can draw a distinction between facts and values;
3. regularities exist in the social as well as the natural world and they can be identified; and
4. empirical validation or falsification is the hallmark of "real" inquiry.

Positivism specifically endorses the use of formal **hypothesis** testing or causal modeling as *methodologies*—modes of research and analysis or a set of rules for the actual practice of investigating IR. This may involve quantitative (use of statistics and mathematical equations) or non-quantitative, so-called qualitative, methods (such as employing in-depth case and comparative case studies) to test empirically the hypotheses we generate. Very often when one hears the term **scientific method,** the reference is to positivism with the focus on that which is observable, empirical, and measurable. This is a convention we will adopt in this book.

    Ontology refers to how each of us views the world—how we see or understand the essence of things around us. Are there, for example, actual structures out there that influence the behavior of actors? If so, is it a material structure consisting of capabilities such as weapons, troops, and economic resources? Or can we also conceive of structure as consisting of internationally shared ideas, beliefs, and norms? Is what we observe caused, facilitated, or impeded by these material or ideational structures (for example, distribution of power or cultures) external to the actors or within which they are immersed? How do we actually view these actors? If they are states, do we see them acting as if they were like rational individuals? Do we assume these actors are more important in explaining IR than the structures? Do we see events or outcomes as effects having discoverable causes? Or can we, by contrast, see events as largely random occurrences? Do we see (or come to see) human beings important as individuals, or do we instead look to larger groups or aggregations of people to find social meaning? Does the individual have a distinct identity, or is the concept of "self" a function of relationships with others and the environment within which one is immersed? Do human beings have the capacity to think and act freely, or are their actions and even their thoughts externally influenced or even determined? Do we see things in good-and-evil terms and thus have a propensity to draw moral distinctions? Or do we see what we observe if not from a morally neutral, then a more or less morally indifferent position?

    The answers to such questions have profound consequences on one's scholarship and even the way we lead our lives. For example, one liberal IR theorist, the late Ernst Haas, described how his work was influenced by an ontological orientation that "avoided fixed dogmas and unchanging universal values" and "highlighted human agency over other causal forces."[1] Another liberal theorist, James Rosenau, sees some of us as ontologically more prone to engage in theorizing than others. In his article appended to this chapter, Rosenau states that one's being "able to assume that human affairs are founded on an underlying order"—an ontological predisposition—is essential to thinking theoretically.

    For their part, the ontologies Kenneth Waltz and many other realists bring to the IR field provide a darker view of the reality they are prone to see, a dimmer view of human beings and their potential than liberals typically hold. It is a tradition steeped in the thought of Thucydides,

Machiavelli, Hobbes, and even James Madison and Alexander Hamilton—the latter two agreeing in the *Federalist Papers* on the term *depravity* to describe the human condition or the natural state in which human beings find themselves. Given such underlying ontologies, the realist image not surprisingly is of a world of competition among self-oriented states as principal actors with different interests and different capabilities or power they bring to bear in the pursuit of these interests.

Waltz describes liberals, by contrast, as (mis)informed by taking the ontological position that "harmony is the natural condition" for human beings, dismissing dissension and strife as supposedly arising from "mistaken belief, inadequate knowledge, and defective governance."[2] Economic structuralists share with realists a dim view of present reality, but one in which exploitation and victimization are the operative words to describe the human condition. **Dialectical materialism** is an example of a theoretical idea drawn from a Marxist, materialist ontology. Economic structuralists vary in their assessments of the future course and effects on the human condition of this historical mechanism. The future may be different from the present and the past. This guarded level of optimism is also evident in the English School where scholars who combine both realist and liberal (Grotian or Kantian) influences write of an international (or even world) society still under construction.

The ontologies we bring to the IR field influence the imagery we construct. **Images** are general perspectives on international relations and world politics that consist of certain assumptions about key actors and processes that influence our theorizing. There is a fine line between how we understand the essence of things (for example, the condition or nature of human beings and the degree to which human beings as agents matter) and the images we have of international or world politics. To say ontologies and images are related, however, is not to say they are the same things.

WHAT IS THEORY?

The word *theory* also means different things to different people. It may even mean different things to the same person. In common parlance, for example, something may be true "in theory" but not in fact or in a particular case or set of circumstances. In this rather loose usage, "in theory" equates to "in principle" or "in the abstract."

■ Explanation and Prediction

Another meaning, more consistent with usage in this volume, views theory as simply a way of making the world or some part of it more intelligible or better understood. Theories dealing with international relations aspire to achieve this goal. Making things more intelligible may, of course, amount to nothing more than better or more precise description of the things we observe. Although accurate description is essential, theory is something more.

For many people with a scientific or positivist bent, theory involves explanation. One goes beyond mere description of phenomena observed and engages in causal explanation based on certain prior occurrences or conditions. To assume this is possible is an ontological assumption about reality or "the world out there." Explanation from the positivist perspective involves establishing the phenomenon it explains as something that was to be expected in the circumstances in which it occurred. This is what Carl Hempel terms the "requirement of explanatory relevance." Information is explanatory only if it "affords good grounds for believing that the phenomenon to be explained does, or did, indeed occur. This condition must be met if we are to be entitled to say 'that explains it—the phenomenon in question was indeed to be expected under the circumstances.'" This information will include one or more laws, as without a knowledge of regularities or patterns in IR, we couldn't expect certain happenings at particular times.[3]

How do we identify these laws? The preferred positivist method is through the development of **hypotheses**—a proposition relating two or more **variables.** Thus, whenever A is present, then B can be expected to follow. "If A, then B" as hypothesis may be subject to empirical test— that is, tested against real-world or factual data to determine its law-like quality. "If states engage in arms races, then the likelihood of war increases" is an example of such an hypothesis. Indeed, formal statement and testing of hypotheses through the use of a statistical methodology is seen by many positivist as central to the theory-building process. Resultant laws or law-like statements, therefore, allow IR theorists to make at least tentative predictions about possible outcomes in IR: "Given these circumstances as validated by our tested hypotheses, we can expect X, Y, or Z."

The primary research strategy that entails invoking laws in a scientific explanation can be called a generalizing or *covering-law* approach. Many realists and liberals are rooted in this tradition, seeking covering laws of such phenomena as war, deterrence, cooperation, and economic integration. The event to be explained is an instance of a certain type of event that follows regularly from the conditions specified. Jack Snyder, for example, has addressed the important question of why the Cold War ended peacefully. His explanation involved establishing the laws and initial conditions that would lead one to believe that given these circumstances, the peaceful collapse of the Soviet empire was to be expected. He posits that expansionist myths coupled with, among other factors, the timing of industrialization provide a framework for understanding the type of collapse experienced by the Soviet Union.[4] Such factors could be applied to other cases.

Another example of positivist social science at work is the ambitious effort of Kenneth Waltz to offer a more formal theory of international politics to explain general tendencies and patterns of behavior among states. To Waltz, "theories explain laws." Waltz identifies a power-based structure of the international system that purportedly explains the behavior of states as the system's principal actors. Having stated "the theory being tested," one proceeds to

> infer hypotheses from it; subject the hypotheses to experimental or observational tests; . . . use the definitions of terms found in the theory being tested; eliminate or control perturbing variables not included in the theory under test; devise a number of distinct and demanding tests; if a test is not passed, ask whether the theory flunks completely, needs repair and restatement, or requires a narrowing of the scope of its explanatory claims.[5]

The commitment to positivism is clear in the last comment that underscores the importance of falsifiability in the testing of theories.

While the covering-law strategy is the most popular for those operating within the positivist framework, there is also a *reconstructive* positivist strategy. In this case, no attempt is made to place the phenomenon under investigation into a larger class. Rather, the event is explained as the expected end-point of a concrete historical sequence, not as an instance of category A, B, or C. Reconstructive explanations also rely on laws, but these are not covering laws but rather component laws—each pertains only to a part of the pathway that led to the event or phenomenon being explained. For example, like Snyder, William Wohlforth attempts to explain the peaceful collapse of the Soviet empire. He does not, however, attempt to "cover" Soviet behavior by showing how we would expect it to be such given the circumstances. Instead he details the sequence of events leading up to the collapse of the Soviet empire. The behavior to be explained emerges from this analysis and historical reconstruction.[6]

In terms of methodology and methods, therefore, some IR scholars prefer a research strategy that relies on the formal construction of hypotheses and theories. These may be tested, for example, through the application of statistical methods. Others prefer to rely on non-quantitative indicators or case and comparative case studies, historical methods, and reasoned argument—the so-called traditional or qualitative approaches to theory building.[7]

Whatever differences international relations scholars might have among themselves, those with a positivist or scientific commitment all tend to agree on one thing: theory is necessary and unavoidable when it comes to explaining and attempting to foresee or predict future outcomes. Because as human beings we are subjective creatures who see and make sense of the world around us from different points of view, even such scientifically oriented scholars approach their subject matter with diverse perspectives, paradigms, **research programs,**[8] theoretical constructs, or images. It is the theory and hypotheses or propositions we are holding (or challenging) that tell us what to focus on and what to ignore in making sense of the world around us. Without theory, we would be overwhelmed and immobilized by an avalanche of mere facts or occurrences around us. In short, the sense we make of what we observe is informed by both the perspectives and theories we hold.

In this admittedly positivist understanding, a *theory* is an intellectual construct composed of a set of interrelated propositions that help one to identify or select facts and interpret them, thus facilitating explanation and prediction concerning the regularities and recurrences or repetitions of observed phenomena. One certainly can think theoretically when it comes to explaining foreign policy processes in general or the foreign policy of a particular state. International relations theorists tend as well to be interested in patterns of behavior *among* diverse state and non-state actors acting internationally or globally. In identifying patterns, the stage is set for making modest predictions about the possible nature and direction of change. To think theoretically, however, is not to engage in point predictions—"*A* will attack *B* the first week of the year"—however much foreign policy, national security, and intelligence analysts may aspire to such precision.

To think theoretically, therefore, is to be interested in central tendencies. As James Rosenau notes in an article appended to this chapter, the theorist views each event as an instance of a more encompassing class or pattern of phenomena. Fitting pieces into a larger whole makes theory building analogous to puzzle solving. In fact, for many theorists, the goal is not merely explanation of patterns of behavior, but explanations of patterns that at first glance seem counterintuitive or different from what one might expect.

War poses a most important puzzle for IR theorists. Why does the phenomenon persist even though wars are extremely costly in terms of lives and treasure lost? Quincy Wright's *A Study of War* and Lewis Richardson's *Statistics of Deadly Quarrels* were pioneering efforts at trying to solve this puzzle through the use of statistical methods or causal modeling. Bruce Bueno de Mesquita's *The War Trap* and John Vasquez's *The War Puzzle* are also examples of work in this genre. Examples of continuing efforts to build better theory by using reasoned argument, historical and comparative cases, or other non-quantitative, qualitative methods include Kenneth Waltz's classic *Man, the State and War,* Michael Howard's *The Causes of Wars,* Stephen Walt's *Revolution and War,* Michael Doyle's *Ways of War and Peace,* and Stephen Van Evera's *Causes of War.*

Theory in a formal, positivist sense specifies relations among variables and ideally would weigh them with the precision one finds in an algebraic equation. Such fully developed theory is less common in the social sciences and certainly not in IR; even positivists wedded to scientific modes of inquiry confess to be operating at a lesser level of theoretical development than are the natural sciences.

General theories that strive to provide a complete account of the causes of war or other phenomena are less common than partial, or middle-range, theories that are more modest in the scope of what is to be explained or predicted. Part of the war puzzle addressed by such middle-range theorists, for example, involves crises and decision making in crises. Are partial theories like building blocks that can at some future date be assembled into a fully developed, general theory of war? Some theorists would say yes and that the most productive enterprise for the present is the development of better middle-range theories. Not everyone would agree. Partial or middle-range theories have tended to be essentially non-additive—they are merely islands of theory without bridges to connect them into a coherent whole. Even if such connections might be made, the result would probably undercut the social science goal of developing theories that are parsimonious—explaining a great deal of behavior through the use of relatively few concepts. Theories that lack parsimony by definition contain too many factors or variables—quickly becoming as complex as or more complex than the reality they purport to explain. If practically everything is portrayed as a cause, then has anything really been found to explain or predict what we observe?

The world of theory is an abstract one. Theories may actually exist apart from facts. Mathematical theorists, for example, deal entirely in the realm of abstraction, whether or not their work has direct relevance to problems of the world in which we live. Practical application for the work of mathematical theorists is sometimes found years later, if ever. From the positivist perspective, however, empirically based theories in the social or natural sciences, by contrast, relate to facts and provide explanation or prediction for observed phenomena. Hypotheses associated with these theories are subject to test against real-world data. The theorist need not have any purpose in developing such empirical theories other than satisfying his or her intellectual curiosity, although many will seek to make their work "policy relevant."

Policy-relevant theories may have explicit purposes that stem from the value preferences of the theorist, such as reducing the likelihood of war or curbing the arms race. Acting on such theories, of course, is the domain of the policymaker, a task separate from that of the empirical theorist. Theorists who become policymakers may well make choices informed by what theories say will be the likely outcomes of implementing one or another alternative. Their choices may be informed by empirical theory or understandings of world events, but the decisions they make are still heavily based on value preferences.

As noted at the outset of this section, a common dismissive attitude toward theory is that while something may be true "in theory," it doesn't apply to the real world. For reasons discussed above, this is a very short-sighted view. By contrast, reflecting on his life's work theorizing in the international relations field, Kenneth Waltz speaks for many theorists with a positivist orientation to IR, confidently telling us that "from theory all else follows." He adds that "theory explains and may at times anticipate or predict outcomes" in what is essentially "a self-help system" of states in international politics. In this regard, "a political theory, if it is any good, not only explains international outcomes, but also provides clues to situations and actions that may produce more of the desired and fewer of the undesired ones."[9] Put another way, there is nothing so practical as a good theory.

Levels of Analysis

Let us assume one is interested in theorizing about the causes of war. Where should one focus one's initial efforts? Does one deal with individual decisionmakers or small groups of individuals engaged in the policy process? How important, for example, are such factors as the correctness of individual perceptions or bargaining skill in determining the decision to go to war? On the other hand, if one looks outside the individual or small decision-making group to the entire state apparatus, society as a whole, or the international political system of states, one is acknowledging the importance of external or environmental factors as well.

The **levels of analysis** constitute a framework designed to organize and assist in systematic thinking about IR. We differentiate the term *levels of analysis* (individual or group, state and society, and "system" as a whole) from **units of analysis,** the latter referring to states, organizations, individuals or groups, classes, and other entities. What one is trying to explain or study (such as the outbreak of war) is known as the **dependent variable.** Factors at different levels of analysis we suspect as being causally related to what we are trying to explain typically are termed **independent variables.** Thus, we can look both "inside" the state as principal unit of analysis in a search for explanatory factors at individual or group and societal levels and "outside" the state to take account of factors that causally affect its actions and interactions with other states at an international "system" level. Work by Kenneth N. Waltz in the 1950s on the causes of war represented a path-breaking effort due to his identification of distinct levels of analysis and his attempt to specify the relations among these levels. Was the cause of war to be found in the nature of individuals? (Are humans innately aggressive?) Or in the nature of states and societies? (Are some types of states more aggressive than others?) Or in the nature of the international system of states? (Is anarchy a "permissive" cause of war, there being no obstacle to the use of force by sovereign states in a world without central governance?)

Each answer reflects a different level of analysis—individual (or group of individuals), state and society, or international (see Figure 1.1). In 1961, the importance of the question of levels of analysis to the study of international relations was further discussed in detail in a then often-cited article by J. David Singer. Singer argued that one's choice of a particular level of analysis determines what one will and will not see. Different levels tend to emphasize different actors, structures, and processes.[10]

For example, it is quite common in IR for the levels of analysis to include (1) the international system (distribution of power among states, geography, technology, and other factors), the capitalist world system (economic structuralists) or an international or world society composed of rules, norms, state and non-state actors (the English School); (2) the state (often treated as a unified actor) and domestic or national society (democratic, authoritarian, etc.); (3) groups as in bureaucratic politics and group dynamics—the domain of social psychology; (4) individuals as in psychology, perception, and belief systems. It is also quite typical for these various levels to be used to explain the foreign policy behavior of states—the dependent variable. The state, in other words, is often the unit of analysis, and explaining its behavior could entail taking into account factors at all of these levels of analysis.

But *which* level of analysis, one may ask, is most important? To take a specific example, let us assume that the foreign policies of most states exhibit relative constancy, or slowness to change. How is this constancy to be explained? Some scholars point to external or exogenous factors such as the distribution or balance of power among states that is relatively slow to change in any major way. Still others instead look internally within the state to the interpretive

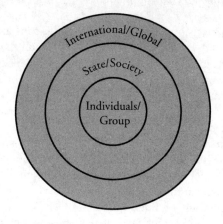

Individual Level (domain of psychology)
    Human nature and psychology
    Leaders and beliefs systems
    Personality of leaders
    Cognition and perception or misperception

Group Level (domain of social psychology)
    Government bureaucracies
    Policymaking groups
    Interest groups
    Other non-governmental organizations

State and Societal (or National) Level
    Governmental
        Structure and nature of political system
        Policymaking process
    Societal (domain of sociology)
        Structure of economic system
        Public opinion
        Nationalism and ethnicity
        Political culture
        Ideology

International—World (or Global) Level
    Anarchic quality of international or world politics
    Number of major powers or poles
    Distribution of power/capabilities among states
    Economic patterns
    Level and diffusion of technology
    Patterns of military alliances
    Patterns of international trade and finance
    International organizations and regimes
    Transnational organizations and networks
    Global norms and international law

FIGURE 1.1   Levels of Analysis: A More Detailed Look

understandings of decisionmakers that may exhibit constancy due to shared world views they hold or approaches they take with incremental or small changes being the rule.

Another example: How are arms races explained? Some scholars point to international factors such as the military expenditures and hostility of other states as well as competition between alliances that lead to an increase in the production of weapons. Other researchers emphasize the importance of domestic factors such as bureaucratic competition between branches of the military services and budgetary processes that encourage a steady increase in expenditures.

The easy answer to the question of which level of analysis should be emphasized is that all levels of analysis should be considered. Such a response is not particularly useful, however, because it suggests that we have to study everything under the sun. Few scholars would even attempt such a task, and the resulting theory, if any, would hardly be parsimonious. Hence, a great deal of the literature on international relations is constantly posing the questions of *what* should be examined *within* each level of analysis, and *how* actors, structures, and other factors or variables relate to one another across levels of analysis and over time.

This issue of levels of analysis also subtly pervades the images and interpretive understandings we identify. Structural or neorealists, for example, note how the overall structure or distribution of power in the international system influences the behavior of states or the perceptions of decisionmakers. Hence, neorealist analysis emphasizes the systems level. Similarly, members of the English School look to international or world society as the principal level of analysis, even as they are quite comfortable crossing the different levels of analysis in seeking explanations. Moreover, certain economic structuralists examine how the historical development of the capitalist world economy generates state actors. Some constructivists argue that international structure can be conceived of ideationally in shared meanings, rules, and norms that facilitate or constrain the actions decisionmakers consider. Despite their differences, many of these scholars tend to start at the systems (or international, world or global society) level of analysis. Those authors associated with the liberal image, however, who examine bureaucracies, interest groups, and individuals tend to emphasize the state-societal and individual levels of analysis. Some liberals and neoliberals, however, are also interested in how the development and spread of international norms influence state behavior—a global system- or world society-level focus.

There is a final important issue that should be mentioned in conjunction with the levels of analysis but that goes well beyond the latter as it raises ontological questions concerning the so-called **agent–structure** problem. As summarized by one author, the problem emerges from two uncontentious claims about social life: first, that human agency is the only moving force behind the actions, events, and outcomes of the social world; and second, that human agency can be realized only in concrete historical circumstances that condition the possibilities for action and influence its course. "People make history," observed Marx in an often-quoted aphorism, "but not in conditions of their own choosing." These claims impose two demands on our scientific explanations: first, that they acknowledge and account for the power of agents; and second, that they recognize the causal relevance of exogenous or "structural factors"—that is, the conditions of action as decisionmakers understand them. The "agent–structure problem" refers to the difficulties of developing theory that successfully meets both demands.[11]

This problem is usually viewed as a matter of ontology, the branch of metaphysics concerned, as noted earlier, with the nature of being. In this case, the ontological issue deals with the nature of both agents (very often viewed as the state or other organizational unit, but also including groups or individuals acting in their personal capacities) and structures (as in international politics), and relations between them. As we will see in the following chapters, a constant theme is how authors deal with the relative importance of human agents and "structural factors," and the extent to which one influences the very nature of the other. Put another way, we ask not only how much **voluntarism** (or freedom of action agents have) or **determinism** (the extent to which they are constrained) there actually is in the world of which we are so integral a part, but also in the theories we construct that purport to explain or predict phenomena in that world. Very often unstated, one's position on this issue—the voluntarism inherent in agency and the determinism that comes from structures—heavily influences how one goes about explaining international politics as well as assessing the possibilities and means of peaceful change.

IMAGES

In Part One of this volume we identify four broad alternative images or perspectives (we use the terms interchangeably) of international relations:

1. *realism* is a term that refers to both classical and neorealism (or structural realism). For the realist, states are the principal or most important actors on the international political stage and represent the key unit of analysis. States are viewed as unitary actors that behave in a generally rational manner. National security issues typically dominate the hierarchy of the international agenda.

2. *liberalism* (and *neoliberal institutionalism*) present a pluralist view of the world composed not just of states and their institutions, but also of multiple non-state actors to include international and non-governmental organizations, individuals, and groups. The state is disaggregated into its component parts and is continually subjected to outside influences. Political-economic issues are a primary research focus, and hence the hierarchy of world issues is not always dominated by matters of military security.

3. *economic structuralism* identifies economic classes and other material structures as well as the broader emphasis on multiple mechanisms of postcolonial domination that maintain the Third World in a subordinate status. For the economic structuralist, all actors must be viewed within the context of an overarching global structure. The defining characteristic of this structure is its capitalist nature; it must be viewed in a historical context. The more recent postcolonial literature provides greater understanding of the way capitalism operates now and in the past.

4. the *English School* tends to see politics occurring in an international society in which one finds operative not only realist, material understandings of power and balance of power, but also the "rational" component of rules (or norms) and institutions. To greater and lesser degrees, all have been influenced by both empiricism and positivism, yet constructivist understandings have informed more recent work. Drawing from both realist and liberal traditions, the English School explores politics, power relations, international law, rules, and institutions in an anarchic international society.

We will examine these images and associated assumptions and concepts in greater detail in subsequent chapters. The image one has of international relations is of critical importance. Images are not theories, but they do inform substantially the way we see the world, thus influencing the formulation of the theories we construct to make better sense of the world around us. Thus, a balance-of-power theory may be informed by the assumptions or premises of a realist image of international relations, but the image itself does not have the standing of a theory.

These images, informed as they are by different ontologies or world views, lead one to ask certain questions, seek certain types of answers, and use certain methodological tools in the construction of theories and testing of hypotheses. The advantage is that such images bring order to the analytical effort and make it more manageable. We are the first, however, to admit that this fourfold classification scheme also has its limitations. Accordingly, we offer several qualifications and clarifications.

First, we concede that the images of IR we identify could be viewed as forms of (or bases for) interpretive understandings. Realism, liberalism, economic structuralism, and the English School are nothing more than constructs that have developed within the IR field, itself a construct that emerged within political science, yet another construct. We need to be humble about claims relating to constructs within constructs! These constructs that scholars have put together do not have an independent existence and, as such, are always subject to challenge. They are merely categories of inquiry or the bases of research programs, their value resting on the degree to which they make the world around us more intelligible, perhaps allowing us to explain or predict more accurately the phenomena we observe. Although the four images are heavily positivist in orientation, subsequent theories that are developed may evince, to varying degrees, aspects of interpretive understandings we discuss in the next section.

Second, the images should be viewed as **ideal** or **pure types** in that each emphasizes what a number of seemingly diverse theoretical approaches have in common. For example, there are substantial differences in the works of Hans J. Morgenthau, John Mearsheimer, and Stephen Walt, to mention just a few. But these and other scholars nevertheless draw from the same realist traditions. What unites them as international relations theorists is more important for our purposes than what divides them.

Third, the overview of key assumptions of each of the four perspectives might give the erroneous impression that these images are mutually exclusive in all respects. This is not the case. Neorealists and neoliberal institutionalists, for example, both utilize rational actor assumptions and tend to treat the identity and interests of their constituent actors as being givens.

Fourth, we acknowledge a certain amount of conceptual eclecticism by scholars in the study of international relations, perhaps reflecting the absence of a single, dominant perspective, much less a single paradigm or set of research programs. For some, conceptual diversity is to be applauded; for others, it is a source of despair. Be that as it may, our focus is primarily on ideas, trends, and both generalized images and interpretive understandings of international relations and only secondarily on the work of particular authors.

Fifth, the images tend to focus more on *what* is studied than on *how* to conduct such studies. Quantitative and non-quantitative methodologies transcend the images we have identified. Statistical methods, formal hypothesis testing, and causal modeling find their adherents within each of the perspectives, as do the more traditional, non-quantitative, historical, philosophical, legal, case study, and comparative case study methods. Our point remains that these are methods, not images of international relations or world politics. Images may influence the choice of methodology or methods employed, but they are not one and the same.

An image of international or world politics influences the selection of units or processes examined and variables identified and operationalized. Thus, for realists, states and state interactions are of key importance; for liberals, institutions as well as transnational interactions to include communications flows across national borders may well be the central focus; for the English School, the ways and means by which order is sustained and security provided in an anarchic international or world society are essential tasks; and for economic structuralists, patterns of class or North–South relations of dominance or dependence are perhaps most important.

Similarly, methods associated with the literature on decision making, game theory, and public- or rational-choice theory—economic or rational models applied to political decision making—transcend the four images we identify. Assumptions made about actors and processes are informed by realist, liberal, English School, and economic structuralist images and color the use a particular method is given. Thus, collective goods theory, game theory, econometrics, and other approaches identified with the interdisciplinary field of political economy find their adherents among scholars holding diverse images or other interpretive understandings and thus are not the exclusive preserve of realists, liberals, the English School, or economic structuralists.

Finally, we wish to reiterate a point made earlier—that the four images we identify are not theories of international relations. Rather, they represent general perspectives on international relations out of which particular theories *may* develop. Assumptions of an image may become part of a theory (such as the realist assumptions of a unified, rational, state-as-actor in some structural-realist works), but more often than not they simply help to orient a scholar's research by highlighting certain units of analysis for investigation in the construction of a theory as well as helping to determine what constitutes evidence in the testing of hypotheses.

INTERPRETIVE UNDERSTANDINGS

What we term **interpretive understandings**—constructivist, critical, postmodern, and feminist thought—share one thing in common: all have taken issue with one or more of the epistemological, methodological, and ontological assumptions that drive positivist theorizing in realism and liberalism in particular. This approach to knowledge assumes that what we know is based on an interpretation of what we think we see, alerting us to the subjective character of all human beings, the institutions or units they construct, and the processes in which they engage. Try as we might to reduce bias, we remain subjective creatures. Pursuit of objectivity and value-free scholarship are at best elusive goals.

Although, as we will see, a number of scholars have contributed to the interpretive understanding approach to IR, the German scholar Max Weber (1864–1920) deserves pride of place. Weber argued that "all knowledge of cultural reality is always knowledge from particular points of view." How research is conducted will be "determined by the evaluative ideas that dominate the investigator and his age."[12] In other words, each individual's work will be influenced by a particular doctrine, image of the world, ideology, paradigm, theory, understanding, or perspective. As a practical matter we try to identify as best we can how this subjective, human dimension affects our scholarship—an attempt to reduce substantially any bias that can adversely affect our theoretical work. Beyond that, the usual remedy is the scrutiny others give our work in what is inherently an inter-subjective process. As he sought to establish the role of ideational factors in explanation by social scientific means, Weber was an important early influence on interpretive understandings—particularly the later development of constructivism.

In the three chapters in Part Two, we build upon this subjective, Weberian tradition of *Verstehen* or interpretive understanding. In Chapter Six we examine constructivism. The rise of constructivism in IR theory has been remarkably fast over the past twenty years, passing economic structuralism, influencing the English School and challenging realism and liberalism in terms of influence on the IR field. Constructivism is less than a theory of IR yet more than an image—it is best characterized as a theoretically informed, interpretive understanding related to the study of IR. While within this approach there are those who could be characterized as positivists and embrace empirical methods, the type of explanation they seek is typically not that of the deductive covering law "out there" driving the behavior of states or non-state actors, but rather causality that takes full account of subjective and inter-subjective, human understandings. Constructivists see states and non-state actors not as mere products of world politics, the international system, or an international or world society, but rather as actually playing a decisive role in shaping it. These actors or agents influence (and are influenced by) the international norms and institutions they construct—activities that sustain or create new interests, values, and the ordering of foreign policy preferences. They take account of the relation between human beings and the organizations they construct as agents and the material and ideational structures that constitute actors and facilitate or constrain their actions. Most constructivists do not reject science or scientific methods associated with positivism, but caution greater humility and care in dealing with concepts that, after all, are of human construction. They can be viewed as occupying the middle ground between positivists seeking causal explanatory theory and those postmodernists or others who reject any such possibility.

Chapter Seven takes up the ongoing debate between those committed to positivist science and their principal critics, the latter who draw heavily from **phenomenology** that describes the phenomena we experience and the subjectivity that defines the essence of human beings. Although critical theorists tend not to reject positivism, they are prone to look under the cover stories governments, organizations, leaders, policy makers, and even theorists use to justify their conduct—an effort to find the underlying power or other realities masked by these narratives. For their part, postmodernists do not focus on some "objective" reality to be discovered "out there," but rather explore the ways human beings "in here" both construct or give meanings to objects, actions, or behaviors and employ narratives or stories that convey these meanings in what is essentially a subjective approach to understanding. Observers cannot be fully autonomous from the objects of their study, and relationships cannot be divided merely into the positivist categories of "causes" and "effects."

We take up feminism in Chapter Eight as an interpretive understanding that brings us to the often overlooked or understated importance and pay-offs of applying the concept of **gender** to IR theorizing. Feminists highlight the dominance or exclusivity of masculinist understandings of the world around us that, they claim, profoundly influence much theoretical work in the IR field. Feminist understandings rest on a centuries-old body of literary and scholarly work that preceded and has been decidedly less-influenced by phenomenology *per se*. Although critical theorists and postmodernists may be found among feminist scholars, some adopt positivist, scientific approaches albeit often informed by constructivist understandings of gender, sexual identity, and related concepts. Put another way, feminist scholarship is inherently interpretive as it challenges theories that either ignore (or marginalize) gender as a variable or, conversely, misuse gender to mask other purposes.

In conclusion, a word of caution in how one approaches the material in this book. One should be wary of sweeping criticisms concerning an entire image or interpretive understanding. It is not particularly difficult to find fault with the work of individual theorists, compile a list of their shortcomings, and then present the results as criticisms of the image or interpretive understanding as a whole. Such selectivity can be distorting and misleading. That is why it is imperative for the serious student of the international relations literature to go to the original sources, evaluate the validity of such criticisms, and assess the value of each approach as the basis for a mode of thinking about international relations.

NORMATIVE THEORY

Part Three of this volume (Chapter Nine) addresses normative theory as a separate line of inquiry in IR that brings us to moral or ethical values rooted in human understandings developed over more than two millennia. Normative IR theory has implications for both interpretive understandings and the images we use to capture the IR field, but it also remains a domain of inquiry in its own right that deals precisely with values and value preferences that inform human judgment. As with empirical theories, we can scrutinize normative theories on logical grounds, looking for flaws in reasoning used to sustain the argument. Unlike empirical theory, however, propositions in normative theory are not subject to empirical tests as a means of establishing their truth or falsehood.

Normative theory deals not so much with what *is*—the domain of empirical theory and the images and interpretive understandings associated with it—but rather with what *should* or *ought to be.* How should the world be ordered, and what value choices should decisionmakers take? Although the bulk of the effort in this volume is allocated to images and interpretive understandings of IR, we consider normative theory to be an important and policy-relevant, if often neglected, enterprise. In dealing with normative theories relevant to international relations and foreign policy choices, we identify normative preferences typically associated with the four images and interpretive understandings of international relations theory.

SUMMATION

We organize this volume on IR theory thematically in three parts—(1) images of the IR field found in realism, liberalism, the English School, and economic structuralism (2) contending interpretive understandings we identify in constructivism, critical theory, postmodernism, and feminism, and (3) normative theory that prescribes how state and non-state actors and their agents ought to behave or conduct themselves, bringing attention to value-oriented, philosophical considerations that also inform our interpretive understandings of IR.

Claims to objectivity in science have been under assault by interpretive understandings that see the acquisition of knowledge as an essentially subjective process. Certain versions of constructivism adopt positivist standards for inquiry, but emphasize subjective and inter-subjective forms of explanation. Critical, postmodern, and feminist critiques question various epistemological, methodological, and ontological aspects of all four of the images we identify.

A case could be made that *images* (particularly realism and liberalism) can be represented as *interpretive understandings* in their own right, as they provide concepts and underlying epistemological and ontological assumptions about how the world works and ways to understand it. But we prefer to reserve the latter term for constructivist, critical theory, postmodern, and feminist understandings. This "image" versus "interpretive understanding" distinction is our way of attempting to bring some taxonomic order to a field replete with "isms" of one kind or another.

Yet we must caution that such a division in particular threatens to make positivist approaches somewhat of a caricature. If we define positivist science as a value-free quest for truth, we have built a straw man relatively easy to demolish. On the other hand, if we add prudent caveats to positivism that make us sensitive to its subjective dimension, we open the door to interpretive and inter-subjective understandings of what we think we know. A more humble approach to "scientific" claims allows positivists to continue practicing their craft even as they must deal with critiques coming from other quarters.

Notes

1. Ernst B. Haas, *Nationalism, Liberalism and Progress,* vol. 2 (Ithaca, NY: Cornell University Press, 2000), 419.
2. Kenneth N. Waltz, "Kant, Liberalism, and War" in Waltz, *Realism and International Politics* (London and New York: Routledge, 2008), 3.
3. What is to be explained—the explanandum—is preceded by certain explanatory sentences—an explanans that "consists of general laws" and "other statements" concerning particular facts. Hempel applied this formalized deductive approach in the formulation of both universal and probabilistic law-like statements. Carl G. Hempel, *Philosophy of Natural Science* (Englewood Cliffs, NJ: Prentice-Hall, 1966), 48, 51.
4. Jack Snyder, "Myths, Modernization, and the Post-Gorbachev World," in Richard Ned Lebow and Thomas Risse-Kappen, eds., *International Relations Theory and the End of the Cold War* (New York: Columbia University Press, 1995), 109–26.
5. Kenneth N. Waltz, *Theory of International Politics* (Reading, MA: Addison-Wesley, 1979), 6, 13.
6. The Snyder and Wohlforth examples are from David Dessler, "Constructivism Within a Positivist Social Science," *Review of International Studies,* 25, 1 (January 1999): 129–30.
7. For an overview of methods, see Stephen Van Evera, *Guide to Methods for Students of Political Science* (Ithaca, NY: Cornell University Press, 1997).
8. Imre Lakatos observed that competitive "research programmes" exist in various fields of scholarly inquiry. See his article in *The Methodology of Scientific Research Programmes: Philosophical Papers* Vol. I, John Worrall and Gregory Currie, eds. (Cambridge, UK: Cambridge University Press, 1978) 8–10, 47–52, 70–72 and 85–93.
9. Kenneth N. Waltz, *Realism and International Politics* (New York and London: Routledge, 2008), vii.
10. Kenneth N. Waltz, *Man, the State and War* (New York: Columbia University Press, 1959); J. David Singer, "The Level-of-Analysis Problem in International Relations," in *International Politics and Foreign Policy,* James N. Rosenau, ed. (New York: Free Press, 1969), 20–29.
11. David Dessler, "What's at Stake in the Agent-Structure Debate?" *International Organization* 43, 3 (Summer 1989).
12. Max Weber, *Methodology of the Social Sciences,* trans. and ed. E. A. Shils and H. A. Finch (New York: Free Press, 1949), 90–93. Cf. Max Weber, *Basic Concepts in Sociology,* trans. H. P. Secher (Westport, CT: Greenwood Press, 1962, 1969), 52–55.

Thinking Theory Thoroughly

JAMES N. ROSENAU

James Rosenau addresses creative theorizing and develops nine principles to guide those who would engage in this enterprise. Indeed, not everyone is prone automatically to think theoretically. Those who are (or develop this orientation to deal comfortably with the abstract) are genuinely puzzled by international phenomena, distrustful of absolutes, and tend to have a high tolerance for ambiguity. Constantly ready to be proven wrong, the theorist typically takes "a playful approach" that facilitates thinking outside the box of conventional understandings. Rosenau's positivism (attempting to separate facts from values) is clear when he cautions us not to confuse empirical and normative or value-oriented theorizing that exist in quite separate domains of inquiry. Further marking his positivist ontological orientation, Rosenau notes an implicit assumption that underlies work by theorists such as himself—that human affairs are founded on an underlying order.

It rarely happens, but now and again in academic life one is jolted into returning to fundamentals, into ascertaining whether one has unknowingly strayed from one's organizing premises. This happened to me recently when a graduate student inquired whether she should take an "independent reading" course under my direction. Noting that my competence was limited, I responded by asking what topics or problems she planned to investigate. Her answer startled me, perhaps partly because it was ungrammatical but mainly because I found it pedagogically challenging. Her answer was simple: "I would like you to teach me to think theory!" I agreed to take on the role of advisor.

At this writing, some eleven weeks, many conversations and much reflection later, I still find the assignment challenging, though now I am beginning to wonder whether the capacity to think theoretically, the inclination to perceive and assess the course of events as suggestive or expressive of larger forces, is a talent that can be taught. It may be, instead, a cast of mind, a personality trait, or a philosophical perspective that some acquire early in life and others do not.

If this is so, there is not much that a professor can do to teach students how to think theoretically. They can be introduced to the nature of theories, taught the various purposes theories can serve, exposed to the controversies over the relative worth of different theories, and instructed on the steps required for the construction of viable theories. And, to solidify the learning of these lessons, they can then be given assignments in which they have to formulate concrete hypotheses and tie them together into an actual theoretical framework. The learning of these skills underlying the design of theories is not, however, the equivalent of learning how to think theoretically. Or, more accurately, it is not the equivalent of what I understood my student as wanting me to teach her. In fact, she may only have been asking instruction on the dos and don'ts of theoretical design. But because of the way she worded her request I interpreted her as seeking more than an introduction to the procedures and techniques essential to creative theorizing. It seemed to me she was looking to acquire not a set of skills, but rather a set of predispositions, a cluster of habits, a way of thinking, a mental lifestyle—or whatever may be the appropriate label for that level of intellectual existence that governs the use of skills and the application of values—that she did not possess and that she thought she valued

James N. Rosenau, *The Scientific Study of Foreign Policy,* rev. ed. London: Frances Pinter, 1980, 19–31. Reprinted by permission.

enough to want to make part of her orientation toward international phenomena. It is this more fundamental dimension of the life of the mind that I now suspect may not be teachable or learnable, a caveat that needs emphasis at the outset because the ensuing analysis amounts to nothing less than a pronouncement on how to think theoretically.

Nine Pre-Conditions for Creative Theorizing

It follows that the task of disciplining ourselves and our students to think theoretically consists, first, of identifying the cognitive inclinations and perceptual impulses from which creative theory springs and, second, of then forming intellectual habits which assure the prevalence of these inclinations and impulses whenever we turn to theory-building endeavors. The central question examined in this paper follows: what are the mental qualities that best enable one to "think theory" and how can their acquisition be best assured? Nine such qualities strike me as especially conducive to the development of good theorists. Each of the nine seems equally important and there is some overlap among them. Accordingly, the sequence of their elaboration here should not be interpreted as implying a rank ordering.

To think theoretically one has to avoid treating the task as that of formulating an appropriate definition of theory.

So as to clarify what is involved in thinking theoretically, let me start with the proposition that the task is not one of developing a clear-cut definition of theory. On balance, it is probably preferable to have a precise conception of the nature of theory rather than a vague one, but definitional exactness is not the only criterion of thinking theoretically and it may not even be a necessary requirement for such thought. I can readily imagine a young student thinking theoretically about international phenomena well before his or her first course on the subject turns to the question of what constitutes theory and the various uses to which it can be put. Indeed, I have had the good fortune of encountering a few students who were, so to speak, born theoreticians. From their very first comments in class as freshmen it was clear that they thought theoretically even though they have never had any methodological training or any exposure to the history of international relations.

Most of us are not so lucky. Most of us have to be trained to think theoretically and then we have to engage in the activity continuously in order to achieve and sustain a genuinely theoretical perspective. Hence, the fact that a few among us can maintain such a perspective without training and practice is a useful reminder that definitional clarity is not a prerequisite to creative theorizing.

The reminder is important because many of us tend to exaggerate the importance of exact definitions. To be clear about the nature of theory is not to guarantee the formulation of meaningful theory. Such clarity can be misleading. It can provide a false sense of security, a misguided confidence that one needs only to organize one's empirical materials in the proper way if one is equipped with a clear-cut definition of theory. It is my impression that much of the writing in our field derives from this premise that good definitions automatically yield good theories, as if the definitions somehow relieve the observer of the need to apply imagination and maintain philosophical discipline.

To be sure, much of the writing also suffers from loose and ambiguous conceptions of theory or from a confusion between theory and method. Such research would, obviously, be more valuable if it proceeded from a tighter and clearer notion of what the theoretical enterprise entails. So, to repeat, I am not arguing against definitional clarity. On the contrary, I believe it is highly appropriate to help students achieve such clarity by introducing them to the vast array of articles and books now available on the dynamics, boundaries, uses, and abuses of theory in the international field. But I am arguing for more than definitional clarity. I am arguing for caution and restraint in the use of definitions: in digesting the literature on theory and building a more elaborate conception of what it involves, one has to be careful not to lean too heavily on definitions and guidance. Also needed is a cast of mind, a mental set that focuses application of the definitions and facilitates creative theorizing.

To think theoretically one has to be clear as to whether one aspires to empirical theory or value theory.

Progress in the study of international affairs depends on advances in both empirical and value theory. But the two are not the same. They may overlap; they can focus on the same problem; and values always underlie the selection of the problems to which empirical theories are addressed. Yet they differ in one overriding way: empirical theory deals essentially with the "is" of international phenomena, with things as they are if and when they are subjected to observation, while value theory deals essentially with the "ought" of international phenomena, with things as they should be if and when they could be subjected to manipulation. This distinction underlies, in turn, entirely different modes of reasoning, a different rhetoric, and different types of evidence.

The habit of making the necessary analytic, rhetorical, and evidential distinctions between empirical and value theory can be difficult for young students to develop. Indeed, it can be weak and elusive for any of us who have strong value commitments and a deep concern for certain moral questions. The more intensive are our values, the more are we tempted to allow our empirical inquiries to be guided by our beliefs rather than by our concern for observation. For this reason I have found that helping students become habituated to the is–ought distinction is among the most difficult pedagogical tasks. They can understand the distinction intellectually and they can even explain and defend it when pressed; but practicing it is another matter and often their empirical analyses slip into moral judgments without their being aware of it. It is as if they somehow fear that their values and the policy goals they want to promote will be undermined if they allow themselves to focus on observable phenomena. Such, of course, is not the case. On the contrary, moral values and policy goals can be well served, even best served, by putting them aside and proceeding detachedly long enough to enlarge empirical understanding of the obstacles that hinder realization of the values and progress toward the goals.

This is the one line of reasoning on behalf of thinking theoretically that my most value-committed students find persuasive. If empirical theory is posited as a tool of moral theory, they can approach it instrumentally and see virtue in habituating themselves to distinguishing between the two. It takes a while, however, before the perceived virtues of habituation are translated into actual habits and, in fact, some never manage to make the transition, hard as they may try. Impatient with the need for change, convinced that time is too scarce to afford the slow pace of empirical inquiry, many simply give up and dismiss the is–ought distinction as one of those picayune obsessions to which some academics fall prey.

It is my impression that impatience with empirical theorizing is likely to be especially intense among Third World students of international relations. The newly developed consciousness of the long-standing injustices built into First World–Third World relationships, the lure of dependency theory, and perhaps a frustration over the central tendencies of social science in the First World have made Third World theorists particularly resistant to detached empirical theorizing. Their resistance gives a First World scholar pause: is his insistence on habituating oneself to the is–ought distinction yet another instance of false superiority, of projecting onto the developing world practices that have worked in industrial societies? It could be. Of late I have become keenly aware of the biases that may underlie my intellectual endeavors and thus I am not prepared merely to brush aside the idea that the is–ought distinction may be inappropriate to theorizing in much of the world. In this particular instance, however, I cannot even begin to break the habit. The relevance of the distinction strikes me as global, as independent of any national biases, as necessary to thinking theoretically wherever and whenever enlarged comprehension is sought. Empirical theory is not superior to moral theory; it is simply preferable for certain purposes, and one of these is the end of deepening our grasp of why international processes unfold as they do.

Aware that my own expertise, such as it may be, lies in the realm of empirical theory, the ensuing discussion makes no pretense of being relevant to thinking theoretically in the moral context. All the precepts that follow are concerned only with those mental qualities that may render us more thoroughgoing in our empirical theorizing.

To think theoretically one must be able to assume that human affairs are founded on an underlying order.

A prime task of empirical theory is to explain why international phenomena are structured as they are and/or behave as they do. To perform this task one must assume that each and every international phenomenon is theoretically explicable, that deeper understanding of its dynamics could be achieved if appropriate instruments for measuring it were available. To assume that everything is potentially explicable is to presume that nothing happens by chance, capriciously, at random, that for every effect there must be a cause. That is, there must be an underlying order out of which international relations springs. If this were not the case, if events could occur for no reason, there would be little point in theorizing. If some events are inherently inexplicable, efforts to build creative theory are bound to fall short to the extent that they embrace phenomena that may occur at random. Indeed, in the absence of the assumption of an underlying order, attempts to fashion theory are futile, pointless exercises, a waste of time that could be better spent writing poetry, playing tennis, or tending the garden.

This is *not* to say that thought only acquires the status of theory when it purports to account for every event. As indicated below, theory is also founded on the laws of probability. Hence it only purports to account for central tendencies, but this claim is unwarranted if an assumption of underlying order is not made. That is, to think theoretically one must presume that there is a cause for every effect even though one does not seek to explain every effect.

I have found that most students have a difficult time becoming habituated to the assumption of an underlying order. They see it as a denial of their own freedom. To presume there is a cause for everything, they reason, is to deprive people of free will, perhaps even to relieve them of responsibility for their actions. The assumption of an underlying order does not, of course, have such implications. One's freedom of choice is not lessened by the fact that the choices made are not random and, instead, derive from some source. Yet, fearful about compromising their own integrity, many students cannot accept this subtlety and insist on the premise that people have the capacity to cut themselves off from all prior experience and to act as they please for no reason whatsoever. To support their resistance to the assumption of an underlying order, they will often cite instances of international history when the unexpected occurred or when a highly deviant, impetuous, and irrational action was undertaken, as if somehow irrationality and impetuosity are capricious and do not stem from any sources.

Besides patiently reassuring dubious students that there are no insidious threats in the assumption of an underlying order, resistance to the idea can be lessened, even broken in some instances, by pointing out how the assumption offers hope for greater understanding and deeper comprehension. To presume that there is a cause of every effect is to assume that everything is potentially knowable, that inquiry can pay off, that one is not necessarily destined to go down an intellectual path that dead ends, leads nowhere. The assumption of an underlying order, in other words, is pervaded with hope. We do not make it to allow ourselves to be hopeful, but it has that consequence. It enables us to view ourselves as totally in charge of our own investigations, limited only by our imaginations and the resources at our disposal. It allows us to approach the chaos we perceive in the world around us as a challenge, as an orderliness that has yet to be identified and traced. It permits us to dare to think theory thoroughly because the affairs of people are patterned and the patterns are susceptible to being uncovered.

> To think theoretically one must be predisposed to ask about every event, every situation, or every observed phenomenon, "Of what is it an instance?"

Of all the habits one must develop to think theoretically, perhaps none is more central than the inclination to ask this question at every opportunity. It must be a constant refrain, a melody that haunts every lurch forward in the process of moving from observations to conclusions. For to see every event as an instance of a more encompassing class of phenomena is to sustain the search for patterns and to avoid treating any phenomenon as inherently unique. To think theoretically is to be at home with abstractions, to generalize, to discern the underlying order that links otherwise discrete incidents, and such a mode of thinking cannot be achieved and maintained unless every observed phenomenon is approached as merely one instance of a recurring sequence.

Again students appear to have a hard time building up this habit. They are inclined to probe for the special meaning of an event, to explore it for what sets it apart from all other events, rather than to treat it as an instance of a larger pattern. They want to understand the Iranian revolution, not revolutions as a social process, and to the extent this is their preference, to that extent do they resist building up the impulse to always reach for more general theoretical insights. Indeed, I have had many students who simply do not know where to begin when asked to indicate of what pattern some event they regard as important is an instance. Their faces turn blank and their tongues turn silent. They are paralyzed. They do not know what it means to treat the event as merely an instance of something, as just part of a larger category. And so they stumble, mumble, or otherwise resist thinking in those elementary terms out of which theorizing springs.

My response here is twofold. First, I try to portray the pleasure, the sheer joy, to be had from taking steps up the ladder of abstraction. Fitting pieces into larger wholes offers, I believe, a special sense of satisfaction, a feeling of accomplishment not unlike that which accompanies solving a puzzle or resolving a mystery. Indeed, theory building can readily be viewed as puzzle solving, as uncovering the dynamics embedded deep in the interstices of human relationships, and there are few students who are not intrigued by the challenge of solving puzzles.

If appealing thus to the curiosity of students does not succeed in getting them to ask habitually "Of what is this an instance?" (and often it is not a sufficient incentive), I revert to a second line of reasoning which, in effect, amounts to an attempt to shame them into the habit. This involves pointing out the implications of stumbling and mumbling, of not being able to discern any larger class of phenomena of which the observed phenomenon is an instance. The implications are unmistakable: to be paralyzed by the question "Of what is this an instance?" is not to know what one is interested in, to be lacking questions that generate and guide one's inquiry, to be confused by the phenomena one claims to be worthy of investigation. Based on the presumption of an underlying order, I believe that no phenomenon exists in isolation, unique only unto itself, and thus I believe that we always have an answer to the of-what-is-this-an-instance question, whether we know it or not. Accordingly, the task is not one of figuring out an answer presently unknown to us; it is rather that of explicating an answer that we have already acquired but have yet to surface. I am arguing, in other words, that we do not get interested in an international phenomenon for no reason, that our interest in it stems from a concern about a more encompassing set of phenomena, and that there is therefore no need to be paralyzed by the question if we press ourselves to move up the ladder of abstraction on which our intellectuality is founded. Once shamed into acknowledging that

their concerns are not confined to the lowest rung on the ladder, most students are willing to begin to venture forth and approach the phenomena they observe as mere instances of something else.

To think theoretically one must be ready to appreciate and accept the need to sacrifice detailed descriptions for broad observations.

One cannot begin to mount the rungs of the ladder of abstraction if one is unable to forgo the detailed account, the elaborated event, the specific minutia. As indicated, the theoretical enterprise is committed to the teasing out of central tendencies, to encompassing ever greater numbers of phenomena, to moving up the ladder of abstraction as parsimoniously as possible. Thus theory involves generalizing rather than particularizing and, in so doing, it requires relinquishing, subordinating, and/or not demonstrating much of one's impulse to expound everything one knows. It means, in effect, that one must discipline one's self to accept simple explanations over complex ones.

These are not easy tasks. Most of us find comfort in detail. The more details we know, the more are we likely to feel we have mastered our subject. To forgo much of the detail, on the other hand, is to opt for uncertainties, to expose ourselves to the criticisms of those who would pick away at our generalizations with exceptions. The temptations to fall back on details are thus considerable and much concentration on the upper rungs of the ladder of abstraction is required if the temptations are to be resisted.

Happily this is less of a problem for beginning students than more mature ones who are introduced late to the theoretical enterprise. The former have yet to acquire extensive familiarity with details and they are therefore not likely to feel threatened by the loss of their knowledge base. They want to focus on the unique, to be sure, but at least it is possible to expose them to the case of theorizing before they find security in endless minutiae. Exactly how more mature scholars accustomed to the comforts of detail can be persuaded to be theoretically venturesome is, I confess, a problem for which I have yet to find anything resembling a solution.

To think theoretically one must be tolerant of ambiguity, concerned about probabilities, and distrustful of absolutes.

To be concerned about central tendencies one needs to be accepting of exceptions, deviations, anomalies, and other phenomena that, taken by themselves, run counter to the anticipated or prevailing pattern. Anomalies ought not be ignored and often explorations of them can lead to valuable, path-breaking insights; but neither can anomalies be allowed to undermine one's focus on central tendencies. Empirical theories deal only with probabilities and not with absolutes, with how most phenomena are likely to respond to a stimulus and not with how each and every phenomenon responds. Theorists simply do not aspire to account for every phenomenon. They know there will be anomalies and exceptions; indeed, they are suspicious of those unlikely occasions when no exceptions are manifest. Rather their goal is to build theories in which the central tendencies encompass the highest possible degree of probability, with certainties and absolutes being left for ideologues and zealots to expound.

Although they engage in it continuously in their daily lives, students tend to be resistant to the necessity of thinking probabilistically when they turn to theorizing. More accurately, they tend to be reluctant to ignore the ambiguity, to be restless with anything less than perfect certainty, as if any exception to the anticipated central tendencies constitutes a negation of their reasoning. I have found this low tolerance of ambiguity difficult to contest. Many students, fearful of uncertainty, seem to get fixated on the exception, and it is very hard at that point to recapture their interest in central tendencies. The very rhetoric of their everyday language—that things are "completely" the case or that an observation is "absolutely" accurate—reinforces their inclinations to be intolerant of deviations. In this mood they recognize only the "whole truth" as valid and regard central tendencies as a partial rather than a legitimate form of knowledge.

I confess to perplexity over how to handle this obstacle to theorizing on the part of students. I have tried elaborating on the many ways in which probabilistic thinking underlies their daily lives. I have tried making analogies between the physicist and the political scientist, pointing out that the former does not aspire to account for the behavior of every atom any more than the latter aspires to accounting for every voter. I have tried sarcasm, stressing the noxious values that derive from a concern with absolutes. Neither alone nor in combination, however, do such techniques seem to have any effect on many students. Whatever its sources, their intolerance of ambiguity is apparently too deep-seated to yield to reasoning or persuasion. So, reluctantly, I have

concluded that students with a low tolerance of ambiguity and a high need for certainty are unlikely to ever think theory thoroughly and that it is probably wasted energy to try to teach them to do so.

To think theoretically one must be playful about international phenomena.

At the core of the theorizing process is a creative imagination. The underlying order of world affairs is too obscure and too complex to yield to pedestrian, constricted, or conventional minds. Only deep penetration into a problem, discerning relationships that are not self-evident and might even be the opposite of what seems readily apparent, can produce incisive and creative theory. Thus to think theoretically one must allow one's mind to run freely, to be playful, to toy around with what might seem absurd, to posit seemingly unrealistic circumstances and speculate what would follow if they were ever to come to pass. Stated differently, one must develop the habit of playing and enjoying the game of "as if"—that is, specifying unlikely conditions and analyzing them as *if* they prevailed.

Put in still another way, it has always seemed to me that good theory ought never be embarrassed by surprises, by unanticipated events that have major consequences for the system on which the theory focuses. A Hitler–Stalin pact, a Nixon resignation, or a Sadat peace initiative should not catch the creative theorist unawares because part of his or her creativity involves imagining the unimaginable. One imagines the unimaginable by allowing one's variables to vary across the entire range of a continuum even if some of its extreme points seem so unlikely as to be absurd. To push one's thinking beyond previously imagined extremes of a continuum is to play the game of "as if," and it involves a playfulness of mind that mitigates against surprises as well as facilitates incisive theorizing.

How one teaches playfulness is, of course, another matter. In some important sense it is an intellectual quality that cannot be taught. One acquires—or perhaps inherits—creativity early in life and no amount of subsequent training can greatly enhance the imaginative powers of those with tunnel vision and inhibited mentalities. On the other hand, encouragement to playfulness can bring out previously untapped talents in some students. Many have become so used to being told what to think that their creative impulses have never been legitimated and, accordingly, they have never even heard of the existence of the "as if" game. So no harm can be done by pressing our students (not to mention ourselves) to be playful and flexible in their thinking, and just conceivably such an emphasis may produce some unexpected results.

To think theoretically one must be genuinely puzzled by international phenomena.

Creative use of the imagination requires humility toward international phenomena. One must be as concerned about asking the right questions about the order underlying world affairs as finding the right answers. To focus only on answers is to be sure about the questions one wants to probe and this, in turn, is to impose unnecessary limits on one's capacity to discern and integrate the deeper structures of global politics. If, on the other hand, one is genuinely puzzled by why events unfold as they do, one is committed to always asking why they occur in one way rather than another and, in so doing, pressing one's theoretical impulses as far as possible.

I do not use the notion of "genuine puzzles" casually. They are not simply open-ended questions but refer, rather, to perplexity over specific and patterned outcomes. To be genuinely puzzled about the declining capacity of governments to govern effectively, for example, one does not ask, "Why do governments do what they do?" Rather, one asks, say, "Why are most governments unable to control inflation?" or "Why do they alter their alliance commitments under specified conditions?" Genuine puzzles, in other words, are not idle, ill-framed, or impetuous speculations. The encompass specified dependent variables for which adequate explanations are lacking. I do not see how one can begin to think theoretically if one does not discern recurrent outcomes that evoke one's curiosity and puzzlement. Some analysts believe they are starting down the road to theory when they start asking what the outcomes are, but such a line of inquiry leads only to deadends, or worse, to endless mazes, because one never knows when one has come upon a relevant outcome. Genuine puzzles can lead us down creative paths, however, because they discipline us to focus on particular patterns.

One cannot teach others to be puzzled. Again it is very much a matter of whether curiosity has been repressed or allowed to flourish at an early age. It is possible, however, to keep after students and colleagues with the simple question, "What genuinely puzzles you about international affairs?" Hopefully repetition of the question will prove to be sufficiently challenging to facilitate a maximum expression of whatever may be the curiosity potential students may possess.

To think theoretically one must be constantly ready to be proven wrong.

Perhaps nothing inhibits the ability to be intellectually puzzled and playful more than the fear of being embarrassed by the inaccuracies of one's theorizing. Many of us have fragile egos that are so sensitive to error as to lead us to prefer sticking close to conventional wisdom rather than risking speculation that may be erroneous. It is as if our stature as students depends upon the soundness of our observations.

Fragile egos are not readily bolstered and some students may never be capable of venturing forth. In my experience, however, there is one line of reasoning that some students find sufficiently persuasive to lessen their fears of appearing ridiculous. It involves the thought that our comprehension of international phenomena can be substantially advanced even if our theories about them prove to be woefully wrong. Such progress can occur in two ways. One is that falsified theory has the virtue of indicating avenues of inquiry which no longer need be traversed. Doubtless egos are best served by theoretical breakthroughs but if one presumes that knowledge is at least partly developed through a process of elimination, there is some satisfaction to be gained from having narrowed the range of inquiry through theory that subsequently proves fallacious.

Secondly, unsound theory can facilitate progress by provoking others into demonstrating its falsity and attempting to show how and why it went astray. Indeed, assuming that the erroneous theory focuses on significant matters, often the more outrageous the theory is, the more it is likely to provoke further investigation. Thus even if one cannot negotiate a theoretical breakthrough on one's own, one can serve one's ego by the possibility that one's errors may sustain the knowledge-building process. This is surely what one astute analyst had in mind when he observed, "it is important to err importantly."[1]

Conclusion: Bringing It All Together

Plainly, there is no easy way to evolve the habit of thinking theoretically. Indeed, if the foregoing nine precepts are well founded, it can be readily argued that theorizing is the hardest of intellectual tasks.

Clearing away the confusion of day-to-day events and teasing out their underlying patterns is not merely a matter of applying one's mental skills. Sustained, disciplined, and uninhibited work is required, and even then theory can be elusive, puzzles difficult to identify, details hard to ignore, and probabilities tough to estimate. And the lures and practices of non-theoretical thinking are always present, tempting us to forgo the insecurities and ambiguities of high levels of abstraction in favor of the comfortable precision available at low levels.

Yet the payoffs for not yielding to the temptations and persisting to think theoretically are considerable. There is an exhilaration, an exquisiteness, to be enjoyed in the theoretical enterprise that virtually defies description. Stimulated by the rarified atmosphere, energized by the freedom to roam uninhibitedly across diverse realms of human experience, one gets giddy at high levels of abstraction. It is that special kind of giddiness that comes from the feeling that one is employing all the resources and talents at one's command, moving beyond anything one has done before. And if one should be so fortunate as actually to achieve a theoretical breakthrough, then the exhilaration, the excitement, and the sense of accomplishment can approach the thrill of discovery that Darwin, Einstein, Freud, and the other great explorers of underlying order must have experienced at their moments of breakthrough.

For all the difficulties it entails, then, thinking theoretically is, on balance, worth the effort. And so, therefore, is the effort to teach others to think thoroughly in this way. The habits of theoretical thinking may not always be teachable, and they may not even be teachable at all; but if our efforts successfully manage to reach only a few students, they are worth undertaking. And it is even conceivable that in trying to teach others to think theoretically, we may refine and enlarge our own capacities for comprehending the underlying order that sustains and alters the human condition.

Note

1. Marion J. Levy, "'Does It Matter If He's Naked?' Bawled the Child," in Klaus Knorr and James N. Rosenau (eds.), *Contending Approaches to International Relations* (Princeton, NJ: Princeton University Press, 1969), 93.

Explaining War: The Levels of Analysis
KENNETH N. WALTZ

In this article excerpted from Man, the State and War, *Professor Waltz provides a causal explanation of war that combines three levels of analysis: individual, state and society, and international system. The permissive cause (providing no obstacle to war) is systemic anarchy; efficient or proximate causes of a given war may also be found at other levels. The systemic argument presented here is the foundation for structural realism developed some twenty years later in his* Theory of International Politics.

Introduction

Asking who won a given war, someone has said, is like asking who won the San Francisco earthquake. That in wars there is no victory but only varying degrees of defeat is a proposition that has gained increasing acceptance in the twentieth century. But are wars also akin to earthquakes in being natural occurrences whose control or elimination is beyond the wit of man? Few would admit that they are, yet attempts to eliminate war, however nobly inspired and assiduously pursued, have brought little more than fleeting moments of peace among states. There is an apparent disproportion between effort and product, between desire and result. The peace wish, we are told, runs strong and deep among the Russian people; and we are convinced that the same can be said of Americans. From these statements there is some comfort to be derived, but in the light of history and of current events as well it is difficult to believe that the wish will father the condition desired.

Social scientists, realizing from their studies how firmly the present is tied to the past and how intimately the parts of a system depend upon each other, are inclined to be conservative in estimating the possibilities of achieving a radically better world. If one asks whether we can now have peace where in the past there has been war, the answers are most often pessimistic. Perhaps this is the wrong question. And indeed the answers will be somewhat less discouraging if instead the following questions are put: Are there ways of decreasing the incidence of war, of increasing the chances of peace? Can we have peace more often in the future than in the past?

Peace is one among a number of ends simultaneously entertained. The means by which peace can be sought are many. The end is pursued and the means are applied under varying conditions. Even though one may find it hard to believe that there are ways to peace not yet tried by statesmen or advocated by publicists, the very complexity of the problem suggests the possibility of combining activities in different ways in the hope that some combination will lead us closer to the goal. Is one then led to conclude that the wisdom of the statesman lies in trying first one policy and then another, in doing what the moment seems to require? An affirmative reply would suggest that the hope for improvement lies in policy divorced from analysis, in action removed from thought. Yet each attempt to alleviate a condition implies some idea of its causes: to explain how peace can be more readily achieved requires an understanding of the causes of war. It is such an understanding that we shall seek in the following pages.

The First Image: International Conflict and Human Behavior

> There is deceit and cunning and from these wars arise.
>
> Confucius

According to the first image of international relations, the focus of the important causes of war is found in the nature and behavior of man. Wars result from selfishness, from misdirected aggressive impulses, from stupidity. Other causes are secondary and have to be interpreted in the light of these factors. If these are the primary causes of war, then the elimination of war must come through uplifting and enlightening men or securing their psychic-social readjustment. This estimate of causes and cures has been dominant in the writings of many serious students of human affairs from Confucius to present-day pacifists. It is the leitmotif of many modern behavioral scientists as well.

Prescriptions associated with first-image analyses need not be identical in content, as a few examples will indicate. Henry Wadsworth Longfellow, moved to poetic expression by a visit to the arsenal at Springfield, set down the following thoughts:

> Were half the power that fills the world with terror,
> Were half the wealth bestowed on camps and courts,
> Given to redeem the human mind from error,
> There were no need of arsenals or forts.

Implicit in these lines is the idea that the people will insist that the right policies be adopted if only they know what the right policies are. Their instincts are good, though their present gullibility may prompt them to follow false leaders. By attributing present difficulties to a defect in knowledge, education becomes the remedy of war. The idea is widespread. Beverly Nichols, a pacifist writing in the 1930s, thought that if Norman Angell "could be made educational dictator of the world, war would vanish like the morning mist, in a single generation."[1] In 1920, a conference of Friends, unwilling to rely upon intellectual development alone, called upon the people of the world to replace self-seeking with the spirit of sacrifice, cooperation, and trust.[2] Bertrand Russell, at about the same time and in much the same vein, saw a decline in the possessive instincts as a prerequisite to peace.[3] By others, increasing the chances of peace has been said to require not so much a change in "instincts" as a channeling of energies that are presently expended in the destructive folly of war. If there were something that men would rather do than fight, they would cease to fight altogether. Aristophanes saw the point. If the women of Athens would deny themselves to husbands and lovers, their men would have to choose between the pleasures of the couch and the exhilarating experiences of the battlefield. Aristophanes thought he knew the men, and women, of Athens well enough to make the outcome a foregone conclusion. William James was in the same tradition. War, in his view, is rooted in man's bellicose nature, which is the product of centuries-old tradition. His nature cannot be changed or his drives suppressed, but they can be diverted. As alternatives to military service, James suggests drafting the youth of the world to mine coal and man ships, to build skyscrapers and roads, to wash dishes and clothes. While his estimate of what diversions would be sufficient is at once less realistic and more seriously intended than that of Aristophanes, his remedy is clearly the same in type.[4]

The prescriptions vary, but common to them all is the thought that in order to achieve a more peaceful world men must be changed, whether in their moral-intellectual outlook or in their psychic-social behavior. One may, however, agree with the first-image analysis of causes without admitting the possibility of practicable prescriptions for their removal. Among those who accept a first-image explanation of war there are both optimists and pessimists, those who think the possibilities of progress so great that wars will end before the next generation is dead and those who think that wars will continue to occur though by them we may all die.

The Second Image: International Conflict and the Internal Structure of States

> However conceived in an image of the world, foreign policy is a phase of domestic policy, an inescapable phase.
>
> Charles Beard, *A Foreign Policy for America*

The first image did not exclude the influence of the state, but the role of the state was introduced as a consideration less important than, and to be explained in terms of, human behavior. According to the first image, to say that the state acts is to speak metonymically. We say that the state acts when we mean that the people in it act, just as we say that the pot boils when we mean that the water in it boils. The preceding [section] concentrated on the contents rather than the container; the present [section] alters the balance of emphasis in favor of the latter. To continue the figure: Water running out of a faucet is chemically the same as water in a container, but once the water is in a container, it can be made to "behave" in different ways. It can be turned into steam and used to power an engine, or, if the water is sealed in and heated to extreme temperatures, it can become the instrument of a destructive explosion. Wars would not exist were human nature not what it is, but neither would Sunday schools and brothels, philanthropic organizations and criminal gangs. Since everything is related to human nature, to explain anything one must consider more than human nature. The events to be explained are so many and so varied that human nature cannot possibly be the single determinant.

The attempt to explain everything by psychology meant, in the end, that psychology succeeded in explaining nothing. And adding sociology to the analysis simply substitutes the error of sociologism for the error of psychologism. Where Spinoza, for example, erred by leaving out of his personal estimate of cause all reference to the causal role of social structures, sociologists have, in approaching the problem of war and peace, often erred in omitting all reference to the political framework within which individual and social actions occur. The conclusion is obvious: to understand war and peace political analysis must be used to supplement and order the findings of psychology and sociology. What kind of political analysis is needed? For possible explanations of the occurrence or nonoccurrence of war, one can look to international politics (since it is in the name of the state that the fighting is actually done). The former approach is postponed [until the next section]; according to the second image, the internal organization of states is the key to understanding war and peace.

One explanation of the second-image type is illustrated as follows. War most often promotes the internal unity of each state involved. The state plagued by internal strife may then, instead of waiting for the accidental attack, seek the war that will bring internal peace. Bodin saw this clearly, for he concludes that "the best way of preserving a state, and guaranteeing it against sedition, rebellion, and civil war is to keep the subjects in amity one with another, and to this end, to find an enemy against whom they can make common cause." And he saw historical evidence that the principle had been applied, especially by the Romans, who "could find no better antidote to civil war, nor one more certain in its effects, than to oppose an enemy to the citizens."[5] Secretary of State William Henry Seward followed this reasoning when, in order to promote unity within the country, he urged upon Lincoln a vigorous foreign policy, which included the possibility of declaring war on Spain and France.[6] Mikhail Skobelev, an influential Russian military officer of the third quarter of the nineteenth century, varied the theme but slightly when he argued that the Russian monarchy was doomed unless it could produce major military successes abroad.[7]

The use of internal defects to explain those external acts of the state that bring war can take many forms. Such explanation may be related to a type of government that is thought to be generically bad. For example, it is often thought that the deprivations imposed by despots upon their subjects produce tensions that may find expressions in foreign adventure. Or the explanation may be given in terms of defects in a government not itself considered bad. Thus it has been argued that the restrictions placed upon a government in order to protect the prescribed rights of its citizens act as impediments to the making and executing of foreign policy. These restrictions, laudable in original purpose, may have the unfortunate effect of making difficult or impossible the effective action of that government for the maintenance of peace in the world.[8] And, as a final example, explanation may be made in terms of geographic or economic deprivation or in terms of deprivations too vaguely defined to be labeled at all. Thus a nation may argue that it has not attained its "natural" frontiers, that such frontiers are necessary to its security, that war to extend the state to its deserved compass is justified or even necessary.[9] The possible variations on this theme have been made familiar by the "have-not" arguments so popular in this century. Such arguments have been used both to explain why "deprived" countries undertake war and to urge the satiated to make the compensatory adjustments thought necessary if peace is to be perpetuated.[10]

The examples just given illustrate in abundant variety one part of the second image, the idea that defects in states cause wars among them. But in just what ways should the structure of states be changed? What definition of the "good" state is to serve as a standard? Among those who have taken this approach to international relations there is a great variety of definitions. Karl Marx defines "good" in terms

of ownership of the means of production; Immanuel Kant in terms of abstract principles of right; Woodrow Wilson in terms of national selfdetermination and modern democratic organization. Though each definition singles out different items as crucial, all are united in asserting that if, and only if, substantially all states reform will world peace result. That is, the reform prescribed is considered the sufficient basis for world peace. This, of course, does not exhaust the subject. Marx, for example, believed that states would disappear shortly after they became socialist. The problem of war, if war is defined as violent conflict among states, would then no longer exist. Kant believed that republican states would voluntarily agree to be governed in their dealings by a code of law drawn up by the states themselves. Wilson urged a variety of requisites to peace, such as improved international understanding, collective security and disarmament, a world confederation of states. But history proved to Wilson that one cannot expect the steadfast cooperation of undemocratic states in any such program for peace.

For each of these men, the reform of states in the ways prescribed is taken to be the *sine quanon* of world peace. The examples given could be multiplied. Classical economists as well as socialists, aristocrats and monarchists as well as democrats, empiricists and realists as well as transcendental idealists—all can furnish examples of men who have believed that peace can be had only if a given pattern of internal organization becomes widespread. Is it that democracies spell peace, but we have had wars because there have never been enough democracies of the right kind? Or that the socialist form of government contains within it the guarantee of peace, but so far there have never been any true socialist governments?[11] If either question were answered in the affirmative, then one would have to assess the merits of different prescriptions and try to decide just which one, or which combination, contains the elusive secret formula for peace. The import of our criticism, however, is that no prescription for international relations written entirely in terms of the second image can be valid, that the approach itself is faulty. Our criticisms of the liberals apply to all theories that would rely on the generalization of one pattern of state and society to bring peace to the world.

Bad states lead to war. As previously said, there is a large and important sense in which this is true. The obverse of this statement, that good states mean peace in the world, is an extremely doubtful proposition. The difficulty, endemic with the second image of international relations, is the same in kind as the difficulty encountered in the first image. There the statement that men make the societies, including the international society, in which they live was criticized not simply as being wrong but as being incomplete. One must add that the societies they live in make men. And it is the same in international relations. The actions of states, or, more accurately, of men acting for states, make up the substance of international relations. But the international political environment has much to do with the ways in which states behave. The influence to be assigned to the internal structure of states in attempting to solve the war–peace equation cannot be determined until the significance of the international environment has been reconsidered.

The Third Image: International Conflict and International Anarchy

> For what can be done against force without force?
>
> Cicero, *The Letters to His Friends*

With many sovereign states, with no system of law enforceable among them, with each state judging its grievances and ambitions according to the dictates of its own reason or desire—conflict, sometimes leading to war, is bound to occur. To achieve a favorable outcome from such conflict a state has to rely on its own devices, the relative efficiency of which must be its constant concern. This, the idea of the third image, is to be examined [here]. It is not an esoteric idea; it is not a new idea. Thucydides implied it when he wrote that it was "the growth of the Athenian power, which terrified the Lacedaemonians and forced them into war."[12] John Adams implied it when he wrote to the citizens of Petersburg, Virginia, that "a war with France, if just and necessary, might wean us from fond and blind affections, which no Nation ought ever to feel towards another, as our experience in more than one instance abundantly testifies."[13] There is an obvious relation between the concern over relative power position expressed by Thucydides and the admonition of John Adams that love affairs between states are inappropriate and dangerous. This relation is made explicit in Frederick Dunn's statement that "so long as the notion of self-help persists, the aim of maintaining the power

position of the nation is paramount to all other considerations."[14]

In anarchy there is no automatic harmony. The three preceding statements reflect this fact. A state will use force to attain its goals if, after assessing the prospects for success, it values those goals more than it values the pleasures of peace. Because each state is the final judge of its own cause, any state may at any time use force to implement its policies. Because any state may at any time use force, all states must constantly be ready either to counter force with force or to pay the cost of weakness. The requirements of state action are, in this view, imposed by the circumstances in which all states exist.

In a manner of speaking, all three images are a part of nature. So fundamental are man, the state, and the state system in any attempt to understand international relations that seldom does an analyst, however wedded to one image, entirely overlook the other two. Still, emphasis on one image may distort one's interpretation of the others. It is, for example, not uncommon to find those inclined to see the world in terms of either the first or the second image countering the oft-made argument that arms breed not war but security, and possibly even peace, by pointing out that the argument is a compound of dishonest myth, to cover the interests of politicians, armament makers, and others, and honest illusion entertained by patriots sincerely interested in the safety of their states. To dispel the illusion, Cobden, to recall one of the many who have argued this way, once pointed out that doubling armaments, if everyone does it, makes no state more secure and, similarly, that none would be endangered if all military establishments were simultaneously reduced by, say, 50 percent.[15] Putting aside the thought that the arithmetic is not necessarily an accurate reflection of what the situation would be, this argument illustrates a supposedly practical application of the first and second images. Whether by educating citizens and leaders of the separate states or by improving the organizations of each of them, a condition is sought in which the lesson here adumbrated becomes the basis for the policies of states. The result?—disarmament, and thus economy, together with peace, and thus security, for all states. If some states display a willingness to pare down their military establishments, other states will be able to pursue similar policies. In emphasizing the interdependence of the policies of all states, the argument pays heed to the third image. The optimism is, however, the result of ignoring some inherent difficulties. [Here Waltz takes up Rousseau's view of man in the early state of nature.—*Ed.*]

In the early state of nature, men were sufficiently dispersed to make any patterns of cooperation unnecessary. But finally the combination of increased numbers and the usual natural hazards posed, in a variety of situations, the proposition: cooperate or die. Rousseau illustrates the line of reasoning with the simplest example. The example is worth reproducing, for it is the point of departure for the establishment of government and contains the basis for his explanation of conflict in international relations as well. Assume that five men who have acquired a rudimentary ability to speak and to understand each other happen to come together at a time when all of them suffer from hunger. The hunger of each will be satisfied by the fifth part of a stag, so they "agree" to cooperate in a project to trap one. But also the hunger of any one of them will be satisfied by a hare, so, as a hare comes within reach, one of them grabs it. The defector obtains the means of satisfying his hunger but in doing so permits the stag to escape. His immediate interest prevails over consideration for his fellows.[16]

The story is simple; the implications are tremendous. In cooperative action, even where all agree on the goal and have an equal interest in the project, one cannot rely on others. Spinoza linked conflict causally to man's imperfect reason. Montesquieu and Rousseau counter Spinoza's analysis with the proposition that the sources of conflict are not so much in the minds of men as they are in the nature of social activity. The difficulty is to some extent verbal. Rousseau grants that if we knew how to receive the true justice that comes from God, "we should need neither government nor laws."[17] This corresponds to Spinoza's proposition that "men in so far as they live in obedience to reason, necessarily live always in harmony one with another."[18] The idea is a truism. If men were perfect, their perfection would be reflected in all of their calculations and actions. Each could rely on the behavior of others, and all decisions would be made on principles that would preserve a true harmony of interests. Spinoza emphasizes not the difficulties inherent in mediating conflicting interests but the defectiveness of man's reason that prevents their consistently making decisions that would be in the interest of each and for

the good of all. Rousseau faces the same problem. He imagines how men must have behaved as they began to depend on one another to meet their daily needs. As long as each provided for his own wants, there could be no conflict; whenever the combination of natural obstacles and growth in population made cooperation necessary, conflict arose. Thus in the stag-hunt example the tension between one man's immediate interest and the general interest of the group is resolved by the unilateral action of the one man. To the extent that he was motivated by a feeling of hunger, his act is one of passion. Reason would have told him that his long-run interest depends on establishing, through experience, the conviction that cooperative action will benefit all of the participants. But reason also tells him that if he forgoes the hare, the man next to him might leave his post to chase it, leaving the first man with nothing but food for thought on the folly of being loyal.

The problem is now posed in more significant terms. If harmony is to exist in anarchy, not only must I be perfectly rational but I must be able to assume that everyone else is too. Otherwise there is no basis for rational calculation. To allow in my calculation for the irrational acts of others can lead to no determinate solutions, but to attempts to act on a rational calculation without making such an allowance may lead to my own undoing. The latter argument is reflected in Rousseau's comments on the proposition that "a people of true Christians would form the most perfect society imaginable." In the first place he points out that such a society "would not be a society of men." Moreover, he says, "For the state to be peaceable and for harmony to be maintained, all the citizens without exception would have to be [equally] good Christians; if by ill hap there should be a single self-seeker or hypocrite . . . The would certainly get the better of his pious compatriots."[19]

If we define cooperative action as rational and any deviation from it irrational, we must agree with Spinoza that conflict results from the irrationality of men. But if we examine the requirements of rational action, we find that even in an example as simple as the stag hunt we have to assume that the reason of each leads to an identical definition of interest, that each will draw the same conclusion as to the methods appropriate to meet the original situation, that all will agree instantly on the action required by any chance incidents that raise the question of altering the original plan, and that each can rely completely on the steadfastness of purpose of all the others. Perfectly rational action requires not only the perception that our welfare is tied up with the welfare of others but also a perfect appraisal of details so that we can answer the question: Just how in each situation is it tied up with everyone else's? Rousseau agrees with Spinoza in refusing to label the act of the rabbit-snatcher either good or bad; unlike Spinoza, he also refuses to label it either rational or irrational. He has noticed that the difficulty is not only in the actors but also in the situations they face. While by no means ignoring the part that avarice and ambition play in the birth and growth of conflict,[20] Rousseau's analysis makes clear the extent to which conflict appears inevitably in the social affairs of men.

In short, the proposition that irrationality is the cause of all the world's troubles, in the sense that a world of perfectly rational men would know no disagreements and no conflicts, is, as Rousseau implies, as true as it is irrelevant. Since the world cannot be defined in terms of perfection, the very real problem of how to achieve an approximation to harmony in cooperative and competitive activity is always with us and, lacking the possibility of perfection, it is a problem that cannot be solved simply by changing men. Rousseau's conclusion, which is also the heart of his theory of international relations, is accurately though somewhat abstractly summarized in the following statement: That among particularities accidents will occur is not accidental but necessary.[21] And this, in turn, is simply another way of saying that in anarchy there is no automatic harmony.

If anarchy is the problem, then there are only two possible solutions: (1) to impose an effective control on the separate and imperfect states; (2) to remove states from the sphere of the accidental, that is, to define the good state as so perfect that it will no longer be particular. Kant tried to compromise by making states good enough to obey a set of laws to which they have volunteered their assent. Rousseau, whom on this point Kant failed to follow, emphasizes the particular nature of even the good state and, in so doing, makes apparent the futility of the solution Kant suggests.[22] He also makes possible a theory of international relations that in general terms explains the behavior of all states, whether good or bad.[23]

In the stag-hunt example, the will of the rabbit-snatcher was rational and predictable from his own point of view. From the point of view of the rest of the group, it was arbitrary and capricious. So of any individual state, a will perfectly good for itself may provoke the violent resistance of other states.[24] The application of Rousseau's theory to international politics is stated with eloquence and clarity in his commentaries on Saint-Pierre and in a short work entitled *The State of War*. His application bears out the preceding analysis. The states of Europe, he writes, "touch each other at so many points that no one of them can move without giving a jar to all the rest; their variances are all the more deadly, as their ties are more closely woven." They "must inevitably fall into quarrels and dissensions at the first changes that come about." And if we ask why they must "inevitably" clash, Rousseau answers: Because their union is "formed and maintained by nothing better than chance." The nations of Europe are willful units in close juxtaposition with rules neither clear nor enforceable to guide them. The public law of Europe is but "a mass of contradictory rules which nothing but the right of the stronger can reduce to order: so that in the absence of any sure clue to guide her, reason is bound, in every case of doubt, to obey the promptings of self-interest—which in itself would make war inevitable, even if all parties desired to be just." In this condition, it is foolhardy to expect automatic harmony of interest and automatic agreement and acquiescence in rights and duties. In a real sense there is a "union of the nations of Europe," but "the imperfections of this association make the state of those who belong to it worse than it would be if they formed no community at all."[25]

The argument is clear. For individuals the bloodiest stage of history was the period just prior to the establishment of society. At that point they had lost the virtues of the savage without having acquired those of the citizen. The late stage of the state of nature is necessarily a state of war. The nations of Europe are precisely in that stage.[26]

What then is cause: the capricious acts of the separate states or the system within which they exist? Rousseau emphasizes the latter:

> Every one can see that what unites any form of society is community of interests, and what disintegrates [it] is their conflict; that either tendency may be changed or modified by a thousand accidents; and therefore that, as soon as a society is founded, some coercive power must be provided to co-ordinate the actions of its members and give to their common interests

and mutual obligations that firmness and consistency which they could never acquire of themselves.[27]

But to emphasize the importance of political structure is not to say that the acts that bring about conflict and lead to the use of force are of no importance. It is the specific acts that are the immediate causes of war,[28] the general structure that permits them to exist and wreak their disasters. To eliminate every vestige of selfishness, perversity, and stupidity in nations would serve to establish perpetual peace, but to try directly to eliminate all the immediate causes of war without altering the structure of the "union of Europe" is utopian.

What alteration of structure is required? The idea that a voluntary federation, such as Kant later proposed, could keep peace among states, Rousseau rejects emphatically. Instead, he says, the remedy for war among states " is to be found only in such a form of federal Government as shall unite nations by bonds similar to those which already unite their individual members, and place the one no less than the other under the authority of the Law."[29] Kant made similar statements only to amend them out of existence once he came to consider the reality of such a federation. Rousseau does not modify his principle, as is made clear in the following quotation, every point of which is a contradiction of Kant's program for the pacific federation:

> The Federation [that is to replace the "free and voluntary association which now unites the States of Europe"] must embrace all the important Powers in its membership; it must have a Legislative Body, with powers to pass laws and ordinances binding upon all its members; it must have a coercive force capable of compelling every State to obey its common resolves whether in the way of command or of prohibition; finally, it must be strong and firm enough to make it impossible for any member to withdraw at his own pleasure the moment he conceives his private interest to clash with that of the whole body.[30]

It is easy to poke holes in the solution offered by Rousseau. The most vulnerable point is revealed by the questions: How could the federation enforce its law on the states that comprise it without waging war against them? and How likely is it that the effective force will always be on the side of the federation? To answer these questions Rousseau argues that the states of Europe are in a condition of balance sufficiently fine to prevent any one state or combination of states from prevailing over the others. For this reason, the necessary margin of force will always rest with the federation itself. The best critical consideration of the inherent weakness of a federation of states in which the law of the federation has to be enforced on the states who are its members is contained in the *Federalist Papers*. The arguments are convincing, but they need not be reviewed here. The practical weakness of Rousseau's recommended solution does not obscure the merit of his theoretical analysis of war as a consequence of international anarchy.

Conclusion

The third image, like the first two, leads directly to a utopian prescription. In each image a cause is identified in terms of which all others are to be understood. The force of the logical relation between the third image and the world-government prescription is great enough to cause some to argue not only the merits of world government but also the ease with which it can be realized.[31] It is of course true that with world government there would no longer be international wars, though with an ineffective world government there would no doubt be civil wars. It is likewise true, reverting to the first two images, that without the imperfections of the separate states there would not be wars, just as it is true that a society of perfectly rational beings, or of perfect Christians, would never know violent conflict. These statements are, unfortunately, as trivial as they are true. They have the unchallengeable quality of airtight tautologies: perfectly good states or men will not do bad things; within an effective organization highly damaging deviant behavior is not permitted. The near perfection required by concentration upon a single cause accounts for a number of otherwise puzzling facts: the pessimism of St. Augustine, the failure of the behavioral scientists as prescribers for peace, the reliance of many liberals on the forces of history to produce a result not conceivably to be produced by the consciously directed efforts of men, the tendency of socialists to identify a corrupting element every time harmony in socialist action fails to appear. It also helps to explain the often rapid alternation of hope and despair among those who most fully adopt a single-cause approach to this or to almost any other problem. The belief that to make the world better requires changing the factors that operate within a precisely defined realm leads to despair whenever it becomes apparent that changes there, if possible at all, will come slowly and with insufficient force. One is constantly defeated by the double problem of demonstrating how the "necessary changes" can be produced and of substantiating the assertion that the changes described as necessary would be sufficient to accomplish the object in view.

The contrary assertion, that all causes may be interrelated, is an argument against assuming that there is a single cause that can be isolated by analysis and eliminated or controlled by wisely constructed policy. It is also an argument against working with one or several hypotheses without bearing in mind the interrelation of all causes. The prescriptions directly derived from a single image are incomplete because they are based upon partial analyses. The partial quality of each image sets up a tension that drives one toward inclusion of the others. With the first image the direction of change, representing Locke's perspective as against Plato's, is from men to societies and states. The second image catches up both elements. Men make states, *and* states make men; but this is still a limited view. One is led to a search for the more inclusive nexus of causes, for states are shaped by the international environments. Most of those whom we have considered in preceding [sections] have not written entirely in terms of one image. That we have thus far been dealing with the consequences arising from differing degrees of emphasis accounts for the complexity of preceding [sections] but now makes somewhat easier the task of suggesting how the images can be interrelated without distorting any one of them.

The First and Second Images in Relation to the Third

It may be true that the Soviet Union poses the greatest threat of war at the present time. It is not true that were the Soviet Union to disappear the remaining states could easily live at peace. We have known wars for centuries; the Soviet Union has existed only for decades. But some states, and perhaps some forms of the state, are more peacefully inclined than others. Would not the multiplication of peacefully inclined states at least warrant the hope that the period

between major wars might be extended? By emphasizing the relevance of the framework of action, the third image makes clear the misleading quality of such partial analyses and of the hopes that are often based upon them. The act that by individual moral standards would be applauded may, when performed by a state, be an invitation to the war we seek to avoid. The third image, taken not as a theory of world government but as a theory of the conditioning effects of the state system itself, alerts us to the fact that so far as increasing the chances of peace is concerned there is no such thing as an act good in itself. The pacification of the Hukbalahaps was a clear and direct contribution to the peace and order of the Philippine state. In international politics a partial "solution," such as one major country becoming pacifistic, might be a real contribution to world peace; but it might as easily hasten the coming of another major war.

The third image, as reflected in the writings of Rousseau, is based on an analysis of the consequences arising from the framework of state action. Rousseau's explanation of the origin of war among states is, in broad outline, the final one so long as we operate within a nation–state system. It is a final explanation because it does not hinge on accidental causes—irrationalities in men, defects in states—but upon his theory of the framework within which *any* accident can bring about a war. That state A wants certain things that it can get only by war does not explain war. Such a desire may or may not lead to war. My wanting a million dollars does not cause me to rob a bank, but if it were easier to rob banks, such desires would lead to much more bank robbing. This does not alter the fact that some people will and some will not attempt to rob banks no matter what the law enforcement situation is. We still have to look to motivation and circumstance in order to explain individual acts. Nevertheless one can predict that, other things being equal, a weakening of law enforcement agencies will lead to an increase in crime. From this point of view it is social structure—institutionalized restraints and institutionalized methods of altering and adjusting interests—that counts. And it counts in a way different from the ways usually associated with the word "cause." What causes a man to rob a bank are such things as the desire for money, a disrespect for social proprieties, a certain boldness. But if obstacles to the operation of these causes are built sufficiently high, nine out of ten would-be bank robbers will live their lives peacefully plying their legitimate trades. If the framework is to be called cause at all, it had best be specified that it is a permissive or underlying cause of war.

Applied to international politics this becomes, in words previously used to summarize Rousseau, the proposition that wars occur because there is nothing to prevent them. Rousseau's analysis explains the recurrence of war without explaining any given war. He tells us that war may at any moment occur, and he tells us why this is so. But the structure of the state system does not directly cause state A to attack state B. Whether or not that attack occurs will depend on a number of special circumstances—location, size, power, interest, type of government, past history and tradition—each of which will influence the actions of both states. If they fight against each other it will be for reasons especially defined for the occasion by each of them. These special reasons become the immediate, or efficient, causes of war. These immediate causes of war are contained in the first and second images. States are motivated to attack each other and to defend themselves by the reason and/or passion of the comparatively few who make policies for states and of the many more who influence the few. Some states, by virtue of their internal conditions, are both more proficient in war and more inclined to put their proficiency to the test. Variations in the factors included in the first and second images are important, indeed crucial, in the making and breaking of periods of peace—the immediate causes of every war must be either the acts of individuals or the acts of states.

If every war is preceded by acts that we can identify (or at least try to identify) as cause, then why can we not eliminate wars by modifying individual or state behavior? This is the line of thinking followed by those who say: To end war, improve men; or: To end war, improve states. But in such prescriptions the role of the international environment is easily distorted. How can some of the acting units improve while others continue to follow their old and often predatory ways? The simplistic assumption of many liberals, that history moves relentlessly toward the millennium, is refuted if the international environment makes it difficult almost to the point of impossibility for states to behave in ways that are progressively more moral. Two points are omitted from the prescriptions we considered under the first and second images: (1) If an effect is produced by two or more causes, the effect is not permanently eliminated by removing one of them. If wars occur because men are less than perfectly rational and because states are less than perfectly formed, to improve only states may do little to decrease the number and intensity of wars. The error here is in identifying one cause where two or more may operate. (2) An endeavor launched against one cause to the neglect of others may make the situation worse instead of better. Thus, as the Western democracies became more inclined to peace, Hitler became more belligerent. The increased propensity to peace of some participants in international politics may increase, rather than decrease, the likelihood of war. This illustrates the role of the permissive cause, the international environment. If there were but two loci of cause involved, men and states, we could be sure that the appearance of more peacefully inclined states would, at worst, not damage the cause of world peace. Whether or not a remedy proposed is truly a remedy or actually worse than none at all depends, however, on the content and timing of the acts of all states. This is made clear in the third image.

War may result because state A has something that state B wants. The efficient cause of the war is the desire of state B; the permissive cause is the fact that there is nothing to prevent state B from undertaking the risks of war. In a different circumstance, the interrelation of efficient and permissive causes becomes still closer. State A may fear that if it does not cut state B down a peg now, it may be unable to do so ten years from now. State A becomes the aggressor in the present because it fears what state B may be able to do in the future. The efficient cause of such a war is derived from the cause that we have labeled permissive. In the first case, conflicts arise from disputes born of specific issues. In an age of hydrogen bombs, no single issue may be worth the risk of full-scale war. Settlement, even on bad grounds, is preferable to self-destruction. The use of reason would seem to require the adoption of a doctrine of "non-recourse to force." One whose reason leads him down this path is following the trail blazed by Cobden when in 1849 he pointed out "that it is almost impossible, on looking back for the last hundred years, to tell precisely what any war was about," and thus implied that Englishmen should never have become involved in them.[32] He is falling into the trap that ensnared A. A. Milne when he explained the First World War as a war in which ten million men died because Austria-Hungary sought, unsuccessfully, to avenge the death of one archduke.[33] He is succumbing to the illusion of Sir Edward Grey, who, in the memoirs he wrote some thirty years ago, hoped that the horrors of the First World War would make it possible for nations "to find at least one common ground on which they should come together in confident understanding: an agreement that, in the disputes between them, war must be ruled out as a means of settlement that entails ruin."[34]

It is true that the immediate causes of many wars are trivial. If we focus upon them, the failure to agree to settlement without force appears to be the ultimate folly. But it is not often true that the immediate causes provide sufficient explanation for the wars that have occurred. And if it is not simply particular disputes that produce wars, rational settlement of them cannot eliminate war. For, as Winston Churchill has written, "small matters are only the symptoms of the dangerous disease, and are only important for that reason. Behind them lie the interests, the passions and the destiny of mighty races of men; and long antagonisms express themselves in trifles."[35] Nevertheless Churchill may be justified in hoping that the fear induced by a "balance of terror" will produce a temporary truce. Advancing technology makes war more horrible and presumably increases the desire for peace; the very rapidity of the advance makes for uncertainty in everyone's military planning and destroys the possibility of an accurate estimate of the likely opposing forces. Fear and permanent peace are more difficult to equate. Each major advance in the technology of war has found its prophet ready to proclaim that war is no longer possible. Alfred Nobel and dynamite, for example, or Benjamin Franklin and the lighter-than-air balloon. There may well have been a prophet to proclaim the end of tribal warfare when the spear was invented and another to make a similar prediction when poison was first added to its tip. Unfortunately, these prophets have all been false. The development of atomic and hydrogen weapons may nurture the peace wish of some, the war sentiment of others. In the United States and else-where after the Second World War, a muted them of foreign-policy debate was the necessity of preventive war—drop the bomb quickly before the likely opponent in a future war has time to make one of his own. Even with two or more states equipped with similar weapon systems, a momentary shift in the balance of terror, giving a decisive military advantage temporarily to one state, may tempt it to seize the moment in order to escape from fear. And the temptation would be proportionate to the fear itself. Finally, mutual fear of big weapons may produce, instead of peace, a spate of smaller wars.

The fear of modern weapons, of the danger of destroying the civilizations of the world, is not sufficient to establish the conditions of peace identified in our discussions of the three images of international relations. One can equate fear with world peace only if the peace wish exists in all states and is uniformly expressed in their policies. But peace is the primary goal of few men or states. If it were the primary goal of even a single state, that state could have peace at any time—simply by surrendering. But, as John Foster Dulles so often warned, "Peace can be a cover whereby evil men perpetrate diabolical wrongs."[36] The issue in a given dispute may not be: Who shall gain from it? It may instead be: Who shall dominate the world? In such circumstances, the best course of even reasonable men is difficult to define; their ability always to contrive solutions without force, impossible to assume. If solutions in terms of none of the three images is presently—if ever—possible, then reason can work only within the frame-work that is suggested by viewing the first and second images in the perspective of the third, a perspective well and simply set forth in the *Federalist Papers,* especially in those written by Hamilton and Jay.

What would happen, Jay asks, if the thirteen states, instead of combining as one state, should form themselves into several confederations? He answers:

> Instead of their being "joined in affection" and free from all apprehension of different "interests," envy and jealousy would soon extinguish confidence and affection, and the partial interests of each confederation, instead of the general interests of all America, would be the only objects of their policy and pursuits. Hence, like most *bordering* nations, they would always be either involved in disputes and war, or live in the constant apprehension of them.[37]

International anarchy, Jay is here saying, is the explanation for international war. But not international anarchy alone. Hamilton adds that to presume a lack of hostile motives among states is to forget that men are "ambitious, vindictive, and rapacious." A monarchical state may go to war because the vanity of its king leads him to seek glory in military victory; a republic may go to war because of the folly of its assembly or because of its commercial interests. That the king may be vain, the assembly foolish, or the commercial interests irreconcilable: none of these is inevitable. However, so many and so varied are the causes of war among states that "to look for a continuation of harmony between a number of independent, unconnected sovereigns in the same neighborhood, would be to disregard the uniform course of human events, and to set at defiance the accumulated experience of the ages."[38]

Jay and Hamilton found in the history of the Western state system confirmation for the conclusion that among separate sovereign states there is constant possibility of war. The third image gives a theoretical basis for the same conclusion. It reveals why, in the absence of tremendous changes in the factors included in the first and second images, war will be perpetually associated with the existence of separate sovereign states. The obvious conclusion of a third-image analysis is that world government is the remedy for world war. The remedy, though it may be unassailable in logic, is unattainable in practice. The third image may provide a utopian approach to world politics. It may also provide a realistic approach, and one that avoids the tendency of some realists to attribute the necessary amorality, or even immorality, of world politics to the inherently bad character of man. If everyone's strategy depends upon everyone else's, then the Hitlers determine in part the action, or better, reaction, of those whose ends are worthy and whose means are fastidious. No matter how good their intentions, policy makers must bear in mind the implications of the third image, which can be stated in summary form as follows: Each state pursues its own interests, however defined, in ways it judges best. Force is a means of achieving the external ends of states because there exists no consistent, reliable process of reconciling the conflicts of interest that inevitably arise among similar units in a condition of anarchy. A foreign policy based on this image of international relations is neither moral nor immoral, but embodies merely a reasoned response to the world about us. The third image describes the framework of world politics, but without the first and second images there can be no knowledge of the forces that determine policy; the first and second images describe the forces in world politics, but without the third image it is imposible to assess their importance or predict their results.

Notes

1. Beverly Nichols, *Cry Havoc!* (New York: Doubleday, Doran & Co., 1933), 164.

2. Margaret E. Hirst, *The Quakers in Peace and War* (London: Swarthmore Press, 1923), 521–25.

3. Bertrand Russell, *Political Ideals* (New York: Century Co., 1917), p. 42. In one way or another the thought recurs in Lord Russell's many writings on international relations.

4. William James, "The Moral Equivalent of War," in *Memories and Studies* (New York: Longmans, Green and Co., 1912), 262–72, 290.

5. Jean Bodin, *Six Books of the Commonwealth,* abridged and trans. M. J. Tooley (Oxford: Basil Blackwell, n.d.), 168.

6. "Some Thoughts for the President's Consideration," Apr. 1, 1861, in *Documents of American History,* ed. Henry Steele Commager, 3d ed. (New York: F. S. Crofts & Co., 1946), 392.

7. Hans Herzfeld, "Bismarck und die Skobelewespisode," *Historische Zeitschrift* 142 (1930): 279–302.

8. Cf. Robert E. Sherwood, *Roosevelt and Hopkins* (New York: Harper and Brothers, 1948), 67–68, 102, 126, 133–36, 272, and esp. 931; and Secretary of State Hay's statement in Henry Adams, *The Education of Henry Adams* (New York: Book League of America, 1928), 374. Note that in this case the fault is one that is thought to decrease the ability of a country to implement a peaceful policy. In the other examples, the defect is thought to increase the propensity of a country to go to war.

9. Cf. Bertrand Russell, who in 1917 wrote: "There can be no good international system until the boundaries of states coincide as nearly as possible with the boundaries of nations" (*Political Ideals,* 146).

10. Frank H. Simonds and Brooks Emery, *The Great Powers in World Politics* (New York: American Book Co., 1939), passim; W. S. Thompson, *Danger Spots in World Population* (New York: Alfred A. Knopf, 1930), esp. the Preface and chaps. 1 and 13.

11. Cf. Vladimir Dedijer, "Albania, Soviet Pawn," *Foreign Affairs* 30 (1961): 104: Socialism, but not Soviet Union state capitalism, means peace.

12. Thucydides, *History of the Peloponnesian War,* trans. B. Jowett, 2d ed. (London: Oxford University Press, 1900), bk. 1, par. 23.

13. John Adams to the citizens of the town of Petersburg, Virginia, June 6, 1798, reprinted in the program for the visit of William Howard Taft, Petersburg, May 19, 1909.

14. Frederick S. Dunn, *Peaceful Change* (New York: Council on Foreign Relations, 1937), 13.

15. Richard Cobden, esp. *Speeches on Peace, Financial Reform, Colonial Reform and Other Subjects Delivered during 1849* (London: James Gilbert, n.d.), 135.

16. Jean Jacques Rousseau, *The Social Contract and Discourses,* trans. G.D.H. Cole, Everyman's Library

Edition (New York: E. P. Dutton and Co., 1950); see esp. *Inequality,* 234 ff.

17.   Ibid., 34.

18.   Benedict de Spinoza, *The Chief Works of Benedict de Spinoza,* trans. R.H.M. Elwes, 2 vols. (New York: Dover Publications, 1951), *Ethics,* pt. 4, prop. 35, proof.

19.   Rousseau, *The Social Contract and Discourses,* 135–36 (bk. 4, chap. 8), italics added. The word "equally" is necessary for and accurate rendering of the French text but does not appear in the translation, cited.

20.   Jean Jacques Rousseau, *A Lasting Peace through the Federation of Europe and the State of War,* trans. C. E. Vaughan (London: Constable and Co., 1917), 72.

21.   This parallels Hegel's formulation: "It is to what is by nature accidental that accidents happen, and the fate whereby they happen is thus a necessity" [G.W.F.] Hegel, *Philosophy of Right,* trans. T. M. Knox (Oxford: Clarendon Press, 1942), sec. 324.

22.   Kant is more willing to admit the force of this criticism than is generally realized.

23.   This is not, of course, to say that no differences in state behavior follow from the different constitutions and situations of states. This point raises the question of the relation of the third image to the second, which will be discussed below.

24.   Rousseau, *The Social Contract and Discourses,* 290–91.

25.   Rousseau, *A Lasting Peace,* 46–48, 58–59.

26.   Ibid., 38, 46–47. On p. 121, Rousseau distinguishes between the "state of war," which always exists among states, and war proper, which manifests itself in the settled intention to destroy the enemy state.

27.   Ibid., 49.

28.   In ibid., 69, Rousseau presents his exhaustive list of such causes.

29.   Ibid., 38–39.

30.   Ibid., 59–60.

31.   Cf. Karl Popper, *The Open Society and Its Enemies* (Princeton: Princeton University Press, 1950), 158–59; and William Esslinger, *Politics and Science* (New York: Philosophical Library, 1955), passim.

32.   Richard Cobden, *Speeches on Questions of Public Policy,* 2 vols., ed. John Bright and James E. Thorold Rogers (London: Macmillan & Co., 1870), 2: 165.

33.   A. A. Milne, *Peace and War* (New York: E. P. Dutton & Co., 1934), 11.

34.   Edward Grey, *Twenty-Five Years,* 2 vols. (New York: Frederick A. Stokes Co., 1925), 2: 285.

35.   Winston Churchill, *The World Crisis,* 1911–1914, 4 vols. (New York: Charles Scribner's Sons, 1923–29), 1: 52.

36.   "Excerpts from Dulles Address on Peace," Washington, D. C., Apr. 11, 1955, in *New York Times,* Apr. 12, 1955, 6.

37.   Alexander Hamilton, John Jay, and James Madison. *The Federalist* (New York: Modern Library, 1941), 23–24 (no. 5).

38.   Ibid., 27–28 (no. 6); cf. 18 (no. 4, Jay) and 34–40 (no. 7, Hamilton).

On Interpretive Understanding

MAX WEBER

Writing in the late-nineteenth and early-twentieth centuries, German sociologist Max Weber raised serious questions about objectivity in the social sciences—that what we know is based on interpretation of what we think we see. That knowledge in the social sciences depends upon interpretive understanding of the phenomena we observe—an insight that some apply to the natural sciences as well—is central to the discussion of theory in this chapter. Constructivism, feminism, postmodernism, and critical theory all emphasize this interpretive understanding we also find in Weber's writing. For their part, realism, liberalism, economic structuralism, and English-School rationalism are themselves framed by the images, standpoints, or perspectives that inform the way they approach international relations theory. We also find in the following piece references to the state as collective actor and the contexts within which human behavior takes place—insights that anticipate the levels of analysis that figure so prominently in present-day international relations theory.

Sociology (in the sense in which this highly ambiguous word is used here) is a science that attempts the interpretive understanding of social action in order thereby to arrive at a causal explanation of its course and effects. In "action" is included all human behavior when and insofar as the acting individual attaches a subjective meaning to it. Action in this sense may be either overt or purely inward or subjective; it may consist of positive intervention in a situation, or of deliberately refraining from such intervention or passively acquiescing in the situation. Action is social insofar as, by virtue of the subjective meaning attached to it by the acting individual (or individuals), it takes account of the behavior of others and is thereby oriented in its course. . . .

For the verifiable accuracy of interpretation of the meaning of a phenomenon, it is a great help to be able to put one's self imaginatively in the place of the actor and thus sympathetically to participate in that person's experiences, but this is not an essential condition of meaningful interpretation. Understandable and non-understandable components of a process are often intermingled and bound up together.

All interpretation of meaning, like all scientific observation, strives for clarity and verifiable accuracy of insight and comprehension. The basis for certainty in understanding can be either rational, which can be further subdivided into logical and mathematical, or it can be of an emotionally empathic or artistically appreciative quality. In the sphere of action things are rationally evident chiefly when we attain a completely clear intellectual grasp of the action-elements in their intended context of meaning. Empathic or appreciative accuracy is attained when, through sympathetic participation, we can adequately grasp the emotional context in which the action took place. . . .

The more we ourselves are susceptible to them the more readily can we imaginatively participate in such emotional reactions as anxiety, anger, ambition, envy, jealousy, love, enthusiasm, pride, vengefulness, loyalty, devotion, and appetites of all sorts, and thereby understand the irrational conduct that grows out of them. Such conduct is "irrational," that is, from the point of view of the rational pursuit of a given end. . . .

[Types of Understanding]

Understanding may be of two kinds: the first is the direct observational understanding of the subjective meaning of a given act as such, including verbal utterances. We thus understand by direct observation, in this sense, the meaning of the proposition 2 + 2 = 4 when we hear or read it. This is a case of the direct rational understanding of ideas. We also understand an outbreak of anger as manifested by facial expression, exclamations or irrational movements. This is direct observational understanding of irrational emotional reactions. We can understand in a similar observational way the action of a woodcutter or of somebody who reaches for the knob to shut a door or who aims a gun at an animal. This is rational observational understanding of actions.

Understanding may, however, be of another sort, namely explanatory understanding. Thus we understand in terms of motive the meaning an actor attaches to the proposition twice two equals four, when . . . we know that he is engaged in balancing a ledger or in making a scientific demonstration, or is engaged in some other task of which this particular act would be an appropriate part. This is rational understanding of motivation—placing the act in an intelligible and more inclusive context of meaning.

Thus we understand the chopping of wood or aiming of a gun in terms of motive in addition to direct observation if we know that the wood-chopper is working for a wage, or is chopping a supply of firewood for his own use, or possibly is doing it for recreation. But he might also be "working off" a fit of rage, an irrational case. Similarly we understand the motive of a person aiming a gun if we know that he has been commanded to shoot as a member of a firing squad, that he is fighting against an enemy, or that he is doing it for revenge. . . .

Finally, we have a motivational understanding of the outburst of anger if we know that it has been provoked by jealousy, injured pride, or an insult. . . . Thus for a science that is concerned with the subjective meaning of action, explanation requires a grasp of the complex of meaning in that an actual course of understandable action thus interpreted belongs. . . .

[Interpretations and Causal Explanations]

Every interpretation attempts to attain clarity and certainty, but no matter how clear an interpretation as such appears to be from the point of view of meaning, it cannot on this account alone claim to be the causally valid interpretation. On this level it must remain only a peculiarly plausible hypothesis. . . . In a large number of cases we know from experience it is not possible to arrive at even an approximate estimate of the relative strength of conflicting motives and very often we cannot be certain of our interpretation . . . [Indeed], a motive is a complex of subjective meaning that seems to the actor himself or to the observer an adequate ground for the conduct in question. . . .

Causal explanation depends on being able to determine that there is a probability, which in the rare ideal case can be numerically stated, but is always in some sense calculable, which a given observable event (overt or subjective) will be followed or accompanied by another event. A correct causal interpretation of a concrete course of action is arrived at when the overt action and the motives have both been correctly apprehended and at the same time their relation has become meaningfully comprehensible. . . .

It may . . . be convenient or even indispensable to treat social collectivities, such as states, associations, business corporations, foundations, as if they were individual persons. Thus they may be treated as the subjects of rights and duties or as the performers of legally significant actions. But for the subjective interpretation of action in sociological work these collectivities must be treated as solely the resultants and modes of organization of the particular acts of individual persons, since these alone can be treated as agents in a course of subjectively understandable action. . . .

Both in legal terminology and in everyday speech the term "state" is used both for the legal concept of the state and for the phenomena of social action to which its legal rules are relevant. . . . When reference is made in a sociological context to a "state," a "nation," a "corporation," a "family," or an "army corps," or to similar collectivities, what is meant is . . . only a certain kind of development of actual or possible social actions of individual persons. . . . It is the method of the so-called "organic" school of sociology to attempt to understand social

interaction by using as a point of departure the "whole" within which the individual acts. . . .

"Objectivity" in Social Science

There is no absolutely "objective" scientific analysis of culture – or . . . of "social phenomena". . . . In the social sciences we are concerned with psychological and intellectual phenomena the empathic understanding of which is naturally a problem of a specifically different type from those that the schemes of the exact natural sciences in general can or seek to solve. . . . We are concerned here not with "laws" in the narrower exact natural-science sense, but with adequate causal relations expressed in rules. . . . The establishment of such regularities is not the end but rather the means of knowledge. . . .

We are cultural beings, endowed with the capacity and the will to take a deliberate attitude toward the world and to lend it significance. . . . All knowledge of cultural reality, as may be seen, is always knowledge from particular points of view. When we require from the historian and social research worker as an elementary presupposition that they distinguish the important from the trivial and that they should have the necessary "point of view" for this distinction, we mean that they must understand how to relate the events of the real world consciously or unconsciously to universal "cultural values," and to select out those relations that are significant for us. . . .

Undoubtedly, all evaluative ideas are *subjective*. . . . The choice of the object of investigation and the extent or depth to which this investigation attempts to penetrate into the infinite causal web are determined by the evaluative ideas that dominate the investigator and his age. In the method of investigation, the guiding "point of view" is of great importance for the construction of the conceptual scheme that will be used in the investigation. In the mode of their use, however, the investigator is obviously bound by the norms of our thought just as much here as elsewhere. For scientific truth is precisely what is valid for all who seek the truth.

SUGGESTIONS FOR FURTHER READING

■ General

Art, Robert J., and Robert Jervis. *International Politics: Enduring Concepts and Contemporary Issues.* New York: HarperCollins, 1992.

Booth, Ken, and Steve Smith, eds. *International Relations Theory Today.* University Park: Pennsylvania State University Press, 1995.

Burchill, Scott et al. *Theories of International Relations.* 2nd ed. New York: Palgrave Macmillan, 2009.

Carlsnaes, Walter, Thomas Risse, and Beth A. Simmons. *Handbook of International Relations.* London: Sage Publications, 2002.

Cox, Michael, Ken Booth, and Tim Dunne, eds. *The Interregnum: Controversies in World Politics 1989–1999.* Cambridge: Cambridge University Press, 1999.

Crane, George T., and Abla Amawi. *The Theoretical Evolution of International Political Economy: A Reader.* New York: Oxford University Press, 1991, 1997.

Dougherty, James E., and Robert L. Pfaltzgraff, Jr. *Contending Theories of International Relations,* 4th ed. New York: Longman, 1997.

Doyle, Michael W., and G. John Ikenberry. *New Thinking in International Relations Theory.* Boulder, CO: Westview, 1997.

Elman, Colin, and Miriam Fendius Elman, eds. *Progress in International Relations Theory: Appraising the Field.* Cambridge, MA: MIT Press, 2003.

Ferguson, Yale H., and Richard W. Mansbach. "Between Celebration and Despair: Constructive Suggestions for Future International Theory." *International Studies Quarterly* 35, 4 (December 1991): 363–496.

_____. *The Elusive Quest: Theory and International Politics.* Columbia: University of South Carolina Press, 1988 and *The Elusive Quest Continues: Theory and Global Politics.* Upper Saddle River, NJ: Prentice Hall, 2003.

Griffiths, Martin. *Fifty Key Thinkers in International Relations.* London: Routledge, 1999.

Groom, A. J. R., and Margot Light, eds. *Contemporary International Relations: A Guide to Theory.* London: Pinter Publishers, 1994.

Hoffmann, Stanley. *Janus and Minerva: Essays in the Theory and Practice of International Politics.* Boulder, CO: Westview Press, 1987.

Hollis, Martin, and Steve Smith. *Explaining and Understanding International Relations.* Oxford, England: Clarendon Press, 1990.

Holsti, K. J. *The Dividing Discipline: Hegemony and Diversity in International Theory.* Boston: Unwin Hyman, 1995.

Kegley, Charles W., ed. *Controversies in International Relations Theory: Realism and the Neoliberal Challenge.* New York: St. Martin's, 1995.

Linklater, Andrew, ed. *International Relations: Critical Concepts in Political Science,* vols. I–V. London: Routledge, 2000.

Morgan, Patrick M. *Theories and Approaches to International Politics.* New Brunswick, NJ: Transaction Books, 1986.

Neuman, Stephanie G., ed. *International Relations Theory and the Third World.* New York: St. Martin's Press, 1998.

Neumann, Iver B., and Ole Weaver, eds. *The Future of International Relations.* London: Routledge, 1997.

Olson, William C., and A. J. R. Groom. *International Relations Then and Now: Origins and Trends in Interpretation.* London: HarperCollins, 1991.

Reus-Smit, Christian, and Duncan Snidal, eds. *The Oxford Handbook of International Relations.* Oxford: Oxford University Press, 2008.

Rothstein, Robert L. *The Evolution of Theory in International Relations.* Columbia: University of South Carolina Press, 1991.

Smith, Steve, Ken Booth, and Marysia Zalewski, eds. *International Theory: Positivism and Beyond.* Cambridge, England: Cambridge University Press, 1996.

Sullivan, Michael P. *Theories of International Relations: Transition vs. Persistence.* New York: Palgrave, 2001 and his earlier *Theories of International Relations: Theories and Evidence.* Englewood Cliffs, NJ: Prentice Hall, 1976.

Thompson, Kenneth W. *Schools of Thought in International Relations*. Baton Rouge: Louisiana State University Press, 1996.

Vasquez, John A. *Classics of International Relations*. 2nd ed. Upper Saddle River, NJ: Prentice Hall, 1986, 1990.

Waltz, Kenneth N. *Realism and International Politics*. New York and London: Routledge, 2008.

On History, Intellectual History, and International Relations

Carr, E. H. *What Is History?* Harmondsworth, England: Penguin Books, 1964.

Dunne, Michael Cox, and Ken Booth, eds. *The Eighty Years' Crisis: International Relations 1919–1999*. Cambridge: Cambridge University Press, 1998.

Howard, Michael. *The Lessons of History*. New Haven: Yale University Press, 1991.

Kauppi, Mark V., and Paul R. Viotti. *The Global Philosophers: World Politics in Western Thought*. Lanham, MD: Lexington Books/Rowman and Littlefield, 1992.

"Symposium: History and Theory." *International Security* 22, 1 (Summer 1997): 5–85.

PART 1

Images of International Relations

CHAPTER 2

Realism: The State and Balance of Power

MAJOR ACTORS AND ASSUMPTIONS

Realism is an image of international relations based on four principal assumptions. Scholars or policymakers who identify themselves as realists, of course, do not all perfectly match the realism ideal type. We find, however, that the four assumptions identified with this perspective are useful as a general statement of the main lines of realist thought and the basis on which hypotheses and theories are developed.

First, states are the principal or most important actors in an **anarchical** world lacking central legitimate governance. States represent the key **unit of analysis,** whether one is dealing with ancient Greek city-states or modern nation-states. The study of international relations is the study of relations among these units. Realists who use the concept of **system** defined in terms of interrelated parts usually refer to an international system of states. What of non-state actors? International organizations such as the United Nations may aspire to the status of independent actor, but from the realist perspective, this aspiration has not in fact been achieved to any significant degree. Realists tend to see international organizations as doing no more than its member states direct. Multinational corporations, terrorist groups, and other transnational and international organizations are frequently acknowledged by realists, but the position of these non-state actors is always one of lesser importance. States remain the dominant actors.

Second, the state is viewed as a unitary actor. For purposes of theory building and analysis, realists view the state as being encapsulated by a metaphorical hard shell or opaque, black box. We need not look much inside this shell or black box. A country faces the outside world as an integrated unit. Indeed, a common assumption associated with realist thought is that political differences within the state are ultimately resolved authoritatively such that the government of the state speaks with one voice for the state as a whole. The state is a unitary actor in that it is usually assumed by realists to have one policy at any given time on any particular issue. To be sure, exceptions occur, but to the realists these are exceptions that demonstrate the rule and that actually support the general notion of the state as an integrated, unitary actor.

Even in those exceptional cases in which, for example, a foreign ministry expresses views different from positions taken by the same country's defense ministry, corrective action is taken in an attempt to bring these alternative views to a common and authoritative statement of policy. "End running" of state authorities by bureaucratic and non-governmental, domestic, and transnational actors is also possible, but it occurs unchecked by state authorities in only those issues in which the stakes are low. From the realist perspective, if the issues are important enough, higher authorities will intervene to preclude bureaucratic end running or action by non-governmental actors that are contrary to centrally directed policy.

Third, given this emphasis on the unitary state-as-actor, realists usually make the further assumption for the purpose of theory building that the state is essentially a rational (or purposive) actor. A rational foreign policy decision-making process would include a statement of objectives, consideration of all feasible alternatives in terms of existing capabilities available to the state, the relative likelihood of attaining these objectives by the various alternatives under consideration, and the benefits or costs associated with each alternative. Following this rational process, governmental decisionmakers select the alternative that maximizes utility (maximizing benefit or minimizing cost associated with attaining the objectives sought) or at least achieves an acceptable outcome. The result is a rank ordering of policy preferences among viable alternatives.

As a practical matter, the realist is aware of the difficulties in viewing the state as a rational actor. Governmental decisionmakers may not have all the factual information or knowledge of cause and effect they need to make value-maximizing decisions. The process may well be clouded by considerable uncertainty as decisionmakers grope for the best solution or approach to an issue. They also have to deal with the problem of human bias and misperception that may lead them astray. In any event, the choice made—if not always the best or value-maximizing choice in fact—is at least perceived to be a satisfactory one. It is a **satisficing** or suboptimal choice—less than a value-maximizing choice, but still good enough in terms of the objectives sought. The assumption of the unitary, rational actor is particularly important in the application of **game theory** and other rational-choice methods to **deterrence,** arms control, balance-of-power, the use of force, and other studies of interest to realists.

Fourth, realists assume that within the hierarchy of issues facing the state, national or international security usually tops the list. Military and related political issues dominate world politics. A realist focuses on actual or potential conflict between state actors and the use of force, examining how international stability is attained or maintained, how it breaks down, the utility of force as a means to resolve disputes, and the prevention of any violation of its territorial integrity. To the realist, military security or strategic issues are sometimes referred to as "high politics," whereas economic and social issues typically are viewed as less important or "low politics." Indeed, the former is often understood to dominate or set the environment within which the latter occurs.

Given the state's objectives, goals, or purposes in terms of security, it seeks and uses **power** (commonly understood in material terms as capabilities relative to other states), which is a key concept to realists as is the **balance of power** among states. The structural realist (or neorealist) puts particular emphasis on the security implications of the distribution of power (or underlying structure) of the international system of states: unipolar (one great power), bipolar (two great powers), or multipolar (three or more great powers). States use the power they have to serve their interests or achieve their objectives. To most realists, the struggle for (or use of) power among states is at the core of international relations. In the words of Hans J. Morgenthau: "International politics, like all politics, is a struggle for power. Whatever the ultimate aims of international politics, power is always the immediate aim or means to an end."[1]

Further comment is necessary concerning assumptions two and three. The important point is that from the standpoint of **methodology,** the image of a unified, rational state is truly an assumption, not a description of the actual world. Realists use such assumptions to build theories, not describe reality. Assumptions should be viewed not in terms of descriptive accuracy, but rather in terms of how fruitful they are in generating insights and valid generalizations about international politics. From this point of view, assumptions are neither true nor false; they are more or less useful in helping the theorist derive testable propositions or hypotheses about international relations. Once hypotheses are developed, they are tested against the real world. The image of the unified, rational state is, therefore, the starting point for realist analysis, not a concluding statement. This is true whether one is a **classical realist** emphasizing the impact of history, international law, and actions taken by political leaders or a more recent **structural** or **neorealist** who believes the basis for a theory of international relations has to have at its core an understanding of the distribution of capabilities across states. Morgenthau, a classical realist, explained the utility of the rational, unitary actor assumption as follows:

> We put ourselves in the position of a statesman who must meet a certain problem of foreign policy under certain circumstances, and we ask ourselves what the rational alternatives are from which a statesman may choose . . . and which of these rational alternatives this particular statesman, acting under these circumstances, is likely to choose. It is the testing of this rational hypothesis against the actual facts and their consequences that gives meaning to the facts of international politics and makes a theory of politics possible.[2]

The point is that neorealist theorizing that focuses primarily on material structure (the distribution of power or capabilities) as the principal explanatory variable depends on the same rationalist assumptions as classical realists. This is despite the fact classical realists are more likely to accept such non-material factors as ideas or norms as part of the theories they develop.

Game theory would be a realist example of the use of such simplifying assumptions as an aid to developing hypotheses and theories about the causes of various international political phenomena. Many works on deterrence and **coercive diplomacy** (or "compellance") also use the rational, unitary actor assumptions as do other explanations of international conflict. The rationality assumption is similarly central to **expected utility models** of international politics. These and similar formulations comprise **rational-choice theorizing.** Not confined to realism, rational choice is also part of theorizing associated with the liberal (particularly neoliberal institutionalist) image discussed in Chapter Three.

As an image of politics, then, realism focuses on power and power politics among states. Neorealists such as Kenneth Waltz, John Mearsheimer, and Christopher Layne emphasize the overall distribution of power among states and are highly skeptical of the extent to which international norms and international institutions can ameliorate competition among states. Classical realists such as Morgenthau, E. H. Carr, and Arnold Wolfers and their present-day followers who could be termed **neoclassical realists** such as Randall Schweller, however, have had a more inclusive approach.[3] While recognizing the importance of balance of power, they also have argued for the serious consideration of how factors at the domestic or societal level of analysis influence international relations. Possible factors include whether a state is revisionist or status-quo oriented as well as the impact of norms and institutions. Hence, as with other images discussed in this book, an adherence to basic realist assumptions can still result in different interpretations and theoretical applications based on these assumptions.

Where did these assumptions of current realist thought come from? They obviously did not appear out of thin air following World War II, the Cold War, or the period since the al Qaeda attacks in 2001 on 9/11. Rather, they represent the culmination of thinking about international relations over the millennia, particularly the last five centuries. We now turn to some of the more notable intellectual precursors who have had a significant impact on the writings of contemporary realists.

INTELLECTUAL PRECURSORS AND INFLUENCES

◾ Thucydides

Thucydides (471–400 B.C.) is usually credited with being the first writer in the realist tradition as well as the founding father of the international relations discipline. Anyone who has taken a class in political philosophy would probably agree that the profound insights of many ancient Greek writers are not easily grasped on first reading. One might initially find this less a problem with Thucydides' *History of the Peloponnesian War* because this famous work chronicles twenty-one of the twenty-eight years of war between Athens and Sparta (and their respective allies) in the fifth century B.C. Taken simply as history, it is a masterful account of this era, filled with tales of heroism and brutality, victory and defeat, brilliance and stupidity, honor and deceit. These human traits are certainly exhibited not only in one particular war, but also in wars throughout the ages. This is what makes the work such a classic.

The task Thucydides set for himself, however, was much more ambitious than simply describing what was occurring. Particular events were dealt with in great and vivid detail, but his goal was to say something significant not only about the events of his own time, but also about the nature of war and why it continually recurs. For Thucydides, the past was the guide for the future. He was less interested in the immediate causes of the Peloponnesian War than he was in the underlying forces at work. Leaders might point to a particular event to justify a policy, but for Thucydides this simply obscured more profound factors that operate throughout history. At heart, for realists *The History of the Peloponnesian War* is a study of the struggle for military and political power.

Thucydides was younger than Socrates and Sophocles and older than Aristophanes. In 424 B.C., during the eighth year of the Peloponnesian War, he was elected an Athenian general. While stationed in Thrace, he failed to prevent the Spartan capture of a city and was punished with twenty years of exile. Athens might have lost a general, but the world gained an historian.

As a member of one of the more notable Athenian families, Thucydides spent the rest of the war observing events, traveling, and interviewing participants. As an exile, he was detached from yet obsessed with politics. Although concerned with accuracy, he gave precedence to understanding the motives and policies of the leaders on all sides of the conflict and used the technique of liberally reconstructing speeches and episodes. His purpose was to draw historical lessons for future statesmen who might read his work. By analyzing the particular, he hoped to illuminate the general.

Why did war break out between Athens and Sparta? Thucydides states:

> I propose first to give an account of the causes of complaint which they had against each other and of the specific instances where their interests clashed [i.e., the immediate causes of the war]: this is in order that there should be no doubt in anyone's mind about what led to this great war falling upon the Hellenes. But the real reason for the war is, in my opinion, most likely to be disguised by such argument. What made war inevitable was the growth of Athenian power and the fear which this caused in Sparta [i.e., this was the underlying cause of the war].[4]

Thus, according to Thucydides, the real or underlying cause of the war was *fear* associated with a shift in the balance of power. Sparta was afraid of losing its preeminent role in the Hellenic world and therefore took countermeasures to build up its military strength and enlist the support of allies. Athens responded in kind. In the ensuing analysis, the situations, events, and policies Thucydides described lend themselves to comparison with such familiar notions as arms races, deterrence, balance of power, alliances, diplomacy, strategy, concern for honor, and perceptions of strengths and weaknesses.

Thucydides' emphasis on fear as a cause of the Peloponnesian War, fear that resulted from the increase in Athenian power relative to that of Sparta, is echoed throughout history. As statesmen perceive the balance of power to be shifting in their disfavor, they make efforts to rectify the situation that in turn causes fear, suspicion, and distrust on the part of their rivals. One could quite easily substitute for Athens and Sparta other historical examples such as France and Britain in the seventeenth and eighteenth centuries, Napoleonic France and the rest of Europe in the early nineteenth century, Germany and Britain after the Franco-Prussian War of 1870, and the Soviet Union and the United States in the four decades following World War II. In all such historical examples, a good case can be made that fear is a dominant characteristic and a motivating factor for arms races and war itself.

One reason Thucydides is deemed a scholar of international relations, however, is that the cause of fear he identifies is not so much innate or basic human nature as it is the nature of interstate politics. Concerning a world in which no superordinate or central authority exists to impose order on all states (whether ancient city-states or modern states often encompassing large expanses of territory), Thucydides relates in a classic statement of **Realpolitik** how Athenians emphasized the overriding importance of power in such a world: "The strong [Athens] do what they have the power to do and the weak [the islanders on Melos] accept what they have to accept."[5] Put even more directly: the strong do what they will; the weak do what they must! Although fear may lead to war, power and capabilities relative to that of others determine the outcome.

Thucydides is sometimes unfairly criticized as an advocate of harsh and brutal wartime policies, one who rationalized such events as he described in the famous Melian dialogue. Thucydides, however, favored the democracy of the Golden Age of Pericles. In fact, the second half of *The History of the Peloponnesian War* is a description of the degeneration of Athenian democracy and the resulting fanaticism that turned the war from a defensive effort to a war of conquest. The Melian dialogue reflects the latter phase of the war and should not be viewed as a personal preference on the part of Thucydides.

Nevertheless, this classic does contain the essential ingredients of the realist perspective described by Thucydides in perhaps its boldest and most extreme form. The Athenians have no interest in whether the demands they make on the Melians are just or moral. It is their relative power and interest that matter. From reading Thucydides we learn quite a lot about the ancient world he knew—insights applicable today concerning honor, perception, neutrality, self-interest, alliances, balance of power, capabilities, and the uncertainty of power calculations.

Machiavelli

By his own admission, the Italian political philosopher Niccolò Machiavelli (1469–1527) drew heavily from his study of ancient, especially Roman, writings. In some respects, the situation in fifteenth- and sixteenth-century Italy, divided as the peninsula was into separate city-states, was similar to the Hellenic world of Thucydides. Machiavelli worked as a civil servant and diplomat until the Republic of Florence fell in 1512. Thought to be a republican counter-revolutionary opposed to the aristocratic Medici family that had assumed power in Florence (as well as in Rome), he was tortured by their interrogators. During his subsequent enforced idleness in a small town south of Florence (Santa Andrea in Percossina), he put his time to good use by reflecting on the chaos and political instability among the Italian city-states influenced as well by French and Spanish interventions.

Like Thucydides, Machiavelli wrote of power, balance of power, formation of alliances and counteralliances, and the causes of conflict between different city-states. His primary focus, however, was on what present-day writers refer to as national security. For Machiavelli, survival of the state (identified with the ruling prince) was paramount. The prince could lose his state by not coping effectively with both internal and external threats to his rule. The German term *Realpolitik,* so central to realist thought, refers to power and power politics among states. Machiavelli's most famous work, *The Prince,* is a practical manual on how to gain, maintain, and expand power. It is dedicated to the ruler of Florence at that time, Lorenzo di Medici.

One of the more controversial parts of Machiavelli's thesis is the notion that the security of the state is so important that it may justify certain acts by the prince that would be forbidden to other individuals not burdened by the princely responsibility of assuring that security. The end—security of the state—is understood to justify any means necessary to achieve that end. Machiavellianism (or Machiavellism) has been condemned by many who consider such a view to be immoral. In fact, Machiavelli never wrote that "the end justifies the means." What he did write was *"si guarda al fine"*—that in decisions and actions the prince should look for or anticipate consequences—wise counsel it would seem, but by no means an assertion that the end justifies any means as he has customarily been (mis)interpreted.

Drawing from Machiavelli, Max Weber and others have argued that the actions of statesmen do (or should) follow a code of conduct different from that of the average citizen. Thus, it has been observed that there are two separate and distinct ethics: first, conventional religious morality concerned with such matters as individual salvation (the ethics of ultimate ends) and, second, by contrast, the moral obligations of rulers who must take actions to provide for national security (the ethics of responsibility).

Following this interpretation, one can understand Machiavelli's view that rulers should be good if they can (good or harmless in the conventional sense) but be willing to cause harm *if necessary* (consistent with their obligations as rulers). Indeed, princes put soldiers in harm's way when they go into battle and these soldiers, in turn, wreak harm upon their adversaries. Machiavelli expressed such choices as invoking *male* (pronounced mah-leh)—the Italian word used to describe evil, harm or negative consequences associated in this context with the decisions and actions of princes.

Although a prince may not wish to be hated, Machiavelli argues "it is much safer to be feared than to be loved, if one must choose." Although the prince may be criticized for being harsh, this is acceptable to Machiavelli so long as the prince keeps his subjects united and loyal. These are the sorts of arguments that have given Machiavellianism a negative connotation, but followers of Machiavelli would respond that the ultimate goal meant to justify particular policies is the security of the state (and its people), not just the security of an individual ruler.

Machiavelli wrote of the world as it *is,* not the world as it *should* or *ought* to be. That is why modern political theorists refer to him as a realist. Ethics or moral norms and the real-world politics he observed are in separate domains. His advice to the prince, following this interpretation, was based on an analysis of history, and of what actually occurs in the political realm, not on abstract ethical principles:

> Many have imagined republics and principalities that have never been seen or known to exist in reality; for how we live is so far removed from how we ought to live, that he who abandons what is done for what ought to be done, will rather learn to bring about his own ruin than his preservation. A man who wishes to make a profession of goodness in everything must necessarily come to grief among so many who are not good.[6]

This is not so much an endorsement of human behavior in politics as it is a statement of what he understands it actually to be. For Machiavelli, in an amoral (if not immoral) world, what meaning, after all, does the preaching of conventional morality have? Indeed, an extreme statement of realist thinking is that considerations of power and power politics are the *only* relevant factors.

In the present-day world, a convenient way to discredit an opponent is to accuse him or her of being Machiavellian. Nevertheless, it must be emphasized that Machiavelli did not encourage rulers to engage in harmful activity or use violence for its own sake. In numerous passages, he advises the prince not to be needlessly cruel because this may eventually undermine his rule. The yardstick one should use is how a particular policy contributes to the security and stability of the state. Indeed, as reading the last few chapters of *The Prince* makes clear, Machiavelli's prescription for Italian security was to be found in unifying the country, thus not only avoiding armed conflict among cities and alliances of cities against one another, but also dissuading interventions or attacks by outside powers, namely France and Spain.

Isn't it interesting that this was the same prescription for American security we find in John Jay's and Alexander Hamilton's *Federalist Papers* 1-9 and later in George Washington's farewell address? The thesis they argued was that unity among the thirteen states under the proposed U.S. Constitution was essential to avoiding war among them and also to securing themselves against invasion by either Britain or Spain. Their concerns proved to have merit: unity helped repel the British in the war of 1812 and failing to keep unity in 1861 resulted in civil war (or war between two coalitions of states).

Hobbes

The political philosophy of the Englishman Thomas Hobbes (1588–1679) was developed during the first fifty turbulent years of the seventeenth century. After attending university in Oxford, Hobbes became a tutor to the son of a nobleman, and throughout his life he remained associated with the family. Identified as a Royalist in a struggle between parliamentarians and the crown, Hobbes left for France in 1641 at a time when Parliament was asserting its power against the monarchy. For three years, he tutored the son of Charles I, the latter eventually being executed in 1649 during the English civil war. Publishing his famous work *Leviathan,* Hobbes returned to England in 1651, pledging loyalty to the newly established republican or parliamentary regime. Indeed, marking the end of divine right of kings, *Leviathan*—the first general theory of politics in English—provided that either a monarch or an assembly (i.e., parliament) could be tasked by the people to assure their security as the primary responsibility of government.

Like Machiavelli, Hobbes had a pessimistic view of human nature. He was informed by his own life experiences. As with others, his life and safety were in jeopardy in the 1640s during the English civil war. In comments to others, he was known frequently to remark: "Fear and I were born twins!" The reference was to his whole life beset by the turmoil of English politics, beginning with his premature birth in 1588 due to the trauma his mother apparently suffered in fear of a Spanish invasion, which was blunted only by English good fortune in its naval battle against Spain—sinking the armada of ships that had been assembled off English shores.

His primary focus in *Leviathan* was domestic politics, and his goal was to make the strongest case possible for the necessity of a powerful, centralized political authority. To illustrate his philosophical points, Hobbes posited that prior to the creation of society, human beings lived in a "state of nature"—a condition of war of "every one against every one." There was in this state of war "a continual fear and danger of violent death; and the life of man, solitary, poor, nasty, brutish, and short."[7]

Hobbes did not argue that such a state of nature had ever really existed. To him, the state of nature was the result of a thought experiment—imagining what the world would be like without governmental authority or any other social structure. Accordingly, he was interested in showing how people could escape from this hypothetical situation—a state of war of everyone against everyone else—by agreeing to place all power in the hands of a sovereign or Leviathan (a state authority, or supreme ruler, either a monarch or parliament) that would end the anarchy of the state of nature, using power to maintain order so essential to daily life. If governmental authority did not already exist, it would have to be created. In his words: "There must be some coercive power to compel men equally to the performance of their covenants, by the terror of some punishment, greater than the benefit they expect by the breach of their covenant."[8] Without order, he argued, civilization and all its benefits are impossible—no economic development, art, knowledge, or anything else of value.

Hobbes's impact on the realist view of international relations stems from an image of states as if they were individuals in a mythical state of nature. Although his focus in *Leviathan* is on domestic societies, his observations are also relevant to international politics and have had a major impact on realism, particulary his assessment of why conflict and violence between individuals or states are to be expected. In the absence of a sovereign or central, superordinate authority, the anarchic world described by Hobbes is a rather dismal one.

Because in international politics as in the state of nature there is no Leviathan or superordinate authority with power to impose order, we find a condition of **anarchy.** For survival, states are left to their own devices in a world in which each state claims to be **sovereign,** each with a right to be independent or autonomous with respect to one another. In Hobbes's words:

> In all times, kings, and persons of sovereign authority, because of their independency, are in continual jealousies, and in the state and posture of gladiators; having their weapons pointing, and

their eyes fixed on one another; that is, their forts, garrisons, and guns upon the frontiers of their kingdoms; and continual spies upon their neighbours; which is a posture of war.[9]

As anarchy prevails in the state of nature, so too is anarchy a dominant characteristic of international politics. In such a world states use power to make their way. Power politics complete with alliances and counter-alliances are the order of the day. Without a Leviathan (or, in the language of contemporary international relations literature, a *hegemonic* power or world state that can maintain order), suspicion, distrust, conflict, and war are seemingly inevitable. There being "no common power"—the absence of any **social contract** among (or authority over) them—states must fend for themselves.

As with Machiavelli's understandings, this rather negative image of international politics offered by Hobbes is central to realist thought. We also find power and balance-of-power politics framed in Machiavellian or Hobbesean terms in English School (see Chapter Five) writings as one source of order in international or world society. This, however, is complemented by the rules states find or make to govern their conduct—a perspective one sees prominently in the writings of Hugo Grotius, the "father" of international law.

■ Grotius

Indeed, Hugo Grotius (1583–1645), a Dutch contemporary of Thomas Hobbes, offered a different view of international relations from that associated with Hobbes and Machiavelli. We also take up Grotian thought in some detail in Chapter Five on the English School. Grotius dealt with the essential anarchy of international relations by calling for the establishment (or acknowledging the existence) of laws or rules accepted by states as binding. That the relations of states *ought* to conform to such rules is a central tenet of the Grotian tradition in international relations. To Grotians, values or norms, particularly when recognized as international law, are important in maintaining order among states.

Grotius dealt with the problems of international relations (including commercial transactions) from a very practical point of view. Given the importance of trade to his native Holland as a seafaring nation, he addressed this subject in his *Law of Prize and Booty* (1604–1605) and questions of freedom of navigation and territorial seas in his *Freedom of the Seas* (1609). Probably his most important work was his *Law of War and Peace* (1625), three volumes that dealt with war and questions of national security—central themes in much realist writing then and now. Grotius has a place alongside Thucydides, Machiavelli, and Hobbes in classical realist thought, although less so in neorealist or structural realist understandings that see international law and global norms or rules as secondary to, or informed by, system structure or the distribution of power among states. Put another way, structural realists put more stock in Hobbes (as in Machiavelli and Thucydides) than in Grotius.

What are the sources of international law? Grotius looked to the use of reason and the "natural law" for general principles. He also looked to customary practice and to rules agreed on by governments that would be binding on states. Such treaties or formal covenants would be binding (in Latin, *pacta sunt servanda*) in the sense that states are obligated to follow them even in the absence of central authority to enforce their adherence. Changing circumstances might lead to the alteration of rules, but the important point is that to Grotians (and many classical realists) order in international relations and matters of war and peace to include commerce involve both power *and* values. In this regard, this Grotian emphasis on norms and laws leads many liberals and neoliberal institutionalists to claim him as one of their own as do those in the English School. For them, the term **rationalist** owes much to rule-oriented, Grotian thought.

Clausewitz

Carl von Clausewitz (1780–1831), a Prussian officer who rose to the rank of general and who served in the Napoleonic wars, thought the military element of a state's power to be extremely important but subordinate always to the political. Consistent with the writings of Machiavelli on war, Clausewitz argued in an oft-quoted phrase that war is "a continuation of political activity by other means." War or the use of force is thus a *means* policy makers may choose rationally to accomplish their state objectives; it decidedly is not an *end* in itself.

Much of Clausewitz's writing took place in the interwar period between the defeat of Napoleon in 1815 and Clausewitz's recall to duty in 1830 for service in East Prussia. Clausewitz died in 1831, never having completed his major work, *On War*. His legacy, nevertheless, remains a central contribution to the realist school thanks to the successful efforts of his wife to publish the manuscript.

The use of force in battle aims to destroy or substantially weaken the war-making capability of an adversary, which undermines (or precludes) the will to continue fighting. Leadership is important, and the commander is crucial in this essentially rational enterprise, adapting to changing circumstances and employing such principles as surprise, mass, and concentration of forces. Attacks effectively directed to an enemy's "center of gravity" (however this may be defined in operational terms) can cause an enemy's capability to collapse. Because one's own military forces are necessarily finite, one is not wasteful in their use—an economy of force essential to sustaining military capabilities against an adversary.

Just as Machiavelli referred to *fortuna* and Thucydides to fate as blunting even the best-laid plans of the prince, Clausewitz identifies the uncertainty that attends decision making in battlefield conditions—the "fog of war." He was also well aware that rationally made plans often run into obstacles or "friction" when actually implemented. He is cautionary when he warns that one ought not take the first step into war without realizing where the last step may lead. These are the kinds of observations one readily finds in present-day strategic literature in the realist genre that owes much to Clausewitz. As significant as his view that the military is properly a political means was his exposition of societal (including social and economic) dimensions of national capabilities. At the same time, his focus on national security problems places him in the mainstream of present-day realist thought.

Carr

Many students of international relations consider Edward Hallett Carr's *The Twenty Years' Crisis, 1919–1939* a classic. Although Carr can be viewed as an intellectual precursor for realists and, as we note in Chapter Five, a forerunner of the present-day English School, his work transcends narrow classification in that he has also been influential, as has Grotius, on the thinking of certain authors whom we would label liberals or neoliberal institutionalists.

The writings of Thucydides, Machiavelli, Hobbes, Grotius, and Clausewitz illustrate how great works are often written during the most difficult times. *The Twenty Years' Crisis* is no exception in that it was completed in the summer of 1939 with the shadow of war looming over Europe. As with other authors we have discussed, Carr was less interested in apportioning blame to particular leaders for the imminent onset of World War II than he was in attempting "to analyse the underlying and significant, rather than the immediate and personal, causes of the disaster." Unless this were done, he argued, we would fail to understand how war could break out twenty short years after the signing of the Versailles Treaty in 1919. He dedicated his book "to the makers of the coming peace." In attempting to understand "the more profound causes of the contemporary international crisis," echoes of Thucydides can be discerned. Carr, for example, placed a great deal of emphasis on the role of fear in explaining World War I.

Throughout *The Twenty Years' Crisis,* Carr refers to the impact of Machiavelli and Hobbes on realist thinking. Although his work is best known as a critique of **utopian** or **idealist** thought, Carr also challenges the more extreme versions of realism that posit the divorce of morality from politics in international relations. He argues that sound political thought must be based on elements of both utopia (i.e., values) and reality (i.e., power). Where utopianism has become a "hollow and intolerable sham," serving merely as a disguise for the privileged, the realist provides a service in exposing it. Pure realism, on the other hand, can offer nothing but "a naked struggle for power which makes any kind of international society impossible." Hence, for Carr, politics is made up of two elements, inextricably intertwined: utopia and reality—values and power.

Consistent with classical-realist understandings that go beyond just power and interest, more than a third of the book is devoted to such Grotian topics as the role of morality in international relations, the foundations of law, the sanctity of treaties, the judicial settlement of international disputes, peaceful change, and the prospects for a new international order. Because Carr critically estimated the strengths and weaknesses of utopianism as well as realism, he can be viewed as an important influence on many contemporary international relations theorists, both realists and non-realists.

◼ Morgenthau

Hans J. Morgenthau (1904–1980) remains one of the most influential IR theorists. Born in Germany, he fled to the United States when the Nazis came to power. While he was a professor at the University of Chicago, his 1948 publication, *Politics Among Nations,* has been viewed by some as a tutorial for post-World War II American statesmen who now led a country of preeminent international power and which could no longer seriously contemplate isolationism from the rest of the world.

Morgenthau posited six principles of political realism: (1) "politics, like society in general, is governed by objective laws that have their roots in human nature"; (2) in international politics, "interest [is] defined in terms of power"; (3) interest defined as power is not endowed with a meaning that is fixed once and for all: "the kind of interest determining political action depends on the political and cultural context within which foreign policy is formulated"; (4) there is "tension between the moral command and the requirements of successful political action," but that as a practical matter "universal moral principles . . . must be filtered through the concrete circumstances of time and place"; (5) "political realism refuses to identify the moral aspirations of a particular nation [such as the United States] with the moral laws that govern the universe"; and (6) "interest defined as power" is an understanding that gives international politics a separate standing and thus emancipates it from other fields of study.[10] Following from this perspective, some scholars give Morgenthau credit, among others, for helping establish the legitimacy of international relations as a separate discipline within political science—and not just a part of history, international law, or philosophy.

This brief overview of the intellectual precursors of contemporary realism illustrates a distinct realist preoccupation with armed conflict or war. A concern with the causes and consequences of conflict helps to explain why the realist perspective is held by statesmen throughout the world: over the centuries leaders have engaged in the very battles and struggles described by authors from Thucydides to Morgenthau. Realism, from the statesman's point of view, is indeed realistic as it tends to correspond to personal experiences both in diplomacy and in war.

Among realists, there are two basic concepts that traditionally have been the foci of analysis at the state and international levels: **power** and **system** in which states are the principal actors. In the following pages, we discuss how realists have attempted to define these terms. We then give examples of how theorists have used these concepts in generating insights and explanations of the causes of war. This is followed by a discussion of how realists deal with the concepts of globalization, interdependence, and change. We conclude with a critique of the realist image of international relations.

POWER

Definitions

In our discussion of several of the more important intellectual precursors of realism, the concept of **power** was mentioned time and again. Any attempt to give the reader a more complete understanding of the realist image of international relations starts with a discussion of this crucial term. Power is *the* core concept for realists.

Having said this, it is rather ironic that even among realists, there is no clear consensus on how to define the term *power*. Some realists understand power to be the sum of military, economic, technological, diplomatic, and other capabilities at the disposal of the state. Others see power not as some absolute value determined for each state as if it were in a vacuum but, rather, as capabilities *relative* to the capabilities of other states. Thus, the power of the United States is evaluated in terms of its capabilities relative to the capabilities of other states.

Both of these definitions—whether treating capabilities of a state in isolation or relative to the capabilities of other states—are termed a **materialist** view. Both also assume a static view of power: it is an attribute of the state that is the sum of its capabilities whether considered alone or relative to other states. An alternative, dynamic definition of power focuses on the interactions of states. A state's influence (or capacity to influence or coerce) is not only determined by its capabilities (or relative capabilities) but also by (1) its willingness (and perceptions by other states of its willingness) to use these capabilities and (2) its control or influence over other states. Power can thus be inferred by observing the behavior of states as they interact. The relative power of states is most clearly revealed by the outcomes of their interactions.

Examples of diverse views of power are the following definitions drawn from the literature: power as the capacity of an individual, group, or nation "to influence the behavior of others in accordance with one's own ends," power as "man's control over the minds and actions of other men," and power as "the ability to prevail in conflict and overcome obstacles." Joseph Nye differentiates between *hard power* as in economic or military capabilities and the *soft power* that comes, for example, from cultural dimensions or the values that define the identity and practices of a state to include the diplomatic capacity to influence other states bilaterally or multilaterally in international organizational contexts. (see his article at the end of this chapter). Others prefer not to dissect it in this fashion, but rather to view power as an integral concept that states apply in different ways in the pursuit of their goals or objectives in international relations.

▮ Measurement

Given these definitional and conceptual disputes, it follows that attempts to measure power will also be divergent for those hoping to apply scientific standards to their work. First, if one understands power as being equivalent to capabilities, one looks for some way to measure military, economic, and other component elements. Even if one assumes that it is possible to measure these capabilities adequately through such indicators as defense expenditures or gross national product, the further problem remains of aggregating or adding up such diverse capabilities into a common measure of power. How can one combine different component capabilities that use different measures such as dollars spent on defense expenditures as opposed to overall gross national product? Even more challenging is how does one measure geographic, technological, or diplomatic factors with any degree of precision? What about the unity and strength of a society? What is the metric? And, if capabilities are difficult to measure, are not *relative* capabilities between and among states even more difficult to specify?

Second, some would say that the view of power as a unitary concept calculated by aggregating component capabilities or relative capabilities misses the key point, which is that the power of a state is dependent on the issue involved. Consider, for example, the argument that some states, such as Japan, have substantial economic power but are militarily weak. Hence, in a particular area, the Japanese are powerful. Conceiving of world politics in terms of separate issue areas or, in the words of Stanley Hoffmann, alternative "chessboards," is one example of awareness among realists of the importance to the state of socioeconomic and other non-military issues. In some respects, Joseph Nye's more recent use of *soft* and *hard power* is a corollary or extension of Hoffmann's observations that use of power by states varies by issue area (his metaphor of states acting differently depending on which chessboard it was engaged).[11] For Nye, "smart power" is the effective combination in policymaking of the hard and soft components he identifies.

Opponents of this disaggregation of power into its component capabilities note that persuasive as it may be on the surface, it is misleading because it overlooks the relations among the various power components. Thus, the economic capabilities of Japan as a global trader are said to be related to its military ties with the United States that assure Japan's freedom to engage in commerce. From this perspective, whether addressing the power of Japan, Europe, or Third World countries, one cannot understand economic, military, political, or other component capabilities of power as if they were factors independent of one another. Much as military ties and divisions among states may define the framework within which economic relations take place, so military capabilities of states are bolstered (or weakened) by the strength or relative strength of their economies.

SYSTEM

In the preceding section, we discussed the concept of power and attempts to measure state power. Using that discussion as a basis, we now move on to a discussion of the concept of **system.** Not all realists portray relations among states in systemic terms, but some (particularly neo- or structural realists) do. When applied to international relations, the term *system* has currency within each of the four images we have identified—realism, liberalism, economic structuralism, and the English School. As one might expect, however, there is considerable diversity among theorists on both the definition of the term and the uses to which it should be put in the construction of international relations theory.

Scholars who understand system to be the set of interactions among states operate from a behavioral methodology. This approach was dominant in the 1960s and 1970s as efforts were made to count, track, and code interactions among states in the hope of identifying patterns of conflict and cooperation. Journals such as *International Studies Quarterly* continue to publish research in this tradition, emphasizing studies that attempt to draw meaning from aggregate numbers and data sets which are amenable to mathematical equations.

Over the past thirty years, however, realist scholars identified as structural or neorealists have argued that counting interactions has provided limited insights on international relations. A more useful starting point, they argue, is the various distributions of power or capabilities among states—unipolar, bipolar, multipolar. The polarity of the system is measured by the number of major powers, and different polarity will have different effects on international relations, including interactions among states.

However *system* may be defined, the uses to which the concept is put vary considerably. Some theorists are content to use systems merely as **taxonomies,** frameworks for organizing knowledge about international relations. Hence one can speak of the international political system, the international economic system, or the international social system. Systems are therefore mental images that may help to describe international phenomena. They are, in effect, superimposed on the real world by a scholar in order to make the real world more intelligible or somewhat easier to understand.

Others are more ambitious and use the system concept to explain and predict outcomes of international relations. In the process of theory building, they may ascribe to systems such properties as equilibrium, or balance, of their component parts (such as among states). Critics, however, find little use in such notions as balancing or "equilibrating tendencies" allegedly to be found in a system of states. The approach of treating a system as if it were a concrete or tangible entity and ascribing properties to it is of questionable validity from this point of view. To do so, according to critics, is to be guilty of the methodological error of **reification**—treating abstractions as if they were real and had a life of their own.

A response by some system theorists to this line of criticism is that dealing in abstractions is useful in the generation of propositions or hypotheses about international relations. These, in turn, can be tested empirically to determine whether or not they have factual support. To the extent, then, that use of the systems concept enables the theorist to describe, explain, or predict international phenomena, the use of the concept is justified.

The reader may or may not wish to visualize international relations or world politics as a system that is defined in terms of patterns of interactions, polarity, equilibrating tendencies, or some other characteristics. Some may share the English School preference for seeing international or global politics as actually occurring in a societal (rather than in a seemingly more mechanical, systemic) context. We do note, however, that the systems concept as an approximation to the nature of world politics is present within the mainstream of contemporary realist thought, even if some (particularly classical) realists avoid its use.

Speaking of abstractions, we admit this discussion has been rather abstract. To lend substance to the concept of system, we next examine the way in which the concept of system has been used by some realists: system as anarchy plus the distribution of capabilities. The intention of scholars has been to explain some aspect of international relations concerning such matters as instability, conflict, and war. In keeping with realist assumptions, the state and state power have been a key focus of analysis and investigation as well as has the analytical assumption of rationality.

■ Game Theory and Anarchy

Game theory is an approach to determining rational choice or optimum strategy in a competitive situation. Each actor tries to maximize gains or minimize losses under conditions of uncertainty and incomplete information which requires each actor to rank order preferences, estimate probabilities, and try to discern what the other actor is going to do. In a two-person zero-sum game, what one competitor wins, the other loses. In a two-person, non-zero-sum or variable sum game, gains and losses are not necessarily equal; it is possible that both sides may gain. This is sometimes referred to as a positive-sum game. In some games, both parties can lose, and by different amounts or to a different degree. So-called *n*-person games include more than two actors or sides. Game theory has contributed to the development of models of deterrence and arms race spirals, but it is also the basis for work concerning the question of how collaboration among competitive states can be achieved: The central problem is that the rational decision for an individual actor such as a state may be to "defect" and go it alone as opposed to taking a chance on collaboration with another state actor.

For many realist writers, game theory is highly relevant to understanding international relations due to the realist emphasis on the conditions of **anarchy** and the distribution of capabilities or power among states. These so-called system-level, structural attributes are viewed as crucial because they act as constraints on decisionmakers. As we will see, the condition of international anarchy is seen by realists as contributing to the amount of distrust and conflict among states. Realists have also been concerned whether particular distributions of capabilities involving various balances of power make war between states more or less likely. We will first take up the concept of anarchy and related terms.

The word *anarchy* brings forth images of violence, destruction, and chaos. For realists, however, anarchy simply refers to the absence of any legitimate authority above states. States are sovereign. They claim a right externally to be independent or autonomous from other states, and they claim a right internally or domestically to exercise complete authority over their own territories. Although states differ in terms of the power they possess or are able to exercise, none may claim the *right* to dominate another sovereign state.

Realists distinguish between *authority* and *power*. When they use the term *anarchy,* they are referring to the absence of any hierarchy of legitimate authority in the international system. There *is* hierarchy of power in international politics, but there is not a hierarchy of authority. Some states are clearly more powerful than others, but there is no recognized authority higher than that of any state.

Anarchy, so understood, is the defining characteristic of the environment within which sovereign states interact. Violence and war may be evident, but so too are periods of relative peace and stability. This absence of any superordinate or central authority over states (such as a world government with authority to enforce rules and to maintain order) is fundamentally different from domestic societies, where an authority exists to maintain order and to act as an arbiter of disputes except in cases of total government collapse or in civil wars when legitimate authority may be unclear.

Realists argue that the absence of a central and overriding authority helps to explain why states come to rely on power, seeking to maintain or increase their power positions relative to other states. For one thing, the condition of anarchy is usually accompanied by a lack of trust among states in this environment. Each state faces a **self-help** situation in which it is dangerous to place the security of one's own country in the hands of another. What guarantee is there against betrayal, however solemn another state's promises may be to an ally? Consistent with the world described by Hobbes, there is really nothing to keep a supposed ally from reneging on a security agreement or any other international pact. There is no world governmental authority to enforce covenants or agreements among states. In such a world, it is logical, rational, and prudent to look out for number one—the security of one's own state. Indeed, this was the same counsel reported by Thucydides when he noted Athenian advice to the Melians not to place their hope for survival in the hands of the Spartans and their allies.

Given international anarchy and the lack of trust in such a situation, states find themselves in what has been called a **security dilemma.**[12] The more one state arms to protect itself from other states, the more threatened these states become and the more prone they are to resort to arming themselves to protect their own national security interests. The dilemma is that even if a state is sincerely arming only for defensive purposes, it is rational in a self-help system to assume the worst in an adversary's intentions and keep pace in any arms buildup. How can one know for certain that a rival is arming strictly for defensive purposes? This is the stuff of arms races. Isn't it best to hedge one's bets by devoting more resources to match a potential adversary's arms buildup? Because a state may not have sufficient resources to be completely self-reliant, it may join an alliance in an attempt to deter aggression by any would-be adversaries.

Given an understanding of the anarchic condition of international politics, one can more easily grasp the game-theoretic dynamics of arms races. All sides involved may sincerely desire peace, but the anarchical nature of international politics leads states to be suspicious of one another and engage in worst-case analyses of one another's intentions. This realist insight, it is argued, is just as applicable to understanding the ancient competition between Sparta and Athens as it is to understanding contemporary international relations. It is a system-level explanation in that the emphasis is placed on the anarchic structure of international politics as a whole, not on the internal nature of a particular state. An example of an explanation that relies on internal factors is the claim that a given country keeps building more and more weapons because of demands from its own military-industrial complex or because of the nature of a national mentality that reflects its regional or global ambitions. External factors such as the anarchic structure of the system or the actions and reactions of other states are ignored.

Even realists, however, disagree on how much weight to accord anarchy as a contributing factor to international conflict. So-called defensive realists, for example, while recognizing the importance of anarchy, caution that analysts should not overstate its importance. They argue that security is readily available, particularly if states adopt defensive strategies. The assumption is made that the international system provides incentives for cautious and restrained behavior on the part of states and that reckless, expansionist behavior is the result of domestic factors, not of systemic conditions such as anarchy.[13]

Finally, an anarchical, self-help system obviously makes cooperation among states difficult to achieve. How are states to act in such a world? Is it inevitable that they will be self-seeking, attempting to maximize their short-term individual or self-interests? Or is it possible that states can upgrade their common (perhaps enlightened) self-interests over both the short and long term? What is the rational thing to do? The informing image for some realists is provided by the allegory of the stag hunt, taken from the writings of the Geneva-born, eighteenth-century philosopher Jean-Jacques Rousseau.[14] It is an excellent example of game theory at work.

Each of five individuals in the state of nature—a world without government or any other form of social structure—has to decide (1) whether to collaborate in the hunting of a stag necessary to meet the hunger needs of all five or (2) to defect from the group to capture a hare. To choose the latter course of action would be to serve one's own self-interest at the expense of the group (see Figure 2.1).

If the individual prefers to serve the common interest (go after the stag), can he or she trust the others to do so? And if one can't trust the others, is it not rational to go for the hare and defect from the group before any of the others do? Or is it possible to develop the basis for collaboration by all five? Scholars who deal with game theory attempt to answer such questions.[15]

How one understands Rousseau's stag hunt fable has a great deal to do with how one sees states interacting in world politics. Some tend to see the state as serving only narrow self interest. Pessimists point to the number, duration, and intensity of wars. They tend to see international politics as sets of competitive games in which decisions or choices may be zero-sum—one side's gains are losses for the other. Those of a more optimistic bent see great potential for collaboration among states, noting how in fact many states live in peace and harmony for decades and even centuries. In competitive settings, the players can find ways in

	Individual interests: pursue the hare	Group/collective interests: pursue the stag
Short run	Serve immediate self-interest	May provide basis for possible future collaboration
Long run	No apparent basis for collaborative behavior	Serve long-term common interest

FIGURE 2.1   The Stag Hunt Fable: A Dilemma of Rational Choice

which all parties can gain, albeit to different degrees—so-called positive- or variable-sum games. When losses have to be taken, optimists argue they can be distributed so as to minimize damage to each party. As such, the payoffs (gains or losses) typically are "asymmetric" or uneven, but still the best that can be achieved for all players.

For international relations theorists, however, it is not simply a matter of having a pessimistic or optimistic nature. Aside from the assumptions that states are unitary and rational actors, structural realists also tend to make the analytical assumption that states are largely concerned with **relative** rather than just **absolute gains.** What is the difference? If a state is concerned with individual, absolute gains, it is indifferent to the gains of others—"As long as I'm doing better, I don't care if others are also increasing their wealth or military power." If, however, a state is concerned with relative gains, it is not satisfied with simply increasing its power or wealth but is concerned with how much those capabilities have kept pace with, increased, or decreased relative to other states.[16]

Differing assumptions about a state's preferences lead to different expectations about the prospects for international conflict and cooperation. For structural realists, the relative gains assumption makes international cooperation in an anarchic world difficult to attain, particularly among great powers prone to improving their relative position or, at least, hold their own in this international competition. Structural realists do not have to rely, therefore, on such classical realist assumptions as found in the works of Machiavelli and Hobbes that man is inherently aggressive. More optimistic about the prospects for international cooperation, English School scholars, neoliberal institutionalists, and social constructivists are much more likely to assume that states may well be satisfied with absolute gains due to the development of international norms, collaborative institutions, and the ability to redefine national interests.

Distribution of Capabilities and the Balance of Power

Realists see anarchy as continuing to be a defining characteristic of the international system unless one state or some kind of superior international authority were constructed to provide a new order to the world through its position of dominance. Within this anarchical environment various distributions of capabilities or power among states emerge in dynamic, competitive relations among states. Indeed, anarchy plus the distribution of capabilities among states define for many realists the international system at any one time, described by them typically as unipolar, bipolar, or multipolar.

As we have seen, many realists begin with the security dilemma in an anarchic world. Where does order come from under such conditions? What keeps states from continually attacking one another? One answer offered by realists is that states find it expedient to band together and pool their capabilities or power whenever one state or group of states appears to be gathering a disproportionate amount of power, thus threatening to dominate the world, or even a portion of it. On the other hand, influenced perhaps by the thought of Hugo Grotius, many classical realists (as well as constructivists and other scholars in the English School) observe some degree of order provided by the development and acceptance over time of international norms and practices, particularly those that come to be codified in international law.

This reasoning—the need to maintain a **balance of power** to avoid the triumph of a dominant power—is a realist concern dating back to the works of Thucydides. It is also found in a report of the British Foreign Office written before World War I:

> History shows that the danger threatening the independence of this or that nation has generally arisen, at least in part, out of the momentary predominance of a neighboring State at once militarily powerful, economically efficient, and ambitious to extend its frontiers or spread its influence. . . . The only check on the abuse of political predominance derived from such a position has always consisted in the opposition of an equally formidable rival, or a combination of several countries forming leagues of defense. The equilibrium established by such a grouping of forces is technically known as the balance of power, and it has become almost an historical truism to identify England's secular policy with the maintenance of this balance by throwing her weight now in this scale and now in that, but ever on the side opposed to the political dictatorship of the strongest single State or group at a given time.[17]

A bipolar balance of power (two states of comparable or relatively equal great power) or a multipolar balance of power (three or more states engaging in checks and balances) are two realist categorizations of particular distributions of capabilities. Such power configurations have occurred in the aftermath of major European wars—the Peace of Westphalia in 1648 following the Thirty Years' War, the Congress of Vienna in 1815 following the defeat of Napoleon, and the settlements following both twentieth-century world wars. Although the post-World War I arrangements bought only twenty years of peace, the Congress of Vienna was more successful in establishing a basis for maintaining a balance of power without general or major war for almost a century. Assessing the efforts of the diplomats at Vienna and subsequent meetings, Henry Kissinger concluded: "Their goal was stability, not perfection, and the balance of power is the classic expression of the lesson of history that no order is safe without physical safeguards against aggression." In short, according to Kissinger, a "new international order came to be created with a sufficient awareness of the connection between power and morality; between security and legitimacy."[18]

Three questions in this regard are subject to debate among realist scholars: (1) Do balances of power automatically occur, or are they created by diplomats or statesmen? (2) Which balance of power—bipolar or multipolar—is more likely to maintain international stability? (3) Is unipolarity a durable condition, or is the single great power's (or hegemon's) typically more assertive actions likely to encourage balancing behaviors by other states resulting over time in the emergence of new balancers of comparable power? This later question is particularly relevant in the current international system with the United States possessing the greatest aggregation of power.

Voluntarism and Determinism. As to the first question, Kissinger (a classical realist) emphasizes **voluntarism**—the balance of power is a foreign policy creation or construction by statesmen; it doesn't just occur automatically. Makers of foreign policy do not act as automatons, prisoners of the balance of power and severely constrained by it. Rather, they are its creators and those charged with maintaining it. They are free to exercise their judgment and their will as agents for their states in the conduct of foreign policy with the expectation that they can have some constructive effect on outcomes.

In contrast to this voluntarist conception is that of Kenneth Waltz, who sees the balance of power as an attribute of the system of states that will occur whether it is willed or not. He argues that "the balance of power is not so much imposed by statesmen on events as it is imposed by events on statesmen."[19] For Waltz, the statesman has much less freedom to maneuver, much less capability to affect the workings of international politics, than Kissinger would allow.

How does Waltz reach this conclusion? Given the assumptions that the state is a rational and a unitary actor that will use its capabilities to accomplish its objectives, states inevitably interact and conflict in the competitive environment of international politics. States may be motivated to improve their own positions so as to dominate others, but such attempts likely will be countered by other states similarly motivated. Waltz observes that in international relations, "the freedom of choice of any one state is limited by the actions of all the others."[20] Thus, a balance of power more often than not occurs as states tend to balance against a rising power as opposed to joining its bandwagon. The structure of the international system itself—anarchy plus the distribution of capabilities—affects the calculations and choices of decisionmakers. Balance-of-power theory so viewed can be used to account for arms races, alliances and counteralliances, coalitions and countercoalitions, and other forms of competitive behavior among states that transcend any particular historical era.

This image of the balance of power, therefore, refers to a recurrent phenomenon characteristic of international relations. It seems to matter little whether the states are democratic or authoritarian; the systemic tendency toward balance or equilibrium is always the same. It is as if states were billiard balls colliding with one another. The faster and larger balls (the major powers) knock the smaller balls (the lesser powers) out of the way, although their own paths may also be deflected slightly by these collisions. These interactions, it is argued, tend toward international equilibrium or stability just as billiard balls eventually come to rest, at least until the balance is upset once again. But then the same tendency toward equilibrium repeats itself, only to be upset again. And so forth. The actors involved in this timeless drama remain the same: states. As Ernst Haas—a critic of the determinism he observed among structural realists and many other balance-of-power theorists—put it: "[They] see the components [of systems, i.e., states] as relatively unchangeable and arrange them in an eternal preprogrammed dance. The rules of the dance may be unknown to the actors and are specified by the theorist. The recurrent patterns discovered by him constitute a super-logic which predicts the future state of the system."[21]

Actor combinations involving two or more states can be observed throughout history as the mechanical workings of the balance of power: multipolar through much of the eighteenth and nineteenth centuries, prior to World War II (1939–1945), and bipolar (the United States and the Soviet Union) in the years following the war. The post–Cold War world has been described as a unipolar system due to the preponderant power of the United States, and this has caused problems for realist balance-of power-theorists, a subject we will subsequently discuss.

In a sense, then, Kissinger and Waltz represent alternative ends of a spectrum of contemporary realists conversant with balance-of-power thinking. Realists such as Waltz who emphasize balance of power as a system tendency have been labeled as "structural realists" or "neorealists" because they have allegedly departed from a realist tradition that granted the statesman or policymaker greater freedom from constraint and thus greater ability to affect international events.

The voluntarism-determinism debate is comparable in some ways to theological dispute over determinism and free will. As we use the term, however, *voluntarism* does not refer only to freedom of choice, but rather to the ability of human beings to influence the course of events. How free are individuals to determine their own fates? How much effective choice do they have? How much are events determined by factors independent of human will exercised by statesmen? In the context of international relations, the question is whether states or their decisionmakers can affect their environment or whether their actions are severely constrained by other states interacting in a system of states. How much is free? How much is determined? Put another way, how much is the behavior of states and other units driven by the international system or its structure and how much is socially constructed by human volition—statesmen and diplomats, institutions and groups, and other human actors?

Kissinger's position is closer to the voluntarist pole, but he definitely would not argue that foreign policymakers are totally free of external constraints. Indeed, their ability to maneuver within these constraints is at least partly a function of their diplomatic skills. Similarly, Waltz would reject the idea that he is in any way a system determinist—that the structure of the international system necessarily determines state behavior. Indeed, he acknowledges the possibility of a state or "unit-level cause negating a structural effect."[22] Nevertheless, his views are far removed from the purely voluntarist pole. The implication of his view of the balance of power is that individual decisionmakers and their states have much less freedom or capability to affect the course of events than others such as Kissinger would assert.

In some respects, the writings of Hans J. Morgenthau were an earlier attempt to combine the two perspectives, thus inviting wrath by proponents of both. Morgenthau acknowledged the balance of power as a tendency within international politics while, at the same time, prescribing what statesmen should do to maintain the balance. He argued that "the balance of power and policies aiming at its preservation are not only inevitable but are an essential stabilizing factor in a society of sovereign nations." Quite apart from the apparent determinism in this statement, Morgenthau assigned to diplomats not just the task of maintaining the balance of power; he also charged them to "create the conditions under which it will not be impossible from the outset to establish a world state."[23]

In short, for Morgenthau, escape from the balance of power and the voluntarist creation of a new world order remained possibilities worthy of pursuit. At the same time, his detractors have noted that, on the one hand, to argue that the balance of power is an inevitable system tendency and, on the other hand, to prescribe what should be done to maintain a balance or transform the system itself is to argue in contradictory terms. Be that as it may, Morgenthau's thinking represents a middle ground between realists who tend toward voluntarist or determinist poles. The present theoretical debate between structural realists and social constructivists is a more recent manifestation of this continuing controversy—the latter far more voluntarist in its formulations, but also understanding that *both* ideational and material structures (or understandings of them) may facilitate or constrain state actions.

Polarity (or system structure). The second question is a long-standing realist debate: Is a bipolar or a multipolar balance of power more conducive to the stability of the international system? Stated another way, is war more likely to occur in a bipolar or a multipolar world?

The best-known statements on the stability of bipolar and multipolar distributions are by Kenneth Waltz on the one hand and J. David Singer and Karl Deutsch on the other.[24] All three agreed that the amount of uncertainty about the consequences of a particular action taken by a state increases as the number of international actors increases. The logic of this assumption is that as the number increases, a state's policymakers have to deal with a greater quantity of information; more international actors mean more information is generated that has to be taken into account in the formulation of foreign policy. Therefore, all three authors concurred that as an international system moves from being bipolar to being multipolar, the amount of overall uncertainty in the system increases. So far, so good.

Where they part company is on the matter of whether an increase in the number of actors (and hence uncertainty) makes war more or less likely. Waltz argued that greater uncertainty makes it *more* likely that a policymaker will misjudge the intentions and actions of a potential foe. Hence, a multipolar system, given its association with higher levels of uncertainty, is less desirable than a bipolar system because multipolarity makes uncertainty and thus the probability of war greater. Singer and Deutsch, however, made the opposite argument, believing that a multipolar system is more conducive to stability because uncertainty breeds caution on the part of states. Caution means following tried and true policies of the past, avoiding deviations. Furthermore, they argued that "the increase in number of independent actors diminishes the share [of attention] that any nation can allocate to any other single actor." This, it is argued, also reduces the probability of war because a state's attention is allocated to a larger number of actors.

Both arguments seem logical. But if both cannot be correct, it is still possible that neither one is correct. This is a proposition put forth by Bruce Bueno de Mesquita. For example, he challenges the assumption that uncertainty is greater in a multipolar world, arguing that "if the system's structure—be it bipolar or multipolar—does not change, there will be little uncertainty" because "learned patterns from prior behavior will aid decision makers to anticipate the likely consequences of similar behaviors under similar circumstances." Hence, "the level of systemic uncertainty, by itself, neither increases nor decreases the likelihood of war. Consequently, neither the number of blocs, nor the magnitude of change in the number of blocs in the system is expected to be associated with the likelihood of war."[25]

This theoretical debate was inconclusive, and there still is no consensus on the issue of bipolarity versus multipolarity in terms of international stability. Other realist work since then, however, has built upon the concept of polarity and addressed two other dimensions at the systemic level of analysis—disparities in capabilities among poles (not simply the number), and the implications if the capability growth rates of states are static or dynamic.[26] Other works delved below the systemic level, examining different factors at the state-societal level of analysis. Ambitious attempts were made to integrate societal and system-level variables (not only polarity but also technology and geography) in the hope of gaining insight on how to explain and predict alliance strategies. In this regard, theorists have identified diverse patterns of state, alliance, and coalition behaviors labeled colorfully as balancing, bandwagoning, free riding, and buck passing.[27] Such a focus is a welcome corrective to traditional realist work on alliances that tended to assume that the distribution of capabilities virtually alone determines a state's international alignment.

Similarly, Stephen Walt has recast balance of power theory (states align against the most powerful states), arguing that a balance of threat theory offers more historically correct explanations.[28] Hence, intentions need to be taken into account (states balance against states that are not only powerful but also threatening). Walt observes that "states are attracted to strength" and "a decline in a state's relative position will lead its allies to opt for neutrality at best or to defect to the other side at worst." Threats matter in Walt's analysis, not just power as such. Thus, one finds that "the greater the threat, the greater the probability that the vulnerable state will seek an alliance."

In this regard, Walt draws a distinction between *balancing* (allying with others against the prevailing threat which is the dominant tendency in international politics) and *bandwagoning* (the opportunistic option of aligning with the source of danger, particularly if it is a strong state). Balancing behavior is more common, tending to reflect "restraint" and, perhaps, an effort to "minimize the threat one poses to others." By contrast, bandwagoning, though less common, typically occurs in a "much more competitive" context.

Walt has also used this theoretical adjustment to balance-of-power theory to analyze how revolutionary domestic changes can increase the risk of international war by intensifying international security competition. Dangers posed by states matter, not just their power or relative power positions *per se*. So understood it is imbalances of threat that cause alliances against the most threatening state. He concludes, then, that balance-of-threat theory provides a stronger explanatory handle than traditional balance-of-power theory offers.

Much as Walt deals with threats or perceptions of danger, Stephen Van Evera adds the ideational—ideas, perceptions, and misperceptions—to the material understandings of power and its distribution.[29] Going beyond gross distinctions captured by the terms *multipolar, bipolar,* and *unipolar,* Van Evera introduces what he labels a "fine-grained structural realism" that takes into account such considerations as the offense-defense balance, the advantage of taking the first move, the size and frequency of power fluctuations, and available resources. Perception (and misperception) matters, and war is more likely when states believe that conquest is easy (whether it is or is not). Other "war-causing ideas" include windows of vulnerability, the hostility of other states, threatening diplomatic tactics (as in coercive diplomacy), and when war is considered cheap or even beneficial.

For his part, John Mearsheimer places emphasis in his structural realism on "offensive" or power-maximizing in contrast to the "defensive" (or "status quo") realism he finds in Waltz and other neorealists. Offensive realism is both a descriptive theory about how states behave as well as a prescriptive one that states ought to follow as "the best way to survive in a dangerous world." He is critical of the defensive realist focus on maintaining the existing balance of power—"preserving power, rather than increasing it." By contrast, offensive realists see states as trying to maximize their power positions—a state's ultimate goal in principle is "to be the hegemon in the system." For Mearsheimer, however, the "best way for a state to survive in anarchy is to take advantage of other states and gain power at their expense."[30] (See his article at the end of this chapter.)

Echoes of Morgenthau's earlier conceptualization of power in international politics can be heard as Mearsheimer characterizes states as maximizing power, not just as "a means to an end(survival) but [also] an end in itself." Great powers pursuing power as an end still come to understand the limits of their power, constrained as it necessarily is by other states pursuing the same ends. In the great game of international politics "the trick for the sophisticated power maximizer is to figure out when to raise and when to fold." Finally, Mearsheimer's form of structural realism is open to cooperation or collaboration among states, enhanced perhaps by the pursuit of absolute as opposed merely to relative gains.[31]

Unipolarity. The third question—is unipolarity a durable condition and if so, for how long—is understandably an important issue of discussion among not only scholars of international relations, but policymakers as well. It is fair to say that realist scholars were caught as unawares as anyone with the collapse of the Soviet Union and the collapse of the bipolar world in the early 1990s. Little, if any, thought had gone into the implications of unipolarity. As one would expect, unipolarity offers the hegemonic power several logical options: isolationism, enhancing the effectiveness of international institutions, and unilateralism in its foreign policy. Whatever a hegemonic state may choose, the underlying logic of realist structural analysis is that unipolarity is inherently unstable and other states will balance against it. There is a consensus among many realists that unipolarity will not last and, in time, the world will become increasingly multipolar—great powers including, for example, a reconstituted Russian Federation, China, Japan, India, and the European Union. Although the United States now holds the predominant position, they see a shift taking place in the distribution of capabilities among states. Furthermore, at least one structural realist has warned that we might come to miss the Cold War for the stability that U.S.-Soviet bipolarity had provided.

For his part, Waltz does not see unipolarity as a permanent condition either. He notes how "World War II destroyed the multipolar structure of international politics that had lasted for three centuries . . . [and] subsequently the demise of the Soviet Union left only one pole standing." Even if unipolarity does not last—the mere exercise of American power inviting balancers—it is what we now have. On whether the adverse American experience in Iraq compared to earlier expectations will moderate U.S. policy, Waltz comments: "It probably will, but not for long. The predicted Vietnam effect lasted only a short time. The concentration of power is a powerful predictor of a state's behavior."[32]

GLOBALIZATION AND INTERDEPENDENCE

To this point, we have discussed some of the intellectual precursors of realism and have then examined two concepts important to the realist analysis of world politics: power and system. In the next section, we discuss the realist view on recent developments within the international relations field involving the concepts of globalization and interdependence.

■ Globalization

There is no doubt that the term **globalization** has captured the imagination of journalists, policymakers, the general public, and writers of textbooks on international relations. Realists generally do not share this enthusiasm, and one would be hard-pressed to find a realist who has utilized the term as an integral part of his or her conceptual framework. Realist skepticism is due to a number of factors.

First, there is the problem of definition. A generally accepted definition of globalization does not exist although it is common to emphasize the continual increase in transnational and worldwide economic, social, and cultural interactions among societies that transcend the boundaries of states, aided by advances in technology. Second, the term is descriptive and lacking in theoretical content. Hence, it hardly qualifies as a "concept" suitable for use in theory-building. Third, the term is trendy, which alone makes realists suspicious. It is rare for academic theoretical concepts to gain such widespread public currency. Fourth, and most important, the literature on globalization assumes the increase in transactions among societies has led to an erosion of sovereignty and the blurring of the boundaries between the state and the international system. For realists anarchy is the distinguishing feature in international relations, and anything that questions the separation of domestic and international politics threatens the centrality of this key realist concept. Finally, globalization has an affinity with another popular concept which came to the fore of the international relations field in the 1970s: interdependence. As with the case of globalization today, some realist scholars were skeptical of the conceptual utility of the concept. How they critiqued and utilized the concept perhaps provides insights on why realists have not embraced the globalization process as the centerpiece of the international relations theory enterprise.

◼ Interdependence and Vulnerability

For those realists who even utilize the concept, **interdependence** is viewed as being between or among states. This is not surprising given the underlying assumptions of realism. They make several related points. First, the balance of power can be understood as a kind of interdependence. To be sure, some realists of a more eclectic sort acknowledge interdependence involving non-state actors such as multinational corporations and try to take them into account. But at the core of realist thought is the image of interactions among states.

Second, for any one state, interdependence among states is not necessarily such a good thing. Rather than being a symmetric relation between coequal parties (which is how many people view the term), interdependence is typically a dominance–dependence relation with the dependent party particularly *vulnerable* (a key realist concept) to the choices of the dominant party. Indeed, interdependence as vulnerability is a source of power of one state over another. To reduce this vulnerability, realists have argued that it is better for the state to be independent or, at least, to minimize its dependency. For example, the state needing to import oil is vulnerable to an embargo or price rise engineered by the state or states exporting the commodity. To reduce this vulnerability would require reducing oil imports by, for example, finding alternative sources.

Third, and following from above, interdependence does not affect all states equally. This applies to the economic realm as much as the military realm. For example, although the economies of most oil-importing countries are affected by dramatic rises in oil prices, they are not all equally vulnerable. Vulnerability is in part a question of what alternatives are available. For example, as a matter of policy, the United States has tried to increase domestic production, create a strategic oil reserve to be drawn from only in emergencies, find other foreign sources of oil, and substitute alternative forms of energy whenever feasible. Given these measures, that many say have not gone far enough, the United States has attempted to reduce somewhat its vulnerability to any new oil embargo or disruption of supply due to war or other regional instabilities in the Middle East or elsewhere. As a practical matter, of course, the United States remains heavily dependent on imported oil.

In any event, if a state wants to be more powerful, it avoids or minimizes economic dependency just as it avoids political or military dependency on other states if this were to amount to a reduction in its relative power position. Dependency on others is to be minimized, whereas dependency of others on one's own state may be desirable to the extent that it increases one's leverage over those other states. In short, in any given issue area, not all states are equally vulnerable. Therefore, the realist is suspicious of such blanket statements as "given increasing globalization, the entire world is increasingly interdependent or interconnected,"—as if this were a good thing—particularly when such claims are supposedly *equally* applicable to all states.

Finally, realists have made interesting arguments concerning interdependence and peace, and it can be inferred they might apply similar observations to the effects of globalization. Interdependence, according to realists, may or may not enhance prospects for peace. Conflict, not cooperation, could just as easily result. Just as in households, sectarian, and community conflicts, one way to establish peace is to eliminate or minimize contact among opponents or potential adversaries. Separation from other units, if that were possible, would mean less contact and thus less conflict. Hence realists would be as unlikely to argue that the increase in globalization among societies has a pacifying effect any more than they would assume interdependence leads to peace.

REALISTS AND INTERNATIONAL COOPERATION

Classical realists perhaps have more faith than structural realists in the ability of international organizations to make a substantive contribution to international stability if not peace; after all, they draw from the same Grotian intellectual wellspring as do those in the English School. But other realists have made a theoretical contribution to our understanding of how under conditions of anarchy international cooperation may be enhanced. For some, this involved the application of game theory and its attendant assumptions of unified, rational state actors.[33] For others the starting point was the systemic distribution of power and the implications of hegemonic leadership.

According to the theory of **hegemonic stability,** the hegemon, or dominant power, assumes leadership, perhaps for the entire globe, in dealing with a particular issue. Thus, Britain was seen as offering leadership in international monetary matters in the nineteenth and early twentieth centuries. The gold standard associated with the international exchange of money was managed from London by the Bank of England. After World War II, the leadership role was finally assumed by the United States.[34]

The absence of hegemony, or leadership, may result in chaos and instability, as happened in the 1930s when the United States was unwilling to assume leadership of the world economy and Britain, given its weakened position, was unable to do so. Competitive depreciation of currencies, erection of trade barriers, and a drastic reduction in the volume of trade were the outcome.

Although not all realists would subscribe to the view, stability is therefore seen by some as enhanced by a concentration of power in international politics; there is virtue in inequality among states. The hegemonic state or states benefit, but so too do other, less powerful states that find a more stable world advantageous. By contrast, the decline of hegemony and the consequent fragmentation of power in international politics is said to produce disorder—a breakdown or unraveling of previously constructed international agreements. Leadership provided by hegemonic states is understood as facilitating achievement of collaboration among states.

Theoretical and empirical controversy in the 1980s and 1990s was mirrored by public debate as to whether or not the United States was a hegemon in decline. The debate was sparked primarily by the work of the historian Paul Kennedy, who examined the rise and fall of great powers over some 500 years. The debate influenced (and was influenced by) discussion already under way mainly among structural realists on how the United States might be able to adapt to hegemonic decline and how stability in the international economic system could be sustained after hegemony. Other writers, including realists, challenged the whole notion of U.S. decline in any absolute sense. After all, U.S. "decline" was *relative* only to the apparent rise of other actors such as Germany and Japan. Notwithstanding all of America's economic problems at the time, this gradual "leveling" of relative standings still left the United States effectively in first position. Moreover, the breakup of the Soviet Union resulted in the United States being the only global superpower—a "unipolar" structure.[35]

Since 2001, work has been done on the implications of nuclear primacy of the United States resulting from the decline in the Russian arsenal, the slow modernization of the Chinese arsenal, and the steady growth of U.S. nuclear counterforce capabilities. While scholars interested in national security have debated the implications for crisis stability, force vulnerability, and the meaning of deterrence in the current environment, an equally important question is: Does nuclear primacy grant the United States real coercive leverage in political disputes? The question is applicable to not only U.S. relations with Russia and China, but also with Iran and North Korea. Stated in terms of international relations theory, what can we anticipate in terms of international outcomes by relying on the realist assumption of the importance of varying distributions of capabilities?

CHANGE

Realists stress the continuity of international relations. Many of the insights of Thucydides are deemed to be as relevant today as they were more than two millennia ago. Looking to modern history, a balance of power involving states has existed at least since the fifteenth and sixteenth centuries—whether viewed as a policy they have pursued or as a recurrent, expected outcome from the interactions of states using power to pursue their own separate interests. Although continuity is the watchword for realists, this does not mean that they are uninterested in change. For many theorists of international relations, understanding the evolution of the international system and predicting its future should be the preeminent research goals. The methods for discovering global patterns may vary. Some scholars have applied quantitative measures to historical data.[36] Others have approached the issue of international political change by attempting to discern cycles of national power and their relation to the outbreak of war.

To illustrate how realists have dealt with the issue of change, we will also briefly discuss the works of Robert Gilpin and George Modelski. As the title of his book suggests, Gilpin is interested in developing a framework for thinking about *War and Change in World Politics*. He believes "it is possible to identify recurrent patterns, common elements, and general tendencies in the major turning points in international history." International political change is the result of efforts of political actors "to change the international system in order to advance their own interests," however these interests may be defined (security, economic gain, ideological goals, etc.). Gilpin lists five assumptions concerning the behavior of states that will guide his analysis. For example, the realist emphasis on the unified, rational actor state is revealed in the second assumption: "A state will attempt to change the international system if the expected benefits exceed the expected costs (i.e., if there is an expected net gain)."

Various periods of history are marked by equilibrium (such as after the Congress of Vienna in 1815) or disequilibrium. As long as the system can adjust to the demands of its constituent states, stability is maintained. What accounts for change and the undermining of the status quo? The key factor, originally identified by Thucydides, "is the tendency in an international system for the powers of member states to change at different rates because of political, economic, and technological developments. In time, the differential growth in power of the various states in the system causes a fundamental redistribution of power in the system."[37] A state with ever-increasing power may determine that the costs involved in attempting to change the nature of the system are outweighed by the benefits if such an endeavor is successful. What has been the principal mechanism of change throughout history? War, because wars determine which states will govern the system. The peace settlement after the war codifies the new status quo. This equilibrium reflects the new distribution of power in the international system until eventually the differential growth in the power of states leads to another attempt to change the system.

Like balance of power theory, therefore, power-transition theory is a systems-level theory. Realist adherents to both theories claim that the distribution of power among states is the key to understanding international relations. Power transition theorists, however, see the international system as hierarchically ordered, with the most powerful state dominating the rest, which are classified as satisfied or dissatisfied with the ordering of the system. But while balance of power theorists argue that the equality of power leads to peace, power-transition theorists such as Gilpin and others claim that war may be more likely when states are relatively equal, particularly when the differential growth in two states' economies brings a challenger close to the reigning hegemon's power.

For his part, George Modelski argued that the global political system goes through distinct and identifiable historical cycles or recurrent patterns of behavior. The global political system dates from about A.D. 1500, and over the years, various world powers have helped to shape and maintain the system. According to Modelski, since A.D. 1500, four states have played dominant roles, each one corresponding to a "long cycle": Portugal (1500 to the end of the sixteenth century), the Netherlands (the seventeenth century), Great Britain (early eighteenth century to the Napoleonic Wars, and a second cycle from 1815 to 1945), and the United States (1945 to the present). As in the case of Gilpin's analysis, war tends to mark the end of one cycle and the beginning of another.

What produces these cycles? Two conditions are critical: (1) the urge of a power to create a global order, and (2) particular properties and weaknesses of the global system. Modelski notes that, as with long-term business cycles, world order is also subject to decay. The dominant power is inevitably faced with the growth of rival power centers, and attempts to maintain territorial control around the globe prove to be a costly task that drains the vitality and energy of the home country. Each cycle, therefore, exhibits a particular nation-state in an ascending and then a descending phase. As Modelski notes, following a major war, one world power

> emerges from that conflict in an advantageous position and organizes the world even as the struggle still goes on and then formalizes its position in the global layer in the peace settlement. For the space of another generation, that new power maintains basic order and is the mainspring of world institutions, often taking transnational forms. But the time comes when the energy that built this order begins to run down. . . . The prominent role of world power attracts competitors (other great powers) . . . ; the system moves into multipolarity. Rivalries among the major powers grow fiercer and assume the characteristics of oligopolistic competition. Gradually, as order dissolves, the system moves toward its original point of departure, that of minimal order and a Babel of conflicting and mutually unintelligible voices.[38]

Modelski and Gilpin present a dynamic view of international politics. Patterns of behavior are evident throughout history. Periods of rapid change alternate with periods of relative stability. Given the emphasis on the importance of war in changing the structure of the system, are we currently experiencing a lull before some sort of global cataclysm? Perhaps this question is too pessimistic. As Modelski notes, it is possible that the international system may be "propelled in a new direction. We have no means of predicting what that new direction might be except that it could be moved away from the present system that relies too heavily on the steady, if long-spaced-out, progression of global wars."[39]

Continuing the work of the late A.F.K. Organski on power-transition theory, Ronald L. Tammen, Jacek Kugler, and their associates see national power as "a function of population, productivity, and relative political capacity."[40] They warn us that periods in which the distribution of power is in transition are more prone to war. When one state is in the process of overtaking the power position of another, the likelihood of war increases markedly. War is least likely when we find the ways and means of satisfying (or, one might add, at least dampening or minimizing dissatisfaction among) the challengers and defenders of existing power positions. The converse—dissatisfied challengers and defenders—is the condition that makes the outbreak of war most likely. How power transitions take place is important, affecting the duration, severity, and consequences of war. Rather than adopting a laissez-faire approach, the authors call for managing alliances, international organizations, levels of satisfaction among states vying for power, the distribution of nuclear weapons, and crises wherever and whenever they emerge.

"Power transition" work on war has been criticized on historical, empirical, and conceptual grounds.[41] Yet this is true of all work which attempts to explain important issues of war and peace. Furthermore, given the ongoing shifts in the distribution of world power and interest in the implications of such rising powers as China, India, and a resurgent Russia, it can be expected that scholars will continue to mine such works for theoretical insights.

REALISTS AND THEIR CRITICS

◼ Realism: The Term Itself

What is perhaps most impressive about the realist image of international politics is its longevity. Although modifications, clarifications, additions, and methodological innovations have been made down through the years, the core elements have remained basically intact.

If realism represents a "realistic" image of international politics—one represented as close to the reality of how things *are* (not necessarily how things *ought* to be), what does that say about competing images? Are they by definition "unrealistic"? In debate and discourse, labels are important. A good example of this involves the period between World War I and World War II during which realists were challenged by advocates of the League of Nations, world federalism, or peace through international law. Many of these individuals came to be known as "idealists" or "utopians" as referred to be E. H. Carr.

The very labels attached to these competing images of world order obviously put the so-called idealists at a disadvantage. Realists could claim that they were dealing with the world as it actually functioned. The idealists, on the other hand, were supposedly more concerned with what ought to be. "Yes," a realist might say, "I too wish the world were a more harmonious place, but that unfortunately is not the case." Those persons who were placed in the idealist camp certainly did not choose this particular label for themselves. Who did? The realists. By so doing, the opposition was stripped of a certain amount of legitimacy. Idealism conjured up images of impractical professors, unsophisticated peace advocates, and utopian schemes.

Realists would respond that realism should be taken at face value; it is an appropriate term precisely because its basic tenets in fact closely approximate the world as it is. This is nothing of which to be ashamed. The longevity of the realist tradition is not simply a function of the expropriation of a particular label but a result of realism's inherent descriptive, explanatory, and predictive strengths.

Another reason for the longevity of realism is that this particular image of the world most closely approximates the image held by practitioners of statecraft. Realism has always had strong policy-prescriptive components, as we have already noted. Machiavelli's *The Prince*, for example, was expressly presented as a guide for the ruler. Nor is it mere coincidence that some of the best known American political scientists who have held national security advisor positions in the White House—Henry A. Kissinger in the Nixon-Ford years, Brent Scowcroft in the Ford and H. W. Bush administrations, Zbigniew Brzezinski in the Carter years, and Condoleeza Rice in the George W. Bush administration—are self-professed (or easily classified as) realists. Indeed, the realist as academic speaks much the same language as the realist as statesman: power, force, national interest, and diplomacy.

It has been argued, however, that some realist writers help to perpetuate the very world they analyze. By describing the world in terms of violence, duplicity, and war, and then providing advice to statesmen as to how statesmen should act, such realists are justifying one particular conception of international relations. Realism becomes a self-fulfilling prophecy. Even efforts to place realism on a stronger theoretical foundation (as in structural realism or neorealism) that favor explanation over policy prescription have the same effect. Critics contend that such realists suffer from a lack of imagination and an inability to consider seriously alternative conceptions of world politics and how these might be achieved.

The realist response is that there is nothing inherently wrong with being policy relevant and helping leaders navigate through dangerous waters. Advice based on wishful thinking and questionable assessments of international forces and trends could lead to disastrous policies, particularly if one is the lone "idealist" leader in a world of realists. Moreover, most criticism is understood to be based on a selective reading of realists, ignoring their genuine concern not only with the causes of war but also with how peace can be achieved or maintained. Finally, not all realists would claim to be particularly interested in providing advice to statesmen. They would rather use realist assumptions and insights to develop better theories of international politics. Being policy relevant or ingratiating oneself with political leaders is not the goal for these realists who merely entertain the scholarly goal of explaining how the world functions.

The System and Determinism

As we have seen, the concept of system is critical to many realist writers. Whether the rather simple notion of anarchy or the more elaborate formulations devised by contemporary realist authors, the system is deemed important for its impact on international actors. It is charged, however, that recent realist writers portray the system as having a life of its own. The system is seemingly independent of the wishes and actions of states, even though it is the result of the preferences and powers of the constituent states. Statesmen are granted too little autonomy and too little room to maneuver, and the decision-making process is seemingly devoid of human volition. Human agents are pawns of a bloodless system that looms over them, a structure whose functioning they do not understand and the mechanics of which they only dimly perceive. Statesmen are faced with an endless array of constraints and few opportunities. It is as if they are engaged in a global game, a game called power politics, and they are unable to change the rules even if they so desire. In sum, critics claim there is a fatalistic, deterministic, and pessimistic undercurrent to much of the realist work.

Realists differ among themselves as to how much explanatory emphasis is to be given the international system. There is disagreement as to what extent the system functions as an independent variable in influencing state behavior. For structural or neorealists, the system is more than the aggregation of state interactions. Rather, it represents a material structure that does indeed influence the behavior of states that are part of the system. It is these scholars who have drawn the most criticism, but they reject the charge that they are structural determinists who ignore actors operating at the unit, or state, level of analysis. One realist who argues that a systemic theory of international politics is composed of "the structure of the system and its interacting units," notes that

> if structure influences without determining, then one must ask how and to what extent the structure of a realm accounts for outcomes and how and to what extent the units [i.e., states] account for outcomes. Structure has to be studied in its own right as do units.

Another realist categorically states that "no neorealist that I have read argues that political structure determines all behavior."[42]

Consistent with Arnold Wolfers, Hans Morgenthau, Henry Kissinger, and others of more recent vintage, traditional or classical realists have often made the distinction between imperialist, revolutionary, or revisionist states on the one hand, and status-quo powers interested in maintaining their own position in a relatively constant regional or global order on the other. "Neoclassical realists" such as Randall Schweller, while appreciating the insights of neorealism, have attempted to incorporate international institutions and explanatory factors at the state-society level of analysis. Similarly, still other realists have examined relations among states (or the interactions level of analysis) that analytically fall between the level of system structure and the level of state and society—arms racing and arms control, and alliance behavior (balancing or bandwagoning). Such factors, it is argued, will affect the stability of either bipolar or multipolar systems and, consequently, the possibility of moving toward a more peaceful world.[43]

Realists therefore differ on the extent to which statesmen impose themselves on events, or vice versa. No realist is completely determinist or voluntarist. It is not a matter of either-or but varying assessments as to how strong are the constraints placed on statesmen and how much room leaders have to maneuver.

Realists and the State

The state is the centerpiece of realist work. Few persons would disagree as to the importance of the state in international affairs. The criticism, however, is that realists are so obsessed with the state that they ignore other actors and other issues not directly related to the maintenance of state security. Other non-state actors—multinational corporations, banks, terrorists, and international organizations—are either excluded, downplayed, or trivialized in the realist perspective. Furthermore, given the national security prism through which realists view the world, other concerns such as the socioeconomic gap between rich and poor societies, international pollution, and the implications of globalization rarely make the realist agenda. At best, such issues are dealt with in a derivative manner. A preoccupation with national security and the state by definition relegates other issues to secondary importance or bans them entirely from the realist agenda.

Realists counter that simply because non-state actors are not dealt with in depth does not mean that they are considered irrelevant. Political scientists, one realist notes, should avoid slipping "into thinking that what an author fails to concentrate his attention upon, he takes to be inconsequential." Similarly, another realist has stated that to argue "that the state . . . is the principal actor in international relations does not deny the existence of other individual and collective actors."[44]

Second, realists contend that theories are constructed to answer certain questions and to explain certain types of international behavior and outcomes. As a result, they purposely limit the types of actors analyzed. A theory concerned with explaining state behavior naturally focuses on states, not multinational corporations or terrorist groups. Similarly, a concern with national security issues by definition makes it unlikely that global welfare and humanitarian issues will receive the same degree of attention.

Finally, it can be argued that focusing on the state is justified on normative grounds. Many scholars, for example, are concerned with how unbridled arms races and military spending contribute to international tension, devastating regional wars, and socioeconomic deprivation. Because it is almost exclusively states that spend this money to buy or produce military hardware, it makes sense to focus on them as the unit of analysis. Hence, far from being enamored of states, many realists are critical of these political entities that are deemed too important to be ignored.

Realists and the Balance of Power

Given the emphasis on the state and the concern with national security issues, we have seen how the concept of balance of power has played a dominant role in realist thought and theory. Although balance of power has been a constant theme in realist writings down through the centuries, it has also come in for a great deal of abuse. Balance of power has been criticized for creating definitional confusion. Hans Morgenthau, a realist himself, discerned at least four definitions: (1) a policy aimed at a certain state of affairs; (2) an objective or actual state of affairs; (3) an approximately equal distribution of power, as when a balance of power exists between the United States and the Soviet Union; and (4) any distribution of power including a preponderance of power, as when the balance of power shifts in favor of either superpower. Another critic found at least seven meanings of the term then in use—(1) distribution of power; (2) equilibrium; (3) hegemony; (4) stability and peace; (5) instability and war; (6) power politics generally; and (7) a universal law of history.[45] Indeed, one is left with the question that if the balance of power means so many different things, can it really mean anything?

Balance of power has also been criticized for leading to war as opposed to preventing it, serving as a poor guide for statesmen, and functioning as a propaganda tool to justify defense spending and foreign adventures. Despite these constant attacks and continual reformulations of the meaning of the term, balance of power remains a crucial concept in the realist vocabulary.

At times, it has appeared that the harshest critics of balance of power as a concept have been the realists themselves. All of these criticisms have been acknowledged and some deemed valid. Attempts have been made, however, to clear up misconceptions and misinterpretations of balance of power, placing it on a more solid conceptual footing. One such effort beginning in the 1970s was made by Kenneth Waltz.[46] Even his formulation, however, was not without its critics, as Waltz soon replaced the late Hans Morgenthau as lightning rod drawing criticism to the realist and structural realist projects. In fact, the debate between Waltz and his critics has been ongoing for more than three decades—the latest rounds involving neoliberal institutionalist, constructivist, critical theory, and postmodern challenges.

Realism and Change

Given the realist view of the international system, the role of the state, and balance of power politics, critics suggest that very little possibility is left for the fundamental and peaceful transformation of international politics. Realists, claim the critics, at best offer analysis aimed at understanding how international stability is achieved, but nothing approaching true peace.

Realist stability reflects a world bristling with weapons, forever on the verge of violent conflict and war. Alternative world futures—scenarios representing a real alternative to the dismal Hobbesian world—are rarely discussed or taken seriously. The timeless quality of international politics, its repetitious nature and cycles of war, and a world in which the strong do as they will and the weak do as they must, dominate the realist image. We are given little information, let alone any hope, say the critics, as to how meaningful and peaceful change can occur and thus help us escape from the security dilemma.

Realists, it is argued, simply assume state interests, but tell us little about how states come to define their interests, or the processes by which those interests are redefined. Interests are not simply "out there" waiting to be discovered, but are constructed through social interaction. Alexander Wendt and other constructivists discussed in Chapter Six claim that international anarchy is what states make of it—interests not being exogenous or given to states, but actually constructed by them.[47]

The issue of change, of course, is intimately connected to that of determinism and to what was referred to in Chapter One as the **agent-structure** problem. Although power politics and the state are central to all realist analyses, this does not mean that fundamental change is impossible or that change is limited to war and the cyclical rise and fall of states. Robert Gilpin argues that

> the state is the principal actor in that the nature of the state and the patterns of relations among states are the most important determinants of the character of international relations at any given moment. This argument does not presume that states need always be the principal actors, nor does it presume that the nature of the state need always be the same and that the contemporary nation-state is the ultimate form of political organization.

What separates realists from some other writers on the question of system change, however, is a belief that "if the nation-state is to disappear . . . it will do so through age-old political processes and not as idealists would wish through a transcendence of politics itself."[48] Hence, realists claim that fundamental change *is* possible and is taken into consideration in their work. Once again, however, the strength of this view varies substantially depending on the author under consideration.

Realism: The Entire Enterprise

Critics of realism have always felt that they have been faced with a difficult task because the image comes close to approaching an impregnable edifice seemingly unscathed by years of criticism. Indeed, scholars who at one time in their careers struggled to devise alternative approaches based on alternative images of international politics have in some instances given up the quest, become converts, or resigned themselves to modifying existing realist explanatory frameworks.

Critics are faced with several problems. First, as noted earlier, given realism's affinity to the real world of policy making, this particular image of the world is automatically imbued with a certain degree of attractiveness and legitimacy. It represents the world out there, not some ivory tower perspective on human events. Not only is the realist perspective the accepted wisdom of the Western foreign policy establishments, but even in the Third World leaders more often than not speak the language of realism as a result of concern over the survival of their regimes and states. Within the halls of academe, realism also has great attractiveness; "peace studies" programs sometimes find it advantageous to change the title to "security and conflict studies" in order to generate student interest. Realism can be as seductive to the academic professional as it can be to the student.

Second, realism is also seductive in that it has been given an increasingly scientific face. Earlier criticisms of the realist literature were very often based on the contention that such concepts as balance of power had less to do with theory building and more to do with ideology and self-justification of one particular approach to conducting international relations. Much of the realist work was, therefore, considered "unscientific." But at least some realists have cast their hunches and insights in the form of hypotheses, testable either quantitatively or with non-quantitative indicators. The work is better grounded scientifically and placed within the context of the positivist view of how we comprehend reality. The positivist approach to knowledge remains prominent in the social as in the natural sciences. Indeed, in some circles any image of international politics that can be presented in the cloak of positivism is immediately granted a certain stature above those that do not.

What realists see as a virtue—a positivist orientation—is viewed by postmodernists and others as erroneous. The heart of their perspective on realism goes to the question of what is this "knowable reality" of international relations that realists claim to be true. This involves serious consideration of the underlying issues of ontology (nature of the actors), epistemology (verification of knowledge claims), and methodology (modes of research and analysis). Is reality simply "out there" waiting to be discovered? Or is reality constructed, for example, by discourse and hence realism is best viewed as simply another perspective or construction of how the world works?

In conclusion, a reminder concerning criticism of any image or interpretive understanding: It is not particularly difficult to find fault with the work of individual theorists and then blanket an entire approach for the supposed sins of an individual author. As this chapter illustrates, although realists may find common ground in terms of basic assumptions and key international actors, there are differences between classical realists and structural or neorealists. Realists of any persuasion may differ in a number of important respects, such as methods they use, levels of analysis they choose, and what they assume about the ability of decisionmakers to influence international outcomes. That is why it is imperative to refer to the original sources.

Notes

1. Hans J. Morgenthau, *Politics Among Nations,* 4th ed. (New York: Knopf, 1966), 25.
2. *Ibid.,* 5
3. See the suggested readings for specific works by these authors.
4. Thucydides, *History of the Peloponnesian War,* trans. Rex Warner (Harmondsworth, England, and New York: Penguin Books, 1982), 49.
5. *Ibid.,* 402.
6. Machiavelli, *The Prince,* Chapter XV, any edition.
7. Thomas Hobbes, *Leviathan,* ed. Michael Oakeshott (New York and London: Collier Macmillan, 1974). These classic citations are drawn from Book 1, Chapter 13.
8. *Ibid.,* Book 1, Chapter 15, 113.
9. *Ibid.,* Book 1, Chapter 13, 101.
10. Morgenthau, *Politics Among Nations,* pp. 4–11.
11. Stanley Hoffmann, "Weighing the Balance of Power," *Foreign Affairs* 50, 4 (July 1972): 618–43.
12. John H. Herz, "Idealist Internationalism and the Security Dilemma," *World Politics* 5, 2 (January 1950): 157–80.

13. See Charles Glaser, "Realists as Optimists: Cooperation as Self-Help," *International Security* 19, 3 (Winter 1994/95): 50–90; Jack Snyder, *Myth of Empire: Domestic Politics and International Ambition* (Ithaca: Cornell University Press, 1991).

14. J. J. Rousseau, "A Discussion on the Origins of Inequality," in *The Social Contract and Discourses*, trans. G. D. H. Cole (New York: E. P. Dutton and Co., 1950), 235–38. Kenneth N. Waltz develops the stag hunt allegory in his *Man, the State and War* (New York: Columbia University Press, 1959), 165–71. For a critique of Waltz's interpretation of Rousseau, see Stanley Hoffmann, "Rousseau on War and Peace," *American Political Science Review* 57, no. 2 (June 1963): 317–33.

15. For a discussion of games such as stag hunt, prisoner's dilemma, deadlock, and chicken, see Robert Axelrod and Robert O. Keohane, "Achieving Cooperation Under Anarchy," *World Politics* 38, 1 (October 1985): 226–54.

16. See Robert Powell, "Absolute and Relative Gains in International Relations Theory," *American Political Science Review* 85 (1991): 1303–1320.

17. Reprinted in Fred A. Sondermann, David S. McClellan, and William C. Olson, eds., *The Theory and Practice of International Relations*, 5th ed. (Englewood Cliffs, NJ: Prentice Hall, 1979), 120.

18. Henry A. Kissinger, *A World Restored: The Politics of Conservatism in a Revolutionary Age* (New York: Grosset & Dunlap, 1964), 317–18.

19. Waltz, *Man, the State and War*, 209

20. *Ibid.*, 204

21. Ernst B. Haas, "On Systems and International Regimes," *World Politics* 27, 2 (January 1975), 151.

22. This is a direct quote from Kenneth Waltz at a roundtable at the Annual Meeting, American Political Science Association, Washington, D.C., August–September 2005.

23. Morgenthau, *Politics Among Nations*, 161 and 519, respectively.

24. Kenneth N. Waltz, "The Stability of a Bipolar World," *Daedalus* 93 (Summer 1964): 881–909; Karl W. Deutsch and J. David Singer, "Multipolar Power Systems and International Stability," *World Politics* 16, 3 (April 1964): 390–406.

25. Bruce Bueno de Mesquita, "Systemic Polarization and the Occurrence and Duration of War," *Journal of Conflict Resolution* 22, 2 (June 1978): 245, 246. See also Michael D. Wallace, *War and Rank Among Nations* (Lexington, MA: D. C. Heath, 1973).

26. See, for example, Randall L. Schweller, *Deadly Imbalances: Tripolarity and Hitler's Strategy of World Conquest* (New York: Columbia University Press, 1997); Edward Mansfield, *Power, Trade, and War* (Princeton: Princeton University Press, 1994); Dale C. Copeland, "Neorealism and the Myth of Bipolar Stability: Toward a New Dynamic Realist Theory of Major War," *Security Studies* 5, 3 (Spring 1996): 29–89. Discussion and references to power transition and power cycle theories are later in this chapter.

27. See, for example, Michael N. Barnett and Jack S. Levy, "Domestic Sources of Alliances and Alignments: The Case of Egypt, 1962–73," *International Organization* 45, 3 (Summer 1991): 369–95; Steven R. David, "Explaining Third World Alignment," *World Politics* 43, 2 (January 1991): 233–55; Thomas J. Christensen and Jack Snyder, "Chain Gangs and Passed Bucks: Predicting Alliance Patterns in Multipolarity," *International Organization* 44, 2 (Spring 1990): 137–68.

28. Stephen Walt, *The Origins of Alliances* (Ithaca: Cornell University Press, 1987) and his *Revolutions and War* (Ithaca: Cornell University Press, 1996).

29. Stephen Van Evera, *Causes of War: Power and the Roots of Conflict* (Ithaca, NY: Cornell University Press, 1999).

30. John J. Mearsheimer, *The Tragedy of Great Power Politics* (New York: W.W. Norton & Company, 2001).

31. For a recent comparison of the conceptions of balance of power of Morgenthau, Waltz, Mearsheimer, and Hedley Bull, see Richard Little, *The Balance of Power in International Relations: Metaphors, Myths, and Models* (Cambridge: Cambridge University Press, 2007).

32. See Kenneth N. Waltz, *Realism and International Politics* (London and New York: Routledge, 2008), x and xiv. Cf. Waltz, "The Emerging Structure of International Politics, "*International Security;* 18, 2 (Fall 1994): 44–79 and John J. Mearsheimer, "Back to the Future: Instability in Europe after the Cold War," *International Security* 15, no. 1 (Summer 1990): 5–56. See also Christopher Layne, "The Unipolar Illusion: Why New Powers Will Arise," *International Security* 17, 4 (1993): 5–51; Michael Mastanduno, "Preserving the Unipolar Moment: Realist Theory and US Grand Strategy After the Cold War," *International Security* 21, 4 (1997): 49–88. For a contrasting view, see William C. Wohlforth, "The Stability of a Bipolar World." *International Security* 24, 1 (1999): 5–41.

33. See the special issue of *World Politics* 38, 1 (October 1985), edited by Kenneth Oye; R. Harrison Wagner, "The Theory of Games and the Problem of International Cooperation," *American Political Science Review* 70, 2 (June 1983): 330–46; Robert Jervis, "Realism, Game Theory, and Cooperation," *World Politics* 40, 3 (April 1988): 317–49; Robert Axelrod, *The Evolution of Cooperation* (New York: Basic Books, 1984).

34. Robert O. Keohane, "The Theory of Hegemonic Stability and Changes in International Economic Regimes, 1967–1977," in Ole R. Holsti, Randolph M. Siverson, and Alexander L. George, eds., *Change in the International System* (Boulder, CO: Westview Press, 1980), 131–62. Charles P. Kindleberger, *The World in Depression, 1929–1939* (Berkeley: University of California Press, 1973); Robert Gilpin, *U.S. Power and the Multinational Corporation* (New York: Basic Books, 1975).

35. Paul Kennedy, *The Rise and Fall of the Great Powers* (New York: Random House, 1987). Cf. the earlier work of the economist Mancur Olson, *The Rise and Decline of Nations* (New Haven: Yale University Press, 1982): Henry R. Nau, *The Myth of America's Decline* (New York: Oxford University Press, 1990); Joseph S. Nye, Jr., *Bound to Lead: The Changing Nature of American Power* (New York: Basic Books, 1990); and Samuel P. Huntington, "The U.S.—Decline or Renewal?" *Foreign Affairs* 67, 2 (Winter 1988/89): 76–96.

36. See the works by Singer and Richardson as listed under "On Power, War, and Peace" under suggested readings.

37. Robert Gilpin, *War and Change in World Politics* (New York: Cambridge University Press, 1981), 3, 10. For other works on power transition, see the works listed under "On Power, War, and Peace."

38. George Modelski, "The Long Cycle of Global Politics and the Nation-State," *Comparative Studies in Society and History* 20, 2 (April 1978): 214–35. The quote is on p. 217. Notice that Modelski does not describe the international system as being anarchic. Although a central authority is lacking, order and authority do exist. It is Modelski's emphasis on the primacy of political factors that places him within the context of the realist as opposed to the economic-structuralist image.

39. *Ibid.*, 235.

40. Ronald L. Tammen, Jacek Kugler *et al.*, *Power Transitions* (New York and London: Chatham House Publishers, 2000).

41. See, for example, Jack S. Levy, "Theories of General War," *World Politics* 37, 3 (April 1985): 344–74; Nathaniel Beck, "The Illusion of Cycles in International Relations," and Joshua S. Goldstein, "The Possibility of Cycles in International Relations," *International Studies Quarterly* 35, 4 (December 1991): 455–80.

42. The first realist we cite is Kenneth N. Waltz, "Letter to the Editor," *International Organization* 36, 3 (Summer 1982): 680, which cites his *Theory of International Politics*, 78 and the other is Robert G. Gilpin, "The Richness of the Tradition of Political Realism," *International Organization* 38, 2 (Spring 1984): 302.

43. Randall L. Schweller and David Priess, "A Tale of Two Realisms: Expanding the Institutions Debate," *Mershon International Studies Review* 41, supplement 1 (May 1997): 1–33, Glenn H. Snyder, "Process Variables in Neorealist Theory," in *Realism: Restatements and Renewal*, ed. Benjamin Frankel, special issue of *Security Studies* 5, 3 (Spring 1996): 167–92, 88.

44. Waltz, "Letter to the Editor," 680; Gilpin, "Richness of Political Realism," 300.

45. Morgenthau, *Politics Among Nations*, 161; Ernst B. Haas, "The Balance of Power: Prescription, Concept or Propaganda? *World Politics* 5, no. 2 (July 1953): 442–77.

46. Waltz, *Theory of International Politics*.

47. Alexander Wendt, *Social Theory of International Politics* (London: Cambridge University Press, 1999).

48. Gilpin, "Richness of Political Realism," 299, 300.

SELECTED READINGS

The Melian Dialogue

THUCYDIDES

This classic contains the essential ingredients of the realist perspective described by Thucydides in perhaps its boldest and most extreme form. The Athenians have no interest in whether the demands they make on the Melians are just or moral. In a classic statement, the Athenians emphasize the overriding importance of power: "The strong do what they have the power to do, and the weak accept what they have to accept." Other important concepts and notions such as honor, perception, neutrality, self-interest, alliances, balance of power, capabilities, and the uncertainty of power calculations are also discussed.

Next summer Alcibiades sailed to Argos with twenty ships and seized 300 Argive citizens who were still suspected of being pro-Spartan. These were put by the Athenians into the nearby islands under Athenian control.

The Athenians also made an expedition against the island of Melos. They had thirty of their own ships, six from Chios, and two from Lesbos; 1,200 hoplites, 300 archers, and twenty mounted archers, all from Athens; and about 1,500 hoplites from the allies and the islanders.

The Melians are a colony from Sparta. They had refused to join the Athenian empire like the other islanders, and at first had remained neutral without helping either side; but afterwards when the Athenians had brought force to bear on them by laying waste their land, they had become open enemies of Athens.

Now the generals Cleomedes, the son of Lycomedes, and Tisias, the son of Tisimachus, encamped with the above force in Melian territory and, before doing any harm to the land, first of all sent representatives to negotiate. The Melians did not invite these representatives to speak before the people, but asked them to make the statement for which they had come in front of the governing body and the few. The Athenian representatives then spoke as follows:

"So we are not to speak before the people, no doubt in case the mass of the people should hear once and for all and without interruption an argument from us which is both persuasive and incontrovertible, and should so be led astray. This, we realize, is your motive in bringing us here to speak before the few. Now suppose that you who sit here should make assurance doubly sure. Suppose that you, too, should refrain from dealing with every point in detail in a set speech, and should instead interrupt us whenever we say something controversial and deal with that before going on to the next point? Tell us first whether you approve of this suggestion of ours."

The Council of the Melians replied as follows:

"No one can object to each of us putting forward our own views in a calm atmosphere. That is perfectly reasonable. What is scarcely consistent with such a proposal is the present threat, indeed the certainty, of your making war on us. We see that you have come prepared to judge the argument yourselves, and that the likely end of it all will be either war, if we prove that we are in the right, and so refuse to surrender, or else slavery."

Athenians: If you are going to spend the time in enumerating your suspicions about the future, or if you have met here for any other reason except to look the facts in the face and on the basis of these facts to consider how you can save your city from destruction, there is no point in our going on with this discussion. If, however, you will do as we suggest, then we will speak on.

Melians: It is natural and understandable that people who are placed as we are should have recourse to all kinds of arguments and different points of view. However, you are right in saying that we are met together here to discuss the safety of our country and, if you will have it so, the discussion shall proceed on the lines that you have laid down.

Athenians: Then we on our side will use no fine phrases saying, for example, that we have a right to our empire because we defeated the Persians, or that we have come against you now because of the injuries you have done us—a great mass of words that nobody would believe. And we ask you on your side not to imagine that you will influence us by saying that you, though a colony of Sparta, have not joined Sparta in the war, or that you have never done us any harm. Instead we recommend that you should try to get what it is possible for you to get, taking into consideration what we both really do think; since you know as well as we do that, when these matters are discussed by practical people, the standard of justice depends on the equality of power to compel and that in fact the strong do what they have the power to do and the weak accept what they have to accept.

Melians: Then in our view (since you force us to leave justice out of account and to confine ourselves to self-interest)—in our view it is at any rate useful that you should not destroy a principle that is to the general good of all men—namely, that in the case of all who fall into danger there should be such a thing as fair play and just dealing, and that such people should be allowed to use and to profit by arguments that fall short of a mathematical accuracy. And this is a principle which affects you as much as anybody, since your own fall would be visited by the most terrible vengeance and would be an example to the world.

Athenians: As for us, even assuming that our empire does come to an end, we are not despondent about what would happen next. One is not so much frightened of being conquered by a power which rules over others, as Sparta does (not that we are concerned with Sparta now), as of what would happen if a ruling power is attacked and defeated by its own subjects. So far as this point is concerned, you can leave it to us to face the risks involved. What we shall do now is to show you that it is for the good of

our own empire that we are here and that it is for the preservation of your city that we shall say what we are going to say. We do not want any trouble in bringing you into our empire, and we want you to be spared for the good both of yourselves and of ourselves.

Melians: And how could it be just as good for us to be the slaves as for you to be the masters?

Athenians: You, by giving in, would save yourselves from disaster; we, by not destroying you, would be able to profit from you.

Melians: So you would not agree to our being neutral, friends instead of enemies, but allies of neither side?

Athenians: No, because it is not so much your hostility that injures us; it is rather the case that, if we were on friendly terms with you, our subjects would regard that as a sign of weakness in us, whereas your hatred is evidence of our power.

Melians: Is that your subjects' idea of fair play—that no distinction should be made between people who are quite unconnected with you and people who are mostly your own colonists or else rebels whom you have conquered?

Athenians: So far as right and wrong are concerned they think that there is no difference between the two, that those who still preserve their independence do so because they are strong, and that if we fail to attack them it is because we are afraid. So that by conquering you we shall increase not only the size but the security of our empire. We rule the sea and you are islanders, and weaker islanders too than the others; it is therefore particularly important that you should not escape.

Melians: But do you think there is security for you in what we suggest? For here again, since you will not let us mention justice, but tell us to give in to your interests, we, too, must tell you what our interests are and, if yours and ours happen to coincide, we must try to persuade you of the fact. Is it not certain that you will make enemies of all states who are at present neutral, when they see what is happening here and naturally conclude that in course of time you will attack them too? Does not this mean that you are strengthening the enemies you have already and are forcing others to become your enemies even against their intensions and their inclinations?

Athenians: As a matter of fact we are not so much frightened of states on the continent. They have their liberty, and this means that it will be a long time before they begin to take precautions against us. We are more concerned about islanders like yourselves, who are still unsubdued, or subjects who have already become embittered by the constraint which our empire imposes on them. These are the people who are most likely to act in a reckless manner and to bring themselves and us, too, into the most obvious danger.

Melians: Then surely, if such hazards are taken by you to keep your empire and by your subjects to escape from it, we who are still free would show ourselves great cowards and weaklings if we failed to face everything that comes rather than submit to slavery.

Athenians: No, not if you are sensible. This is no fair fight, with honour on one side and shame on the other. It is rather a question of saving your lives and not resisting those who are far too strong for you.

Melians: Yet we know that in war fortune sometimes makes the odds more level than could be expected from the difference in numbers of the two sides. And if we surrender, then all our hope is lost at once, whereas, so long as we remain in action, there is still a hope that we may yet stand upright.

Athenians: Hope, that comforter in danger! If one already has solid advantages to fall back upon, one can indulge in hope. It may do harm, but will not destroy one. But hope is by nature an expensive commodity, and those who are risking their all on one cast find out what it means only when they are already ruined; it never fails them in the period when such a knowledge would enable them to take precautions. Do not let this happen to you, you who are weak and whose fate depends on a single movement of the scale. And do not be like those people who, as so commonly happens, miss the chance of saving themselves in a human and practical way, and, when every clear and distinct hope has left them in their adversity, turn to what is blind and vague, to prophecies and oracles and such things which by encouraging hope lead men to ruin.

Melians: It is difficult, and you may be sure that we know it, for us to oppose your power and fortune, unless the terms be equal. Nevertheless we trust that the gods will give us fortune as good as yours, because we are standing for what is right against what is wrong; and as for what we lack in power, we trust that it will be made up for by our alliance with the Spartans, who are bound, if for no other reason, than for honour's sake, and because we are their kinsmen, to come to our help. Our confidence, therefore, is not so entirely irrational as you think.

Athenians: So far as the favour of the gods is concerned, we think we have as much right to that as you have. Our aims and our actions are perfectly consistent with the beliefs men hold about the gods and with the principles which govern their own conduct. Our opinion of the gods and our knowledge of men lead us to conclude that it is a general and necessary law of nature to rule whatever one can. This is not a law that we made ourselves, nor were we the first to act upon it when it was made. We found it already in existence, and we shall leave it to exist forever among those who come after us. We are merely acting in accordance with it, and we know that you or anybody else with the same power as ours would be acting in precisely the same way. And therefore, so far as the gods are concerned, we see no good reason why we should fear to be at a disadvantage. But with regard to your views about Sparta and your confidence that she, out of a sense of honour, will come to your aid, we must say that we congratulate you on your simplicity but do not envy you your folly. In matters that concern themselves for their own constitution the Spartans are quite remarkably good; as for their relations with others, that is a long story, but it can be expressed shortly and clearly by saying that of all people we know the Spartans are most conspicuous for believing that what they like doing is honourable and what suits their interests is just. And this kind of attitude is not going to be of much help to you in your absurd quest for safety at the moment.

Melians: But this is the very point where we can feel most sure. Their own self-interest will make them refuse to betray their own colonists, the Melians, for that would mean losing the confidence of their friends among the Hellenes and doing good to their enemies.

Athenians: You seem to forget that if one follows one's self-interest one wants to be safe, whereas the path of justice and honour involves one in danger. And, where danger is concerned, the Spartans are not, as a rule, very venturesome.

Melians: But we think that they would even endanger themselves for our sake and count the risk more worth taking than in the case of others, because we are so close to the Peloponnese that they could operate more easily, and because they can depend on us more than on others, since we are of the same race and share the same feelings.

Athenians: Good will shown by the party that is asking for help does not mean security for the prospective ally. What is looked for is a positive pre-ponderance of power in action. And the Spartans pay attention to this point even more than others do. Certainly they distrust their own native resources so much that when they attack a neighbour they bring a great army of allies with them. It is hardly likely therefore that, while we are in control of the sea, they will cross over to an island.

Melians: But they still might send others. The Cretan sea is a wide one, and it is harder for those who control it to intercept others than for those who want to slip through to do so safely. And even if they were to fail in this, they would turn against your own land and against those of your allies left unvisited by Brasidas. So, instead of troubling about a country which has nothing to do with you, you will find trouble nearer home, among your allies, and in your own country.

Athenians: It is a possibility, something that has in fact happened before. It may happen in your case, but you are well aware that the Athenians have never yet relinquished a single siege operation through fear of others. But we are somewhat shocked to find that, though you announced your intention of dis-cussing how you could preserve yourselves, in all this talk you have said absolutely nothing which could justify a man in thinking that he could be pre-served. Your chief points are concerned with what you hope may happen in the future, while your ac-tual resources are too scanty to give you a chance of survival against the forces that are opposed to you at this moment. You will therefore be showing an ex-traordinary lack of common sense if, after you have asked us to retire from this meeting, you still fail to reach a conclusion wiser than anything you have mentioned so far. Do not be led astray by a false sense of honour—a thing which often brings men to ruin when they are faced with an obvious danger that somehow affects their pride. For in many cases men have still been able to see the dangers ahead of them, but this thing called dishonour, this word, by its own force of seduction, has drawn them into a state where they have surrendered to an idea, while in fact they have fallen voluntarily into irrevocable disaster, in dishonour that is all the more dishon-ourable because it has come to them from their own folly rather than their misfortune. You, if you take the right view, will be careful to avoid this. You will see that there is nothing disgraceful in giving way to the greatest city in Hellas when she is offering you

such reasonable terms—alliance on a tribute-paying basis and liberty to enjoy your own property. And, when you are allowed to choose between war and safety, you will not be so insensitively arrogant as to make the wrong choice. This is the safe rule—to stand up to one's equals, to behave with deference towards one's superiors, and to treat one's inferiors with moderation. Think it over again, then, when we have withdrawn from the meeting, and let this be a point that constantly recurs to your minds—that you are discussing the fate of your country, that you have only one country, and that its future for good or ill depends on this one single decision which you are going to make.

The Athenians then withdrew from the discus-sion. The Melians, left to themselves, reached a con-clusion which was much the same as they had indicated in their previous replies. Their answer was as follows:

"Our decision, Athenians, is just the same as it was at first. We are not prepared to give up in a short moment the liberty which our city has enjoyed from its foundation for 700 years. We put our trust in the fortune that the gods will send and which has saved us up to now, and in the help of men—that is, of the Spartans; and so we shall try to save ourselves. But we invited you to allow us to be friends of yours and enemies to neither side, to make a treaty which shall be agreeable to both you and us, and so to leave our country."

The Melians made this reply, and the Athenians, just as they were breaking off the discussion, said:

"Well, at any rate, judging from this decision of yours, you seem to us quite unique in your ability to consider the future as something more certain than what is before your eyes, and to see uncertainties as realities, simply because you would like them to be so. As you have staked most on and trusted most in Spartans, luck, and hopes, so in all these you will find yourselves most completely deluded."

The Athenian representatives then went back to the army, and the Athenian generals, finding that the Melians would not submit, immediately com-menced hostilities and built a wall completely round the city of Melos, dividing the work out among the various states. Later they left behind a garrison of some of their own and some allied troops to block-ade the place by land and sea, and with the greater part of their army returned home. The force left behind stayed on and continued with the siege.

About the same time the Argives invaded Phliasia and were ambushed by the Phliasians and the exiles from Argos, losing about eighty men.

Then, too, the Athenians at Pylos captured a great quantity of plunder from Spartan territory. Not even after this did the Spartans renounce the treaty and make war, but they issued a proclamation saying that any of their people who wished to do so were free to make raids on the Athenians. The Corinthians also made some attacks on the Athenians because of private quarrels of their own, but the rest of the Peloponnesians stayed quiet.

Meanwhile the Melians made a night attack and captured the part of the Athenian lines opposite the market-place. They killed some of the troops, and then, after bringing in corn and everything else useful that they could lay their hands on, retired again and made no further move, while the Athenians took measures to make their blockade more efficient in the future. So the summer came to an end.

In the following winter the Spartans planned to invade the territory of Argos, but when the sacrifices for crossing the frontier turned out unfavourably, they gave up the expedition. The fact that they had intended to invade made the Argives suspect certain people in their city, some of whom they arrested, though others succeeded in escaping.

About this same time the Melians again captured another part of the Athenian lines where there were only a few of the garrison on guard. As a result of this, another force came out afterwards from Athens under the command of Philocrates, the son of Demeas. Siege operations were now carried on vigorously and, as there was also some treachery from inside, the Melians surrendered unconditionally to the Athenians, who put to death all the men of military age whom they took, and sold the women and children as slaves. Melos itself they took over for themselves, sending out later a colony of 500 men.

On Princes and the Security of Their States

NICCOLÒ MACHIAVELLI

In this selection from The Prince, *Machiavelli makes a number of his famous observations on how a prince should rule. Although a prince may not wish to be hated, Machiavelli argues "it is much safer to be feared than to be loved, if one must choose." Although the prince may be criticized for being harsh, this is acceptable to Machiavelli so long as the prince keeps his subjects united and loyal. These are the sorts of argument that have given Machiavellianism a negative connotation, but followers of Machiavelli would respond that the ultimate goal meant to justify particular policies is the security of the state, not just the security of an individual ruler.*

On Things for Which Men, and Particularly Princes, Are Praised or Blamed

We now have left to consider what should be the manners and attitudes of a prince toward his subjects and his friends. As I know that many have written on this subject I feel that I may be held presumptuous in what I have to say, if in my comments I do not follow the lines laid down by others.

Since, however, it has been my intention to write something which may be of use to the understanding reader, it has seemed wiser to me to follow the real truth of the matter rather than what we imagine it to be. For imagination has created many principalities and republics that have never been seen or known to have any real existence, for how we live is so different from how we ought to live that he who studies what ought to be done rather than what is

From Niccolò Machiavelli, *The Prince,* translated and edited by Thomas G. Bergin. Reprinted by permission.

done will learn the way to his downfall rather than to his preservation. A man striving in every way to be good will meet his ruin among the great number who are not good. Hence it is necessary for a prince, if he wishes to remain in power, to learn how not to be good and to use his knowledge or refrain from using it as he may need.

Putting aside then the things imagined as pertaining to a prince and considering those that really do, I will say that all men, and particularly princes because of their prominence, when comment is made of them, are noted as having some characteristics deserving either praise or blame. One is accounted liberal, another stingy, to use a Tuscan term—for in our speech avaricious (*avaro*) is applied to such as are desirous of acquiring by rapine whereas stingy (*misero*) is the term used for those who are reluctant to part with their own—one is considered bountiful, another rapacious; one cruel, another tenderhearted; one false to his word, another trustworthy; one effeminate and pusillanimous, another wild and spirited; one humane, another haughty; one lascivious, another chaste; one a man of integrity and another sly; one tough and another pliant; one serious and another frivolous; one religious and another skeptical, and so on. Everyone will agree, I know, that it would be a most praiseworthy thing if all the qualities accounted as good in the above enumeration were found in a Prince. But since they cannot be so possessed nor observed because of human conditions which do not allow of it, what is necessary for the prince is to be prudent enough to escape the infamy of such vices as would result in the loss of his state; as for the others which would not have that effect, he must guard himself from them as far as possible but if he cannot, he may overlook them as being of less importance. Further, he should have no concern about incurring the infamy of such vices without which the preservation of his state would be difficult. For, if the matter be well considered, it will be seen that some habits which appear virtuous, if adopted would signify ruin, and others that seem vices lead to security and the well-being of the prince.

Cruelty and Clemency and Whether It Is Better to Be Loved or Feared

Now to continue with the list of characteristics. It should be the desire of every prince to be considered merciful and not cruel, yet he should take care not to make poor use of his clemency. Cesare Borgia was regarded as cruel, yet his cruelty reorganized Romagna and united it in peace and loyalty. Indeed, if we reflect, we shall see that this man was more merciful than the Florentines who, to avoid the charge of cruelty, allowed Pistoia to be destroyed.[1] A prince should care nothing for the accusation of cruelty so long as he keeps his subjects united and loyal; by making a very few examples he can be more truly merciful than those who through too much tender-heartedness allow disorders to arise whence come killings and rapine. For these offend an entire community, while the few executions ordered by the prince affect only a few individuals. For a new prince above all it is impossible not to earn a reputation for cruelty since new states are full of dangers. Virgil indeed has Dido apologize for the inhumanity of her rule because it is new, in the words:

> Res dura et regni novitas me talia cogunt Moliri et late fines custode tueri.

Nevertheless a prince should not be too ready to listen to talebearers nor to act on suspicion, nor should he allow himself to be easily frightened. He should proceed with a mixture of prudence and humanity in such a way as not to be made incautious by overconfidence nor yet intolerable by excessive mistrust.

Here the question arises; whether it is better to be loved than feared or feared than loved. The answer is that it would be desirable to be both but, since that is difficult, it is much safer to be feared than to be loved, if one must choose. For on men in general this observation may be made: they are ungrateful, fickle, and deceitful, eager to avoid dangers, and avid for gain, and while you are useful to them they are all with you, offering you their blood, their property, their lives, and their sons so long as danger is remote, as we noted above, but when it approaches they turn on you. Any prince, trusting only in their words and having no other preparations made, will fall to his ruin, for friendships that are bought at a price and not by greatness and nobility of soul are paid for indeed, but they are not owned and cannot be called upon in time of need. Men have less hesitation in offending a man who is loved than one who is feared, for love is held by a bond of obligation which, as men are wicked, is broken whenever personal advantage suggests it, but fear is accompanied by the dread of punishment which never relaxes.

Yet a prince should make himself feared in such a way that, if he does not thereby merit love, at least he may escape odium, for being feared and not hated may well go together. And indeed the prince may attain this end if he but respect the property and the women of his subjects and citizens. And if it should become necessary to seek the death of someone, he should find a proper justification and a public cause, and above all he should keep his hands off another's property, for men forget more readily the death of their father than the loss of their patrimony. Besides, pretexts for seizing property are never lacking, and when a prince begins to live by means of rapine he will always find some excuse for plundering others, and conversely pretexts for execution are rarer and are more quickly exhausted.

A prince at the head of his armies and with a vast number of soldiers under his command should give not the slightest heed if he is esteemed cruel, for without such a reputation he will not be able to keep his army united and ready for action. Among the marvelous things told of Hannibal is that, having a vast army under his command made up of all kinds and races of men and waging war far from his country, he never allowed any dissension to arise either as between the troops and their leaders or among the troops themselves, and this both in times of good fortune and bad. This could only have come about through his most inhuman cruelty which, taken in conjunction with his great valor, kept him always an object of respect and terror in the eyes of his soldiers. And without the cruelty his other characteristics would not have achieved this effect. Thoughtless writers have admired his actions and at the same time deplored the cruelty which was the basis of them. As evidence of the truth of our statement that his other virtues would have been insufficient let us examine the case of Scipio, an extraordinary leader not only in his own day but for all recorded history. His army in Spain revolted and for no other reason than because of his kind-heartedness, which had allowed more license to his soldiery than military discipline properly permits. His policy was attacked in the Senate by Fabius Maximus, who called him a corrupter of the Roman arms. When the Locrians had been mishandled by one of his lieutenants, his easy-going nature prevented him from avenging them or disciplining his officer, and it was à propos of this incident that one of the senators remarked, wishing to find an excuse for him, that there were many men who knew better how to avoid error themselves than to correct it in others. This characteristic of Scipio would have clouded his fame and glory had he continued in authority, but as he lived under the government of the Senate, its harmful aspect was hidden and it reflected credit on him.

Hence, on the subject of being loved or feared I will conclude that since love depends on the subjects, but the prince has it in his own hands to create fear, a wise prince will rely on what is his own, remembering at the same time that he must avoid arousing hatred, as we have said.

Note

1. By unchecked rioting between opposing factions (1502).

Of the Natural Condition of Mankind

THOMAS HOBBES

Hobbes analyzes why conflict and violence between individuals or states are to be expected. Although his focus in Leviathan is on domestic societies, his observations are also relevant to international politics and have had a major impact on realism. In the absence of a sovereign or central, superordinate authority, the anarchic world described by Hobbes is a rather dismal one in which the life of the individual is "solitary, poor, nasty, brutish, and short" and "kings . . . because of their independency, are in continual jealousies, and in the state and posture of gladiators."

From Thomas Hobbes, *Leviathan*, introduction by Richard S. Peters. New York: Macmillan/Collier Books, 1962.

Men by Nature Equal.   Nature hath made men so equal, in the faculties of the body, and mind; as that though there be found one man sometimes manifestly stronger in body, or of quicker mind than another; yet when all is reckoned together, the difference between man, and man, is not so considerable, as that one man can thereupon claim to himself any benefit, to which another may not pretend, as well as he. For as to the strength of body, the weakest has strength enough to kill the strongest, either by secret machination, or by confederacy with others, that are in the same danger with himself.

And as to the faculties of the mind, setting aside the arts grounded upon words, and especially that skill of proceeding upon general, and infallible rules, called science; which very few have, and but in few things; as being not a native faculty, born with us; nor attained, as prudence, while we look after somewhat else, I find yet a greater equality amongst men, than that of strength. For prudence, is but experience; which equal time, equally bestows on all men, in those things they equally apply themselves unto. That which may perhaps make such equality incredible, is but a vain conceit of one's own wisdom, which almost all men think they have in a greater degree, than the vulgar; that is, than all men but themselves, and a few others, whom by fame, or for concurring with themselves, they approve. For such is the nature of men, that howsoever they may acknowledge many others to be more witty, or more eloquent, or more learned; yet they will hardly believe there be many so wise as themselves; for they see their own wit at hand, and other men's at a distance. But this proveth rather that men are in that point equal, than unequal. For there is not ordinarily a greater sign of the equal distribution of any thing, than that every man is contented with his share.

From Equality Proceeds Diffidence. From this equality of ability, ariseth equality of hope in the attaining of our ends. And therefore if any two men desire the same thing, which nevertheless they cannot both enjoy they become enemies; and in the way to their end, which is principally their own conservation, and sometimes their delectation only, endeavour to destroy, or subdue one another. And from hence it comes to pass, that where an invader hath no more to fear, than another man's single power; if one plant, sow, build, or possess a convenient seat, others may probably be expected to come prepared with forces united, to dispossess, and deprive him, not only of the fruit of his labour, but also of his life, or liberty. And the invader again is in the like danger of another.

From Diffidence War.   And from this diffidence of one another, there is no way for any man to secure himself, so reasonable, as anticipation; that is, by force, or wiles, to master the persons of all men he can, so long, till he see no other power great enough to endanger him: and this is no more than his own conservation requireth, and is generally allowed. Also because there be some, that taking pleasure in contemplating their own power in the acts of conquest, which they pursue farther than their security requires; if others, that otherwise would be glad to be at ease within modest bounds, should not by invasion increase their power, they would not be able, long time, by standing only on their defence, to subsist. And by consequence, such augmentation of dominion over men being necessary to a man's conservation, it ought to be allowed him.

Again, men have no pleasure, but on the contrary a great deal of grief, in keeping company, where there is no power able to overawe them all. For every man looketh that his companion should value him, at the same rate he sets upon himself: and upon all signs of contempt, or undervaluing, naturally endeavours, as far as he dares, (which amongst them that have no common power to keep them in quiet, is far enough to make them destroy each other), to extort a greater value from his contemners, by damage; and from others, by the example.

So that in the nature of man, we find three principal causes of quarrel. First, competition; secondly, diffidence; thirdly, glory.

The first, maketh men invade for gain; the second, for safety; and the third, for reputation. The first use violence, to make themselves masters of other men's persons, wives, children, and cattle; the second, to defend them; the third, for trifles, as a word, a smile, a different opinion, and any other sign of undervalue, either direct in their persons, or by reflection in their kindred, their friends, their nation, their profession, or their name.

Out of Civil States, There Is Always War of Every One against Every One.   Hereby it is manifest, that during the time men live without a common power to keep them all in awe, they are in that condition which is called war; and such a war, as is of every man, against every man. For WAR, consisteth not in battle only, or the act of fighting; but in a tract of time, wherein the will to content by battle is sufficiently known: and therefore the notion of *time*, is to be considered in the nature of war; as it is in the nature of weather. For as the nature of foul weather, lieth not in a shower or two of rain; but in an inclination thereto of many days together: so the nature of war, consisteth not in actual fighting; but in the known disposition thereto, during all the time there is no assurance to the contrary. All other time is PEACE.

The Incommodities of Such a War. Whatsoever therefore is consequent to a time of war, where every man is enemy to every man; the same is consequent to the time, wherein men live without other security, than what their own strength, and their own invention shall furnish them withal. In such condition, there is no place for industry; because the fruit thereof is uncertain: and consequently no culture of the earth; no navigation, nor use of the commodities that may be imported by sea; no commodious building; no instruments of moving, and removing, such things as require much force; no knowledge of the face of the earth; no account of time; no arts; no letters; no society; and which is worst of all, continual fear, and danger of violent death; and the life of man, solitary, poor, nasty, brutish, and short.

It may seem strange to some man, that has not well weighed these things; that nature should thus dissociate, and render men apt to invade, and destroy one another; and he may therefore, not trusting to this inference, made from the passions, desire perhaps to have the same confirmed by experience. Let him therefore consider with himself, when taking a journey, he arms himself, and seeks to go well accompanied; when going to sleep, he locks his doors; when even in his house he locks his chests; and this when he knows there be laws, and public officers, armed, to revenge all injuries shall be done him; what opinion he has of his fellow-subjects, when he rides armed; of his fellow citizens, when he locks his doors; and of his children, and servants, when he locks his chests. Does he not there as much accuse mankind by his actions, as I do by my words? But neither of us accuse man's nature in it. The desires, and other passions of man, are in themselves no sin. No more are the actions, that proceed from those passions, till they know a law that forbids them: which till laws be made they cannot know: nor can any law be made, till they have agreed upon the person that shall make it.

It may peradventure be thought, there was never such a time, nor condition of war as this; and I believe it was never generally so, over all the world: but there are many places, where they live so now. For the savage people in many places of America, except the government of small families, the concord whereof dependeth on natural lust, have no government at all; and live at this day in the brutish manner, as I said before. Howsoever, it may be perceived what manner of life there would be, where there were no common power to fear, by the manner of life, which men that have formerly lived under a peaceful government, use to degenerate into, in a civil war.

But though there had never been any time, wherein particular men were in a condition of war one against another; yet in all times, kings, and persons of sovereign authority, because of their independency, are in continual jealousies, and in the state and posture of gladiators; having their weapons pointing, and their eyes fixed on one another; that is, their forts, garrisons, and guns upon the frontiers of their kingdoms; and continual spies upon their neighbours; which is a posture of war. But because they uphold thereby, the industry of their subjects; there does not follow from it, that misery, which accompanies the liberty of particular men.

In Such a War Nothing Is Unjust. To this war of every man, against every man, this also is consequent; that nothing can be unjust. The notions of right and wrong, justice and injustice have there no place. Where there is no common power, there is no law: where no law, no injustice. Force, and fraud, are in war the two cardinal virtues. Justice, and injustice are none of the faculties neither of the body, nor mind. If they were, they might be in a man that were alone in the world, as well as his senses, and passions. They are qualities, that relate to men in society, not in solitude. It is consequent also to the same condition, there there be no propriety, no dominion, no *mine* and *thine* distinct; but only that to be every man's, that he can get: and for so long, as he can keep it. And thus much for the ill condition, which man by mere nature is actually placed in; though with a possibility to come out of it, consisting partly in the passions, partly in his reason.

The Passions That Incline Men to Peace. The passions that incline men to peace, are fear of death; desire of such things as are necessary to commodious living; and a hope by their industry to obtain them. And reason suggesteth convenient articles of peace, upon which men may be drawn to agreement.

The State of War: Confederation as Means to Peace in Europe

JEAN-JACQUES ROUSSEAU

Rousseau observes that "man is naturally peaceful and shy." He takes issue with the Hobbesian view of man's nature, contesting the idea that it could be so negative. At the same time, it is the "liberty" that states have in relation to one another that results in "accidental and specific wars." He portrays states as unitary and rational (purposive) actors that may come into conflict, engaging in warfare with one another. War does not depend upon the nature of man. For Rousseau war is the product of a social context within which the state (or body politic) finds itself—one in which there is no authority higher than the state itself. Rousseau does not reject the view that a European confederation could produce peace, but considers it unlikely that such a restructuring of politics will be achieved. This selection is key to understanding realist and structural realist views; note his reference to the "absolute independence" of states and how, in order to add to one's "relative power," one must "seek out only exclusive gains." See also the discussion of Rousseau's stag hunt fable on pages 29–30 of this book.

When I reflect upon the condition of the human race, the first thing that I notice is a manifest contradiction in its constitution. As individuals we live in a civil state and are subject to laws, but as nations each enjoys the liberty of nature. The resulting continual vacillation makes our situation worse than if these distinctions were unknown. For living simultaneously in the social order and in the state of nature, we are subjected to the evils of both without gaining the security of either. The perfections of the social order consists, it is true, in the conjunction of force and law. But for this it is necessary that law direct force. According to the notion that princes must be absolutely independent, however, force alone, which appears as law to its own citizens and "raison d'état" to foreigners, deprives the latter of the power and the former of the will to resist, so that in the end the vain name of justice serves only to safeguard violence.

As for what is called the law of nations, it is clear that without any real sanction these laws are only illusions that are more tenuous even than the notion of natural law. The latter at least addresses itself to the heart of individuals, whereas decisions based on the law of nations, having no other guarantee than the utility of the one who submits to them, are respected only as long as those decisions confirm one's own self-interest. In the double condition in which we find ourselves, by doing too much or too little for whichever of the two systems we happen to prefer, we in fact have done nothing at all, and thereby have put ourselves in the worst possible position. This, it seems to me, is the true origin of public calamities.

For a moment, let us put these ideas in opposition to the horrible system of Hobbes. We will find, contrary to his absurd doctrine, that far from the state of war being natural to man, war is born out of peace, or at least out of the precautions men have taken to assure themselves of peace....

Critique of the Perpetual Peace Project

As the most worthy cause to which a good man might devote himself, the *Project for Perpetual Peace* must also have been, among all the projects of the Abbé de Saint-Pierre, the one that he thought about the most and the one that he pursued with the greatest obstinancy. For how else could one explain the missionary zeal with which he clung to this project—despite the obvious impossibility of its success, the ridicule that it brought upon him every day, and the hostility that he was made continually to suffer. It seems that this humane soul was so single-mindedly focused on the public good that he measured the efforts that he gave things solely on the basis of their usefulness, without ever letting himself be discouraged by obstacles and without ever thinking about his own personal self-interest.

If ever a moral truth has been demonstrated, it seems to me that it is the general and the specific usefulness of this project. The advantages that would result from its formation both for each prince and for each nation, as well as for Europe as a whole, are immense, clear, and uncontestable. One cannot imagine anything more solid and more precise than the arguments with which the author supports his case. Indeed, so much would the experience allow each individual to gain from the common good, that to realize the European Republic for one day would be enough to make it last forever. However, these same princes who would defend the European Republic with all their might once it existed would now be opposed even to its being set up, and they would invariably prevent it from being established with just as much energy as they would prevent it from being destroyed. The work of the Abbé de Saint-Pierre thus would seem both ineffectual for producing peace and superfluous for maintaining it. Some impatient reader will say that it is therefore nothing but vain speculation. No, it is a solid and sensible book, and it is very important that it exists.

Let us begin by examining the difficulties of those who do not judge arguments with reason but only with events and who have nothing to object to in this project other than that it has not been tried. In effect, they doubtlessly will say, if the advantages are so real, why have the sovereigns of Europe not adopted them already? Why do they neglect their own self-interest, if this self-interest has now been made so clear? Do we see them rejecting all the other ways of increasing their revenues and their power? If this project were as good for that purpose as is claimed, is it plausible that they would be less impressed with it than with those which have failed them so many times before, or that they would prefer a thousand risky chances to one sure gain?

Clearly, all this is plausible unless we pretend that the wisdom of all these sovereigns is equal to their ambition and that the more strongly they desire their own advantages the better they can see them. Instead, the great penalty for excessive *amour propre* is forever to resort to the means that abuse it, and the very heat of the passions is what almost always prevents them from reaching their goal. We must distinguish, then, in politics as well as in morality, real interest from apparent interest. The first is to be found in perpetual peace—that has been demonstrated in the *Project.* The second can be found in the condition of absolute independence that draws sovereigns away from the rule of law in order to submit them to the rule of chance—like a mad sailor who, to show off his knowledge and intimidate his crew, would prefer to drift dangerously among the reefs during a storm than to secure his ship with an anchor. . . .

We must add, in considering the great commercial advantages that would result from a general and perpetual peace, that while they are obviously in themselves certain and incontestable, being common to all they would not be relative advantages to anyone. Since advantage is usually only sensed by virtue of difference, to add to one's relative power one must seek out only exclusive gains.

Ceaselessly deceived by the appearance of things, princes will therefore reject this peace when judging it by their own self-interest. Just think, then, what will happen when they leave such judgments to their ministers, whose interests are always opposed to those of the people and almost always opposed to those of the prince. Ministers need war to make themselves necessary, to precipitate the prince into crises that he cannot get out of without them, and to cause the loss of the state, if it is necessary, rather than the loss of their jobs. They need war to harass the people in the guise of public safety, to find work for their protégés, to make money on the markets, and to form a thousand corrupt monopolies in secret. They need it to satisfy their passions and to push each other out of office. They need it to preoccupy the prince and remove him from the court while dangerous intrigues arise among them. Such resources would all be lost to them if there were a perpetual peace. And the public keeps on demanding why, if the project is possible, it has not been adopted! They fail to see that there is nothing impossible about the project except its adoption. And what will the ministers do to oppose it? What they have always done—they will turn it to ridicule.

Nor is it possible to believe along with the Abbé de Saint-Pierre that, even with the good will which neither princes nor ministers will ever have, it would be easy to find a favorable moment to set this system in motion. For that it would be necessary that the sum of individual interests would not outweigh the common interest, and that each one would believe that he had found in the good of all the greatest good that he could hope for for himself. Now this would require a convergence of wisdom among so many different minds and a convergence of aims among so many different interests that one could hardly hope to get the happy agreement of all these necessary circumstances simply by chance. The only way to make up for the failure of this agreement to come about by chance would be to make it come about by force. Then it would no longer be a question of persuading but of compelling, and then what would be needed is not to write books but to levy troops.

Thus, although the project was very wise, the means of putting it into effect reflect the naiveté of the author. He innocently imagined that all you would need to do is to assemble a committee, propose his articles, have everyone sign them, and that would be it. We must conclude that, as with all the projects of this good man, he could envision quite well the effect of things after they had been established, but he judged with too little sophistication the methods for getting them established in the first place. . . .

We may not say, therefore, that if his system has not been adopted, it is because it was not good; on the contrary, we must say that it was too good to be adopted. For evil and abuse, which so many men profit from, happen by themselves, but whatever is useful to the public must be brought by force—seeing as special interests are almost always opposed to it. Doubtless perpetual peace is at present a project that seems absurd. . . .

We will not see federative leagues establishing themselves except by revolution, and, on this principle, who would dare to say whether this European league is to be desired or to be feared? It would perhaps cause more harm in one moment than it could prevent for centuries to come.

Hard and Soft Power in American Foreign Policy

JOSEPH S. NYE, JR.

Using the United States as his principal case, the author sees the power of a state as including both hard and soft components—the former economic and military and the latter composed of cultural dimensions or the values that define the identity and practices of a state. Combining hard and soft power assets effectively—"smart" power as Nye now calls it—is essential to attaining national objectives and affecting the behavior of others. Soft power becomes manifest in international institutions (listening to others) and in foreign policy (promoting peace and human rights). An advocate of multilateralism, the author sees sustaining American power as dependent upon "strategic restraint, reassuring partners and facilitating cooperation," not just "because of unmatched American hard power." Consistent with classical realism, we find in this article, then, an argument that addresses the ideational, not just the material dimensions of power. He also addresses the supposed desirability of a multipolar balance of power versus hegemonic power.

"Hard and Soft Power in American Foreign Policy" from *The Paradox of American Power* by Joseph S. Nye, Jr., 2003. Reprinted by permission of Oxford University Press, Inc.

The ability to obtain the outcomes one wants is often associated with the possession of certain resources, and so we commonly use shorthand and define power as possession of relatively large amounts of such elements as population, territory, natural resources, economic strength, military force, and political stability. Power in this sense means holding the high cards in the international poker game. If you show high cards, others are likely to fold their hands. Of course, if you play your hand poorly or fall victim to bluff and deception, you can still lose, or at least fail to get the outcome you want. For example, the United States was the largest power after World War I, but it failed to prevent the rise of Hitler or Pearl Harbor. Converting America's potential power resources into realized power requires well-designed policy and skillful leadership. But it helps to start by holding the high cards.

Traditionally, the test of a great power was "strength for war."[1] War was the ultimate game in which the cards of international politics were played and estimates of relative power were proven. Over the centuries, as technologies evolved, the sources of power have changed. In the agrarian economies of seventeenth- and eighteenth-century Europe, population was a critical power resource because it provided a base for taxes and the recruitment of infantry (who were mostly mercenaries), and this combination of men and money gave the edge to France. But in the nineteenth century, the growing importance of industry benefited first Britain, which ruled the waves with a navy that had no peer, and later Germany, which used efficient administration and railways to transport armies for quick victories on the Continent (though Russia had a larger population and army). By the middle of the twentieth century, with the advent of the nuclear age, the United States and the Soviet Union possessed not only industrial might but nuclear arsenals and intercontinental missiles.

Today the foundations of power have been moving away from the emphasis on military force and conquest. Paradoxically, nuclear weapons were one of the causes. As we know from the history of the Cold War, nuclear weapons proved so awesome and destructive that they became muscle bound— too costly to use except, theoretically, in the most extreme circumstances.[2] A second important change was the rise of nationalism, which has made it more difficult for empires to rule over awakened populations. In the nineteenth century, a few adventurers conquered most of Africa with a handful of soldiers, and Britain ruled India with a colonial force that was a tiny fraction of the indigenous population. Today, colonial rule is not only widely condemned but far too costly, as both Cold War superpowers discovered in Vietnam and Afghanistan. The collapse of the Soviet empire followed the end of European empires by a matter of decades.

A third important cause is societal change inside great powers. Postindustrial societies are focused on welfare rather than glory, and they loathe high casualties except when survival is at stake. This does not mean that they will not use force, even when casualties are expected—witness the 1991 Gulf War or Afghanistan today. But the absence of a warrior ethic in modern democracies means that the use of force requires an elaborate moral justification to ensure popular support (except in cases where survival is at stake). Roughly speaking, there are three types of countries in the world today: poor, weak preindustrial states, which are often the chaotic remnants of collapsed empires; modernizing industrial states such as India or China; and the postindustrial societies that prevail in Europe, North America, and Japan. The use of force is common in the first type of country, still accepted in the second, but less tolerated in the third. In the words of British diplomat Robert Cooper, "A large number of the most powerful states no longer want to fight or to conquer."[3] War remains possible, but it is much less acceptable now than it was a century or even half a century age.[4]

Finally, for most of today's great powers, the use of force would jeopardize their economic objectives. Even nondemocratic countries that feel fewer popular moral constraints on the use of force have to consider its effects on their economic objectives. As Thomas Friedman has put it, countries are disciplined by an "electronic herd" of investors who control their access to capital in a globalized economy.[5] And Richard Rosecrance writes, "In the past, it was cheaper to seize another state's territory by force than to develop the sophisticated economic and trading apparatus needed to derive benefit from commercial exchange with it."[6] Imperial Japan used the former approach when it created the Greater East Asia Co-prosperity Sphere in the 1930s, but Japan's post–World War II role as a trading state turned out to be far more successful, leading it to become the second largest national economy in the world. It is difficult now to imagine a scenario in which Japan would try to colonize its neighbors, or succeed in doing so.

As mentioned above, none of this is to suggest that military force plays no role in international politics today. For one thing, the information revolution has yet to transform most of the world. Many states are unconstrained by democratic societal forces, as Kuwait learned from its neighbor Iraq, and terrorist groups pay little heed to the normal constraints of liberal societies. Civil wars are rife in many parts of the world where collapsed empires left power vacuums. Moreover, throughout history, the rise of new great powers has been accompanied by anxieties that have sometimes precipitated military crises. In Thucydides's immortal description, the Peloponnesian War in ancient Greece was caused by the rise to power of Athens and the fear it created in Sparta.[7] World War I owed much to the rise of the kaiser's Germany and the fear that created in Britain.[8] Some foretell a similar dynamic in this century arising from the rise of China and the fear it creates in the United States.

Geoeconomics has not replaced geopolitics, although in the early twenty-first century there has clearly been a blurring of the traditional boundaries between the two. To ignore the role of force and the centrality of security would be like ignoring oxygen. Under normal circumstances, oxygen is plentiful and we pay it little attention. But once those conditions change and we begin to miss it, we can focus on nothing else.[9] Even in those areas where the direct employment of force falls out of use among countries—for instance, within Western Europe or between the United States and Japan—nonstate actors such as terrorists may use force. Moreover, military force can still play an important political role among advanced nations. For example, most countries in East Asia welcome the presence of American troops as an insurance policy against uncertain neighbors. Moreover, deterring threats or ensuring access to a crucial resource such as oil in the Persian Gulf increases America's influence with its allies. Sometimes the linkages may be direct; more often they are present in the back of statesmen's minds. As the Defense Department describes it, one of the missions of American troops based overseas is to "shape the environment."

With that said, economic power *has* become more important than in the past, both because of the relative increase in the costliness of force and because economic objectives loom large in the values of postindustrial societies.[10] In a world of economic globalization, all countries are to some extent dependent on market forces beyond their direct control. When President Clinton was struggling to balance the federal budget in 1993, one of his advisors stated in exasperation that if he were to be reborn, he would like to come back as "the market" because that was clearly the most powerful player.[11] But markets constrain different countries to different degrees. Because the United States constitutes such a large part of the market in trade and finance, it is better placed to set its own terms than is Argentina or Thailand. And if small countries are willing to pay the price of opting out of the market, they can reduce the power that other countries have over them. Thus American economic sanctions have had little effect, for example, on improving human rights in isolated Myanmar. Saddam Hussein's strong preference for his own survival rather than the welfare of the Iraqi people meant that crippling sanctions failed for more than a decade to remove him from power. And economic sanctions may disrupt but not deter non-state terrorists. But the exceptions prove the rule. Military power remains crucial in certain situations, but it is a mistake to focus too narrowly on the military dimensions of American power.

Soft Power

In my view, if the United States wants to remain strong, Americans need also to pay attention to our soft power. What precisely do I mean by soft power? Military power and economic power are both examples of hard command power that can be used to induce others to change their position. Hard power can rest on inducements (carrots) or threats (sticks). But there is also an indirect way to exercise power. A country may obtain the outcomes it wants in world politics because other countries want to follow it, admiring its values, emulating its example, aspiring to its level of prosperity and openness. In this sense, it is just as important to set the agenda in world politics and attract others as it is to force them to change through the threat or use of military or economic weapons. This aspect of power—getting others to want what you want—I call soft power.[12] It co-opts people rather than coerces them.

Soft power rests on the ability to set the political agenda in a way that shapes the preferences of others.

At the personal level, wise parents know that if they have brought up their children with the right beliefs and values, their power will be greater and will last longer than if they have relied only on spankings, cutting off allowances, or taking away the car keys. Similarly, political leaders and thinkers such as Antonio Gramsci have long understood the power that comes from setting the agenda and determining the framework of a debate. The ability to establish preferences tends to be associated with intangible power resources such as an attractive culture, ideology, and institutions. If I can get you to *want* to do what I want, then I do not have to force you to do what you do *not* want to do. If the United States represents values that others want to follow, it will cost us less to lead. Soft power is not merely the same as influence, though it is one source of influence. After all, I can also influence you by threats or rewards. Soft power is also more than persuasion or the ability to move people by argument. It is the ability to entice and attract. And attraction often leads to acquiescence or imitation.

Soft power arises in large part from our values. These values are expressed in our culture, in the policies we follow inside our country, and in the way we handle ourselves internationally. The government sometimes finds it difficult to control and employ soft power. Like love, it is hard to measure and to handle, and does not touch everyone, but that does not diminish its importance. As Hubert Védrine laments, Americans are so powerful because they can "inspire the dreams and desires of others, thanks to the mastery of global images through film and television and because, for these same reasons, large numbers of students from other countries come to the United States to finish their studies."[13] Soft power is an important reality.

Of course, hard and soft power are related and can reinforce each other. Both are aspects of the ability to achieve our purposes by affecting the behavior of others. Sometimes the same power resources can affect the entire spectrum of behavior from coercion to attraction.[14] A country that suffers economic and military decline is likely to lose its ability to shape the international agenda as well as its attractiveness. And some countries may be attracted to others with hard power by the myth of invincibility or inevitability. Both Hitler and Stalin tried to develop such myths. Hard power can also be used to establish empires and institutions that set the agenda for smaller states— witness Soviet rule over the countries of Eastern Europe. But soft power is not simply the reflection of hard power. The Vatican did not lose its soft power when it lost the Papal States in Italy in the nineteenth century. Conversely, the Soviet Union lost much of its soft power after it invaded Hungary and Czechoslovakia, even though its economic and military resources continued to grow. Imperious policies that utilized Soviet hard power actually undercut its soft power. And some countries such as Canada, the Netherlands, and the Scandinavian states have political clout that is greater than their military and economic weight, because of the incorporation of attractive causes such as economic aid or peacekeeping into their definitions of national interest. These are lessons that the unilateralists forget at their and our peril.

Britain in the nineteenth century and America in the second half of the twentieth century enhanced their power by creating liberal international economic rules and institutions that were consistent with the liberal and democratic structures of British and American capitalism—free trade and the gold standard in the case of Britain, the International Monetary Fund, World Trade Organization, and other institutions in the case of the United States. If a country can make its power legitimate in the eyes of others, it will encounter less resistance to its wishes. If its culture and ideology are attractive, others more willingly follow. If it can establish international rules that are consistent with its society, it will be less likely to have to change. If it can help support institutions that encourage other countries to channel or limit their activities in ways it prefers, it may not needed as many costly carrots and sticks.

In short, the universality of a country's culture and its ability to establish a set of favourable rules and institutions that govern areas of international activity are critical sources of power. The values of democracy, personal freedom, upward mobility, and openness that are often expressed in American popular culture, higher education, and foreign policy contribute to American power in many areas. In the view of German journalist Josef Joffe, America's soft power "looms even larger than its economic and military assets. U.S. culture, low-brow or high, radiates outward with an intensity last seen in the days of the Roman Empire—but with a novel twist. Rome's and Soviet Russia's cultural sway stopped exactly at their military borders. America's soft power, though, rules over an empire on which the sun never sets."[15]

Of course, soft power is more than just cultural power. The values our government champions in its behavior at home (for example, democracy), in international institutions (listening to others), and in foreign policy (promoting peace and human rights) also affect the preferences of others. We can attract (or repel) others by the influence of our example. But soft power does not belong to the government in the same degree that hard power does. Some hard power assets (such as armed forces) are strictly governmental, others are inherently national (such as our oil and gas reserves), and many can be transferred to collective control (such as industrial assets that can be mobilized in an emergency). In contrast, many soft power resources are separate from American government and only partly responsive to its purposes. In the Vietnam era, for example, American government policy and popular culture worked at cross-purposes. Today popular U.S. firms or nongovernmental groups develop soft power of their own that may coincide or be at odds with official foreign policy goals. That is all the more reason for our government to make sure that its own actions reinforce rather than undercut American soft power. [A]ll these sources of soft power are likely to become increasingly important in the global information age of this new century. And, at the same time, the arrogance, indifference to the opinions of others, and narrow approach to our national interests advocated by the new unilateralists are a sure way to undermine our soft power.

Power in the global information age is becoming less tangible and less coercive, particularly among the advanced countries, but most of the world does not consist of postindustrial societies, and that limits the transformation of power. Much of Africa and the Middle East remains locked in preindustrial agricultural societies with weak institutions and authoritarian rulers. Other countries, such as China, India, and Brazil, are industrial economies analogous to parts of the West in the mid-twentieth century.[16] In such a variegated world, all three sources of power—military, economic, and soft—remain relevant, although to different degrees in different relationships. However, if current economic and social trends continue, leadership in the information revolution and soft power will become more important in the mix. Table 2.1 provides a simplified description of the evolution of power resources over the past few centuries.

Power in the twenty-first century will rest on a mix of hard and soft resources. No country is better endowed than the United States in all three dimensions—military, economic, and soft power. Our greatest mistake in such a world would be to fall into one-dimensional analysis and to believe that investing in military power alone will ensure our strength.

Balance or Hegemony?

America's power—hard and soft—is only part of the story. How others react to American power is equally important to the question of stability and governance in this global information age. Many realists

Table 2.1 Leading States and Their Power Resources, 1500–2000

Period	State	Major Resources
Sixteenth century	Spain	Gold bullion, colonial trade, mercenary armies, dynastic ties
Seventeenth century	Netherlands	Trade, capital markets, navy
Eighteenth century	France	Population, rural industry, public administration, army, culture (soft power)
Nineteenth century	Britain	Industry, political cohesion, finance and credit, navy, liberal norms (soft power), island location (easy to defend)
Twentieth century	United States	Economic scale, scientific and technical leadership, location, military forces and alliances, universalistic culture and liberal international regimes (soft power)
Twenty-first century	United States	Technological leadership, military and economic scale, soft power, hub of transnational communications

extol the virtues of the classic nineteenth-century European balance of power, in which constantly shifting coalitions contained the ambitions of any especially aggressive power. They urge the United States to rediscover the virtues of a balance of power at the global level today. Already in the 1970s, Richard Nixon argued that "the only time in the history of the world that we have had any extended periods of peace is when there has been a balance of power. It is when one nation becomes infinitely more powerful in relation to its potential competitors that the danger of war arises."[17] But whether such multipolarity would be good or bad for the United States and for the world is debatable. I am skeptical.

War was the constant companion and crucial instrument of the multipolar balance of power. The classic European balance provided stability in the sense of maintaining the independence of most countries, but there were wars among the great powers for 60 percent of the years since 1500.[18] Rote adherence to the balance of power and multipolarity may prove to be a dangerous approach to global governance in a world where war could turn nuclear.

Many regions of the world and periods in history have seen stability under hegemony—when one power has been preeminent. Margaret Thatcher warned against drifting toward "an Orwellian future of Oceania, Eurasia, and Eastasia—three mercantilist world empires on increasingly hostile terms. . . . In other words, 2095 might look like 1914 played on a somewhat larger stage."[19] Both the Nixon and Thatcher views are too mechanical because they ignore soft power. America is an exception, says Josef Joffe, "because the 'hyperpower' is also the most alluring and seductive society in history. Napoleon had to rely on bayonets to spread France's revolutionary creed. In the American case, Munichers and Muscovites *want* what the avatar of ultra-modernity has to offer."[20]

The term "balance of power" is sometimes used in contradictory ways. The most interesting use of the term is as a predictor about how countries will behave; that is, will they pursue policies that will prevent any other country from developing power that could threaten their independence? By the evidence of history, many believe, the current preponderance of the United States will call forth a countervailing coalition that will eventually limit American power. In the words of the self-styled realist political scientist Kenneth Waltz, "both friends and foes will react as countries always have to threatened or real predominance of one among them: they will work to right the balance. The present condition of international politics is unnatural."[21]

In my view, such a mechanical prediction misses the mark. For one thing, countries sometimes react to the rise of a single power by "bandwagoning" — that is, joining the seemingly stronger rather than weaker side—much as Mussolini did when he decided, after several years of hesitation, to ally with Hitler. Proximity to and perceptions of threat also affect the way in which countries react.[22] The United States benefits from its geographical separation from Europe and Asia in that it often appears as a less proximate threat than neighboring countries inside those regions. Indeed, in 1945, the United States was by far the strongest nation on earth, and a mechanical application of balancing theory would have predicted an alliance against it. Instead, Europe and Japan allied with the Americans because the Soviet Union, while weaker in overall power, posed a greater military threat because of its geographical proximity and its lingering revolutionary ambitions. . . . Nationalism can also complicate predictions. For example, if North Korea and South Korea are reunited, they should have a strong incentive to maintain an alliance with a distant power such as the United States in order to balance their two giant neighbors, China and Japan. But intense nationalism resulting in opposition to an American presence could change this if American diplomacy is heavy-handed. Non-state actors can also have an effect, as witnessed by the way cooperation against terrorists changed some states' behavior after September 2001.

A good case can be made that inequality of power can be a source of peace and stability. No matter how power is measured, some theorists argue, an equal distribution of power among major states has been relatively rare in history, and efforts to maintain a balance have often led to war. On the other hand, inequality of power has often led to peace and stability because there was little point in declaring war on a dominant state. . . . Robert Gilpin has argued that "*Pax Britannica* and *Pax Americana*, like the *Pax Romana*, ensured an international system of relative peace and security" And the economist Charles Kindleberger claimed that "for the world economy to be stabilized, there has to be a stabilizer, one stabilizer[23] Global governance requires a large state to take the lead. But how much and what kind of inequality of power is necessary—or tolerable—and for how long? If the leading country possesses soft power and behaves in a manner that benefits others, effective counter-coalitions may be slow to arise. If, on the other hand, the leading country defines its interests narrowly and uses its weight arrogantly, it increases the incentives for others to coordinate to escape its hegemony.

Some countries chafe under the weight of American power more than others. *Hegemony* is sometimes used as a term of opprobrium by political leaders in Russia, China, the Middle East, France, and others. The term is used less often or less negatively in countries where American soft power is strong. If hegemony means being able to dictate, or at least dominate, the rules and arrangements by which international relations are conducted, as Joshua Goldstein argues, then the United States is hardly a hegemon today.[24] It does have a predominant voice and vote in the International Monetary Fund, but it cannot alone choose the director. It has not been able to prevail over Europe and Japan in the World Trade Organization. It opposed the Land Mines Treaty but could not prevent it from coming into existence. The U.S. opposed Russia's war in Chechnya and civil war in Colombia, but to no avail. If hegemony is defined more modestly as a situation where one country has significantly more power resources or capabilities than others, then it simply signifies American preponderance, not necessarily dominance or control.[25] Even after World War II, when the United States controlled half the world's economic production (because all other countries had been devastated by the war), it was not able to prevail in all of its objectives.[26]

Pax-Britannica in the nineteenth century is often cited as an example of successful hegemony, even though Britain ranked behind the United States and Russia in GNP. Britain was never as superior in productivity to the rest of the world as the United States has been since 1945, but Britain also had a degree of soft power. Victorian culture was influential around the globe, and Britain gained in reputation when it defined its interests in ways that benefited other nations (for example, opening its markets to imports or eradicating piracy). America lacks a global territorial empire like Britain's, but instead possesses a large, continental-scale home economy and has greater soft power. These differences between Britain and America suggest a greater staying power for American hegemony. Political scientist William Wohlforth argues that the United States is so far ahead that potential rivals find it dangerous to invite America's focused enmity, and allied states can feel confident that they can continue to rely on American protection.[27] Thus the usual balancing forces are weakened.

Nonetheless, if American diplomacy is unilateral and arrogant, our preponderance would not prevent other states and non-state actors from taking actions that complicate American calculations and constrain our freedom of action.[28] For example, some allies may follow the American bandwagon on the largest security issues but form coalitions to balance American behavior in other areas such as trade or the environment. And diplomatic maneuvering short of alliance can have political effects. As William Safire observed when presidents Vladimir Putin and George W. Bush first met, "Well aware of the weakness of his hand, Putin is emulating Nixon's strategy by playing the China card. Pointedly, just before meeting with Bush, Putin traveled to Shanghai to set up a regional cooperation semi-alliance with Jiang Zemin and some of his Asian fellow travelers."[29] Putin's tactics, according to one reporter, "put Mr. Bush on the defensive, and Mr. Bush was at pains to assert that America is not about to go it alone in international affairs."[30]

Pax Americana is likely to last not only because of unmatched American hard power but also to the extent that the United States "is uniquely capable of engaging in 'strategic restraint,' reassuring partners and facilitating cooperation."[31] The open and pluralistic way in which our foreign policy is made can often reduce surprises, allow others to have a voice, and contribute to our soft power. Moreover, the impact of American preponderance is softened when it is embodied in a web of multilateral institutions that allows others to participate in decisions and that act as a sort of world constitution to limit the capriciousness of American power. That was the lesson we learned as we struggled to create an antiterrorist coalition in the wake of the September 2001 attacks. When the society and culture of the hegemon are attractive, the sense of threat and need to balance it are reduced.[32] Whether other countries will unite to balance American power will depend on how the United States behaves as well as the power resources of potential challengers.

Notes

1. A. J. Taylor, *The Struggle for Mastery in Europe, 1848–1918* (Oxford: Oxford University Press, 1954), xxix.

2. Whether this would change with the proliferation of nuclear weapons to more states is hotly debated among theorists. Deterrence should work with most states, but the prospects of accident and loss of control would increase. For my views, see Joseph S. Nye Jr., *Nuclear Ethics* (New York: Free Press, 1986).

3. Robert Cooper, *The Postmodern State and the World Order* (London: Demos, 2000), 22.

4. John Mueller, *Retreat from Doomsday: The Obsolescence of Major War* (New York: Basic Books, 1989).

5. Thomas Friedman, *The Lexus and the Olive Tree: Understanding Globalization* (New York: Farrar, Straus and Giroux, 1999), chapter 6.

6. Richard N. Rosecrance, *The Rise of the Trading State* (New York: Basic Books, 1986), 16, 160.

7. Thucydides, *History of the Peloponnesian War,* trans. Rex Warner (London: Penguin, 1972), book I, chapter 1.

8. And in turn, as industrialization progressed and railroads were built, Germany feared the rise of Russia.

9. Henry Kissinger portrays four international systems existing side by side: the West (and Western Hemisphere), marked by democratic peace; Asia, where strategic conflict is possible; the Middle East, marked by religious conflict; and Africa, where civil wars threaten weak post-colonial states. "America at the Apex," *The National Interest,* summer 2001, 14.

10. Robert O. Keohane and Joseph S. Nye Jr., *Power and Interdependence,* 3rd ed. (New York: Longman, 2000), chapter 1.

11. James Carville quoted in Bob Woodward, *The Agenda: Inside the Clinton White House* (New York: Simon and Schuster, 1994), 302.

12. For a more detailed discussion, see Joseph S. Nye Jr., *Bound to Lead: The Changing Nature of American Power* (New York: Basic Books, 1990), chapter 2. This builds on what Peter Bachrach and Morton Baratz called the "second face of power" in "Decisions and Nondecisions: An Analytical Framework," *American Political Science Review,* September 1963, 632–42.

13. Védrine, *France in an Age of Globalization,* 3.

14. The distinction between hard and soft power is one of degree, both in the nature of the behavior and in the tangibility of the resources. Both are aspects of the ability to achieve one's purposes by affecting the behavior of others. Command power—the ability to change what others do—can rest on coercion or inducement. Co-optive power—the ability to shape what others want—can rest on the attractiveness of one's culture and ideology or the ability to manipulate the agenda of political choices in a manner that makes actors fail to express some preferences because they seem to be too unrealistic. The forms of behavior between command and co-optive power range along a continuum: command power, coercion, inducement, agenda setting, attraction, co-optive power. Soft power resources tend to be associated with co-optive power behavior, whereas hard power resources are usually associated with command behavior. But the relationship is imperfect. For example, countries may be attracted to others with command power by myths of invincibility, and command power may sometimes be used to establish institutions that later become regarded as legitimate. But the general association is strong enough to allow the useful shorthand reference to hard and soft power.

15. Josef Joffe, "Who's Afraid of Mr. Big?" *The National Interest,* summer 2001, 43.

16. See Cooper, *Postmodern State;* Bell, *The Coming of Post-Industrial Society.*

17. Nixon quoted in James Chace and Nicholas X. Rizopoulos, "Towards a New Concert of Nations: An American Perspective," *World Policy Journal,* fall 1999, 9.

18. Jack S. Levy, *War in the Modern Great Power System, 1495–1975* (Lexington: University Press of Kentucky, 1983), 97.

19. Margaret Thatcher, "Why America Must Remain Number One," *National Review,* July 31, 1995, 25.

20. Josef Joffe, "Envy," *The New Republic,* January 17, 2000, 6.

21. Kenneth Waltz, "Globalization and American Power," *The National Interest,* spring 2000, 55–56.

22. Stephen Walt, "Alliance Formation and the Balance of Power," *International Security,* spring 1985.

23. Robert Gilpin, *War and Change in World Politics* (New York: Cambridge University Press, 1981), 144–45; Charles Kindleberger, *The World in Depression, 1929–1939* (Berkely: University of California Press, 1973), 305.

24. Joshua S. Goldstein, *Long Cycles: Prosperity and War in the Modern Age* (New Haven: Yale University Press, 1988), 281.

25. See Robert O. Keohane, *After Hegemony: Cooperation and Discord in the World Political Economy* (Princeton: Princeton University Press, 1984), 235.

26. Over the years, a number of scholars have tried to predict the rise and fall of nations by developing a general historical theory of hegemonic transition. Some have tried to generalize from the experience of Portugal, Spain, the Netherlands, France, and Britain. Others have focused more closely on Britain's decline in the twentieth century as a predictor for the fate for the United States. None of these approaches has been successful. Most of the theories have predicted that America would decline long before now. Vague definitions and arbitrary schematizations alert us to the inadequacies of such grand theories. Most try to squeeze history into procrustean theoretical beds by focusing on particular power resources while ignoring

others that are equally important. Hegemony can be used as a descriptive term (though it is sometimes fraught with emotional overtones), but grand hegemonic theories are weak in predicting future events. See Immanuel Wallerstein, *The Politics of the World Economy: The States, the Movements, and the Civilizations: Essays* (New York: Cambridge University Press, 1984), 38, 41; George Modelski, "The Long Cycle of Global Politics and the Nation-State," *Comparative Studies in Society and History,* April 1978; George Modelski, *Long Cycles in World Politics* (Seattle: University of Washington Press, 1987). For a detailed discussion, see Nye, *Bound to Lead,* chapter 2.

27. William Wohlforth, "The Stability of a Unipolar World," *International Security* 24, 1 (summer 1999): 5–41.

28. Stephen Walt, "Keeping the World 'Off-Balance': Self-Restraint and US Foreign Policy," Kennedy School Research Working Paper Series 00–013, October 2000.

29. William Safire, "Putin's China Card," *New York Times,* June 18, 2001, A29.

30. Patrick Tyler, "Bush and Putin Look Each Other in the Eye," *New York Times,* June 17, 2001, A10.

31. Ikenberry, "Institutions, Strategic Restraint," 47; also Ikenberry, "Getting Hegemony Right," *The National Interest,* spring 2001, 17–24.

32. Josef Joffe, "How America Does It," *Foreign Affairs,* September–October 1997.

Tragedy of Great Power Politics

JOHN J. MEARSHEIMER

Mearsheimer is a structural or neorealist, but one who places emphasis on offensive or power-maximizing in contrast to the defensive (or "status quo") realism he finds in Kenneth Waltz and other structural realists. Mearsheimer argues offensive realism is both a descriptive theory about how states behave as well as a prescriptive one that states ought to follow as the best way to survive in a dangerous world. He discusses such concepts as anarchy, self-help, and relative gains.

This [article] offers a realist theory of international politics that challenges the prevailing optimism about relations among the great powers. That enterprise involves three particular tasks.

I begin by laying out the key components of the theory, which I call "offensive realism." I make a number of arguments about how great powers behave toward each other, emphasizing that they look for opportunities to gain power at each others expense. Moreover, I identify the conditions that make conflict more or less likely. For example, I argue that multipolar systems are more war-prone than are bipolar systems, and that multipolar systems that contain especially powerful states—potential hegemons—are the most dangerous systems of all. But I do not just assert these various claims; I also attempt to provide compelling explanations for the behaviors and the outcomes that lie at the heart of the theory. In other

words, I lay out the causal logic, or reasoning, which underpins each of my claims.

The theory focuses on the great powers because these states have the largest impact on what happens in international politics. The fortunes of all states—great powers and smaller powers alike—are determined primarily by the decisions and actions of those with the greatest capability. For example, politics in almost every region of the world were deeply influenced by the competition between the Soviet Union and the United States between 1945 and 1990. The two world wars that preceded the Cold War had a similar effect on regional politics around the world. Each of these conflicts was a great-power rivalry, and each cast a long shadow over every part of the globe.

Great powers are determined largely on the basis of their relative military capability. To qualify as a great power, a state must have sufficient military assets to put up a serious fight in an all-out conventional war against the most powerful state in the world. The candidate need not have the capability to defeat the leading state, but it must have some reasonable prospect of turning the conflict into a war of attrition that leaves the dominant state seriously weakened, even if that dominant state ultimately wins the war. In the nuclear age great powers must have a nuclear deterrent that can survive a nuclear strike against it, as well as formidable conventional forces. In the unlikely event that one state gained nuclear superiority over all of its rivals, it would be so powerful that it would be the only great power in the system. The balance of conventional forces would be largely irrelevant if a nuclear hegemon were to emerge. . . .

Theories encounter anomalies because they simplify reality by emphasizing certain factors while ignoring others. Offensive realism assumes that the international system strongly shapes the behavior of states. Structural factors such as anarchy and the distribution of power, I argue, are what matter most for explaining international politics. The theory pays little attention to individuals or domestic political considerations such as ideology. It tends to treat states like black boxes or billiard balls. For example, it does not matter for the theory whether Germany in 1905 was led by Bismarck, Kaiser Wilhelm, or Adolf Hitler, or whether Germany was democratic or autocratic. What matters for the theory is how much relative power Germany possessed at the time. These omitted factors, however, occasionally dominate a state's decision-making process; under these circumstances, offensive realism is not going to perform as well. In short, there is a price to pay for simplifying reality.

Furthermore, offensive realism does not answer every question that arises in world politics, because there will be cases in which the theory is consistent with several possible outcomes. When this occurs, other theories have to be brought in to provide more precise explanations. Social scientists say that a theory is "indeterminate" in such cases, a situation that is not unusual with broad-gauged theories like offensive realism. . . .

It should be apparent from this discussion that offensive realism is mainly a descriptive theory. It explains how great powers have behaved in the past and how they are likely to behave in the future. But it is also a prescriptive theory. States *should* behave according to the dictates of offensive realism, because it outlines the best way to survive in a dangerous world.

One might ask, if the theory describes how great powers act, why is it necessary to stipulate how they *should* act? The imposing constraints of the system should leave great powers with little choice but to act as the theory predicts. Although there is much truth in this description of great powers as prisoners trapped in an iron cage, the fact remains that they sometimes—although not often—act in contradiction to the theory. . . . As we shall see, such foolish behavior invariably has negative consequences. In short, if they want to survive, great powers should always act like good offensive realists.

The Pursuit of Power

Enough said about theory. More needs to be said about the substance of my arguments, which means zeroing in on the core concept of "power." For all realists, calculations about power lie at the heart of how states think about the world around them. Power is the currency of great-power politics, and states compete for it among themselves. What money is to economics, power is to international relations. . . .

Realism

In contrast to liberals, realists are pessimists when it comes to international politics. Realists agree that creating a peaceful world would be desirable, but they see no easy way to escape the harsh world of security competition and war. Creating a peaceful world is surely an attractive idea, but it is not a practical one. "Realism," as Carr notes, "tends to emphasize the irresistible strength of existing forces and the inevitable character of existing tendencies, and to insist that the highest wisdom lies in accepting, and adapting oneself to these forces and these tendencies."[1]

This gloomy view of international relations is based on three core beliefs. First, realists, like liberals, treat states as the principal actors in world politics. Realists focus mainly on great powers, however, because these states dominate and shape international politics and they also cause the deadliest wars. Second, realists believe that the behavior of great powers is influenced mainly by their external environment, not by their internal characteristics. The structure of the international system, which all states must deal with, largely shapes their foreign policies. Realists tend not to draw sharp distinctions between "good" and "bad" states, because all great powers act according to the same logic regardless of their culture, political system, or who runs the government. It is therefore difficult to discriminate among states, save for differences in relative power. In essence, great powers are like billiard balls that vary only in size.

Third, realists hold that calculations about power dominate states' thinking, and that states compete for power among themselves. That competition sometimes necessitates going to war, which is considered an acceptable instrument of statecraft. To quote Carl von Clausewitz, the nineteenth-century military strategist, war is a continuation of politics by other means. Finally, a zero-sum quality characterizes that competition, sometimes making it intense and unforgiving. States may cooperate with each other on occasion, but at root they have conflicting interests. . . .

Defensive realism, which is frequently referred to as "structural realism," came on the scene in the late 1970s with the appearence of Waltz's *Theory of International Politics*. Unlike Morgenthau, Waltz does not assume that great powers are inherently aggressive because they are infused with a will to power; instead he starts by assuming that states merely aim to survive. Above all else, they seek security. Nevertheless, he maintains that the structure of the international system forces great powers to pay careful attention to the balance of power. In particular, anarchy forces security-seeking states to compete with each other for power, because power is the best means to survival. Whereas human nature is the deep cause of security competition in Morgenthau's theory, anarchy plays that role in Waltz's theory.

Waltz does not emphasize, however, that the international system provides great powers with good reasons to act offensively to gain power. Instead, he appears to make the opposite case: that anarchy encourages states to behave defensively and to maintain rather than upset the balance of power. "The first concern of states," he writes, is "to maintain their position in the system." There seems to be, as international relations theorist Randall Schweller notes, a "status quo bias" in Waltz's theory.[2]

Waltz recognizes that states have incentives to gain power at their rivals' expense and that it makes good strategic sense to act on that motive when the time is right. But he does not develop that line of argument in any detail. On the contrary, he emphasizes that when great powers behave aggressively, the potential victims usually balance against the aggressor and thwart its efforts to gain power. For Waltz, in short, balancing checkmates offense. Furthermore, he stresses that great powers must be careful not to acquire too much power, because "excessive strength" is likely to cause other states to join forces against them, thereby leaving them worse off than they would have been had they refrained from seeking additional increments of power.

Waltz's views on the causes of war further reflect his theory's status quo bias. There are no profound or deep causes of war in his theory. In particular, he does not suggest that there might be important benefits to be gained from war. In fact, he says little about the causes of war, other than to argue that wars are largely the result of uncertainty and miscalculation. In other words, if states knew better, they would not start wars.

Robert Jervis, Jack Snyder, and Stephen Van Evera buttress the defensive realists' case by focusing attention on a structural concept known as the offense-defense balance. They maintain that military power at any point in time can be categorized as favoring either offense or defense. If defense has a clear advantage over offense, and conquest is therefore difficult, great powers will have little incentive to use force to gain power and will concentrate instead on protecting what they have. When defense has the advantage, protecting what you have should be a relatively easy task. Alternatively, if offense is easier, states will be sorely tempted to try conquering each other, and there will be a lot of war in the system. Defensive realists argue, however, that the offense-defense balance is usually heavily tilted toward defense, thus making conquest extremely difficult. In sum, efficient balancing coupled with the natural advantages of defense over offense should discourage great powers from pursuing aggressive strategies and instead make them "defensive positionalists."

My theory of offensive realism is also a structural theory of international politics. As with defensive realism, my theory sees great powers as concerned mainly with figuring out how to survive in a world where there is no agency to protect them from each other; they quickly realize that power is the key to their survival. Offensive realism parts company with defensive realism over the question of how much power states want. For defensive realists, the international structure provides states with little incentive to seek additional increments of power; instead it pushes them to maintain the existing balance of power. Preserving power, rather than increasing it, is the main goal of states. Offensive realists, on the other hand, believe that status quo powers are rarely found in world politics, because the international system creates powerful incentives for states to look for opportunities to gain power at the expense of rivals, and to take advantage of those situations when the benefits outweigh the costs. A state's ultimate goal is to be the hegemon in the system. . . .

Competition for Power

Great powers, I argue, are always searching for opportunities to gain power over their rivals, with hegemony as their final goal. This perspective does not allow for status quo powers, except for the unusual state that achieves preponderance. Instead, the system is populated with great powers that have revisionist intentions at their core. This [article] presents a theory that explains this competition for power. Specifically, I attempt to show that there is a compelling logic behind my claim that great powers seek to maximize their share of world power. . . .

Why States Pursue Power

My explanation for why great powers vie with each other for power and strive for hegemony is derived from five assumptions about the international system. None of these assumptions alone mandates that states behave competitively. Taken together, however, they depict a world in which states have considerable reason to think and sometimes behave aggressively. In particular, the system encourages states to look for opportunities to maximize their power vis-à-vis other states. . . .

Bedrock Assumptions

The first assumption is that the international system is anarchic, which does not mean that it is chaotic or riven by disorder. It is easy to draw that conclusion, since realism depicts a world characterized by security competition and war. By itself, however, the realist notion of anarchy has nothing to do with conflict; it is an ordering principle, which says that the system comprises independent states that have no central authority above them. Sovereignty, in other words, inheres in states because there is no higher ruling body in the international system. There is no "government over governments."

The second assumption is that great powers inherently possess some offensive military capability, which gives them the wherewithal to hurt and possibly destroy each other. States are potentially dangerous to each other, although some states have more military might than others and are therefore more dangerous. A state's military power is usually identified with the particular weaponry at its disposal, although even if there were no weapons, the individuals in those states could still use their feet and hands to attack the population of another state. After all, for every neck, there are two hands to choke it.

The third assumption is that states can never be certain about other states' intentions. Specifically, no state can be sure that another state will not use its offensive military capability to attack the first state. This is not to say that states necessarily have hostile intentions. Indeed, all of the states in the system may be reliably benign, but it is impossible to be sure of that judgement because intentions are impossible to divine with 100 percent certainty. There are many possible causes of aggression, and no state can be sure that another state is not motivated by one of them. Furthermore, intentions can change quickly, so a state's intentions can be benign one day and hostile the next. Uncertainty about intentions is unavoidable, which means that states can never be sure that other states do not have offensive intentions to go along with their offensive capabilities.

The fourth assumption is that survival is the primary goal of great powers. Specifically, states seek to maintain their territorial integrity and the autonomy of their domestic political order. Survival dominates other motives because, once a state is conquered, it is unlikely to be in a position to pursue other aims. Soviet leader Josef Stalin put the point well during a war scare in 1927: "We can and must build socialism in the [Soviet Union]. But in order to do so we first of all have to exist." [3] States can and do pursue other goals, of course, but security is their most important objective.

The fifth assumption is that great powers are rational actors. They are aware of their external environment and they think strategically about how to survive in it. In particular, they consider the preferences of other states and how their own behavior is likely to affect the behavior of those other states, and how the behavior of those other states is likely to affect their own strategy for survival. Moreover, states pay attention to the long term as well as the immediate consequences of their actions.

As emphasized, none of these assumptions alone dictates that great powers as a general rule *should* behave aggressively toward each other. There is surely the possibility that some state might have hostile intentions, but the only assumption dealing with a specific motive that is common to all states says that their principal objective is to survive, which by itself is a rather harmless goal. Nevertheless, when the five assumptions are married together, they create powerful incentives for great powers to think and act offensively with regard to each other. In particular, three general patterns of behavior result: fear, self-help, and power maximization.

State Behavior

Great powers fear each other. They regard each other with suspicion, and they worry that war might be in the offing. They anticipate danger. There is little room for trust among states. For sure, the level of fear varies across time and space, but it cannot be reduced to a trivial level. From the perspective of any one great power, all other great powers are potential enemies. This point is illustrated by the reaction of the United Kingdom and France to German reunification at the end of the Cold War. Despite the fact that these three states had been close allies for almost forty-five years, both the United Kingdom and France immediately began worrying about the potential dangers of a united Germany.

The basis of this fear is that in a world where great powers have the capability to attack each other and might have the motive to do so, any state bent on survival must be at least suspicious of other states and reluctant to trust them. Add to this the "911" problem—the absence of a central authority to which a threatened state can turn for help—and states have even greater incentive to fear each other. Moreover, there is no mechanism, other than the possible self-interest of third parties, for punishing an aggressor. Because it is sometimes difficult to deter potential aggressors, states have ample reason not to trust other states and to be prepared for war with them.

The possible consequences of falling victim to aggression further amplify the importance of fear as a motivating force in world politics. Great powers do not compete with each other as if international politics were merely an economic marketplace. Political competition among states is a much more dangerous business than mere economic intercourse; the former can lead to war, and war often means mass killing on the battlefield as well as mass murder of civilians. In extreme cases, war can even lead to the destruction of states. The horrible consequences of war sometimes cause states to view each other not just as competitors, but as potentially deadly enemies. Political antagonism, in short, tends to be intense, because the stakes are great.

States in the international system also aim to guarantee their own survival. Because other states are potential threats, and because there is no higher authority to come to their rescue when they dial 911, states cannot depend on others for their own security. Each state tends to see itself as vulnerable and alone, and therefore it aims to provide for its own survival. In international politics, God helps those who help themselves. This emphasis on self-help does not preclude states from forming alliances. But alliances are only temporary marriages of convenience: today's alliance partner might be tomorrow's enemy, and today's enemy might be tomorrow's alliance partner. For example, the United States fought with China and the Soviet Union against Germany and Japan in World War II, but soon thereafter flip-flopped enemies and partners and allied with West Germany and Japan against China and the Soviet Union during the Cold War.

States operating in a self-help world almost always act according to their own self-interest and do not subordinate their interests to the interests of other states, or to the interests of the so-called international community. The reason is simple: it pays to be selfish in a self-help world. This is true in the short term as well as in the long term, because if a state loses in the short run, it might not be around for the long haul.

Apprehensive about the ultimate intentions of other states, and aware that they operate in a self-help system, states quickly understand that the best way to ensure their survival is to be the most powerful state in the system. The stronger a state is relative to its potential rivals, the less likely it is that any of those rivals will attack it and threaten its survival. Weaker states will be reluctant to pick fights with more powerful states because the weaker states are likely to suffer military defeat. Indeed, the bigger the gap in power between any two states, the less likely it is that the weaker will attack the stronger. Neither Canada nor

Mexico, for example, would countenance attacking the United States, which is far more powerful than its neighbors. The ideal situation is to be the hegemon in the system. As Immanuel Kant said, "It is the desire of every state, or of its ruler, to arrive at a condition of perpetual peace by conquering the whole world, if that were possible."[4] Survival would then be almost guaranteed.

Consequently, states pay close attention to how power is distributed among them, and they make a special effort to maximize their share of world power. Specifically, they look for opportunities to alter the balance of power by acquiring additional increments of power at the expense of potential rivals. States employ a variety of means—economic, diplomatic, and military—to shift the balance of power in their favor, even if doing so makes other states suspicious or even hostile. Because one state's gain in power is another state's loss, great powers tend to have a zero-sum mentality when dealing with each other. The trick, of course, is to be the winner in this competition and to dominate the other states in the system. Thus, the claim that states maximize relative power is tantamount to arguing that states are disposed to think offensively toward other states, even though their ultimate motive is simply to survive. In short, great powers have aggressive intentions.

Even when a great power achieves a distinct military advantage over its rivals, it continues looking for chances to gain more power. The pursuit of power stops only when hegemony is achieved. The idea that a great power might feel secure without dominating the system, provided it has an "appropriate amount" of power, is not persuasive, for two reasons. First, it is difficult to assess how much relative power one state must have over its rivals before it is secure. Is twice as much power an appropriate threshold? Or is three times as much power the magic number? The root of the problem is that power calculations alone do not determine which side wins a war. Clever strategies, for example, sometimes allow less powerful states to defeat more powerful foes.

Second, determining how much power is enough becomes even more complicated when great powers contemplate how power will be distributed among them ten or twenty years down the road. The capabilities of individual states vary over time, sometimes markedly, and it is often difficult to predict the direction and scope of change in the balance of power. Remember, few in the West anticipated the collapse of the Soviet Union before it happened. In fact, during the first half of the Cold War, many in the West feared that the Soviet economy would eventually generate greater wealth than the American economy, which would cause a marked power shift against the United States and its allies. What the future holds for China and Russia and what the balance of power will look like in 2020 is difficult to foresee.

Given the difficulty of determining how much power is enough for today and tomorrow, great powers recognize that the best way to ensure their security is to achieve hegemony now, thus eliminating any possibility of a challenge by another great power. Only a misguided state would pass up an opportunity to be the hegemon in the system because it thought it already had sufficient power to survive. But even if a great power does not have the wherewithal to achieve hegemony (and that is usually the case), it will still act offensively to amass as much power as it can, because states are almost always better off with more rather than less power. In short, states do not become status quo powers until they completely dominate the system.

All states are influenced by this logic, which means that not only do they look for opportunities to take advantage of one another, they also work to ensure that other states do not take advantage of them. After all, rival states are driven by the same logic, and most states are likely to recognize their own motives at play in the actions of other states. In short, states ultimately pay attention to defense as well as offense. They think about conquest themselves, and they work to check aggressor states from gaining power at their expense. This inexorably leads to a world of constant security competition, where states are willing to lie, cheat, and use brute force if it helps them gain advantage over their rivals. Peace, if one defines that concept as a state of tranquility or mutual concord, is not likely to break out in this world.

The "security dilemma," which is one of the most well-known concepts in the international relations literature, reflects the basic logic of offensive realism. The essence of the dilemma is that the measures a state takes to increase its own security usually decrease the security of other states. Thus, it is difficult for a state to increase its own chances of survival without threatening the survival of other states. John Herz first introduced the security dilemma in a 1950 article in the journal *World Politics*. After discussing the anarchic nature of international politics, he writes, "Striving to attain security from . . . attack, [states] are driven to acquire more and more power in order to escape the impact of the power of others. This, in turn, renders the others more insecure and compels them to prepare for the worst. Since none can ever feel entirely secure in such a world of competing units, power competition ensues, and the vicious circle of security and power accumulation is on."[5] The implication of Herz's analysis is clear: the best way for a state to survive in anarchy is to take advantage of other states and gain power at their expense. The best defense is a good offense. Since this message is widely understood, ceaseless security competition ensues. Unfortunately, little can be done to ameliorate the security dilemma as long as states operate in anarchy.

It should be apparent from this discussion that saying that states are power maximizers is tantamount to saying that they care about relative power, not absolute power. There is an important distinction here, because states concerned about relative power behave differently than do states interested in absolute power. States that maximize relative power are concerned primarily with the distribution of material capabilities. In particular, they try to gain as large a power advantage as possible over potential rivals, because power is the best means to survival in a dangerous world. Thus, states motivated by relative power concerns are likely to forgo large gains in their own power, if such gains give rival states even greater power, for smaller national gains that nevertheless provide them with a power advantage over their rivals. States that maximize absolute power, on the other hand, care only about the size of their own gains, not those of other states. They are not motivated by balance-of-power logic but instead are concerned with amassing power without regard to how much power other states control. They would jump at the opportunity for large gains, even if a rival gained more in the deal. Power, according to this logic, is not a means to an end (survival), but an end in itself. . . .

Calculated Aggression

There is obviously little room for status quo powers in a world where states are inclined to look for opportunities to gain more power. Nevertheless, great powers cannot always act on their offensive intentions, because behavior is influenced not only by what states want, but also by their capacity to realize these desires. Every state might want to be king of the hill, but not every state has the wherewithal to compete for that lofty position, much less achieve it. Much depends on how military might is distributed among the great powers. A great power that has a marked power advantage over its rivals is likely to behave more aggressively, because it has the capability as well as the incentive to do so.

By contrast, great powers facing powerful opponents will be less inclined to consider offensive action and more concerned with defending the existing balance of power from threats by their more powerful opponents. Let there be an opportunity for those weaker states to revise the balance in their own favor, however, and they will take advantage of it. Stalin put the point well at the end of World War II: "Everyone imposes his own system as far as his army can reach. It cannot be otherwise."[6] States might also have the capability to gain advantage over a rival power but nevertheless decide that the perceived costs of offense are too high and do not justify the expected benefits.

In short, great powers are not mindless aggressors so bent on gaining power that they charge headlong into losing wars or pursue Pyrrhic victories. On the contrary, before great powers take offensive actions, they think carefully about the balance of power and about how other states will react to their moves. They weigh the costs and risks of offense against the likely benefits. If the benefits do not outweigh the risks, they sit tight and wait for a more propitious moment. Nor do states start arms races that are unlikely to improve their overall position. . . . States sometimes limit defense spending either because spending more would bring no strategic advantage or because spending more would weaken the economy and undermine the state's power in the long run. To paraphrase Clint Eastwood, a state has to know its limitations to survive in the international system.

Nevertheless, great powers miscalculate from time to time because they invariably make important decisions on the basis of imperfect information. States hardly ever have complete information about any situation they confront. There are two dimensions to this problem. Potential adversaries have incentives to misrepresent their own strength or weakness, and to conceal their true aims. For example, a weaker state trying to deter a stronger state is likely to exaggerate its own power to discourage the potential aggressor from attacking. On the other hand, a state bent on aggression is likely to emphasize its peaceful goals while exaggerating its military weakness, so that the potential victim does not build up its own arms and thus leaves itself vulnerable to attack. Probably no national leader was better at practicing this kind of deception than Adolf Hitler.

But even if disinformation was not a problem, great powers are often unsure about how their own military forces, as well as the adversary's, will perform on the battlefield. For example, it is sometimes difficult to determine in advance how new weapons and untested combat units will perform in the face of enemy fire. Peacetime maneuvers and war games are helpful but imperfect indicators of what is likely to happen in actual combat. Fighting wars is a complicated business in which it is often difficult to predict outcomes. . . .

Great powers are also sometimes unsure about the resolve of opposing states as well as allies. For example, Germany believed that if it went to war against France and Russia in the summer of 1914, the United Kingdom would probably stay out of the fight. Saddam Hussein expected the United States to stand aside when he invaded Kuwait in August 1990. Both aggressors guessed wrong, but each had good reason to think that its initial judgment was correct. In the 1930s, Adolf Hitler believed that his great-power rivals would be easy to exploit and isolate because each had little interest in fighting Germany and instead was determined to get someone else to assume that burden. He guessed right. In short, great powers constantly find themselves confronting situations in which they have to make important decisions with incomplete information. Not surprisingly, they sometimes make faulty judgments and end up doing themselves serious harm.

Some defensive realists go so far as to suggest that the constraints of the international system are so powerful that offense rarely succeeds, and that aggressive great powers invariably end up being punished. As noted, they emphasize that 1) threatened states balance against aggressors and ultimately crush them, and 2) there is an offense-defense balance that is usually heavily tilted toward the defense, thus making conquest especially difficult. Great powers, therefore, should be content with the existing balance of power and not try to change it by force. After all, it makes little sense for a state to initiate a war that it is likely to lose; that would be self-defeating behavior. It is better to concentrate instead on preserving the balance of power. Moreover, because aggressors seldom succeed, states should understand that security is abundant, and thus there is no good strategic reason for wanting more power in the first place. In a world where conquest seldom pays, states should have relatively benign intentions toward each other. If they do not, these defensive realists argue, the reason is probably poisonous domestic politics, not smart calculations about how to guarantee one's security in an anarchic world.

There is no question that systemic factors constrain aggression, especially balancing by threatened states. But defensive realists exaggerate those restraining forces. Indeed, the historical record provides little support for their claim that offense rarely succeeds. One study estimates that there were 63 wars between 1815 and 1980, and the initiator won 39 times, which translates into about a 60 percent success rate. Turning to specific cases, Otto von Bismarck unified Germany by winning military victories against Denmark in 1864, Austria in 1866, and France in 1870, and the United States as we know it today was created in good part by conquest in the nineteenth century. Conquest certainly paid big dividends in these cases. Nazi Germany won wars against Poland in 1939 and France in 1940, but lost to the Soviet Union between 1941 and 1945. Conquest ultimately did not pay for the Third Reich, but if Hitler had restrained himself after the fall of France and had not invaded the Soviet Union, conquest probably would have paid handsomely for the Nazis. In short, the historical record shows that offense sometimes succeeds and sometimes does not. The trick for a sophisticated power maximizer is to figure out when to raise and when to fold.

Hegemony's Limits

Great powers, as I have emphasized, strive to gain power over their rivals and hopefully become hegemons. Once a state achieves that exalted position, it becomes a status quo power. More needs to be said, however, about the meaning of hegemony.

A hegemon is a state that is so powerful that it dominates all the other states in the system. No other state has the military wherewithal to put up a serious fight against it. In essence, a hegemon is the only great power in the system. A state that is substantially more powerful than the other great powers in the system is not a hegemon, because it faces, by definition, other great powers. The United Kingdom in the mid-nineteenth century, for example, is sometimes called a hegemon. But it was not a hegemon, because there were four other great powers in Europe at the time—Austria, France, Prussia, and Russia—and the United Kingdom did not dominate them in any meaningful way. In fact, during that period, the United Kingdom considered France to be a serious threat to the balance of power. Europe in the nineteenth century was multipolar, not unipolar.

Hegemony means domination of the system, which is usually interpreted to mean the entire world. It is possible, however, to apply the concept of a system more narrowly and use it to describe particular regions, such as Europe, Northeast Asia, and the Western Hemisphere. Thus, one can distinguish between *global hegemons,* which dominate the world, and *regional hegemons,* which dominate distinct geographical areas. The United States has been a regional hegemon in the Western Hemisphere for at least the past one hundred years. No other state in the Americas has sufficient military might to challenge it, which is why the United States is widely recognized as the only great power in its region.

My argument . . . is that except for the unlikely event wherein one state achieves clear-cut nuclear superiority, it is virtually impossible for any state to achieve global hegemony. The principal impediment to world domination is the difficulty of projecting power across the world's oceans onto the territory of a rival great power. The United States, for example, is the most powerful state on the planet today. But it does not dominate Europe and Northeast Asia the way it does the Western Hemisphere, and it has no intention of trying to conquer and control those distant regions, mainly because of the stopping power of water. Indeed, there is reason to think that the American military commitment to Europe and Northeast Asia might wither away over the next decade. In short, there has never been a global hegemon, and there is not likely to be one anytime soon.

The best outcome a great power can hope for is to be a regional hegemon and possibly control another region that is nearby and accessible over land. . . . States that achieve regional hegemony seek to prevent great powers in other regions from duplicating their feat. Regional hegemons, in other words, do not want peers. Thus the United States, for example, played a key role in preventing imperial Japan, Wilhelmine Germany, Nazi Germany, and the Soviet Union from gaining regional supremacy. Regional hegemons attempt to check aspiring hegemons in other regions because they fear that a rival great power that dominates its own region will be an especially powerful foe that is essentially free to cause trouble in the fearful great power's backyard. Regional hegemons prefer that there be at least two great powers located together in other regions, because their proximity will force them to concentrate their attention on each other rather than on the distant hegemon.

Furthermore, if a potential hegemon emerges among them, the other great powers in that region might be able to contain it by themselves, allowing the distant hegemon to remain safely on the sidelines. Of course, if the local great powers were unable to do the job, the distant hegemon would take the appropriate measures to deal with the threatening state. The United States, as noted, has assumed that burden on four separate occasions in the twentieth century, which is why it is commonly referred to as an "offshore balancer."

In sum, the ideal situation for any great power is to be the only regional hegemon in the world. That state would be a status quo power, and it would go to considerable lengths to preserve the existing distribution of power. The United States is in that enviable position today; it dominates the Western Hemisphere and there is no hegemon in any other area of the world. But if a regional hegemon is confronted with a peer competitor, it would no longer be a status quo power. Indeed, it would go to considerable lengths to weaken and maybe even destroy its distant rival. Of course, both regional hegemons would be motivated by that logic, which would make for a fierce security competition between them.

Cooperation Among States

One might conclude from the preceding discussion that my theory does not allow for any cooperation among the great powers. But this conclusion would be wrong. States can cooperate, although cooperation is sometimes difficult to achieve and always difficult to sustain. Two factors inhibit cooperation: considerations about relative gains and concern about cheating. Ultimately, great powers live in a fundamentally competitive world where they view each other as real, or at least potential, enemies, and they therefore look to gain power at each other's expense.

Any two states contemplating cooperation must consider how profits or gains will be distributed between them. They can think about the division in terms of either absolute or relative gains (recall the distinction made earlier between pursuing either absolute power or relative power; the concept here is the same). With absolute gains, each side is concerned with maximizing its own profits and cares little about how much the other side gains or loses in the deal. Each side cares about the other only to the extent that the other side's behavior affects its own prospects for achieving maximum profits. With relative gains, on the other hand, each side considers not only its own individual gain, but also how well it fares compared to the other side.

Because great powers care deeply about the balance of power, their thinking focuses on relative gains when they consider cooperating with other states. For sure, each state tries to maximize its absolute gains; still, it is more important for a state to make sure that it does no worse, and perhaps better, than the other state in any agreement. Cooperation is more difficult to achieve, however when states are attuned to relative gains rather than absolute gains. This is because states concerned about absolute gains have to make sure that if the pie is expanding, they are getting at least some portion of the increase, whereas states that worry about relative gains must pay careful attention to how the pie is divided, which complicates cooperative efforts.

Concerns about cheating also hinder cooperation. Great powers are often reluctant to enter into cooperative agreements for fear that the other side will cheat on the agreement and gain a significant advantage. This concern is especially acute in the military realm. . . . Such a development could create a window of opportunity for the state that cheats to inflict a decisive defeat on its victim.

These barriers to cooperation notwithstanding, great powers do cooperate in a realist world. Balance-of-power logic often causes great powers to form alliances and cooperate against common enemies. . . . Rivals as well as allies cooperate. After all, deals can be struck that roughly reflect the distribution of power and satisfy concerns about cheating. The various arms control agreements signed by the superpowers during the Cold War illustrate this point.

The bottom line, however, is that cooperation takes place in a world that is competitive at its core—one where states have powerful incentives to take advantage of other states. This point is graphically highlighted by the state of European politics in the forty years before World War I. The great powers cooperated frequently during this period but that did not stop them from going to war on August 1, 1914. The United States and the Soviet Union also cooperated considerably during World War II, but that cooperation did not prevent the outbreak of the Cold War shortly after Germany and Japan were defeated. Perhaps most amazingly, there was significant economic and military cooperation between Nazi Germany and the Soviet Union during the two years before the Wehrmacht attacked the Red Army. No amount of cooperation can eliminate the dominating logic of security competition. Genuine peace, or a world in which states do not compete for power, is not likely as long as the state system remains anarchic.

In sum, my argument is that the structure of the international system, not the particular characteristics of individual great powers, causes them to think and act offensively and to seek hegemony. I do not adopt Morgenthau's claim that states invariably behave aggressively because they have a will to power hardwired into them. Instead, I assume that the principal motive behind great-power behavior is survival. In anarchy, however, the desire to survive encourages states to behave aggressively. Nor does my theory classify states as more or less aggressive on the basis of their economic or political systems. Offensive realism makes only a handful of assumptions about great powers, and these assumptions apply equally to all great powers. Except for differences in how much power each state controls, the theory treats all states alike. . . .

Notes

1. E. H. Carr, *The Twenty Years' Crisis,* 2nd ed. (London: Macmillan, 1962), p. 10.
2. Randall L. Schweller, "Neorealism's Status Quo Bias: What Security Dilemma?" *Security Studies* 5, No. 3 (Spring 1996, special issue): 90–121.
3. Quoted in Jon Jacobson, *When the Soviet Union Entered World Politics* (Berkeley: University of California Press, 1994), p. 271.

4. Quoted in Martin Wight, *Power Politics* (London: Royal Institute of International Affairs, 1946), p. 40.

5. John H. Herz, "Idealist Internationalism and the Security Dilemma," *World Politics* 2, No. 2 (January 1950): 157.

6. Quoted in Marc Trachtenberg, *A Constructed Peace: The Making of the European Settlement, 1945–1963* (Princeton, NJ: Princeton University Press, 1999), p. 36.

SUGGESTIONS FOR FURTHER READING

REALISM: Suggested Readings

Below are lists of works on realism categorized by theme; these lists only scratch the surface of a very rich, extensive literature. As with any such taxonomy, the categories overlap as do the works within them. Nevertheless, we offer this as an initial cut that we hope will be of help to those approaching IR seen through this image. The categories we have selected in order of the listing below are (1) classical realism; (2) realism and structural realism (or neorealism); (3) balance of power, anarchy, and security; (4) war, its causes and remedies; (5) leadership, hegemony, and hegemonic stability; (6) power, war, and peace; (7) deterrence; (8) anarchy and cooperation under anarchy; (9) empires; (10) international political economy; (11) long cycles, history, and international relations theory; (12) other, earlier work in the field; and (13) realist critiques, challenges, and modifications.

◾ On Classical Realism

Bell, Duncan. *Political Thought and International Relations: Variations on a Realist Theme.* New York: Oxford University Press, 2008.

Carr, Edward H. *The Twenty Year's Crisis.* New York: Palgrave, 2001.

Clausewitz, Carl von. *On War.* (Various editions.)

Clinton, David. *The Realist Tradition and Contemporary International Relations.* Baton Rouge, LA: Louisiana State University Press, 2007.

Doyle, Michael. *The Ways of War and Peace.* New York: Norton, 1997. [Part One addresses Realism.]

Frankel, Benjamin. *Roots of Realism.* London: Routledge, 1997.

Gulick, Edward. *Europe's Classical Balance of Power.* New York: W. W. Norton, 1995.

Haslam, Jonathan. *No Virtue like Necessity: Realist Thought in International Relations Since Machiavelli.* New Haven, CT: Yale University Press, 2002.

Herz, John. "Political Realism Revisited." *International Studies Quarterly* 25, 2, *Symposium in Honor of Hans J. Morgenthau* (June 1981): 182–97.

Hobbes, Thomas. *Leviathan.* New York: Cambridge University Press, 1991.

Kissinger, Henry. *Diplomacy.* New York: Simon & Schuster, 1994.

———. *A World Restored; Metternich, Castlereagh and the Problems of Peace, 1812–22.* Boston, MA: Houghton Mifflin, 1957.

Lebow, Richard Ned. "Classical Realism." In *International Relations Theories: Discipline and Diversity,* eds. Tim Dunne, Milja Kurki, and Steve Smith. New York: Oxford University Press, 2007.

Liska, George. *The Ways of Power.* Cambridge, England: Basil Blackwell, 1990.

Lowell, Gustafson, ed. *Thucydides' Theory of International Relations: A Lasting Possession.* Baton Rouge, LA: Louisiana State University Press, 2000.

Lukes, Steven. *Power: A Radical View.* London: Macmillan, 1974.

Machiavelli, Niccolo. *The Prince, The Discourses, The Art of War* and *History of Florence.* Various translations and editions.

Morgenthau, Hans, and Kenneth Thompson. *Politics Among Nations: The Struggle for Power and Peace.* Brief 6th ed. New York: Knopf, 1985.

Thucydides. *The Peloponnesian War.* New York: The Modern Library, 1951.

Waltz, Kenneth N. *Man, the State and War.* New York: Columbia University Press, 1959.

Williams, Michael. *Realism Reconsidered.* New York: Oxford University Press, 2007.

On Realism and Structural Realism (Neorealism)

Brecher, Michael, and Frank Harvey. *Realism and Institutionalism in International Studies*. Ann Arbor, MI: University of Michigan Press, 2002.

Buzan, Barry, Charles Jones, and Richard Little. *The Logic of Anarchy: Neorealism to Structural Realism*, New York: Columbia University Press, 1993.

Crawford, Robert. *Idealism and Realism in International Relations: Beyond the Discipline*. Taylor and Francis, 2007.

Donnelly, Jack. *Realism and International Relations*. Boston: Cambridge University Press, 2000.

Frankel, Benjamin, ed. *Realism: Restatements and Renewal*. London: Frank Cass and Company, 1996.

Gilpin, Robert. *War and Change in World Politics*. Boston: Cambridge University Press, 2003.

Griffiths, Martin. *Realism, Idealism and International Politics*. New York: Taylor and Francis, 2007.

Griffiths, Martin, and Terry O'Callaghan. "Realism." In *An Introduction to International Relations: Australian Perspectives,* eds. Devetak Richard, Anthony Burke and Jim George. New York: Cambridge University Press, 2007.

Hanami, Andrew, ed. *Perspectives on Structural Realism*. New York: Palgrave Macmillan, 2003.

Jervis, Robert. *System Effects*. New Jersey: Princeton University of Press, 1998.

Layne, Christopher. "The Unipolar Illusion: Why New Great Powers Will Rise," *International Security* 17, 4 (Spring 1993): 5 51.

Lobell, Steven, Ripsman Norrin, and Jeffrey Taliaferro, eds. *Neoclassical Realism, the State, and Foreign Policy*. New York: Cambridge University Press, 2009.

Kapstein, Ethan, and Michael Mastanduno, eds. *Unipolar Politics: Realism and State Strategies after the Cold War*. New York: Columbia University Press, 1999.

Kolodziej, Edward. *Security and International Relations*. New York: Cambridge University Press, 2005, Ch. 4.

Mastanduno, Michael. "Preserving the Unipolar Moment. Realist Theories and US Grand Strategy after the Cold War." *International Security* 21, 4 (Spring 1997): 49–88.

Mearsheimer, John. "Structural Realism." In *International Relations Theories: Discipline and Diversity,* eds. Tim Dunne, Milja Kurki, and Steve Smith. New York: Oxford University Press, 2007.

———. *The Tragedy of Great Power Politics*. New York: W. W. Norton and Company, 2001.

Powell, Robert. "Absolute and Relative Gains in International Relations Theory," *American Political Science Review* 85, 4 (December 1991): 1303–20.

Pressman, Jeremy. *Warring Friends: Alliance Restraints in International Politics*. Ithaca, NY: Cornell University Press, 2008.

Rose, Gideon. "Neoclassical Realism and Theories of Foreign Policy." *World Politics* 51, 1(October 1998): 144–72.

Rosecrance, Richard. "Has Realism Become Cost-Benefit Analysis? A Review Essay." *International Security* 26, 2 (Fall 2001): 132–54.

Rosenau, James, and Mary Durfee. *Thinking Theory Thoroughly: Coherent Approaches to an Incoherent World* 2nd ed. Boulder, CO: Westview Press, 2000, Ch. 3.

Ruggie, John. "Continuity and Transformation in the World Polity: Toward a Neorealist Synthesis," *World Politics,* 35, 2 (January 1983): 261–85.

Schroeder, Paul. "Historical Reality vs. Neo-Realist Theory," *International Security,* 19, 1 (Summer 1994): 108–48.

Taliaferro, Jeff. *Realism and U.S. Foreign Policy: The Primacy of Politics*. London: Routledge, 2009.

Vazquez, John, and Colin Elman, eds. *Realism and the Balancing of Power: A New Debate*. Upper Saddle River, NJ: Prentice Hall, 2003.

Walt, Stephen. *The Origins of Alliances*. New York: Cornell University Press, 1990.

———. "The Progressive Power of Realism." *American Political Science Review* 91, 4 (December 1997): 931–35.

———. *Revolution and War*. New York: Cornell University Press, 1997.

———. "Why Alliances Endure or Collapse." *Survival* 39, 1 (Spring 1997): 156–79.

Waltz, Kenneth. *Realism and International Politics*. London: Routledge, 2008

———. "Realist Thought and Neorealist Theory." *Journal of International Affairs* 44 (Spring/Summer 1990): 21–37.

———. "Structural Realism after the Cold War." *International Security* 25, 1 (Summer 2000): 5–41.

———. "The Emerging Structure of International Politics." *International Security* 18, 2 (Fall 1993): 45–73.

———. "The New World Order." *Millennium* 22 (1993): 187–95.

———. *Theory of International Politics.* New York: McGraw-Hill (first published by Addison-Wesley), 1979.

———. "Theory of International Relations." In *Handbook of Political Science,* Vol. 8, ed. Nelson W. Polsby and Fred I. Greenstein. Reading, MA: Addison-Wesley, 1975.

Williams, Michael. *The Realist Tradition and the Limits of International Relations.* New York: Cambridge University Press, 2005.

———. "What is the National Interest? The Neoconservative Challenge in IR Theory." *European Journal of International Relations* 11, 3 (2005): 307–37.

Wohlforth, William. "Realism." In *The Oxford Handbook of International Relations,* eds. Reus-Smit Christian and Duncan Snidal. New York: Oxford University Press, 2008.

———. "The Stability of a Unipolar World." *International Security* 24, no. 1 (Summer 1999): 5–41.

On Power, Balance of Power, Anarchy, and Security

Art, Robert, and Robert, Jervis. *International Politics: Enduring Concepts and Contemporary Issues,* 7th ed. New York: Longman, 2005. Selected articles from Kenneth Waltz, Robert Jervis, Stephen Walt, and John Mearsheimer.

Berenskoetter, Felix, and M. J. Williams, eds. *Power in World Politics.* New York: Routledge, 2007, Ch. 3–4.

Brooks, Stephen, and William Wohlforth. *Worlds Out of Balance: International Relations and the Challenge of American Primacy.* Princeton, NJ: Princeton University Press, 2008, Ch. 1, 2, 3, and 7.

Brooks, Stephen G. "Dueling Realisms." *International Organization* 51, 3 (Summer 1997): 445–77.

Brown, Michael, Sean M. Lynn-Jones, and Steven Miller, eds. *Perils of Anarchy: Contemporary Realism and International Security.* Cambridge, MA: The MIT Press, 1995.

Cederman, Lars-Erik. "Emerging Polarity: Analyzing State-Formation and Power Politics." *International Studies Quarterly* 38, 4 (December 1994): 501–33.

Christensen, Thomas, and Jack Snyder. "Chain Gangs and Passed Bucks: Predicting Alliance Patterns in Multipolarity." *International Organization* 44, 2 (Spring 1990): 137–68

Grieco, Joseph. "Anarchy and the Limits of Cooperation: A Realist Critique of the Newest Liberal Institutionalism," *International Organization* 42, 3 (Summer 1988): 485–307.

Gulick, Edward. *The Time Is Now: Strategy and Structure for World Governance.* Lanham, MD: Lexington Books, 1999, Ch. 2.

Haas, Ernst. "The Balance of Power: Prescription, Concept or Propaganda?" *World Politics* 5, 4 (July 1953): 442–77.

Jervis, Robert. "Cooperation under the Security Dilemma," *World Politics* 30, 2 (January 1978): 167–214.

———. "Realism, Game Theory, and Cooperation." *World Politics* 40, 3 (April 1988): 317–49

———. "Realism, Neoliberalism, and Cooperation." *International Security* 24, 1 (Summer 1999): 42–63.

Jervis, Robert and Jack Snyder, eds. *Dominoes and Bandwagons.* New York: Oxford University Press, 1991.

Katzenstein, Peter J. *The Culture of National Security.* New York: Columbia University Press, 1996.

Kegley, Charles W., Jr. and Gregory A. Raymond. *A Multipolar Peace? Great-Power Politics in the Twenty-first Century.* New York: St. Martin's, 1994.

Krasner, Stephen D. *Problematic Sovereignty.* New York: Columbia University, 2001.

———. *Sovereignty.* Princeton, NJ: Princeton University Press, 1999.

Lake, David. "Anarchy, Hierarchy, and the Variety of International Relations." *International Organization* 50, 1 (Winter 1996): 1–34.

———. "Beyond Anarchy: The Importance of Security Institutions." *International Security* 26, 1 (Summer 2001): 129–60.

Layne, Christopher. "The Unipolar Illusion Revisited: The Coming End of the United States' Unipolar Moment." *International Security* 31, 2 (Fall 2006): 7–41.

Lebow, Richard Ned, and Thomas Risse-Kappen. *International Relations Theory and the End of the Cold War.* New York: Columbia University Press, 1995.

Little, Richard. "Balance of Power." In *Contending Images of World Politics,* eds. Greg Fry and Jacinta O'Hagan. New York: St. Martin's Press, 2000.

———. *The Balance of Power in International Relations: Metaphors, Myths and Models*. New York: Cambridge University Press, 2007, Ch. 4–7.

Mearsheimer, John. "The False Promise of International Institutions." *International Security* 19, 3 (Winter 1994–1995): 5–49.

———. *The Tragedy of Great Power Politics*. New York: W.W. Norton, 2001.

Milner, Helen. "The Assumption of Anarchy in International Relations Theory: A Critique." In *Neorealism and Neoliberalism: The Contemporary Debate*, ed. David Baldwin. New York: Columbia University Press, 1993.

Moens, Alexander, Lenard J. Cohen, and Allen G. Sens. *NATO and European Security: Alliance Politics from the End of the Cold War to the Age of Terrorism*. Westport, CT: Praeger, 2003.

Molloy, Seán. *The Hidden History of Realism: A Genealogy of Power Politics*. New York: Palgrave Macmillan, 2006.

Montgomery, Evan. "Breaking Out of the Security Dilemma: Realism, Reassurance, and the Problem of Uncertainty." *International Security* 31, 2 (Fall 2006): 151–85.

Mowle, Thomas, and David Sacko. *The Unipolar World: An Unbalanced Future*. New York: Palgrave Macmillan, 2007.

Niou, Emerson, and Peter, Ordeshook. "Stability in Anarchic International Systems." *American Political Science Review*, 4 (December 1990): 1207–34.

Niou, Emerson, Peter, Ordeshook, and Rose Gregory, eds. *The Balance of Power*. Cambridge: Cambridge University Press, 1989.

Odgaard, Liselotte. *The Balance of Power in Asia-Pacific Security: US-China Policies on Regional Order*. London: Routledge, 2007.

Paul, T. V., James Wirtz, and Michel Fortman, eds. *Balance of Power: Theory and Practice in the 21st Century*. Palo Alto, CA: Stanford University Press, 2004.

Rendall, Mathew. "Defensive Realism and the Concert of Europe." *Review of International Studies* 32 (2006): 523–40.

Schweller, Randall. "Bandwagoning for Profit: Bringing the Revisionist State Back In." *International Security* 19, 1 (Summer 1994): 72–107.

———. *Deadly Imbalances*. New York: Columbia University Press, 1998.

———. "Unanswered Threats: A Neoclassical Realist Theory of Underbalancing." *International Security* 29, 2 (Fall 2004): 159–201.

———. *Unanswered Threats: Political Constraints on the Balance of Power*. Princeton, NJ: Princeton University Press, 2006.

Snyder, Glenn. "Mearsheimer's World-Offensive Realism and the Struggle for Security." *International Security* 27, 1 (Summer 2002): 149–73.

Stein, Arthur. *Why Nations Cooperate: Circumstance and Choice in International Relations*. Ithaca, New York: Cornell University Press, 1990.

Taliaferro, Jeffrey. "Security Seeking under Anarchy: Defensive Realism Revisited." *International Security* 25, 3 (Winter 2000–2001): 128–61.

Wagner, Harrison. "The Theory of Games and the Balance of Power." *World Politics* 38, 4 (July 1986): 546–76.

———. "What Was Bipolarity," *International Organization* 47, 1 (Winter 1993): 77–106.

Walt, Stephen. *Taming American Power: The Global Response to U.S. Primacy*. New York: Norton, 2005.

Wendt, Alexander, and Michael N. Barnett. "Dependent State Formation and Third World Militarization." *Review of International Studies* 19 (1993): 321–47.

Wohlforth, William. "The Stability of a Unipolar World." *International Security* 24, 1 (Summer 1999): 5–41.

On War, Its Causes, and Remedies

Aron, Raymond. *On War*. London: Secker and Warburg, 1958.

———. *Peace and War*. Garden City, NY: Doubleday, 1966.

Brodie, Bernard. *War and Politics*. New York: Macmillan, 1973.

Brown, Michael, ed. *Theories of War and Peace*. Cambridge, MA: MIT Press, 1998.

Brown, Seyom. *The Causes and Prevention of War*. New York: St. Martin's, 1987.

Copeland, Dale. *The Origins of Major War*. Ithaca, NY: Cornell University Press, 2000.

Doyle, Michael W. *Ways of War and Peace*. New York: W. W. Norton, 1997.

Fearon, James D. "Rationalist Explanations for War." *International Organization* 49, 3 (Summer 1995): 379–414.

George, Alexander, and Richard Smoke. *Deterrence in American Foreign Policy.* New York: Columbia University Press, 1974.

George, Alexander L. *Bridging the Gap: Theory and Practice in Foreign Policy.* Washington, DC: U.S. Institute of Peace, 1993.

Gilpin, Robert. *War and Change in World Politics.* Cambridge, England: Cambridge University Press, 1981.

Hoffmann, Stanley. *The State of War.* New York: Praeger, 1965.

Hoffmann, Stanley, and David Fidler. *Rousseau on International Relations.* Oxford, England: Clarendon Press, 1991.

Holsti, Kalevi J. *Peace and War: Armed Conflicts and International Order, 1648–1989.* New York: Cambridge University Press, 1991.

———. *The State, War, and the State of War.* New York: Cambridge University Press, 1996.

Howard, Michael. *The Causes of War and Other Essays.* Cambridge, MA: Harvard University Press, 1983.

———. *War and the Liberal Conscience.* New Brunswick, NJ: Rutgers University Press, 1978.

Jervis, Robert. *American Foreign Policy in a New Era.* New York: Routledge, 2005, Ch. 1.

Lebow, Richard Ned. *Between Peace and War.* Baltimore: The Johns Hopkins University Press, 1981.

Miller, Benjamin. *States, Nations, and the Great Powers: The Sources of Regional War and Peace.* New York: Cambridge University Press, 2007.

Mueller, John. *Quiet Cataclysm: Reflections on the Recent Transformation of World Politics.* New York: HarperCollins, 1995.

———. *Retreat from Doomsday: The Obsolescence of Major War.* New York: Basic Books, 1989.

Sagan, Scott, and Kenneth N. Waltz. *The Spread of Nuclear Weapons: A Debate.* New York: W. W. Norton, 1995. [Waltz presents a realist case and Sagan responds with more of a pluralist understanding that relies on organization theory.]

Schelling, Thomas S. *Arms and Influence.* New Haven, CT: Yale University Press, 1966.

———. *The Strategy of Conflict.* New York: Oxford University Press, 1960.

Stoessinger, John G. *Why Nations Go to War.* New York: St. Martin's, 1978.

Thompson, William R. *On Global War: Historical-Structural Approaches to World Politics.* Columbia: University of South Carolina Press, 1990.

Van Evera, Stephen. *Causes of War: Power and the Roots of Conflict.* Ithaca, NY: Cornell University Press, 1999.

———. "Hypotheses on Nationalism and War." *International Security* 18, 4 (Spring 1994): 5–39.

Wagner, Harrison. *War and the State: The Theory of International Politics.* Ann Arbor, MI: University of Michigan Press, 2007.

Walt, Stephen M. *Revolution and War.* Ithaca, NY: Cornell University Press, 1996.

Waltz, Kenneth N. "Kant, Liberalism, and War." *American Political Science Review* 56 (June 1962): 331–40.

———. *Man, the State and War.* New York: Columbia University Press, 1959.

Wright, Quincy. *A Study of War.* Chicago: University of Chicago Press, 1964.

■ On Leadership, Hegemony, and Hegemonic Stability

Keohane, Robert O. *After Hegemony: Cooperation and Discord in the World Political Economy.* Princeton, NJ: Princeton University Press, 1984.

Lebow, Richard Ned, and Barry S. Strauss, eds. *Hegemonic Rivalry: From Thucydides to the Nuclear Age.* Boulder, CO: Westview Press, 1991.

Lepgold, Joseph. *The Declining Hegemon.* New York: Praeger, 1990.

Nau, Henry. *The Myth of America's Decline.* New York: Oxford University Press, 1990.

Nye, Joseph S. *Bound to Lead: The Changing Nature of American Power.* New York: Basic Books, 1990.

Strange, Susan. "The Persistent Myth of Lost Hegemony." *International Organization* 41, 4 (Autumn 1987): 551–74.

■ On Power, War, and Peace: Rational Choice and Statistical Analyses

Alt, James, Randall Calvert, and Biran Humes. "Reputation and Hegemonic Stability: A Game-Theoretic Analysis," *American Political Science Review* 82, 2 (June 1996): 445–66.

Bueno de Mesquita, Bruce. "Risk, Power Distributions, and the Likelihood of War." *International Studies Quarterly* 25, 4 (December 1981): 541–68.

————. *The War Trap*. New Haven, CT: Yale University Press, 1981.

————. "The War Trap Revisited: A Revised Expected Utility Model." *American Political Science Review* 79, 1 (March 1985): 156–73.

Bueno de Mesquita, Bruce, and David Lalman. "Empirical Support for Systemic and Dyadic Explanations of International Conflict." *World Politics* 41, 1 (October 1988): 1–20.

————. *War and Reason: Domestic and International Imperatives*. New Haven: Yale University Press, 1992.

Bueno de Mesquita, Bruce, James Morrow, and Ethan Zorick. "Capabilities, Perception, and Escalation." *American Political Science Review* 91, 1 (March 1997): 15–27.

Bueno de Mesquita, Bruce, and Randolph M. Siverson. "War and the Survival of Political Leaders." *American Political Science Review* 89, 4 (December 1995): 841–55.

Bueno de Mesquita, Bruce, Randolph M. Siverson, and Gary Woller. "War and the Fate of Regimes." *American Political Science Review* 86 (1992): 638–46.

Bueno de Mesquita, Bruce, et al., "Capabilities, Perception and Escalation." *American Political Science Review* 91, 1 (March 1997): 15–27.

Choucri, Nazli, and Robert C. North. *Nations in Conflict*. San Francisco: W. H. Freeman, 1975.

Cioffi-Revilla, Claudio. *The Scientific Measurement of International Conflict*. Boulder, CO: Lynne Rienner, 1990.

Fearon, James. "Rationalist Explanations of War," *International Organization* 49, 3 (Summer 1995): 379–414.

Geller, Daniel. "Capability Concentration, Power Transition, and War." *International Interactions* 17, 3 (May 1992): 269–84.

Gilpin, Robert. "The Theory of Hegemonic War," *Journal of Interdisciplinary History* 18 (Spring 1988): 591–614.

————. *War & Change in World Politics*. Cambridge University Press, 1981.

Hagan, Joe D. "Domestic Political Systems and War Proneness." *Mershon International Studies Review* 38 (1994): 183–207.

James, Patrick. "Structural Realism and the Causes of War." *Mershon International Studies Review* 39, 2 (October, 1995): 181–208.

Kugler, Jacek, and Douglas Lemke, eds. *Parity and War: Evaluations and Extensions of the War Ledger*. Ann Arbor: University of Michigan Press, 1996.

Lemke, Douglas, and Jacek Kugler. "The Evolution of the Power Transition Perspective." In *Parity and War*, eds. Jacek Kugler and Douglas Lemke. Michigan: University of Michigan Press, 1996.

Lemke, Douglas, and Suzanne Werber. "Power Parity, Commitment to Change, and War." *International Studies Quarterly* 40, 2 (June 1996): 235–60.

Levy, Jack. "Alliance Formation and War Behavior: An Analysis of the Great Powers, 1495–1975." *Journal of Conflict Resolution* 25, 4 (December 1981): 581–613.

————. "Prospect Theory, Rational Choice, and International Relations." *International Studies Quarterly* 41, 1 (March 1997): 87–112.

————. "The Diversionary Theory of War." ed. In Manus Midlarsky, *Handbook of War Studies*. Boston: Unwin Hyman, 1989.

————. "Theories of General War." *World Politics* 37, 3 (April 1985): 344–74.

Mansfield, Edward D. *Power, Trade, and War*. Princeton, NJ: Princeton University Press, 1994.

————. "The Concentration of Capabilities and the Onset of War." *Journal of Conflict Resolution* 36, 1 (March 1992): 3–24.

Mearsheimer, John. "Back to the Future: Instability in Europe after the Cold War." *International Security* 15, 1 (Summer 1990): 5–56.

Midlarsky, Manus, ed. *Handbook of War Studies*. Boston: Unwin Hyman, 1989.

————. *The Evolution of Inequality: War, State Survival, and Democracy in Comparative Perspective*. Stanford, CA: Stanford University Press, 1999.

————. *The Killing Trap: Genocide in the Twentieth Century*. Cambridge, UK: Cambridge University Press, 2005.

————. *The Onset of World War*. Boston: Unwin Hyman, 1988.

Morrow, James. "Alliances and Asymmetry: An Alternative to the Capability Aggregation Model of Alliances," *American Journal of Political Science* 35, 4 (November 1991): 904–33.

Powell, Robert. "Stability and the Distribution of Power." *World Politics* 48, 2 (January 1996): 239–67.

Rapoport, Anatol. *The Origins of Violence*. New Brunswick, NJ: Transaction Publishers, 1989, 1995.

Reiter, Dan. "Learning, Realism, and Alliances: The Weight of the Shadow of the Past." *World Politics* 46, 4 (July 1994): 490–526.

Richardson, Lewis F. *Arms and Insecurity.* Pittsburg, PA: Boxwood, 1960.

———. *Statistics of Deadly Quarrels.* Chicago: Quadrangle Books, 1960.

Rummel, Rudolph. *Dimensions of Nations.* Beverly Hills, CA: Sage Publications, 1972.

———. *Understanding Conflict and War* (5 volumes). Beverly Hills, CA: Sage Publications, 1975–81.

Singer, J. David, Stuart Bremer, and John Stuckey. "Capability Distribution, Uncertainty, and Major Power War, 1820–1965." In *The Scientific Study of Peace and War,* eds. John Vazquez and Marie Henehan. New York: Macmillan/Lexington Books, 1992, Ch. 2.

Singer, J. David, and P. F. Diehl. *Measuring the Correlates of War.* Ann Arbor: University of Michigan Press, 1993.

Singer, J. David, and Melvin Small. *The Wages of War, 1816–1965.* New York: John Wiley, 1972.

Small, Melvin, and J. David Singer, eds. *International War: An Anthology and Study Guide.* Homewood, IL: Dorsey Press, 1985.

Smith, Alastair. "Alliance Formation and War." *International Studies Quarterly* 39, 4 (December 1995): 405–25.

Sullivan, Michael P. *Power in Contemporary International Politics.* Columbia: University of South Carolina Press, 1990.

Vasquez, John A. "The Realist Paradigm and Degenerate Versus Progressive Research Programs: An Appraisal of Neotraditional Research on Waltz's Balancing Proposition." *American Political Science Review* 91, 4 (December 1997): 899–912.

———. "The Steps to War: Toward a Scientific Explanation of the Correlates of War Findings." *World Politics* 40, 1 (October 1987): 108–45.

———. *The War Puzzle.* Cambridge, England: Cambridge University Press, 1993.

Wagner, Harrison. "Peace, War, and the Balance of Power." *American Political Science Review* 88, 3 (September 1994): 593–607.

Wohlforth, William. "Realism and the End of the Cold War." *International Security* 19, 3 (Winter 1994–1995): 91–129.

Woosang, Kim, and James Morrow. "When Do Power Shifts Lead to War?" *American Journal of Political Science* 36, 4 (November 1992): 896–922.

On Deterrence

Achen, Christopher, and Duncan Snidal. "Rational Deterrence Theory and Comparative Case Studies." *World Politics* 41, 2 (January 1989): 143–69.

Adams, Karen. "Attack and Conquer? International Anarchy and the Offense-Defense-Deterrence Balance." *International Security* 28, 3 (Winter 2003–04): 45–83.

Coleman, David, and Joseph Siracusa. *Real-World Nuclear Deterrence: The Making of International Strategy.* Westport, CT: Praeger Security International, 2006.

Danilovic, Vesna. *When the Stakes Are High: Deterrence and Conflict among Major Powers.* Ann Arbor, MI: University of Michigan Press, 2002.

Downs, George. "The Rational Deterrence Debate," *World Politics* 41, 2 (January 1989): 225–37.

Downs, George, and David Rocke. "Tacit Bargaining and Arms Control," *World Politics* 39, 3 (April 1987): 297–325.

Fearon, James. "Signaling Versus the Balance of Power and Interests: An Empirical Test of a Crisis Bargaining Model." *Journal of Conflict Resolution* 38, 2 (June 1994): 236–69.

Freedman, Lawrence. *Deterrence.* Cambridge, MA: Polity Press, 2004.

George, Alexander, and Richard Smoke. "Deterrence and Foreign Policy." *World Politics* 41, 2 (January 1989): 170–82.

Glaser, Charles. "When Are Arms Races Dangerous? Rational Versus Suboptimal Arming." *International Security* 28, 4 (Spring 2004): 44–84.

Gray, Colin. *Maintaining Effective Deterrence.* Carlisle, PA: Strategic Studies Institute, U.S. Army War College, 2003.

Huth, Paul, Christopher Gelpi, and Scott Bennet. "The Escalation of Great Power Militarized Disputes: Testing Rational Deterrence Theory and Structural Realism." *The American Political Science Review* 87, 3 (September 1993): 609–23.

Huth, Paul, and Bruce, Russett. "General Deterrence between Enduring Rivals: Testing Three Competing Models." *American Political Science Review* 87, 1(March 1993): 61–73.

Jervis, Robert. *Perception and Misperception in International Politics.* Princeton, NJ: Princeton University Press, 1976.

———. "Rational Deterrence: Theory and Evidence." *World Politics* 41, 2 (January 1989): 183–207.

Kenyon, Ian, and John Simpson. *Deterrence and the New Global Security Environment.* New York: Routledge, 2006.

Lebow, Richard, and Janice Stein. "Rational Deterrence Theory: I Think, Therefore I Deter." *World Politics* 41, 2 (January 1989): 208–24.

Morrow, James. "A Spatial Model of International Conflict." *American Political Science Review* 80, 4 (December 1986): 1131–50.

———. "Signaling Difficulties with Linkage in Crisis Bargaining." *International Studies Quarterly* 36, 1 (March 1992): 153–72.

Ochmanek, David, and Lowell Schwartz. *The Challenge of Nuclear-Armed Regional Adversaries.* Santa Monica, CA: Rand Corp., 2008.

Schelling, Thomas. *The Strategy of Conflict.* Cambridge: Harvard University Press, 1980.

Weber, Steven. "Realism, Detente, and Nuclear Weapons." *International Organization* 44, 1 (Winter 1990): 55–82.

Zagare, Frank. "Rationality and Deterrence." *World Politics* 42, 2 (January 1990): 238–60.

On Anarchy and Cooperation under Anarchy

Brown, Michael E., Sean M. Lynn-Jones, and Steven E. Miller, eds. *The Perils of Anarchy: Contemporary Realism and International Security.* Cambridge, MA: MIT Press, 1995.

Bull, Hedley. *The Anarchical Society: A Study of Order in World Politics.* New York: Columbia University Press, 1977.

Buzan, Barry, Richard Little, and Charles Jones. *The Logic of Anarchy: Neorealism to Structural Realism.* New York: Columbia University Press, 1993.

Grieco, Joseph M. "Anarchy and the Limits of Cooperation." *International Organization* 42, 3 (Summer 1988): 485–506.

———. *Cooperation among Nations.* Ithaca, NY: Cornell University Press, 1990.

Oye, Kenneth A., ed. *Cooperation under Anarchy.* Princeton, NJ: Princeton University Press, 1986.

Stein, Arthur. *Why Nations Cooperate: Circumstance and Choice in International Relations.* Ithaca, NY: Cornell University Press, 1993.

On Empires

Bacevich, Andrew J. *American Empire: The Realities and Consequences of U.S. Diplomacy.* Cambridge, MA: Harvard University Press, 2002.

Chomsky, Noam. *Hegemony or Survival: America's Quest for Global Dominance.* New York: Henry Holt, Metropolitan Books, 2003 and 2004.

———. *Failed States: The Abuse of Power and the Assault on Democracy.* New York: Henry Holt, Metropolitan Books, 2006.

———. *Imperial Ambitions: Conversations on the Post-9/11 World.* New York: Henry Holt, Metropolitan Books, 2005.

Daalder, Ivo, and James Lindsay. *America Unbound: The Bush Revolution in Foreign Policy.* Hoboken, NJ: Wiley, 2005.

Doyle, Michael. *Empires.* New York: Cornell University Press, 1986.

Elliott, J. H. *Empires of the Atlantic World.* New Haven, CT: Yale University Press, 2006.

Ferguson, Niall. *Empire: How Britain Made the Modern World.* London: Penguin, 2004.

———. *Empire: The Rise and Demise of the British World Order and the Lessons for Global Power.* New York: Basic Books, 2004.

Gordon, Michael, and General Bernard E. Trainor. *Cobra II: The Inside Story of the Invasion and Occupation of Iraq.* New York: Pantheon, 2006.

Harvey, David. *The New Imperialism.* Oxford and New York: Oxford University Press, 2003.

Howe, Stephen. *Empire: A Very Short Introduction.* Oxford and New York: Oxford University Press, 2002.

Huntington, Samuel. *The Clash of Civilizations and the Remaking of the World Order.* New York: Simon & Schuster, 1996.

Ikenberry, John, ed. *America Unrivaled.* Ithaca, NY: Cornell University Press, 2002. [See in particular the Introduction and Part I on the Durability of Unipolarity (Waltz, Kupchan, & Wohlforth).]

———. "America's Imperial Ambition" in Art & Waltz, *Use of Force.* 6th ed. Lanham, MD: Rowman and Littlefield, 2003.

Joffe, Josef. *Überpower: The Imperial Temptation of America.* New York: Norton, 2006.

Johnson, Chalmers. *A Trilogy: Nemesis: The Last Days of the American Republic* (2007); *The Sorrows of Empire: Militarism, Secrecy and the End of the Republic* (2004); and *Blowback: The Costs and Consequences of American Empire* (2000 and 2004). New York: Henry Holt, Metropolitan Books.

Kinzer, Stephen. *Overthrow: America's Century of Regime Change from Hawaii to Iraq.* New York: Times Books, 2006.

Kupchan, Charles A. *The Vulnerability of Empire.* Ithaca, NY: Cornell University Press, 1994.

Layne, Christopher, and Bradley A. Thayer. *American Empire: A Debate.* London: Routledge, 2006.

———. *The Peace of Illusions: American Grand Strategy from 1940 to the Present.* Ithaca, NY: Cornell University Press, 2007.

Mearsheimer, John. *The Tragedy of Great Power Politics.* New York: W. W. Norton and Company, 2001.

Peters, Ralph. *New Glory: Expanding America's Global Supremacy.* New York: Penguin Group, 2005.

Ricks, Thomas E. *Fiasco: The American Military Adventure in Iraq.* New York: Penguin, 2006.

Snyder, Jack. *Myths of Empire: Domestic Politics and International Ambition.* Ithaca, NY: Cornell University Press, 1991.

Tucker, Robert W., and David Hendrickson. *The Imperial Temptation: The New World Order & America's Purpose.* New York: NYU Press, 1992.

Walt, Stephen M. *Taming American Power: The Global Response to U.S. Primacy.* New York: W.W. Norton, 2006.

On International Political Economy

Gilpin, Robert. *Global Political Economy: Understanding the International Economic Order.* Andhra Pradesh, India: Orient Longman, 2003.

———. *The Political Economy of International Relations.* Princeton, NJ: Princeton University Press, 1987.

———. *U.S. Power and the Multinational Corporation.* New York: Basic Books, 1975.

Grieco, Joseph M. *Cooperation among Nations: Europe, America, and Non-Tariff Barriers to Trade.* Ithaca, NY: Cornell University Press, 1990.

Grieco, Joseph M., and G. John Ikenberry. *State Power and World Markets: The International Political Economy.* New York: W. W. Norton & Company, 2002.

Katzenstein, Peter J. *Small States in World Markets.* Ithaca, NY: Cornell University Press, 1985.

Kindleberger, Charles P. *World Economic Primacy, 1500–1900.* New York: Oxford University Press, 1996.

Knorr, Klaus. *The Power of Nations: The Political Economy of International Relations.* New York: Basic Books, 1975.

Krasner, Stephen D. *Structural Conflict: The Third World against Global Liberalism.* Berkeley: University of California Press, 1985.

Mastanduno, Michael. "Do Relative Gains Matter? America's Response to Japanese Industrial Policy." In *Neorealism and Neoliberalism.* ed. David Baldwin. New York: Columbia University Press, 1993: 250–66.

Olson, Mancur. *The Rise and Decline of Nations.* New Haven, CT: Yale University Press, 1982.

Rosecrance, Richard. *The Rise of the Trading State.* New York: Basic Books, 1986.

Strange, Susan. *States and Markets.* London: Pinter, 1988, 1994.

Zysman, John. *Governments, Markets and Growth.* Ithaca, NY: Cornell University Press, 1983.

On Long Cycles, History, and International Relations Theory

Goldstein, Joshua S. *Long Cycles: Prosperity and War in the Modern Age.* New Haven: Yale University Press, 1988.

———. "The Possibility of Cycles in International Relations." *International Studies Quarterly* 35, 4 (December 1991): 477–80.

Kennedy, Paul. *The Rise and Fall of the Great Powers.* New York: Random House, 1987.

Modelski, George. *Exploring Long Cycles*. Boulder, CO: Lynne Rienner, 1987.

Modelski, George, and W. R. Thompson. *Leading Sectors and World Powers*. Columbia: University of South Carolina Press, 1996.

———. *Seapower in Global Politics, 1494–1993*. Seattle: University of Washington Press, 1988.

Rasler, Karen A., and William R. Thompson. *The Great Powers and Global Struggle, 1490–1990*. Lexington: University Press of Kentucky, 1994.

Rosecrance, Richard. "Long Cycle Theory in International Relations." *International Organization* 41, 2 (Spring 1987): 283–301.

Thompson, William R. "Long Waves, Technological Innovation, and Relative Decline." *International Organization* 44, 2 (Spring 1990): 201–33.

Other, Earlier Work in the Field

Claude, Inis. *Power and International Relations*. New York: Random House, 1962.

Herz, John. *Political Realism and Political Idealism*. Chicago: University of Chicago Press, 1951.

———. "Political Realism Revisited." *International Studies Quarterly* 25, 2 (June 1981): 182–241.

Hoffmann, Stanley. "Raymond Aron and the Theory of International Relations." *International Studies Quarterly* 29, 1 (March 1985): 13–27.

Iklé, Fred C. *How Nations Negotiate*. New York: Harper & Row, 1964.

Kaplan, Morton. *System and Process in International Politics*. New York: John Wiley, 1957.

Kissinger, Henry. *A World Restored*. New York: Grosset and Dunlap, 1964.

Liska, George. *Nations in Alliance*. Baltimore: Johns Hopkins University Press, 1968.

Mackinder, Halford J. "The Round World and the Winning of the Peace." *Foreign Affairs* 21, 4 (July 1943): 595–605.

Morgenthau, Hans. J. *In Defense of the National Interest*. New York: Knopf, 1951.

———. *Politics among Nations*, 5th ed. New York: Knopf, 1978.

Osgood, Robert E. *Alliances and American Foreign Policy*. Baltimore: Johns Hopkins University Press, 1967.

Osgood, Robert E., and Robert W. Tucker. *Force, Order and Justice*. Baltimore: Johns Hopkins University Press, 1967.

Riker, William H. *A Theory of Political Coalitions*. New Haven, CT: Yale University Press, 1962.

Rosecrance, Richard. *Action and Reaction in World Politics*. Boston: Little, Brown, 1963.

Russett, Bruce M. *International Regions and the International System*. Chicago: Rand McNally, 1967.

Tucker, Robert W. *The Inequality of Nations*. New York: Basic Books, 1977.

Waltz, Kenneth N. *Foreign Policy and Democratic Politics*. Boston: Little, Brown, 1967.

Wolfers, Arnold. *Discord and Collaboration*. Baltimore: Johns Hopkins University Press, 1962.

Wright, Quincy. *The Study of International Relations*. New York: Appleton-Century-Crofts, 1955.

Realist Critiques, Challenges, and Modifications

Ashley, Richard K. "Political Realism and Human Interests." *International Studies Quarterly* 25, 2 (June 1981): 204–36.

Baldwin, David A., ed. *Neorealism and Neoliberalism: The Contemporary Debate*. New York: Columbia University Press, 1993.

Beer, Francis A., and Robert Hariman, eds. *Post-Realism: The Rhetorical Turn in International Relations*. East Lansing, MI: Michigan State University Press, 1996.

Grieco, Joseph M. "Anarchy and the Limits of Cooperation: A Realist Critique of the Newest Liberal Institutionalism." *International Organization* 42, 3 (Summer 1988): 485–506.

———. *Cooperation among Nations*. Ithaca, NY: Cornell University Press, 1990.

———. "The Relative-Gains Problem for International Cooperation." *American Political Science Review* 87, 3 (September 1993): 729–35.

Haas, Ernst B. "The Balance of Power: Prescription, Concept or Propaganda?" *World Politics* 5, 4 (July 1953): 442–77.

Hoffmann, Stanley. "Obstinate or Obsolete? The Fate of the Nation-State and the Case of Western Europe." *Daedalus* 95 (Summer 1966): 862–915.

Kegley, Charles W., ed. *Controversies in International Relations Theory: Realism and the Neoliberal Challenge.* New York: St. Martin's, 1995.

Keohane, Robert O. *After Hegemony: Cooperation and Discord in the World Political Economy.* Princeton, NJ: Princeton University Press, 1984.

———. *International Institutions and State Power.* Boulder, CO: Westview, 1989.

———. ed. *Neorealism and Its Critics.* New York: Columbia University Press, 1986.

———. "The Theory of Hegemonic Stability and Changes in International Economic Regimes." In *Change in the International System,* ed. Ole Holsti, Randolph M. Siverson, and Alexander George. Boulder, CO: Westview, 1980.

———. "Theory of World Politics: Structural Realism and Beyond." In *Political Science: State of the Discipline,* ed. Ada W. Finifter. Washington, DC: American Political Science Association, 1983.

Keohane, Robert O., and Joseph S. Nye. *Power and Interdependence.* Boston: Little, Brown, 1977.

Lyons, Gene M., and Michael Mastanduno, eds. *Beyond Westphalia: State Sovereignty and International Intervention.* Baltimore: Johns Hopkins University Press, 1995.

Nye, Joseph S. "Neorealism and Neoliberalism." *World Politics* 40, 2 (January 1988): 235–51.

Patomäki, Heikki. *After International Relations: Critical Realism and the (Re)construction of World Politics.* London; New York: Routledge, 2002.

Powell, Robert. "Absolute and Relative Gains in International Relations Theory." *American Political Science Review* 85 (1991): 1303–20.

———. "Anarchy in International Relations Theory: The Neorealist-Neoliberal Debate." *International Organization* 48 (1994): 313–44.

Rapoport, Anatol. *Strategy and Conscience.* New York: Schocken Books, 1969.

Rosecrance, Richard, and Arthur Stein. *The Domestic Bases of Grand Strategy.* Ithaca, NY: Cornell University Press, 1993.

Snidal, Duncan. "Relative Gains and the Pattern of International Cooperation." *American Political Science Review* 85, 3 (September 1991): 701–26.

Spruyt, Hendrik. *The Sovereign State and Its Competitors.* Princeton, NJ: Princeton University Press, 1994.

Vasquez, John A. "The Realist Paradigm and Degenerative Versus Progressive Research Programs: An Appraisal of Neotraditional Research on Waltz's Balancing Proposition." *American Political Science Review* 91, 4 (December 1997): 899–912.

———. *The War Puzzle.* Cambridge, England: Cambridge University Press, 1993.

Waltz, Kenneth N. "Reflections on *Theory of International Politics:* Response to My Critics." In ed. Robert O. Keohane, *Neorealism and Its Critics.* New York: Columbia University Press, 1986.

Wendt, Alexander E. "The Agent-Structure Problem in International Relations Theory." *International Organization* 41, 3 (Summer 1987): 335–70.

3

Liberalism: Interdependence and Global Governance

MAJOR ACTORS AND ASSUMPTIONS

The liberal image of international relations has influenced many theoretical research programs ranging from democratic peace theory to neoliberal institutionalism, the latter sharing several key assumptions with realism. In part to distinguish themselves from liberal thinkers focused on new world orders that minimized (or even eliminated) states as major players in international politics—as if state sovereignty could so easily be put at bay—some liberal theorists prefer to use the prefix *neo*, which captures their view that states and institutions still matter. Global governance to **neoliberal institutionalists** does not mean world government, but rather the ways and means by which both state and non-state actors act authoritatively to deal with issues on the global agenda. Institutional actors (and the ideas embedded in them) are important whether they be components of states or international and non-governmental organizations to include multinational or global corporations.

Underlying liberalism—the liberal image of international relations taken as a whole—are four key assumptions. First, states as well as non-state, transnational actors are important entities in world politics. International organizations, for example, may on certain issues be independent actors in their own right. Similarly, other non-governmental, transnational organizations such as multinational corporations (MNCs) and human rights and environmental groups play important roles in world politics. On occasions even individuals can have a significant impact. The growth of transnational networks oriented around common strategies and goals epitomizes the rapid expansion of "sovereignty-free" actors and the coining of the term **global civil society.** On the other hand, terrorist and criminal organizations could be viewed as the dark-side of globalization, posing various degrees of threats to states and peoples.

The liberal image really is a pluralist one in which multiple kinds of state and non-state actors play substantial roles in world politics. Indeed, many liberals prefer *world* or *global* rather than *international* politics since the latter term tends to privilege the state over international and non-governmental organizations, groups, and individuals. To these liberals, referring to international politics is really a euphemism for interstate politics—an understanding more suited to realists.

Second, the state is not always a unitary actor, and the worst aspects of anarchy can be overcome as institutions and ideas matter to both states and non-state actors that operate transnationally across state borders. The staff of a particular international organization, for example, may play an important role in implementing, monitoring, and adjudicating disputes arising from decisions made by constituent states. Or the organization may have a great deal of power in terms of agenda setting as well as in providing information that may influence how states define their interests.

Liberals, particularly neoliberal institutionalists, do not reject the rational-actor model for either state or non-state actors, but see such purposive choices affected by calculations and complex interactions among them and by the bureaucracies or institutions that operate both within states and across national borders. State preferences are therefore not a given but rather influenced by these factors, which in turn influence state behavior. Calculations of interest or utility—gains and losses—can also be affected by misunderstanding or misperceptions on the part of decisionmakers as a result of incomplete information, bias, stress, or uncertainty about cause and effect relations related to policy options under consideration. Particular policies may enhance the bureaucratic power, prestige, and standing of one organization or institution at the expense of others or of the state as a whole. Decision-making processes associated with coalition and countercoalition building, bargaining, and compromising may not yield a best or optimal decision for a particular state.

Compared to structural realists and many economic structuralists in particular, liberals therefore tend to be voluntarists. Human agency matters. While globalization is not without its costs, liberals tend to be cautiously optimistic that international collaboration or partial global goverance is achievable.

Even in the absence of an international organization, collaboration is possible where principles, norms, and actors' expectations converge on a particular issue area. Liberalism therefore takes from **game theory** a **positive-sum** perspective—the size of the pie can be increased. Absolute gains (all can win) are opposed to the realist assumption of **relative gains** that supposedly drives interstate competition—when one gains or loses disproportionately more than others or when one's gain is another's loss—a **zero-sum** outcome. Despite their differences, functionalist, regime, and neoliberal institutionalist theories all examine the possibilities of upgrading the common interest to include the impact of non-material factors such as ideas in general and norms in particular. Hence some liberals incorporate social constructivist understandings within their work.

Third, liberals see economic or other forms of interdependence or interconnectedness among both state and non-state actors as tending to have if not a pacifying, then at least a moderating effect on state behavior. As the world is ever more closely bound with a veritable cobweb not only of economic, but also social, cultural, and political or transnational ties, the literature on economic interdependence naturally flows into discussion of the process of globalization. In an increasingly globalized world, liberals see states, international and non-governmental organizations, multinational corporations, groups and individuals operating in complex arrays of overlapping or cross-cutting coalitions and networks.

Finally, for liberals the state-society relation is critical to understanding international relations and, as a result, the agenda of international politics is extensive. The liberal rejects the notion that the agenda of international politics is dominated only by military-security issues.

The distinction between **high** and **low politics** is falsely drawn. Economic and social issues also matter. Sometimes they also can be understood as security issues in their own right, perhaps even more salient than other security matters.

As opposed to structural realists with their "top-down" view on how anarchy and the distribution of capabilities affect state behavior, some liberals take an "inside-out" view that examines how factors at the state-society and individual levels of analysis affect international relations. For its part, democratic peace theory attempts to show how political culture, values, and domestic political structures influence the prospects for international peace. Other work examines the role of perception, small group behavior, and decision-making processes.

Agents matter as we take into account how they relate to the material or ideational factors that may facilitate or constrain their conduct. Liberal theorists dealing with agency may refer to states, international and non-governmental organizations as actors, but they also are prone to look within the state or other institutions to find agency at the human level of individuals and small groups. While cognizant of the impact of system-level influences, these efforts challenge the realist assumption of a rational, unified decisionmaker. The liberal approach to theory, then, can be characterized as building separate islands of theory (each explaining some things but not others), perhaps with the eventual goal of connecting them together within a more general theory of international politics.

INTELLECTUAL PRECURSORS AND INFLUENCES

With realism it was relatively easy to identify intellectual precursors. In the case of liberalism, however, the impact of particular theorists has tended to be more indirect. Many of these writers have not been observers of international relations *per se* but have been economists, social scientists, theologians, or political scientists primarily interested in domestic politics. Their one common denominator, however, has been an interest in not simply the state, but also the individual or group. Agency—a focus on actors—is an important theme among these intellectual precursors even as they also have examined the impact societal, systemic, or structural factors have had on agents and vice versa. Although some aspects of liberal thought have also influenced realist scholars, we focus here on those aspects of liberalism that have informed work on transnationalism, interdependence, democratic peace theory, global governance, and decision making. First, however, we discuss briefly the tradition of political thought known as Stoicism.

Stoicism

Realism emphasizes what separates political entities and people. **Idealism** is another tradition of political thought that emphasizes what unites people. From this perspective, ideas are an important factor that significantly influences how we live our lives, how we relate to others, and the institutions we construct. Idealism—an important, underlying influence on contemporary liberal thought—can be traced back in western philosophy to stoicism, a school of thought that arose in Greece around 300 B.C. Today the term **stoicism** is generally associated with the idea that one should bravely face life's adversities, accept pain with grace, and persevere despite all odds. More importantly for our purposes, however, the Stoics also argued that we are all part of a larger community of humankind, regardless of our different political communities and cultures. Stoic ideas were very influential in republican and imperial Rome—Emperor Marcus

Aurelius and Paul of Tarsus (the Christian St. Paul) were among those identified as stoics. The universalism in stoic thought anticipated the worldviews of the seventeenth-century Dutch legal writer Hugo Grotius and the nineteenth-century German scholar Immanuel Kant.

For the Stoics, the ability to reason is a quality shared by all humans. It is this reasoning or thinking capacity that distinguishes *homo sapiens* from other animals. Reason is a divine spark, a reflection of the God within us. Many followers of stoicism thought of the divine as the source of the laws of nature. Humanity's universal ability to reason and the universal applicability of these laws of nature led the Stoics to emphasize the essential equality of people and the factors that unite them as opposed to what divides them, whether those divisions are geographic, cultural, ethnic, or political. Although they did not use the term, stoicism had a very transnationalist perspective.

Classical Liberalism

Influenced directly or indirectly by thought rooted in stoicism, **liberalism** is a tradition of political thought composed of a set of practical goals and ideals. For classical liberal theorists, the individual is the most important unit of analysis and the claimant of rights. The state is to play a minimal role in a liberal society, principally acting as arbiter in disputes between individuals and ensuring the maintenance of conditions under which individuals can enjoy their rights to the fullest. There are important differences among liberal theorists. They agree, however, on the primacy of the individual in political life and on the role of the state as being limited to maintaining a stable political, social, and economic environment within which individuals can interact and pursue their chosen ends. This emphasis on the individual and the limited state is perhaps best exemplified in John Locke's *Second Treatise on Government*, published in England in 1689.

Liberalism as an ideology came to dominate much of the political and economic thought in the eighteenth and nineteenth centuries, particularly in Great Britain and the United States. Liberal concerns for the individual were reinforced by Adam Smith's and David Ricardo's works in economics. They emphasized the important role of the individual entrepreneur who should be relatively unconstrained by a minimalist state—a major theme in early capitalist writings. David Hume's contribution to logic and the philosophy of science similarly stressed the importance of the individual as the unit of analysis. The nineteenth-century essays of such **utilitarians** as Jeremy Bentham viewed people as rational, calculating individuals capable of deciding what was best for themselves without much government interference. Liberalism reigned supreme, virtually unchallenged in the United States and Great Britain until the twentieth century.

The spirit of liberalism and its emphasis on the individual pervaded all spheres of life and thought—scientific, political, economic, social, and religious. The Industrial Revolution, however, eventually resulted in modifications of liberal doctrine which, although retaining an emphasis on the individual, now allowed the state to be given a more activist role in order to mitigate the most harmful effects of unrestrained economic competition. Still elevating the individual, this new strain of *social* liberalism also brought to bear the resources of government to help individuals realize their potential. Whether of the classical or social variety, individuals (and individualism) mattered to liberals of all stripes.

For classical liberals, the minimal state was a possibility (and necessity) because it was assumed that no particular government had a monopoly on sound judgment. Just as the competition of the marketplace would produce the best goods, so too would the marketplace of political ideas eventually produce the best governance, the balance held by the governed. Consistent with this logic, liberals emphasized the positive role played by public opinion in providing guidance to state officials and producing good public policy, including foreign policy. The state, therefore, was not some unitary, solitary actor pursuing its own course independently of the public. To the contrary, it was composed of numerous persons representing a multitude of interests. Out of the clash of ideas and interests would come political consensus. The attainment of this consensus, therefore, presumed faith that an underlying harmony of interests existed for the greater good to the benefit of the greatest number.

Immanuel Kant

This view of the domestic polity was carried over into the international realm. Liberals recognized that war was a defining characteristic of international politics. They also agreed with realists that the state of anarchy that characterized world (as opposed to domestic) politics contributed to suspicion and distrust among states, posing an obstacle to cooperation and peace. But just as it was assumed that there could be a harmony of interests among individuals within a given state, so too did liberal theorists argue that a harmony of interests among states was possible. The most famous argument in this genre of thought was made by the German scholar Immanuel Kant (1724–1804) whose writings have influenced some contemporary democratic peace theorists.

The stoic roots of Kant's thoughts on world politics are quite clear as evidenced by his universalism, his concept of world citizenship, and his advocacy of a federation among states as a means to peace. Kant's vision is of a diverse world in which human beings can live freely and without war. Kant was no head-in-the-clouds idealist, and he realized the transformation of world politics was neither imminent nor easy to achieve. The sovereign state was a reality, and any plan to deal with international anarchy had to take states into account. Even if it were possible to eliminate states and create an empire, this would not solve the problem of war because warring groups could still arise within any such empire.

Kant proposed instead something less than an empire—a league or federation of nations constituted as republics (representative democracies)—an arrangement that would leave sovereign states intact, but alter their collective character. How did Kant reach this conclusion? On the one hand, he recognized the continuous threat of war due to the condition of anarchy in international relations. On the other hand, Kant disagreed with Thomas Hobbes in that he believed that the gradual transformation of human beings and international society was possible. Over time, Kant maintained, discord among human beings will lead them to learn ways to avoid future wars. As reasoning beings concerned with self-preservation and self-improvement, people will learn that states are necessary to secure internal peace. This emphasis on learning is also shared by many present-day liberals.

Clearly reflecting the democratic and social-contract influence of Jean-Jacques Rousseau, Kant claimed that the best way to ensure progress toward peace is to encourage the growth of republics that manifest the popular will. In a statement echoed by many political leaders to this day, Kant argued that a federation of republics would be inclined toward peace and more likely to take international law seriously than would monarchies or empires. As the number of republics gradually increased, the world would move ever closer to a "perpetual peace." By transforming the state, the violent manifestations of international anarchy can eventually be overcome. Just as the ethical standing of individuals can improve by their subscription to universal principles to guide their behavior, so too can states constituted as republics (and their agents) choose to act morally—opting for peace rather than war—in their relations with other states. The idealism in Kant is clear.

Richard Cobden

Economics and the welfare of human beings also matter to liberals. Richard Cobden (1804–1865) was the foremost exponent of what could be called commercial liberalism. Other prominent eighteenth- and nineteenth-century writers associated with this perspective include Adam Smith, Jeremy Bentham, Jean-Jacques Rousseau, Montesquieu, and John Stuart Mill. Cobden made three ambitious claims concerning the impact of free trade on peace. First, he asserted that most wars were fought by states to achieve their mercantilist goals. Free trade as part of a capitalist system would show leaders a much more effective—and peaceful—means to achieve national wealth. Second, even in the case of wars not arising from commercial rivalry, states with domestic interests that would suffer from the interruption of free trade caused by war would be less inclined to resort to hostilities because of the losses they would suffer. Finally, Cobden argued that with an expansion of free trade, contact and communication among peoples would expand. This in turn would encourage international friendship and understanding. This posited relation between increased economic interdependence and international peace has been a recurrent proposition in works we will examine subsequently.

Joseph Schumpeter

Kant's belief in the power of democracy combined with Cobden's faith that unrestricted capitalism would enhance the possibility of international harmony came together in the works of Joseph Schumpeter (1883–1950). Contrary to the arguments of Marxist-Leninists, while arms sellers or "merchants of death" might register some narrow, short-term gains, the net effect of war is to destroy capital—the productive capacity of economies. Because it is the capitalists who own this productive capacity, their real interest is in protecting and expanding capital, not destroying it. According to this reasoning, peace is served by the spread of capitalism and commercial values that displace heroism, gallantry, glory, and other obsolete, war-oriented values of an earlier pre-capitalist or feudal period. In sum, democratic capitalism leads to peace. The arguments of Kant, Cobden, and Schumpeter have one thing in common: it is the nature of state and society or the political and economic regime and the ideas underpinning them that are responsible for increasing or decreasing the likelihood of war.

Interest Group Liberalism

We have to be careful in thinking about societal or structural representations so that we don't overlook agents at the individual and small-group levels of analysis that also matter in liberal understandings. Indeed, the liberalism we find among many American and European scholars is not unrelated to the way they also see domestic politics. Often it is the same ontologies or domestic lenses that inform liberals as they look at world politics beyond their national borders.

It is a multi-actor pluralism of individuals in groups interacting, forming coalitions, and counter-coalitions in the domestic arenas of politics that many liberal scholars project as capturing the essence of politics across the entire globe as well. From this perspective, international political processes are not all that different from, and may even be considered an extension of, those conducted within the boundaries of a given state. As a result, many liberals reject the realist distinction between "international" and "domestic" politics. For the liberal, one is an extension of the other. This perspective is quite evident in much of the literature on decision making and transnationalism that disaggregates the state-as-actor into its component parts, placing particular emphasis on agency—the decisionmakers themselves.

The connection of interest group liberalism to earlier currents in eighteenth- and nineteenth-century liberal thought is apparent. Theodore Lowi observes that interest group liberalism assumes the "role of government is one of assuring access to the most effectively organized, and of ratifying the agreements and adjustments worked out among competing leaders and their claims." Second, there is a "belief in a natural harmony of group competition." Finally, interest group liberalism defines both "the policy agenda and the public interest . . . in terms of the organized interests in society."[1] All three observations are consistent with the liberal notions of (1) the state as neutral arbiter, (2) the potential for a natural harmony of interest, in this case among groups of individuals, and (3) public concern for, and participation in, a policy process not restricted to elites.

In the image of politics held by adherents of interest group liberalism, conflict and competition as well as cooperation and collaboration among interest groups thus play an important role. There is a proliferation of interest groups. Individuals form interest groups in attempts to outmaneuver, end-run, or overwhelm opposing groups or coalitions. Viewed in this way, politics is a game, but a game with very real stakes to be won or lost. Authoritative choices (or decisions) are made by government decisionmakers as the outcome of this process.

David Truman (1913–2003), whose writings are in the school of interest group liberalism, acknowledges his intellectual debt to Arthur F. Bentley (1870–1957), whose 1908 volume *The Process of Government* served as "the principal bench mark for my thinking." Truman observes that "the outstanding characteristic of American politics" is the "multiplicity of co-ordinate or nearly co-ordinate points of access to governmental decisions." He proceeds to describe the conflictual nature of American politics, but comments that "overlapping membership among organized interest groups" provides "the principal balancing force in the politics of a multi-group society such as the United States."

The writings of Harold Lasswell (1902–78) and Robert Dahl (b. 1915) are also illustrative of this image. Dahl describes American politics as a "system in which all the active and legitimate groups in the population can make themselves heard at some crucial stage in the process of decision." Noting that it is a decentralized system, he observes that "decisions are made by endless bargaining." Groups are central to the process. Rather than either majority rule or minority rule, Dahl argues that the term *minorities rule* is the more accurate. Politically active groups—minorities—are the most influential.

Thus, the image of politics that interest group liberals hold is of a fragmented political system, one in which multiple actors compete. Agents matter to liberals at least as much (and for many a good deal more) than societal factors, systems, or structures do. The image is shared by most American political scientists even though their views may differ greatly on other conceptual and normative matters. The scholars mentioned are not, of course, creators of this image of American politics. Certainly *The Federalist Papers,* especially the writings of James Madison and later those of the Frenchman Alexis de Tocqueville, expose one to a good dose of this pluralist view of American domestic politics.

In sum, what the group is to the interest group liberal, the individual is to the liberal philosopher. What they have in common is agreement on the fragmented nature of the state and society and the potential for harmony to develop out of competition and conflict. The state is not an independent, coherent, autonomous actor separated or aloof from society. Its primary function is as arbiter of conflicting demands and claims, or as an arena for the expression of such interests. Furthermore, the focus of analysis is less on the state and more on both competition and cooperation among individuals and groups as agents of both state and non-state actors in world politics.

INTEGRATION

The League of Nations established in the aftermath of World War I as an effort to maintain the peace drew upon European diplomatic experience—the post-Napoleonic peace found in a Concert of Europe—and reflected liberal ideas found in Kant and others. Influenced among others by American President Woodrow Wilson's liberal thought—he was not alone in these views as is often suggested—negotiators moved away from alliances (and secret agreements among them that were thought to have triggered World War I), power, and the balance of power. These were understood to be more the cause of war than a mechanism for maintaining the peace. It was instead to be a **collective security** based on the rule of law. Aggression was prohibited (and war later declared illegal). Law-abiding states in these collective security arrangements were to come together as collective law enforcers against any state committing aggression. Realist critics observed that such idealism posed no effective obstacles to stop aggression by Germany, Italy, Japan, and other states joining with them.

This failed experience with collective security through the rule of law was at the root of the realist-idealist debate in the interwar period that continued after World War II. On security matters, the new United Nations retained collective security (see Chapter 7, particularly Article 42 of the U.N. Charter), but augmented it with **collective defense**—a euphemism for bringing alliances back into the mix (see Articles 51 and 52) as a supplement to a sovereign state's right to self-defense under international law. In practice, then, liberal and realist conceptions came together in the multilateral security mechanism constituted under the authority of the U.N. Security Council. In other respects, liberal ideas became embedded in a wide variety of U.N.-affiliated and other international organizations—the World Bank, International Monetary Fund, The General Agreement on Tariffs and Trade and later the World Trade Organization, the International Telecommunications Union, the International Civil Aviation and Maritime Organizations, the World Health Organization, the Food and Agricultural Organization, the International Labor Organization, and the U.N. High Commission on Human Rights, to mention just a few.

The present-day story of liberalism and IR theory, then, begins in Europe in the aftermath of World War II. Notwithstanding embedded liberalism in international organizations, with the advent of the Cold War realism secured a preeminent place in the study of international relations. But while headlines focused on crises in Berlin and the rise in East-West tensions, Europe was also the test bed for theories in the liberal tradition. The economic rebuilding of Western Europe was not simply a humanitarian priority, but a political one as well. The fear was that a failure to rebuild Europe would make communist subversion and political unrest more likely, particularly in Germany. Furthermore, the hope was that a rebuilt Europe would eventually tie together states such as France and Germany into a web of interdependencies in order to reduce the likelihood of another devastating war. In keeping with liberal theory, increased economic ties would play a major role.

The first scholar to explicate the hope and logic of **integration** was David Mitrany in his theory of **functionalism.** Mitrany argued that modern society faced a myriad of technical problems that can best be resolved by experts as opposed to politicians. This is true within states as well as among states in multilateral arrangements. Indeed, he saw the proliferation of common problems logically requiring collaborative responses from states. Hence, these essentially non-political problems (economic, social, scientific) should be assigned to non-political experts from the affected countries for resolution.

Mitrany reasoned that successful collaboration in one particular technical field would lead to further collaboration in other related fields. Governments would recognize the common benefits to be gained by such cooperative endeavors and so would encourage or allow for a further expansion of collaborative tasks. In effect, Mitrany saw a way to sneak up on the authority of the sovereign state. As states and societies became increasingly integrated due to the expansion of collaboration in technical areas in which all parties made absolute gains, the cost of breaking these functional ties would be great and hence give leaders reason to pause before doing so.

The interest in Mitrany's functionalist theory—and integration in general—was spurred by the successful creation of the European Coal and Steel Community (ECSC) in 1952 and formation of the European Economic Community (EEC) or Common Market in the 1956 Treaty of Rome. The EEC even seemed to hold out promise for the eventual political integration of Western Europe. Furthermore, the EEC's initial successes in the realm of economic integration increased interest in the more general question: Under what conditions is integration among states possible? Scholars noted that what was occurring in Western Europe did not match the Hobbesian image of states constantly prepared to go to war, an image that included little faith in the possibility of collaborative behavior among sovereign states.

Karl Deutsch pioneered in developing the idea of a security community in Europe—an approach still underway in a continent and its islands in what some now refer to as a zone of peace. A separate enterprise has been building a secure Europe through collaboration in economic and social activities—first establishing what would come to be called webs of interdependence and interconnectedness across an increasingly integrated Europe.

The most prominent theorist of regional integration was Ernst Haas (1924–2003) whose work and that of his colleagues was referred to as **neofunctionalism.** Mitrany's functionalist logic of technical tasks driving the creation of international organizations had discounted the importance of politics. Neofunctionalists now put politics back in center stage. The prefix *neo* was added to the term *functionalism* precisely to acknowledge how integral politics is to integration processes. While acknowledging his intellectual debt to Mitrany, Haas and fellow neofunctionalists parted company with Mitrany, rejecting the notion that one somehow can separate technical tasks from politics. For integration to occur, Haas argued that it must be perceived by politically connected elites to be in their interest to pursue such aims—whether they be experts in economics and finance, agriculture, health, environment, telecommunications, one or another scientific field, education, or any other specialization.

An early constructivist (even before the term came into common usage), Haas saw ideas grounded in the interests of the actors as driving forces in politics. The assigning of tasks to an international organization—even if this involves a seemingly technical function such as supervising an international mail system—will be attained and sustained only if actors believe their interests are best served by making a political commitment to constructing and maintaining such institutions. Applying game theory to neofunctional understandings, politics can produce a variable- or positive-sum outcome for all actors. Stated another way, the perspective on Rousseau's stag hunt fable discussed in Chapter Two is that collaborative behavior is possible and in the enlightened self-interest of states. Rather than just compete in ongoing zero-sum contests, optimizing short-term self-interest at the expense of others, they can upgrade service of their common and long-term interests through cooperative and collaborative efforts reflected in international institutions—the organizations they construct and the processes they establish.

Integration—the focal point of most neofunctional thought—can be understood as moving from surface-level cooperation down a progressive ladder into deeper forms of collaboration. At the surface level—or, more precisely, the first step down our ladder of integration—is establishing a free trade area—in principle removing all tariffs and other barriers to trade as has been underway since the North American Free Trade Agreement (NAFTA) came into effect in 1994. Even taking this first step down into deeper integration is difficult—witness challenges faced in economic integration efforts in the Caribbean, Central and South America, and various parts of Africa.

By contrast, European integration has gone much deeper than any other regional effort. A customs union adds an additional, important step down on the integration ladder—going beyond merely free trade among participating countries to agreements among them on common external tariffs charged against imports from outside the union. A step yet further down to deeper integration is to establish free movement of land (resources), labor, and capital—the factors of production—in a common market. A final step down this ladder—the deepest level of economic integration—is constructing an economic and monetary union with a common currency and central bank. Although politics have always been part of the process of deepening levels of integration, at this point integration has moved substantially into the political realm—the domain of macroeconomic (fiscal and monetary) policy, although treasuries and political authority over them still remain in national hands. The degree of integration of foreign policy, defense, and other, often local matters remains a matter of choice—some functions reserved by design to states and lower institutional levels within states where, in principle, they can be performed more effectively (a principle sometimes referred to as **subsidiarity**).

Rather than just gloss over integration theory merely as an artifact of liberalism in IR from past decades, we think it useful to survey briefly the European case here, assessing its theoretical implications. The internal logic of neofunctionalism applied to the European case led theorists to anticipate how increased integration in particular economic sectors would "spill over" into other related sectors—a process carried by politically connected elites seeing positive gains to be found in increased collaboration as states became increasingly integrated economically. Six European states (Germany, France, Italy, Belgium, Netherlands, Luxembourg) agreed in 1958 to move beyond the coal-and-steel community (ECSC) established in 1953 to establish two additional communities—one for atomic energy (EURATOM) and the other a European Economic Community (EEC)—a full customs union that finally was achieved by 1967.

Early predictions of further progress in regional integration did not occur, at least not to the extent anticipated. In the 1960s and 1970s, strong nationally oriented leaders were able to block transfers of too much more authority to the three European Communities (EC). Moreover, politically powerful farm interests in some countries made trying to facilitate trade by hammering out price arrangements across heavily subsidized domestic agricultural sectors extraordinarily difficult. If that were not enough, agreement on agricultural pricing using the then fixed exchange rate of the U.S. dollar as the common measure became unglued when the United States decided in 1971 to let the dollar float. The need for an independent European monetary measure became apparent, which in practice soon took the form of a carefully selected "basket" of currencies, stability in the measure assured when upward movements of some currencies were offset by downward movement by others.

By the early 1970s integration seemed to have stalled. The internal logic of spillover from one economic sector to another no longer seemed to be driving European integration. Rather than expecting further "spillover" in further progress to greater integration, some worried about "spillback"—reversing earlier gains. It was, in fact, increased competition the EC countries faced in the 1980s from the United States, Japan, and other rising economies—a factor external to Europe that Haas saw reigniting the integration engine and calls in 1987 to move toward a full common market by 1992. Bringing Europe together would achieve economies of scale, allowing Europe to compete globally in production of goods and services increasingly dependent upon ever higher technologies.

Achieved with much fanfare, the EC countries renamed themselves the European Union (EU) in 1992 and set their sights on a full economic and monetary union by the dawn of the new century. Some members, guarding their national prerogatives, chose not to go all the way down to this deepest level of integration, but most did. Critics now observed that European integration had become *à la carte*, allowing members to pick and choose the level of integration that suited their fancy. The problem has grown with the expansion of the EU, incorporating European states of great diversity in levels of economic development—critics of "widening" the membership noting that doing so would make "deepening" of integration ever more difficult. Be that as it may, the overall level of integration that has been achieved was thought decades earlier as highly unlikely, if not impossible to achieve in so short a period of time.

How did this occur? Politically connected elites still mattered in driving this process; some key players in institutionalized settings like the European Commission in Brussels (in effect the EU's executive branch) cultivated their counterparts in European governments and elites in the non-governmental or private sectors as well. To Haas and others who shared his views, this external focus on worldwide competitors and carving out a competitive position for Europe as a whole had displaced the intra-European, inward-looking logic that neofunctionalists had seen as advancing the earlier stages of regional integration.

Integration as a robust research program has faded, no longer enjoying the luster it once had. Haas himself concluded that regional integration theories should be subordinated to a broader theory of interdependence which did not anticipate a transfer of state sovereignty to regional organizations. As we look back, however, we can find within the neofunctional and integration research program the seeds of the still unresolved agency-structure debates that remain prominent in the IR field, particularly among constructivists. How ideas relate to material considerations in the heads of agents and how they relate to ideational and material structures that enable or constrain them are not new topics. Referring to the 1970s, when Ernst Haas and others were grappling with such questions, John Ruggie has commented that we were all constructivists then but didn't know it—the term not yet having entered the IR field.

For his part, Haas held to the position that agency matters. Individuals need not be captives of system structure, but can in fact influence the course of events. Changing knowledge, for example, can lead to redefining interests. Organizations composed of thinking people can adapt, learn, and innovate in changing circumstances. Nevertheless, they still face enormous challenges that theorists can reflect upon. Cognitive challenges—the apparent turbulence confronting decisionmakers in the present time—stem, according to Haas, from "confused and clashing perceptions of organizational actors which find themselves in a setting of great social complexity." Not only must agents deal with a large number of fellow actors, but each may be pursuing "a variety of objectives which are mutually incompatible," compounded by uncertainty surrounding "trade-offs between the objectives."[2]

Though not an integration theorist, much of James Rosenau's work also has been focused on the important roles played by both state and non-state actors in world politics. Like Haas, Rosenau also identifies turbulence as a substantial challenge.[3] In this regard, Rosenau reveals his ontology as one seeing two competing "worlds"—the first he describes as state-centric and the other multicentric involving diverse state and non-state actors. The agency-structure issue is reflected in the distinction he draws between parameters at micro-level (individual) and macro-level (system structure) and the "relational one" that tries to put the micro and macro together. Change is propelled by the dynamics of technology, the emergence of complex issues, the reduced capacity of states to deal effectively with many contemporary problems, and the emergence of "subgroupism" and individuals who are analytically ever more capable and diverse in orientation. Agents obviously still matter to Rosenau, as they also did to Haas.

TRANSNATIONALISM

By the early 1970s, just as neofunctional understandings of regional integration were losing conceptual steam, the concept of transnationalism entered the mainstream IR theory lexicon. Attention turned to the increasing role of multinational corporations abroad and the challenge they posed to the sovereign prerogatives of states as they transited across national boundaries in the daily conduct of their business transactions. Interest in international political economy increased substantially. The unilateral decision by the United States in 1971 to go off the gold-exchange standard of $35 an ounce (a rate the Treasury had maintained since 1934) and allow the dollar's value to float caused turmoil in international currency markets. Similar disruption of the status quo occurred when major oil-producing countries in the Organization of Petroleum Exporting Countries (OPEC) cartel dramatically raised the cost of oil by regulating its supply to global markets. Economics now seemed to be "high politics" as opposed to merely "low politics."

Even on security matters things seemed to be changing. Zero-sum calculations and relative gains prominent in realist thought were augmented by positive-sum understandings more common among liberals. An initial thawing of U.S.-Soviet relations in the late 1960s—still in the midst of Cold War—had produced *détente,* or a relaxation of tensions between the two superpowers, a climate conducive to arms control. Explicitly intended as balance-of-power politics vis-à-vis the Soviet Union, Washington also played its "China card" and reached out to Beijing, setting in motion a process that would lead to normalization of relations between the two Cold War adversaries. At the same time, power-based realist ideas—that the strong do what they will and the weak do what they must—had difficulty accounting for why a superpower like the United States could get bogged down and eventually lose a war in Vietnam, forced to evacuate its remaining forces in 1975.

These events in the late 1960s and early 1970s contributed to ferment in the IR field, setting the stage for new developments in both realist and liberal theories in IR. In 1971 and 1972 two works raised the question of the conceptual adequacy of the realist approach to international relations. John W. Burton argued in *World Society* that a "cobweb" model of multiple state and non-state actors better captured the nature of current reality than did the realist "billiard ball" model merely of states interacting with one another. He also asserted that the idea of a "world society" was descriptively more accurate than the concept of international relations.

Also published at this time was the seminal work *Transnational Relations and World Politics* by Joseph Nye, Jr. and Robert Keohane.[4] This work brought attention to multinational corporations and other non-governmental, transnational organizations as well as bureaucratic agencies, departments, or other components of governments that in their own right operate transnationally across state boundaries, sometimes even forming **transgovernmental** coalitions and countercoalitions with their counterparts in other countries. Thus diplomats and civil servants in the U.S. State Department might find common ground with fellow professionals in Germany or the United Kingdom on an issue like arms control that might be at odds with views in their respective defense ministries.

Liberal theories now moved to center stage within the IR field. The term *transnational* itself was used to describe either an actor (i.e., MNC) or a pattern of behavior (i.e., "MNCs act transnationally"). The new focus was on studying these actors, their interactions, and the coalitions they form across state boundaries that involved diverse non-governmental actors such as multinational corporations (MNCs), banks, churches, and eventually human rights, environmental, and terror or criminal networks. Transgovernmental links at the level of bureaucracies were also a new item on the liberal agenda, challenging realist claims to the state as unitary actor. Links or coalitions between non-governmental organizations and transgovernmental actors also became a subject of some interest.

Was there in fact a chipping-away or leakage of state sovereignty to be studied? Just as the regional integration literature posited the possibility of going beyond the nation-state, so, too, did much of the transnational literature leave the impression that states, assuming they survived as actors over the long term, would become ensnared like Gulliver in Jonathan Swift's classic political novel *Gulliver's Travels*.

A problem with this new transnational literature, however, was that in most cases the work was highly descriptive, lacking in theoretical content. A realist response—reasserting the enduring importance of the state and capabilities or power among states—was soon heard from Kenneth Waltz initially in his "Theory of International Relations" and later in *Theory of International Politics* discussed in Chapter Two.

INTERDEPENDENCE

In 1977 Keohane and Nye published their influential *Power and Interdependence: World Politics in Transition*. The title says it all: to develop the concept of interdependence and make it analytically useful, power must be taken into consideration. For Nye and Keohane, interdependence is simply defined as mutual dependence resulting from the types of international transactions catalogued by transnationalists—flows of money, goods, services, people, communications, etc. Interdependence exists when there are "reciprocal [though not necessarily symmetrical] effects among countries or among actors in different countries."[5] There is, in other words, sensitivity in Country *B* to what is going on in or emanating from Country *A*. Although there are costs associated with interdependence, as it by definition restricts autonomy, benefits to either or both parties may outweigh these costs. Thus, interdependence is not necessarily only a matter of country *B*'s vulnerability to Country *A*, which is the realist perspective. While Nye and Keohane fully recognized the importance of vulnerability interdependence such as when one country can manipulate the flow of oil to other countries, their interests lay elsewhere.

The centerpiece of their work was the concept of **complex interdependence**—an ideal type constructed to analyze situations involving transnational issues. In a situation of complex interdependence, multiple channels connect societies, there is an absence of hierarchy among issues, and military force is not used by governments against other governments involved in the interdependent relation. While some enthusiasts greeted *Power and Interdependence* as a challenge to realist conceptions of international relations, Nye and Keohane have always asserted that the work was rather designed to provide analytical insights and a research program in areas that the traditional realist focus on matters of military security and force tended to discount.

INTERNATIONAL REGIMES

Keohane and Nye's work on complex interdependence did not displace the state as principal focus of study. As noted, interdependence involves reciprocal effects among countries or other actors in different countries. Furthermore, even most of the elements of the complex interdependence model involved states—states' goals varied by issue area, states could use their power resources to manipulate interdependent relations, and it was states that would experience difficulties in linking issues together.

One important area that was highlighted, however, was that of international organizations. IOs were not just institutions composed of state members, but also actors that could set agendas, encourage coalition-formation, and act as arenas for political action even by small, relatively weaker states. Non-governmental organizations were also quite capable of establishing their own ties with these inter-governmental organizations. Instead of viewing the policies of these international organizations simply as the dependent variable (decisions or actions to be explained), they and their agents (leaders and staffs) came to be understood as independent variables in their own right, sometimes with substantial influence on states.

This was a new "institutionalism" that found its way into the IR field even before such studies became prominent in other political science fields during the 1980s. In liberal IR scholarship, the institutional turn took the form of a robust research program on the role of **international regimes**—rules agreed to by states (some with the binding character of international law) concerning their conduct in specific issue areas (trade, monetary exchange, navigation on the high seas or in the air, non-proliferation of weapons of mass destruction, etc.) and often associated with international and non-governmental organizations linked to these regimes.

The regime literature has focused, then, on the ways and means of constructing and maintaining or managing interdependent relations found in these multilateral, institutionalized arrangements. The term *regime* was borrowed from domestic politics, where it refers typically to an existing governmental or constitutional order (democratic, authoritarian, or otherwise). In its international context, given the absence of a superordinate or overarching central authority, these rules are voluntarily established by states to provide some degree of order in international relations. Thus, there is a strong Grotian strain in liberal thought, particularly when talk turns to managing interdependence through the construction of regimes.

As sets of principles, norms, rules, and procedures, international regimes are not the same as international organizations (although they usually are associated with them)—they do not require a mailing address or possess the capacity to act. In IR theory they are merely analytical constructs defined by observers. Action remains with states and both international and non-governmental organizations. Furthermore, an organization associated with a particular regime (e.g., the International Telecommunications Union that regulates the global distribution of frequencies) also may concern itself with other regimes covering diverse issue areas in a global context within what is referred to as the United Nations "system" of international organizations.

The regime literature, then, is concerned with such basic questions as: How and why are international regimes formed? What accounts for rule-based cooperation? How do regimes affect state behavior and collective outcomes in particular issue areas? How and why do regimes evolve or dissolve? There are several schools of thought on such questions.[6]

Power-based realist theories. These theories emphasize, not surprisingly, the role of anarchy and the impact of the relative distribution of capabilities. The best-known realist regime theory, hegemonic stability, was discussed in Chapter 2. The basic argument is that regimes are established and maintained when a state holds a preponderance of power resources, as did the United States after World War II. Once this hegemonic power declines and power is spread more equally among states, if regimes do not adapt themselves to changed circumstances, they can be expected to decline. While a few realists are completely dismissive of international regimes and organizations, most would accept Stephen Krasner's view that regimes help states avoid uncoordinated action and in some cases can actually be a source of power for weaker states.[7]

Knowledge-based cognitive regime theories. Scholars associated with these theories have been critical of both realist (hegemonic stability) and the neoliberal institutionalist perspective discussed below. Cognition theorists (some identified as constructivists we discuss in Chapter Six) argue that state interests are not given, but rather created. This leads them to examine the role of normative and causative beliefs of decisionmakers in explaining preferences and interest formation. In other words, the focus is less on overt behavior and more on intersubjective understandings. Learning matters as when a change in beliefs or understandings influences subsequent behavior. Cognition theorists attempt to demonstrate that states can redefine their interests without any shift in the overall systemic distribution of power and use regimes and institutions to "lock in" to their advantage the learning that has occurred.

One way knowledge might come to be shared by decisionmakers is through the influence of transnational, **epistemic communities,** defined as "network[s] of professionals with recognized expertise and competence in a particular domain and an authoritative claim to policy-relevant knowledge within that domain."[8] Epistemic communities (for example, environmentalists, scientists, international economists, and other specialists), it is argued, can influence the creation and maintenance of international regimes in a number of ways.

Path-breaking work on epistemic communities by Peter Haas, Emanuel Adler, and others has had a substantial impact on liberal understandings of how ideas carried by transnational groups of specialists impact policy processes. These communities are composed of politically connected elites one also finds in the earlier work on integration by Ernst Haas. Common understandings and ideas held by these communities of professionals or experts have global impact on how policies are made in diverse institutional contexts. Peter Haas observes that "members of epistemic communities not only hold in common a set of principled and causal beliefs, but also have shared notions of validity and a shared policy enterprise." When called upon by policymakers, these specialists bring their socially constructed interpretations of facts or knowledge and causality to the questions at issue. Studying the roles played and influence on policy by epistemic communities is itself a major research program.

International regimes are embedded in the broader normative structures of international society and, as a result, states typically are not free to ignore institutional commitments without paying a price. A focus on self-interest alone will not explain regime maintenance. Regimes have more than a regulative function that requires states to behave in accordance with certain norms and rules. They also create a common social world that interprets the meaning of international behavior. In other words, regimes have what is called a "constitutive" dimension— they are socially constructed— and hence cognitive regime theorists have advocated opening "the positivist epistemology to more interpretive strains, more closely attuned to the reality of regimes."[9]

This view of regimes can therefore be placed in the broader social constructivist approach to international relations. As discussed in Chapter Six, the focus is on the social construction of world politics and identities in particular. It is argued that actors in international politics make decisions based upon what the world appears to be and how they conceive their roles in it. These conceptions derive from systemic, intersubjective shared understandings and expectations. In terms of regimes, it logically follows that rule-governed cooperation can, over time, lead actors to change their beliefs about who they are and how they relate to the rest of the world. Cooperative and collaborative behaviors can become a matter of habit.

NEOLIBERAL INSTITUTIONALISM

Perhaps the most widely cited approach to regime theory was developed by Robert Keohane, his colleagues, and students in the 1980s. In fact, for Keohane, "regime theory" is too limiting a term to describe his approach to the conditions under which international cooperation can be achieved. He has developed the broader concept of "institutions" that he defines as "persistent and connected sets of rules (formal and informal) that prescribe behavioral roles, constrain activity, and shape expectations."[10] Thus defined, international institutions can take one of three forms:

1. *Formal Intergovernmental or Cross-national, Non-governmental Organizations:* These are purposive entities, bureaucratic organizations with explicit rules and missions. The United Nations is a prime example of the former, the International Committee of the Red Cross (ICRC) of the latter.
2. *International Regimes:* Institutionalized rules explicitly agreed upon by governments, that deal with a particular set of issues. Examples would include the international monetary regime established in 1944 but adapted to changing circumstances since then, the Law of the Sea regime developed in the 1970s, and the various arms control agreements between the United States and the Soviet Union during the Cold War.
3. *Conventions:* Informal institutions (or customary norms and practices) with implicit rules and understandings. These implicit understandings allow actors to understand one another and coordinate their behavior. Not only do they facilitate coordination, but they also affect actors' incentives not to defect in those situations where at least in the short term it might be in their interest to do so. "Reciprocity" is an example of a convention—political leaders expect reciprocal treatment in international dealings, both positive and negative, and anticipate costs of one kind or another if they violate the convention. Diplomatic immunity is an example of a convention that existed for centuries before it was codified in formal agreements in the 1960s.

The point to keep in mind is that Keohane's neoliberal institutionalist formulation is not restricted to formal organizations and regimes. It is a counter within liberal thought to what some perceived as the intellectual hegemony of neorealist writings within the IR field. Keohane's starting point is the proposition that "variations in the institutionalization of world politics exert significant impacts on the behavior of governments. In particular, patterns of cooperation and discord can be understood only in the context of the institutions that help define the meaning and importance of state action."[11]

His first stab at a theory of institutions was in *Power and Interdependence* in what he and Nye referred to as the international organization model of regime change. Subsequent work in the 1980s was done against the backdrop of rising challengers to the primacy of the United States in world politics. Much to the consternation of a number of scholars associated with regime theory and global civil society, Keohane's *After Hegemony* (1984) in fact adopts several realist premises. They include a desire to explain behavioral regularities in a decentralized international system, yet epistemologically sensitive to the fact that while theories can and must be tested, it is naïve to believe that reality can be objectively known. Furthermore, state power must be taken seriously, and it is assumed that leaders of states calculate the costs and benefits of contemplated courses of action. Finally, he also shares with neorealists an interest in the applicability to IR of economic theories of market behavior. With these premises as a starting point, he addresses the puzzle of why even self-interested, rational egoists—individuals seeking to maximize gains—would pursue multilateral, cooperative behavior.

Yet Keohane argues that despite these affinities with neorealism, neoliberal institutionalism is a distinct school of thought. First, neorealists and neoliberal institutionalists agree that international relations or world politics lack a stable hierarchy due to its anarchic or decentralized character. Neoliberals, however, are much more emphatic that there is no necessary logical link between the condition of anarchy and war. If any connection does exist between warfare and lack of harmony among states, it is conditional on the nature of prevailing expectations among actors to include those held by institutions.

Second, some realists, particularly neorealists, claim that in a condition of anarchy, relative gains are more important than absolute gains. States, therefore, are concerned with preventing others from achieving advances in their relative capabilities. So even though two states may both make material gains such as enhancing their military capabilities, the important question to most realists is who gained more? Is the power gap widening? This realist formulation seems to characterize U.S.-Soviet relations during the Cold War (and, perhaps, between India and Pakistan at present).

Neoliberals counter that this realist understanding does not accurately describe U.S. policy toward Europe or Japan in which the United States actively promoted economic recovery and development, and at least in the case of Europe pleaded for greater defense spending as the senior partner in the North Atlantic Treaty Organization (NATO). Nor does the neorealist formulation explain the peaceful relations among members of the European Union where, despite economic integration favoring some states more than others, members across the board are willing to accept an asymmetric distribution of absolute gains—some clearly gaining more than others. Neoliberals concede, of course, that this absolute gains argument may be more applicable in conditions where substantial mutual gains can be achieved and governments do not expect others will threaten to use force against them.

As with all propositions in international relations theory, such statements are conditional. But conditionality for neoliberals is a function of prevailing rules and expectations.

States use international institutions for self-interested reasons—institutions perform important tasks that enhance cooperation. For example, the transaction costs—making, monitoring, and enforcing rules—are reduced when institutions provide information to all parties and facilitate the making of credible commitments. What, however, are the guarantors of compliance to the commitments made by states? Reputation is one. Reciprocity is another, which includes threats of retaliation as well as promises of reciprocal cooperation.

While Keohane's interest in trade, monetary, and energy issues deals with material self-interest in which reciprocity plays a key role, he argues that the same framework works with environmental issues that often include a normative dimension and the role of principled ideas. His work with Judith Goldstein underscores the importance of ideas as a significant independent variable in explanations of foreign policy.[12] World views, principled beliefs, and causal beliefs are ideas that become embedded in institutions and impact the making of policy by acting as cognitive road maps. Ideas define the universe of possibilities for action. To Keohane "interests are incomprehensible without an awareness of the beliefs that lie behind them." These ideas shape agendas and, as a result, directly affect outcomes. When ideas become institutionalized, they assume a life of their own as socially embedded norms. Ideas linked to interests do influence the making of foreign policy choices.

Neoliberals like Keohane claim that institutions and regimes matter because they enable states to do things they otherwise *could not do*. With rising levels of interdependence and interconnectedness in world politics, it is hypothesized that states likely will rely more heavily on regimes for their own selfish reasons. Hence, while realists tend to view regimes as constraints on state behavior, neoliberals view regimes more positively as actually enabling states to achieve mutually beneficial outcomes.

Such thinking brings us back to Rousseau's stag hunt allegory discussed in Chapter Two and the possibilities of upgrading the common interest, despite the underlying condition of anarchy. In sum, the literature on international organizations, regimes, and institutions in the liberal tradition offers insight on how states may accommodate differences and upgrade the interests they share in common. Consistent with Rousseau's stag hunt fable, the actors may agree to collaborate in certain circumstances in hunting the stag rather than serve only narrowly defined, short-term self-interest. Absolute gains for all are possible as policymakers learn the benefits of cooperation in areas of interest to them.

GLOBAL GOVERNANCE

The increasing complexity of issues on the global agenda brings neoliberal institutionalists to the question of global governance. Governance involves the processes and institutions, both formal and informal, that guide and restrain the collective activities of groups. Keohane describes a "partially globalized world" as one with "thick networks of interdependence in which boundaries and states nevertheless matter a great deal."[13] With increasing interdependence in this partially globalized world, Keohane sees greater institutionalization as the world becomes more like a polity with governance essential to trade, finance, environment, security, and other matters of global import.

Keohane does not see global governance as if it were the same as world government—a new, unitary super state. It is merely a design that integrates "networks among agents and norms—standards of expected behavior—that are widely accepted among agents." Devising better, more effective global institutions to serve the needs of humankind is an imperative. On this, Keohane boldly asserts that "the challenge for American political science resembles that of the founders of the United States: how to design institutions for a polity of unprecedented size and diversity."[14]

He notes that "increased interdependence among human beings produces discord, since self-regarding actions affect the welfare of others." Moreover, he is concerned that institutional approaches to problems may not always be benign. Indeed, left to their own devices, they "can foster exploitation or even oppression." He observes that "the stakes in the mission" of establishing the ways and means of global governance are high—that "if global institutions are designed well, they will promote human welfare, but if we bungle the job, the results could be disastrous."[15]

To avoid adverse outcomes, we need instead to draw insights "from a variety of perspectives, including game theory, the study of political culture, and work on the role that ideas play in politics"—learning "how important beliefs are in reaching equilibrium solutions and how institutionalized beliefs structure situations of political choice." It is indeed a large order for applied theory to fill! As Keohane puts it: "From traditional political theory we are reminded of the importance of normative beliefs for the practice of politics . . . , from historical institutionalism and political sociology we understand how values and norms operate in society . . . [and] from democratic theory we discover the crucial roles of accountability, participation, and especially persuasion in creating legitimate political institutions."[16]

In sum, most issues on the global governance agenda cannot be managed unilaterally even if states wished to do so. Global economy, health, human rights, and the environment are among the issues on global-governance agendas of both governmental and non-governmental organizations. Developing consensus on what is to be done is by no means an easy task, much less finding resources that can be allocated to these matters. Quite apart from opposition to proposed remedies by those whose economic or other interests would be adversely affected are genuine disagreements over outcomes to be sought as well as confusion about the "science" associated with particular problems—understanding cause-effect relations associated with different options under consideration.

Green Politics and the Environment

In J. D. Thompson's classic study of organizations, he noted how uncertainties can make decision making difficult.[17] If we apply his insights to global governance concerns such as global warming, we find a consensus that it is in fact occurring, but still great uncertainty among atmospheric scientists about the relative importance of different causes, proposed remedies, and possible outcomes (whether it can be slowed and its effects managed through adaptation or whether we face a real danger of sudden, accelerated warming—cataclysmic climate change with disastrous consequences for human and other forms of life on the planet). As a practical matter, these uncertainties make it extraordinarily difficult to form a global political consensus on what is to be done and how fast we need to do it, especially since proposed remedies are usually very costly. Confounding the problem of finding consensus among those genuinely committed to finding effective remedies, of course, is political opposition to environmentally friendly measures by those whose interests lie in the continued mass consumption of fossil fuels.

Thompson's matrix (Figure 3.1) may help us understand these problems analytically since building political consensus nationally and globally on appropriate environmental remedies is central to global governance. The debate that began in the late 1980s on carbon-emissions caps was accompanied over the next two decades by politically motivated naysayers who either

Preferences Regarding Possible Outcomes

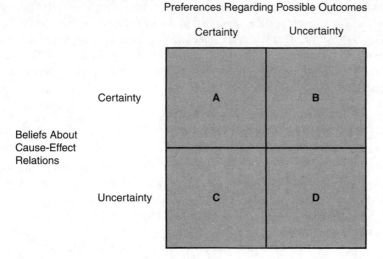

FIGURE 3.1 Decision-Making Matrix

Source: J. D. Thompson, *Organizations in Action* (New York: McGraw-Hill, 1967), 134–135.

denied global warming was occurring or discounted its effects. Even those who saw global warming as a problem were not entirely certain about the magnitude of the effect—how many degrees the Earth would warm over coming decades, what the effects would be on various parts of the Earth, and what impact various remedies would have on efforts to slow global warming.

Long stuck in cell D, there has been movement more recently on global warming toward greater understanding of cause-effect relations as well as greater agreement on preferences regarding possible outcomes. Facilitating the formation of an emerging "green" consensus, of course, is the interest some have in securing market share in one or another of the proposed remedies (alternative energy sources; more efficient engineering of automobiles, public transportation, and power plants; new technologies for trapping carbon emissions and "sequestering" them from release to the atmosphere, etc.).

By contrast to global warming, the scientific understanding of ozone-layer depletion caused by chlorofluorocarbon (CFC) emissions has been far clearer and agreement on preferred outcomes easier to forge—a position in cell A, making a political consensus on remedies to be implemented much easier to achieve. The initial result was agreement in the Montreal Protocol, which eliminates or tries at least to reduce CFC emissions substantially. Somewhere in between global warming and ozone-layer depletion in terms of degree of uncertainty is the case of increased acidification of precipitation—acid rain.

The matrix gives us a convenient way to categorize our understanding (or lack of understanding) of any number of issues on global agendas. It may be even more helpful to array degrees of certainty or uncertainty as a continuum rather than as either-or cells in a matrix. Be that as it may, Thompson's matrix focuses our attention on objectives, means and ends that are too often discounted, overlooked, or dismissed as too hard to solve. Making decisions collectively in global governance is by no means an easy process when we are uncertain not only about what is to be done, but also about the implications of different courses of action or inaction.

In the final analysis, of course, decisions on such matters are political choices. Even the best of ideas likely will go nowhere unless grounded in the interests of the relevant players. This seems as true in global governance as it is in all other levels of politics. When ideas enjoy interest-based support, agreements can be reached and implemented on even the most difficult of issues on global agendas. Put another way, liberals do not leave the concept of *interest* only to realists. It remains an integral part of their work as well.

ECONOMIC INTERDEPENDENCE AND PEACE

The eighteenth- and nineteenth-century argument associating increased trade among states with peace is reflected in Richard Rosecrance's *The Rise of the Trading State*.[18] Rosecrance contrasts the realist military-political world with the liberal trading world, utilizing game theory to highlight their respective constant-sum or variable-sum characters. His essential argument is that the rise of a new "trading world" offers the possibility of escaping major international conflicts and establishing new patterns of cooperation among states. The benefits of trade greatly exceed those of military competition and territorial aggrandizement as exemplified by such countries as Japan.

In fact, territorial acquisition may actually harm the ability of a state to increase its national wealth. Rosecrance does not deny that traditional military competition will continue, but rather suggests states will calculate out of self-interest that an open international trading system will allow them to find a productive niche in the structure of world commerce. Part of the reason for such an opportunity is that since 1945 the threat of an all-out nuclear war made major wars less likely to occur if not, in the words of another author, obsolete.[19]

Following this logic, the prevalence of the trading option since 1945 increases peaceful possibilities among states that were lacking in the late nineteenth century and in the 1930s when competitive economic policies helped to drive the world into depression. As economic interdependence spreads, economic development through trade and foreign investment becomes a self-reinforcing process and an integral part of state strategy. Rosecrance thus expands our theoretical focus by including trade and commerce in strategic understandings, not just confining strategy to the military sector.

Realists have been skeptical if not outright hostile to the peace-through-economic interdependence proposition. Kenneth Waltz and John Mearsheimer, for example, have noted that the late nineteenth-century western trading system had extremely high levels of interdependence, but this did not prevent the disaster of World War I—national security concerns trumped economic interests. If states feel threatened, they will take whatever military action is required despite the costs of breaking economic ties. This is even more the case if an aggressive great power attempts to upset the territorial status quo and embarks on a series of cumulative military conquests.

The question of how shifts in the international economy can affect international security relations has been rejoined in the past decade as the scope of international economic integration has been examined under the increasingly popular rubric of "globalization." An intriguing work in this genre is Stephen Brooks' *Producing Security: Multinational Corporations, Globalization, and the Changing Calculus of Conflict*.[20] His focus is not on the traditional debate concerning the hypothesized pacification of interstate relations through international trade, but rather the impact of the globalization of production on great power security relations and security relations among states in general (see his article later in this chapter). Brooks argues that an historically unprecedented development has been left out of the debate: the geographic dispersion of production by multinational corporations. Where and how these MNCs organize their international production activities are now the key integrating force of global commerce, not trade *per se*.

Unlike the work on MNCs in the 1970s that focused on the extraction of raw materials from exploited Third World states, his study on the globalization of production examines broader international security implications. Rather than focusing on a dependent variable and seeking to explain a particular case (such as the outbreak of World War I) or a general class of events (such as interstate wars), Brooks uses his independent variable—the globalization of production—and examines how it could influence security calculations. He does not assume that such production is a force for peace, but wishes to leave this an open question.

Brooks examines three major means by which the international economy can influence security—changing capabilities, incentives, and the nature of the actors. The capabilities issue addresses whether the globalization of production has changed the parameters of weapons production—is self-sufficiency still possible? He concludes that autarkic, go-it-alone arms production is in decline. To remain on the cutting edge of military technology requires engagement in the production of weaponry beyond one's borders. In terms of incentives, has the geographic dispersion of MNC production reduced the benefits of the physical conquest of other states? He concludes while there are exceptions, the economic benefits of military conquest have been greatly reduced, at least among the advanced industrial states. Finally, with regard to actors, has dispersed MNC production positively influenced the prospects for regional integration? He states it has, even where traditional security rivalries have existed. While perhaps not the primary cause of such integration, it can help deepen it. These three mechanisms are the primary focus of his book, although he examines others as well.

His conclusion is that the influence of the globalization of production is most evident in terms of great powers relations. While cognizant of other explanations such as democratic peace theory, Brooks believes his evidence strengthens the argument that international commerce indeed acts as a force for peace among great powers. As for the rest of the world, there is a differential impact. The security implications of the globalization of production is a mixed bag between the great powers and developing countries, and actually negative among developing countries.

THE DEMOCRATIC PEACE

As noted earlier, for liberals the likelihood of war is reduced not only through the expansion of free trade, but also democracy. Particularly with the end of the Cold War in 1991, scholars have attempted to answer empirically the question "Are democracies more peaceful in their foreign relations?" The collapse of communism and the rise of an increasing number of fledgling democracies to replace authoritarian regimes provided a good test bed for democratic peace theory. Following in the tradition of Immanuel Kant, scholars such as Michael Doyle, Rudolph Rummel, and Bruce Russett have argued that liberal democracies are unique in that they are able to establish peaceful relations among themselves based upon their shared values and common approach to establishing legitimate domestic political orders.

Democracies tend not to go to war with each other.[21] Doyle brought renewed attention to this Kantian idea of democratic peace, re-examining the traditional liberal claim that governments founded on a respect for individual liberty exercise restraint and peaceful intentions in their foreign policies (see his article later in this chapter). Despite the contradictions between liberal pacifism and liberal imperialism (both found in democratic practice), liberalism nevertheless does leave us with a coherent legacy on foreign affairs. Liberal states are different and indeed more peaceful, yet they also are prone to use force when they see it as in their interest to do so, albeit not in wars with each other.

Democracies certainly fight authoritarian regimes—sometimes representing themselves as "arsenals of democracy" as the United States did in its military campaign against fascism in World War II. As with authoritarian regimes, democracies have engaged historically in violent imperial expansions that also have provided opportunities to spread their own liberal, democratic ideologies. Furthermore, recent empirical work suggests that newly emerging democratic states may even be *more* prone to start wars than either long-established democracies or authoritarian regimes.[22] The key adjective or qualifier here is *emerging*.

The democratic peace literature's claims have spawned a substantial research program in liberal IR that seeks to identify and explain patterns of behavior exhibited by democracies throughout the world. Indeed, some years ago one scholar commented that "the absence of war between democracies comes as close as anything to an empirical law in international relations." Another observed that the democratic peace proposition is "one of the strongest nontrivial or non-tautological generalizations that can be made about international relations."[23]

The excitement generated, particularly during the 1990s, fueled an increasingly robust research program. While the proposition dates back at least to Immanuel Kant, it was the collapse of the Soviet Union and breakup of the Warsaw Pact that produced a wave of new democracies and promised new empirical possibilities to test the theory. For liberals, here was a proposition that seemed to undermine the neorealist argument that it is the structure of the international system (not the nature of governments or societies) that explains a state's policies. To democratic-peace theorists, state and society do matter as do the people that compose them.

The theory has even been used (many would say "misused") by politicians since the end of the Cold War to make optimistic predictions concerning the future of international politics. Much to the dismay of many liberal scholars, the virtues of the theory were invoked by neoconservatives who added democratization to the list of reasons used to justify the American invasion of Iraq in 2003. A democratic Iraq would not only bring benefit to the Iraqi people, but also would provide a model for all of Araby—a positive domino effect on the rest of this troubled region. A liberal theory embraced in this way by policy elites for their own purposes is hardly a blessing.

As in most new research programs, scholarship has taken different directions on both complementary and contradictory research paths. Key concepts are defined in different ways, and different variables are utilized. Consider, for example, the basic question of how one defines democracy. Critics complain that democratic peace theorists are all over the lot in defining their independent variable. Democracy (or states with democratic regimes) purportedly explain the propensity for peaceful relations with other democracies, but what constitutes a democracy is not entirely clear.

To begin with, Immanuel Kant argued that republics made for more peaceful international relations, not democracies *per se*. Republicanism as we now understand it is *representative* democracy supported by the rule of law and respect for basic freedoms or rights in civil society. It is not direct democracy in which the popular will (or the majority) necessarily prevails. People may not even choose to be active participants in day-to-day politics, effectively leaving such matters to their representatives with varying degrees of accountability to the electorate.

If we are not clear or lack consensus on what constitutes a democracy (or liberal republic), testing democratic-peace hypotheses becomes problematic. Highly inclusive definitions compete with those excluding a large number of cases. After all, it takes more than just having elections to make a democracy. It is not the forms of democratic practice (even dictatorships can use elections to mask their authoritarian designs) that count, it is the *substance* that matters. Fully developed, enduring democracies are buttressed by social structures, economies, and cultures of shared values conducive to democratic practice that are often lacking in emerging regimes we refer loosely to as democracies.

Even when we agree on what counts as a democracy, how are we to define the dependent variable, whether war or peace? How is it to be operationalized—measured or counted? If war, does that include armed interventions with marines landing on the beach, or only major and long, drawn-out conflicts involving widespread death and destruction such as occurred in World Wars I and II? Similarly, if one wishes to utilize "peace" as the dependent variable, how is that defined? Is peace simply the absence of war? If so, are we left with a Hobbesian view that international anarchy is inherently a state of war and that the only remedy, then, is to eliminate anarchy, perhaps by establishing an all-powerful Leviathan or world government as the means to maintaining peace? How far must global governance go? Or can we rely more simply on peace-oriented norms of behavior—values shared by democracies?

Beyond such questions, what is the time period we need to examine to test democratic-peace hypotheses? Different historical time periods result in different findings as in some periods certain cases are included and others not. Finally, is the attribute of democracy the only explanatory factor as to why democratic states do not fight one another? Is democracy not only necessary, but also sufficient to provide explanation of peace? Or are other factors of equal or even greater importance?

Take, for example, the fact that states in western Europe have not engaged in war or exhibited warlike behaviors amongst themselves since 1945. Is that due to the logic of the democratic peace? Or due to the fact that the Soviet threat from 1945–91 bound these states together under a U.S. security umbrella that provided a comfortable deterrent effect against would-be invaders? Or perhaps historical memories of the devastation caused by two world wars on the continent are enough to discourage war? Or, as suggested above, are the pacifying effects of economic interdependence and the integration process the key to peace in the European context?

Given these and other theoretical and empirical challenges, democratic peace theorists still have their work cut out for them.[24] They find themselves in what Imre Lakatos termed a "progressive research program," seeking new insights in the pursuit of answers to central questions on matters of war and peace. Will future efforts expand beyond a single variable effectively integrating other causal factors in the development of a more comprehensive model of the relation between democracy and peace? Will the program turn as well to broader questions of global governance? Quite apart from their normative preferences, should studies of democratic peace be augmented or expanded to include questions of distributive justice as Doyle and others have done? What can be said about justice and its relation to peace in "one world" composed of "many peoples?"[25]

DECISION MAKING

Perhaps the most important liberal insight on international relations is the centrality of state-society relations. This is most evident in the democratic peace literature. Instead of viewing the state as a rational, unified actor, the state is composed of diverse societal actors. Ideas, group interests, institutions, and individuals shape state preferences; they are not a given. When combined with the reality of the impact of interdependence and globalization, the liberal IR theorist has a catalog of independent variables that helps to account for state behavior in any particular issue area.

Pathbreaking work in the early 1960s on *Foreign Policy Decision-Making* by Richard Snyder, H.W. Bruck, and Burton Sapin set the stage for substantial work in this genre that looked inside the state and society, disaggregating the neorealist rational, unified actor. It reflects and parallels the perspectives of the authors summarized under the heading on Interest Group Liberalism discussed earlier. Included in the Snyder, Bruck, and Sapin (SBS) taxonomy were bureaucracies, interest groups, and both psychological and social-psychological factors that influence decisionmakers. Valerie Hudson has led a re-examination of work by SBS, tracing its impact over the decades and on more recent work that would follow in this genre.[26]

SBS were well aware of the agent-structure issue. The debate is not really new. They wanted "to avoid deterministic explanations" and what they saw as "the awkward problems of the objective-subjective dilemma" by turning their attention to the agent—an "attempt to see the world through the decision-maker's eyes."[27] The state-as-actor has meaning only when we look within the state to the decisionmakers themselves and examine how they are influenced by domestic factors and how they relate to their decision-making counterparts in other states. Material and ideational factors intersect not at the abstract level of the state, but rather at the decision-making level. Real people make decisions. Both situational and biographical factors influence foreign policy choices.

Following the SBS lead, Hudson is impatient with "the supposed incommensurability of rational choice and *verstehen*" methods. There is complementarity between "thin" rationality found in rational choice theories and "'thick' analysis of world views and values." The two are not mutually exclusive. Beyond that, Hudson clearly stakes out her position in the agency-structure debate. She thinks it "theoretically foolish to retain a primary focus on system-level variables, or even on enduring structural constraints." Indeed, she comments how "humans appear to have almost an infinite capacity for wriggling out of macro-level structures and constraints." Finally, since "ideas do matter in international affairs," we need to focus "below the state level to find the unit of analysis that can think of those ideas"—the human beings who are the decisionmakers.[28]

Agency is important in this classic understanding. The state-as-actor has meaning only when we look within the state to the decisionmakers themselves and examine how they are influenced by domestic factors and how they relate to their decision-making counterparts in other states. Much has been accomplished over the decades since SBS first appeared, but much is left to be done. The renewed SBS research program thus raises many still unanswered questions that can be the subject of ongoing studies: (1) the interplay between cognition and emotion; (2) personal relations and trust; (3) the role of speeches and policy entrepreneurs in the policy process; (4) perceiving opportunities; and (5) the role of time constraints on decision making.[29]

Work in psychology and social psychology has contributed substantially to our knowledge of how and why decisionmakers act. The cognitive orientations and ontologies decisionmakers have directly influence their perceptions and the meanings they ascribe to or infer from what they observe. Under what conditions are decisionmakers blinded from realities that contradict their prior expectations? Are our perceptions affected by what Leon Festinger called cognitive dissonance—we tend not to see what we don't expect to see?[30] If so, this can lead to intelligence failures and adversely affect decision making whether in crisis or non-crisis conditions.

Perceptions thus clearly play a particularly important role in times of crisis as argued by Robert Jervis in his classic *Perception and Misperception in International Politics*. Individuals relate the images they have to the facts or at least to the information they have before them. Richard Ned Lebow tested similar ideas in his *Between Peace and War*. Content analysis of documents has been utilized to explore the pattern of decisions, mindsets, and assumptions that led to the outbreak, for example, of World War I. Ole Holsti's work on crisis decision making built upon this foundation, identifying how stress during crises compounded by the short time to receive and assess a large quantity of information can reduce span of attention, result in cognitive rigidity, and cause dysfunctions that adversely affect decision-making tasks.[31]

Group dynamics can also result in dysfunctions with adverse effects on decision making. In *Victims of Groupthink*, Irving Janis noted how consensus building and team play within a group—normally considered a plus—can lead the group to screen out information at odds with the consensus view. Any naysayers that challenge the common wisdom are likely to be ostracized or pay some high price for taking a contrary position.[32]

In *Essence of Decision*, Graham Allison challenged the rational-actor approach to explaining foreign policy choices.[33] The book expanded upon an earlier journal article on conceptual models and the Cuban Missile Crisis that almost led to war between the United States and the Soviet Union in October 1962. He and his colleagues questioned the conventional, realist assumption of rationality (referred to as Model I)—that states specify their objectives consistent with national interests, identify alternatives, and choose the options most likely to achieve these purposes.

By contrast, in Model II he asked whether organizational processes affect decisions—the routines or standard operating procedures organizations employ and the ethos or perspectives that define their organizational essence and ways of doing the business of government. Allison has acknowledged that this insight owes much to Max Weber's perspective on bureaucratic rationality defined as routinizing recurrent functions in efforts to achieve efficiencies. Finally, in Allison's Model III, bureaucratic politics were added to the mix—coalition and countercoalition formation and the pulling-and-hauling of day-to-day struggles within and among bureaucracies.

By the 1980s, there was an evident decline in the amount of literature devoted to decision making. Nevertheless, cognitive factors remained part of the discourse with attention given to the role of ideas in foreign policy as reflected in work by Robert Keohane and Judith Goldstein. Goldstein also argues that in order to understand U.S. trade policies over the years, a reliance on international structural or domestic economic interests is insufficient. Rather, one must also take into account actors' causal beliefs as to which economic policies can best achieve preferred interests. For his part, Ernst Haas also underscored the importance of cognitive factors and ideas in his book *When Knowledge Is Power*.[34] As discussed in Chapter Six, the role of ideas is also critical in constructivist theorizing about international relations and foreign policy.

Recent years have seen a revival of interest in the perception literature as applied to international relations. Dominic Johnson, for example, in his *Overconfidence and War* revisits the perennial question of why states are susceptible to exaggerated ideas of their ability to control events and foresee future outcomes, particularly when differences in power would seem to suggest it is foolish to go to war.[35] He examines the power of "positive illusions" and overconfidence in case studies of World War I, the Munich Crisis of 1939, Vietnam, and Iraq. He draws on a diverse body of theoretical and empirical work to include not only psychology, but also evolutionary biology and international conflict.

Another good example is Dominic Johnson teaming with Dominic Tierney in *Failing to Win: Perceptions of Victory and Defeat in International Politics*.[36] It is evident that the decision-making literature has invariably focused on the decision to go to war or factors influencing decisions during a crisis. Johnson and Tierney, however, are interested in evaluations of success or failure once the shooting has stopped or the crisis is resolved. The question they pose is: "What are the psychological, political, and cultural factors that predispose observers (whether leaders, the public, or the media) to perceive outcomes of international disputes as victories or defeats?" They argue that there is often a huge gap between perceptions (observers' personal interpretations) and reality. Sometimes perceptions and reality of events on the battlefield match, as in the case of the Fall of Berlin to the Soviet Union in April 1945. But other times they do not, or different observers judge similar events very differently. Why?

Johnson and Tierney note that evaluating winners and losers in wars and crises is not simply a matter of answering the question of which country made the greatest gains or achieved its stated goals. Quite often, "people end up evaluating outcomes on the basis of factors that are largely independent of the battlefield: their preexisting beliefs, the symbolism of events, and manipulation by elites and the media." By way of example, the War of 1812 between the United States and Great Britain was basically a draw on the ground and a return to the pre-war status quo. Yet in the United States it was trumpeted as a great triumph, despite the failed U.S. attempt to annex Canada, the burning of the White House, and divisions among Americans themselves.

Conversely, the U.S. involvement in the African country of Somalia in 1993 is deemed a failure, etched in most people's minds as the infamous "Blackhawk Down" firefight in which eighteen American soldiers died. What is forgotten is that the initial relief operation—a humanitarian effort (UNITAF/Operation Restore Hope)—saved, by varying estimates, anywhere from tens of thousands to one million Somali lives. The initial mission was to stabilize the security environment to make humanitarian relief efforts possible, and many refugees were able to return home. Subsequent failures overshadowed these successes, and the result was political leaders and the U.S. public souring on the idea of humanitarian interventions. This contributed to the lack of U.S. action several months later when in Rwanda the systematic genocide of Tutsis and moderate Hutus resulted in the deaths of 800,000 people in a few short months. Other in-depth cases examined by the authors include the Cuban Missile Crisis (1962), the Tet Offensive in Vietnam (1968), and the Yom Kippur (or October) War between Egypt and Israel (1973).

Perceptions of victory and defeat are obviously important for leaders in democratic societies who are concerned with political survival. But perceived defeat, in particular, can have a traumatic effect on society at large, potentially defining a country's self-image for years to come. Furthermore, perceptions of success and failure can shape current and future foreign policy options and decisions.

Johnson and Tierney devise a conceptual framework to explain the dependent variable: people's perceptions of victory and defeat. First, they examine the conventional wisdom hypothesis that people's judgments of victory and defeat simply reflect the material outcome. They refer to this as score-keeping and provide five possible definitions of "victory" that can serve as empirically verifiable metrics. Second, the authors attempt to explain why the observed gains and losses made by each side often fail to explain people's perceptions of victory in wars or crises, arguing that the score-keeping approach fails to answer this question adequately. The explanatory concept they develop is termed "match-fixing" and relies on the vast body of literature on informational and psychological biases to include cognitive processes, affective processes, learning theory, and cultural influences.

No one would deny that the study of ideas, perceptions, and organizations is important if we wish to improve our understanding of foreign policy or national security decision making. Two important questions, however, are (1) How much emphasis should be placed on the domestic level of analysis as opposed to the international level when attempting to explain international outcomes and patterns? and (2) How can theorists link the two levels to provide a complete accounting of the phenomena under consideration? The challenge is to develop theories that account simultaneously for the interaction of domestic and international factors—more easily said than done.

CHANGE AND GLOBALIZATION

Liberals note that while a great deal of international relations involves continuity, change is also a constant. The Soviet Union collapsed. American domination of the international economy has eroded. Radical Islam, the power of religion in general, and international terrorism did not loom large on the radar screen of IR scholars even fifteen years ago. To explain such changes by reference to shifts in the global distribution of power begs the question of how to explain those shifts in the first place. It is safe to say that of all of the images discussed in this book, liberalism is most open (and expectant) of change. This is in part due to its emphasis on the voluntarism end of the determinism—voluntarism spectrum.

The concept of **globalization** captures the sort of changes that are associated with transnationalism, interdependence, and interconnectedness. Nevertheless, the concept has not moved to the forefront of liberal theorizing any more than it has with the other three images. This is perhaps because globalization appears to cover just about everything that crosses borders to include ideas, individuals, material goods, communications, financial transactions, and trade whether primarily the result of actions by states, international organizations, or economic processes.

LIBERALS AND THEIR CRITICS

■ Anarchy

As noted, liberals argue that the role of anarchy and the security dilemma is overemphasized in explaining international relations, or argue that its worst aspects can be overcome through purposeful collaborative behavior to include international organizations, institutions, and regimes. It has been argued by realists, however, that any analysis of world politics must begin with the anarchical structure of the system being taken into account. How is it possible to assess realistically the possibilities for cooperation and peace between states unless the role of anarchy in creating suspicion and distrust is recognized? The realist would contend that if one ignores or reduces the importance of such considerations, thinking can quickly become utopian with little relation to reality. Furthermore, realists argue that states often have fundamentally different interests in which the drive for relative material gains makes conflict inevitable and part of the eternal landscape of international relations.

A liberal response is that placing so much emphasis on the security dilemma loads the dice against any change from the status quo. To see the world as nothing more than competition and conflict born of mistrust among states is itself a distortion of reality, or even a self-fulfilling prophecy. One's acts, if born of suspicion and distrust, will tend to produce similar responses in others, thus confirming one's initial suspicions.

Furthermore, the history of world politics is a history not only of conflict but also of collaboration. To study instances of when the security dilemma has been overcome is just as important as studying instances when it has contributed to the onset of war. Liberals claim they have the conceptual tools to do so whether it is integration, interdependence, neoliberal institutionalism, regime theory, or the democratic peace and the role of ideas in accounting for actor preferences.

Theory Building

Realists have argued that much of the work in the liberal tradition is highly descriptive and lacking theoretical content. Hence the generally disparaging attitude toward a term such as *globalization* that is more of a popular buzzword than a theoretically useful concept. Realists claim that by describing the world in greater and greater detail, descriptive accuracy increases at the expense of developing *parsimonious* theories of international relations that can explain patterns of behavior. In other words, theories should be as simple as possible. Understanding increases by moving *away* from the real world, not by moving closer to it. At first, this statement might seem counterintuitive or different from what one might expect. But ambitious theories aim at producing valid generalizations by viewing the forest as a whole, not individual trees. By faithfully cataloguing the complexity of the world, many liberals, according to critics, are in danger of remaining in the realm of merely describing things as opposed to explaining why things happen the way they do.

Scholars operating within the liberal image make a number of rebuttals. First, one only has to point to neoliberal institutionalism to rebut the charge of description at the expense of theoretical parsimony. The work of Robert Keohane and his colleagues has often been characterized as a theoretical counterpoint to neorealist approaches to international relations, despite the fact that both research agendas employ rational actor assumptions and positivist standards of evidence.

Second, liberals note this obsession with parsimony is really most attributable to neo or structural realists. Classical realists such as Haas Morgenthau and Arnold Wolfers examined the role of a multitude of factors at various levels of analysis, just as more recent scholars in the classical realist tradition seek to understand the reciprocal interactive effects of the state and the international system.

Finally, the liberal research agenda in recent years has perhaps offered more theories and testable hypotheses than any other image of international politics, contributing to the ultimate social science goal of cumulative knowledge. In particular, varying liberal research agendas tend to coalesce around the unifying theme of the pacifying effects of democracy, economic interdependence, and international institutions. Far from being unrelated research agendas, these three topics reinforce one another. Yes, it is admitted, the diversity of approaches under the liberal image is not as neat and streamlined as the realist image with its traditional focus on issues of conflict among states. The liberal image consists of a number of different actors operating within and across state boundaries that makes for complexity, but theories of international relations should aspire to deal with such complexity and not pretend that it does not exist. How adequate are theories that fail to deal with and explain many of the changes that have occurred in the nature of world politics over the past half-century? While realism is a useful "first cut" at understanding world politics, too much is left out: the role of institutions, transnational relations, domestic politics, and ideas.

The Democratic Peace

With the demise of the Soviet Union in the early 1990s, Francis Fukuyama in his *End of History* stated that liberal democracy had no serious ideological rival and hence it was "the end point of mankind's ideological evolution" and the "final form of human government."[37] Indeed democracy seemed to be gaining adherents, not only in states of the former Soviet empire in East Europe, but also in areas of the Third World where nascent democratic transitions were occurring. Realists, to put it mildly, were skeptical, not only doubting how long the expanded zone of democratic peace would last in the new Europe, but also pointing to the conflict in the Balkans, conflict among a number of African states, India-Pakistan tensions, and the gradual rise of China as a global economic, political, and military power.

Liberals responded that the democratic zone of peace in Europe is no small achievement, and since the 1990s there has been no hint of a possible interstate war within Europe. Even if it is subject to debate how much the spread of democracy contributes to the explanation of this situation as opposed to the economic interdependence and enticements provided by membership in the European Union, the fact remains that realist predictions of an incessant drive for domination and the supposed built-in systemic incentives for armed conflict have not threatened the European peace. As for the Third World, few liberals have claimed this to be an appropriate test bed for democratic peace theory. Indeed, the Third World is more often characterized as a zone of conflict where internal conflicts and weak states now seem more the norm than interstate conflict.

Voluntarism

If realists have been criticized for being excessively pessimistic concerning the human condition and the ability of individuals to control international events and forces, liberals can be criticized for their heavy reliance on the assumption of voluntarism, or effective free will. Their emphasis on agency over structure reflects the voluntarism in much of liberal theory. Some liberal writings leave one with the impression that international harmony can be achieved if only leaders really wanted it—that it is a simple matter of human volition, a mere matter of desiring cooperation as opposed to competition. Hence, the transformation of the nature of world politics is seen to be desirable as well as attainable. Either "bad and ignorant leaders" or "bad governments" stand in the way; if they could be educated or removed, the world would be a better place. Once again, the influence of the liberal philosophy is evident, and once again, the realist evaluation would be that this view of international change and how it can be achieved ignores constraints placed on all leaders and states by the anarchical nature of the international system, the drive for relative gains, and the balance of power. Moreover, some realists would argue that people are indeed aggressive with a proclivity toward warlike behavior; it is part of human nature to behave so.

The emphasis on voluntarism is not always acknowledged in liberal writings. Nor is it necessarily a function of a philosophical commitment to a belief in free will that can influence outcomes. It could also derive from the fact that the focus of analysis for many liberals happens to be factors operating at the domestic level of analysis which involves the study of actual institutions, individual actors, and collective belief systems held by flesh and blood policymakers. When one studies real individuals within real institutions, it is obvious that agency matters. World politics takes on a human face, understandably resulting in a reliance on the assumption of voluntarism.

Notes

1. Theodore J. Lowi, *The End of Liberalism: Ideology, Policy, and the Crisis of Public Authority* (New York: Norton, 1969), 48 and 71. Subsequent quotes are from David Truman, *The Governmental Process* (New York: Knopf, 1959), ix, 519–20; Robert A. Dahl, *A Preface to Democratic Theory* (Chicago: University of Chicago Press, 1963), 173; see also Harold D. Lasswell, *Politics: Who Gets What, When, How* (New York: McGraw-Hill, 1936).

2. Ernst B. Haas, "Turbulent Fields and the Theory of Regional Integration," *International Organization*, 30, 2 (Spring 1976), 179.

3. See the full argument in James N. Rosenau, *Turbulence in World Politics* (Princeton, NJ: Princeton University Press, 1990).

4. John W. Burton, *World Society* (Cambridge, England: Cambridge University Press, 1972); Robert O. Keohane and Joseph S. Nye, Jr., eds. *Transnational Relations and World Politics* (Cambridge, MA: Harvard University Press, 1971). Examples of later works in this genre include Margaret E. Keck and Kathryn Sikkink, *Activists beyond Borders: Advocacy Networks in International Politics* (Ithaca, NY: Cornell University Press, 1998); and Sanjeev Khagram, James A. Riker, and Kathryn Sikkink, eds., *Restructuring World Politics: Transnational Movements, Networks, and Norms* (Minneapolis: University of Minnesota Press, 2002).

5. Robert O. Keohane and Joseph S. Nye, Jr., *Power and Interdependence: World Politics in Transition* (Boston: Little Brown, 1977), 8.

6. Andreas Hansenclever, Peter Mayer, and Volker Rittberger, "Interests, Power, Knowledge: The Study of International Regimes," *Mershon International Studies Review* 40, 2 (October 1996): 177–228.

7. Stephen D. Krasner, "Global Communications and National Power: Life on the Pareto Frontier," *World Politics* 43 (1991): 363.

8. Peter M. Haas, "Introduction: Epistemic Communities and International Policy Coordination," *International Organization* 46 (1992): 3. Subsequent quote also from this article.

9. Friedrich V. Kratochwil and John Gerard Ruggie, "International Organization: A State of the Art on an Art of the State," *International Organization* 40 (1986): 764, 766.

10. Robert O. Keohane, "Neoliberal Institutionalism: A Perspective on World Politics," in *International Institutions and State Power: Essays in International Relations Theory*, ed. Robert O. Keohane (Boulder, CO: Westview Press, 1989), 3. The rest of this section draws on this chapter of Keohane's collected essays as well as his *After Hegemony: Cooperation and Discord in the World Political Economy* (Princeton, NJ: Princeton University Press, 1984).

11. Keohane, "Neoliberal Institutionalism: A Perspective on World Politics," 2.

12. See Judith Goldstein and Robert O. Keohane, eds., *Ideas and Foreign Policy: Beliefs, Institutions, and Political Change* (Ithaca, NY: Cornell University Press, 1993).

13. Robert O. Keohane, *Power and Governance in a Partially Globalized World* (New York and London: Routledge, 2002), 258.

14. *Ibid.*, 16, 208, and 245.

15. *Ibid.*, 266 and 246.

16. *Ibid.*, 266.

17. See J.D. Thompson, *Organizations in Action* (New York: McGraw-Hill, 1967), 134–35.

18. Richard Rosecrance, *The Rise of the Trading State: Commerce and Conquest in the Modern World.* (New York: Basic Books, 1986).

19. John Mueller, *Retreat from Doomsday: The Obsolescence of Major War* (New York: Basic Books, 1989).

20. Stephen G. Brooks, *Producing Security: Multinational Corporations, Globalization, and the Changing Calculus of Conflict* (Princeton, NJ: Princeton University Press, 2005, 2007).

21. Michael W. Doyle, "Liberalism and World Politics," *American Political Science Review,* 80, 4 (1986): 1151–69. For a survey of the literature, see Edward Mansfield and Brian Pollins, "The Study of Interdependence and Conflict: Recent Advances, Open Questions, and Directions for Future Research," *Journal of Conflict Resolution* 45, 6 (2001): 834–59. Cf. Larry Diamond, *The Spirit of Democracy: The Struggle to Build Free Societies Throughout the World* (New York: Times Books-Henry Holt, 2008).

22. Edward D. Mansfield and Jack Snyder, *Electing to Fight: Why Emerging Democracies Go to War* (Boston: MIT Press, 2005).

23. Jack Levy, "The Causes of War: A Review of Theories and Evidence," in Phillip E. Tetlock, et.al., eds. *Behavior, Society, and Nuclear War,* vol. 1 (New York: Oxford University Press, 1989), 270.

24. See, for example, David Kinsella, "No Rest for the Democratic Peace," *American Political Science Review,* 99, 3 (August 2005): 453–72.

25. See Michael W. Doyle, "One World, Many Peoples: International Justice in John Rawls's *The Law of Peoples,*" *Perspectives on Politics,* 4, 1 (March 2006): 109–20.

26. See Valerie M. Hudson, Derek H. Chollet, and James M. Goldgeier, *Foreign Policy Decision-Making (Revisited)* including the original text by Richard C. Snyder, H.W. Bruck, and Burton Sapin (New York: Palgrave, 2002).

27. *Ibid.,* 5.

28. *Ibid.,* 7–9.

29. *Ibid.,* 165.

30. Leon Festinger, *Theory of Cognitive Dissonance* (Stanford: Stanford University Press, 1957).

31. Robert Jervis, *Perception and Misperception in International Politics* (Princeton, NJ: Princeton University Press, 1976); Richard Ned Lebow, *Between Peace and War: The Nature of International Crisis* (Baltimore MD: The Johns Hopkins University Press, 1984); see Ole Holsti's article on crisis decision making in Paul Gordon Lauren, *Diplomacy: New Approaches in History, New Approaches in History, Theory and Policy* (New York, Free Press, 1979).

32. Irving Janis, *Victims of Groupthink* (Boston: Houghton Mifflin, 1972).

33. Graham Allison, *Essence of Decision: Explaining the Cuban Missile Crisis,* 2nd ed. (New York: Longman, 1971, 1999).

34. Judith Goldstein, *Ideas, Interests, and American Trade Policy* (Ithaca: Cornell University Press, 1994); Ernst B. Haas, *When Knowledge Is Power: Three Modes of Change in International Politics* (Berkeley, CA: University of California Press, 1990).

35. Dominic Johnson, *Overconfidence and War* (Cambridge MA: Harvard University Press, 2004).

36. Dominic Johnson and Dominic Tierney, *Failing to Win: Perceptions of Victory and Defeat in International Politics.* (Cambridge, MA: Harvard University Press, 2006).

37. Francis Fukuyama, *The End of History and the Last Man* (New York: Free Press, 1992), xi–xii.

SELECTED READINGS

Liberalism and World Politics

MICHAEL W. DOYLE

In this article, the author makes a major contribution to the literature on the "democratic peace" by re-examining the traditional liberal claim that governments founded on a respect for individual liberty exercise restraint and peaceful intentions in their foreign policy. He looks at three distinct theoretical traditions of liberalism, attributable to three theorists: Schumpeter, Machiavelli, and Kant. Despite the contradictions of liberal pacifism and liberal imperialism, Professor Doyle finds, with Kant and other democratic republicans, that liberalism does leave a coherent legacy on foreign affairs. Liberal states are different and indeed peaceful, yet they are also prone at times to make war. Building upon Doyle's work and the theorists he cites, scholars in recent years have conceptually developed and empirically tested some of the arguments presented in this article, which is an excellent introduction to the "democratic peace" literature.

I look at three distinct theoretical traditions of liberalism, attributable to three theorists: Schumpeter, a brilliant explicator of . . . liberal pacifism . . . ; Machiavelli, a classical republican whose glory is an imperialism we often practice; and Kant.

Despite the contradictions of liberal pacifism and liberal imperialism, I find, with Kant and other liberal republicans, that liberalism does leave a coherent legacy on foreign affairs. Liberal states are different. They are indeed peaceful, yet they are also prone to make war. . . . Liberal states have created a separate peace, as Kant argued they would, and have also discovered liberal reasons for aggression, as he feared they might. I conclude by arguing that the differences among liberal pacifism, liberal imperialism, and Kant's liberal internationalism are not arbitrary but rooted in differing conceptions of the citizen and the state.

Liberal Pacifism

There is no canonical description of liberalism. What we tend to call *liberal* resembles a family portrait of principles and institutions, recognizable by certain characteristics—for example, individual freedom, political participation, private property, and equality of opportunity—that most liberal states share, although none has perfected them all. Joseph Schumpeter clearly fits within this family when he considers the international effects of capitalism and democracy.

Schumpeter's "Sociology of Imperialisms," published in 1919, made a coherent and sustained argument concerning the pacifying (in the sense of nonaggressive) effects of liberal institutions and principles (Schumpeter, 1955; see also Doyle, 1986, pp. 155–59). Unlike some of the earlier liberal theorists who focused on a single feature such as trade or failed to examine critically the arguments they were advancing, Schumpeter saw the interaction of capitalism and democracy as the foundation of liberal pacifism, and he tested his arguments in a sociology of historical imperialisms.

He defines *imperialism* as "an objectless disposition on the part of a state to unlimited forcible expansion" (Schumpeter, 1955, p. 6). Excluding imperialisms that were mere "catchwords" and those that were "objectful" (e.g., defensive imperialism), he traces the roots of objectless imperialism to three sources, each an atavism. Modern imperialism,

"Liberalism and World Politics" by Michael W. Doyle from *American Political Science Review*, Vol. 80 (December 1986), pp. 1151–1169. Reprinted with the permission of Cambridge University Press.

according to Schumpeter, resulted from the combined impact of a "war machine," warlike instincts, and export monopolism.

Once necessary, the war machine later developed a life of its own and took control of a state's foreign policy: "Created by the wars that required it, the machine now created the wars it required" (Schumpeter, 1995, p. 25). Thus, Schumpeter tells us that the army of ancient Egypt, created to drive the Hyksos out of Egypt, took over the state and pursued militaristic imperialism. Like the later armies of the courts of absolutist Europe, it fought wars for the sake of glory and booty, for the sake of warriors and monarchs—wars *gratia* warriors.

A warlike disposition, elsewhere called "instinctual elements of bloody primitivism," is the natural ideology of a war machine. It also exists independently; the Persians, says Schumpeter (1955, pp. 25–32), were a warrior nation from the outset.

Under modern capitalism, export monopolists, the third source of modern imperialism, push for imperialist expansion as a way to expand their closed markets. The absolute monarchies were the last clear-cut imperialisms. Nineteenth-century imperialisms merely represent the vestiges of the imperialisms created by Louis XIV and Catherine the Great. Thus, the export monopolists are an atavism of the absolute monarchies, for they depend completely on the tariffs imposed by the monarchs and their militaristic successors for revenue (Schumpeter, 1955, pp. 82–83). Without tariffs, monopolies would be eliminated by foreign competition.

Modern (nineteenth-century) imperialism, therefore, rests on a atavistic war machine, militaristic attitudes left over from the days of monarchical wars, and export monopolism, which is nothing more than the economic residue of monarchical finance. In the modern era, imperialists gratify their private interests. From the national perspective, their imperialistic wars are objectless.

Schumpeter's theme now emerges. Capitalism and democracy are forces for peace. Indeed, they are antithetical to imperialism. For Schumpeter, the further development of capitalism and democracy means that imperialism will inevitably disappear. He maintains that capitalism produces an unwarlike disposition; its populace is "democratized, individualized, rationalized" (Schumpeter, 1955, p. 68). The people's energies are daily absorbed in production. The disciplines of industry and the market train people in "economic rationalism"; the instability of industrial life necessitates calculation. Capitalism also "individualizes"; "subjective opportunities" replace the "immutable factors" of traditional, hierarchical society. Rational individuals demand democratic governance.

Democratic capitalism leads to peace. As evidence, Schumpeter claims that throughout the capitalist world an opposition has arisen to "war, expansion, cabinet diplomacy"; that contemporary capitalism is associated with peace parties; and that the industrial worker of capitalism is "vigorously anti-imperialist." In addition, he points out that the capitalist world has developed means of preventing war, such as the Hague Court and that the least feudal, most capitalist society—the United States—has demonstrated the least imperialistic tendencies (Schumpeter, 1955, pp. 95–96). An example of the lack of imperialistic tendencies in the U.S., Schumpeter thought, was our leaving over half of Mexico unconquered in the war of 1846–48.

Schumpeter's explanation for liberal pacifism is quite simple: Only war profiteers and military aristocrats gain from wars. No democracy would pursue a minority interest and tolerate the high costs of imperialism. When free trade prevails, "no class" gains from forcible expansion because

> raw materials and food stuffs are as accessible to each nation as though they were in its own territory. Where the cultural backwardness of a region makes normal economic intercourse dependent on colonization it does not matter, assuming free trade, which of the "civilized" nations undertakes the task of colonization. (Schumpeter, 1955, pp. 75–76)

Schumpeter's arguments are difficult to evaluate. In partial tests of quasi-Schumpeterian propositions, Michael Haas (1974, pp. 464–65) discovered a cluster that associates democracy, development, and sustained modernization with peaceful conditions. However, M. Small and J. D. Singer (1976) have discovered that there is no clearly negative correlation between democracy and war in the period 1816–1965—the period that would be central to Schumpeter's argument.

Later in his career, in *Capitalism, Socialism, and Democracy*, Schumpeter (1950, pp. 127–28) acknowledged that "almost purely bourgeois commonwealths were often aggressive when it seemed to pay—like the

Athenian or the Venetian commonwealths." Yet he stuck to his pacifistic guns, restating the view that capitalist democracy "steadily tells . . . against the use of military force and for peaceful arrangements, even when the balance of pecuniary advantage is clearly on the side of war which, under modern circumstances, is not in general very likely" (Schumpeter, 1950, p. 128). A . . . study by R. J. Rummel (1983) of "libertarianism" and international violence is the closest test Schumpeterian pacifism has received. "Free" states (those enjoying political and economic freedom) were shown to have considerably less conflict at or above the level of economic sanctions than "nonfree" states. The free states, the partly free states (including the democratic socialist countries such as Sweden), and the nonfree states accounted for 24%, 26%, and 61%, respectively, of the international violence during the period examined.

These effects are impressive but not conclusive for the Schumpeterian thesis. The data are limited, in this test, to the period 1976 to 1980. It includes, for example, the Russo-Afghan War, the Vietnamese invasion of Cambodia, China's invasion of Vietnam, and Tanzania's invasion of Uganda but just misses the U.S., quasi-covert intervention in Angola (1975) and our not so covert war against Nicaragua. More importantly, it excludes the cold war period, with its numerous interventions, and the long history of colonial wars (the Boer War, the Spanish-American War, the Mexican Intervention, etc.) that marked the history of liberal, including democratic capitalist, states.

The discrepancy between the warlike history of liberal states and Schumpeter's pacifistic expectations highlights three extreme assumptions. First, his "materialistic monism" leaves little room for noneconomic objectives, whether espoused by states or individuals. Neither glory, nor prestige, nor ideological justification, nor the pure power of ruling shapes policy. These nonmaterial goals leave little room for positive-sum gains, such as the comparative advantages of trade. Second, and relatedly, the same is true for his states. The political life of individuals seems to have been homogenized at the same time as the individuals were "rationalized, individualized, and democratized." Citizens—capitalists and workers, rural and urban—seek material welfare. Schumpeter seems to presume that ruling makes no difference. He also presumes that no one is prepared to take those measures (such as stirring up foreign quarrels to preserve a domestic ruling coalition)

that enhance one's political power, despite detrimental effects on mass welfare. Third, like domestic politics, world politics are homogenized. Materially monistic and democratically capitalist, all states evolve toward free trade and liberty together. Countries differently constituted seem to disappear from Schumpeter's analysis. "Civilized" nations govern "culturally backward" *regions.* These assumptions are not shared by Machiavelli's theory of liberalism.

Liberal Imperialism

Machiavelli argues, not only that republics are not pacifistic, but that they are the best form of state for imperial expansion. Establishing a republic fit for imperial expansion is, moreover, the best way to guarantee the survival of a state.

Machiavelli's republic is a classical mixed republic. It is not a democracy—which he thought would quickly degenerate into a tyranny—but is characterized by social equality, popular liberty, and political participation (Machiavelli, 1950, bk. 1, chap. 2, p. 112). The consuls serve as "kings," the senate as an aristocracy managing the state, and the people in the assembly as the source of strength.

Liberty results from "disunion"—the competition and necessity for compromise required by the division of powers among senate, consuls, and tribunes (the last representing the common people). Liberty also results from the popular veto. The powerful few threaten the rest with tyranny Machiavelli says because they seek to dominate. The mass demands not to be dominated, and their veto thus preserves the liberties of the state (Machiavelli, 1950, bk. 1, chap. 5, p. 122). However, since the people and the rulers have different social characters, the people need to be "managed" by the few to avoid having their recklessness overturn or their fecklessness undermine the ability of the state to expand (Machiavelli, 1950, bk. 1, chap. 53, pp. 249–50). Thus the senate and the consuls plan expansion, consult oracles, and employ religion to manage the resources that the energy of the people supplies.

Strength, and then imperial expansion, results from the way liberty encourages increased population and property, which grow when the citizens know their lives and goods are secure from arbitrary seizure. Free citizens equip large armies and provide soldiers who fight for public glory and the common good because these are, in fact, their own (Machiavelli,

1950, bk. 2, chap. 2, pp. 287–90). If you seek the honor of having your state expand, Machiavelli advises, you should organize it as a free and popular republic like Rome, rather than as an aristocratic republic like Sparta or Venice. Expansion thus calls for a free republic.

"Necessity"—political survival—calls for expansion. If a stable aristocratic republic is forced by foreign conflict "to extend her territory, in such a case we shall see her foundations give way and herself quickly brought to ruin"; if, on the other hand, domestic security prevails, "the continued tranquility would enervate her, or provoke internal dissensions, which together, or either of them separately, will apt to prove her ruin" (Machiavelli, 1950, bk. 1, chap. 6, p. 129). Machiavelli therefore believes it is necessary to take the constitution of Rome, rather than that of Sparta or Venice, as our model.

Hence, this belief leads to liberal imperialism. We are lovers of glory, Machiavelli announces. We seek to rule or, at least, to avoid being oppressed. In either case, we want more for ourselves and our states than just material welfare (materialistic monism). Because other states with similar aims thereby threaten us, we prepare ourselves for expansion. Because our fellow citizens threaten us if we do not allow them either to satisfy their ambition or to release their political energies through imperial expansion, we expand.

There is considerable historical evidence for liberal imperialism. Machiavelli's (Polybius's) Rome and Thucydides' Athens both were imperial republics in the Machiavellian sense (Thucydides, 1954, bk. 6). The historical record of numerous U.S. interventions in the postwar period supports Machiavelli's argument, but the current record of liberal pacifism, weak as it is, calls some of his insights into question. To the extent that the modern populace actually controls (and thus unbalances) the mixed republic, its diffidence may outweigh elite ("senatorial") aggressiveness.

We can conclude either that (1) liberal pacifism has at least taken over with the further development of capitalist democracy, as Schumpeter predicted it would or that (2) the mixed record of liberalism—pacifism and imperialism—indicates that some liberal states are Schumpeterian democracies while others are Machiavellian republics. Before we accept either conclusion, however, we must consider a third apparent regularity of modern world politics.

Liberal Internationalism

Modern liberalism carries with it two legacies. They do not affect liberal states separately, according to whether they are pacifistic or imperialistic, but simultaneously.

The first of these legacies is the pacification of foreign relations among liberal states.[1] During the nineteenth century, the United States and Great Britain engaged in nearly continual strife; however, after the Reform Act of 1832 defined actual representation as the formal source of the sovereignty of the British parliament, Britain and the United States negotiated their disputes. They negotiated despite, for example, British grievances during the Civil War against the North's blockade of the South, with which Britain had close economic ties. Despite severe Anglo-French colonial rivalry, liberal France and liberal Britain formed an entente against illiberal Germany before World War I. And from 1914 to 1915, Italy, the liberal member of the Triple Alliance with Germany and Austria, chose not to fulfill its obligations under that treaty to support its allies. Instead, Italy joined in an alliance with Britain and France, which prevented it from having to fight other liberal states and then declared war on Germany and Austria. Despite generations of Anglo-American tension and Britain's wartime restrictions on American trade with Germany, the United States leaned toward Britain and France from 1914 to 1917 before entering World War I on their side.

Beginning in the eighteenth century and slowly growing since then, a zone of peace, which Kant called the "pacific federation" or "pacific union," has begun to be established among liberal societies. More than 40 liberal states currently make up the union. Most are in Europe and North America, but they can be found on every continent.

Here the predictions of liberal pacifists (and President Reagan) are borne out: liberal states do exercise peaceful restraint, and a separate peace exists among them. This separate peace provides a solid foundation for the United States' crucial alliances with the liberal powers, e.g., the North Atlantic Treaty Organization and our Japanese alliance. This foundation appears to be impervious to the quarrels with our allies that bedeviled the Carter and Reagan administrations. It also offers the promise of a continuing peace among liberal states, and as the number of liberal states increases, it announces the possibility of global peace this side of the grave or world conquest.

Of course, the probability of the outbreak of war in any given year between any two given states is low. The occurrence of a war between any two adjacent states, considered over a long period of time, would be more probable. The apparent absence of war between liberal states, whether adjacent or not, for almost 200 years thus may have significance. Similar claims cannot be made for feudal, fascist, communist, authoritarian, or totalitarian forms of rule (Doyle, 1983a, pp. 222), nor for pluralistic or merely similar societies. More significant perhaps is that when states are forced to decide on which side of an impending world war they will fight, liberal states all wind up on the same side despite the complexity of the paths that take them there. These characteristics do not prove that the peace among liberals is statistically significant nor that liberalism is the sole valid explanation for the peace.[2] They do suggest that we consider the possibility that liberals have indeed established a separate peace—but only among themselves.

Liberalism also carries with it a second legacy: international "imprudence" (Hume, 1963, pp. 346–47). Peaceful restraint only seems to work in liberals' relations with other liberals. Liberal states have fought numerous wars with non-liberal states.

Many of these wars have been defensive and thus prudent by necessity. Liberal states have been attacked and threatened by nonliberal states that do not exercise any special restraint in their dealings with the liberal states. Authoritarian rulers both stimulate and respond to an international political environment in which conflicts of prestige, interest, and pure fear of what other states might do all lead states toward war. War and conquest have thus characterized the careers of many authoritarian rulers and ruling parties, from Louis XIV and Napoleon to Mussolini's fascists, Hitler's Nazis, and Stalin's communists.

Yet we cannot simply blame warfare on the authoritarians or totalitarians, as many of our more enthusiastic politicians would have us do. Most wars arise out of calculations and miscalculations of interest, misunderstandings, and mutual suspicions, such as those that characterized the origins of World War I. However, aggression by the liberal state has also characterized a large number of wars. Both France and Britain fought expansionist colonial wars throughout the nineteenth century. The

United States fought a similar war with Mexico from 1846 to 1848, waged a war of annihilation against the American Indians, and intervened militarily against sovereign states many times before and after World War II. Liberal states invade weak nonliberal states and display striking distrust in dealings with powerful nonliberal states (Doyle, 1983b).

Neither realist (statist) nor Marxist theory accounts well for these two legacies. While they can account for aspects of certain periods of international stability, neither the logic of the balance of power nor the logic of international hegemony explains the separate peace maintained for more than 150 years among states sharing one particular form of governance—liberal principles and institutions. Balance-of-power theory expects—indeed is premised upon—flexible arrangements of geostrategic rivalry that include preventive war. Hegemonies wax and wane, but the liberal peace holds. Marxist "ultra-imperialists" expect a form of peaceful rivalry among capitalists, but only liberal capitalists maintain peace. Leninists expect liberal capitalists to be aggressive toward nonliberal states, but they also (and especially) expect them to be imperialistic toward fellow liberal capitalists.

Kant's theory of liberal internationalism helps us understand these two legacies. The importance of Immanuel Kant as a theorist of international ethics has been well appreciated, but Kant also has an important analytical theory of international politics. *Perpetual Peace,* written in 1795 (Kant, 1970, pp. 93–130), helps us understand the interactive nature of international relations. Kant tries to teach us methodologically that we can study neither the systemic relations of states nor the varieties of state behavior in isolation from each other. Substantively, he anticipates for use the ever-widening pacification of a liberal pacific union, explains this pacification, and at the same time suggests why liberal states are not pacific in their relations with nonliberal states. Kant argues that perpetual peace will be guaranteed by the ever-widening acceptance of three "definitive articles" of peace. When all nations have accepted the definitive articles in a metaphorical "treaty" of perpetual peace he asks them to sign, perpetual peace will have been established.

The First Definitive Article requires the civil constitution of the state to be republican. By *republican* Kant means a political society that has solved the problem of combining moral autonomy, individualism, and social order. A private property and market-oriented economy partially addressed that dilemma in the private sphere. The public, or political, sphere was more troubling. His answer was a republic that preserved juridical freedom—the legal equality of citizens as subjects—on the basis of a representative government with a separation of powers. Juridical freedom is preserved because the morally autonomous individual is by means of representation a self-legislator making laws that apply to all citizens equally, including himself or herself. Tyranny is avoided because the individual is subject to laws he or she does not also administer (Kant, *PP*, pp. 99–102).[3]

Liberal republics will progressively establish peace among themselves by means of the pacific federation, or union (*foedus pacificum*), described in Kant's Second Definitive Article. The pacific union will establish peace within a federation of free states and securely maintain the rights of each state. The world will not have achieved the "perpetual peace" that provides the ultimate guarantor of republican freedom until "a late stage and after many unsuccessful attempts" (Kant, *UH*, p. 47). At that time, all nations will have learned the lessons of peace through right conceptions of the appropriate constitution, great and sad experience, and good will. Only then will individuals enjoy perfect republican rights or the full guarantee of a global and just peace. In the meantime, the "pacific federation" of liberal republics—"an enduring and gradually expanding federation likely to prevent war"—brings within it more and more republics—despite republican collapses, backsliding, and disastrous wars—creating an ever-expanding separate peace (Kant, *PP*, p. 105).[4] Kant emphasizes that

> it can be shown that this idea of federalism, extending gradually to encompass all states and thus leading to perpetual peace, is practicable and has objective reality. For if by good fortune one powerful and enlightened nation can form a republic (which is by nature inclined to seek peace), this will provide a focal point for federal association among other states. These will join up with the first one, thus securing the freedom of each state in accordance with the idea of international right, and the whole will gradually spread further and further by a series of alliances of this kind. (Kant, *PP*, p. 104)

The pacific union is not a single peace treaty ending one war, a world state, nor a state of nations. Kant finds the first insufficient. The second and third are impossible or potentially tyrannical. National sovereignty precludes reliable subservience to a state of nations; a world state destroys the civic freedom on which the development of human capacities rests (Kant, *UH*, p. 50). Although Kant obliquely refers to various classical interstate confederations and modern diplomatic congresses, he develops no systematic organizational embodiment of this treaty and presumably does not find institutionalization necessary. He appears to have in mind a mutual non-aggression pact, perhaps a collective security agreement, and the cosmopolitan law set forth in the Third Definitive Article.[5]

The Third Definitive Article establishes a cosmopolitan law to operate in conjunction with the pacific union. The cosmopolitan law "shall be limited to conditions of universal hospitality." In this Kant calls for the recognition of the "right of a foreigner not to be treated with hostility when he arrives on someone else's territory." This "does not extend beyond those conditions which make it possible for them [foreigners] to attempt to enter into relations [commerce] with the native inhabitants" (Kant, *PP*, p. 106). Hospitality does not require extending to foreigners either the right to citizenship or the right to settlement, unless the foreign visitors would perish if they were expelled. Foreign conquest and plunder also find no justification under this right. Hospitality does appear to include the right of access and the obligation of maintaining the opportunity for citizens to exchange goods and ideas without imposing the obligation to trade (a voluntary act in all cases under liberal constitutions).

Perpetual peace, for Kant, is an epistemology, a condition for ethical action, and, most importantly, an explanation of how the "mechanical process of nature visibly exhibits the purposive plan of producing concord among men, even against their will and indeed by means of their very discord" (Kant, *PP*, p. 108; *UH*, pp. 44–45). Understanding history requires an epistemological foundation, for without a teleology, such as the promise of perpetual peace, the complexity of history would overwhelm human understanding (Kant, *UH*, pp. 51–53). Perpetual peace, however, is not merely a heuristic device with which to interpret history. It is guaranteed, Kant explains in the "First Addition" to *Perpetual Peace*

("On the Guarantee of Perpetual Peace"), to result from men fulfilling their ethical duty or, failing that, from a hidden plan.[6] Peace is an ethical duty because it is only under conditions of peace that all men can treat each other as ends, rather than means to an end (Kant, *UH*, p. 50). In order for this duty to be practical, Kant needs, of course, to show that peace is in fact possible. The widespread sentiment of approbation that he saw aroused by the early success of the French revolutionaries showed him that we can indeed be moved by ethical sentiments with a cosmopolitan reach (Kant, *CF*, pp. 181–82). This does not mean, however, that perpetual peace is certain ("prophesiable"). Even the scientifically regular course of the planets could be changed by a wayward comet striking them out of orbit. Human freedom requires that we allow for much greater reversals in the course of history. We must, in fact, anticipate the possibility of backsliding and destructive wars—though these will serve to educate nations to the importance of peace (Kant, *UH*, pp. 47–48).

In the end, however, our guarantee of perpetual peace does not rest on ethical conduct. As Kant emphasizes.

> we now come to the essential question regarding the prospect of perpetual peace. What does nature do in relation to the end which man's own reason prescribes to him as a duty, i.e., how does nature help to promote his *moral purpose?* And how does nature guarantee that what man ought to do by the laws of his freedom (but does not do) will in fact be done through nature's compulsion, without prejudice to the free agency of man? . . . This does not mean that nature imposes on us a *duty* to do it, for duties can only be imposed by practical reason. On the contrary, nature does it herself, whether we are willing or not: *facta volentem ducunt, nolentem tradunt.* (*PP*, p. 112)

The guarantee thus rests, Kant argues, not on the probable behavior of moral angels, but on that of "devils, so long as they possess understanding" (*PP*, p. 112). In explaining the sources of each of the three definitive articles of the perpetual peace, Kant then tells us how we (as free and intelligent devils) could be motivated by fear, force, and calculated advantage to undertake a course of action whose outcome we could reasonably anticipate to be perpetual peace. Yet while it is possible to conceive of the Kantian road to peace in these terms, Kant himself

recognizes and argues that social evolution also makes the conditions of moral behavior less onerous and hence more likely (*CF*, pp. 187–89). In tracing the effects of both political and moral development, he builds an account of why liberal states do maintain peace among themselves and of how it will (by implication, has) come about that the pacific union will expand. He also explains how these republics would engage in wars with nonrepublics and therefore suffer the "sad experience" of wars that an ethical policy might have avoided.

The first source of the three definitive articles derives from a political evolution—from a constitutional law. Nature (providence) has seen to it that human beings can live in all the regions where they have been driven to settle by wars. (Kant, who once taught geography, reports on the Lapps, the Samoyeds, the Pescheras.) "Asocial sociability" draws men together to fulfill needs for security and material welfare as it drives them into conflicts over the distribution and control of social products (Kant, *UH*, pp. 44–45; *PP*, pp. 110–11). This violent natural evolution tends towards the liberal peace because "asocial sociability" inevitably leads toward republican governments, and republican governments are a source of the liberal peace.

Republican representation and separation of powers are produced because they are the means by which the state is "organized well" to prepare for and meet foreign threats (by unity) and to tame the ambitions of selfish and aggressive individuals (by authority derived from representation, by general laws, and by nondespotic administration) (Kant, *PP*, pp. 112–13). States that are not organized in this fashion fail. Monarchs thus encourage commerce and private property in order to increase national wealth. They cede rights of representation to their subjects in order to strengthen their political support or to obtain willing grants of tax revenue.

Kant shows how republics, once established, lead to peaceful relations. He argues that once the aggressive interests of absolutist monarchies are tamed and the habit of respect for individual rights engrained by republican government, wars would appear as the disaster to the people's welfare that he and the other liberals thought them to be. The fundamental reason is this:

> If, as is inevitably the case under this constitution, the consent of the citizens is required to

decide whether or not war should be declared, it is very natural that they will have a great hesitation in embarking on so dangerous an enterprise. For this would mean calling down on themselves all the miseries of war, such as doing the fighting themselves, supplying the costs of the war from their own resources, painfully making good the ensuing devastation, and, as the crowning evil, having to take upon themselves a burden of debts which will embitter peace itself and which can never be paid off on account of the constant threat of new wars. But under a constitution where the subject is not a citizen, and which is therefore not republican, it is the simplest thing in the world to go to war. For the head of state is not a fellow citizen, but the owner of the state, and war will not force him to make the slightest sacrifice so far as his banquets, hunts, pleasure palaces and court festivals are concerned. He can thus decide on war, without any significant reason, as a kind of amusement, and unconcernedly leave it to the diplomatic corps (who are always ready for such purposes) to justify the war for the sake of propriety. (Kant, *PP*, p. 100)

Yet these domestic republican restraints do not end war. If they did, liberal states would not be warlike, which is far from the case. They do introduce republican caution—Kant's "hesitation"—in place of monarchical caprice. Liberal wars are only fought for popular, liberal purposes. The historical liberal legacy is laden with popular wars fought to promote freedom, to protect private property, or to support liberal allies against nonliberal enemies. Kant's position is ambiguous. He regards these wars as unjust and warns liberals of their susceptibility to them (Kant, *PP*, p. 106). At the same time, Kant argues that each nation "can and ought to" demand that its neighboring nations enter into the pacific union of liberal states (*PP*, p. 102). Thus to see how the pacific union removes the occasion of wars among liberal states and not wars between liberal and nonliberal states, we need to shift our attention from constitutional law to international law, Kant's second source.

Complementing the constitutional guarantee of caution, international law adds a second source for the definitive articles: a guarantee of respect. The separation of nations that a social sociability encourages is reinforced by the development of separate languages and religions. These further guarantee a world of separate states—an essential condition needed to avoid a "global, soul-less despotism." Yet, at the same time, they also morally integrate liberal states: "as culture grows and men gradually move towards greater agreement over their principles, they lead to mutual understanding and peace" (Kant, *PP*, p. 114). As republics emerge (the first source) and as culture progresses, an understanding of the legitimate rights of all citizens and of all republics comes into play; and this, now that caution characterizes policy, sets up the moral foundations for the liberal peace. Correspondingly, international law highlights the importance of Kantian publicity. Domestically, publicity helps ensure that the officials of republics act according to the principles they profess to hold just and according to the interests of the electors they claim to represent. Internationally, free speech and the effective communication of accurate conceptions of the political life of foreign peoples is essential to establishing and preserving the understanding on which the guarantee of respect depends. Domestically just republics, which rest on consent, then presume foreign republics also to be consensual, just, and therefore deserving of accommodation. The experience of cooperation helps engender further cooperative behavior when the consequences of state policy are unclear but (potentially) mutually beneficial. At the same time, liberal states assume that nonliberal states, which do not rest on free consent, are not just. Because nonliberal governments are in a state of aggression with their own people, their foreign relations become for liberal governments deeply suspect. In short, fellow liberals benefit from a presumption of amity; nonliberals suffer from a presumption of enmity. Both presumptions may be accurate; each, however, may also be self-confirming.

Lastly, cosmopolitan law adds material incentives to moral commitments. The cosmopolitan right to hospitality permits the "spirit of commerce" sooner or later to take hold of every nation, thus impelling states to promote peace and to try to avert war. Liberal economic theory holds that these cosmopolitan ties derive from a cooperative international division of labor and free trade according to comparative advantage. Each economy is said to be better off than it would have been under autarky; each thus acquires an incentive to avoid policies that would lead the other to break these economic ties. Because keeping open markets rests upon the assumption that the next set of transactions will also be determined by prices rather than coercion, a sense of mutual security is vital to avoid security-motivated searches for economic autarky. Thus, avoiding a challenge to another liberal state's security or even enhancing each others' security by means of alliance naturally follows economic interdependence.

A further cosmopolitan source of liberal peace is the international market's removal of difficult decisions of production and distribution from the direct sphere of state policy. A foreign state thus does not appear directly responsible for these outcomes, and states can stand aside from, and to some degree above, these contentious market rivalries and be ready to step in to resolve crises. The interdependence of commerce and the international contacts of state officials help create crosscutting transnational ties that serve as lobbies for mutual accommodation. According to modern liberal scholars, international financiers and transnational and transgovernmental organizations create interests in favor of accommodation. Moreover, their variety has ensured that no single conflict sours an entire relationship by setting off a spiral of reciprocated retaliation (Brzezinski and Huntington, 1963, chap. 9; Keohane and Nye, 1977, chap. 7; Neustadt, 1970; Polanyi, 1944, chaps. 1–2). Conversely, a sense of suspicion, such as that characterizing relations between liberal and nonliberal governments, can lead to restrictions on the range of contacts between societies, and this can increase the prospect that a single conflict will determine an entire relationship.

No single constitutional, international, or cosmopolitan source is alone sufficient, but together (and only together) they plausibly connect the characteristics of liberal polities and economies with sustained liberal peace. Alliances founded on mutual strategic interest among liberal and nonliberal states have been broken; economic ties between liberal and nonliberal states have proven fragile; but the political bonds of liberal rights and interests have proven a remarkably firm foundation for mutual nonaggression. A separate peace exists among liberal states.

In their relations with nonliberal states, however, liberal states have not escaped from the insecurity caused by anarchy in the world political system considered as a whole. Moreover, the very constitutional restraint, international respect for individual rights, and shared commercial interests that establish grounds for peace among liberal states establish grounds for additional conflict in relations between liberal and nonliberal societies.

Conclusion

Kant's liberal internationalism, Machiavelli's liberal imperialism, and Schumpeter's liberal pacifism rest on fundamentally different views of the nature of the human being, the state, and international relations.[7] Schumpeter's humans are rationalized, individualized, and democratized. They are also homogenized, pursuing material interests "monistically." Because their material interests lie in peaceful trade, they and the democratic state that these fellow citizens control are pacifistic. Machiavelli's citizens are splendidly diverse in their goals but fundamentally unequal in them as well, seeking to rule or fearing being dominated. Extending the rule of the dominant elite or avoiding the political collapse of their state, each calls for imperial expansion.

Kant's citizens, too, are diverse in their goals and individualized and rationalized, but most importantly, they are capable of appreciating the moral equality of all individuals and of treating other individuals as ends rather than as means. The Kantian state thus is governed publicly according to law, as a republic. Kant's is the state that solves the problem of governing individualized equals, whether they are the "rational devils" he says we often find ourselves to be or the ethical agents we can and should become. Republics tell us that

> in order to organize a group of rational beings who together require universal laws for their survival, but of whom each separate individual is secretly inclined to exempt himself from them, the constitution must be so designed so that, although the citizens are opposed to one another in their private attitudes, these opposing views may inhibit one another in such a way that the public conduct of the citizens will be the same as if they did not have such evil attitudes. (Kant, *PP*, p. 113)

Unlike Machiavelli's republics, Kant's republics are capable of achieving peace among themselves because they exercise democratic caution and are capable of appreciating the international rights of foreign republics. These international rights of republics derive from the representation of foreign individuals who are our moral equals. Unlike Schumpeter's capitalist democracies, Kant's republics—including our own—remain in a state of war with nonrepublics. Liberal republics see themselves as threatened by aggression from nonrepublics that are not constrained by representation. Even though wars often cost more than the economic return they generate, liberal republics also are prepared to protect and promote—sometimes forcibly—democracy, private property, and the rights of individuals overseas against nonrepublics, which, because they do not authentically represent the rights of individuals, have no rights to noninterference. These wars may liberate oppressed individuals overseas; they also can generate enormous suffering.

Preserving the legacy of the liberal peace without succumbing to the legacy of liberal imprudence is both a moral and a strategic challenge. The bipolar stability of the international system, and the near certainty of mutual devastation resulting from a nuclear war between the superpowers, have created a "crystal ball effect" that has helped to constrain the tendency toward miscalculation present at the outbreak of so many wars in the past (Carnesale, Doty, Hoffmann, Huntington, Nye, and Sagan, 1983, p. 44; Waltz, 1964). However, this "nuclear peace" appears to be limited to the super-powers. It has not curbed military interventions in the Third World. Moreover, it is subject to a desperate technological race designed to overcome its constraints and to crises that have pushed even the super-powers to the brink of war. We must still reckon with the war fevers and moods of appeasement that have almost alternately swept liberal democracies.

Yet restraining liberal imprudence, whether aggressive or passive, may not be possible without threatening liberal pacification. Improving the strategic acumen of our foreign policy calls for introducing steadier strategic calculations of the national interest in the long run and more flexible responses to changes in the international political environment. Constraining the indiscriminate meddling of our foreign interventions calls for a deeper appreciation of the "particularism of history, culture, and membership" (Walzer, 1983, p. 5), but both the improvement in strategy and the constraint on intervention seem, in turn, to require an executive freed from the restraints of a representative legislature in the management of foreign policy and a political culture indifferent to the universal rights of individuals. These conditions, in their turn, could break the chain of constitutional guarantees, the respect for representative government, and the web of transnational contact that have sustained the pacific union of liberal states.

Perpetual peace, Kant says, is the end point of the hard journey his republics will take. The promise of perpetual peace, the violent lessons of war, and the experience of a partial peace are proof of the need for and the possibility of world peace. They are also the grounds for moral citizens and statesmen to assume the duty of striving for peace.

Notes

1. Clarence Streit (1938, pp. 88, 90–92) seems to have been the first to point out (in contemporary foreign relations) the empirical tendency of democracies to maintain peace among themselves, and he made this the foundation of his proposal for a (non-Kantian) federal union of the 15 leading democracies of the 1930s. . . . I use the term *liberal* in a. . . . Kantian sense. . . . (Doyle, 1983a). In that essay, I survey the period from 1790 to the present and find no war among liberal states.

2. Babst (1972) did make a preliminary test of the significance of the distribution of alliance partners in World War I. He found that the possibility that the actual distribution of alliance partners could have occurred by chance was less than 1% (Babst, 1972, p. 56). However, this assumes that there was an equal possibility that any two nations could have gone to war with each other, and this is a strong assumption. Rummel (1983) has a further discussion of the issue of statistical significance as it applies to his libertarian thesis.

3. All citations from Kant are from *Kant's Political Writings* (Kant, 1970), the H. B. Nisbet translation edited by Hans Reiss. The works discussed and the abbreviations by which they are identified in the text are as follows:

PP *Perpetual Peace* (1795)
UH *The Idea for a Universal History with a Cosmopolitan Purpose* (1784)
CF *The Contest of Faculties* (1798)
MM *The Metaphysics of Morals* (1797)

4. I think Kant meant that the peace would be established among liberal regimes and would expand by ordinary political and legal means as new liberal regimes appeared. By a process of gradual extension the peace would become global and then perpetual; the occasion

for wars with nonliberals would disappear as nonliberal regimes disappeared.

5. Kant's *foedus pacificum* is thus neither a *pactum pacis* (a single peace treaty) nor a *civitas gentium* (a world state). He appears to have anticipated something like a less formally institutionalized League of Nations or United Nations. One could argue that in practice, these two institutions worked for liberal states and only for liberal states, but no specifically liberal "pacific union" was institutionalized. Instead, liberal states have behaved for the past 180 years as if such a Kantian pacific union and treaty of perpetual peace had been signed.

6. In the *Metaphysics of Morals* (the *Rechtslehre*) Kant seems to write as if perpetual peace is only an epistemological device and, while an ethical duty, is empirically merely a "pious hope" (*MM*, pp. 164–75)—though even here he finds that the pacific union is not "impracticable" (*MM*, p. 171). In the *Universal History* (*UH*), Kant writes as if the brute force of physical nature drives men toward inevitable peace....

7. For a comparative discussion of the political foundations of Kant's ideas, see Shklar (1984, pp. 232–38).

References

Babst, Dean V. 1972. A Force for Peace. *Industrial Research*. 14 (April): 55–58.

Brzezinski, Zbigniew, and Samuel Huntington. 1963. *Political Power: USA/USSR*. New York: Viking Press.

Carnesale, Albert, Paul Doty, Stanley Hoffmann, Samuel Huntington, Joseph Nye, and Scott Sagan. 1983. *Living With Nuclear Weapons*. New York: Bantam.

Doyle, Michael W. 1983a. Kant, Liberal Legacies, and Foreign Affairs: Part 1. *Philosophy and Public Affairs* 12: 205–35.

Doyle, Michael W. 1983b. Kant, Liberal Legacies, and Foreign Affairs: Part 2. *Philosophy and Public Affairs* 12: 323–53.

Hume, David. 1963. Of the Balance of Power. *Essays: Moral, Political, and Literary*. Oxford: Oxford University Press.

Kant, Immanuel. 1970. *Kant's Political Writings*. Hans Reiss, ed. H. B. Nisbet, trans. Cambridge: Cambridge University Press.

Keohane, Robert, and Joseph Nye. 1977. *Power and Interdependence*. Boston: Little Brown.

Neustadt, Richard. 1970. *Alliance Politics*. New York: Columbia University Press.

Polanyi, Karl. 1944. *The Great Transformation*. Boston: Beacon Press.

Rummel, Rudolph J. 1983. Libertarianism and International Violence. *Journal of Conflict Resolution*, 27: 27–71.

Schumpeter, Joseph. 1950. *Capitalism, Socialism, and Democracy*. New York: Harper Torchbooks.

Schumpeter, Joseph. 1955. The Sociology of Imperialism. In *Imperialism and Social Classes*. Cleveland: World Publishing Co. (Essay originally published in 1919.)

Shklar, Judith. 1984. *Ordinary Vices*. Cambridge, MA: Harvard University Press.

Streit, Clarence. 1938. *Union Now: A Proposal for a Federal Union of the Leading Democracies*. New York: Harpers.

Thucydides. 1954. *The Peloponnesian War*. Rex Warner, ed. and trans. Baltimore: Penguin.

Waltz, Kenneth. 1964. The Stability of a Bipolar World. *Daedalus*, 93: 881–909.

Walzer, Michael. 1983. *Spheres of Justice*. New York: Basic Books.

From Interdependence and Institutions to Globalization and Governance

ROBERT O. KEOHANE

The author provides his understanding of how the world works that is "both individualist and institutionalist." He summarizes much of his earlier work on interdependence and subsequently on institutions and ideas rooted in liberalism. With increasing globalization (albeit in a still only partially globalized world), he sees greater institutionalization as the world becomes more like a polity with governance essential to trade, finance, environment, security, and other matters of global import. Devising better, more effective global institutions to serve the needs of humankind is an imperative.

The . . . conception . . . of how the world works is both individualist and institutionalist, regarding institutions both as created by human action and as structuring that action.[1] The principal motor of action in this view is self-interest, guided by rationality, which translates structural and institutional conditions into payoffs and probabilities, and therefore incentives. But my conceptions of self-interest and rationality are broad ones. Self-interest is not simply material; on the contrary, it encompasses one's interest in being thought well of, and in thinking well of oneself. One's self-interest is not divorced from one's principled ideas or identity but closely connected with them. Furthermore, not all action is necessarily self-interested: actions such as those of firemen rushing into the burning World Trade Center on September 11, 2001, reflect commitment and courage rather than interest.

The resulting conception of how the world works is complex, seeking to take into account subjectivity as well as objectivity, primal urges for power as well as institutional constraints, principled beliefs and worldviews that cannot be validated as well as rational calculation. It therefore lacks parsimony. The core of my contribution to this view of the world has been to explore how international institutions operate, in the context of interdependence. But my exploration of institutions and interdependence has taken place in the context of an awareness of how they are affected by other, broader factors. Hence, I do not assume that institutions and interdependence are the most important aspects of contemporary world politics, that they somehow contain the unique key to history. Indeed, they only make sense if they are fit into the larger puzzle. . . .

From Interdependence to Institutional Theory

Over thirty years ago, astute observers of the world political economy began to comment on striking increases in economic connections among societies and the growing role of multinational corporations. Meanwhile, the literature on the European Community, pioneered by Ernst B. Haas, focused on how economic interdependence affected arrangements for governance. Nye and I picked up on these themes, beginning with our edited special issue of *International Organization* on transnational relations

(1972), a term that we did not invent but that we did insert into the literature on world politics.

At that time the buzzword for these changes was "interdependence." In the 1970s, Nye and I built a theory elucidating the notion of "complex interdependence," an ideal type for analyzing situations of multiple transnational issues and contacts in which force is not a useful instrument of policy. We defined interdependence itself more broadly, to encompass strategic issues involving force as well as economic ones. In our analysis, interdependence is frequently asymmetrical and highly political: indeed, asymmetries in interdependence generate power resources for states, as well as for non-state actors. *Power and Interdependence,* published first in 1977, elaborated this theory and applied it to fifty years of history (1920–1970) in two issue-areas (oceans and money) and two country relationships (US–Australia and US–Canada). There were a number of gaps in our analysis, some of which we acknowledged a decade later,[2] but the analysis of the relationship between asymmetrical interdependence and power continues to be useful. . . .

Power and Interdependence contained an incipient theory of institutions, in the form of what Nye and I called an international organization model of regime change (1977). But this theory was not well-developed. What preoccupied me for seven years after the publication of *Power and Interdependence* was the puzzle of why states establish international regimes—rule-oriented institutions that limit their Members' legal freedom of action. In *After Hegemony: Cooperation and Discord in the World Political Economy* (1984), I presented a theory of international institutions based on rationalist theory, in particular economic theories of the firm and of imperfect markets. I argued that institutions perform important tasks for states, enabling them to cooperate. In particular, institutions reduce the costs of making, monitoring, and enforcing rules—transaction costs—provide information, and facilitate the making of credible commitments. In this theory, the principal guarantors of compliance with commitments are reciprocity (including both threats of retaliation and promises of reciprocal cooperation) and reputation. . . .

My formulation of institutional theory has often been referred to as "liberal institutionalism" or "neo-liberal institutionalism." These labels do not appeal to me, not just because they are awkward. My theory does have its roots in liberalism . . . , but the connotations of liberalism are multiple and misleading. My theory has nothing to do with the view that commerce leads necessarily to peace; that people are basically good; or that progress in human history is inevitable—all propositions sometimes associated with liberalism. Nor is it connected with the view that liberty should have priority over equality and social justice, much less with the "neoliberalism" of the past decade: the so-called "Washington Consensus" that dictated the dismantling of much governmental regulation of markets in developing countries. My liberalism is more pessimistic about human nature and more cautious about causal connections running from economics to politics than some versions of classical liberalism; and I have never been a supporter of the "Washington Consensus" in its strong neo-liberal form. Since attaching a "liberal label" to my perspective generates such a need for explication, it seems better to leave it off entirely.

"Institutionalist" is descriptive of my work, since it emphasizes the significance of institutions and seeks to explain them. Using this term is not meant as a claim to intellectual hegemony. Indeed, there are many other institutionalist theories, often with quite different concepts, and implications, than my own. However, I regard my own formulation as having as good a claim to the adjective "institutionalist" as any of its competitors. When I refer below to "institutionalist theory," I refer to my own version of institutionalism.

The theory in *After Hegemony* was rather stylized: as in *Power and Interdependence,* differences in domestic politics were deliberately overlooked for purposes of simplification. This is not to say that the importance of domestic politics was denied: quite the contrary. But the theory did not encompass domestic politics. Indeed, the theoretical gap created by the omission from the theory of domestic politics was sufficiently wide to drive many dissertations through it. Some of my former students have been leaders in this effort. They have analyzed the impact of domestic politics on world politics, in the context of a sophisticated understanding of interstate politics and the roles played by international institutions and non-state actors.[3]

The fact that my former students have written over a dozen books linking domestic politics and international relations is not only gratifying to me personally; it illustrates a broader aspect of American graduate education that is often overlooked. The resumés of scholars normally include only their own work. But the puzzles that they recognize but fail to address may be as important to their own students, and to their field as a whole, as their own contributions. Paths that lead through open doors may beckon more strongly to aspiring scholars than imposing intellectual edifices, no matter how impressive. And the explorations of graduate students instruct their professors. Graduate education is a process of interchange, not merely of transmission.

The theory developed in *After Hegemony* and closely related writings was strongly affected by my research on trade, monetary, and energy issues—all questions of material self-interest in which reciprocity played a substantial role. On the whole, the same framework fits environmental issues quite well. Perhaps this congruity should not be surprising, since similar questions arise of cross-border externalities and economic competition. On both sets of issues, monitoring of agreements is important and is carried out largely under the auspices of international institutions, while enforcement takes place through state action, legitimated through such institutions.

Environmental issues do have a moral dimension that is largely missing from the economic questions emphasized in *After Hegemony.* Principled ideas, concerned with right and wrong, play a significant role in mobilizing publics on issues such as ozone depletion, pollution of the oceans, and global warming. Such principled ideas play an even more prominent role on questions of human rights. And causal ideas, specifying connections between cause and effect, are important in policy debates in both issue-areas, as well as in other arenas of world politics.

Intrigued by the role of ideas, and their connections to rationalistic frameworks of analysis, Judith Goldstein and I began to explore the role of ideas on policy in the early 1990s. The role of ideas, of course, has been a long-standing theme in the work of a number of distinguished students of international relations, including my own mentor, Stanley Hoffmann, Hedley Bull, and Martin Wight. Goldstein and I, however, were particularly interested in reconciling theories of rational choice, with which we were sympathetic, with our view that ideas are significant in world politics. We distinguished among three types of beliefs: worldviews, principled beliefs, and causal beliefs. Worldviews are illustrated by religion, principled beliefs by doctrines of human rights, and causal beliefs by Keynesian or monetarist theories of macroeconomics. All three types of belief affect policy, but they do so differently.

Goldstein and I went on to suggest that ideas exert effects along three causal pathways: (1) as "roadmaps," (2) as focal points where there is no unique equilibrium, and (3) as embedded elements of institutions. Our essay is not reprinted here both because it is well-known and easily accessible, and because it forms an integral part of an edited volume to which it served as an introduction. But my thinking since the early 1990s has been deeply affected by my appreciation, heightened by work on this project, of the role of ideas in world politics. As noted below, my recent work on international law seeks to explore how the ideas incorporated in legal thinking affect persuasion and practice in world politics.

As these remarks imply, I disagree with the frequently-heard criticism that the role of ideas is necessarily de-emphasized by a view of the world that is based on an individualist ontology and a neo-positivist epistemology. It is individuals who have beliefs, although of course these beliefs are formed through social processes, and are perpetuated through societies that outlive individuals. As social scientists, we can investigate the impact of these beliefs through theoretical and empirical work, exploring how variations in ideas—between individuals and between groups—help to account for variations in behavior. Of course we have to be alert to the operation of social norms and practices, and shared memories—so we should not adopt an unsocialized, atomistic notion of human beings. Man, as Aristotle pointed out, is a social animal. But in my view we should focus on individuals as the principal unit of analysis, as long as we keep in mind their interactions in society, and the historical and cultural contexts within which they live. This means that the analyst goes back and forth between individual and society, regarding both seriously, but always seeking to explain individual behavior, and aggregate it upward, rather than to theorize about society without considering whether the resulting propositions are consistent with patterns of individual behavior. In this way, we can give our theories micro-foundations and avoid the reification of abstract concepts or the positing of a collective consciousness for which there seems to be little scientific evidence.

The most important work on the role of ideas in world politics has been done not by me but others. The politics of human rights are not well-explained by the reciprocity-based logic of institutionalist theory: states do not retaliate for human rights violations by others by abridging human rights themselves. On other issues, such as the use of weapons of mass destruction, principled ideas and organizational cultures seem to have played an important a role in accounting for behavior. "Constructivist" writing on world politics has emphasized, as did work drawing on psychology earlier, the importance of subjectivity: the beliefs by which our images of the world are constructed in shaping world politics. Major work on the role of ideas has also been done by such scholars as Goldstein, Martha Finnemore, Margaret Keck, Friedrich Kratochwil, Henry R. Nau, my former student Daniel Philpott, Thomas Risse, John Gerard Ruggie, and Kathryn Sikkink.

Institutional and Realist Theory

It should be clear from this discussion that I do not claim that institutional theory is a comprehensive theory of world politics. I still believe it to be superior to a crude realism that fails to incorporate international institutions as important entities. But as Peter Katzenstein, Stephan Krasner and I have argued, a stylized competition between realism and institutionalism is not particularly conducive to new insights, now, in our field. Sophisticated versions of realism—both of the classical and structural varieties—share a great deal with my version of institutionalism, epistemologically and ontologically. They are all concerned with issues of power, including state power. Indeed, it is one of the silliest criticisms of my own work that it ignores power, as the titles of my major works from the 1970s and 1980s make clear.[4] Realism and institutionalism, in my formulation, are actor-oriented, individualist theories whose practitioners follow neo-positivist standards of evidence. They are by no means incommensurate paradigms; rather they are labels for loosely grouped interpretations that differ along a variety of dimensions. These dimensions include the intensity of competition in world politics, the role of rules and norms, the nature of information available to actors, and the linkages and separations between issue-areas.

Realism is a useful "first cut" at understanding world politics, but its vision of the field is too limited to make it a good comprehensive doctrine. Too much is left out: not only institutions, but also transnational relations, domestic politics and the role of ideas. Realism is long on structure, short on process.

Due to its limitations, realism is a poor candidate to correct the flaws in much institutionalist work that have been noted above: failure to theorize domestic politics, and an under-emphasis on the role of ideas. Realists cannot correct these flaws because it shares them, even in a more pronounced way. Waltz's *Theory of International Politics* (1979) abstracts away from domestic politics, just as my own book of the mid-1980s, *After Hegemony* (1984) does. This is not to say that either Professor Waltz or I were unaware of its importance: Waltz, for instance, wrote a whole book on the subject before developing his system-oriented theory (Waltz 1967). But it is difficult to construct a theory that simultaneously takes into account relations between states and relations within them, and that remains parsimonious.[5]

Classical realism—as in the hands of Carr and Morgenthau—has discussed the role of ideas, but more recent structural realism, as notably developed by Waltz and Robert Gilpin, has omitted it. The lack of extensive and sophisticated understanding of the role of ideas in world politics—which would have to include Nazism, communism and fundamentalism as well as human rights thinking and environmental awareness—hampers us particularly now in the wake of the September 11, 2001 attacks on the United States. These attacks illustrate the role of religion—overlooked by both of these secular approaches—in world politics. What Nye labeled "soft power" in the 1990s is not a monopoly of secular society, much less of the United States. . . .

The implication of these remarks is that two major trends in the study of world politics during the 1990s need to be continued and extended: the analysis of how domestic and world politics interact, and the investigation of the role of ideas in world politics. The brand of liberalism represented by the work of Andrew Moravcsik and Anne-Marie Slaughter is a valuable way to analyze the former; constructivist theory offers promise in understanding how ideas matter.

In breaking into the theoretically complacent world of realist thinking, it was expedient to emphasize the distinctive value of institutionalist theory, even while recognizing the contributions of realism.

And in the heat of subsequent controversy, it has been all too easy to overstate differences between institutional and realist theory, and perhaps to over-emphasize the superiority of the former. No perspective has a monopoly on wisdom: realism, theories focusing on domestic politics, and theories emphasizing subjective beliefs all have a role to play. Contestation between different approaches can play a positive role in social science scholarship, pushing advocates to sharpen their theories and to test them in more convincing ways. But if the contending approaches become conflicting schools of warring scholars, with graduate students signed up as in one camp or another, they become what Albert Hirschman once called "paradigms as hindrances to understanding."[6]

Institutionalism and the Puzzle of Compliance

The institutionalist theory that I developed in *After Hegemony* created only a promissory note on a major issue: that of compliance. In a world without centralized government, why should states comply with obligations that had become inconvenient? One set of problems might arise from deliberate deception, although prudence on the part of others could limit those dangers. A more pervasive set of problems could arise as a result of time: events may adversely change the cost-benefit calculus of state compliance. Why, one asks, should states guided by rational self-interest comply with obligations that have become inconvenient?

I sought in the late 1980s and 1990s to explore these questions in an historically oriented inquiry focused on United States foreign policy. I learned a great deal in the process, but failed to come up with either a comprehensive theory or satisfactory systematic evidence. On the theoretical side, my initial hunch was that concerns about reputation would ensure fairly regular compliance. In the record of United States foreign policy I did indeed find much concern with reputation, but I also found a consistent pattern, when commitments were inconvenient, of ingenious attempts to design policies to avoid reputational constraints. . . .

Although I am naturally somewhat chagrined by my own failure to solve the puzzle of compliance with commitments, I gain considerable satisfaction from the fact that at least for some issues it is being analyzed successfully within the framework of a rational-institutionalist theory. What matters for the fruitfulness of a theory is not the work of an individual, but the effort of a research community that is sufficiently intrigued or inspired by the theory to develop it creatively and test its implications systematically. There emerges a division of labor within this community among those who create the original theoretical intuitions, who specify the theory, who test it systematically, and who explore the wider implications of the findings that emerge. Since these capabilities are rarely all found in a single person, it is shortsighted to make any one of them the litmus test for productive scholarship. It is clear from my career that I am better at proposing new explanations, beginning to specify them as a theory, and exploring their wider implications, than at formalizing or testing hypotheses systematically. In a sense, then, my contributions can only be validated by others, which makes me very grateful to them for their creativity, intelligence, and effort. The fact that many of the major contributors to the institutionalist research program are former students of mine, naturally imbues this gratitude with feelings of pride.

If pride in one's own accomplishments and those of one's colleagues increases over time, even more does humility. Humility is probably not a positive attribute for a young scholar: one has to believe that one's own ideas are superior to conventional wisdom in certain areas, which requires, for an untested scholar, a certain arrogance. Certainly few colleagues who encountered me during my 30s would have listed humility as one of my virtues. Over time, however, one's personal failure to solve certain problems or keep up with certain technical advances does induce humility. So does the broader recognition that one's own theory—in my case, institutional theory—is only a partial approach to world politics, which needs to be combined with other perspectives.

Liberalism, Sovereignty and Security

One way of thinking about institutions and interdependence is to view interdependence as the context within which international institutions operate. Institutions are, in this view, a response to interdependence. The tradition of modern thought that is most conducive to this framing of the issue is that of liberalism.... Liberalism as an approach to international relations emphasizes individuals, seeks to understand collective decisions, and, in an ethical sense, promotes human rights and validates attempts to ameliorate the human condition. Sophisticated liberalism combines strands of commercialism, republicanism and regulatory politics. Attempts to regulate transnational activity occur as a response to economic interdependence, in the context of pluralistic democracy. Liberalism reaffirms the attempt of institutionalists to seek to understand politics for the sake of designing institutions that will promote cooperation, welfare, and human rights.

As I indicated above, liberalism has many variants, not all of which are consistent with one another. Hence as a general perspective, it does not offer specific normative guidance. My own form of liberalism ... emphasizes that interdependence among human beings produces discord, which generates a need for institutions. But it also stresses that institutions can be oppressive. My brand of liberalism is therefore hardly the naively overoptimistic doctrine caricatured by Voltaire in *Candide,* whose hero goes from disaster to disaster proclaiming that he is in "the best of all possible worlds." My liberalism recognizes the arguments of Judith Shklar's "liberalism of fear," while still holding out hope for progress. My intellectual heroes include James Madison, for his recognition that institutions must be designed to check one another, and John Rawls, for his construction of a moral theory based on adopting a standpoint of impartiality. I believe that institutions, including international institutions, should be accountable to those they govern. It is also desirable that they rest insofar as possible on honest persuasion rather than on coercion or bargaining based on asymmetrical resources; and that they encourage public participation. My own liberalism, while resolutely anti-utopian, nevertheless offers normative as well as positive guidance for public policy.

Sovereignty is important from this perspective because it illuminates a central tension in contemporary liberalism. Commercial liberalism emphasizes the benefits of the division of labor, hence favors greater openness and the institutions needed to assure openness. Republican liberalism, on the contrary, stresses the importance of self-determination and democracy within well defined boundaries, so that the public can exercise effective control over self-seeking private actors. From the standpoint of commercial liberalism, sovereignty is a problem; from the standpoint of republican liberalism, it is an essential guarantee. It is therefore not surprising that contemporary debates about openness often pit proponents of sovereignty against opponents of it, and divide the traditional right as well as the traditional left.

During the 1980s, theories of world politics were rather sharply subdivided into those dealing with security and those concerned with issues of political economy. In fact, the field virtually bifurcated into two specialties, which were often seen as having little relationship to one another. In *After Hegemony* I even defended "abstracting from military issues" as a way of focusing more clearly on "the economic origins of change."

Even during the Cold War, this view was quite problematic, as the impact of Ronald Reagan's military buildup on Soviet power, and indirectly on the world economy, was soon to demonstrate. The end of the Cold War made this separation between political-military issues and political-economic ones even more untenable. In *Bound to Lead,* Nye developed a persuasive argument about the centrality of American power, which linked security tightly to political economy. Some work I did with colleagues at Harvard on international institutions after the Cold War reinforced my interest in explaining how institutional theory could illuminate security issues. . . .

The transaction costs–informational theories of international institutions developed in *After Hegemony* also pertain to security issues in which the participants have common or complementary interests. States that seek to cooperate on security issues also need to devise institutions that facilitate cooperation by making promises credible, providing information, and reducing other costs of agreement. Once successful institutions have been developed, it is easier to adapt them to respond to change than to create entirely new ones, particularly if the institutions have a "hybrid" quality, with practices that can be transferred at relatively low cost to new situations. . . .

From Institutions to Law

In the later 1980s and early 1990s a few innovative legal scholars began to use institutionalist theory. Kenneth Abbott systematically reviewed and commented on institutionalist theory in a major law review article. Anne-Marie Slaughter, writing under her former name of Burley, essentially argued that political scientists were speaking legal prose without recognizing it: that we were theorizing about institutions that generations of legal scholars had described, though not explained. Both in the world of ideas and in the real world of international institutions, the separation between institutions and law seemed more and more tenuous.

My own aversion to international law had been forged in graduate school, when the "world peace through world law" work of Louis Sohn and Grenville Clark had seemed utterly divorced from Cold War reality. More influential in my own training were the critiques of legalism by the realists E.H. Carr and George F. Kennan. Perhaps as a reaction to my own tendency toward personal moralism, I have always been allergic to preaching as a substitute for analysis. But by the early 1990s I had recognized that international law did not have to be textual, formalistic and separated from real political problems and ethnical dilemmas. . . .

I think that the analysis of legalization undertaken by my colleagues and myself is consistent with my overall framework for the analysis of world politics. I begin with actors—individuals and organizations—pursuing their interests as they see them, and guided by the values they internalize. These actors use resources at their disposal, including force, material capabilities, and persuasive ideas, to seek to achieve their objectives. The actors are located in structures of power that provide incentives for action, by affecting the payoffs of various strategies; they are also located within organizations, which delegate authority to various agents. Individuals respond to incentives in a broadly rational way; organizations may do so also, depending on how they are structured. Rationality does not mean full information, or the ability to calculate perfectly; instead, it is the "bounded rationality" of Herbert Simon. In contemporary world politics, states are usually the most important actors, although they are by no means alone. They have to contend with transnational actors, and with structures of transnational as well as interstate relationships. Both sets of actors, state and non-state, also deal with institutions in two important senses: as inherited patterns of rules and relationships that can affect beliefs and expectations, and as potential tools for the pursuit of their own objectives.

To understand politics within this framework, one first looks for the key bargains that create policies and establish coalitions. One can think of these bargains as reflecting the equilibria of games, which create institutions, which then, in turn, establish or solidify equilibria so that these institutions, and particular policies, persist. The viability of these institutionalized agreements, however, depends not merely on the interests, capacities, and beliefs of the participants, and on the nominal rules of the institutions, but also on their consistency with broader sets of beliefs and expectations held by other actors or coalitions that control political resources.

Legalized institutions, with precise obligations interpreted by third parties, often impose particularly strong constraints on political actors, as well as providing opportunities for innovative strategies that involve legal action. The success of these strategies is frequently dependent on whether implicit coalitions can be formed, and bargains made, among actors playing well-defined legal roles, including judges. Strategic interaction is central both to politics and to law. Beliefs and institutions, as well as material capabilities, are crucial to strategic interaction. Indeed, the outcomes of strategic interactions may depend as much on how rules are interpreted—a key focus of international legal scholarship—as on the wording of the rules themselves. World politics and the processes of international law can only be understood, therefore, from multiple perspectives, which encompass issues of state power, non-state action, domestic politics, institutions, processes of interpretation, coalitions and bargaining, and the persuasiveness of competing sets of ideas. Understanding how international legal scholars work helps one see issues of interpretation and persuasion in a more subtle way.

From Interdependence to Globalism

. . . When a new buzzword comes to our faddish field, it is more effective to redefine and reinterpret it than to ignore it. Interdependence was the buzzword of the 1970s, but it had been used in sloppy ways that limited thought. In *Power and Interdependence,* Nye and I sought to redefine and reinterpret it as an analytically useful concept. We disparaged "rhetorical" uses of the phrase and

defined interdependence as referring to situations characterized by reciprocal costly effects among actors. We explicitly rejected the view that interdependence was necessarily benign and declared our skepticism about the naïve view that "rising interdependence is creating a brave new world of cooperation to replace the bad old world of international conflict." We therefore sought to make interdependence into a useful analytical tool that did not prejudge conclusions.

When globalization became the buzzword of the 1990s, my first reaction was to regard it as journalistic hype: interdependence in flashier but less revealing garb. Indeed, Helen Milner and I entitled a book that we edited in 1996, "internationalization and domestic politics," rather than "globalization and domestic politics," since "globalization" seemed to imply an answer to the question we were asking about convergence or divergence of national policies. But it is frustrating to try to row against a strong tide, or to sail directly into the wind. To be heard, the scholar has to speak to the concerns of his era in the language of his era. Doing so gets people hooked; then one can proceed to the analysis that may increase their understanding, or at least raise questions about their preconceptions.

At one level, then, "interdependence" was simply overtaken by "globalization" as the fashionable language to describe increases in economic openness and integration. But at a deeper level, changes in terminology reflect changes in reality. The most comprehensive work on globalization of which I am aware defines it as a set of processes that embody "a transformation in the spatial organization of social relations and transactions" generating transcontinental flows and networks, . . . four aspects of globalization [being] extensity (the stretching of space), intensity, velocity, and impact. Globalization moves beyond linkages between separate societies to the reorganization of social life on a transnational basis. As John Ruggie [once] commented . . . : globalization is to interdependence as Federal Express is to the exchange of letters between separate national post offices.

We should notice, however, the semantic differences between these two terms. Interdependence refers to a *state of the world,* whereas globalization describes a *trend* of increasing transnational flows and increasingly thick networks of interdependence. For the terms to be comparable, we need to use a different term: "globalism," which describes a state of the world. Both interdependence and globalism can be viewed as matters of degree; both can increase or decline over time. Globalization, by contrast, implies increases in globalism. It makes more sense to speak of a "decline in globalism" (as, for instance, with economic globalism between 1914 and 1945) than a "decline in globalization."

Despite the differences, the complexities of interdependence, as Nye and I and others had worked them out in the 1970s, are crucial to a coherent and realistic understanding of globalism and globalization. In particular, interdependence was not just economic, but also strategic, environmental, and ideational. Globalism, . . . is also multidimensional. We differentiate economic, social, environmental and military globalization, each of which has political dimensions. Globalism involves thick networks of interdependence, organized on a transnational basis. Each strand of interdependence involves specific actors, whereas globalism refers to the aggregate pattern produced by all of these strands, and by their organization on a global scale.

From Institutions to Governance

Finally, how does "governance" enter this picture? . . . What explains the apparent shift in my emphasis from institutions to governance? The answer to this question parallels my answer to the last one. As networks of interdependence intensify, they become more important to domestic publics. And as they thicken into globalism, the connections between them also become more intense. It is less and less feasible to regard issues of trade, finance, environment, and security as separable, each with its own institution devoted to it. The world system looks more and more like a polity. Successful polities have governance structures in which the institutions are well-articulated with one another; but the world polity, if one can call it that, has disarticulated and fragmented institutions. Hence the problem arises of governance, which is defined . . . as "the processes and institutions, both formal and informal, that guide and restrain the collective activities of a group." Globally, the question of governance is one of how the various institutions and processes of global society could be meshed more effectively, in a way that would be regarded as legitimate by attentive publics controlling access to key resources.

In this context, what Nye and I . . . call the "club model" of international organizations becomes less and less tenable. In the half-century after World War II, a practice developed by which a limited set of elites from different countries came together within the confines of an international organization to bargain over a limited set of issues. These clubs were not very transparent and they kept outsiders at arms' length, but they often succeeded, as in trade or in the European Union, in negotiating important agreements that promoted openness. Yet with the growth in sophistication and activism of both developing countries and non-governmental actors, and in the context of a democratic political culture in their leading members, the club model has lost legitimacy. In particular, demands have been raised for accountability within the organizations—demands that are inconsistent with club practices, as well as with the interests of the developing countries as they perceive them. Legitimacy in terms of outputs—liberalized trade, widely beneficial to all, including the poor—may be inconsistent with legitimacy in terms of inputs, involving transparency and accountability. It is still unclear what form of governance on issues related to trade could be developed that would be sufficiently transparent and participatory to be legitimate, yet effective enough to solve pressing problems of inefficiency and the poverty that is accentuated by inefficiency.

The key issues, in my view, involve governance in a partially globalized world. . . . A partially globalized world is a world of thick networks of interdependence, in which boundaries, and states, nevertheless matter a great deal. Even the quite open US–Canadian border has a strong impact on economic activity. And as much work has demonstrated, globalization has not produced convergence of national welfare-state policies.

To understand governance in such a world, we have to understand institutions, which arise in the first instance from demands by political actors and from bargaining. To an extent they are the product of rational egoism; but simple functional theories that derive outcomes from need or purpose over-look both a variety of perverse incentives that often stand in the way, and the potential for public-spirited action. Institutions have paradoxical effects: they are essential for the good life, but they may also institutionalize bias in ways that make the good life impossible to attain for many people.

One response is to recognize that even if most people behave in self-interested ways most of the time, self-interest can be defined in more or less enlightened ways, and many people are not purely egotistical. Another response is to stress the role of prevailing expectations and beliefs in structuring even self-interested behavior. If just principles are generally accepted in a society, even self-interested people may have more incentives to act justly. Normatively, thinking about institutionalized governance raises issues of institutional design: in particular, fostering accountability, participation and persuasion by providing incentives for those practices to flourish. In the face of globalization, the essay concludes, our challenge is similar to that of the founders of the United States: "to design working institutions for a polity of unprecedented size and diversity."

Such institutions can only operate smoothly in a world free from threats of terror, just as threats of terror are only likely to be minimized in a world of well-functioning global institutions. What Nye and I referred to as "complex interdependence" in 1977—a world of multiple interactions in which recourse to force is excluded—is a condition for deep cooperation, which creates potential vulnerabilities as societies become intertwined. Relationships in which terror is employed involve interdependence, but are obviously not relationships of "complex interdependence." Hence, the attacks on the United States of September 11, 2001, reinforce the caution that Nye and I have consistently expressed about the spread of complex interdependence. As Nye likes to say, "security is like oxygen." You are only aware of it when it is absent. Global governance during the next decades will have to deal with threats of force as well as with economic interdependence. . . .

The attacks on the United States of September 11 [2001] did not focus on the world political economy, nor were international institutions directly involved. Perspectives from realism and political philosophy shed light on these events, but so do approaches with their origins in the study of interdependence and institutions. I do not claim that my perspectives on these issues are more important than other perspectives, but I do believe that theories linking asymmetrical interdependence to power, and institutional analysis, both contribute productively to the analysis of the globalization of informal violence.

We students of world politics did not choose our subject because it is aesthetically pleasing, nor because clear propositions about it can be developed and tested easily, using scientific methods. We should aspire to be scientific in the best sense; but neither the experimental nor statistical methods are easy to apply to a world of strategic interactions, by a limited number of players, that are not subject to our control. We choose our subject because it is vitally important: a matter of life and death, wealth and poverty. Surely the events of September 11 indicate anew its crucial significance. We face a moral imperative to understand world politics better. Better understanding should enable people to design better policies and institutions, although it is no guarantee of such improvements. Better institutions would enable ordinary human beings to live lives of their own choosing, free from fear. Under such conditions, people could devise their own ways to love and respect other people and to value the natural world on which we all depend.

Notes

1. I am indebted to Nannerl O. Keohane, Joseph S. Nye, and John Gerard Ruggie for comments on an earlier version of this introduction, and to my editor, Craig Fowlie, both for encouraging me to write this introduction and for comments on an earlier draft.

2. See Keohane and Nye (1987), reprinted in the second and third editions of *Power and Interdependence*, 1989 and 2001.

3. I have had so many able students that I would hesitate to create an exhaustive list, for fear of omitting some important work by people I respect very much.

4. *Power and Interdependence* (1977), *After Hegemony* (1984), *International Institutions and State Power* (1989).

5. See Kenneth N. Waltz, *Foreign Policy and Democratic Politics* (Boston: Little Brown, 1967).

6. The volume that I edited in 1986a, *Neorealism and Its Critics*, has been widely used and is still in print, but I have mixed feelings about it. It helpfully brought together Kenneth Waltz's seminal statements of neo-realist thinking, together with some of the major early critiques of his work. But it probably contributed to the "us versus them" tone of the discussion for much of the following decade.

Producing Security

STEPHEN G. BROOKS

Brooks observes that the issue of the relation between international commerce and war and peace goes back several thousands of years. The traditional focus and debate has been on economic interdependence defined in terms of trade between states. In an era of economic globalization, however, the key focus of analysis should be the impact of the globalization of production, in particular the international production strategies of multinational corporations. The issue is to what extent the globalization of production acts as a significant force for stability among great powers, between great powers and other states, and among states with secondary international power capabilities. He directly takes on John Mearsheimer's pessimistic view of international relations among great powers.

Scholars and statesmen have debated the influence of international commerce on war and peace for thousands of years. Around A.D. 100, Plutarch maintained that international commerce brought about "cooperation and friendship" and that the cessation of commercial exchange would cause the life of man to be "savage and destitute."[1] This line of reasoning became particularly prominent in the eighteenth and nineteenth centuries with the writings of philosophers such as Adam Smith, Jeremy Bentham, Immanuel Kant, Thomas Paine, Jean-Jacques Rousseau, Montesquieu, and John Stuart Mill.[2] These men were united in their belief that enhanced international commerce made war among states more costly and, thus, that "the natural effect of commerce is to lead to peace,"[3] as Montesquieu maintained in 1748. Many of them also believed that commerce was a dynamic force having a progressively stronger stabilizing effect over time. In the eyes of Kant, "the spirit of commerce, which is incompatible with war, sooner or later gains the upper hand in every state."[4]

This sanguine view of commerce as having a strong, positive effect on interstate relations has not been universally embraced. Indeed, many have argued the opposite is true. Perhaps the most prominent early pessimistic statement in this regard was advanced by Alexander Hamilton. Writing in 1787, he devotes most of Federalist 6 to critiquing the notion that the "spirit of commerce has a tendency to soften the manners of men and to extinguish those inflammable humors which have so often kindled into wars." After running through a series of historical examples. Hamilton ultimately concludes that numerous wars were "founded upon commercial motives" and that "spirit of commerce in many instances administered new incentives" for conflict.[5] Another prominent early pessimist is Frederick List, who argued during the middle of the nineteenth century that reducing participation in international commerce is, in the absence of a universal republic, the surest route to enhancing a state's security.[6] At the dawn of the twentieth century, John Hobson famously maintained that the business activities of firms led to imperialism; a few years later, Lenin then took one step further, emphasizing that not just imperialism but eventually war among capitalist states would be the inevitable result of capitalism.[7]

The belief that international commerce can strongly shape security relations is reflected not just in the writings of scholars over the centuries, but in policy discussions and governmental decisions. Over the years, the optimistic perspective on commerce and security has most strongly and directly shaped policy. David Lloyd George, Cordell Hull, Woodrow Wilson, Richard Cobden, William Gladstone, and Bill Clinton are prominent examples of politicians who have advanced policies premised on the notion that international commerce can promote peace.[8] As we move into the twenty-first century, this view continues to significantly influence important aspects of policy. In the United States, the decision to push for China's entry into the World Trade Organization is the most prominent recent example. In his 28 January 2000 State of Union Address, President Bill Clinton exhorted: "Congress should support the agreement we negotiated to bring China into the WTO, by passing Permanent Normal Trade Relations with China as soon as possible . . . [because] it will plainly advance the cause of peace in Asia." While the foreign policy approaches of the Clinton and George W. Bush administrations differ greatly on many issues, a key common theme is the notion that promoting economic globalization throughout the world can foster a stable security environment.[9]

Despite the prominence of the view among scholars and policymakers that international commerce significantly influences security relations, up until the 1990s essentially no empirical analysis of this issue existed.[10] In the final phase of the Cold War, prominent scholars such as Richard Rosecrance and Kenneth Waltz continued the centuries-old debate on the effects of commerce on peace, but this discussion was confined to the level of theory.[11] The rapidly growing scope of international economic integration, termed "globalization," has over the past decade led international relations scholars to renew their attention to how shifts in the international economy affect states' security behavior. Unlike almost all previous scholarship on this general subject, the most recent wave of investigations was empirically focused.[12] The general finding emerging from this literature—that trade linkages between states reduce the likelihood of conflict—is important in its own right and, more generally, indicates that the centuries-old contention that the business activities of firms can significantly shape security affairs is, in fact, valid.[13]

Bringing in the Globalization of Production

Given the great importance of economic globalization in the international environment, it is crucial to carefully evaluate its influence on security. The recent literature examining how the international economy influences security has produced important new insights, but it suffers from a major

limitation: it neglects the most significant feature of today's global economy. Over the centuries, scholars have generally treated the questions "Does international commerce influence security?" and "Do trade flows influence security?" as synonymous. Not surprisingly, virtually all studies in this recent wave of scholarship examine the security repercussions of international trade flows.[14] In the past, such an overarching focus on the security implications of trade made sense. It no longer does. Until recently, trade was "the primary means of organizing international economic transactions."[15] Today, however, trade is a second-order phenomenon: where and how multinational corporations (MNCs) organize their production activities is now the key integrating force in global commerce.[16]

MNC international production strategies have changed in a variety of fundamental ways over the past three decades. These new strategies are characterized by an increased cross-border dispersion of production. For this reason, analysts commonly use the short-hand term *globalization of production* as a descriptor of these recent changes in MNC production—a practice I will also adopt here.[17] As will be shown, MNCs are geographically dispersing production activities both internally and externally—that is, within the firm itself as well as through the development of more extensive interfirm linkages across borders. More specifically, MNCs have greatly enhanced the intrafirm international division of the production process through a new role for foreign affiliates: at the same time, they have pursued deeper relationships with foreign suppliers and cooperative partners located abroad through international subcontracting and international interfirm alliances.

Although analysts use the language of globalization in describing these shifts, the geographic dispersion of MNC production activities is not truly global in scope. These shifts in MNC production have had powerful effects on some states, but have largely bypassed many others. Specifically, it is among the economically most advanced states that the geographic dispersion of MNC production has been most prominent; the rise of international interfirm alliances, for example, is a trend largely restricted to North America, Western Europe, and Japan. It is also important to recognize that the geographic dispersion of MNC production is not occurring equally across all industries. . . . [I]nternationalization strategies have become prominent only in certain sectors.

The unprecedented nature of the globalization of production is a key feature distinguishing it from international trade. Many analysts argue that what we call economic globalization resembles the international economy during the "golden age" of capitalism from 1870 to 1914. However, this similarity is strong only if we treat economic globalization as an aggregate; when we break economic globalization into its constituent parts, we reach a very different answer. The globalization of production clearly represents an ongoing qualitative change in the international economy; trying to advance the same claim about the other two economic globalization trends—of international trade and international financial markets, respectively—is more problematic. In the end, the geographic dispersion of MNC production is the most historically novel aspect of contemporary economic globalization.

Despite the substantive significance and historical novelty of the globalization of production, there has so far been no systematic empirical analysis of its implications for security relations among states. The last detailed empirical examination of how international production by MNCs can influence security affairs was written in 1935.[18] A number of prominent analysts have recently noted that changes in MNC production strategies may have significant repercussions for security affairs, but this is not a primary focus of their analysis, and they do not empirically evaluate the notions they advance.[19] Because systematic data on the geographic dispersion of MNC production does not exist, there is a dearth of quantitative studies of international conflict that use measures of this global production shift.[20] A significant literature did develop in the middle and late 1980s that analyzed the United States' increased reliance upon foreign suppliers for parts and components of military weapons systems.[21] However, this literature, as well as the studies following in its wake, focuses almost exclusively on the consequences of the globalization of production for U.S. defense policy or the structure of the U.S. economy rather than upon the repercussions for international security more generally. This literature also centers upon increases in international subcontracting, which is only one element of the geographic dispersion of MNC production.

Empirical analyses of the security repercussions of trade flows can no longer eclipse examinations of how the globalization of production affects security relations. This book is the first systematic study of how this unprecedented change in the global economy influences international security. Since the geographic dispersion of MNC production is a novel and dramatic shift in the international environment, it is critical to know how it changes the prospects for peace. This analysis shows that the globalization of production has led to major changes in the global security environment that collectively improve the security climate in some regions while decreasing it in others.

The Globalization of Production Leads to Changes in Capabilities, Incentives, and Actors

Within the literature that examines how the international economy can influence security, scholars outline a wide variety of arguments. In practice, these disparate arguments can be boiled down to three general mechanisms: the global economy can influence security by changing capabilities, incentives, and the nature of the actors. This book shows that the globalization of production has reshaped the global security environment via each of these three general mechanisms.

Regarding capabilities, the key puzzle is whether the globalization of production has fundamentally changed the parameters of weapons production. As Richard Bitzinger notes, throughout history, "most countries traditionally have preferred to be self-sufficient in arms production."[22] The reasons are straight-forward: "going it alone" in defense production makes it possible to guard against vulnerability to supply interruptions and to ensure that strategic competitors do not have easy access to the same vital military technologies. States continue to have a preference for relying on their own resources for weapons production; the key question is how capable they are of pursuing this strategy. Analysts agree that going it alone has become harder in defense production in recent years.[23] Until now, however, we have lacked an understanding of exactly how much more difficult it has become. The analysis in this book reveals that the scales have decisively shifted against a strategy of autarkic defense production: no state, including the great powers, can now effectively remain on the cutting edge in military technology if it does not pursue significant internationalization in the production of weaponry.

Concerning incentives, the key unanswered question is whether the geographic dispersion of MNC production has changed the economic benefits of conquest. Economic gain has historically been a significant motivating force for conflict, and wars of conquest unfortunately still occur, as is demonstrated by Iraq's 1991 invasion of Kuwait and the occupation of western Congo by Uganda, Burundi, and Rwanda from 1998 to 2002. Irrespective of the motivation for war, the prospects for stability—that is, peacefulness—will decrease if aggressors are able to extract significant economic resources from newly occupied territory. The current benchmark study of the economic benefits of conquest concludes that conquerors are still in a position to effectively extract economic resources from vanquished wealthy countries.[24] In order to determine whether this is truly the case, we need to investigate how recent economic transformations within the most advanced countries affect the economic benefits of conquest. Until now, this key issue has been neglected in the literature. This analysis reveals that while conquerors are still in a position to effectively extract economic resources from a subset of wealthy countries, they can no longer do so from most. Specifically, I find that the globalization of production has greatly reduced the economic benefits of military conquest among the most advanced countries.

With respect to shifts in the nature of the actors, the primary puzzle is whether the geographic dispersion of MNC production can reshape security by influencing the prospects for regional economic integration. Because regional integration can alter the interests of the group's respective members, scholars conclude that such institutions can play a significant role in the development of stable, peaceful security relationships.[25] Although this line of argument is compelling, a key question remains: under what conditions will states with security tensions be able to consolidate integration in the first place? All the theory we have indicates that it is the consolidation of deep regional economic integration, and not simply the formation of an agreement, that has significant positive security repercussions. And yet, scholars who study international co-operation generally agree that states with security tensions will be least likely to engage in deep economic cooperation.[26] We need to examine whether the globalization of production can exert sufficient pressure to induce even those states with a history of security

rivalry to consolidate regional integration. The analysis here shows that it can. I find that this global production shift can, under certain conditions, enhance the prospects for peace by contributing to the consolidation of deep regional economic integration among long-standing security rivals.

The globalization of production has significant ramifications for security affairs by virtue of the fact that it has altered the parameters of weapons development, the economic benefits of conquest, and the prospects for regional economic integration among security rivals. These three mechanisms are the focus of this book both because of their significance in the literature and because they can be directly examined empirically. However, these mechanisms are not the only means by which the geographic dispersion of MNC production can potentially influence security; in total, there are *five other mechanisms, all of which I analyze in this book. . . . [T]hese five other mechanisms are all prospective in nature: they have the potential to influence security relations in the future, but do not appear to have yet played a role. The bottom line is that the globalization of production has already reshaped the international security environment in dramatic ways and may have an even greater influence in the years ahead.

The Globalization of Production Acts as a Significant Force for Great Power Stability

The influence of the globalization of production on security is clearest and also most consequential with respect to great power relations. A massive amount of literature within international relations is devoted to examining the most dangerous potential outcome in the system: a great power that attempts to fundamentally upset the territorial status quo and is successful in doing so because the gains of military conquest are cumulative. The possibility of this outcome has cast a long shadow over researchers working within every different approach and method in the field.[27] This focus is not surprising. Although great power war is not an everyday occurrence, it is one that holds great peril: in World War II, over 50 million were killed, and the possibility that the nature of the system could be transformed by the Axis powers was far from remote. Moreover, the mere threat of great power revisionism is grave and consequential: the U.S. effort to contain the Soviet threat to the system during the Cold War was incredibly expensive in economic terms (for decades America committed between 5 and 14 percent of its GDP to defense spending), and U.S presidents repeatedly engaged in brinkmanship that ran the risk of escalation to global thermonuclear destruction.

Many different factors influence the prospects for great power stability.[28] What is crucial is to identify which factors are important and whether they are likely to have a positive or negative influence. The findings of this book collectively indicate that the globalization of production now acts as a force for stability among the great powers. Put most precisely, the conclusion of this study is that the increased geographic dispersion of MNC production will, ceteris paribus, increase the stability of great power relations.

Of course, some say that the rise of what we now call economic globalization is partly due to the "long peace" that emerged among the great powers after 1945.[29] This is true. There are many different sources of this long peace, which, in turn, provided a favorable environment for the onset and acceleration of economic globalization. This book is not about the causes of the long peace, nor the genesis of economic globalization. Instead, the motivation for this study is to understand the repercussions of the globalization of production for security relations throughout the world in recent years and in the years to come. With the fading of Cold War security structures, a number of prominent analysts now see an increased threat of security competition among great powers.[30] This is where the geographic dispersion of MNC production enters in. As this study will show, now that the globalization of production is here, it works independently to reinforce stability among the great powers in a positive feedback loop via a specific set of mechanisms.

This analysis, in short, greatly strengthens the argument that international commerce now acts as a force for peace among the great powers. This book's conclusion—that the production activities of MNCs contributes to stability in a way that is different from and stronger than trade—undercuts those who advance pessimistic projections about the great powers in the years ahead. Significantly, these analysts all maintain that international commerce now provides no reason for optimism about the future. The most forceful proponent of this gloomy perspective, John Mearsheimer, certainly does recognize that economic globalization is a significant force in world politics

that has the potential to dramatically influence security affairs, but ultimately concludes that it does not reduce the force of his pessimistic predictions. Mearsheimer asserts there is essentially no difference between the nature and extent of international commerce in today's global economy and that of the pre-1914 era; he then reasons that if extensive international commerce did not prevent World War I, "a highly interdependent world economy does not make great-power war more or less likely" and that we ultimately have no reason to think that the current wave of economic globalization will act as a significant constraint on the severity of conflict among the great powers in the years ahead.[31]

Mearsheimer's treatment of economic globalization suffers from the standard problem in the security field at large: an overly narrow and static conceptualization of international commerce. Trade linkages before World War I were very extensive, to be sure. But trade comprises only one part of what international commerce now consists of, a minority portion at that. Before World War I, there was nothing like the geographic dispersion of MNC production that exists today. Given that the globalization of production is historically novel and is now the pivotal driver of international commerce, analyses such as Mearsheimer's that dismiss the current security repercussions of economic globalization of parallels with pre–World War I trade make no sense. Indeed, they are biased.

It turns out that once we factor in the globalization of production, Mearsheimer's pessimistic argument concerning the future of great power security relations loses steam. In his analysis, whether substantial power gains can be accrued through military conquest has a fundamental influence on the prospects for great power conflict.[32] Much of the basis for Mearsheimer's overall pessimism is a reflection of this in combination with his assessment that great power conquerors can, in fact, still effectively extract the economic wealth of those societies they vanquish on the battlefield and forcibly occupy.[33] As recently as World War II, it appears that great powers were in a position to conquer other great powers and effectively extract economic benefits from occupation.[34] This is no longer the case: a key finding of this book is that the globalization of production has greatly lowered the economic benefits of conquest in the most economically advanced states, and hence among all of the current and future great powers. This alone significantly undercuts Mearsheimer's pessimistic portrait of great power security relations in the years ahead.

The reasons why Mearsheimer places great stress on the economic benefits of conquest as an influence on great power stability are, of course, particular to his specific analysis. However, we need not agree with his particular theory of world politics to appreciate why the reduction in the economic benefits of conquest among the most advanced countries caused by the globalization of production significantly enhances stability among the great powers. Numerous other scholars employing approaches very different from Mearsheimer's similarly emphasize the economic benefits of conquest as a key influence on great power stability.[35] Irrespective of why a state seizes territory beyond its borders, the prospects for stability are greatly reduced when a great power can use one military conquest as a springboard for the next. During World War II, for example, the Nazis achieved great initial success and were hard to defeat in large part because they were able to effectively extract economic resources from the territory they occupied; these resources provided capacity that the Nazis could use to protect captured territory and acquire more. Had the Nazis been unable to effectively extract economic resources from vanquished territory, then their strategic vulnerability would have increased as they extended themselves militarily. This example makes it evident why a reduction in the economic benefits of conquest among the most advanced countries would enhance stability among the great powers.

Through its influence on the economic benefits of conquest, the geographic dispersion of MNC production acts as a force for continued peacefulness among the great powers. Although significant, this is not the only reason why this global production shift promotes great power stability. This study's finding that great powers can no longer effectively go it alone in defense-related production points in the same direction. While the consequences of a change in the benefits of conquest for great power stability has received extensive scholarly treatment, the potential significance of a shift in the ability of states to pursue an autarkic defense production strategy has not yet been examined. There is good reason for this, since until very recently great powers retained the ability to be self-sufficient in defense production.

To put it simply for now, this book's finding that an autarkic defense production strategy has been fundamentally undermined augurs well for peaceful security relations among the great powers for two basic reasons.[36] First, consider what would happen if a great power were to go it alone in defense production in the current environment. Any state that pursues this course will not have leading-edge military equipment and will thus be in a weaker position to pursue revisionist aims. Modern history makes clear the significance of this development: the three main revisionist great powers from the past 75 years (imperial Japan and Nazi Germany in World War II, and the Soviet Union during the Cold War) were largely closed off from the international economy at the time they challenged the status quo.

Second, the finding that states can no longer effectively produce leading-edge military technologies on their own means that any great power that makes a fundamental challenge to the territorial status quo will be easier to subdue; this is the case irrespective of which defense production strategy is pursued. The great powers that have made fundamental challenges to the status quo over the past century all acted largely on their own and provoked a counterbalancing coalition that imposed a supply cutoff upon them. The problem is that these supply cutoffs were far from effective in reducing the ability of the revisionist great power to develop and produce competitive military weaponry.[37] The world of today is much less threatening in this regard: the globalization of production greatly magnifies the degree to which a supply cutoff like those imposed in World War II would degrade the military capacity of a revisionist great power that acts alone.

The marked reduction in the benefits of conquest among the most advanced countries and the change in the parameters of weapons development caused by the globalization of production are both stabilizing for security relations among the great powers on their own. Of key importance, however, is that these changes overlap and reinforce each other: as chapter 7 shows, these two shifts in combination make less acute the most dangerous threat in the system. Significantly, this is true regardless of what motivates great powers. No matter whether the ultimate goal is power, security, prestige, or wealth, the geographic dispersion of MNC production has structurally shifted the scales against any great power that tries to overturn the fundamental nature of the system through force. Given that the globalization of production is a major, historically novel shift in the international environment, we are fortunate that it has a stabilizing influence on great power relations.

Is the Globalization of Production Leading to Universal Peace?

The view that economic shifts can influence the political world is one of the most enduring notions within political science and the social sciences more generally. Although sometimes viewed as being exclusively associated with Marxist theory, it is an intellectual project of incredible diversity. Unfortunately, many analysts go so far as to advance economic determinist arguments.[38] A prominent example of this tendency with respect to international security is John Stuart Mill's argument in 1848: "It is commerce which is rapidly rendering war obsolete, by strengthening and multiplying the personal interests which are in natural opposition to it. . . . [Commerce is] the principal guarantee of the peace of the world."[39]

Mill's optimistic forecast that international commerce was rendering war obsolete, like many similar predictions that followed in its wake, proved to be greatly in error.[40] His understanding was not simply wrong at the time; it necessarily will always be wrong.[41] The simple reason is that international commerce is only one of the variables that influences the likelihood of war. This study is motivated by the need to better understand whether international commerce now has a positive or negative influence on security relations; in pursuing this goal, I recognize that it does not serve as a master variable.

Although the globalization of production does not provide any guarantee of peace among the great powers, it does act as a force for stability among them. This raises a key question: does this global production shift have beneficial repercussions for security throughout the world or only in certain regions? For many, the term *globalization* connotes a system or process that encompasses all countries and industries. As stressed above, the globalization of production is not, in fact, 'global' but instead remains bounded in important respects: it is an ongoing process, not an end point.[42] It is, consequently, vital to examine the nature of this production change in its current form rather than to speculate about some hypothetical future international economy that is perfectly globalized.[43] Once we do so, it becomes clear that there is no reason to expect that the geographic dispersion of MNC production will have a uniform effect on security relations throughout the world.

The unfortunate conclusion of this book is that while the geographic dispersion of MNC production is stabilizing among the great powers, it will not promote peace elsewhere in the world. Indeed, the analysis in the concluding section of the book shows that this global production shift is likely to have a net negative influence on security relations among developing countries. As will be seen, this is partly because developing countries have not yet participated in the globalization of production to nearly the same extent that the great powers have. Far from acting as a general force for improved security relations, as some prominent analysts aver is the case, the positive influence of the globalization of production. I conclude, will be geographically circumscribed for the foreseeable future.

Notes

1. Irwin 1996, 11.
2. See the discussion in Silberner 1946; and Doyle 1997. chap. 7.
3. Montesquieu 1989, 338.
4. Kant 1957, 32.
5. Hamilton 1961, 56, 57.
6. See Silberner 1946, chaps. 8 and 9.
7. Hobson 1902; and Lenin 1917.
8. See Way 1998, chap. 1.
9. On this point, see Rose 2003.
10. On this point, see, for example, Levy 1989, 261–62.
11. Rosecrance (1986) argues that commerce promotes stability, whereas Waltz (1979, esp. 138) advances the opposite position.
12. For useful reviews of this recent literature, see McMillan 1997; Barbieri and Schneider 1999; and Mansfield and Pollins 2001.
13. This is not to say that there is uniform agreement concerning how trade linkages influence security behavior. The prevailing view is that higher levels of trade interdependence lower the likelihood of conflict (on this point, see, for example, the discussion in Mansfield and Pollins 2001).
14. A partial list of these studies includes Oneal and Russett 1997, 1999; Russett and Oneal 2000; Oneal et al. 1996. For a full set of citations, see the bibliographies in Barbieri and Schneider 1999; McMillan 1997; and Mansfield and Pollins 2001.
15. Kobrin 1995, 26.

16. A multinational corporation is a firm that owns, coordinates, or controls value-adding activities in more than one country.

17. See, for example, Dunning 1992, 128–32. The "geographic dispersion of MNC production" is a more accurate, but also more cumbersome, short-hand descriptor that I will also sometimes use.

18. See Staley 1935.

19. See, for example, Rosecrance 1999.

20. For useful discussions of the limitations of data on the International production activities of MNCs, see OECD: Economic Outlook 71, 2002, 159.

21. Much of this literature is discussed in Moran 1990.

22. Bitzinger 1994, 172.

23. See, for example, Moran 1990; Bitzinger 1994.

24. See Liberman 1996.

25. See, for example, Wendt 1994; Deutsch et al. 1957; Nye 1971; and Russett and Oneal 2000. chap. 5.

26. See, for example, Grieco, Powell, and Snidal 1993.

27. Mearsheimer 2001; Rosecrance 1999; and Stam and Smith 2001 are recent examples.

28. The most significant recent empirical analysis emphasizing this point is Bennett and Stam 2003.

29. For this argument, see, for example, Buzan 1984. On the long peace, see Gaddis 1987.

30. See Mearsheimer 2001; Kupchan 2002; Waltz 2000; and Huntington 1993.

31. See Mearsheimer 2001, 371. This is the same line of argument advanced in Waltz 2000; and Kupchan 2002, esp. 103. Huntington goes one step further, arguing that commerce is now destabilizing among the great powers; see Huntington 1993, 25–27.

32. Of the four strategies Mearsheimer identifies for states to enhance their power, it is conquest that plays by far the most significant role in his account and in the historical record: see Mearsheimer 2001, esp. 147–55.

33. Mearsheimer 2001, esp. 148–50.

34. See Liberman 1996, chap. 3.

35. Three of the strongest recent statements in this regard are Van Evera 1999, chap. 5; Stam and Smith 2001; and Rosecrance 1999, esp. 17, 81.

36. A more detailed version of this argument is presented in chapter 7 of the book.

37. For a useful overview, see Mearsheimer 2001, 90–96.

38. Here, economic determinism is taken to mean that "the tendencies, forces, and outcomes of economic processes exert an independent, determining influence on other aspects of social development, such as political organization and cultural beliefs" (Bimber 1994, 91).

39. Mill 1920, 582.

40. The most famous of these forecasts was advanced by Norman Angell; Angell 1910.

41. See the discussion in Keohane and Nye 1998, 81.

42. On this point, see Dicken 1998, 5.

43. Some globalization proponents are more extreme in this respect; see, for example, Reich 1991; and Ohmae 1995.

References

Angell, Norman. 1910. *The Great Illusion: A Study of the Relationship of Military Power in Nations to Their Economic and Social Advantage.* London: William Henemann.

Barbieri, Katherine, and Gerald Snyder. 1999. Globalization and Peace: Assessing New Directions in the Study of Trade and Conflict. *Journal of Peace Research* 36.

Bennett, D. Scott, and Allan Stam. 2003. *The Behavioral Origins of War.* Ann Arbor: University of Michigan Press.

Bimber, Bruce. 1994. Three Faces of Technological Determinism. In *Does Technology Drive History?* edited by M. Smith and L. Marx. Cambridge: MIT Press.

Bitzinger, Richard A. 1994. The Globalization of the Arms Industry: The Next Proliferation Challenge. *International Security* 19 (2).

Buzan, Barry. 1984. Economic Structure and International Security: The Limits of the Liberal Case. *International Organization, 38.*

Deutsch, Karl., et.al. 1957. *Political Community and the North Atlantic Area.* Princeton: Princeton University Press.

Dicken, Peter. 1998. *Global Shift: Transforming the World Economy.* 3rd ed. New York: Guilford Press.

Doyle, Michael W. 1997. *Ways of War and Peace: Realism, Liberalism, and Socialism.* New York: Norton.

Dunning, John. 1992. *Multinational Enterprises and the Global Economy.* Reading, Mass.: Addison Wesley.

Gaddis, John. 1987. *The Long Peace: Inquiries Into the History of the Cold War.* New York: Oxford University Press.

Grieco, Joseph, Robert Powell, and Duncan Snidal. 1993. The Relative Gains Problem for International Cooperation. *American Political Science Review* 87.

Hamilton, Alexander (Publius). 1961. The Federalist No. 6 in *The Federalist Papers.*

Hobson, John. 1965. *Imperialism: A Study.* Ann Arbor: University of Michigan Press.

Huntington, Samuel. 1993. The Clash of Civilizations? *Foreign Affairs* 72 (3).

Irwin, Douglas. 1996. *Against the Tide: An Intellectual History of Free Trade.* Princeton: Princeton University Press.

Kant, Immanuel. 1957. *Perpetual Peace.* Translated by Lewis White Beck. New York: Bobbs-Merrill.

Keohane, Robert O., and Joseph S. Nye Jr. 1998. Power and Interdependence in the Information Age *Foreign Affairs* 77 (5).

Kobrin, Stephen. 1995. Regional Integration in a Globally Networked Economy. *Transnational Corporations* 4 (2).

Kupchan, Charles. 2002. *The End of the American Era: U.S. Foreign Policy and the Geopolitics of the Twenty-first Century.* New York: Knopf.

Lenin, Vladimir. 1917. *Imperialism: The Highest Stage of Capitalism.* New York: International Publishers.

Levy, Jack S. 1989. The Causes of War: A Review of Theories and Evidence. In *Behavior, Society, and Nuclear War,* edited by P. Tetlock et al. New York: Oxford University Press.

Liberman, Peter. 1996. *Does Conquest Pay? The Exploitation of Occupied Industrial Societies.* Princeton: Princeton University Press.

Mansfield, Edward, and Brian Pollins. 2001. The Study of Interdependence and Conflict: Recent Advances. Open Questions, and Directions for Future Research. *Journal of Conflict Resolution* 45 (6).

McMillan Susan M. 1997. Interdependence and Conflict. *Mershon International Studies* 41.

Mearsheimer, John J. 2001. *The Tragedy of Great Power Politics.* New York: Norton.

Mill, John Stuart. 1920. *Principles of Political Economy.* London: Longman, Green.

Montesquieu, Charles de Secondat. 1989. *The Spirit of the Laws.* Cambridge: Cambridge University Press.

Moran, Theodore H. 1990. The Globalization of America's Defense Industries. *International Security* 15 (1).

Nye, Joseph S., Jr. 1971. *Peace in Parts: Integration and Conflict in Regional Organization.* Boston: Little Brown.

Ohmae, Kenichi. 1995. *The End of the Nation State: The Rise of the Regional Economies.* New York: Free Press.

Oneal, John, France Oneal, Zeev Maoz, and Bruce M. Russett. 1996. The Liberal Peace: Interdependence, Democracy, and International Conflict, 1950–85. *Journal of Peace Research* 33 (1).

———. 1999. Assessing the Liberal Peace with Alternative Specifications: Trade Still Reduces Conflict. *Journal of Peace Research* 36 (4).

Reich, Robert. 1991. *The Work of Nations.* New York: Alfred A. Knopf.

Rose, Gideon. 2003. Imperialism: The Highest Stage of Capitalism. *National Interest,* spring.

Rosecrance, Richard. 1986. *The Rise of the Trading State.* New York: Basic Books.

———. 1996. The Rise of the Virtual State. *Foreign Affairs* 75 (4).

———. 1999. *The Rise of the Virtual State: Wealth and Power in the Coming Century.* New York: Basic Books.

Russett, Bruce M., and John R. Oneal. 2000. *Triangulating Peace: Democracy, Interdependence, and International Organizations.* New York: Norton.

Silberner, Edmund. 1946. *The Problem of War in Nineteenth Century Economic Thought.* Princeton: Princeton University Press.

Staley, Eugene. 1935. War and Private Investor. Garden City, New York: Doubleday, 1935.

Stam, Allan C., and Alastair Smith. 2001. Issues, Stakes, and the Nature of War. Paper presented to the Annual Meeting of the American Political Science Association, San Francisco.

Van Evera, Stephen. 1990–91. Primed for Peace: Europe after the Cold War. *International Security* 15.

Vernon, Raymond, and Ethan B. Kapstein. 1991. National Needs, Global Resources. *Daedalus* 120 (4).

Waltz, Kenneth N. 1979. *Theory of International Politics.* Reading, Mass.: Addison-Wesley.

———. 1993. The Emerging Structure of International Politics. *International Security* 18.

———. 2000. Globalization and American Power. *National Interest,* spring.

Way, Christopher. 1998. Manchester Revisited: A Theoretical and Empirical Evaluation of Commercial Liberalism. Ph.D. dissertation, Stanford University.

Wendt, Alexander. 1992. Anarchy Is What States Make of It: The Social Construction of Power Politics. *International Organization* 46.

———. 1994. Collective Identity Formation and the International State. *American Political Science Review* 88.

SUGGESTIONS FOR FURTHER READING

▪ On Transnationalism and Interdependence

Burton, John W. *World Society.* Cambridge, England: Cambridge University Press, 1972.

Guidry, John A, Michael D. Kennedy, and Mayer N. Zald, eds. *Globalizations and Social Movements: Culture, Power, and the Transnational Public Sphere.* Ann Arbor: University of Michigan Press, 2000.

Keck, Margaret E., and Kathryn Sikkink. *Activists beyond Borders: Advocacy Networks in International Politics.* Ithaca, NY: Cornell University Press, 1998.

Keohane, Robert O., and Joseph Nye, Jr. *Power and Interdependence: World Politics in Transition.* Boston: Little, Brown and Company, 1977.

Keohane, Robert O., and Joseph S. Nye, Jr., eds. *Transnational Relations and World Politics.* Cambridge, MA: Harvard University Press, 1972.

Khagram, Sanjeev, James A. Riker, and Kathryn Sikkink, eds., *Restructuring World Politics: Transnational Movements, Networks, and Norms.* Minneapolis: University of Minnesota Press, 2002.

Nye, Joseph S., and Robert O. Keohane. "Transnational Relations and World Politics: An Introduction" *International Organization* 25, 3(Summer 1971): 329–49.

Rosecrance, Richard. *The Rise of the Trading State: Commerce and Conquest in the Modern World.* New York: Basic Books, 1986.

———. *The Rise of the Virtual State: Wealth and Power in the Coming Century.* New York: Basic Books, 1999.

Smith, Jackie, Charles Chatfield, and Ron Pagnucco, eds. *Transnational Social Movements and Global Politics: Solidarity Beyond the State.* Syracuse: Syracuse University Press, 1997.

Tarrow, Sidney. *The New Transnational Activism.* Cambridge: Cambridge University Press, 2005.

On International Institutions and Organizations

Alvarez, José. "International Organizations: Then and Now." *The American Journal of International Law* 100, 2 (April 2006): 324–47.

Axelrod, Robert. "The Emergence of Cooperation among Egoists." *American Political Science Review* 75, 2 (June 1981): 306–18.

———. *The Evolution of Cooperation.* New York: Basic Books, 1984.

Barnett, Michael, and Raymond Duvall. *Power in Global Governance.* Cambridge: Cambridge University Press, 2005.

Botcheva, Liliana, and Lisa L. Martin. "Institutional Effects on State Behavior: Convergence and Divergence." *International Studies Quarterly* 45, 1 (March 2001): 1–26.

Campbell, John L., and Ove K. Pedersen, eds. *The Rise of Neoliberalism and Institutional Analysis.* Princeton: Princeton University Press, 2001.

Colas, Alejandro. "Neoliberalism, Globalization and International Relations." In *Neoliberalism: A Critical Reader,* ed. Saad-Filho, Alfredo and Deborah Johnston London. Ann Arbor, MI: Pluto Press, 2005.

Fearon, James. "Bargaining, Enforcement, and International Cooperation." *International Organization* 52, 2 (Spring 1998): 269–306.

Foot, Rosemary, S. Neil MacFarlane, and Michael Mastanduno, eds. *U.S. Hegemony and International Organizations: The United States and Multilateral Institutions.* Oxford: Oxford University Press, 2003.

Frieden, Jeffrey. "Actors and Preferences in International Relations." In *Strategic Choice and International Relations,* eds. David Lake and Robert Powell. Princeton, NJ: Princeton University Press, 1999.

Haas, Ernst. *Beyond the Nation-State.* Stanford, CA.: Stanford University Press, 1964.

———. *The Uniting of Europe: Political, Social, and Economic Forces, 1950–1957.* New ed. South Bend, IN: University of Notre Dame Press, 2004 [first published 1958]).

———. *When Knowledge Is Power: Three Modes of Change in International Organization.* Berkeley, CA: University of California Press, 1990.

Holsti, Kalevi. *Taming the Sovereigns: Institutional Change in International Politics.* Cambridge: Cambridge University Press, 2004.

Ikenberry, John, and Takashi Inoguchi. *The Uses of Institutions: The US, Japan, and Governance in East Asia.* New York: Palgrave Macmillan, 2007.

Katzenstein, Peter, Robert O. Keohane, and Stephen Krasner. "International Organization and the Study of World Politics." *International Organization* 52, 4 (Autumn 1998): 645–85.

Keohane, Robert. "Global Governance and Democratic Accountability." In *Taming Globalization: Frontiers of Governance,* eds. David Held and Mathias Koenig-Archibugi. London: Polity Press, 2003, 130–59.

———. "Governance in a Partly Globalized World." *American Political Science Review* 95, 1 (March 2001): 1–15.

———. "Institutional Theory in International Relations." In *Realism and Institutionalism in International Studies,* eds. Michael Brecher, and Frank Harvey. Ann Arbor: University of Michigan Press, 2002.

———. *International Institutions and State Power: Essays in International Relations Theory.* Westview, 1989.

————. "International Institutions: Two Approaches, *International Studies Quarterly* 32, 4 (December 1988): 379–96.

————. *Power and Governance in a Partially Globalized World*. London: Routledge, 2002.

Keohane, Robert, and Allen Buchanan. "The Legitimacy of Global Governance Institutions." *Ethics and International Affairs* 20, 4 (December 2006).

Keohane, Robert, Helga Haftendorn, and Celeste Wallander, eds. *Imperfect Unions: Security Institutions Across Time and Space*. Oxford: Oxford University Press, 1999.

Keohane, Robert, and Lisa L. Martin. "The Promise of Institutionalist Theory." *International Security* 20, 1 (Summer 1995): 39–51.

Koremenos, Barbara, Charles Lipson, and Duncan Snidal. "The Rational Design of International Institutions," *International Organization* 55, 4 (Autumn 2001): 761–99.

Liberman, Peter. *Democratic Commitments: Legislatures and International Cooperation*. Princeton: Princeton University Press, 2000.

————. "Interests, Power and Multilateralism." *International Organization* 46, 4 (Autumn 1992): 765–92.

————. *International Institutions in the New Global Economy*. Cheltenham, UK: Edward Elgar Publishing, 2005.

————. "Trading with the Enemy: Security and Relative Economic Gains." *International Security* 21, 1 (Summer 1996): 147–65.

Martin, Lisa. "The President and International Agreements: Treaties as Signaling Devices." *Presidential Studies Quarterly* 35, 3 (September 2005): 440–65.

Martin, Lisa, and Beth Simmons, eds. *International Institutions: An International Organization Reader*. Cambridge, MA.: MIT Press, 2001.

————. "Theories and Empirical Studies of International Institutions." *International Organization* 52, 4 (Autumn 1998): 729–57.

Martin, Lisa, and Robert Keohane. "Institutional Theory, Endogeneity, and Delegation." In *Progress in International Relations Theory: Appraising the Field,* eds. Colin Elman and Miriam Elman. Cambridge, MA: MIT Press, 2003, 71–107.

Matthews, John C. "Current Gains and Future Outcomes: When Cumulative Relative Gains Matter." *International Security* 21, 1 (Summer 1996): 112–46.

Milner, Helen, and B. Peter Rosendorff. "The Optimal Design of International Institutions: Why Escape Clauses Are Essential." In *The Rational Design of International Institutions,* eds. C. Lipson, B. Koremenos, and D. Snidal. New York: Cambridge University Press, 2004.

Mitrany, David. *A Working Peace System*. Chicago: Quadrangle Books, 1966.

Moravcsik, Andrew. "Taking Preferences Seriously: A Liberal Theory of International Relations." *International Organization* 51, 4 (Autumn 1997): 513–53.

————. *The Paradox of American Power: Why the World's Only Superpower Can't Go it Alone*. Oxford: Oxford University Press, 2003.

Nye, Jr., Joseph. *Soft Power: The Means to Success in World Politics*. New York: Public Affairs, 2004.

Oye, Kenneth. "Explaining Cooperation under Anarchy: Hypotheses and Strategies." In *Cooperation under Anarchy,* ed. Kenneth Oye. Princeton, NJ: Princeton University Press, 1986.

Powell, Robert. "Absolute and Relative Gains in International Relations Theory," *American Political Science Review* 85, 4 (December 1991): 1303–20.

Rochester, Martin. "Coordination Versus Prisoner's Dilemma: Implications for International Cooperation and Regimes." *American Political Science Review* 79, 4 (December 1985): 923–42.

————. "The Rise and Fall of International Organization as a Field of Study." *International Organization* 40, 4 (Autumn 1986): 773–813.

Ruggie, John. "Multilateralism: The Anatomy of an Institution." *International Organization* 46, 3 (Summer 1992): 561–98.

Simmons, Beth. "Capacity, Commitment, and Compliance: International Institutions and Territorial Disputes." *The Journal of Conflict Resolution* 46, 6. (December 2002): 829–56.

Snidal, Duncan. "The Game Theory of International Politics." In *Cooperation Under Anarchy,* ed. Kenneth Oye. Princeton, NJ: Princeton University Press, 1986.

Steffek, Jens. *Embedded Liberalism and Its Critics: Justifying Global Governance in the American Century*. New York: Palgrave Macmillan, 2006.

■ On International Regimes

Breitmeier, Helmut, Oran Young and Michael Zurn. *Analyzing International Environmental Regimes.* Cambridge, MA: The MIT Press, 2007.

Donnelly, Jack. "International Human Rights: A Regime Analysis." *International Organization,* 40, 3 (Summer 1986): 599–642.

———. "Why Collaborate?: Issue-Linkage and International Regimes." *World Politics* 32, 3 (April 1980): 357–405.

Haas, Ernst. "Words Can Hurt You; Or, Who Said What to Whom about Regimes." *International Organization* 36, 2 (Spring 1982): 207–43.

Haggard, Stephen, and Beth Simmons. "Theories of International Regimes." *International Organization* 41, 3 (Summer 1987): 491–517.

Hasenclever, Andreas, Peter Mayer, and Volker Rittberger. *Theories of International Regimes.* New York: Cambridge University Press, 1997.

Helm, Carsten, and Detlef Sprinz. "Measuring the Effectiveness of International Environmental Regimes." *The Journal of Conflict Resolution* 44, 5 (October 2000): 630–52.

Keohane, Robert. "The Demand for International Regimes." *International Organization,* 36, 2 (Spring 1982): 325–55.

Krasner, Stephen. *International Regimes.* Ithaca, NY: Cornell University Press, 1983.

———. "Regimes and the Limits of Realism: Regimes as Autonomous Variables." *International Organization* 36, 2 (Spring 1982): 497–510.

———. "Structural Causes and Regime Consequences: Regimes as Intervening Variables." *International Organization* 36, 2 (Spring 1982): 185–205.

Levy, Marc, Oran Young, and Michael Zürn. "The Study of International Regimes." *European Journal of International Relations* 1, 3(1995): 267–331.

Milner, Helen. "International Regimes and World Politics: Comments on the Articles by Smouts, de Senarclens and Jönsson," *International Social Science Journal* 45, 1 (November 1993): 491–97.

Milner, Helen, Edward Mansfield, and Peter Rosendorff. "Replication, Realism, and Robustness: Analyzing Political Regimes and International Trade." *American Political Science Review* 96, 1 (March 2002): 167–69.

Rittberger, Volker, and Peter Mayer, eds. *Regime Theory and International Relations.* New York: Oxford University Press, 1995.

Ruggie, John. "International Regimes, Transactions, and Change: Embedded Liberalism in the Postwar Economic Order." *International Organization* 36, 2 (Spring 1982): 379–415.

Snidal, Duncan. "Coordination Versus Prisoners' Dilemma: Implications for International Cooperation and Regimes." *The American Political Science Review* 79, 4 (December 1985): 923–42.

Stein, Arthur. "Coordination and Collaboration: Regimes in an Anarchic World." *International Organization* 36, 2 (Spring 1982): 299–324.

Stokke, Olav. "Regimes as Governance Systems." In *Global Governance—Drawing Insights from the Environmental Experience,* ed. Oran Young. Cambridge: The MIT Press, 1997.

Strange, Susan. "Cave! Hic Dragones: A Critique of Regime Analysis." *International Organization* 36, 2 (Spring 1982): 479–96.

Young, Oran. "Regime Dynamics: The Rise and Fall of International Regimes." *International Organization* 36, 2 (Spring 1982): 277–97.

■ On Economic Interdependence

Barbieri, Katherine, and Gerald Snyder. "Sleeping with the Enemy: The Impact of War on Trade." *Journal of Peace Research* 36 (1999).

Brooks, Stephen. *Producing Security: Multinational Corporations, Globalization, and the Changing Calculus of Conflict.* Princeton: Princeton University Press, 2005.

Mansfield, Edward, and Brian Pollins. "The Study of Interdependence and Conflict: Recent Advances, Open Questions, and Directions for Future Research." *Journal of Conflict Resolution* 45, 6 (2001).

McMillan, Susan. "Interdependence and Conflict." *Mershon International Studies* 41 (1997).

Oneal, John, and Bruce M. Russett. "Assessing the Liberal Peace with Alternative Specifications: Trade Still Reduced Conflict." *Journal of Peace Research* 36, 4 (1999).

————. "The Classical Liberals Were Right: Democracy, Interdependence, and Conflict, 1950–1985." *International Studies Quarterly* 41 (1997).

Rosecrance, Richard. *The Rise of the Trading State: Commerce and Conquest in the Modern World.* New York: Basic Books, 1986.

Symposium on "Producing Security" *Security Studies* 16, 4 (October–December 2007): 583–649.

On Democratic Peace Theory

Axelrod, Robert. "Promoting Democracy through International Organizations." In *Reforming the United Nations for Peace and Security,* ed. Ernesto Zedillo. New Haven: Yale Center for the Study of Globalization, 2005, 19–38.

Cederman, Lars-Erik. "Back to Kant: Reinterpreting the Democratic Peace as a Macrohistorical Learning Process," *American Political Science Review* 95, 1 (2001): 15–31.

Cederman, Lars-Erik, and Rao Mohan. "Exploring the Dynamics of the Democratic Peace." *The Journal of Conflict Resolution* 45, 6 (Dec. 2001): 818–33.

Chan, Steve. "In Search of Democratic Peace: Problems and Promises." *Mershon International Studies Review* 40, 1 (May 1997): 59–91.

Chernoff, Fred. "The Study of Democratic Peace and Progress in International Relations." *International Studies Review* 6, 1 (Spring 2004): 49–78.

Diamond, Larry. "Kant, Liberal Legacies, and Foreign Affairs." *Philosophy and Public Affairs* 12, 3 (Summer 1983): 205–35.

————. *The Spirit of Democracy: The Struggle to Build Free Societies Throughout the World.* New York: Times Books-Henry Holt, 2008.

Doyle, Michael. "Liberalism and World Politics." *American Political Science Review* 80, 4 (December 1986): 1151–69.

————. *Ways of War and Peace.* New York: W.W. Norton, 1997.

Farnham, Barbara. "The Theory of Democratic Peace and Threat Perception." *International Studies Quarterly* 47, 3 (September 2003): 395–415.

Gartzke, Erik. "Preferences and the Democratic Peace." *International Studies Quarterly* 44, 2 (June 2000): 191–212.

————. "The Capitalist Peace." *American Journal of Political Science* 51, 1 (January 2007): 166–91.

Hasenclever, Andreas, and Brigitte Weiffen. "International Institutions Are the Key: A New Perspective on the Democratic Peace." *Review of International Studies* 32 (2006): 563–85.

Hensel, Paul, Gary Goertz, and Paul Diehl. "The Democratic Peace and Rivalries." *The Journal of Politics* 62, 4 (November 2000): 1173–88.

Kadera, Kelly, Mark Crescenzi, and Megan Shannon. "Democratic Survival, Peace, and War in the International System." *American Journal of Political Science* 47, 2 (April 2003): 234–47.

Kegley, Charles and Margaret Hermann. "Military Intervention and the Democratic Peace," *International Interactions* 21, 1 (1995): 1–21.

Lake, David. "Powerful Pacifists: Democratic States and War." *American Political Science Review* 86, 1 (March 1992): 24–37.

Linklater, Andrew, ed. *International Relations: Critical Concepts in Political Science,* v. III, section 5. London: Routledge, 2000.

MacMillan, John. "Beyond the Separate Democratic Peace." *Journal of Peace Research* 40, 2 (March 2003): 233–43.

Mansfield, Edward, and Jon C. Pevehouse. "Democratization and International Organizations." *International Organization* 60, 1 (Winter 2006): 137.

———— and Brian Pollins. "The Study of Interdependence and Conflict: Recent Advances, Open Questions, and Directions for Future Research." *Journal of Conflict Resolution* 45, 6 (2001): 834–59.

———— and Jack Snyder. "Democratization and the Danger of War," *International Security* 20, 1 (Summer 1995): 5–38.

Moaz, Zeev. "The Controversy over the Democratic Peace." *International Security* 22, no. 1 (Summer 1997):162–198.

Moaz, Zeev, and Bruce Russett. "Normative and Structural Causes of Democratic Peace, 1946–1986." *American Political Science Review* 87, 3 (September 1993): 624–38.

Mousseau, Michael. "The Nexus of Market Society, Liberal Preferences, and Democratic Peace: Interdisciplinary Theory and Evidence." *International Studies Quarterly* 47, 4 (December 2003): 483–510.

Oneal, John, and Bruce Russett. "Clear and Clean: The Fixed Effects of the Liberal Peace." *International Organization* 55, 2 (Spring 2001): 469–85.

Owen, John. "How Liberalism Produces Democratic Peace." *International Security* 19, 2 (Fall 1994): 87–125.

Pevehouse, Jon. "Interdependence Theory and the Measurement of International Conflict." *The Journal of Politics* 66, 1 (February 2004): 247–66.

Rasler, Karen, and William Thompson. "Rivalries and the Democratic Peace in the Major Power Subsystem." *Journal of Peace Research* 38, 6 (November 2001): 659–83.

Rosato, Sebastian. "Democracies Are Less Warlike than Other Regimes." *European Journal of International Relations* 1 (December 1995): 457–79.

———. "The Flawed Logic of Democratic Peace Theory." *The American Political Science Review* 97, 4 (November 2003): 585–602.

Rummel, Rudolph. "Libertarianism and International Violence." *Journal of Conflict Resolution* 27 (1983): 27–71.

Russett, Bruce. "Bushwhacking the Democratic Peace." *International Studies Perspectives* 6, 4 (November 2005): 395–408.

———. "Can a Democratic Peace Be Built?" *International Interactions* 18, 3 (Spring 1993): 277–82.

———. *Grasping the Democratic Peace: Principles for a Post-Cold War World* Princeton: Princeton University Press, 1993.

Russett, Bruce, and John Oneal. *Triangulating Peace: Democracy, Interdependence, and International Organizations.* New York: W. W. Norton and Company, 2001.

Schultz, Kenneth. "Do Democratic Institutions Constrain or Inform? Contrasting Two Institutional Perspectives on Democracy and War." *International Organization* 53, 2 (Spring 1999): 233–66.

Schweller, Randall. "Domestic Structure and Preventive War: Are Democracies More Pacific?" *World Politics* 44, 2 (January 1992): 235–69.

Silverson, Randolph, and Juliann Emmons. "Birds of a Feather: Democratic Political Systems and Alliance Choices in the 20th Century." *Journal of Conflict Resolution* 35, 2 (June 1991): 285–306.

Starr, Harvey. "Democracy and Integration: Why Democracies Don't Fight Each Other." *Journal of Peace Research* 34, 2 (May 1997): 153–62.

Ward, Michael, and Kristian Gleditsch. "Democratizing for Peace." *The American Political Science Review* 92, 1 (March 1998): 51–61.

Weitsman, Patricia, and George Shambaugh. "International Systems, Domestic Structures, and Risk." *Journal of Peace Research* 39, 3 (May 2002): 289–312.

On Bureaucracies and Decision Making in Foreign Policy

Allison, Graham, and Philip Zelikow. *Essence of Decision: Explaining the Cuban Missile Crisis,* 2nd ed. New York: Longman, 1999.

Beasley, Ryan, Juliet Kaarbo, Jeffrey Lantis, and Michael Snarr, eds. *Foreign Policy in Comparative Perspective: Domestic and International Influences on State Behavior.* Washington, DC: Congressional Quarterly Press, 2001.

Bendor, Jonathan. "Rethinking Allison's Models." *American Political Science Review* 86, 2 (June 1992): 301–22.

Bueno de Mesquita, Bruce. "Domestic Politics and International Relations." *International Studies Quarterly* 46, 1 (March 2002): 1–9.

Byman, Daniel L., and Kenneth M. Pollack. "Let Us Now Praise Famous Men: Bringing the Statesman Back In." *International Security* 25, 4 (Spring 2001): 107–46.

Clapp, Priscilla, and Morton Halperin. *Bureaucratic Politics and Foreign Policy,* 2nd ed. Washington, DC: Brookings Institute Press, 2007.

Drezner, Daniel. "Ideas, Bureaucratic Politics, and the Crafting of Foreign Policy." *American Journal of Political Science* 44, 3 (October 2000): 733–49.

Gallhofer, Irmtraud N., and Willem E. Saris. *Collective Choice Processes: A Qualitative and Quantitative Analysis of Foreign Policy Decision-making.* New York: Praeger, 1997, 3–49, 149–196.

George, Alexander. *Bridging the Gap: Theory and Practice in Foreign Policy.* Washington, DC: United States Institute of Peace Press, 1993.

————. "The Operational Code: A Neglected Approach to the Study of Political Leaders and Decision-Making." *International Studies Quarterly* 13, 2 (June 1969): 190–222.

Foyle, Douglas. "Public Opinion and Foreign Policy: Elites Beliefs as a Mediating Variable." *International Studies Quarterly* 41, 1 (March 1997): 141–69.

Hermann, Margaret, and Charles Hermann. "Who Makes Foreign Policy Decisions and How: An Empirical Inquiry." *International Studies Quarterly* 33, 4 (December 1989): 361–87.

Herrick, Christopher, and Patricia McRae. *Issues in American Foreign Policy.* New York: Longman, 2002.

Hill, Christopher. *The Changing Politics of Foreign Policy.* New York: Palgrave Macmillan, 2003.

Holsti, Ole. *Crisis, Escalation, and War.* Montreal and London: McGill-Queen's University Press, 1972.

Holsti, Ole, and James Rosenau. "The Foreign Policy Beliefs of American Leaders: Some Further Thoughts on Theory and Method." *International Studies Quarterly* 30, 4 (December 1986): 375–409 and 473–84.

Hudson, Valerie. *Foreign Policy Analysis: Classic and Contemporary Theory.* Lanham, MD: Rowman and Littlefield, 2006.

Ikenberry, John. *American Foreign Policy: Theoretical Essays.* 4th ed. New York: Longman, 2004.

Janis, Irving. *Victims of Groupthink.* Boston: Houghton Mifflin, 1972.

Jervis, Robert. *Perception and Misperception in International Politics.* Princeton, NJ: Princeton University Press, 1976.

Jervis, Robert, Richard Ned Lebow, and Janice Stein. *Psychology and Deterrence.* Baltimore: Johns Hopkins University Press, 1985.

Johnson, Dominic D.P., *Overconfidence and War: The Havoc and Glory of Positive Illusions.* Cambridge, MA: Harvard University Press, 2004.

Johnson, Dominic D.P., and Dominic Tierney, *Failing to Win: Perceptions of Victory and Defeat in International Politics.* Cambridge, MA: Harvard University Press, 2006.

Lebow, Richard Ned. *Between Peace and War: The Nature of International Crisis.* Baltimore: Johns Hopkins University Press, 1981.

Levy, Jack S. "Misperception and the Causes of War." *World Politics* 36, 1 (October 1983): 76–99.

————. "Organization Routines and the Causes of War." *International Studies Quarterly* 30, 2 (June 1986): 193–222.

————. "Prospect Theory, Rational Choice, and International Relations." *International Studies Quarterly* 41, 1 (March 1997): 87–112.

Maoz, Zeev. "Framing the National Interest: The Manipulation of Foreign Policy Decisions in Group Settings." *World Politics* 43, 1 (Oct. 1990): 77–110.

————. *National Choices and International Processes.* Cambridge: Cambridge University Press, 1990.

Maoz, Zeev, and Ben D. Mor. *Bound by Struggle: The Strategic Evolution of Enduring International Rivalries.* Ann Arbor, MI: University of Michigan Press, 2002, 27–84, 256–88.

Milner, Helen. *Interests, Institutions and Information: Domestic Politics and International Relations.* Princeton, NJ: Princeton University Press, 1997.

Neustadt, Richard, and Ernest May. *Thinking in Time: The Uses of History for Decision-Makers.* New York: Free Press, 1986.

Putnam, Robert. "Diplomacy and Domestic Politics: The Logic of Two-Level Games." *International Organization* 42, 3 (Summer 1988): 427–60.

Raiffa, Howard. *Negotiation Analysis: The Science and Art of Collaborative Decision Making.* Cambridge, MA: Harvard University Press, 2002, 3–52.

Renshon, Stanley, and Deborah Larson. *Good Judgment in Foreign Policy.* Lanham, MD: Rowman and Littlefield, 2003.

Risse-Kappen, Thomas. "Public Opinion, Domestic Structure, and Foreign Policy in Liberal Democracies." *World Politics* 43, 4 (July 1991): 479–512.

Schaffer, Mark, and Scott Crichlow. "The Process-Outcome Connection in Foreign Policy Decision Making: A Quantitative Study Building on Groupthink." *International Studies Quarterly* 46, 1 (March 2002): 45–68.

Snyder, Jack. *Myths of Empire: Domestic Politics and International Ambition.* Ithaca, NY: Cornell University Press, 1991, Ch. 7.

Snyder, Richard, H.W. Bruck, and Burton Sapin. *Foreign Policy Decision-Making* (Revisited). New York: Palgrave Macmillan, 2002.

4

Economic Structuralism: Global Capitalism and Postcolonialism

MAJOR ACTORS AND ASSUMPTIONS

We have seen how many realists organize their work around the basic question: How can stability or order be maintained in an anarchic world? Many liberals or neoliberal institutionalists ask how peaceful change can be promoted in a world that is increasingly interdependent politically, militarily, socially, and economically. Economic structuralism concentrates on the broad question of why so many **Third World** states in Latin America, Africa, and Asia have been unable to develop. For some economic structuralists, this question is part of a larger effort to develop a theory of world capitalist development. Hence, for them, globalization is not a new phenomenon but can be traced back several centuries. Given this context, we include commentary here on a growing literature on **postcolonialism**—a term that captures not only the period since the formal end of colonialism following World War II, but one that also takes us back to the imperial and colonial experiences that have so many implications for the present day. We have avoided the label **Marxism** because there are both Marxists (and neo-Marxists) as well as non-Marxists who work within what we have chosen to call an economic-structuralist image. Indeed, some economic structuralists decidedly avoid Marxian modes of analysis.

Since the end of the Cold War, there have been decidedly fewer theoretical and empirical challenges levied against economic structuralist approaches to international relations theory. Indeed, they tended to be ignored in mainstream literature. This may be due in part to the demise of the Soviet Union and other Leninist regimes in Eastern Europe, which dampened scholarly interest in this mode of scholarly analysis, particularly in the United States. This is ironic, however, for one could argue that at least the capitalist world-system perspective was quite prescient, anticipating the continual unfolding of the logic of capitalism and its inexorable spread to virtually every nook and cranny around the globe. Hence we note that economic structuralism as an image of international relations or world politics—particularly the capitalist world-system approach—remains highly relevant. Particularly at times of global economic hardship, one witnesses a revival in interest in approaches we place under the economic structuralist umbrella.

As an intellectual image informing the development of theory, economic structuralism has always been independent of the rise and fall of particular regimes occurring within a capitalist mode of production. Indeed, from this perspective, the still-surviving self-professed communist regimes (China, North Korea, Vietnam, and Cuba) are best understood by their different adaptations to domination within a capitalist world-system. Finally, in recent years much of the scholarly literature and debate dealing with economic, political, and social crises in the developing world are cast in the wider net of postcolonialism theorizing. As we will see, while this literature accommodates economic structuralist approaches, it has had relatively little impact on the debates occurring within mainstream IR journals.

Economic structuralists are guided by four key assumptions. First, it is necessary to understand the global context within which states and other entities interact. Economic structuralists argue that to explain behavior at any and all **levels of analysis** (the individual; group, class, bureaucratic or institutional units; state and society as a whole; and between or among states or societies) one must first understand the overall **structure** of the global system within which such behavior takes place. As with structural or neorealists discussed in Chapter Two, most economic structuralists believe that the starting point of analysis should be the international or for them, the capitalist world-system. To a large extent, the behavior of individual actors is explained by a system that provides both opportunities and constraints. The essential difference between structural realists and economic structuralists, of course, is focus by the former on structure as the distribution of power among states, the latter on global economic structures—whether expressed as North vs. South, First vs. Third worlds, **core** vs. **periphery,** or capital-owning bourgeois vs. toiling (working or peasant) classes.

Second, economic structuralists stress the importance of historical analysis in comprehending the international system. It is this historical focus that postcolonial studies also bring to economic-structuralist understandings. Only by tracing the historical evolution of the system is it possible to understand its current structure. The key historical factor and defining characteristic of the system as a whole is **capitalism.** This particular economic system or mode of production works to the benefit of some individuals, states, and societies but at the expense of others. Even the few remaining socialist states must operate within a capitalist world economy that significantly constrains their options. Hence, for economic structuralists, the East-West division during the height of the Cold War was not nearly as important as the North-South divide and competition among such advanced capitalist states as Germany, Japan, and the United States.

Third, economic structuralists assume that particular mechanisms of domination exist that keep Third World states from developing, contributing to worldwide **uneven development.** To understand these mechanisms requires an examination of dependency relations between the "northern" industrialized, capital-rich states (principally those in Europe and North America, Japan, Australia and New Zealand) and their capital-poorer neighbors in the southern hemisphere (Africa, Latin America, Asia, and the Pacific island states). Although most capital-poor countries are located south of Europe, North America, and Japan, the North-South designation is more figurative than geographic since much of Asia lies in the northern hemisphere as do Central America, the Caribbean, and the northern part of South America—not to mention that Australia and New Zealand are in the southern hemisphere.

In economic-structuralist discourse, which we take up later in this chapter, the First World or northern, capital-rich countries are often referred to as constituting the core of global capitalism. The Third World or southern, capital-poor countries are set at the periphery of this capitalist world-system, a residual category reserved for those somewhere in between core and periphery—the semiperiphery. What is most important in economic-structural analyses, however, is the capital position that describes the level of economic development or productive capacity a country has achieved regardless of its geographic location.

For this reason some prefer still to refer to the capital-rich countries as **First World** and capital poor as Third World. The reference to "third" has its origins in French-socialist discourse in the early 1960s that saw the term *Third World* as capturing the aspirations for a better life where most people on Earth live, much as in French revolutionary history the term *third estate* referred broadly to the downtrodden popular classes—the masses of the people (the other two estates being the upper rungs of eighteenth-century French society—the nobility or aristocracy and clergy). Calling these poor countries "third" world, then, was not intended to be a put-down as if somehow they were third rate. To the contrary, that ultimately the people will triumph was the hopeful implication of this "Third World" label.

Whether core or periphery, North or South, First or Third Worlds as designations of the structural components of dominance mechanisms, economic structuralist theory also must take account of newly industrializing states like China, South Korea, and Vietnam that also have accumulated substantial capital, adding yet another category to the complexity of uneven development. Quite apart from its global position, China has a decidedly uneven development internally that combines both First and Third World dimensions in a dual economy. Some 20–25% of its 1.4 billion people are participants in (and to varying degrees beneficiaries of) economic development, the remaining 75–80% still living in essentially Third World circumstances in both the countryside and urban areas of China.

Changes in the global economy since the end of the Cold War have had their impact on economic-structuralist analyses, requiring adaptation of concepts and terms more readily used in a Cold War world. The demise of Soviet and other Leninist regimes and their command economies in eastern Europe at the end of the Cold War, coupled with the embrace of capitalist modes of economic development by regimes in China and Vietnam, have made the "Second World" designation as obsolete as "East vs. West"—both terms now artifacts of the past and thus rarely in discussions about the present-day world order. The term **Second World** (sometimes called **socialist** or **communist**) once captured a large number of countries—a category generally separate from those linked within the **dependency** mechanism in which the capital-poor, Third World countries and classes in the South are dominated by the capital-rich, First World countries and classes in the North.

Finally, and as should be apparent from the discussion thus far, economic structuralists assume that economic factors are absolutely critical in explaining the evolution and functioning of the international or capitalist world-system and the relegation of Third World states to a subordinate position. These factors have important impact on political, social, cultural, ethnic, and gender issues, which also are captured in the more recent postcolonialism literature.

The economic-structuralist approach does share some commonalities with the other three images, although differences clearly outweigh any similarities. As noted, both economic structuralists and structural realists (neorealists) place greater emphasis on the importance of the system level, or world as a whole, in affecting actors' behavior than do liberals and scholars in the English School. But they differ in terms of ontology as to how they characterize system-level components. Thus, economic structuralists tend to focus on economic structure (e.g., classes or blocs, core vs. periphery, North vs. South, etc.) within a capitalist mode of production, while for neorealists structure is to be found in the distribution of aggregate power among states (e.g., unipolar, bipolar, and multipolar labels for structure). Furthermore, economic structuralists are much more likely than realists to emphasize the intimate connection between the international or capitalist world-system and domestic politics. State and society are never viewed as being encapsulated by a metaphorical hard shell. Class structure, for example, transcends the boundaries of states and their component societies.

Economic structuralists and liberals share at least three commonalities that can be viewed as criticisms of the realist perspective. First, both stress an approach to international relations grounded in **political economy.** The distinction between high politics and low politics (the relative importance of political-military as compared to economic factors) is rejected—if not totally reversed for certain economic structuralists. For the economic structuralist, various manifestations of political and military power generally reflect the driving force of underlying economic factors. Politics depends on economics; it is not an autonomous realm.

Second, both economic structuralists and liberals are much more attuned to events, processes, institutions, and actors operating both within and between states; the impermeable billiard ball (the unitary, rational actor common in many realist understandings) is broken down into its component parts. Both approaches tend to range up and down the levels of analysis and focus on a greater variety of actors, but economic structuralists place a much greater emphasis on the context (i.e., the capitalist nature of the international system) within which these actors operate than do liberals. Agency matters less to economic structuralists who generally focus on factors external to particular actors than liberals are prone to do. There is decidedly more voluntarism in liberal understandings, more determinism in economic-structuralist theorizing.

Third, both the economic structuralists and those liberals who write in the **transnationalist** tradition emphasize socioeconomic or welfare issues. A number of liberals have a normative commitment to peaceful change. International relations do not have to be viewed and played as a **zero-sum game** with winners and losers, but can be seen as a **positive-sum game** in which the restructuring of interstate relations is achieved through bargaining and compromise, allowing all parties to gain. Although economic structuralists are also concerned with the welfare of less developed countries (LDCs), they are not so optimistic about the possibility of peaceful change. The hierarchical nature of world politics with South subordinated to North and the economic dictates of the capitalist world-system make it unlikely that the northern industrialized states will make any meaningful concessions to the Third World. Change, peaceful or revolutionary, is problematic until the capitalist world-system reaches a point of systemic crisis. In sum, there are indeed major differences between economic structuralists and liberals. There is also little in common between economic structuralism and the English School—the latter more of a middle path between realism on the one hand, liberalism and idealism on the other.

Although the economic structuralists are primarily concerned with the question of why the euphemistically termed "developing world" or "emerging economies" can't develop, answering such a query is difficult. How and why did capitalism develop in Europe? How did it expand outward to other continents? As an international phenomenon, how has capitalism changed over the centuries? What are the specific mechanisms of dependency that allow for the maintenance of exploitative relations? What are the relations between the elites of the wealthy, capital-rich *center* countries (the First World) and the elites of the poorer periphery? Is it possible for an LDC to break out of a dependent situation? Economic structuralist answers to such questions are addressed in the subsequent pages in this chapter.

INTELLECTUAL PRECURSORS AND INFLUENCES

■ Karl Marx

All economic structuralists have been influenced either directly or indirectly by the works of Karl Marx (1818–1883). This is certainly not to suggest that all economic structuralists are Marxists (any more than alleging that all Marxists accept without qualification the sum total of Marx's efforts). It is simply to acknowledge that they all owe an intellectual debt to him in terms of their methods of analysis and certain critical insights into the functioning, development, and expansion of the capitalist mode of production. Marx focused attention on unequal and exploitative relations and thus set an important backdrop or context for scholarship by economic structuralists, whether they be Marxist, neo-Marxist, or non-Marxist in orientation. To appreciate Marx as scholar, one does not have to ascribe to the views of Marx as revolutionary. Similarly, Marx could claim the title of the original critical theorist. Current work in this genre, however, sharply differs from Marx due to his essential neglect of gender, racial, and religious inequalities.

Karl Marx's work concerns humankind's historical growth process and movement toward final self-realization and fulfillment in a society he called *communist*. For Marx, history was not so much the story of the rise and fall of particular city-states, empires, and nation-states as it was the story of **class conflict** generated by the advance of technology from ancient times to present-day economic modernization. Preceded by a **feudal** system in the Middle Ages, a change in mode of production occurred over time—often accompanied by violence—with market capitalism reigning supreme in the nineteenth-century Europe in which Marx lived. Marx argued that capitalism—which involves market exchanges, labor as a commodity, and the **means of production** typically held in private hands—produced particular political, social, and cultural effects. Marx's discussion and analysis of capitalism, then, have influenced economic structuralists in at least three ways.

First, Marx was concerned with exploitation of the many by the few, in particular the patterns and mechanisms of exploitation in different modes of economic production. He no doubt recognized the historically progressive role played by capitalists (the **proletarian revolution** would not be possible until after the establishment of a capitalist system), but his personal sympathies were with the downtrodden who were alienated from the means of production.

Second, according to Marx, capitalism exhibited certain law-like qualities in terms of its development and expansion. He viewed capitalism as part of a world historical process unfolding dialectically, an economic system riddled with clashing contradictions or internal tensions that could be resolved only by a revolutionary transformation into a socialist mode of production. While recognizing the important role of human agency in moving history forward, he felt that historical economic and social realities were paramount in explaining outcomes. As he argued, "Men make their own history, but they do not make it just as they please; they do not make it under circumstances chosen by themselves, but under circumstances directly found, given, and transmitted from the past. The tradition of all dead generations weighs heavily like a nightmare on the brain of the living."[1]

Finally, Marx insisted that a society must be studied in its totality, not piecemeal. An analyst must be aware of how various parts of society were interrelated, including those aspects not so apparent to the casual observer. As Robert L. Heilbroner states: "The entire contribution of Marxism to social thought rests ultimately on its effort to penetrate the veil of appearances to discover the hidden essence of things, the web of relations that is the real ground of reality and not the surface manifestations that are its facade."[2]

This perspective has deeply influenced the economic structuralists, some of whom earlier in their careers had little use for history and were preoccupied almost exclusively with such **units of analysis** as states or individuals. As two leading economic structuralists have argued: "If there is one thing which distinguishes a world-system perspective from any other, it is its insistence that the unit of analysis is a *world*-system defined in terms of *economic* processes and links, and not any units defined in terms of juridical, political, cultural, geographical, or other criteria."[3] Although such units of analysis are not ignored by the economic structuralists, they take on connotations different from those of the realist, liberal, or English School theorist. The state, for example, is not viewed in terms of its being a sovereign entity preoccupied with security concerns. Rather, it derives its significance from the role it plays in actively aiding or hindering the capitalist accumulation process. Any one particular state is not viewed in isolation but in terms of how it fits into the overall global capitalist system.

In sum, Marx has influenced contemporary scholars working within the economic structuralist image by virtue of his emphasis on exploitation, discernible historical patterns of capitalist development and expansion, and the importance of understanding the "big picture" and then asking how individual parts fit into the whole.

Hobson and Imperialism

Marx saw capitalism as a worldwide mode of production. His observations on capitalism in the nineteenth century were applied subsequently in various theories of **imperialism.** Imperialism assumes an international, hierarchical division of labor between rich and poor regions of the world, but the relation is not one of mutually beneficial **comparative advantage.** Rather, it is one of exploitation.

Ironically, perhaps one of the most significant theories of imperialism was devised by a non-Marxist, the English economist John A. Hobson (1858–1940). Near the turn of the century, Hobson noted that capitalist societies were faced with three basic interrelated problems: overproduction, underconsumption by workers and other classes, and oversavings on the part of capitalists. As the capitalist owners of industry continued to exploit workers and pay the lowest possible wages, profits mounted and goods began to pile up. But who was to purchase the excess goods? Given the low wages, not the mass of the working class, because members of this class did not have sufficient purchasing power. The efficiency of the capitalist mode of production resulted, however, in the relentless production of more and more goods the society was unable to consume.

What could capitalists have done with excess goods and profits, and how could they have resolved the problem of underconsumption? Redistribute wealth? Highly unlikely. Because capitalist European and North American powers were experiencing overproduction and domestic underconsumption, investment opportunities in other developed countries remained limited.

The solution reached by capitalists was to invest in what are now known as Third World countries. The result was imperialism: "the endeavor of the great controllers of industry to broaden the channel for the flow of their surplus wealth by seeking foreign markets and foreign investments to take off the goods and capital they cannot sell or use at home." Hobson argued against "the supposed inevitability of imperial expansion." He stated that it is "not inherent in the nature of things that we should spend our natural resources on militarism, war, and risky, unscrupulous diplomacy, in order to find markets for our goods and surplus capital."[4] Hobson hence rejected the determinism so often found in the work of Marxist scholars who write on imperialism.

For Hobson, imperialism did not benefit the home country as a whole. Instead, selected groups such as industrialists, financiers, and the individuals who staffed the colonial empires profited. Furthermore, because the flag followed trade, large military expenditures were required to protect the imperialist system. The drive for capitalist profits by securing overseas territories led to competition and rivalry among European powers. Hence, imperialism was to Hobson a major cause of war, and Hobson suggested that capitalists might indeed profit from such conflicts.

Lenin

V. I. Lenin's (1870–1924) *Imperialism: The Highest Stage of Capitalism* is his most important theoretical work of interest to economic structuralists. Writing in the midst of World War I (1916), Lenin developed a theory that claimed to explain the necessity for capitalist exploitation of lesser developed countries and the causes of war among advanced capitalist states. He drew heavily upon the works of Hobson and the German Social Democrat, Rudolph Hilferding (1877–1941).

From Hobson, Lenin accepted the key argument that underconsumption and overproduction caused capitalists to scramble for foreign markets beyond Europe and to engage in colonialism. From Hilferding, Lenin took the notion that imperialist policies reflected the existence of monopoly and finance capital, or the highest stage of capitalism. In other words, capitalism had developed such that oligopolies and monopolies controlled the key sectors of the economy, squeezing out or taking over smaller firms and milking domestic markets dry. The result was a need to look elsewhere for investment opportunities. This logically entailed the creation of overseas markets. As markets expanded, they required more economic inputs such as raw materials, which encouraged the further spread of imperialism to secure such resources.

Marx had seen that rates of profits would decline because of overproduction and underconsumption and that greater misery for the working class would result because more and more people would be out of jobs or receive even less in wages. Proletarian, or working-class, consciousness would grow, leading ultimately to revolution in all capitalist countries. For Lenin, imperialism explained why Marx's prediction of proletarian revolution in Europe had failed to come about. Economic contradictions inherent in the capitalist mode of production still existed, but imperialism allowed capitalists a breathing space. Imperialism provided the European working class a taste or small portion of the spoils derived from the exploitation of overseas territories—new markets, cheap labor, and natural resources. By buying off the European working class in the short term through higher wages, imperialism delayed the inevitable revolution. But an important trade-off was involved. Domestic stability was achieved at the cost of wars among the capitalist powers that resulted from the continual struggle for overseas markets. Once the globe had been effectively divided up, further expansion could come about only at the expense of a capitalist rival.

For Lenin, imperialism was therefore driven by economic forces, and it was inevitable that such exploitation and eventual conflict would occur. Hence, he disagreed with Hobson and later theorists (e.g., Joseph Schumpeter) who argued that other factors such as primitive or irrational instincts or an enjoyment of struggle and conquest also played a role in explaining imperialist policies resulting in warfare. He also disagreed with writers who argued that imperialism was simply the chosen policy of capitalists and hence was subject to change. Lenin rejected this line of thinking. For him, imperialism was not a matter of choice but of inevitability. The capitalists could not save themselves any other way than to pursue imperialist policies. Imperialism was the direct result of the attainment of monopoly capital. The resulting competition among states, reflecting the domination of capitalist class interests and the differential growth rates of capitalist economies (i.e., uneven development), unavoidably led to world wars such as the one being experienced at the time of Lenin's writing.

Although Lenin's theory of imperialism has been subject to a great deal of both empirical and conceptual criticism over the years, Lenin was writing not just as a theorist, but also as a revolutionary whose writings were designed to mobilize support for a socialist revolution. He is a prime example of a writer blending theory and practice. In combination with his works on the importance of revolutionary leadership and organization, Lenin's *Imperialism* has had a great deal of influence since his time on revolutionaries throughout the Third World.

Strictly as a theorist, Lenin has particularly influenced the economic structuralist literature with his emphasis on the global nature of capitalism and its inherent exploitativeness that primarily benefits the **bourgeoisie** in advanced capitalist states at the expense of poorer countries. Although there is arguably a good deal of determinism in his theory of imperialism, his work as a revolutionary (like that of Marx) reflected considerable voluntarism in practice. Agency mattered to Lenin as apparent in his call for a "vanguard of the proletariat" led by a communist party to push history down its revolutionary path. This was an idea he developed not only in theory but in practice as well. The actions of revolutionaries were at the very least to serve as catalysts to the worldwide proletarian revolution whenever the objective conditions of working class exploitation were ripe or had reached their revolutionary stage.[5]

■ Luxemburg and Revolution vs. Reform

Not to be seduced by the appeal of peaceful, gradual change or reformism, Rosa Luxemburg (1870–1919) expressed deep commitment to revolution as the only effective means of transforming society. She wrote as a critic of Eduard Bernstein's late nineteenth-century German Social Democratic Party politics of **reformism.** She saw reformism as an abandonment of Marxist principles, however helpful such policies might appear to be for the workers in the short run. Luxemburg argued vociferously the necessity for revolution to effect "removal of obstacles that a privileged minority places in the path of social progress." By contrast, she believed that reformism involves compromise with the bourgeoisie, strengthening the hand of the capitalist class: "Only the hammer blow of revolution, that is to say, the conquest of political power by the proletariat," or working class, "can break down this wall" of opposition posed by capitalists to "socialist society." She also described the negative impact of imperialism on colonies.[6]

The issue of whether the kinds of changes anticipated by many economic structuralists can be achieved by reformist tactics or whether they can be achieved only through revolutionary violence remains a matter for dispute. Many economic structuralists are reform-minded, non-Marxists. Economic structuralists who claim to be Marxists are divided. There are reform-minded Marxists in the tradition of Eduard Bernstein who are opposed by those who see revolution as the only effective means to change the existing world order. Even the latter disagree: When will the revolution occur, or when should it occur? Does one wait until objective conditions are ripe, or does one take some affirmative action to move the process along? Are revolutions inevitable, or must they be made—the subjective component? How much is the result of voluntary action, and how much is determined by "historical inevitabilities"? The agency-structure, subjective-objective debate is clearly not new to economic structuralists. The one point on which these theorists tend to agree, however, is the desirability of change from the present unjust order.[7]

Antonio Gramsci

The Italian Marxist Antonio Gramsci (1891–1937) departed from more hard-line, Marxist-Leninist formulations and offered a volitional approach to both theory and practice. Written in prison during the fascist period in Italy under Mussolini, his Prison Notebooks are a rich source of his views. Gramsci's emphasis on political voluntarism—the subjective—clearly has roots in his study of Machiavelli, who understood the importance of practical action. A key concept in his work that influences some present-day economic structuralist scholarship is the historical and ideological *bloc,* which may well be a *bloc* or obstacle to social change, thus maintaining a pattern of dominance in society or even on a global scale.[8] We note that such blocs are social constructions that serve dominant class interests. The historic bloc (*blocco storico*) is an instrument of hegemony. To Gramsci, it is decisive, composed as it is of both structures and superstructures, the objective and the subjective, respectively.

Gramsci's influence is apparent in Robert Cox's work on social forces, relating as he does ideas to global economic and political structures with the goal of avoiding the limitations of state-centric IR theory. For Cox, realism and liberalism underestimate how economic production shapes state power and strategic interaction among states. For his part, Craig Murphy sees a Gramsci-style, North–South historical *bloc* composed of an "Atlantic" or "Trilateral" ruling class, some of the subordinate classes within advanced industrial states, and a rising governing class, or "organizational bourgeoisie" in dependent Third World states that maintain a collective position of dominance over those subordinate to them. To be sure, the bloc has many interrelated or interconnected, reinforcing faces—economic, political, and cultural—that facilitate maintenance of this dominance.[9]

DEPENDENCY THEORISTS

ECLA and UNCTAD Arguments

Some of the more provocative work in the economic-structuralist tradition was pioneered by Latin American scholars in the 1960s and 1970s. Representing various branches of the social sciences, they came to be known collectively as dependency theorists. Several of these writers were associated in the 1960s with the Economic Commission on Latin America (ECLA) and the United Nations Conference on Trade and Development (UNCTAD). They were concerned with the important problem of explaining why Latin America and other Third World regions were not developing as anticipated. North American social science models had predicted an economic takeoff for LDCs. What had gone wrong? What explained economic stagnation, **balance of payments** difficulties, and deteriorating **terms of trade?** Why wasn't the North American–Western European experience being repeated?

One response came from mainstream *modernization* writers. This modernization literature attempted to answer these questions by exploring the difficulties of LDCs in moving from "traditional" to "modern" societies. The tradition–modernity dichotomy has been used in one form or another by social scientists as a tool of analysis since the nineteenth century.

The ethos and organization of a traditional society, it is argued, are both a cause and an expression of underdevelopment. The cultural values of a traditional society are postulated to be a hindrance to modernization. The LDCs are wedded to their pasts, reflecting a lack of entrepreneurial spirit that was found in European society during the rise of capitalism in the sixteenth century.[10]

This view of development and underdevelopment as the outcomes of internal processes has been criticized on a number of grounds. Two important criticisms are, first, that the modernization writers assume that the tradition–modernity dichotomy is universally applicable. But is the Latin American experience really so similar to the European experience? Are there really no significant historical differences between the African and European (or American) experiences? Of course, there are and they are substantial. Second, the modernization literature usually neglects a state's or a society's external environment, particularly international political and economic factors. Instead, modernization writers have tended to focus internally or within particular states or societies, generally ignoring that state's or society's place in the world capitalist order. Is there any society, even in the European historical experience, that is immune to outside influences? Very unlikely, respond the dependency theorists, who place particular emphasis on Latin America's colonial heritage and an historical legacy of exploitation also experienced in Africa.

The focus of the ECLA and UNCTAD economists was initially quite narrow. They examined the unequal terms of trade between LDCs that exported raw materials and northern industrialized countries that exported finished manufactured goods. They questioned the supposed benefits of free trade. The ECLA at one point favored the diversification of exports, advising that LDCs produce goods instead of importing them. This policy did not result in the anticipated amount of success and in fact increased the influence of foreign multinational corporations brought in to facilitate domestic production.

Did all countries fail to experience economic growth? No, some economies did grow, but growth tended to occur in an LDC only when the developed countries had a need for a particular raw material or agricultural product. Because many LDCs are dependent on only a few of these commodities for their foreign exchange earnings, a drastic decline in the demand for one of them (perhaps caused by a recession in North America) would have a calamitous impact on an LDC's economy. Or, alternatively, a bumper crop in several LDCs heavily dependent on one particular export (such as coffee or sugar) would also cause prices to fall.

The volatility of prices for minerals and agricultural products and the generally downward tendency of those prices contrast sharply with more stable and gradually increasing prices for manufactured items produced by industrial countries. Thus, the terms of trade are thought to be stacked against those Third World states that export farm products or natural resources.

◼ Radical Critiques

Writers in ECLA and UNCTAD (e.g., Argentine economist Raúl Prebisch, 1901–1986), although critical of the more conservative views of development, nevertheless tended to restrict their analyses to economic dimensions and to cast their arguments in terms of nationalism and the need for state-guided capitalism.[11] Other writers, however, more boldly emphasized political and social factors within the context of a capitalist economic system that bind Latin America to North America. Development, it was argued, is not autonomous. If it occurs at all, it is reflexive—subject to the vagaries and ups and downs of the world's advanced economies.

Choices for Latin American countries are restricted or constrained not only as a result of the dictates of capitalism, but also due to supporting political, social, and cultural relations. The result is a structure of domination. This multifaceted web of dependency reinforces unequal exchange between the northern and southern parts of the hemisphere. Opportunities for LDCs are few and far between because LDCs are allocated a subordinate role in world capitalism.

That various states and societies produce those things of which they are relatively the most efficient producers or sell those items in which they have a comparative advantage is seen by dependency theorists as a "one-way advantage." Economic exploitation of LDCs by the industrialized states is not an accident or simply an additional means by which these states enrich themselves. Rather, economic exploitation is an integral part of the capitalist system and is required to keep it functioning.

The result is a condition of dependency, succinctly defined as a "situation in which a certain number of countries have their economy conditioned by the development and expansion of another . . . , placing the dependent countries in a backward position exploited by the dominant countries."[12] The modernization experience of a particular society should not be seen in isolation, "but as part of the development of an internationalist capitalist system, whose dynamic has a determining influence on the local processes." As a result, underdevelopment is not "a moment in the evolution of a society which has been economically, politically and culturally autonomous and isolated."[13] Instead, Latin American and other Third World countries are attempting to develop under historical conditions quite different from those of the northern industrialized states.

Some economic structuralists use Marxist terminology and Leninist insights to explain this situation of dependency. More important than relations between states are transnational class coalitions linking elites in industrially developed countries (the center or core) with their counterparts in the South (or periphery). This version of class analysis emphasizes how transnational ties within the global bourgeois or capitalist class work to the disadvantage of workers and peasants in the periphery. The multinational corporation (MNC) and international banks, therefore, are viewed from a much different perspective than that of the realist or liberal. To the liberal or English School scholar, MNCs and international banks appear merely as other, potentially benign, actors in world politics or global society. To the realist, they tend to be of secondary importance because of the emphasis on the state-as-actor. To the economic structuralist, however, they are central players in establishing and maintaining dependency relations. To economic structuralists of Marxist persuasion, MNCs and banks are agents *par excellence* of the international bourgeoisie. They represent two of the critical means by which Third World states are maintained in their subordinate position within the world-capitalist economy.

■ Domestic Forces

Dependency theorists dealt not only with external factors (such as foreign states, multinational corporations, international banks, multilateral lending institutions, foreign control of technology, and an international bourgeoisie). They also examined internal constraints on development (such as patterns of land tenure, social structures, class alliances, and the role of the state). These internal factors tend to reinforce instruments of foreign domination. It is argued, for example, that the inability to break out of a dependent situation is often strengthened by citizens of a Latin American country who accrue selfish benefits at the expense of the country as a whole. This so-called **comprador class,** or national bourgeoisie, aids in the exploitation of its own society.

Allied with foreign capitalists, this class and its self-serving policies encourage the expansion of social and economic inequality, which may take the form of an ever-widening rural–urban gap. Although limited development may occur in a few urban centers, the countryside stagnates and is viewed only as a provider of cheap labor and raw materials. These exploiters, therefore, have more in common with the elites of the center countries than they do with their fellow citizens of the periphery.

Such arguments are rather sweeping in scope. The importance of internal dimensions, however, will vary depending on the particular country under examination. Class coalitions, for example, will differ and may relate to external actors in a variety of ways. As two noted dependency theorists have stated:

> We conceive the relationship between external and internal forces as forming a complex whole whose structural links are not based on mere external forms of exploitation and coercion, but are rooted in coincidence of interests between local dominant classes and international ones.[14]

In some cases, this "coincidence of interests" might even involve portions of the working class.

As a result of the interplay of external and internal factors, the nature of the development or underdevelopment of a society will vary. Changes in the international economy will affect LDCs in different ways. Dependency theorists, therefore, do not claim that economic stagnation in LDCs is always and inevitably the norm. They argue, however, that development benefits some at the expense of others, increases social inequalities, and leads to greater foreign control over Third World economies.

The dependency literature had its academic moment in the sun. But the concept virtually disappeared in the literature by the 1990s. This was not only a function of empirical and theoretical criticism (discussed at the end of this chapter), but many governments in Latin America were pursuing free market economic policies with at least some degree of initial success. One prominent scholar, Fernando Henrique Cardoso, even became president of Brazil for eight years—setting aside his earlier sociological work on dependency and pursuing in office conservative fiscal policies he saw as central to the country's economic development. In the field as a whole, dependency insights and arguments were subsumed under the broader concept of the capitalist world-system literature and the even broader postcolonialism research programs.

THE CAPITALIST WORLD-SYSTEM

The dependency theorists pointed the way for scholars who write from what is known as the capitalist world-system perspective. This perspective is truly economic structuralist and differs from dependency in two ways.

First, advocates of the capitalist world-system perspective not only are concerned with the lack of Third World development, but also wish to understand the economic, political, and social development of regions throughout the *entire* world. Developed and underdeveloped states, winners and losers, are all examined in attempts to explain the global existence of uneven development.

Second, the goal is to understand the fate of various parts of the world at various times in history within the larger context of a developing world political economy. Latin America, for example, is not unique. Its experience is an integral part of the capitalist world-system. Third World underdevelopment and exploitation are central to maintaining the present structure of dominance in the capitalist world-system. The first priority, therefore, is to understand this global system in historical perspective. Only then can the fates of particular societies or regions of the globe be understood.

The writings of Immanuel Wallerstein represent the most ambitious of economic-structuralist work and have been the catalyst for an extensive amount of subsequent research. In attempting to understand the origins and dynamics of the modern world economy and the existence of worldwide uneven development, he and his followers aspire to no less than an historically based theory of global development, which he terms *world-system theory*.[15]

Wallerstein begins by analyzing the emergence of capitalism in Europe, tracing its development into a capitalist world-system that contains a *core,* a *periphery,* and a *semi-periphery*—a decidedly different understanding of globalization from that offered by liberals. The core areas historically have engaged in the most advanced economic activities: banking, manufacturing, technologically advanced agriculture, and ship building. The periphery has provided raw materials such as minerals and timber to fuel the core's economic expansion. Unskilled labor is repressed, and the peripheral countries are denied advanced technology in those areas that might make them more competitive with core states. The semi-periphery is involved in a mix of production activities, some associated with core areas and others with peripheral areas. The semi-periphery also serves a number of other functions such as being an outlet for investment when wages in core economies become too high. Over time, particular regions of the world may gravitate between core, peripheral, and semi-peripheral status.

Class structure varies in each zone depending on how the dominant class relates to the world economy. Contrary to the liberal economic notion of specialization based on comparative advantage, this division of labor requires increases in inequality between regions. States in the periphery are weak in that they are unable to control their fates, whereas states in the core are economically, politically, and militarily dominant. The basic function of the state is to ensure the continuation of the capitalist mode of production.

Wallerstein's explanatory goals are breathtaking in scope, and his debt to Marx and other economic structuralist intellectual precursors is evident. He deals with such topics as the cause of war among states and factors leading to the rise and fall of core powers. These issues are discussed in the context of the creation and expansion of capitalism as an historical world system. The focus is first and foremost on economic processes and how they in turn influence political and security considerations.

■ System

Wallerstein and other economic structuralists insist that in order to understand the development of global economic, political, and social processes, we must keep our eyes on the development of capitalism. Capitalism is a system-wide or global phenomenon. We should not concentrate on individual states and national economies and then extrapolate from their experiences. Instead, we should examine capitalism as an integrated, historically expanding system that transcends any particular political or geographic boundaries. By first understanding capitalism as a truly integrated world-system, we then can understand better the fate of particular countries. This emphasis on the system as the key to understanding may sound familiar. It should; some realists also claim that to develop a true theory of international relations, one must give precedence to the system as opposed to focusing on individual states. Do economic structuralists operating from the world-system perspective in fact share the realist view as to what constitutes the international system? There are some interesting parallels, particularly if one closely examines Wallerstein's work.

First, some realists acknowledge that Wallerstein is attempting to develop a systems-level theory, although he emphasizes economic factors over political variables.[16]

Second, Wallerstein explicitly recognizes the importance of **anarchy**, a concept of critical importance to many realist writers. Recall that anarchy simply refers to the absence of a superordinate or central political authority. Wallerstein notes that "the absence of a single political authority makes it impossible for anyone to legislate the general will of the world-system and hence to curtail the capitalist mode of production."[17] Anarchy, therefore, is defined in political terms for both Wallerstein and those realists who discuss the importance of the absence of any central authority in the world.

The implications of anarchy for the realist and economic structuralist are quite different, however, as evidenced by the latter part of the quotation: "to curtail the capitalist mode of production." For the realist, anarchy leads one to examine international political stability, war, and balance-of-power politics involving major states. For the economic structuralist, the economic ramifications of political anarchy are paramount. The political anarchy of the interstate system facilitates the development and expansion of world capitalism because no single state can control the *entire* world economy. The result is an economic division of labor involving a core, a periphery, and a semi-periphery that is the focal point of economic-structuralist analysis. Political anarchy becomes a backdrop for an extensive analysis of capitalist dynamics.

Finally, Wallerstein addresses the issue of the international distribution of capabilities or power. Once again, it would appear that Wallerstein has much in common with realists. The following quotation is illustrative:

> Of course, we shall find on closer inspection that there are periods where one state is relatively quite powerful and other periods where power is more diffuse and contested, permitting weaker states broader ranges of action. We can talk then of the relative tightness or looseness of the world-system as an important variable and seek to analyze why this dimension tends to be cyclical in nature, as it seems to have been for several hundred years.[18]

There is, however, a major difference in how realists and Wallerstein use this notion of a distribution of capabilities.

For Wallerstein, the very existence of a particular distribution of power or capabilities cannot be explained without reference to the underlying economic order. In other words, he would argue that realists spend a great deal of time talking about the balance of power but that they fail to appreciate that there are important economic processes at work that are critical in accounting for the particular distribution of capabilities or balance of power in the first place!

In sum, despite sharing a similar systems vocabulary, the use and relative importance of these concepts is quite different. For an economic structuralist such as Wallerstein, merely focusing on the distribution of capabilities among states is insufficient if one wishes to comprehend fully the nature of the world-system. The international system has always been composed of weak and strong political units. Differential power alone is not the defining characteristic of the system. Once again, what is critical for the Wallersteinian economic structuralist is the fact that the key aspect of the system is its capitalist nature, the existence of global class relations, and the various functions states and societies perform in the world economy. Capitalism has been the defining attribute of the international system since the sixteenth century. It is capitalism that helps to account for a core, a periphery, and a semi-periphery. It is capitalism that provides the critical environment in which states and classes operate by constraining, shaping, and channeling behavior. Some states and classes are rewarded. Others are doomed to play subordinate roles in a worldwide division of labor determined by the dictates of capitalism. So, although states and politics are certainly important to the economic structuralist, they must be analyzed in the context of the capitalist world-system. To Wallerstein and his followers, material structure clearly matters more than agency.

In a post–Cold War volume, Wallerstein puts the events of 1989 and since in historical perspective, taking a long, multicentury view of global capitalism. Liberalism—an ideology he identifies as associated with the capitalist world-system—has served as a "legitimating geoculture." On North–South relations, he depicts the North's wealth as largely "the result of a transfer of surplus value from the South." Vulnerability in a capitalist world economy comes from "ceaseless accumulation of capital" that approaches its limit "to the point where none of the mechanisms for restoring the normal functioning of the system can work effectively any longer." Grossly unequal distribution of material gains contributes to "multiple strains on the system" and undermines "state structures," notably "their ability to maintain order in a world of widespread civil warfare, both global and [at the] state level."[19]

■ Political, Economic, and Social Factors

As noted in earlier chapters, realists understand the importance of economic factors, but they focus on power, the balance of power, and political explanations of international relations. Liberals interested in transnationalism emphasize political, economic, and social factors, depending on the issue. The English School tends to subordinate economic factors to their concern with elaborating the concept of "international society." As noted, economic structuralists tend to stress economic factors as underlying or driving politics in a capitalist world economy or system.

These are generalizations, and as with all generalizations, they are subject to qualification. All economic structuralists emphasize economic factors in their conceptions of the world-system, but the degree of their emphasis varies. There even has been recent debate as to whether the capitalist mode of production has been overemphasized. At one extreme, there is Wallerstein, who is claimed by critics to have reduced the derivation and operation of the state system (or system of states) to economics. Other economic structuralists, although accepting the logic of the capitalist world-system approach, stress the interdependence of political and economic variables.

Christopher Chase-Dunn, for example, argues that "the capitalist mode of production exhibits a single logic in which both political-military power" and exploitative economic processes "play an integrated role." Patrick McGowan states that "distinctions between economic and political processes represent false dichotomies. . . . Accumulation, imperialism, and conflict can be considered part of a single dynamic whereby a hegemonic core state in an increasingly competitive world-system attempts to ensure its own stability, prosperity, and primacy."[20] Political processes, however, are still basically derivative of the world capitalist mode of production, or they are placed in the context of economic structures and processes. Chase-Dunn, for example, develops the argument that "both the attempts and the failures of imperium can be understood as responses to the pressures of uneven development in the world-economy. . . . The interstate system is dependent on the institutions and opportunities presented by the world market for its survival."[21]

Johan Galtung went one step further in his perspective on imperialism, which had a major impact on economic structuralists.[22] In examining the mechanisms of imperialism that cause and perpetuate the tremendous inequality within and among nations, Galtung parted company with Marx and Lenin in that for him, imperialism was not simply an economic relation arising out of capitalism. Imperialism is a structural relation of dominance defined in political, economic, military, cultural, and communications terms. These types of imperialism have to be seen in their totality. It is not enough for international relations scholars to be preoccupied with only political and military factors, or economists to restrict their focus to economic factors. The entire structure of dominance has to be comprehended.

Equally important, Galtung argued that one must look *inside* societies to understand the effects of interactions *among* them. Imperialism means, for example, that elites in center (or core) nations dominate and collaborate with elites in periphery nations to the disadvantage of the majority of people in the latter. This would be a political effect of imperialism. Economic effects would include the production of only a few commodities by a periphery state, trade being concentrated with a particular center state. Equal emphasis, however, is given to other forms of imperialism.

CHANGE AND GLOBALIZATION

Many international relations scholars are interested in understanding system change. A common distinction is between changes *of* the system and lesser changes *within* an existing system that retains its basic characteristics. For economic structuralists, changes within the world-system appear to fall into three categories. First, there are changes in the actors' positions within the capitalist world economy. As Wallerstein states: "There is constant and patterned movement between groups of economic actors as to who shall occupy various positions in the hierarchy of production, profit, and consumption."[23] The Dutch empire of the seventeenth century, for example, gave way to British domination, and eventually the United States rose to prominence in the twentieth century. Despite different core powers, however, the hierarchical nature of the system remains the same.

Second, some scholars identify phases or cycles of capitalist growth and contraction that affect all societies. A period of relative social stability and economic stagnation precedes twenty or thirty years of rapid economic growth. This is then followed by another two or three decades of economic decline, followed again by expansion. Overproduction, a key factor discussed by Hobson, is central to the interplay of economic, social, and political forces.[24]

Third, there is what has been termed a **structural transformation** of the system. This term refers to the historical and geographical expansion of the capitalist world-system, incorporating new areas of the globe and non-integrated sectors of the world economy.[25] Although the term *transformation* is used, these changes could still be viewed as changes within the system because the capitalist mode of production, although perhaps changing its character, is still capitalist. In sum, the economic structuralist view of the capitalist world-system is hardly static. The world-system is dynamic, reflecting a myriad of activities and changes.

But what about changes *of* the capitalist system? Is globalization a new transforming force, or is it the mere continuation of long-established capitalist trends? World-system theorists point to one major historical transformation occurrence: the movement from feudalism into capitalism in sixteenth-century Europe. For world-system theorists, therefore, they claim that they have been talking about globalization long before the word was even coined and became popularized. Indeed, the process of globalization goes back to the aforementioned sixteenth century and the rise of capitalism. Globalization is not just a twentieth and twenty-first century phenomenon.

What are the chances of going beyond capitalism? Economic structuralists are ambivalent on this point. Wallerstein may title one article "The Rise and Future Demise of the World Capitalist System," but he also refers to "The Limited Possibilities of Transformation within the Capitalist World Order." Similarly, in the early 1980s, a number of theorists discussed how Eastern European and socialist states might succumb to the powerful forces of the capitalist world-system. Their analysis proved accurate.[26] Other economic structuralists point to possible transformational processes that might make significant system change possible. Such non-Marxist scholars as Hayward Alker and Johan Galtung, for example, downplayed the notion of constraints that supposedly limit the evolution of alternative world orders. Alker saw change occurring through the dialectical clash of world forces and different visions of world futures. These contradictory world-order contenders (capitalist power balancing, socialism, collective self-reliance, and corporatist authoritarianism) make system transformation possible. For his part, Galtung saw the international system as open and subject to change. He even speculated on the decline not only of the nation-state, but also of multinational corporations and even any world government that may be constructed in the distant future.[27] Although neither used the term *globalization*, much of what they discussed would fall under the common contemporary conceptions of globalization.

What role does human volition play in system change? At one extreme, there are scholars who apparently see large-scale historical processes as relatively immune from the actions of human beings. A strong dose of determinism seems to be reflected in their work. They are challenged by critics who downplay constraints. Some of these critics call for revolutions to end capitalist exploitation. They argue that despite the "particularity" of Latin America or other Third World regions that is emphasized by dependency theorists, these areas remain consistent with the patterns of capitalist development discussed by Marx. The "subordinated classes," they claim, have been neglected by some economic structuralists in favor of a focus on exchange relations among societies. Such critics state that class contradictions and the intensification of class conflict still make possible the type of worker revolution discussed by Marx. Hence, these authors have taken the more voluntarist position in a long-standing Marxist debate on the potential for revolution in the Third World—that revolutionaries can help produce world-system change.[28] Do agents merely have to wait for objective conditions to be ripe, perhaps serving as catalysts when they are, or can they do something subjectively to effect these conditions? With the collapse of the Soviet Union and China's embrace of capitalism, however, less has been heard from these writers in recent years.

Some world-system theorists have taken an intermediate position. Powerful "structures of domination" are acknowledged, but so also is the permanent struggle among classes. As Cardoso stated of dependency theory: "Instead of accepting the existence of a determined course in history, there is a return to conceiving of it as an open-ended process. Thus, if structures delimit the range of oscillation, the actions of humans, as well as their imagination, revive and transfigure these structures and may even replace them with others that are not predetermined."

Similarly, Terence Hopkins and Immanuel Wallerstein have argued that the study of the capitalist world economy is the "theoretical side of the practical work of transforming the modern world-system into the socialist world-order that modern social change has made at once politically necessary and historically possible."[29] In this formulation, there is room for human political will to effect transformation. Thus, if one accepts economic structuralists at their word (and some critics do not), economic structuralist theory is not determinist. It allows for (and even requires) political action.

In recent years, a good deal of interesting work has been done under the heading of **neostructuralism.** In keeping with the economic structuralist emphasis, these authors are critical of the realist reliance on the unitary, rational, state-as-actor. While they recognize the importance of earlier dependency and world-system work, their influences also include Fernand Braudel, Karl Polanyi, and Antonio Gramsci. Neostructuralism is interested in understanding how global processes interact with other processes of state and social transformation occurring at many other levels of analysis of the world-system. The study of international relations, therefore, is not limited to foreign policy or patterns of distributions of capabilities, nor confined to reducing international relations to economic variables. Given the fact that the focus of analysis is on transformative processes, states as well as economic and social forces have to be taken into account. A web of relations and forces are intricately linked, transcending all levels of analysis. Nevertheless, neostructuralists are consistent with the economic structuralist tradition in that governments play a secondary role to socioeconomic structures and forces when it comes to explaining world politics.

POSTCOLONIALISM

There is a vast, diverse, and ever-expanding literature that falls under the heading of "postcolonialism" and effectively subsumes the approaches discussed above. As with realism and liberalism, there are divergences in terms of focus and assumptions, leading to lively debates. Nevertheless, to generalize, postcolonialism emphasizes an interdisciplinary perspective that encompasses economic, political, social, and cultural aspects of decolonization and highlights the importance of race, gender, and ethnicity in understanding anti-colonial struggles. Furthermore, a good deal of the work is interested in examining the impact of decolonization on both the metropolitan (usually Western) and colonized societies. Hence under the conceptual umbrella of postcolonialism, one finds not only Wallerstein's capitalist world-system, but also postmodern critiques and the focus on discourse as discussed in Chapter Seven. With this caution in mind concerning the breadth and diversity of the literature, what follows is an attempt to give the reader at least a flavor of the postcolonial perspective and its internal debates that encompass academic disciplines ranging from history, political science, and economics to sociology, cultural anthropology, and linguistics.

For their part, Third World countries at the Bandung Conference in Indonesia in 1958 established the non-aligned movement. This was followed a decade later in 1966 by the Tricontinental Conference in Havana that identified the movement as spanning Latin America, Africa, and Asia. These activities provided a foundation for the call for a new international economic order (NIEO) in the 1970s and later a "postcolonial politics" or "grass roots movement to fight a system of injustice and gross material inequality that is sustained by powerful local interests and international power structures of banks, businesses and investment funds."[30]

One ongoing debate within the literature involves the basic question of definition of key concepts. This is true of all the theories and images we examine in this book. Such concepts as **imperialism, colonialism,** and certainly **postcolonialism** are hotly contested and reflect differing theoretical positions and political values. Can there be, for example, only "formal" imperialism, meaning a country forfeits its sovereignty and is incorporated into an empire? Or can there be "informal" imperialism? If so, is that the same as "neo-colonialism"? What about cases where an indigenous elite work with the foreign imperial power to exploit their own people? Would this be an example of "internal colonialism"? Can one speak of a postcolonial "hegemonic" power?

This latter issue brings in the matter of how to characterize the United States. Can and should the United States be viewed as an imperial power? The answer depends on how a particular author defines imperialism and associated terms. Conventional historians have tended to reinforce the narrative that the United States is not an imperial power due to its own historical struggle for independence from British colonialism and the supposed resultant anti-imperialist culture. Only in the late nineteenth century as in the Spanish-American War (1898) would we find a brief imperial turn in American policy, albeit one that would continue in the early twentieth century.

Not surprisingly many postcolonialist writers view this story merely as myth, part of the "American exceptionalism" tale, augmented as well by President Woodrow Wilson's championing of "national self-determination" for oppressed peoples after World War I. If anything, American imperialism dates at least from the time of the Monroe Doctrine (1823) when hegemony was proclaimed over Latin America. The Vietnam war only reinforced this perspective in the minds of many postcolonial historians and theorists. Other postcolonial works take a different view, simply assigning the United States as an imperial power as part of the West in general. U.S. continental expansion and the dealings with indigenous native Americans are often considered a separate phenomenon that may not be captured by concepts such as "colonialism" devised to explain the European experience in Africa, Asia, and the Middle East, but are still part of the imperial project engaged in by the United States in its own sphere.

While colonialism in terms of the physical occupation of a state is no longer the hallmark of the international system, empire and imperialism, postcolonialists argue, are alive and well. Hence, while the term *postcolonial* presumes going beyond the era of "colonialism," it is not clear what constitutes the temporal dividing line. In fact a number of postcolonial theorists question the utility of even trying to pinpoint the divide between the colonial and postcolonial eras, instead viewing the period from at least the fifteenth century to today as a seamless web of relations between the West and what has variously been termed the "non-West," Third World, developing world, or the South. In other words, while formal empires may have disintegrated, strategies were developed to retain Western power and influence before and during the decolonization process and are still in existence today in the postcolonial world. Earlier approaches designed to maintain power during direct colonial rule (exploiting ethnic and racial divisions among subject people, co-opting activists into colonial administrations, and extending judicious concessions in trade) have been supplemented by more subtle mechanisms of domination ranging from the use of the International Monetary Fund and World Bank to the manipulation of language designed to encourage "mental colonialism."[31]

Put another way, as it is by some, the postcolonial world still exhibits **neocolonial** forms of cultural, economic, and even political-military dominance over these former colonies. Independence has not really brought liberation when former colonies are still so linked to the metropole—the seat of power in the former colonial country. Thus, to understand politics in any African country, it remains important to identify the "former" colonial power, whether Britain, France, Belgium, the Netherlands, Spain or Portugal. Neocolonial patterns of dominance remain important in the postcolonial period. One can see this even in trade and other economic arrangements the European Union has with former colonies in Africa, the Caribbean, and the Pacific (the so-called ACP countries) that keep these states in relations that still work to the net advantage of the metropole.

An interesting aspect of the postcolonial literature concerns an increased focus on the recipients of colonial policies. Early work on imperialism and colonialism had a distinct Western focus. Great Britain, in particular, tended to be the favorite object of analysis. Much of the historical work emphasized the motives and mechanisms of British imperialism and colonialism and delved deeply into archival material. The French experience, particularly in Africa and southeast Asia, has also been a wellspring of academic study. It is not surprising that a large number of postcolonial theorists and historians are also from British and French universities. One of the major contributions they have made is to draw attention to the perspectives and experiences of those people who were on the receiving end of British, French, or other colonial and imperial policies. By giving voice to them (often in creative ways), scholars have highlighted what has been obscured in more mainstream work on colonialism: the attempts to resist military, political, economic and cultural repression and oppression. As one writer who acknowledges the voices and experiences of the downtrodden puts it: "Postcolonialism claims the right of all people on this earth to the same material and cultural well-being." It is the "politics of 'the subaltern,' that is, subordinated classes and peoples."[32]

As noted above, much of the post-World War II work on imperialism such as dependency theory was informed by the concepts and arguments of Marx, Lenin, and Hobson. Interest in the impact of capitalism on the Third World, however, was not limited to Marxists. Some authors pursued detailed case studies of colonial policies and relations between Great Britain and a single colonized people. Others took a more global approach, tracing capitalist development and its global expansion over the centuries. Wallerstein's work is a good example, and the emphasis on economic drivers continues to be a primary concern of many postcolonialist theorists.

Some theorists within the postcolonial perspective, however, have argued that capitalism should not be conflated with imperialism. Older, pre-capitalist empires have existed throughout recorded history, certainly well before the rise of capitalism as a mode of production. Whatever the era under investigation, the hallmark of all empires is the subjugation of a weaker people. This is true whether the empire was Roman, Ottoman, British, or French. Why privilege the capitalism-imperialism nexus as opposed to placing it under a broader perspective on imperialism?

But scholars who emphasize the critical role of capitalism in terms of the development of the modern world offer the rebuttal that while ancient empires came and went, those empires that emerged in conjunction with the rise of capitalism exhibited unique characteristics linked to particular intellectual, technological, and scientific innovations. These characteristics, often placed under the heading of "modernity," were most evident in what has been termed the New Imperialism that emerged in the nineteenth century and is associated with Western Europe and eventually the United States. Certainly, weapons technology and firepower were critical factors to explain the success of imperialist policies, but so, too, were intellectual and ideological claims ("white man's burden," social Darwinism) that accompanied, were used to justify, and perhaps even motivate imperial policies.

Aside from equating capitalist expansion with imperialism, a second point made is that a "Eurocentric" analytical perspective tends to restrict capitalism as an economic mode of production to Europe. Far from being some sort of European miracle, it has been argued that African-Asian market and capitalist practices existed prior to developments in Europe. India, China, and Japan were as advanced as Europe prior to the eighteenth century. As one postcolonialist scholar has written:

> [T]here is something puzzling about the excitement with which European historians hail the arrival of cities, trade, regular taxation, standing armies, legal codes, bureaucracies . . . and other common appurtenances of civilized societies as if they were unique and self-evident stepping stones to modernity: to the non-European they simply indicated that Europe had finally joined the club.[33]

Many cities in Asia in particular were larger than any eighteenth-century European city. There is agreement, however, that with the development of long-distance trading networks in the late fifteenth century and the beginning of overseas colonization, the advantage turned to Europe. This was not a function, it has been argued, of European superiority, but rather the coalescing of political, economic, environmental, cultural, and population changes that enabled capitalism and modernity to emerge. This facilitated, as it does today, the dominance of the global political economy.[34] The most advanced European empires such as France, Holland, and Great Britain were either the most economically advanced or most influenced by modernity as stimulated by the ideas of the Enlightenment. Spain stagnated in semi-feudalism and Russia declined to second-tier imperial status.[35]

A final point of contention within the postcolonial literature in recent years involves the concept of *globalization* and its relation to imperialism and the postcolonial era, however defined. For some, globalization is simply a new stage in Western imperialism and has deepened racial, class, and gender hierarchies and inequalities. There is total rejection of the idea that globalization could be of benefit to any peoples except those in dominant positions of power. Others argue that while there might be an increase in economic interdependence, politically the world is breaking into blocs characterized by different forms and mutations of capitalism. World-system theorists wonder what all the fuss is about. For them, globalization is not new but can be traced back to the origins of capitalism. This global world-system was essentially completed in the twentieth century, but has moved into a prolonged period of crisis that in time will bring the system to its end.

ECONOMIC STRUCTURALISTS AND THEIR CRITICS

The economic structuralist literature has been either subject to a great deal of criticism by specialists in international relations and comparative politics or simply ignored. In particular, the postcolonial literature is rarely even referenced in mainstream IR journals. Much of the criticism is harsh, particularly of dependency theorists and Immanuel Wallerstein's ambitious work. While some of this criticism undoubtedly reflects divergent ontological and epistemological issues as reflected in the positivist-postmodern divide, there is perhaps also an element of ideological preference. We first discuss some of the more telling critiques and then present rebuttals from economic structuralists.[36]

The Question of Causality

Some critics question whether dependency creates and sustains underdevelopment (as economic structuralists claim) or whether it is this lesser level of development that leads to a situation of dependency. In short, there is no agreement on causality—whether dependency is the *cause* of underdevelopment or whether it is the *effect* of this condition.

Reliance on Economics

Critics have argued that some economic structuralists have reduced the operation of the international system down to the process of capital accumulation and related dynamics. What of other, non-economic explanations of imperialism and relations among states? Are not political and strategic motives equally or even more important? For example, how can one account for nineteenth-century European states scrambling for economically low-value pieces of terrain such as present-day Chad or lifeless Pacific atolls? What was the economic motive? If the competitive interstate system is derived from the capitalist mode of production, how does one explain similar competitive behavior among political units in precapitalist eras before the fifteenth century? For example, recall Thucydides' discussion of the Peloponnesian War that lends support to the validity of such notions as anarchy and the security dilemma. This suggests the autonomy of the political realm and a distinctly political dynamic involving competition among sovereign units well before the emergence of a capitalist world-system.

      The economic variable, critics claim, cannot carry the very great explanatory weight assigned to it. Insights generated from the contemplation of international relations over the centuries should not be ignored. Structural realists, for example, would argue that if anything, it is the international political-security system that largely determines the international economic system, not the other way around.

System Dominance

Despite economic structuralist references to internal factors, it is fair to ask if there is an excessive reliance on international economic factors in explaining poverty and dependence in the periphery and that domestic variables at the societal level of analysis are downplayed. The cruder dependency work, it is argued, is too sweeping in its claims, blaming virtually every Third World political, economic, and social problem on the northern industrialized states. Lack of economic growth, social unrest, and repressive governments are all laid at the doorstep of the richer capitalist countries. Critics see structure as occupying too central a role, effectively marginalizing agency in what is essentially a system-dominant, if not system-determined theoretical enterprise.

Theoretical Rigidity

The criticism of economics and system dominance as bases for causality logically leads to the following: individual cases are examined solely in terms of general theoretical constructs such as the "capitalist world-system." A society's experiences are reduced to (or explained in terms of) one or two concepts. Major political, economic, and social changes all supposedly fall under the general explanatory logic of a term such as *dependency*. Furthermore, rather than modifying the theories or concepts in light of empirical evidence (often supposedly lacking) or questions raised by case studies, it is claimed that case studies are used by economic structuralists only when they appear to provide evidence to support the line of argument. There is no tension between theory and findings, little questioning of the framework, and an unwillingness to consider alternative hypotheses. Such criticisms, of course, are also often leveled at work associated with realists and liberals.

■ Accounting for Anomalies

Economic structuralists have trouble accounting for Third World countries that have been relatively successful economically despite their ups and downs: Taiwan, Venezuela, Brazil, Singapore, South Korea. In addition, there are the greatest success stories of any non-European, non-North American country: Japan and now China. What is it about these countries that has allowed them either to escape abject poverty or, at least in the case of China, make such amazing strides forward? Neither are examples of autonomous development. In fact, they seem to have benefited greatly from being enmeshed in the global capitalist system.

In response, it should be noted that no theory or approach can be expected to explain everything. The virtue of good theorizing is that it points out and accounts for commonalities, what particular cases have in common. Anomalies are expected and do not detract from the utility of the theory if it can be adequately explained why a unique case does not fit the general pattern.

Critics comment, however, that economic structuralists such as Wallerstein simply group all anomalies under the concept of the semi-periphery, a theoretically and empirically poorly defined concept. Furthermore, what of the insights of authors who argue that there are certain advantages to backwardness when a state is trying to catch up economically with more advanced states? What of the work by scholars who emphasize the importance of different types of state structures, political and social coalitions, and shifting alliances in accounting for the differential modernization success of various countries?[37] Such literature is ignored, it is argued, because the economic structuralist perspective refuses to give due consideration to domestic factors that are not the result of capitalist dynamics.

■ Defining Alternatives and Science as Ideology

It is argued that some economic structuralists have done a poor job in defining reasonable alternative world futures, let alone strategies, for LDCs to pursue. What is meant, for example, by the call for "autonomous development"? Is such as goal feasible? How is it to be achieved? Would redistributive policies of government be combined with political repression and the abuse of power?

Critics also charge that value preferences infuse economic structuralist work. Economic structuralists, however, are not apologetic for their normative commitment to fundamental changes in the relations between the North and the South. As one noted writer has stated, in analyses of dependency relations "there is no presumption of scientific neutrality." Such works are considered to be "more true because they assume that, by discerning which are the historical agents capable of propelling a process of transformation . . . , these analyses thus grasp the meaning of historical movement and help to negate a given order of domination."[38]

▪ Responses

Why has the economic structuralist literature—when it has not been totally ignored—received such a great deal of criticism? Is it simply because it is deserving of such critical scrutiny? Three comments are in order.

First, it is not surprising that most of the criticism comes from scholars working within mainstream North American social science. The vocabulary of the economic-structuralist literature is alien to many of these scholars. Analyses based on Marxian insights and categories are generally viewed with distrust in North American universities and often dismissed out of hand. And although some of the economic-structuralist work is characterized as being ideological, economic structuralists have similarly surmised that the attacks on them are based less on dispassionate critiques and more on the value preferences of the reviewer. Ideological biases are wrapped in the cloak of supposedly objective criticisms.

Second, it was pointed out that a number of critics charge that the dependency literature in particular has been insufficiently empirical, failing to marshal evidence based on the canons of positivist science. Where's the data, they ask? In fact, it is claimed that the empirical testing of selective hypotheses from the dependency literature indicates that these hypotheses simply do not hold up.[39]

Dependency theorists respond that such a charge is based on the assumption that the rationalist or positivist methods are the only means to comprehend reality. In point of fact, as noted in Chapter One, there are alternative epistemological premises or assumptions from which one can start that question the value of formal hypothesis testing with its often exclusive focus on what can be measured, counted, and added. As one theorist notes:

> The divergence is not merely methodological-formal. It is, rather, at the very heart of studies of dependency. If these studies do in fact have any power of attraction at all, it is not merely because they propose a methodology to substitute for a previously existing paradigm or because they open up a new set of themes. It is principally because they do this from a *radically critical* viewpoint.[40]

Even from the perspective of a positivist approach to knowledge, however, a hallmark of much of the world-system literature is its conspicuously empirical, cross-national focus. And while much of the broader postcolonial literature does not engage in statistical analysis, it does rely heavily on detailed case studies drawing on in-depth archival research.

To conclude, judging by the international relations textbooks currently on the market in the United States, it is apparent that the economic-structuralist perspective is not considered mainstream. Realist, liberal, and constructivist perspectives dominate the literature, but this certainly does not mean that the economic-structuralist image of international relations is unimportant or undeserving of attention. Its contribution to increased understanding of the world around us should not be seen only as a function of its degree of popularity at a particular point in time. By providing a very different, challenging, and provocative perspective on world politics, it still remains in our view worthy of attention. This is particularly true as it directly addresses the problems faced by the Third World.

After all, dominant scientific paradigms or research programs of one particular period have a tendency to decay. What is at one time considered to be heretical or at the fringes of "normal science" may one day itself become the prevailing orthodoxy.[41] At a minimum, the economic-structuralist perspective should encourage the student of international relations to analyze critically the realist, liberal, and English School rationalist images and the assumptions on which they are based. At the maximum, economic-structuralist writers have provided challenging hypotheses and insights concerning the dynamics and development of international relations and world politics that still constitute an important, if less prominent image.

Notes

1. Karl Marx, "The Eighteenth Brumaire of Louis Bonaparte" in *The Marx-Engels Reader*, ed. Robert C. Tucker (New York: Norton, 1972), 436.
2. Robert Heilbroner, *Marxism: For and Against* (New York: Norton, 1980), 49. See also Andrew Gamble, David Marsh, and Tony Tant, eds., *Marxism and Social Science* (Champaign, IL: University of Illinois Press, 1999).
3. Terence K. Hopkins, Immanuel Wallerstein, and Associates, "Patterns of Development of the Modern World-System," in *World-System Analysis: Theory and Methodology*, ed. Hopkins, Wallerstein, and associates (Beverly Hills, CA: Sage Publications, 1982), 72.
4. John A. Hobson, *Imperialism: A Study* (Ann Arbor: University of Michigan Press, 1965), 85–86.
5. For example, see Lenin's "What Is to Be Done?" in *The Lenin Anthology*, ed. Robert C. Tucker (New York: Norton, 1975), 12–114. Others who would later write in this tradition would argue that revolutionaries play more of a role than mere catalysts. They can actually create the conditions for revolution; the "subjective" can create the "objective." This is most explicit in the writings, for example, of Che Guevara, although one also finds shades of it in Mao Zedong's writings on guerrilla warfare.
6. Rosa Luxemburg, *Reform or Revolution* (New York: Pathfinder Press, 1970, 1973), 72, 29.
7. For important early discussions, see Leon Trotsky, *The Russian Revolution* (New York: Doubleday, 1959); N. I. Bukharin, *Imperialism and World Economy* (New York: International Publishers, 1929); and Eduard Bernstein, *Evolutionary Socialism* (New York: B. W. Huebsch, 1911).
8. See Quintin Hoare and Geoffrey Nowell Smith, eds. *Selections from the Prison Notebooks.* (New York: International Publishers, 1971), especially Part II, ch. 1 on the Modern Prince, Machiavelli, Marx, voluntarism, and Social Masses, 123–205. On Gramsci, see the three-volume set of his *Prison Notebooks*, trans. and ed. Joseph A. Buttigieg (New York: Columbia University Press, published serially in 1991, 1996 and 2007).
9. Robert W. Cox, "Social Forces, States, and World Orders" in *Neorealism and Its Critics,* (ed.) Robert O. Keohane (New York: Columbia University Press, 1986). See also Craig Murphy. "Freezing the North–South Bloc(k) After the East–West Thaw," *Socialist Review* 20, 3 (July–September 1990): 25–46.
10. The classic statement is found in Max Weber, *The Protestant Ethic and the Spirit of Capitalism* (New York: Scribner's, 1958).
11. Raúl Prebisch, *Towards a Dynamic Development Policy for Latin America* (New York: United Nations, 1963).
12. Theotonio dos Santos, "La crisis del desarrollo, las relaciones de dependencia en America Latina," in *La Dependencia politico-economica de America Latina*, ed. H. Jaguaribe et al. (Mexico, 1970), 180, as cited in J. Samuel Valenzuela and Arturo Valenzuela, "Modernization and Dependency: Alternative Perspectives in the Study of Latin American Underdevelopment," *Comparative Politics* 10, 4 (July 1978): 544.
13. Osvaldo Sunkel, "Big Business and Dependencia: A Latin American View," *Foreign Affairs* 50, 3 (1972): 519–20. Sunkel's more recent work can be found in several volumes co-edited by Hettne, Bjorn, Andras Inotai, and Osvaldo Sunkel to include *Globalism and the New Regionalism* (New York: Palgrave Macmillan, 2000).
14. Fernando Henrique Cardoso and Enzo Faletto, *Dependency and Development in Latin America* (Berkeley: University of California Press, 1979), xvi. See Cardoso's more recent *The Accidental President of Brazil: A Memoir* (New York: Public Affairs, 2007).
15. Immanuel Wallerstein, *The Modern World-System I: Capitalist Agriculture and the Origins of the European World-Economy in the Sixteenth Century* (New York: Academic Press, 1974); and *The*

Modern World-System II: Mercantilism and the Consolidation of the European World-Economy, 1600–1750 (New York: Academic Press, 1980).

16. Kenneth N. Waltz, *Theory of International Politics* (Reading, MA: Addison-Wesley, 1979), 38.

17. Immanuel Wallerstein, *The Capitalist World-Economy* (Cambridge, England: Cambridge University Press, 1979), 69.

18. *Ibid.*, 25.

19. Immanuel Wallerstein, *After Liberalism* (New York: New Press, 1995).

20. Christopher Chase-Dunn, "Interstate System and Capitalist World-Economy: One Logic or Two?" in *World System Structure: Continuity and Change*, ed. W. Ladd Hollist and James N. Rosenau (Beverly Hills, CA: Sage Publications, 1981), 31. Cf. the more recent Christopher Chase-Dunn and Salvatore J. Babones, eds. *Global Social Change: Historical and Comparative Perspectives.* (Baltimore MD: The Johns Hopkins University Press, 2006); Chase-Dunn and Tom Hall, *Rise and Demise: Comparing World Systems* (Boulder, CO: Westview Press, 1997). Patrick J. McGowan with Bohdan Kordan, "Imperialism in World-System Perspective: Britain 1870–1914," in *World System Structure*, ed. Hollist and Rosenau, 78.

21. Christopher Chase-Dunn, "Interstate System and Capitalist World-Economy," 50–51.

22. Johan Galtung, "A Structural Theory of Imperialism," *Journal of Peace Research* 2 (1971): 81–98.

23. Wallerstein, *Capitalist World-Economy*, 67.

24. Hopkins and Wallerstein, "Structural Transformations of the World-Economy," in *World-System Analysis*, 121–122. For a discussion of cycles, see also Wallerstein, *Modern World-System II*, Chapter 1.

25. *Ibid.*, 123.

26. Immanuel Wallerstein, "The Rise and Future Demise of the World Capitalist System," *Comparative Studies in Society and History* 16, 4 (September 1974): 387–415, and his "Dependence in an Interdependent World: The Limited Possibilities of Transformation Within the Capitalist World Economy," *African Studies Review* 18, 1 (April 1974): 1–26. Christopher Chase-Dunn, ed., *Socialist States in the World-System* (Beverly Hills, CA: Sage Publications, 1982).

27. Hayward R. Alker, Jr., "Dialectical Foundations of Global Disparities," in *World System Structure*, eds. Hollist and Rosenau, 80–109; Johan Galtung, "Global Processes and the World in the 1980s," in *World System Structure*, eds. Hollist and Rosenau, 110–138. Chase-Dunn (also in Hollist and Rosenau, 43) states that transformation might involve the dissolution of states, the elimination of economic exchanges between national territories, or the creation of a world state.

28. Augustin Cueva, "A Summary of Problems and Perspectives of Dependency Theory," *Latin American Perspectives* 3, 4 (Fall 1976): 12–16. On the need to build a revolutionary party, see Raul A. Fernandez and Jose F. Ocampo, "The Latin American Revolution: A Theory of Imperialism, Not Dependence," *Latin American Perspectives* 1 (Spring 1974): 30–61.

29. Fernando Henrique Cardoso, "The Consumption of Dependency Theory in the United States," *Latin American Research Review* 12, 3 (1977): 10–11; Hopkins and Wallerstein, *World-System Analysis*, 8.

30. Robert J.C. Young, *Postcolonialism: An Historical Introduction* (Oxford: Blackwell, 2001); 17 and 18. Cf. Barbara Bush, *Imperialism and Postcolonialism* (Harlow, England: Longman, 2006); Leela Gandhi, *Postcolonial Theory: A Critical Introduction* (Edinburgh: Edinburgh University Press, 1998).

31. Jurgen Osterhammel, *Colonialism* (Princeton and Kingston: Marcus Weiner/Ian Randle, 1997), 119.

32. Young, 2 and 6.

33. Patricia Crone, *Pre-Industrial Societies: Anatomy of the Pre-modern World* (Oxford: Blackwell, 1989), 148, as cited by Bush, *Imperialism and Postcolonialism*, 80.

34. Kenneth Pomerantz, *The Great Divergence: Europe, China and the Making of the Modern World Economy* (Princeton, NJ: Princeton University Press, 2000), 17–19.

35. Bush, *Imperialism and Postcolonialism*, 80.

36. See, for example, Robert A. Packenham, *The Dependency Movement: Scholarship in Development Studies* (Cambridge: Harvard University Press, 1992); Andreas Velasco, "The Dustbin of History: Dependency Theory," *Foreign Affairs* (November-December 2002): 44–45; Tony Smith, "The Underdevelopment of Development Literature: The Case of Dependency Theory," *World Politics*, 31, 2 (January 1979): 247–88; Daniel Garst, "Wallerstein and His Critics," *Theory and Society*, 14, 4 (July 1985): 469–95.

37. See, for example, Alexander Gerschenkron, *Economic Backwardness in Historical Perspective* (New York: Praeger, 1965); Barrington Moore, *Social Origins of Dictatorship and Democracy* (Boston: Beacon Press, 1966); Theda Skocpol, *States and Social Revolutions* (New York: Cambridge University Press, 1979).

38. Henrique Cardoso, "The Consumption of Dependency Theory," 16. See also the comments by James A. Caporaso, "Introduction," *International Organization* 32, no. 1 (Winter 1978): 2–3. A special issue on dependence and dependency. Cf. Cardoso, Fernando and Enzo Faletto. *Dependency and Development in Latin America* (Berkeley, CA: University of California Press, 1979).

39. Velasco, "The Dustbin of History," 45.

40. Cardoso, "The Consumption of Dependency Theory," 16.

41. Thomas S. Kuhn, *The Structure of Scientific Revolutions* (Chicago: University of Chicago Press, 1970).

SELECTED READINGS

The Economic Taproot of Imperialism

J. A. HOBSON

John Hobson discusses the economic taproot, or driving force, of imperialism. A high rate of savings and the power of production outstrip consumption. Industrialists and manufacturers therefore seek foreign sources of investment and markets in Third World countries to solve these problems. Although Hobson was not a Marxist, his views nevertheless had direct influence on Lenin and others who would be highly critical of imperialism as an advanced stage of capitalism.

No mere array of facts and figures adduced to illustrate the economic nature of the new imperialism will suffice to dispel the popular delusion that the use of national force to secure new markets by annexing fresh tracts of territory is a sound and a necessary policy for an advanced industrial country like Great Britain. It has indeed been proved that recent annexations of tropical countries, procured at great expense, have furnished poor and precarious markets, that our aggregate trade with our colonial possessions is virtually stationary, and that our most profitable and progressive trade is with rival industrial nations, whose territories we have no desire to annex, whose markets we cannot force, and whose active antagonism we are provoking by our expansive policy.

But these arguments are not conclusive. It is open to Imperialists to argue thus: "We must have markets for our growing manufactures, we must have new outlets for the investment of our surplus capital and for the energies of the adventurous surplus of our population: such expansion is a necessity of life to a nation with our great and growing powers of production. An ever larger share of our population is devoted to the manufactures and commerce of towns, and is thus dependent for life and work upon food and raw materials from foreign lands. In order to buy and pay for these things we must sell our goods abroad. During the first three-quarters of the nineteenth century we could do so without difficulty by a natural expansion of commerce with continental nations and our colonies, all of which were far behind us in the main arts of manufacture and the carrying trades. So long as England held a virtual monopoly of the world markets for certain important classes of manufactured goods, Imperialism was unnecessary. After 1870 this manufacturing and trading supremacy was greatly impaired: other nations, especially Germany, the United States, and Belgium, advanced with great rapidity, and while they have not crushed or even stayed the increase of our external trade, their competition made it more and more difficult to dispose of the full surplus of our manufactures at a profit. The encroachments made by these nations upon our old markets, even in our own possessions, made it most urgent that we should take energetic means to secure new markets. These new markets had to lie in hitherto undeveloped countries, chiefly in the tropics, where vast populations lived capable of growing economic needs which our manufacturers and merchants could supply. Our rivals were seizing and annexing territories for similar purposes, and when they had annexed them closed them to our trade. The diplomacy and the arms of Great Britain had to be used in order to compel the owners of the new markets to deal with us: and experience showed that the safest means of securing and developing such markets is by establishing 'protectorates' or by annexation. The

"The Economic Taproot of Imperialism" from *Imperialism* by John A. Hobson, 1902, John Nesbit & Co., Ltd, and later Allen & Unwin, pp. 71–93.

value in 1905 of these markets must not be taken as a final test of the economy of such a policy; the process of educating civilized needs which we can supply is of necessity a gradual one, and the cost of such Imperialism must be regarded as a capital outlay, the fruits of which posterity would reap. The new markets might not be large, but they formed serviceable outlets for the overflow of our great textile and metal industries, and, when the vast Asiatic and African populations of the interior were reached, a rapid expansion of trade was expected to result.

"Far larger and more important is the pressure of capital for external fields of investment. Moreover, while the manufacturer and trader are well content to trade with foreign nations, the tendency for investors to work towards the political annexation of countries which contain their more speculative investments is very powerful. Of the fact of this pressure of capital there can be no question. Large savings are made which cannot find any profitable investment in this country; they must find employment elsewhere, and it is to the advantage of the nation that they should be employed as largely as possible in lands where they can be utilized in opening up markets for British trade and employment for British enterprise.

"However costly, however perilous, this process of imperial expansion may be, it is necessary to the continued existence and progress of our nation; if we abandoned it we must be content to leave the development of the world to other nations, who will everywhere cut into our trade, and even impair our means of securing the food and raw materials we require to support our population. Imperialism is thus seen to be, not a choice, but a necessity."

The practical force of this economic argument in politics is strikingly illustrated by the later history of the United States. Here is a country which suddenly broke through a conservative policy, strongly held by both political parties, bound up with every popular instinct and tradition, and flung itself into a rapid imperial career for which it possessed neither the material nor the moral equipment, risking the principles and practices of liberty and equality by the establishment of militarism and the forcible subjugation of peoples which it could not safely admit to the condition of American citizenship.

Was this a mere wild freak of spread-eaglism, a burst of political ambition on the part of a nation coming to a sudden realization of its destiny? Not at all. The spirit of adventure, the American "mission of civilization," were as forces making for Imperialism, clearly subordinate to the driving force of the economic factor. The dramatic character of the change is due to the unprecedented rapidity of the industrial revolution in the United States from the eighties onward. During that period the United States, with her unrivalled natural resources, her immense resources of skilled and unskilled labour, and her genius for invention and organization, developed the best equipped and most productive manufacturing economy the world has yet seen. Fostered by rigid protective tariffs, her metal, textile, tool, clothing, furniture, and other manufactures shot up in a single generation from infancy to full maturity, and, having passed through a period of intense competition, attained, under the able control of great trustmakers, a power of production greater than has been attained in the most advanced industrial countries of Europe.

An era of cut-throat competition, followed by a rapid process of amalgamation, threw an enormous quantity of wealth into the hands of a small number of captains of industry. No luxury of living to which this class could attain kept pace with its rise of income, and a process of automatic saving set in upon an unprecedented scale. The investment of these savings in other industries helped to bring these under the same concentrative forces. Thus a great increase of savings seeking profitable investment is synchronous with a stricter economy of the use of existing capital. No doubt the rapid growth of a population, accustomed to a high and an always ascending standard of comfort, absorbs in the satisfaction of its wants a large quantity of new capital. But the actual rate of saving, conjoined with a more economical application of forms of existing capital, exceeded considerably the rise of the national consumption of manufactures. The power of production far outstripped the actual rate of consumption, and, contrary to the older economic theory, was unable to force a corresponding increase of consumption by lowering prices.

This is no mere theory. The history of any of the numerous trusts or combinations in the United States sets out the facts with complete distinctness. In the free competition of manufactures preceding combination the chronic condition is one of "overproduction," in the sense that all the mills or factories can only be kept at work by cutting prices down towards a point where the weaker competitors are forced to close down, because they cannot sell their goods at a price which covers the true cost of production. The first result of the successful formation of a trust or combine is to close down the worse equipped or worse placed mills, and supply the entire market from the better equipped and better placed ones. This course may or may not be attended by a rise of price and some restriction of consumption: in some cases trusts take most of their profits by raising prices, in other cases by reducing the costs of production through employing only the best mills and stopping the waste of competition.

For the present argument it matters not which course is taken; the point is that this concentration of industry in "trusts," "combines," etc. at once limits the quantity of capital which can be effectively employed and increases the share of profits out of which fresh savings and fresh capital will spring. It is quite evident that a trust which is motivated by cut-throat competition, due to an excess of capital, cannot normally find inside the "trusted" industry employment for that portion of the profits which the trust-makers desire to save and to invest. New inventions and other economies of production or distribution within the trade may absorb some of the new capital, but there are rigid limits to this absorption. The trustmaker in oil or sugar must find other investments for his savings: if he is early in the application of the combination principles to his trade, he will naturally apply his surplus capital to establish similar combinations in other industries, economising capital still further, and rendering it ever harder for ordinary saving men to find investments for their savings.

Indeed, the conditions alike of cut-throat competition and of combination attest the congestion of capital in the manufacturing industries which have entered the machine economy. We are not here concerned with any theoretic question as to the possibility of producing by modern machine methods more goods than can find a market. It is sufficient to point out that the manufacturing power of a country like the United States would grow so fast as to exceed the demands of the home market. No one acquainted with trade will deny a fact which all American economists assert, that this is the condition which the United States reached at the end of the century, so far, as the more developed industries are concerned. Her manufactures were saturated with capital and could absorb no more. One after another they sought refuge from the waste of competition in "combines" which secure a measure of profitable peace by restricting the quantity of operative capital. Industrial and financial princes in oil, steel, sugar, railroads, banking, etc. were faced with the dilemma of either spending more than they knew how to spend, or forcing markets outside the home area. Two economic courses were open to them, both leading towards an abandonment of the political isolation of the past and the adoption of imperialist methods in the future. Instead of shutting down inferior mills and rigidly restricting output to correspond with profitable sales in the home markets, they might employ their full productive power, applying their savings to increase their business capital, and, while still regulating output and prices for the home market, may "hustle" for foreign markets, dumping down their surplus goods at prices which would not be possible save for the profitable nature of their home market. So likewise they might employ their savings in seeking investments outside their country, first repaying the capital borrowed from Great Britain and other countries for the early development of their railroads, mines and manufactures, and afterwards becoming themselves a creditor class to foreign countries.

It was this sudden demand for foreign markets for manufactures and for investment which was avowedly responsible for the adoption of Imperialism as a political policy and practice by the Republican party to which the great industrial and financial chiefs belonged, and which belonged to them. The adventurous enthusiasm of President Theodore Roosevelt and his "manifest destiny" and "mission of civilization" party must not deceive us. It was Messrs. Rockefeller, Pierpont Morgan, and their associates who needed Imperialism and who fastened it upon the shoulders of the great Republic of the West. They needed Imperialism because they desired to use the public resources of their country to find profitable employment for their capital which otherwise would be superfluous. . . .

It is this economic condition of affairs that forms the taproot of Imperialism. If the consuming public in this country raised its standard of consumption to keep pace with every rise of productive powers, there could be no excess of goods or capital clamorous to use Imperialism in order to find markets: foreign trade would indeed exist, but there would be no difficulty in exchanging a small surplus of our manufactures for the food and raw material we annually absorbed, and all the savings that we made could find employment, if we chose, in home industries. . . .

Gramsci, Hegemony,
and International Relations

ROBERT W. COX

Cox examines the implications of Antonio Gramsci's concept of hegemony for IR. The historic bloc (blocco storico) to Gramsci is decisive, composed as it is of both "structures and superstructures"—the objective and the subjective, respectively. Thus, Cox tells us we find in the bloc "the juxtaposition and reciprocal relationships of the political, ethical, and ideological spheres of activity with the economic sphere." The bloc becomes the instrument of hegemony. Hegemony at the International level extends beyond states. It is an order within the world economy exhibiting a dominant mode of production that penetrates all countries. It also consists of complex social relations, connecting classes among different countries. World hegemony, therefore, consists of mutually reinforcing social, political, and economic structures. One expression and mechanism of world hegemony are international organizations. Prospects for the creation of counter-hegemonic blocks are most likely to be at the national, not the international level.

Some time ago I began reading Gramsci's *Prison Notebooks*. In these fragments, written in a fascist prison between 1929 and 1935, the former leader of the Italian Communist Party was concerned with the problem of understanding capitalist societies in the 1920s and 1930s, and particularly with the meaning of fascism and the possibilities of building an alternative form of state and society based on the working class. What he had to say centered upon the state, upon the relationship of civil society to the state, and upon the relationship of politics, ethics, and ideology to production. Not surprisingly, Gramsci did not have very much to say directly about international relations. Nevertheless, I found that Gramsci's thinking was helpful in understanding the meaning of international organization with which I was then principally concerned. Particularly useful was his concept of hegemony, but valuable also were several concepts which he had worked out for himself or developed from others. This essay sets forth my understanding of what Gramsci meant by hegemony and these related concepts, and suggests how I think they may be adapted, retaining his essential meaning, to the understanding of problems of world order. It does not purport to be a critical study of Gramsci's political theory but merely a derivation from it of some ideas useful for a revision of current international relations theory.[1] . . .

Gramsci and Hegemony

Gramsci's concepts were all derived from history–both from his own reflections upon those periods of history which he thought helped to throw an explanatory light upon the present, and from his personal experience of political and social struggle. These included the workers' councils movement of the early 1920s, his participation in the Third International, and his opposition to fascism. Gramsci's ideas have always to be related to his own historical context. Moreover, he was constantly adjusting his concepts to specific historical circumstances. The concepts cannot usefully be considered in abstraction from their applications, for when they are so abstracted different usages of the same concept appear to contain contradictions or ambiguities.[2] A concept, in Gramsci's thought, is loose and elastic and attains precision only when brought into contact with a particular situation which it helps to explain, a contact which also develops the meaning of the concept. This is the strength of Gramsci's historicism and therein lies its explanatory power.

Robert W. Cox, "Gramsci, Hegemony, and International Relations" in Robert W. Cox and Timothy J. Sinclair, *Approaches to World Order* (Cambridge, UK: Cambridge University Press, 1996), 124–41. Reprinted by permission.

The term "historicism" is however, frequently mis-understood and criticized by those who seek a more abstract systematic, universalistic, and non-historical form of knowledge.[3]

Gramsci geared his thought consistently to the practical purpose of political action. In his prison writings, he always referred to Marxism as "the phi-losophy of praxis."[4] Partly at least, one may surmise, it must have been to underline the practical revolu-tionary purpose of philosophy. Partly too, it would have been to indicate his intention to contribute to a lively developing current of thought, given impetus by Marx but not forever circumscribed by Marx's work. Nothing could be further from his mind than a Marxism which consists in an exegesis of the sacred texts for the purpose of refining a timeless set of categories and concepts.

Origins of the Concepts of Hegemony

There are two main strands leading to the Grams-cian idea of hegemony. The first ran from the debates within the Third International concerning the strat-egy of the Bolshevik Revolution and the creation of a Soviet socialist state, the second from the writings of Machiavelli. In tracing the first strand, some commentators have sought to contrast Gramsci's thought with Lenin's by aligning Gramsci with the idea of a hegemony of the proletariat and Lenin with a dictatorship of the proletariat. Other commenta-tors have underlined their basic agreement.[5] What is important is that Lenin referred to the Russian pro-letariat as both a dominant and a directing class, dominance implying dictatorship and direction im-plying leadership with the consent of allied classes (notably the peasantry). Gramsci, in effect, took over an idea that was current in the circles of the Third International: the workers exercised hegemony over the allied classes and dictatorship over enemy classes. Yet this idea was applied by the Third Inter-national only to the working class and expressed the role of the working class in leading an alliance of workers, peasants, and perhaps some other groups potentially supportive of revolutionary change.[6]

Gramsci's originality lies in his giving a twist to this first strand: he began to apply it to the bour-geoisie, to the apparatus or mechanisms of hege-mony of the dominant class.[7] This made it possible for him to distinguish cases in which the bourgeoisie had attained a hegemonic position of leadership over

other classes from those in which it had not. In north-ern Europe, in the countries where capitalism had first become established, bourgeois hegemony was most complete. It necessarily involved concessions to subordinate classes in return for acquiescence in bourgeois leadership, concessions which could lead ultimately to forms of social democracy which pre-serve capitalism while making it more acceptable to workers and the petty bourgeoisie. Because their hegemony was firmly entrenched in civil society, the bourgeoisie often did not need to run the state themselves. Landed aristocrats in England, Junkers in Prussia, or a renegade pretender to the mantle of Napoleon I in France, could do it for them so long as these rulers recognized the hegemonic structures of civil society as the basic limits of their political action.

This perception of hegemony led Gramsci to enlarge his definition of the state. When the admin-istrative, executive, and coercive apparatus of gov-ernment was in effect constrained by the hegemony of the leading class of a whole social formation, it became meaningless to limit the definition of the state to those elements of government. To be mean-ingful, the notion of the state would also have to include the underpinnings of the political structure in civil society. Gramsci thought of these in concrete historical terms: the church, the educational system, the press, all the institutions which helped to create in people certain modes of behavior and expec-tations consistent with the hegemonic social order. For example, Gramsci argued that the Masonic lodges in Italy were a bond amongst the government officials who entered into the state machinery after the unification of Italy, and therefore must be con-sidered as part of the state for the purpose of assess-ing its broader political structure. The hegemony of a dominant class thus bridged the conventional categories of state and civil society, categories which retained a certain analytical usefulness but ceased to correspond to separable entities in reality.

As noted above, the second strand leading to the Gramscian idea of hegemony came all the way from Machiavelli and helps to broaden even further the potential scope of application of the concept. Gramsci had pondered what Machiavelli had writ-ten, especially in *The Prince*, concerning the prob-lem of founding a new state. Machiavelli, in the fifteenth century, was concerned with finding the leadership and the supporting social basis for a united Italy; Gramsci, in the twentieth century, with the leadership and supportive basis for an alternative to fascism. Where Machiavelli looked to the individual prince, Gramsci looked to the modern prince: the revolutionary party engaged in a continuing and developing dialogue with its own base of support. Gramsci took over from Machiavelli the image of power as a centaur: half man, half beast, a necessary combination of consent and coercion.[8] To the extent that the consensual aspect of power is in the forefront, hegemony prevails. Coercion is always latent but is only applied in marginal, deviant cases. Hegemony is enough to ensure conformity of behavior in most people most of the time. The Machiavellian connection frees the concept of power (and of hegemony as one form of power) from a tie to historically specific social classes and gives it a wider applicability to relations of dominance and subordination, including, as will be suggested below, relations of world order. It does not, however, sever power relations from their social basis (i.e., in the case of world-order relations by making them into relations among states narrowly conceived), but directs attention towards deepening an awareness of this social basis.

War of Movement and War of Position

In thinking through the first strand of his concept of hegemony, Gramsci reflected upon the experiences of the Bolshevik Revolution and sought to determine what lessons might be drawn from it for the task of revolution in western Europe.[9] He came to the conclusion that the circumstances in western Europe differed greatly from those in Russia. To illustrate the differences in circumstances, and the consequent differences in strategies required, he had recourse to the military analogy of wars of movement and wars of position. The basic difference between Russia and western Europe was in the relative strengths of state and civil society. In Russia, the administrative and coercive apparatus of the state was formidable but proved to be vulnerable, while civil society was undeveloped. A relatively small working class led by a disciplined vanguard was able to overwhelm the state in a war of movement and met no effective resistance from the rest of civil society. The vanguard party could set about founding a new state through a combination of applying coercion against recalcitrant elements and building consent among others. (This analysis was

particularly apposite to the period of the New Economic Policy before coercion began to be applied on a larger scale against the rural population.)

In western Europe, by contrast, civil society, under bourgeois hegemony, was much more fully developed and took manifold forms. A war of movement might conceivably, in conditions of exceptional upheaval, enable a revolutionary vanguard to seize control of the state apparatus; but because of the resiliency of civil society such an exploit would in the long run be doomed to failure. Gramsci described the state in western Europe (by which we should read state in the limited sense of administrative, governmental, and coercive apparatus and not the enlarged concept of the state mentioned above) as "an outer ditch, behind which there stands a powerful system of fortresses and earthworks."

> In Russia, the State was everything, civil society was primordial and gelatinous; in the West, there was a proper relation between State and civil society, and when the State trembled a sturdy structure of civil society was at once revealed.[10]

Accordingly, Gramsci argued that the war of movement could not be effective against the hegemonic state-societies of western Europe. The alternative strategy is the war of position which slowly builds up the strength of the social foundations of a new state. In western Europe, the struggle had to be won in civil society before an assault on the state could achieve success. Premature attack on the state by a war of movement would only reveal the weakness of the opposition and lead to a reimposition of bourgeois dominance as the institutions of civil society reasserted control.

The strategic implications of this analysis are clear but fraught with difficulties. To build up the basis of an alternative state and society upon the leadership of the working class means creating alternative institutions and alternative intellectual resources within existing society and building bridges between workers and other subordinate classes. It means actively building a counterhegemony within an established hegemony while resisting the pressures and temptations to relapse into pursuit of incremental gains for subaltern groups within the framework of bourgeois hegemony. This is the line between war of position as a long-range revolutionary strategy and social democracy as a policy of making gains within the established order.

Passive Revolution

Not all western European societies were bourgeois hegemonies. Gramsci distinguished between two kinds of societies. One kind had undergone a thorough social revolution and worked out fully its consequences in new modes of production and social relations. England and France were cases that had gone further than most others in this respect. The other kind were societies which had so to speak imported or had thrust upon them aspects of a new order created abroad, without the old order having been displaced. These last were caught up in a dialectic of revolution-restoration which tended to become blocked as neither the new forces nor the old could triumph. In these societies, the new industrial bourgeoisie failed to achieve hegemony. The resulting stalemate with the traditionally dominant social classes created the conditions that Gramsci called "passive revolution," the introduction of changes which did not involve any arousal of popular forces.[11]

One typical accompaniment to passive revolution in Gramsci's analysis is caesarism: a strong man intervenes to resolve the stalemate between equal and opposed social forces. Gramsci allowed that there were both progressive and reactionary forms of caesarism: progressive when strong rule presides over a more orderly development of a new state, reactionary when it stabilizes existing power. Napoleon I was a case of progressive caesarism, but Napoleon III, the exemplar of reactionary caesarism, was more representative of the kind likely to arise in the course of passive revolution. Gramsci's analysis here is virtually identical with that of Marx in *The Eighteenth Brumaire of Louis Bonaparte*: the French bourgeoisie, unable to rule directly through their own political parties, were content to develop capitalism under a political regime which had its social basis in the peasantry, an inarticulate and unorganized class whose virtual representative Bonaparte could claim to be.

In late nineteenth-century Italy, the northern industrial bourgeoisie, the class with the most to gain from the unification of Italy, was unable to dominate the peninsula. The basis for the new state became an alliance between the industrial bourgeoisie of the north and the landowners of the south—an alliance which also provided benefits for petty-bourgeois clients (especially from the south) who staffed the new state bureaucracy and political parties and became the intermediaries between the various population groups and the state. The lack of any sustained and widespread popular participation in the unification movement explained the "passive revolution" character of its outcome. In the aftermath of World War I, worker and peasant occupations of factories and land demonstrated a strength which was considerable enough to threaten yet insufficient to dislodge the existing state.[12] There took place then what Gramsci called a "displacement of the basis of the state" towards the petty bourgeoisie, the only class of nationwide extent, which became the anchor of fascist power. Fascism continued the passive revolution, sustaining the position of the old owner classes yet unable to attract the support of worker or peasant subaltern groups.

Apart from caesarism, the second major feature of passive revolution in Italy Gramsci called *trasformismo*. It was exemplified in Italian politics by Giovanni Giolitti, who sought to bring about the widest possible coalition of interests and who dominated the political scene in the years preceding fascism. For example, he aimed to bring northern industrial workers into a common front with industrialists through a protectionist policy. *Trasformismo* worked to co-opt potential leaders of subaltern social groups. By extension *trasformismo* can serve as a strategy of assimilating and domesticating potentially dangerous ideas by adjusting them to the policies of the dominant coalition and can thereby obstruct the formation of class-based organized opposition to established social and political power. Fascism continued *trasformismo*. Gramsci interprets the fascist state corporatism as an unsuccessful attempt to introduce some of the more advanced industrial practices of American capitalism under the aegis of the old Italian management.

The concept of passive revolution is a counterpart to the concept of hegemony in that it describes the condition of a nonhegemonic society, one in which no dominant class has been able to establish a hegemony in Gramsci's sense of the term. Today this notion of passive revolution, together with its components, caesarism and *trasformismo*, is particularly apposite to industrializing Third World countries.

Historic Bloc (*Blocco Storico*)

Gramsci attributed the source of his notion of the historic bloc (*blocco storico*) to Georges Sorel, though Sorel never used the term or any other in precisely the sense Gramsci gave to it.[13] Sorel did, however, interpret revolutionary action in terms of social myths through which people engaged in action perceived a confrontation of totalities—in which they saw a new order challenging an established order. In the course of a cataclysmic event, the old order would be overthrown as a whole and the new be freed to unfold.[14] While Gramsci did not share the subjectivism of this vision, he did share the view that state and society together constituted a solid structure and that revolution implied the development within it of another structure strong enough to replace the first. Echoing Marx, he thought this could come about only when the first had exhausted its full potential. Whether dominant or emergent, such a structure is what Gramsci called an historic bloc.

For Sorel, social myth, a powerful form of collective subjectivity, would obstruct reformist tendencies. These might otherwise attract workers away from revolutionary syndicalism into incrementalist trade unionism or reformist party politics. The myth was a weapon in struggle as well as a tool for analysis. For Gramsci, the historic bloc similarly had a revolutionary orientation through its stress on the unity and coherence of sociopolitical orders. It was an intellectual defense against cooptation by *trasformismo*.

The historic bloc is a dialectical concept in the sense that its interacting elements create a larger unity. Gramsci expressed these interacting elements sometimes as the subjective and the objective, sometimes as superstructure and structure.

> Structures and superstructures form an "historic bloc." That is to say the complex contradictory and discordant *ensemble* of the superstructures is the reflection of the *ensemble* of the social relations of production.[15]

The juxtaposition and reciprocal relationships of the political, ethical, and ideological spheres of activity with the economic sphere avoid reductionism. It avoids reducing everything either to economics (economism) or to ideas (idealism). In Gramsci's historical materialism (which he was careful to distinguish from what he called "historical economism" or a narrowly economic interpretation of history), ideas and material conditions are always bound together, mutually influencing one another, and not reducible one to the other. Ideas have to be understood in relation to material circumstances. Material circumstances include both the social relations and the physical means of production. Superstructures of ideology and political organization shape the development of both aspects of production and are shaped by them.

An historic bloc cannot exist without a hegemonic social class. Where the hegemonic class is the dominant class in a country or social formation, the state (in Gramsci's enlarged concept) maintains cohesion and identity within the bloc through the propagation of a common culture. A new bloc is formed when a subordinate class (e.g., the workers) establishes its hegemony over other subordinate groups (e.g., small farmers, marginals). This process requires intensive dialogue between leaders and followers within the would-be hegemonic class. Gramsci may have concurred in the Leninist idea of a vanguard party which takes upon itself the responsibility for leading an immature working class, but only as an aspect of a war of movement. Because a war-of-position strategy was required in the western countries, as he saw it, the role of the party should be to lead, intensify, and develop dialogue within the working class and between the working class and other subordinate classes which could be brought into alliance with it. The "mass line" as a mobilization technique once developed by the Chinese Communist Party is consistent with Gramsci's thinking in this respect.

Intellectuals play a key role in the building of an historic bloc. Intellectuals are not a distinct and relatively classless social stratum. Gramsci saw them as organically connected with a social class. They perform the function of developing and sustaining the mental images, technologies, and organizations which bind together the members of a class and of an historic bloc into a common identity. Bourgeois intellectuals did this for a whole society in which the bourgeoisie was hegemonic. The organic intellectuals of the working class would perform a similar role in the creation of a new historic bloc under working-class hegemony within that society. To do this they would have to evolve a clearly distinctive culture, organization, and technique, and do so in constant interaction with the members of the emergent block. Everyone, for Gramsci, is in some part an intellectual, although only some perform full-time the social function of an intellectual. In this task, the party was, in his conception, a "collective intellectual."

In the movement towards hegemony and the creation of an historic bloc, Gramsci distinguished three levels of consciousness: the economico-corporative, which is aware of the specific interests of a particular group; the solidarity or class consciousness, which extends to a whole social class but remains at a purely economic level; and the hegemonic, which brings the interests of the leading class into harmony with those of subordinate classes and incorporates these other interests into an ideology expressed in universal terms.[16] The movement towards hegemony, Gramsci says, is a "passage from the structure to the sphere of the complex superstructures," by which he means passing from the specific interests of a group or class to the building of institutions and elaboration of ideologies. If they reflect a hegemony, these institutions and ideologies will be universal in form, i.e., they will not appear as those of a particular class, and will give some satisfaction to the subordinate groups while not undermining the leadership or vital interests of the hegemonic class.

Hegemony and International Relations

We can now make the transition from what Gramsci said about hegemony and related concepts to the implications of these concepts for international relations. First, however, it is useful to look at what little Gramsci himself had to say about international relations. Let us begin with this passage:

> Do international relations precede or follow (logically) fundamental social relations? There can be no doubt that they follow. Any organic innovation in the social structure, through its technical-military expressions, modifies organically absolute and relative relations in the international field too.[17]

By "organic" Gramsci meant that which is structural, long-term, or relatively permanent, as opposed to the short-term or "conjunctural." He was saying that basic changes in international power relations or world order, which are observed as changes in the military-strategic and geopolitical balance, can be traced to fundamental changes in social relations.

Gramsci did not in any way bypass the state or diminish its importance. The state remained for him the basic entity in international relations and the place where social conflicts take place—the place also, therefore, where hegemonies of social classes can be built. In these hegemonies of social classes, the particular characteristics of nations combine in unique and original ways. The working class, which might be considered to be international in an abstract sense, nationalizes itself in the process of building its hegemony. The emergence of new worker-led blocs at the national level would, in this line of reasoning, precede any basic restructuring of international relations. However, the state, which remains the primary focus of social struggle and the basic entity of international relations, is the enlarged state which includes its own social basis. This view sets aside a narrow or superficial view of the state which reduces it, for instance, to the foreign-policy bureaucracy or the state's military capabilities.

From his Italian perspective, Gramsci had a keen sense of what we would now call dependency. What happened in Italy he knew was markedly influenced by external powers. At the purely foreign-policy level, great powers have relative freedom to determine their foreign policies in response to domestic interests; smaller powers have less autonomy.[18] The economic life of subordinate nations is penetrated by and intertwined with that of powerful nations. This is further complicated by the existence within countries of structurally diverse regions which have distinctive patterns of relationship to external forces.[19]

At an even deeper level, those states which are powerful are precisely those which have undergone a profound social and economic revolution and have most fully worked out the consequences of this revolution in the form of state and of social relations. The French Revolution was the case Gramsci reflected upon, but we can think of the development during the Cold War of U.S. and Soviet power in the same way. These were all nation-based developments which spilled over national boundaries to become internationally expansive phenomena. Other countries have received the impact of these developments in a passive way, an instance of what Gramsci described at the national level as a passive revolution. This effect comes when the impetus to change does not arise out of a "vast local economic development . . . but is instead the reflection of international developments which transmit their ideological currents to the periphery."[20]

The group which is the bearer of the new ideas, in such circumstances, is not an indigenous social group which is actively engaged in building a new economic base with a new structure of social relations. It is an intellectual stratum which picks up ideas originating from a prior foreign economic and social revolution. Consequently, the thought of this group takes an idealistic shape ungrounded in a domestic economic development; and its conception of the state takes the form of "a rational absolute."[21] Gramsci criticized the thought of Benedetto Croce, the dominant figure of the Italian intellectual establishment of his own time, for expressing this kind of distortion.

Hegemony and World Order

Is the Gramscian concept of hegemony applicable at the international or world level? Before attempting to suggest how this might be done, it is well to rule out some usages of the term which are common in international relations studies. Very often "hegemony" is used to mean the dominance of one country over others, thereby tying the usage to a relationship strictly among states. Sometimes "hegemony" is used as a euphemism for imperialism. When Chinese political leaders used to accuse the Soviet Union of "hegemonism," they seem to have had in mind some combination of these two. These meanings differ so much from the Gramscian sense of the term that it is better, for purposes of clarity in this chapter, to use the term "dominance" to replace them.

In applying the concept of hegemony to world order, it becomes important to determine when a period of hegemony begins and when it ends. A period in which a world hegemony has been established can be called hegemonic and one in which dominance of a nonhegemonic kind prevails, nonhegemonic. To illustrate, let us consider the past century and a half as falling into four distinguishable periods, roughly.[22] 1845–1875, 1875–1945, 1945–1965, and 1965 to the present.[a]

The first period (1845–75) was hegemonic there was a world economy with Britain as its center. Economic doctrines consistent with British supremacy but universal in form—comparative advantage, free trade, and the gold standard—spread gradually outward from Britain. Coercive strength underwrote this order. Britain held the balance of power in Europe, thereby preventing any challenge to hegemony from a land-based power. Britain ruled supreme at sea and had the capacity to enforce obedience by peripheral countries to the rules of the market.

In the second period (1875–1945), all these features were reversed. Other countries challenged British supremacy. The balance of power in Europe became destabilized, leading to two world wars. Free trade was superseded by protectionism; the gold standard was ultimately abandoned; and the world economy fragmented into economic blocs. This was a nonhegemonic period.

In the third period, following World War II (1945–65), the United States founded a new hegemonic world order similar in basic structure to that dominated by Britain in middle of the nineteenth century but with institutions and doctrines adjusted to a more complex world economy and to national societies more sensitive to the political repercussions of economic crises. Sometime from the later 1960s through the early 1970s it became evident that this US-based world order was no longer working well. During the uncertain times which followed, three possibilities of structural transformation of world order opened up: a reconstruction of hegemony with a broadening of political management on the lines envisaged by the Trilateral Commission; increased fragmentation of the world economy around big-power-centered economic spheres; and the possible assertion of a Third World-based counterhegemony with the concerted demand for the New International Economic Order as a forerunner.

---

[a] In *Production, Power, and World Order*, three successive structures of world order are substituted for the periodization given above, based on the dialectical relation of production, forms of state, and different configurations of world order. These three structures are: (1) the liberal international economy (1789–1873); (2) the era of rival imperialisms (1873–1945); and (3) the neoliberal world order (post–World War II). See Robert W. Cox, *Production, Power, and World Order: Social Forces in the Making of History* (New York: Columbia University Press, 1987), 107–109.

On the basis of this tentative notation, it would appear that, historically, to become hegemonic, a state would have to found and protect a world order which was universal in conception, i.e., not an order in which one state directly exploits others but an order which most other states (or at least those within reach of the hegemony) could find compatible with their interests. Such an order would hardly be conceived in inter-state terms alone, for this would likely bring to the fore oppositions of state interests. It would most likely give prominence to opportunities for the forces of civil society to operate on the world scale (or on the scale of the sphere within which hegemony prevails). The hegemonic concept of world order is founded not only upon the regulation of inter-state conflict but also upon a globally conceived civil society, i.e., a mode of production of global extent which brings about links among social classes of the countries encompassed by it.

Historically, hegemonies of this kind are founded by powerful states which have undergone a thorough social and economic revolution. The revolution not only modifies the internal economic and political structures of the state in question but also unleashes energies which expand beyond the state's boundaries. A world hegemony is thus in its beginnings an outward expansion of the internal (national) hegemony established by a dominant social class. The economic and social institutions, the culture, the technology associated with this national hegemony become patterns for emulation abroad. Such an expansive hegemony impinges on the more peripheral countries as a passive revolution. These countries have not undergone the same thorough social revolution, nor have their economies developed in the same way, but they try to incorporate elements from the hegemonic model without disturbing old power structures. While peripheral countries may adopt some economic and cultural aspects of the hegemonic core, they are less able to adopt its political models. Just as fascism became the form of passive revolution in the Italy of the interwar period, so various forms of military-bureaucratic regime supervise passive revolution in today's peripheries. In the world-hegemonic model, hegemony is more intense and consistent at the core and more laden with contradictions at the periphery.

Hegemony at the international level is thus not merely an order among states. It is an order within a world economy with a dominant mode of production which penetrates into all countries and links into other subordinate modes of production. It is also a complex of international social relationships which connect the social classes of the different countries. World hegemony can be described as a social structure, an economic structure, and a political structure; and it cannot be simply one of these things but must be all three. World hegemony, furthermore, is expressed in universal norms, institutions, and mechanisms which lay down general rules of behavior for states and for those forces of civil society that act across national boundaries, rules which support the dominant mode of production.

The Mechanisms of Hegemony: International Organizations

One mechanism through which the universal norms of a world hegemony are expressed is the international organization. Indeed, international organization functions as the process through which the institutions of hegemony and its ideology are developed. Among the features of international organization which express its hegemonic role are the following: (1) the institutions embody the rules which facilitate the expansion of hegemonic world orders; (2) they are themselves the product of the hegemonic world order; (3) they ideologically legitimate the norms of the world order; (4) they co-opt the elites from peripheral countries; and (5) they absorb counterhegemonic ideas.

International institutions embody rules which facilitate the expansion of the dominant economic and social forces but which at the same time permit adjustments to be made by subordinated interests with a minimum of pain. The rules governing world monetary and trade relations are particularly significant. They are framed primarily to promote economic expansion. At the same time they allow for exceptions and derogations to take care of problem situations. They can be revised in the light of changed circumstances. The Bretton Woods institutions provided more safeguards for domestic social concerns like unemployment than did the gold standard, on condition that national policies were consistent with the goal of a liberal world economy. The current system of floating exchange rates also gives scope for national actions while maintaining the principle of a prior commitment to harmonize national policies in the interests of a liberal world economy.

International institutions and rules are generally initiated by the state which establishes the hegemony. At the very least they must have that state's support. The dominant state takes care to secure the acquiescence of other states according to a hierarchy of powers within the inter-state structure of hegemony. Some second-rank countries are consulted first and their support is secured. The consent of at least some of the more peripheral countries is solicited. Formal participation may be weighed in favor of the dominant powers as in the International Monetary Fund and World Bank, or it may be on a one-state–one-vote basis as in most other major international institutions. There is an informal structure of influence reflecting the different levels of real political and economic power which underlies the formal procedures for decisions.

International institutions perform an ideological role as well. They help define policy guidelines for states and legitimate certain institutions and practices at the national level. They reflect orientations favorable to the dominant social and economic forces. The Organization for Economic Cooperation and Development, in recommending monetarism, endorsed a dominant consensus of policy thinking in the core countries and strengthened those who were determined to combat inflation this way against others who were more concerned about unemployment. The International Labor Organization, by advocating tripartism, legitimates the social relations evolved in the core countries as the desirable model for emulation.

Elite talent from peripheral countries is co-opted into international institutions in the manner of *trasformismo*. Individuals from peripheral countries, though they may come to international institutions with the idea of working from within to change the system, are condemned to work within the structures of passive revolution. At best they will help transfer elements of "modernization" to the peripheries but only as these are consistent with the interests of established local powers. Hegemony is like a pillow: it absorbs blows and sooner or later the would-be assailant will find it comfortable to rest upon. Only where representation in international institutions is firmly based upon an articulate social and political challenge to hegemony—upon a nascent historic bloc and counterhegemony—could participation pose a real threat. The co-optation of outstanding individuals from the peripheries renders this less likely.

Trasformismo also absorbs potentially counter-hegemonic ideas and makes these ideas consistent with hegemonic doctrine. The notion of self-reliance, for example, began as a challenge to the world economy by advocating endogenously determined autonomous development. The term has now been transformed to mean support by the agencies of the world economy for do-it-yourself welfare programs in the peripheral countries. These programs aim to enable the rural populations to achieve self-sufficiency, to stem the rural exodus to the cities, and to achieve thereby a greater degree of social and political stability amongst populations which the world economy is incapable of integrating. Self-reliance in its transformed meaning becomes complementary to and supportive of hegemonic goals for the world economy.

Thus, one tactic for bringing about change in the structure of world order can be ruled out as a total illusion. There is very little likelihood of a war of movement at the international level through which radicals would seize control of the superstructure of international institutions. Daniel Patrick Moynihan notwithstanding, Third World radicals do not control international institutions.[b] Even if they did, they could achieve nothing by it. These superstructures are inadequately connected with any popular political base. They are connected with the national hegemonic classes in the core countries and, through the intermediacy of these classes, have a broader base in these countries. In the peripheries, they connect only with the passive revolution.

The Prospects for Counterhegemony

World orders—to return to Gramsci's statement cited earlier in this essay—are grounded in social relations. A significant structural change in world order is, accordingly, likely to be traceable to some fundamental change in social relations and in the national political orders which correspond to national structures of social relations. In Gramsci's thinking, this would come about with the emergence of a new historic bloc.

---

[b] Moynihan was US ambassador to the UN during the Carter administration. He made speeches deploring that the United States was "in opposition" in the UN, which he represented as being run by a majority of Third World countries. See *New York Times*, January 28, 1976.

We must shift the problem of changing world order back from international institutions to national societies. Gramsci's analysis of Italy is even more valid when applied to the world order; only a war of position can, in the long run, bring about the structural changes, and a war of position involves building up the sociopolitical base for change through the creation of new historic blocs. The national context remains the only place where an historic bloc can be founded, although world-economy and world-political conditions materially influence the prospects for such an enterprise.

The prolonged crisis in the world economy (the beginning of which can be traced to the late 1960s and early 1970s) is propitious for some developments which could lead to a counterhegemonic challenge. In the core countries, those policies which cut into transfer payments to deprive social groups and generate high unemployment open the prospects of a broad alliance of the disadvantaged against the sectors of capital and labor which find common ground in international production and the monopoly-liberal world order. The policy basis for this alliance would most likely be post-Keynesian and neomercantilist. In peripheral countries, some states are vulnerable to revolutionary action, as events from Iran to Central America suggest. Political preparation of the population in sufficient depth may not, however, be able to keep pace with revolutionary opportunity and this diminishes the prospect for a new historic bloc. An effective political organization (Gramsci's modern prince) would be required in order to rally the new working classes generated by international production and build a bridge to peasants and urban marginals. Without this, we can only envisage a process where local political elites, even some which are the product of abortive revolutionary upheavals, would entrench their power within a monopoly-liberal world order. A reconstructed monopoly-liberal hegemony would be quite capable of practicing *trasformismo* by adjusting to many varieties of national institutions and practices, including nationalization of industries. The rhetoric of nationalism and of socialism could then be brought into line with the restoration of passive revolution under new guise in the periphery.

In short, the task of changing world order begins with the long, laborious effort to build new historic blocs within national boundaries.

Notes

This text was first published in *Millennium: Journal of International Studies*, vol. 12, no. 2 (Summer 1983), 162–175. An earlier version was presented to the Panel on Hegemony and International Relations, convened by the caucus for a New Political Science at the 1981 annual meeting of the American Political Science Association, New York, September 1981.

1. For citation here, I refer where possible to Antonio Gramsci, *Selections from the Prison Notebooks*, edited and trans. by Quintin Hoare and Geoffrey Nowell Smith (New York: International Publishers, 1971), hereafter cited as *Selections*. The full critical edition, *Quaderni del carcere* (Turin: Einaudi, 1975), is cited as *Quaderni*.

2. This seems to be the problem underlying Perry Anderson's "The Antinomies of Antonio Gramsci," *New Left Review*, no. 100 (November 1976–January 1977), which purports to find inconsistencies in Gramsci's use of concepts.

3. On this point see E. P. Thompson, "The Poverty of Theory," in his *The Poverty of Theory and Other Essays* (London: Merlin Press, 1978), which represents an historicist position analogous to that of Gramsci's in opposition to the abstract philosophical Marxism of Louis Althusser. For Althusser's position see "Marxism is not Historicism," in Louis Althusser and Etienne Balibar, *Reading Capital*, trans. by Hen Brewster (London: New Left Books, 1979).

4. It is said that this was to avoid confiscation of his notes by the prison censor, who, if this is true, must have been particularly slow-witted.

5. Christine Buci-Gluckmann, *Gramsci et l'état. Une théorie matérialiste de la philosophie* (Paris: Fayard, 1975), places Gramsci squarely in the Leninist tradition. Hughes Portelli, *Gramsci et le bloc historique* (Paris: Fayard, 1972), and Maria Antonietta Macciocchi, *Pour Gramsci* (Paris: Fayard, 1973), both contrast Gramsci with Lenin. Buci-Gluckmann's work seems to me to be more fully thought through. See also Chantal Mouffe and Anne Showstack Sassoon, "Gramsci in France and Italy—A Review of the Literature," *Economy and Society*, 6, 1 (February 1977), 31–68.

6. This notion fitted well with Gramsci's assessment of the situation in Italy in the early 1920s; the working class was by itself too weak to carry the full burden of revolution and could only bring about the founding of a new state by an alliance with the peasantry and some petty bourgeois elements. In fact, Gramsci considered the workers' council movement as a school for leadership of such a coalition and his efforts prior to his imprisonment were directed towards building this coalition.

7. See Buci-Gluckmann, *Gramsci et l'état*, 63.

8. Machiavelli, *The Prince*, Norton Critical Edition, edited by Robert M. Adams (New York: W. W. Norton, 1977), 49–50; and Gramsci, *Selections*, 169–170.

9. The term "western Europe" refers here to the Britain, France, Germany and Italy of the 1920s and 1930s.

10. Gramsci, *Selections*, 238.

11. Gramsci borrowed the term "passive revolution" from the Neopolitan historian Vincenzo Cuocco (1777–1823), who was active in the early stages of the Risorgimento. In Cuocco's interpretation, Napoleon's armies had brought a passive revolution to Italy.

12. Buci-Gluckmann, *Gramsci el l'étal*, 121.

13. Gramsci, *Quaderni*, vol. IV, 2632.

14. See Sorel's discussion of myth and the "Napoleonic battle" in the letter to Daniel Halévy which introduces his *Reflections on Violence*, trans. by T. E. Hulme (New York: Peter Smith, 1941).

15. Gramsci, *Selections*, 366

16. *Ibid.*, 180–195.

17. *Ibid.*, 176.

18. *Ibid.*, 264.

19. *Ibid.*, 182.

20. *Ibid.*, 116.

21. *Ibid.*, 117.

22. The dating is tentative and would have to be refined by enquiry into the structural features proper to each period as well as into factors deemed to constitute the breaking points between one period and another. These are offered here as mere notations for a revision of historical scholarship to raise some questions about hegemony and its attendant structures and mechanisms.

Imperialism, which has taken different forms in these periods, is a closely related question. In the first, *pax britannica*, although some territories were directly administered, control of colonies seems to have been incidental to rather than necessary for economic expansion. Argentina, a formally independent country, had essentially the same relationship to the British economy as Canada, a former colony. This, as George Lichtheim noted, may be called the phase of "liberal imperialism." In the second period, the so-called "new imperialism" brought more emphasis on direct political controls. It also saw the growth of capital exports and of the finance capital identified by Lenin as the very essence of imperialism. In the third period, which might be called that of the neoliberal or monopoly-liberal imperialism, the internationalizing of production emerged as the preeminent form, supported also by new forms of finance capital (multinational banks and consortia). There seems little point in trying to define some unchanging essence of imperialism, but it would be useful to describe the structural characteristics of the imperialisms which correspond to successive hegemonic and nonhegemonic world orders.

The Modern World System as a Capitalist World-Economy

IMMANUEL WALLERSTEIN

Professor Wallerstein outlines key concepts and propositions associated with the capitalist world-system. A present-day Marxist scholar, Wallerstein sees capitalism as best understood as a global, system-wide phenomenon. We like this presentation of his work because it is a formal, succinct statement of his theoretical understanding of capitalist world-economy.

The world in which we are now living, the modern world-system, had its origins in the sixteenth century. This world-system was then located in only a part of the globe, primarily in parts of Europe and the Americas. It expanded over time to cover the whole globe. It is and has always been a *world-economy*. It is and has always been a *capitalist* world-economy. We should begin by explaining what these two terms, world-economy and capitalism, denote. It will then be easier to appreciate the historical contours of the modern world-system—its origins, its geography, its temporal development, and its contemporary structural crisis.

Immanuel Wallerstein, *World-Systems Analysis: An Introduction* (Durham: Duke University Press, 2004), 23–41. Reprinted by permission.

What we mean by a world-economy (Braudel's *économie-monde*) is a large geographic zone within which there is a division of labor and hence significant internal exchange of basic or essential goods as well as flows of capital and labor. A defining feature of a world-economy is that it is *not* bounded by a unitary political structure. Rather, there are many political units inside the world-economy, loosely tied together in our modern world-system in an interstate system. And a world-economy contains many cultures and groups—practicing many religions, speaking many language, differing in their everyday patterns. This does not mean that they do not evolve some common cultural patterns, what we shall be calling a geoculture. It does mean that neither political nor cultural homogeneity is to be expected or found in a world-economy. What unifies the structure most is the division of labor which is constituted within it.

Capitalism is not the mere existence of persons or firms producing for sale on the market with the intention of obtaining a profit. Such persons or firms have existed for thousands of years all across the world. Nor is the existence of persons working for wages sufficient as a definition. Wage-labor has also been known for thousands of years. We are in a capitalist system only when the system gives priority to the *endless* accumulation of capital. Using such a definition, only the modern world-system has been a capitalist system. Endless accumulation is a quite simple concept: it means that people and firms are accumulating capital in order to accumulate still more capital, a process that is continual and endless. If we say that a system "gives priority" to such endless accumulation, it means that there exist structural mechanisms by which those who act with other motivations are penalized in some way, and are eventually eliminated from the social scene, whereas those who act with the appropriate motivations are rewarded and, if successful, enriched.

A world-economy and a capitalist system go together. Since world-economies lack the unifying cement of an overall political structure or a homogeneous culture, what holds them together is the efficacy of the division of labor. And this efficacy is a function of the constantly expanding wealth that a capitalist system provides. Until modern times, the world-economies that had been constructed either fell apart or were transformed *manu militari* into world-empires. Historically, the only world-economy to have survived for a long time has been the modern world-system, and that is because the capitalist system took root and became consolidated as its defining feature.

Conversely, a capitalist system cannot exist within any framework except that of a world-economy. We shall see that a capitalist system requires a very special relationship between economic producers and the holders of political power. If the latter are too strong, as in a world-empire, their interests will override those of the economic producers, and the endless accumulation of capital will cease to be a priority. Capitalists need a large market (hence mini-systems are too narrow for them) but they also need a multiplicity of states, so that they can gain the advantages of working with states but also can circumvent states hostile to their interests in favor of states friendly to their interests. Only the existence of a multiplicity of states within the overall division of labor assures this possibility.

A capitalist world-economy is a collection of many institutions, the combination of which accounts for its processes, and all of which are intertwined with each other. The basic institutions are the market, or rather the markets; the firms that compete in the markets; the multiple states, within an interstate system; the households; the classes; and the status-groups (to use Weber's term, which some people in recent years have renamed the "identities"). They are all institutions that have been created within the framework of the capitalist world-economy. Of course, such institutions have some similarities to institutions that existed in prior historical systems to which we have given the same or similar names. But using the same name to describe institutions located in different historical systems quite often confuses rather than clarifies analysis. It is better to think of the set of institutions of the modern world-system as contextually specific to it.

Let us start with markets, since these are normally considered the essential feature of a capitalist system. A market is both a concrete local structure in which individuals or firms sell and buy goods, and a virtual institution across space where the same kind of exchange occurs. How large and wide-spread any virtual market is depends on the realistic alternatives that sellers and buyers have at a given time. In principle, in a capitalist world-economy the virtual market exists in the world-economy as a whole. But as we shall see, there are often interferences with these boundaries, creating narrower and more "protected" markets. There are of course separate virtual markets for all commodities as well as for capital and different kinds of labor. But over time, there can also be said to exist a single virtual world market for all the factors of production combined, despite all the barriers that exist to its free functioning. One can think of this complete virtual market as a magnet for all producers and buyers, whose pull is a constant political factor in the decision-making of everyone—the states, the firms, the households, the classes, and the status-groups (or identities). This complete virtual world market is a reality in that it influences all decision making, but it never functions fully and freely (that is, without interference). The totally free market functions as an ideology, a myth, and a constraining influence, but never as a day-to-day reality.

One of the reasons it is not a day-to-day reality is that a totally free market, were it ever to exist, would make impossible the endless accumulation of capital. This may seem a paradox because it is surely true that capitalism cannot function without markets, and it is also true that capitalists regularly say that they favor free markets. But capitalists in fact need not totally free markets but rather markets that are only partially free. The reason is clear. Suppose there really existed a world market in which all the factors of production were totally free, as our textbooks in economics usually define this—that is, one in which the factors flowed without restriction, in which there were a very large number of buyers and a very large number of sellers, and in which there was perfect information (meaning that all sellers and all buyers knew the exact state of all costs of production). In such a perfect market, it would always be possible for the buyers to bargain down the sellers to an absolutely minuscule level of profit (let us think of it as a penny), and this low level of profit would make the capitalist game entirely uninteresting to producers, removing the basic social underpinnings of such a system.

What sellers always prefer is a monopoly, for then they can create a relatively wide margin between the costs of production and the sales price, and thus realize high rates of profit. Of course, perfect monopolies are extremely difficult to create, and rare, but quasi-monopolies are not. What one needs most of all is the support of the machinery of a relatively strong state, one which can enforce a quasi-monopoly. There are many ways of doing this.

One of the most fundamental is the system of patents which reserves rights in an "invention" for a specified number of years. This is what basically makes "new" products the most expensive for consumers and the most profitable for their producers. Of course, patents are often violated and in any case they eventually expire, but by and large they protect a quasi-monopoly for a time. Even so, production protected by patents usually remains only a quasi-monopoly, since there may be other similar products on the market that are not covered by the patent. This is why the normal situation for so-called leading products (that is, products that are both new and have an important share of the overall world market for commodities) is an oligopoly rather than an absolute monopoly. Oligopolies are however good enough to realize the desired high rate of profits, especially since the various firms often collude to minimize price competition.

Patents are not the only way in which states can create quasi-monopolies. State restrictions on imports and exports (so-called protectionist measures) are another. State subsidies and tax benefits are a third. The ability of strong states to use their muscle to prevent weaker states from creating counter-protectionist measures is still another. The role of the states as large-scale buyers of certain products willing to pay excessive prices is still another. Finally, regulations which impose a burden on producers may be relatively easy to absorb by large producers but crippling to smaller producers, an asymmetry which results in the elimination of the smaller producers from the market and thus increases the degree of oligopoly. The modalities by which states interfere with the virtual market are so extensive that they constitute a fundamental factor in determining prices and profits. Without such interferences, the capitalist system could not thrive and therefore could not survive.

Nonetheless, there are two inbuilt anti-monopolistic features in a capitalist world-economy. First of all, one producer's monopolistic advantage is another producer's loss. The losers will of course struggle politically to remove the advantages of the winners. They can do this by political struggle within the states where the monopolistic producers are located, appealing to doctrines of a free market and offering support to political leaders inclined to end a particular monopolistic advantage. Or they do this by persuading other states to defy the world market monopoly by using their state power to sustain competitive producers. Both methods are used. Therefore, over time, every quasi-monopoly is undone by the entry of further producers into the market.

Quasi-monopolies are thus self-liquidating. But they last long enough (say thirty years) to ensure considerable accumulation of capital by those who control the quasi-monopolies. When a quasi-monopoly does cease to exist, the large accumulators of capital simply move their capital to new leading products or whole new leading industries. The result is a cycle of leading products. Leading products have moderately short lives, but they are constantly succeeded by other leading industries. Thus the game continues. As for the once-leading industries past their prime, they become more and more "competitive," that is, less and less profitable. We see this pattern in action all the time.

Firms are the main actors in the market. Firms are normally the competitors of other firms operating in the same virtual market. They are also in conflict with those firms from whom they purchase inputs and those firms to which they sell their products. Fierce intercapitalist rivalry is the name of the game. And only the strongest and the most agile survive. One must remember that bankruptcy, or absorption by a more powerful firm, is the daily bread of capitalist enterprises. Not all capitalist entrepreneurs succeed in accumulating capital. Far from it. If they all succeeded, each would be likely to obtain very little capital. So, the repeated "failures" of firms not only weed out the weak competitors but are a condition sine qua non of the endless accumulation of capital. That is what explains the constant process of the concentration of capital.

To be sure, there is a downside to the growth of firms, either horizontally (in the same product), vertically (in the different steps in the chain of production), or what might be thought of as orthogonally (into other products not closely related). Size brings down costs through so-called economies of scale. But size adds costs of administration and coordination, and multiplies the risks of managerial inefficiencies. As a result of this contradiction, there has been a repeated zigzag process of firms getting larger and then getting smaller. But it has not at all been a simple up-and-down cycle. Rather, worldwide there has been a secular increase in the size of firms, the whole historical process taking the form of a ratchet, two steps up then one step back, continuously. The

size of firms also has direct political implications. Large size gives firms more political clout but also makes them more vulnerable to political assault—by their competitors, their employees, and their consumers. But here too the bottom line is an upward ratchet, toward more political influence over time.

The axial division of labor of a capitalist world-economy divides production into core-like products and peripheral products. Core-periphery is a relational concept. What we mean by core-periphery is the degree of profitability of the production processes. Since profitability is directly related to the degree of monopolization, what we essentially mean by core-like production processes is those that are controlled by quasi-monopolies. Peripheral processes are then those that are truly competitive. When exchange occurs, competitive products are in a weak position and quasi-monopolized products are in a strong position. As a result, there is a constant flow of surplus-value from the producers of peripheral products to the producers of core-like products. This has been called unequal exchange.

To be sure, unequal exchange is not the only way of moving accumulated capital from politically weak regions to politically strong regions. There is also plunder, often used extensively during the early days of incorporating new regions into the world-economy (consider, for example, the conquistadores and gold in the Americas). But plunder is self-liquidating. It is a case of killing the goose that lays the golden eggs. Still, since the consequences are middle-term and the advantages short-term, there still exists much plunder in the modern world-system, although we are often "scandalized" when we learn of it. When Enron goes bankrupt, after procedures that have moved enormous sums into the hands of a few managers, that is in fact plunder. When "privatizations" of erstwhile state property lead to its being garnered by mafia-like businessmen who quickly leave the country with destroyed enterprises in their wake, that is plunder. Self-liquidating, yes, but only after much damage has been done to the world's productive system, and indeed to the health of the capitalist world-economy.

Since quasi-monopolies depend on the patronage of strong states, they are largely located—juridically, physically, and in terms of ownership—within such states. There is therefore a geographical consequence of the core-peripheral relationship. Core-like processes tend to group themselves in a few states and to constitute the bulk of the production activity in such states.

Peripheral processes tend to be scattered among a large number of states and to constitute the bulk of the production activity in these states. Thus, for shorthand purposes we can talk of core states and peripheral states, so long as we remember that we are really talking of a relationship between production processes. Some states have a near even mix of core-like and peripheral products. We may call them semiperipheral states. They have, as we shall see, special political properties. It is however not meaningful to speak of semiperipheral production processes.

Since, as we have seen, quasi-monopolies exhaust themselves, what is a core-like process today will become a peripheral process tomorrow. The economic history of the modern world-system is replete with the shift, or downgrading, of products, first to semiperipheral countries, and then to peripheral ones. If circa 1800 the production of textiles was possibly the preeminent core-like production process, by 2000 it was manifestly one of the least profitable peripheral production processes. In 1800 these textiles were produced primarily in a very few countries (notably England and some other countries of northwestern Europe); in 2000 textiles were produced in virtually every part of the world-system, especially cheap textiles. The process has been repeated with many other products. Think of steel, or automobiles, or even computers. This kind of shift has no effect on the structure of the system itself. In 2000 there were other core-like processes (e.g. aircraft production or genetic engineering) which were concentrated in a few countries. There have always been new core-like processes to replace those which become more competitive and then move out of the states in which they were originally located.

The role of each state is very different vis-à-vis productive processes depending on the mix of core-peripheral processes within it. The strong states, which contain a disproportionate share of core-like processes, tend to emphasize their role of protecting the quasi-monopolies of the core-like processes. The very weak states, which contain a disproportionate share of peripheral production processes, are usually unable to do very much to affect the axial division of labor, and in effect are largely forced to accept the lot that has been given them.

The semiperipheral states which have a relatively even mix of production processes find themselves in the most difficult situation. Under pressure from core states and putting pressure on peripheral states, their major concern is to keep themselves from slipping into the periphery and to do what they can to advance themselves toward the core. Neither is easy, and both require considerable state interference with the world market. These semiperipheral states are the ones that put forward most aggressively and most publicly so-called protectionist policies. They hope thereby to "protect" their production processes from the competition of stronger firms outside, while trying to improve the efficiency of the firms inside so as to compete better in the world market. They are eager recipients of the relocation of erstwhile leading products, which they define these days as achieving "economic development." In this effort, their competition comes not from the core states but from other semiperipheral states, equally eager to be the recipients of relocation which cannot go to all the eager aspirants simultaneously and to the same degree. In the beginning of the twenty-first century, some obvious countries to be labeled semiperipheral are South Korea, Brazil, and India—countries with strong enterprises that export products (for example steel, automobiles, pharmaceuticals) to peripheral zones, but that also regularly relate to core zones as importers of more "advanced" products.

The normal evolution of the leading industries—the slow dissolution of the quasi-monopolies—is what accounts for the cyclical rhythms of the world-economy. A major leading industry will be a major stimulus to the expansion of the world-economy and will result in considerable accumulation of capital. But it also normally leads to more extensive employment in the world-economy, higher wage-levels, and a general sense of relative prosperity. As more and more firms enter the market of the erstwhile quasi-monopoly, there will be "overproduction" (that is, too much production for the real effective demand at a given time) and consequently increased price competition (because of the demand squeeze), thus lowering the rates of profit. At some point, a buildup of unsold products results, and consequently a slowdown in further production.

When this happens, we tend to see a reversal of the cyclical curve of the world-economy. We talk of stagnation or recession in the world-economy. Rates of unemployment rise worldwide. Producers seek to reduce costs in order to maintain their share of the world market. One of the mechanisms is relocation of the production processes to zones that have historically lower wages, that is, to semiperipheral countries. This shift puts pressure on the wage levels in the processes still remaining in core zones, and wages there tend to become lower as well. Effective demand which was at first lacking because of overproduction now becomes lacking because of a reduction in earnings of the consumers. In such a situation, not all producers necessarily lose out. There is obviously acutely increased competition among the diluted oligopoly that is now engaged in these production processes. They fight each other furiously, usually with the aid of their state machineries. Some states and some producers succeed in "exporting unemployment" from one core state to the others. Systemically, there is contraction, but certain core states and especially certain semiperipheral states may seem to be doing quite well.

The process we have been describing—expansion of the world-economy when there are quasi-monopolistic leading industries and contraction in the world-economy when there is a lowering of the intensity of quasi-monopoly—can be drawn as an up-and-down curve of so-called A-(expansion) and B-(stagnation) phases. A cycle consisting of an A-phase followed by a B-phase is sometimes referred to as a Kondratieff cycle, after the economist who described this phenomenon with clarity in the beginning of the twentieth century. Kondratieff cycles have up to now been more or less fifty to sixty years in length. Their exact length depends on the political measures taken by the states to avert a B-phase, and especially the measures to achieve recuperation from a B-phase on the basis of new leading industries that can stimulate a new A-phase.

A Kondratieff cycle, when it ends, never returns the situation to where it was at the beginning of the cycle. That is because what is done in the B-phase in order to get out of it and return to an A-phase changes in some important way the parameters of the world-system. The changes that solve the immediate (or short-run) problem of inadequate expansion of the world-economy (an essential element in maintaining the possibility of the endless accumulation of capital) restore a middle-run equilibrium but begin to create problems for the structure in the long run. The result is what we may call a secular trend. A secular trend should be thought of as a curve whose abscissa (or x-axis) records time and

whose ordinate (or y-axis) measures a phenomenon by recording the proportion of some group that has a certain characteristic. If over time the percentage is moving upward in an overall linear fashion, it means by definition (since the ordinate is in percentages) that at some point it cannot continue to do so. We call this reaching the asymptote, or 100 percent point. No characteristic can be ascribed to more than 100 percent of any group. This means that as we solve the middle-run problems by moving up on the curve, we will eventually run into the long-run problem of approaching the asymptote.

Let us suggest one example of how this works in a capitalist world-economy. One of the problems we noted in the Kondratieff cycles is that at a certain point major production processes become less profitable, and these processes begin to relocate in order to reduce costs. Meanwhile, there is increasing unemployment in core zones, and this affects global effective demand. Individual firms reduce their costs, but the collectivity of firms finds it more difficult to find sufficient customers. One way to restore a sufficient level of world effective demand is to increase the pay levels of ordinary workers in core zones, something which has frequently occurred at the latter end of Kondratieff B-periods. This thereby creates the kind of effective demand that is necessary to provide sufficient customers for new leading products. But of course higher pay levels may mean lesser profits for the entrepreneurs. At a world level this can be compensated for by expanding the pool of wage workers elsewhere in the world, who are willing to work at a lower level of wages. This can be done by drawing new persons into the wage-labor pool, for whom the lower wage represents in fact an increase in real income. But of course every time one draws "new" persons into the wage-labor pool, one reduces the number of persons remaining outside the wage-labor pool. There will come a time when the pool is diminished to the point where it no longer exists effectively. We are reaching the asymptote. We shall return to this issue in the last chapter when we discuss the structural crisis of the twenty-first century.

Obviously, a capitalist system requires that there be workers who provide the labor for the productive processes. It is often said that these laborers are proletarians, that is, wage-workers who have no alternative means of support (because they are landless and without monetary or property reserves). This is not quite accurate. For one thing, it is unrealistic to think of workers as isolated individuals. Almost all workers are linked to other persons in household structures that normally group together persons of both sexes and of different age-levels. Many, perhaps most, of these household structures can be called families, but family ties are not necessarily the only mode by which households can be held together. Households often have common residences, but in fact less frequently than one thinks.

A typical household consists of three to ten persons who, over a long period (say thirty years or so), pool multiple sources of income in order to survive collectively. Households are not usually egalitarian structures internally nor are they unchanging structures (persons are born and die, enter or leave households, and in any case grow older and thus tend to alter their economic role). What distinguishes a household structure is some form of obligation to provide income for the group and to share in the consumption resulting from this income. Households are quite different from clans or tribes or other quite large and extended entities, which often share obligations of mutual security and identity but do not regularly share income. Or if there exist such large entities which are income-pooling, they are dysfunctional for the capitalist system.

We first must look at what the term "income" covers. There are in fact generically five kinds of income in the modern world-system. And almost all households seek and obtain all five kinds, although in different proportions (which turns out to be very important). One obvious form is wage-income, by which is meant payment (usually in money form) by persons outside the household for work of a member of the household that is performed outside the household in some production process. Wage-income may be occasional or regular. It may be payment by time employed or by work accomplished (piece-work). Wage-income has the advantage to the employer that it is "flexible" (that is, continued work is a function of the employer's need), although the trade union, other forms of syndical action by workers, and state legislation have often limited employers' flexibility in many ways. Still, employers are almost never obligated to provide lifetime support to particular workers. Conversely, this system has the disadvantage to the employer that when more workers are needed, they may not be readily available for employment, especially if the economy is expanding. That is, in a system of wage-labor, the employer is trading not being required to pay workers in periods when they are not needed for the guarantee that the workers are available when they are needed.

A second obvious source of household income is subsistence activity. We usually define this type of work too narrowly, taking it to mean only the efforts of rural persons to grow food and produce necessities for their own consumption without passing through a market. This is indeed a form of subsistence production, and this kind of work has of course been on a sharp decline in the modern world-system, which is why we often say that subsistence production is disappearing. By using such a narrow definition, we are however neglecting the numerous ways in which subsistence activity is actually increasing in the modern world. When someone cooks a meal or washes dishes at home, this is subsistence production. When a homeowner assembles furniture bought from a store, this is subsistence production. And when a professional uses a computer to send an e-mail which, in an earlier day, a (paid) secretary would have typed, he or she is engaged in subsistence production. Subsistence production is a large part of household income today in the most economically wealthy zones of the capitalist world-economy.

A third kind of household income we might generically call petty commodity production. A petty commodity is defined as a product produced within the confines of the household but sold for cash on a wider market. Obviously, this sort of production continues to be very widespread in the poorer zones of the world-economy but is not totally absent anywhere. In richer zones we often call it free-lancing. This kind of activity involves not only the marketing of produced goods (including of course intellectual goods) but also petty marketing. When a small boy sells on the street cigarettes or matches one by one to consumers who cannot afford to buy them in the normal quantity that is packaged, this boy is engaged in petty-commodity production, the production activity being simply the disassembly of the larger package and its transport to the street market.

A fourth kind of income is what we can generically call rent. Rent can be drawn from some major capital investment (offering urban apartments for rent, or rooms within apartments) or from locational advantage (collecting a toll on a private bridge) or from capital ownership (clipping coupons on bonds, earning interest on a savings account). What makes it rent is that it is ownership and not work of any kind that makes possible the income.

Finally, there is a fifth kind of income, which in the modern world we call transfer payments. These may be defined as income that comes to an individual by virtue of a defined obligation of someone else to provide this income. The transfer payments may come from persons close to the household, as when gifts or loans are given from one generation to the other at the time of birth, marriage, or death. Such transfer payments between households may be made on the basis of reciprocity (which in theory ensures no extra income over a lifetime but tends to smooth out liquidity needs). Or transfer payments may occur through the efforts of the state (in which case one's own money may simply be returning at a different moment in time), or through an insurance scheme (in which one may in the end benefit or lose), or through redistribution from one economic class to another.

As soon as we think about it, we all are familiar with the income-pooling that goes on in households. Picture a middle-class American family, in which the adult male has a job (and perhaps moonlights at a second), the adult female is a caterer operating out of her home, the teenage son has a paper route, and the twelve-year-old daughter babysits. Add in perhaps the grandmother who draws a widow's pension and who also occasionally babysits for a small child, and the room above the garage that is rented out. Or picture the working-class Mexican household in which the adult male has migrated to the United States illegally and is sending home money, the adult female is cultivating a plot at home, the teenage girl is working as a domestic (paid in money and in kind) in a wealthy Mexican's home, and the subteen boy is peddling small items in the town market after school (or instead of school). Each of us can elaborate many more such combinations.

In actual practice, few households are without all five kinds of income. But one should notice right away that the persons within the household who tend to provide the income may correlate with sex or age categories. That is to say, many of these tasks are gender- and age-defined. Wage-labor was for a long time largely considered the province of males between the ages of fourteen or eighteen to sixty or sixty-five. Subsistence and petty-commodity production have been for the most part defined as the province of adult women and of children and the aged. State transfer income has been largely linked to wage earning, except for certain transfers relating to child rearing. Much political activity of the last hundred years has been aimed at overcoming the gender specificity of these definitions.

As we have already noted, the relative importance of the various forms of income in particular households has varied widely. Let us distinguish two major varieties: the household where wage-income accounts for 50 percent or more of the total lifetime income, and the household where it accounts for less. Let us call the former a "proletarian household" (because it seems to be heavily dependent on wage-income, which is what the term proletarian is supposed to invoke); and let us then call the latter a "semiproletarian house-hold" (because there is doubtless at least some wage-income for most members of it). If we do this, we can see that an employer has an advantage in employing those wage-laborers who are in a semiproletarian household. Whenever wage-labor constitutes a substantial component of household income, there is necessarily a floor for how much the wage-earner can be paid. It must be an amount that represents at least a proportionate share of the reproduction costs of the household. This is what we can think of as an *absolute* minimum wage. If, however, the wage-earner is ensconced in a household that is only semiproletarian, the wage-earner can be paid a wage *below* the absolute minimum wage, without necessarily endangering the survival of the household. The difference can be made up by additional income provided from other sources and usually by other members of the household. What we see happening in such cases is that the other producers of income in the household are in effect transferring surplus-value to the employer of the wage-earner over and above whatever surplus-value the wage-earner himself is transferring, by permitting the employer to pay less than the absolute minimum wage.

It follows that in a capitalist system employers would in general prefer to employ wage-workers coming from semiproletarian households. There are however two pressures working in the other direction. One is the pressure of the wage-workers themselves who seek to be "proletarianized," because that in effect means being better paid. And one is the contradictory pressure on the employers themselves.

Against their individual need to lower wages, there is their collective longer-term need to have a large enough effective demand in the world-economy to sustain the market for their products. So over time, as a result of these two very different pressures, there is a slow increase in the number of households that are proletarianized. Nonetheless, this description of the long-term trend is contrary to the traditional social science picture that capitalism as a system requires primarily proletarians as workers. If this were so, it would be difficult to explain why, after four to five hundred years, the proportion of proletarian workers is not much higher than it is. Rather than think of proletarianization as a capitalist necessity, it would be more useful to think of it as a locus of struggle, whose outcome has been a slow if steady increase, a secular trend moving toward its asymptote.

There are classes in a capitalist system, since there are clearly persons who are differently located in the economic system with different levels of income who have differing interests. For example, it is obviously in the interest of workers to seek an increase in their wages, and it is equally obviously in the interest of employers to resist these increases, at least in general. But, as we have just seen, wage-workers are ensconced in households. It makes no sense to think of the workers belonging to one class and other members of their household to another. It is obviously households, not individuals, that are located within classes. Individuals who wish to be class-mobile often find that they must withdraw from the households in which they are located and locate themselves in other households, in order to achieve such an objective. This is not easy but it is by no means impossible.

Classes however are not the only groups within which households locate themselves. They are also members of status-groups or identities. (If one calls them status-groups, one is emphasizing how they are perceived by others, a sort of objective criterion. If one calls them identities, one is emphasizing how they perceive themselves, a sort of subjective criterion. But under one name or the other, they are an institutional reality of the modern world-system.) Status-groups or identities are ascribed labels, since we are born into them, or at least we usually think we are born into them. It is on the whole rather difficult to join such groups voluntarily, although not impossible. These status-groups or identities are the numerous "peoples" of which all of us are members—nations, races, ethnic groups, religious

communities, but also genders and categories of sexual preferences. Most of these categories are often alleged to be anachronistic leftovers of pre-modern times. This is quite wrong as a premise. Membership in status-groups or identities is very much a part of modernity. Far from dying out, they are actually growing in importance as the logic of a capitalist system unfolds further and consumes us more and more intensively.

If we argue that households locate themselves in a class, and all their members share this location, is this equally true of status-groups or identities? There does exist an enormous pressure within households to maintain a common identity, to be part of a single status-group or identity. This pressure is felt first of all by persons who are marrying and who are required, or at least pressured, to look within the status-group or identity for a partner. But obviously, the constant movement of individuals within the modern world-system plus the normative pressures to ignore status-group or identity membership in favor of meritocratic criteria have led to a considerable mixing of original identities within the framework of households. Nonetheless, what tends to happen in each household is an evolution toward a single identity, the emergence of new, often barely articulated status-group identities that precisely reify what began as a mixture, and thereby reunify the household in terms of status-group identities. One element in the demand to legitimate gay marriages is this felt pressure to reunify the identity of the household.

Why is it so important for households to maintain singular class and status-group identities, or at least pretend to maintain them? Such a homogenization of course aids in maintaining the unity of a household as an income-pooling unit and in overcoming any centrifugal tendencies that might arise because of internal inequalities in the distribution of consumption and decision making. It would however be a mistake to see this tendency as primarily an internal group defense mechanism. There are important benefits to the overall world-system from the homogenizing trends within household structures.

Households serve as the primary socializing agencies of the world-system. They seek to teach us, and particularly the young, knowledge of and respect for the social rules by which we are supposed to abide. They are of course seconded by state agencies such as schools and armies as well as by religious institutions and the media. But none of these come close to the households in actual impact. What however determines how the households will socialize their members? Largely how the secondary institutions frame the issues for the households, and their ability to do so effectively depends on the relative homogeneity of the households—that is, they have and see themselves as having a defined role in the historical social system. A household that is certain of its status-group identity—its nationality, its race, its religion, its ethnicity, its code of sexuality—knows exactly how to socialize its members. One whose identity is less certain but that tries to create a homogenized, even if novel, identity can do almost as well. A household that would openly avow a permanently split identity would find the socialization function almost impossible to do, and might find it difficult to survive as a group.

Of course, the powers that be in a social system always hope that socialization results in the acceptance of the very real hierarchies that are the product of the system. They also hope that socialization results in the internalization of the myths, the rhetoric, and the theorizing of the system. This does happen in part but never in full. Households also socialize members into rebellion, withdrawal, and deviance. To be sure, up to a point even such antisystemic socialization can be useful to the system by offering an outlet for restless spirits, provided that the overall system is in relative equilibrium. In that case, one can anticipate that the negative socializations may have at most a limited impact on the functioning of the system. But when the historical system comes into structural crisis, suddenly such antisystemic socializations can play a profoundly unsettling role for the system.

Thus far, we have merely cited class identification and status-group identification as the two alternative modes of collective expression for households. But obviously there are multiple kinds of status-groups, not always totally consonant one with the other. Furthermore, as historical time has moved on, the number of kinds of status-groups has grown, not diminished. In the late twentieth century, people often began to claim identities in terms of sexual preferences which were not a basis for household construction in previous centuries. Since we are all involved in a multiplicity of status-groups or identities, the question arises whether there is a priority order of identities. In case of conflicts, which should prevail? Which does prevail? Can a household be homogeneous in terms of one identity but not in

terms of another? The answer obviously is yes, but what are the consequences?

We must look at the pressures on households coming from outside. Most of the status-groups have some kind of trans-household institutional expression. And these institutions place direct pressure on the households not merely to conform to their norms and their collective strategies but to give them priority. Of the trans-household institutions, the states are the most successful in influencing the households because they have the most immediate weapons of pressure (the law, substantial benefits to distribute, the capacity to mobilize media). But wherever the state is less strong, the religious structures, the ethnic organizations, and similar groups may become the strongest voices insisting on the priorities of the households. Even when status-groups or identities describe themselves as antisystemic, they may still be in rivalry with other antisystemic status-groups or identities, demanding priority in allegiance. It is this complicated turmoil of household identities that underlies the roller coaster of political struggle within the modern world-system.

The complex relationships of the world-economy, the firms, the states, the households, and the trans-household institutions that link members of classes and status-groups are beset by two opposite—but symbiotic—ideological themes; universalism on the one hand and racism and sexism on the other.

Universalism is a theme prominently associated with the modern world-system. It is in many ways one of its boasts. Universalism means in general the priority to general rules applying equally to all persons, and therefore the rejection of particularistic preferences in most spheres. The only rules that are considered permissible within the framework of universalism are those which can be shown to apply directly to the narrowly defined proper functioning of the world-system.

The expressions of universalism are manifold. If we translate universalism to the level of the firm or the school, it means for example the assigning of persons to positions on the basis of their training and capacities (a practice otherwise known as meritocracy). If we translate it to the level of the household, it implies among other things that marriage should be contracted for reasons of "love" but not those of wealth or ethnicity or any other general particularism. If we translate it to the level of the state, it means such rules as universal suffrage and equality before the law. We are all familiar with the mantras, since they are repeated with some regularity in public discourse. They are supposed to be the central focus of our socialization. Of course, we know that these mantras are unevenly advocated in various locales of the world-system (and we shall want to discuss why this is so), and we know that they are far from fully observed in practice. But they have become the official gospel of modernity.

Universalism is a positive norm, which means that most people assert their belief in it, and almost everyone claims that it is a virtue. Racism and sexism are just the opposite. They too are norms, but they are negative norms, in that most people deny their belief in them. Almost everyone declares that they are vices, yet nonetheless they are norms. What is more, the degree to which the negative norms of racism and sexism are observed is at least as high as, in fact for the most part much higher than, the virtuous norm of universalism. This may seem to be an anomaly. But it is not.

Let us look at what we mean by racism and sexism. Actually these are terms that came into widespread use only in the second half of the twentieth century. Racism and sexism are instances of a far wider phenomenon that has no convenient name, but that might be thought of as anti-universalism, or the active institutional discrimination against all the persons in a given status-group or identity. For each kind of identity, there is a social ranking. It can be a crude ranking, with two categories, or elaborate, with a whole ladder. But there is always a group on top in the ranking, and one or several groups at the bottom. These rankings are both worldwide and more local, and both kinds of ranking have enormous consequences in the lives of people and in the operation of the capitalist world-economy.

We are all quite familiar with the worldwide rankings within the modern world-system: men over women, Whites over Blacks (or non-Whites), adults over children (or the aged), educated over less educated, heterosexuals over gays and lesbians, the bourgeois and professionals over workers, urbanites over rural dwellers. Ethnic rankings are more local, but in every country, there is a dominant ethnicity and then the others. Religious rankings vary across the world, but in any particular zone everyone is aware of what they are. Nationalism often takes the form of

constructing links between one side of each of the antinomies into fused categories, so that, for example, one might create the norm that adult White heterosexual males of particular ethnicities and religions are the only ones who would be considered "true" nationals.

There are several questions which this description brings to our attention. What is the point of professing universalism and practicing anti-universalism simultaneously? Why should there be so many varieties of anti-universalism? Is this contradictory antinomy a necessary part of the modern world-system? Universalism and anti-universalism are in fact both operative day to day, but they operate in different arenas. Universalism tends to be the operative principle most strongly for what we could call the cadres of the world-system—neither those who are at the very top in terms of power and wealth, nor those who provide the large majority of the world's workers and ordinary people in all fields of work and all across the world, but rather an in-between group of people who have leadership or supervisory roles in various institutions. It is a norm that spells out the optimal recruitment mode for such technical, professional, and scientific personnel. This in-between group may be larger or smaller according to a country's location in the world-system and the local political situation. The stronger the country's economic position, the larger the group. Whenever universalism loses its hold even among the cadres in particular parts of the world-system, however, observers tend to see dysfunction, and quite immediately there emerge political pressures (both from within the country and from the rest of the world) to restore some degree of universalistic criteria.

There are two quite different reasons for this. On the one hand, universalism is believed to ensure relatively competent performance and thus make for a more efficient world-economy, which in turn improves the ability to accumulate capital. Hence, normally those who control production processes push for such universalistic criteria. Of course, universalistic criteria arouse resentment when they come into operation only after some particularistic criterion has been invoked. If the civil service is only open to persons of some particular religion or ethnicity, then the choice of persons within this category may be universalistic but the overall choice is not. If universalistic criteria are invoked only at the time of choice while ignoring the particularistic criteria by which individuals have access to the necessary prior training, again there is resentment. When, however, the choice is truly universalistic, resentment may still occur because choice involves exclusion, and we may get "populist" pressure for untested and unranked access to position. Under these multiple circumstances, universalistic criteria play a major social-psychological role in legitimating meritocratic allocation. They make those who have attained the status of cadre feel justified in their advantage and ignore the ways in which the so-called universalistic criteria that permitted their access were not in fact fully universalistic, or ignore the claims of all the others to material benefits given primarily to cadres. The norm of universalism is an enormous comfort to those who are benefiting from the system. It makes them feel they deserve what they have.

On the other hand, racism, sexism, and other anti-universalistic norms perform equally important tasks in allocating work, power, and privilege within the modern world-system. They seem to imply exclusions from the social arena. Actually they are really modes of inclusion, but of inclusion at inferior ranks. These norms exist to justify the power ranking, to enforce the lower ranking, and per-

versely even to make it somewhat palatable to those who have the lower ranking. Anti-universalistic norms are presented as codifications of natural, eternal verities not subject to social modification. They are presented not merely as cultural verities but, implicitly or even explicitly, as biologically rooted necessities of the functioning of the human animal.

They become norms for the state, the workplace, the social arena. But they also become norms into which households are pushed to socialize their members, an effort that has been quite successful on the whole. They justify the polarization of the world-system. Since polarization has been increasing over time, racism, sexism, and other forms of anti-universalism have become ever more important, even though the political struggle against such forms of anti-universalism has also become more central to the functioning of the world-system.

The bottom line is that the modern world-system has made as a central, basic feature of its structure the simultaneous existence, propagation, and practice of both universalism and anti-universalism. This antinomic duo is as fundamental to the system as is the core-peripheral axial division of labor.

SUGGESTIONS FOR FURTHER READING

◾ General

Boggs, Carl. *Gramsci's Marxism.* London: Pluto Press, 1976.

Cohen, Benjamin. *The Question of Imperialism.* New York: Basic Books, 1973.

Doyle, Michael W. *Ways of War and Peace.* New York: W. W. Norton, 1997. [Part Three addresses Marxism, Leninism, and Socialism.]

Evans, Peter B. *Embedded Autonomy: States and Industrial Production.* Princeton NJ: Princeton University Press, 1995.

Gamble, Andrew, David Marsh, and Tony Tant, eds. *Marxism and Social Science.* Champaign, IL: University of Illinois Press, 1999.

Gill, Stephen. *Gramsci, Historical Materialism and International Relations.* Cambridge, UK: Cambridge University Press, 1993.

———. *Power and Resistance in the New World Order.* New York: Palgrave Macmillan, 2003.

Gilpin, Robert. "Three Models of the Future," *International Organization,* 29, 1 (1975): 37–60.

Gramsci, Antonio. *Selections from the Prison Notebooks,* ed. Quentin Hoare and Geoffrey Nowell Smith. New York: International Publishers, 1971.

Gramsci, Antonio. Trans. and ed. Joseph A. Buttigieg. *Prison Notebooks,* New York: Columbia University Press, Vol. 1, 1991; Vol. 2, 1996; Vol. 3, 2007.

Heilbroner, Robert. *The Nature and Logic of Capitalism.* New York: W. W. Norton, 1985.

———. *21st Century Capitalism.* New York: W. W. Norton, 1993.

Hobsbawm, Eric. *On Empire: America, War, and Global Supremacy.* Pantheon Books, 2008.

———. with David Forgacs. Ed. *The Antonio Gramsci Reader: Selected Writings 1916–1935.* New York: NYU Press, 2000.

Holm, Hans-Henrik, and Georg Sorensen. *Whose World Order? Uneven Globalization and the End of the Cold War.* Boulder: Westview, 1995.

Jones, Steven J. *Antonio Gramsci.* London: Routledge, 2006.

Morton, Adam David. *Unravelling Gramsci: Hegemony and Passive Revolution in the Global Political Economy.* London: Pluto Press, 2007.

Murphy, Craig N., ed. *Egalitarian Politics in the Age of Globalization.* New York: Palgrave Macmillan, 2002.

———. *Global Institutions, Marginalization and Development.* (London: Routledge, 2005).

———. *International Organization and Industrial Change.* New York: Oxford University Press, 1994.

———. *The United Nations Development Programme: A Better Way?* Cambridge, UK: Cambridge University Press, 2006.

Murphy, Craig N., and Roger Tooze, eds. *The New International Political Economy.* Boulder, CO: Lynne Rienner, 1991.

Pala, Ronen P., and Barry Gills, eds. *Transcending the State-Global Divide: A Neostructuralist Agenda in International Relations.* Boulder, CO: Lynne Rienner, 1994.

Rostow, W. W. 1960. *The Stages of Economic Growth, a Non-Communist Manifesto.* Cambridge, UK: Cambridge University Press, 1960.

On Capitalism and the Capitalist World-System

Amin, Samir. *Empire of Chaos.* New York: Monthly Review Press, 1992.

Archer, Margaret. "The Dubious Guarantees of Social Science: A Reply to Wallerstein." *International Sociology* 13, 1 (March 1998): 5–17.

Arrighi, Giovanni. "Capitalism and the Modern World-System: Rethinking the Nondebates of the 1970s." *Review* 21, 1 (Winter 1998): 113–29.

———. *The Long 20th Century: Money, Power, and the Origins of Our Times* (New York: Verso, 1995).

Bergesen, Albert. *Studies of the Modern World-System.* New York: Academic Press, 1980.

Boswell, Terry, and Immanuel Wallerstein, eds. *Revolution in the World System.* Westport, CT: Greenwood, 1989.

———. *The Spiral of Capitalism and Socialism: Toward Global Democracy.* Boulder CO: Lynne Rienner Publishers, 2000.

Chase-Dunn, Christopher. *Global Formation: Structures of the World Economy.* Oxford, England: Blackwell, 1989; rev. ed. Lanham MD: Rowman & Littlefield Publishers, 1998.

———. ed. *The Historical Evolution of the International Political Economy.* Cheltenham Glos, UK: Edward Elgar Publishing, 1995.

Chase-Dunn, Christopher, and Salvatore J. Babones, eds. *Global Social Change: Historical and Comparative Perspectives.* Baltimore MD: The Johns Hopkins University Press, 2006.

Chase-Dunn, Christopher, and Peter Grimes. "World-Systems Analysis." *Annual Review of Sociology.* 21 (1995): 387–417.

Chase-Dunn, Christopher, and Thomas D. Hall, eds. *Core-Periphery Relations in Pre-Capitalist Worlds.* Boulder, CO: Westview, 1991.

Chase-Dunn, Christopher, with Charles Tilly and Scott McNail, eds. *Rise and Demise: Comparing World Systems.* Boulder CO: Westview Press, 1997.

Chew, Sing C., and Robert A. Denemark, eds. *The Underdevelopment of Development: Essays in Honor of André Gunder Frank.* Thousand Oaks, CA: Sage Publications, 1999.

Chirot, Daniel, and Thomas D. Hall. "World-System Theory." *Annual Review of Sociology.* 8 (1982): 81–106.

Cox, Robert. "Ideologies and the New International Economic Order," *International Organization* 33, 2 (1979): 257–302.

Cox, Robert W. *The Political Economy of a Plural World: Critical Reflections on Power, Morals and Civilization.* London: Taylor & Francis, 2007.

———. *Power, Production, and World Order.* New York: Columbia University Press, 1987.

Cox, Robert W., and Timothy J. Sinclair. *Approaches to World Order.* Cambridge, UK: Cambridge University Press, 1996.

Evans, Peter. *States Versus Markets in the World System.* ed. Peter B. Evans. Beverly Hills, CA : Sage, 1985.

Frank, André Gunder. *Capitalism and Underdevelopment in Latin America*. New York and London: Monthly Review Press, 1969.

———. "The Modern World System Revisited: Rereading Braudel and Wallerstein." In ed. Stephen Sandersons, *Civilizations and World-Systems: Studying World-Historical Change*. Walnut Creek, CA: AltaMira Press, 1995, 163–94.

———. "A Plea for World System History." *Journal of World History* 2, 1 (Winter 1991).

———. *ReORIENT: Global Economy in the Asian Age*. Berkeley, CA: University of California Press, 1998.

———. *World Accumulation, 1492–1789*. New York: Algora Publishing, 2003.

Friedmann, Harriet. "Rethinking Capitalism and Hierarchy." *Review* 13, 2 (Spring1990): 255–64.

Friedmann, Jonathan, and Christopher Chase-Dunn. *Hegemonic Decline: Present and Past*. Boulder CO: Paradigm Publishers, 2005.

Galtung, Johan. "A Structural Theory of Imperialism." *Journal of Peace Research*, 2 (1971): 81–98.

Gill, Stephen, and Isabella Bakker-Power. *Production and Social Reproduction: Human In/security in the Global Political Economy*. New York: Palgrave Macmillan, 2004.

Gasiorowski, Mark. "The Structure of Third World Economic Interdependence," *International Organization* 39, 2 (1985): 331–42.

Goldfrank, Walter L. "Paradigm Regained? The Rules of Wallerstein's World-System Method." *Journal of World-Systems Research* 6, 2 (2000): 150–95.

Hall, Thomas D. "The World-System Perspective: A Small Sample from a Large Universe," *Sociological Inquiry* 66, 4 (Fall1996): 440–54.

Jaguaribe, Hélio. *Economic & Political Development*. Cambridge, MA: Harvard University Press, 1968.

Klink, Frank F. "Rationalizing Core-Periphery Relations." *International Studies Quarterly* 34, 2 (June 1990): 183–209.

Morton, Adam David. *Unravelling Gramsci: Hegemony and Passive Revolution in the Global Political Economy*. London: Pluto Press, 2007.

Murphy, Craig N. "Freezing the North–South Bloc(k) After the East–West Thaw." *Socialist Review* 20, 3 (July–September 1990): 25–46.

Nurkse, R. *Problems of Capital Formation in Underdeveloped Countries*. Oxford: Blackwell, 1953.

Pomerantz, Kenneth. *The Great Divergence: Europe, China and the Making of the Modern World Economy* Princeton, NJ: Princeton University Press, 2000.

Roudometof, Victor, and Roland Robertson. "Globalization, World-System Theory, and the Comparative Study of Civilizations: Issues of Theoretical Logic in World-Historical Sociology." In ed., Stephen Sandersons, *Civilizations and World-Systems: Studying World-Historical Change*. Walnut Creek, CA: AltaMira Press, 1995, 273–300.

Schaeffer, Robert K., and Immanuel Wallerstein, eds. *War in the World-System*. Westport, CT: Greenwood, 1989.

Shannon, Thomas Richard. *An Introduction to the World-System Perspective*, 2nd ed. Boulder, CO: Westview 1989, 1996.

Skocpol, Theda. "Wallerstein's World Capitalist System: A Theoretical and Historical Critique." *American Journal of Sociology* 82, 5 (March 1977): 1075–90.

Terlouw, C. P. "The Elusive Semiperiphery: A Critical Examination of the Concept Semiperiphery." *International Journal of Comparative Sociology* 34, 1–2 (January–April 1993): 87–102.

Thompson, William R. *Contending Approaches to World System Analysis*. Beverly Hills, CA: Sage, 1983.

Van Rossem, Ronan. "The World System Paradigm as General Theory of Development: A Cross-National Test." *American Sociological Review* 61, 3 (June1996): 508–27.

Wallerstein, Immanuel. *Africa: The Politics of Independence and Unity*. [Combines earlier works from 1961, 1967 and 1971.] Lincoln NE: University of Nebraska Press, 2005.

———. *After Liberalism*. New York: New Press, 1995.

———. *The Capitalist World Economy*. Cambridge, England: Cambridge University Press, 1979.

———. *The End of the World As We Know It: Social Science for the Twenty-First Century*. Minneapolis MN: University of Minnesota Press, 2001.

———. *The Essential Wallerstein*. New York: New Press, 2000.

———. *European Universalism: The Rhetoric of Power*. New York: New Press, 2006.

———. *Geopolitics and Geoculture: Essays on the Changing World System*. New York: Cambridge University Press, 1991.

———. *Historical Capitalism*. London: Verso, 1983.

————. *The Modern World System* I: *Capitalist Agriculture and the Origins of the European World-Economy in the Sixteenth Century*. New York: Academic Press, 1974.

————. *The Modern World System* II: *Mercantilism and the Consolidation of the European World-Economy, 1600–1750*. New York: Academic Press, 1980.

————. *The Modern World System* III: *The Second Era of Great Expansion of the Capitalist World-Economy, 1730–1840s*. New York: Academic Press, 1988.

————. *The Politics of the World-Economy*. New York: Cambridge University Press, 1984.

————. "The Rise and Future Demise of the World Capitalist System." *Comparative Studies in Society and History* 16, 4 (September 1974): 387–415.

————. "Systeme Mondiale contre Systeme-Monde." *Sociologie et Societe* 22, 2 (October 1990).

————. *World-Systems Analysis: An Introduction*. Durham, NC: Duke University Press, 2004.

Walton, John, and Charles Ragin. "Global and National Sources of Political Protest: Third World Responses to the Debt Crisis." *American Sociological Review* 55, 6 (December 1990): 876–90.

Yo, Alvin. *Social Change and Development: Modernization, Dependency and World-Systems Theories*. Newbury Park, CA: Sage Library of Social Research, 2005.

■ On Dependency

Berger, Mark T. *Under Northern Eyes: Latin American Studies and U.S. Hegemony in the Americas, 1898–1990*. Bloomington: Indiana University Press, 1995.

Caporaso, James. "Dependence, Dependency, and Power in the Global System: A Structural and Behavioral Analysis," *International Organization*, 32, 1 (1978): 13–44.

————. "Dependency Theory: Continuities and Discontinuities in Development Studies." *International Organization* 34, 4 (Autumn 1980): 605–28. [A review essay.]

————. "Introduction to the Special Issue of International Organization on Dependence and Dependency in the Global System," *International Organization*, 32, 1 (1978): 1–12.

Cardoso, Fernando Henrique. *The Accidental President of Brazil: A Memoir*. New York: Public Affairs, 2007.

————. "Associated-Dependent Development." In *Authoritarian Brazil*, ed. Alfred Stepan. New Haven, CT: Yale University Press, 1973.

————. "The Consumption of Dependency Theory in the United States." *Latin American Research Review* 12, 3 (1977): 7–24.

————. "Dependency and Development in Latin America." *New Left Review* 74 (July–August 1972): 83–95.

————. "Imperialism and Dependency in Latin America." In *Structures of Dependency*, ed. Frank Bonilla and Robert Girling. Stanford, CA: Stanford Institute of Political Studies, 1973.

Cardoso, Fernando, and Enzo Faletto. *Dependency and Development in Latin America*. Berkeley, CA: University of California Press, 1979.

Chilcote, Ronald. "Theories of Development and Underdevelopment." In *Theories of Comparative Politics: In Search of a Paradigm Reconsidered*. Boulder, CO: Westview Press, 1994.

Collier, David. "Timing of Economic Growth and Regime Characteristics in Latin America," *Comparative Politics* 7, 3 (1975): 331–59.

dos Santos, Theotonio. "The Structure of Dependence." *American Economic Review* 60, 2 (May 1970): 231–36.

————. "The Structure of Dependency" in *The Theoretical Evolution of International Political Economy*, eds. George Crane and Abla Amawi. New York: Oxford University Press, 1990.

————. *Teoria de la Dependencia*. Barcelona, Spain: Plaza y Janes, 2003.

dos Santos, Theotonio, and Randall Laura. "The Theoretical Foundations of the Cardoso Government: A New Stage of the Dependency-Theory Debate," *Latin American Perspectives* 25, 1 (January 1998): 53–70.

Dussel, Enrique, and Yanez Anibal. "Marx's Economic Manuscripts of 1861–63 and the 'Concept' of Dependency." *Latin American Perspectives* 17, 2, Post-Marxism, the Left, and Democracy. (Spring, 1990): 62–101.

Duvall, Raymond. "Dependence and Dependencia Theory," *International Organization* 31, 1 (1978): 51–78.

Evans, Peter. *Dependent Development: The Alliance of Multinational, State and Local Capital in Brazil*. Princeton, NJ: Princeton University Press, 1979.

Fagen, Richard. "A Funny Thing Happened on the Way to the Market: Thoughts on Extending Dependency Ideas," *International Organization* 32, 1 (1978): 287–300.

————. "Studying Latin American Politics: Some Implications of a Dependencia Approach," *Latin American Research Review*, 12, 3 (1977).

Fagen, Richard, Carmen D. Deere, and Jose L. Coraggio, eds. *Transition and Development: Problems of Third World Socialism*. New York: Monthly Review Press, 1986.

Frank, Andre Gunder. *Capitalism and Underdevelopment in Latin America*. London: Penguin, 1971.

———. *Dependent Accumulation and Underdevelopment*. London: Macmillan, 1978.

Ghosh, B.N. *Dependency Theory Revisited*. London: Ashgate Publishing, 2001.

Grieco, Joseph. "Between Dependency and Autonomy: India's Experience with the International Computer Industry," *International Organization* 36, 3 (1982): 609–32.

Halebsky, Sandor, and Richard L. Harris. *Capital, Power and Inequality in Latin America*. Boulder, CO: Westview, 1995.

Hettne, Bjorn, Andras Inotai, and Osvaldo Sunkel, eds. *Comparing Regionalisms: Implications for Global Development*. New York: Palgrave Macmillan, 2000.

———. *Globalism and the New Regionalism*. New York: Palgrave Macmillan, 2000.

———. *National Perspectives on the New Regionalism in the North*. New York: Palgrave Macmillan, 2000.

———. *National Perspectives on the New Regionalism in the South*. New York: Palgrave Macmillan, 2000.

———. *The New Regionalism and the Future of Security and Development*. New York: Palgrave Macmillan, 2000.

Kauffman, Robert, Harry Chernotsky, and Daniel Geller. "A Preliminary Test of the Theory of Dependency," *Comparative Politics* 7, 3 (1975): 202–330.

Klink, Frank. "Rationalizing Core-Periphery Relations: The Analytical Foundations of Structural Inequality in World Politics," *International Studies Quarterly* 34, 2 (June 1990): 183–209.

Larrain, Jorge. *Theories of Development: Capitalism, Colonialism and Dependency*. Cambridge, UK: Polity, 1991.

Love, Joseph. "The Origins of Dependency Analysis." *Journal of Latin American Studies* 22, 1 (1990): 143–68.

———. "The Rise and Decline of Economic Structuralism in Latin America: New Dimensions," *Latin American Research Review* 40, 3 (2005): 100–25.

Martin-Jones, David. "Peasant Revolutions, Dependencia and Developmental States." In *The Image of China in Western Social and Political Thought*. New York: Palgrave, 2001.

McGowan, Patrick, and Dale Smith. "Economic Dependency in Black Africa: An Analysis of Competing Theories," *International Organization* 32, 1 (1978): 179–235.

Moran, Theodore. *Harnessing Foreign Direct Investment for Development: Policies for Developed and Developing Countries*. Washington, DC: Center for Global Development, 2006.

———. "Multinational Corporations and Dependency, A Dialogue for Dependentistas and Non-Dependentistas," *International Organization*, 32, 1 (1978): 79–100.

Packenham, Robert. *The Dependency Movement: Scholarship and Politics in Development Studies*. Cambridge, MA: Harvard University Press, 1992.

Prebisch, Raul. "The Economic Development of Latin America and Its Principal Problems," *Economic Bulletin for Latin America*, 7, 1962, 1–22. (First published by ECLA in Spanish in 1949).

———. *Towards a Dynamic Development Policy for Latin America*. New York: United Nations, 1963.

Smith, Tony. "The Underdevelopment of Development Literature: The Case of Dependency Theory." *World Politics* 31, 2 (January 1979): 247–88.

Sunkel, Osvaldo. "Big Business and Dependencia." *Foreign Affairs* 50 (April 1972): 317–531.

———. *Development from Within: Toward a Neostructuralist Approach for Latin America*. Boulder, CO: Lynne Rienner Publishers, 1993.

———. "National Development Policy and External Dependence in Latin America." *Journal of Development Studies* 61 (1969): 23–48.

Tetreault, Mary Ann, and Charles Frederick Abel, eds. *Dependency Theory and the Return of High Politics*. Westport, CT: Greenwood, 1986.

Topik, Steven. "Dependency Revisited: Saving the Baby from the Bathwater." *Latin American Perspectives* 25, 6 (November, 1998), 95–99.

Valenzuela, J. Samuel, and Arturo Valenzuela. "Modernization and Dependency." *Comparative Politics* 10 (July 1978): 535–57.

Valenzuela, J., and Valenzuela, Arturo. "Modernization and Dependency: Alternative Perspectives in the Study of Latin American Underdevelopment," *Comparative Politics*, 10, 4 (1978): 535–57.

Wendt, Alexander, and Michael Barnett. "Dependent State Formation and Third World Militarization." *Review of International Studies* 19 (1993): 321–47.

On Postcolonialism

Abernethy, David. *The Dynamics of Global Dominance: European Empires Overseas, 1415–1980*. New Haven and London: Yale University Press, 2000.

Adam, Ian, and Helen Tiffin, eds. *Past the Last Post: Theorizing Post-Colonialism and Post-Modernism*. Hemel Hempstead: Harvester Wheatsheaf, 1991.

Ahmad, Aijaz. "Postcolonialism: What's in a Name?" in eds. *Late Imperial Culture*. Roman de la Campa, E. Ann Kaplan, and Michael Sprinkler, London: Verso, 1995.

Alcock, Susan, et al., eds. *Empires: Perspectives from Archeology and History*. Cambridge: Cambridge University Press, 2002.

Birmingham, David. *The Decolonisation of Africa*. London: UCL Press, 1995.

Boahen, A. Adu. *African Perspectives on Colonialism*. Baltimore: Johns Hopkins University Press, 1987.

Buraway, Michael, et al. *Globalisation and New Identities: A View From the Middle*. Johannesburg: Jacana Media, 2007.

Bush, Barbara. *Imperialism and Postcolonialism*. Harlow, England: Longman, 2006.

Cain, Peter, and Mark Harrison, eds. *Imperialism: Critical Concepts in Historical Studies*. London: Routledge, 2001. 3 vols.

Eschl, C. *Critical Theories, IR and 'the Anti-Globalisation Movement': The Politics of Global Resistance*. London: Routledge, 2005.

Gandhi, Leela. *Postcolonial Theory: A Critical Introduction*. Edinburgh: Edinburgh University Press, 1998.

Gills, Barry, ed. *Globalisation and the Politics of Resistance*. London: Taylor and Francis, 1997.

Goldberg, David, and Ato Quayson, eds. *Relocating Postcolonialism*. Oxford: Blackwell, 2002.

Harvey, David. *The New Imperialism*. Oxford: Oxford University Press, 2003.

Held, David, and Anthony McGrew, eds. *The Global Transformation Reader*. Cambridge: Polity Press, 2003.

Howe, Stephen. "Review Article: When—If Ever—Did Empire End? Recent Studies of Imperialism and Decolonisation." *Journal of Contemporary History*. 40, 3 (2005): 585–99.

Kiely, Ray. *The Clash Of Globalisations: Neo-Liberalism, The Third Way and Anti-Globalisation*. Boston: Brill Academic Publishers, 2005.

LeSeur, James, ed. *The Decolonisation Reader*. London: Routledge, 2004.

Loomba, Ania. *Colonialism/Postcolonialism*. London: Routledge, 1998.

Marchand, M. *Gender and Global Restructuring: Sightings, Sites, and Resistances*. London: Routledge, 2000.

McLeod, John. *Beginning Postcolonialism*. Manchester: Manchester University Press, 2000.

Misha, Vijay, and Bob Hodge. "What is Post(-)colonialism?" in eds. *Colonial Discourse and Postcolonial Theory: A Reader*. Patrick Williams and Laura Chrisman. New York, London: Harvester Wheatsheaf, 1993.

Pieterse, Jan Nederveen. *Globalisation and Culture*. Lanham, MD: Rowan and Littlefield, 2004.

Prakash, Gyan, ed. *After Colonialism: Imperial Histories and Postcolonial Displacements*. Princeton: Princeton University Press, 1995.

Robertson, Roland. *Globalisation: Social Theory and Global Culture*. London: Sage, 1992.

Said, Edward. *Culture and Imperialism*. London: Vintage, 1994.

Said, Edward. *Orientalism: Western Conceptions of the Orient*. Harmondsworth: Penguin, 1986, 1979.

Wolfe, Patrick. "History and Imperialism: A Century of Theory, from Marx to Postcolonialism." *American Historical Review*. 102, 2 (April 1997): 388–420.

Young, Robert and J. C. Young. *Postcolonialsm: An Historical Introduction*. Oxford: Blackwell, 2001.

CHAPTER 5

The English School: International Society and Grotian Rationalism

The primary research task of the English School has been to trace the history and development of international society and to uncover its nature and functioning. The English School is an interesting blend of realist understandings of power and balance of power and the liberal perspective of the ways international law, rules, norms, and institutions operate internationally. In terms of methodology, it emphasizes an historical sociological approach and, most recently, interpretive understandings that reflect deep skepticism about the scientific and causal approach to IR theorizing. The English School can be understood, then, as a synthesis drawn principally from both classical realist and liberal (as well as idealist) understandings—or, as some prefer to put it, a middle path or *via media* between the two traditions. Hence, perspectives on international politics associated with Machiavelli, Hobbes, but particularly Grotius and Kant have all influenced the development of the English School. Even more so than the case with other images discussed in this book, there is therefore a good amount of diversity among scholars who associate themselves with the English School.

It is interesting to note that although the formal origins as a "school" were the 1950s, its obituary as an approach to IR was written by some in the early 1990s. But with the end of the Cold War a decade later, the English School's nuanced conceptual eclecticism seemed well suited to an era of change and globalization. As Barry Buzan noted in 2001, the English School is an "underutilized research resource. The time is ripe to develop and apply its historicist, constructivist, and methodologically pluralist approach to IR."[1]

MAJOR ACTORS AND ASSUMPTIONS

The first assumption underlying the English School image is that the world can be understood as an international or anarchical society in which both states and non-state actors operate. The emphasis is on the concept of "society" which realists would tend not to pair with "anarchical." An anthology of papers published in 1968 indicates quite clearly that the frame of reference from the outset was "international society."[2] As later succinctly stated by Adam Watson and Hedley Bull, an international society is

> [A] group of states (or, more generally, a group of independent political communities) which not merely form a system, in the sense that the behavior of each is a necessary factor in the calculations of the others, but also have established by dialogue and consent common rules and institutions for the conduct of their relations, and recognize their common interest in maintaining these arrangements.[3]

Although recognizing the importance of the historical existence of an "international system of states" (as realists frequently use the term), it is the overarching term **international society** that captures the essence of English School thinking. As a result, English School scholars are skeptical of the domestic analogy whereby it is assumed that because the international system lacks a common power to keep citizens in awe, we cannot speak of an international society but rather only a system of states.

Second, for the English School the concept of **order** in the anarchical society plays an important theoretical role. Order, however, results not simply from power and the balance of power, but also from the acceptance of rules and institutional arrangements that are in the enlightened, rational self-interest of states and other actors. Like classical realists, those in the English School understand the importance in international affairs of both power—the material component—and ideas, values, and norms. The reliance on the tradition of international law is particularly evident. As noted in Chapters Two and Three, realists, liberals, and neoliberal institutionalists often use the concept of "rationality" as an underlying or simplifying assumption that contributes to the development of parsimonious theories. **"Rationalist"** in the English School, however, has a different meaning. Invoking a tradition associated with Grotius—the "father of international law"—English School rationalism refers to the rules, laws, and institutional arrangements states have established to provide some degree of order to an anarchic international society. Hence, as opposed to the realist emphasis defining structure in terms of polarity or the distribution of capabilities, structure is more closely associated with this broadly conceived rule-based institutional framework.

Finally, the English School recognizes the importance of Kantian ethical and moral understandings, but this is balanced by a pragmatic view of the anarchical society as one in which considerations of power and interest remain important. The concept of **world society** in English School usage is reserved for this Kantian or "revolutionist" (some would say utopian) strain of thought—realizing a universal cosmopolitanism and thus transforming the world as we know it into a society based on norms with broad moral acceptance. This English School usage of world society is decidedly different from the liberal view of world or global society. For liberals, world society goes beyond international or interstate relations to encompass a complex array of state, non-state, and transnational actors that engage with each other globally. Put another way, the concept of international society reflects the Grotian rationalist influence so central to the English School, while world society is reserved in the English School for the "revolutionist" usage influenced by Kant.

In sum, the English School has avoided a parochial perspective on world politics. As noted by Martin Wight, all three perspectives—realist (international system), rationalist (international society), and revolutionist (world society) are important to understanding world politics. The traditions are not like "railroad tracks running into infinity." Rather, "they are streams, with eddies and cross-currents, sometimes interlacing and never for long confined to their own river bed."[4] The idea that international system, international society, and world society perspectives can all exist simultaneously as understandings of reality and subject to analysis is core to the English School.

INTELLECTUAL PRECURSORS AND INFLUENCES

◼ Grotius

Hugo Grotius (Huig de Groot, 1583–1645), as noted above and in Chapters Two and Three, is the generally recognized "father" of international law and as such he looked beyond the power and balance-of-power politics we read in the Florentine Niccolò Machiavelli (1469–1527) or the Englishman Thomas Hobbes (1588–1679). The norms or rules (many of which have standing as international law and form the "rational" bases of international or world politics) are observed by states because they produce some degree of order or security that is in their enlightened self-interest. It is this interest-driven, rule-following dimension that led Martin Wight (1913–72) to adopt the term *rationalism*, which his follower Hedley Bull (1932–85) later placed in the context of a still anarchic, international society of states.

Grotius did not ignore power and power politics among states. Indeed, conflict among states including the use of force were central to his discussion on the *Law of War and Peace* (*De jure belli ac pacis*). Similarly, his treatment in other works of economic activities to include freedom of navigation on the high seas provided the intellectual basis for what would become international commercial law. Notwithstanding the independence of sovereign states, it was in their (rational) interest to follow rules that set the parameters of international relations in peacetime and even provided criteria for resort to (and conduct of) war. The result, he hoped, was perhaps to make the use of force somewhat less barbarous than it otherwise would be.

Both scholar and a very practical man living in the Dutch commercial town of Delft, Grotius turned his attention to these concerns—commercial issues and matters of war and peace—of governments, trading companies, and businesses of newly formed states in his day. Writing with the horrors of the Thirty Years' War in mind, Grotius offered formulations of law drawn from several sources. One can see the influence on Grotius of the philosophical and historical legacy of a Roman imperial *jus gentium* (a law to govern relations among diverse peoples in the ancient Roman empire) as well as natural law thinking.

Natural law is a philosophical view that claims there are laws inherent in nature that transcend any laws made by mere mortals. Such thinking is closely tied to the writings of Augustine, Aquinas, and other Christian writers of the late Roman Empire and Middle Ages. Grotius also knew how to make general principles and customary practice central to his constructions of legal rules-of-the-road for states in a newly emerging, state-based European society. Later colonial and imperial extension of European states in the eighteenth, nineteenth, and twentieth centuries resulted in Grotian conceptions of international law becoming global in the scope of their application, particularly as the European construct of the sovereign state spread worldwide.

Aided by new transportation and communications technologies, territorial states became the principal actors in this new international societal order. Following Grotius and other writers, international law developed rapidly in diplomacy. For example, the territorial sea came to be defined by a three-mile limit from the shoreline of the coastal state. The reason three miles was chosen was a practical one—artillery technology of the time limited the range of a cannonball to about three miles, the practical distance that any country could expect to defend from the shore without actually going to sea. Principles of **just war** (limits on, resort to, and conduct in warfare) developed by Cicero, Augustine, Aquinas, Gentili, Vitoria, Suarez, and other philosophers over more than 1,500 years of Western civilization now became matters of international law, not just moral preachings. Ideas concerning mutual respect for the welfare of foreign diplomats and their embassies and consulates also became legal obligations based on the customary practice of states.

Kant

In contrast to Grotius, with some exceptions founders of the English School clearly were not as persuaded by the writings of the East Prussian, Immanuel Kant (1724–1804). Martin Wight, for example, made no secret of his characterization of Kantians as "revolutionists" who try to substitute moral principle for the realities of politics. For his part, Edward Hallett Carr (1892–1982) rejected any Kantian invocation of morality as transforming international relations somehow independent of power and interest. Kant's major influence is most evident in concerns about justice in international society. This is particularly true with the follow-on generation of English School scholars interested in establishing global, cosmopolitan norms in a transformed international or, more precisely, world society.[5]

Carr

Although not a formal member of the "British Committee" that was established in the 1950s, E. H. Carr (usually categorized as a classical realist) is now widely acknowledged as an intellectual precursor to the emergence of the English School. For Carr, "the inner meaning of the modern international crises" experienced in the interwar period (1919–39) was "the collapse of the whole structure of utopianism based on the concept of the harmony of interests."[6] International politics involves a continuing tension between power and interest on the one hand and moral considerations on the other. Thus, Carr rejected as utopian the pure idealism of focusing only on moral values and trying to exclude power and interest. Similarly, he found unrealistic any so-called "realism" that pretends values somehow can be dropped from the political equation. Carr's observation of the inherent tension in IR between interest and power on the one hand and moral considerations on the other set the intellectual stage for development within the English School for a rationalist middle path. This can be traced back to Grotius who falls between the realism of a Machiavelli or Hobbes and the idealism (or "revolutionism") in Kant.

THE DIVERGENCE OF BRITISH AND AMERICAN SCHOLARSHIP

How did the English School emerge as having a distinct, societal-based, rationalist image of international relations? We begin to find an answer to this question in the divergence that took place in the decades following World War II between British and American scholarship on politics in general, international politics in particular. Still wedded to the strengths to be found in classical understandings and more traditional methods of analysis, British scholars did not embrace the behavioral movement that in the 1950s and 1960s was gradually overtaking American political science albeit somewhat more slowly in the IR field.

Classical scholarship in both American and British studies of diplomacy and international politics—influenced by historically based understandings and drawing as well from philosophy, law and institutional studies—had indeed been challenged by the behavioral movement that emerged in American social sciences by the 1930s. This movement gained steam in the years after World War II and began establishing a prominent position in the international relations field by the 1960s when realism still occupied center stage. Debate in the inter-war period (1919–1939) and after had occurred between realists who preferred to focus on the "realities" of power and interest and those who, given the devastation of world war, wished to change this business-as-usual approach by turning to greater reliance on international law and institutions as a substitute for the brutality of **Realpolitik,** or power politics.

More troubling for many classically trained scholars was the attempt within the behavioral movement to make the social "sciences" more scientific, emulating the natural sciences and adopting (or at least trying to adapt) their methodologies to include formal hypothesis testing and quantitative methods of analysis. The divergence within Anglo-American scholarship in international relations was clearly identified in Hedley Bull's critique in the late 1960s of the direction American scholarship was taking. Indeed, he argued the case for a "classical approach" and opposed "the scientific approach [that] has contributed and is likely to contribute very little to the theory of international relations." Moreover, he observed that "in so far as it is intended to encroach upon and ultimately displace the classical approach, it is positively harmful."[7]

In a call for continued reliance on judgment that scholars should bring to the theory of international relations, Bull took exception to "confining [our]selves to what can be logically or mathematically proved or verified according to strict procedures." He was skeptical about "scientific" claims made by Americans wedded to these methods: "The practitioners of the scientific approach are unlikely to make progress of the sort to which they aspire." He hastened to add that "where practitioners of the scientific approach have succeeded in casting light upon the subject, it has been by stepping beyond the bounds of that approach and employing the classical method." In this critique Bull rejected the "construction and manipulation of so-called 'models'" entertained by the "scientific school" and warned against the dogmatism that can be found among modelers—"attributing to the model a connection with reality it does not have," sometimes "distorting the model itself by importing additional assumptions about the world in the guise of logical axioms." Similarly, he also objected to the work of the scientific school that in some cases he found to be "distorted and impoverished by a fetish for measurement."

Still calling for rigor and precision in the theory of international politics, Bull found these accommodated readily enough within the classical approach, which "should undoubtedly attempt to be scientific in the sense of being a coherent, precise, and orderly body of knowledge, and in the sense of being consistent with the philosophical foundations of modern science." Offensive to Bull was the arrogance of practitioners of the scientific approach who "by cutting themselves off from history and philosophy, have deprived themselves of the means of self-criticism." He observed that the consequence is that they "have a view of their subject that is callow and brash."

Bull was representing in this discourse not only his own views, but also those shared by many of his colleagues in the yet unnamed, still emerging English School. His comments were pointedly directed to American scholars and reflective of the divergence then well underway between British and American methodological and epistemological approaches in the international relations field. The earlier convergence in Anglo-American approaches around history, law, and institutional studies was clearly giving way in the United States to positivist, quantitative approaches to which Bull was objecting.

British scholarship would retain traditional approaches in the field even as their own "school" substantially developed a societal focus in studying international relations and world politics—one that not only found a middle path between realism and idealism as well as between realism and liberalism, but also opened itself to both historical sociology and constructivist understandings.

THE GENESIS OF THE ENGLISH SCHOOL

To find the genesis of what would become the English School, our journey actually starts in the United States. In 1954 with sponsorship of the Rockefeller Foundation, an initiative led by Dean Rusk (later to be Secretary of State in the Kennedy-Johnson administrations) and Kenneth Thompson (a student and then colleague of Hans Morgenthau) established an American Committee of academic and policy-oriented realists.[8] Other members included William T. R. Fox, Hans Morgenthau, Reinhold Niebuhr, Paul Nitze, Arnold Wolfers—the senior generation—and Kenneth Waltz, then about thirty (and one of Fox's students while at Columbia). Institutionally located in New York at Columbia University, the focus of this American Committee was to develop a theory to comprehend, explain, and guide the study of international relations and the formulation of foreign policy. Given deep divisions among these realists on theory and policy, however, the American Committee did not last long.

It was Thompson who reached out across the Atlantic in 1954 to his friend and colleague, historian Herbert Butterfield at Cambridge University, to see about forming a parallel group. After considerable discussion, Butterfield turned initially to diplomatic historian Desmond Williams. In 1958 international relations scholar Martin Wight, then in his mid-forties and at the London School of Economics (LSE), was invited to join them in forming what became the British Committee, locating it at Cambridge. Bringing academics and policy-oriented scholars together, other members included Adam Watson from the British Foreign Office, William Armstrong from the Treasury, military historian Michael Howard from the University of London (later at Oxford), Donald Mackinnon of Aberdeen University, and Wight's protégé at the LSE, the Australian Hedley Bull, then just twenty-six years of age.

Two prominent scholars not invited to join were E. H. Carr (apparently because, given his stature, it was thought his presence would become too dominant a force in the group) and F. H. Hinsley (whom Adam Watson later portrayed as seeing "Europe, and the world, as more of an anarchy and less of a society than Bull or myself"). This quote is quite telling, given the direction that the British Committee would take in the decades to follow under the successor-generation leadership of Watson and Bull as well as Bull's mentee and follower, R. J. Vincent. As Tim Dunne comments: "Both [Bull and Vincent] had an interest in strategic studies . . . , both deployed Wight's three traditions [the realism of Machiavelli or Hobbes, the rationalism of Grotius, and the revolutionism of Kant] as a means to engage with classical theorists, and most significantly of all, they shared a theoretical investigation into the nature of order and justice in international society."[9]

Viewing international relations and world politics primarily as a society rather than a system (the latter characterization then prominent among American scholars to include Kenneth Waltz) became a central understanding within the English School. Of course, one can speak in English School parlance of a system of states, but any such "system" lacks the bonds, common norms, or cohesion one finds usually in international society. The interesting question for English School theorists is how a system of states can be transformed into an international society and how the latter can slip back into a system of states.

Hedley Bull followed Wight's lead in his now classic *The Anarchical Society: A Study of Order in World Politics.*[10] A central question in Bull's work is where order comes from in such an anarchical international society. Is it from the operation of power and the balance of power as Hobbesean realists would have it? Or does it spring at least as much from the rules or law that have been constructed in international society as Grotian rationalists would be prone to claim? Finally, is order to be found as Kantian understandings of moral principle that come to be accepted in a progressive improvement not only of states themselves, but also in their relations with other states? For his part, Bull takes us beyond the realism inherent in Hobbes to find in Grotian internationalism the rules or norms that are a source of order in international society. Bull thus exemplifies in his rule-oriented construction the *via media* between the Hobbesian realism of power and balance of power and the Kantian idealism of universal moral principle.

LEVELS OF ANALYSIS AND THEORY

Given the three key concepts (international system, international society, world society), it is not surprising that the primary level of analysis is the global or systems level. States are the major actors in the international society, even in an era of globalization. This is perhaps not surprising as the historical-sociological approach emphasized the rise of the European state and societal systems. This development led to the spread of Western conceptions such as sovereignty to the rest of the world. As we will see below, the expansion of the concept of world society has in recent years opened up other units and levels of analysis to include individuals, groups, and transnational organizations.

Ontological primacy is given to the English School's conception of international society. The impact of constructivism with its emphasis on social relations and the agent-structure debate (see Chapter Six) have lent substance and nuance to this scholarly orientation. In terms of methodology, the English School generally prefers the more "traditional" approaches defended by Bull. These entail developing a set of interrelated concepts and categories to guide research and help structure questions that guide scholarly inquiry. The emphasis on historical sociology is also important and can be seen as a rebuttal to the apparent ahistoricism of some neorealist conceptions of IR. Causal theorizing based on positivism, associated with realism and liberalism in particular, found few advocates among the early English School theorists. Yet younger scholars have avoided the positivist explanatory versus interpretive understanding dichotomy and offered a synthesis of different perspectives and concepts. Hence this chapter is appropriately placed in the middle of this book between IR images that, for the most part, have spawned positivist theories and the interpretive understandings that also guide much of contemporary IR theorizing.

CHANGE

◼ From System to International Society

Realists emphasize the continuity of IR throughout history; the insights of Thucydides are as relevant today as in the fifth century B.C. Liberals have faith that change is possible, with much of their work focused on the role of institutions, regimes, and norms particularly since the end of World War II. Economic structuralists have a normative commitment to change yet are cognizant of the restraints resulting from the capitalist world-system. The fact that English School theorists situate their work in the context of the realist, rationalist, and revolutionist framework shows a sensitivity and recognition of both the possibilities and limitations of change in IR and world politics.

The interest in applying an historical-sociological approach to the development of international society is another indicator of English School interest in understanding change. Adam Watson took up the mantle of Martin Wight in conducting in-depth studies of the historical development of systems of states. From Hedley Bull, he adopted the distinction between a system of states (an impersonal network of pressures and interests that bind states together and essentially operates outside the will of the members) and a society of states (a set of common rules, institutions, codes of conduct, and values that states agree to be bound by). While realist writings on systems of states tend to revolve around the issue of power and the struggle for power among states, the English School is particularly interested in the societal aspects of systems, which includes an emphasis on how authority is developed and the manner in which practitioners have contributed to the development and monitoring of rules of the game. How can we understand the current international system and the extent to which it represents an international society unless we understand how it came into being? Furthermore, such an historical assessment might also provide insight into how the current system may change in the future.

Such an investigation requires casting one's net beyond Europe, which is exactly what Watson does in his *The Evolution of International Society*.[11] He investigates ancient state systems such as Sumer, Assyria, Persia, Macedonia, India, China, Rome, and Islam as well as the development of the European international society through case studies of medieval Europe, renaissance Italy, the Hapsburg empire, the rise of the modern Westphalian commonwealth of states, and the Napoleonic empire. Each system varies along a continuum of hegemony or dominance by one political entity as opposed to a system characterized by relative autonomy or decentralization of power and authority.

Such case studies provide insight on the English School's concern with the conditions for international order—how did these systems regulate their political entities? How did the societal aspects of the system develop over time? Can we learn from their trial and errors? His analysis therefore takes issue with the realist conception of IR being characterized by a repetitive condition of anarchy through recorded history, and instead claims that relations among states can be viewed through the lens of international societies regulated by rules and practices. These are not based on some idealist conception of what the world should be, but rather the result of actual experience. By placing the current international system in historical context, he raises the question of how permanent it is and how it might change in the future.

The English School's interest in continuity and change in IR can also be stated as an interest in the relation between international order and the aspiration for human justice. This concern is particularly evident among younger scholars associated with the English School who have responded to changes in IR since the end of the Cold War. While Watson examined the expansion of international society, others have studied the phenomenon of failed states and the resultant human cost. Contrasting if not clashing views of what constitutes international society from the point of view of non-Westerners has also been investigated. Similarly, some scholars have joined liberals and constructivists in examining the changing relations among state sovereignty, human rights, and the norms of humanitarian intervention. Other research topics that received less attention in the English School such as European integration, international political economy, and global environmental politics are now being investigated.[12]

From International Society to World Society

This renaissance of the English School is remarkable in that its obituary and even a call for its disbandment were suggested in the early 1980s.[13] One scholar who is responsible for the resurrection and reformulation of the English School approach to IR is Barry Buzan. Buzan engaged in one of the most extensive critiques of the English School as exemplified by Wight, Bull, and Butterfield. He noted internal debates, inconsistencies, and conceptual and empirical voids. For Buzan, the rise of constructivism deserves credit for reinvigorating the English School's important yet underdeveloped emphasis on the social or societal dimension of IR.[14]

Buzan notes that the English School actually consists of several complementary elements that are not always made explicit in the first generation of theorizing: the School as a set of ideas to be found in the minds of statesmen; a set of ideas in the minds of political theorists; and a set of externally imposed concepts that define material and social structures of the international system. It is the latter that is his main concern, particularly the key goal of addressing the conceptually weak concept of world society, the third element of the English School triad.

The traditional discussion within the English School was generally limited to a debate between a "pluralist" versus a "solidarist" conception of international society, a topic of concern to Hedley Bull in particular. The debate centered on the actual and potential extent of shared norms, rules, institutions, and international law within international society. The pluralist view finds states have relatively little in common other than the calculations of interest. This is a "thin morality" in which states can agree to a framework of international order that allows for mutually advantageous cooperation. At best, it is a world of enlightened self-interest in which states are most concerned with security and maintaining order under anarchy. Practical policies emphasize mutual recognition of sovereignty, diplomacy, and maintaining the non-intervention principle in terms of the domestic affairs of states. This reflects more of a realist influence.

The opposing solidarist view sees the world in cosmopolitan terms, arguing international society has a relatively high degree of shared norms, rules, and institutions among states. This is a "thick morality" with the capacity even to enforce universalist ethics. As a result, ideas of individual rights and the extent to which a community of humankind exists inevitably enter into consideration. This reflects a Kantian influence. Whether viewed as a dichotomy or a spectrum, the traditional debate among English School theorists was essentially conducted *within* the international society framework, the flagship concept, as opposed to a realist international system or a Kantian-style world society.

Buzan's contribution to reformulating the English School was to argue that the world society concept was really more of a set of normative goals for theorists, but conceptually and analytically has remained at the margins. He aimed to correct this by examining world society from the perspective of norms and ideas as forms of social structure (hence the interest in constructivism). In other words, his interest is in a theory about norms as opposed to normative theory. Such an approach closes the gap, discussed above, between the English School view of theory as simply a way to organize and structure questions, concepts, and categories systematically and the positivist emphasis on causal explanations.

Buzan argued that a conceptually robust concept of world society could become the best approach to coming to grips with the phenomenon of globalization, a challenge for IR theory in general. The relation between international society and world society is not only the biggest weakness of existing English School theory, but also where the biggest theoretical if not practical gains can be made. Working out the relation between order and a more cosmopolitan culture in "international" society is one of the unfinished legacies of Bull's work. A revised English School theory, therefore, has potential to improve how globalization is conceptualized, but only if world society can be developed as a coherent theoretical concept.[15]

Buzan argues that the English School's triad of concepts captures key aspects of globalization to include the simultaneous existence of state and non-state systems to include transnational actors such as non-governmental organizations. Just as Watson examined the historical relation and transition between systems of states and international societies (Hobbes and Grotius, realism and rationalism), the development of the world society concept can help us understand the potential and obstacles for transitioning to post-Westphalian world politics. Unless the weakness of world society as a pillar of English School thought is overcome, further progress within the English School is constrained. Constructivist insights and its approach to social relations can provide a useful tool.

In the process of his ambitious effort to rethink the English School in an era of globalization, therefore, Buzan (a) retools the international system, international society, and world society triad; (b) reconstructs the pluralist-solidarist debate; (c) thinks through the analytical and normative implications of the world society concept; and (d) examines the concept of institutions that is the underpinning of order in IR. In terms of the final task, he compares and contrasts the English School approach to institutions to the ways realists, neoliberal institutionalists, and regime theorists deal with the concept.

THE ENGLISH SCHOOL, LIBERALS, AND SOCIAL CONSTRUCTIVISTS

Given the English School emphasis on an anarchical or international society, it is important to note similarities with liberalism discussed in Chapter Three and social constructivism in Chapter Six. Norms that become established in the form of either tacitly accepted understandings or explicitly agreed-upon rules (some of which have the binding quality of international law) lie at the foundation of **international régimes**. For liberals, such régimes consist of voluntarily agreed sets of principles, norms, rules, and procedures concerning diverse issues—human rights, war and peace, commercial transactions, and the like—and their servicing institutions, both governmental and non-governmental organizations.

These régimes and institutions are the outcome of human design efforts over centuries of time intended to provide an authoritative basis for regulating or at least influencing the behavior of both state and non-state actors. So understood, the development of international society can be viewed as a constructivist enterprise. As noted in Chapter Six, social constructivists portray self-help, power politics, sovereignty, and similar concepts as having been socially constructed or having evolved under the anarchy of international relations and world politics. They are not inevitable or essential attributes of international politics, but rather have been socially constructed. The key point is that international relations and world politics do not have an independent existence; they are what people make (or have made) of them. Ideas, culture, and norms matter and can influence behavior, including the creation of multilateral institutions.

An example of overlapping interest in all three approaches to IR involves human rights. In the case of English School theorists, it is scholars sympathetic to the solidarist perspective who have examined human rights and humanitarian intervention. Similar interest has been expressed with regard to the global environment.[16] Such concerns to date, however, have reflected more normative aspirations and less conceptual and empirical development within the English School.

THE ENGLISH SCHOOL AND ITS CRITICS

Methodological Muddle

The affinity between aspects of liberalism, constructivism, and the English School is reflected in the fact that friendly criticism of the English School has come from both liberals and constructivists. Martha Finnemore, for example, has written widely on humanitarian intervention from a constructivist perspective. She argues that improving the visibility of the English School among American IR academics would enrich the latter's scholarship due to the English School's historical and normative orientation. Unfortunately, "the School's lack of clarity about both method and theoretical claims has made it difficult for American scholars to incorporate it into their research. . . . For many American scholars, simply figuring out what its methods *are* is a challenge" as "English School authors . . . almost never provide systematic discussion about rules of evidence."[17]

Historical Knowledge

As noted, the historical-sociological approach is a hallmark of the English School. It is one thing to claim, as do Bull and Watson, that historical knowledge is important. But the question is *why* is this so? Is it because the present and the future are part of an historical narrative or story slowly unfolding from time past? Is what we observe today in international society grounded in historical developments over centuries in time? Or is historical knowledge important because the present and the future are similar to the past, all subject to similar types of forces? Or is the past a guide to predicting the future? Or an indispensable tool for speculating about future options?[18]

Political Economy, the Environment, and Gender

The economy and the global environment as integral to international and world society was a topic conspicuously absent from the work of early English School authors. On the one hand, perhaps they were more concerned with the "high politics" of diplomacy, collective security, and alliance politics, discounting the salience of political-economic and environmental issues. As Barry Buzan has stated: "The English school's founding fathers . . . were too much in thrall to universalist principles of order and justice derived from debates in political theory and were too disinterested in international political economy."[19] Although the founders may have given less attention to the international economy, the environment, and human rights, successor generations in the English School are examining the possibilities and limitations of integrating such concerns into the English School's triad and its understanding of international society.[20]

The English School shares with other images presented in this book almost a complete lack of knowledge or interest in the feminist gender perspective on IR. As Jacqui True argues, "This neglect of gender reveals the concept of international society to be neither open nor sufficiently dynamic enough to capture or explain the social sources and dimensions of interstate behavior, and world politics more broadly." To do so requires a serious examination of the question "Where are women in international society?"[21]

Conceptual and Philosophical Eclecticism

As noted, the English School image of international relations has been influenced by works ranging from Hobbes and Machiavelli to Grotius and (to a lesser extent) Kant. As such, scholars operating from alternative perpsectives of international relations can find much with which to identify. Realists can applaud the English School recognition of anarchy, just as realists as well as liberals can agree on the importance of Grotius to our understanding of international relations. Social constructivists find English School discussions of the evolution of international society and the development of norms to be quite compatible with their world view. Alexander Wendt's description of Lockean culture, discussed in Chapter Six, comes close to the Grotian rationalist perspective in the English School. Hence, recognition of diverse traditions of thought can be appealing as there is a bit of something for everyone.

But such an eclectic intellectual heritage can also lead to criticism. This is particularly the case for those positivists who aspire to develop parsimonious, deductively based theories. If one is a structural or neorealist, for example, then the English School smorgasbord is unappealing. While they may agree with Hedley Bull's critique of behavioralism, they question to what extent a truly "classical" and historical-sociological approach to understanding international relations can help in developing new explanatory theories. Even neoliberal institutionalists who rely on the rationality assumption in attempting to account for the conditions under which institutions can aid international cooperation might find the English School and its assumptions too diverse.

The fact of the matter, however, is that the English School is attempting to do something that is at odds with the warring conceptual camps of IR theory from the 1960s onward: integration of the field. Positivist and interpretive understandings compete. Images clash based upon diverse underlying assumptions. Professors have trouble deciding which theories or approaches to emphasize in a ten- to fifteen-week class, and students have to wrestle with the problem of coming to terms with vast amounts of material for upcoming exams.

One could argue that this is not a burning issue, and in fact a multiplicity of interests, methods, paradigms, images, concepts, and value preferences is actually beneficial and should be applauded. Greater unity, it is feared, could result in uniformity and the intellectual tyranny of a dominant paradigm or school of thought. Hence, from this point of view, eclecticism is to be encouraged, and any signs of uniformity regarded with suspicion. No one would argue against diversity *per se*—it is the lifeblood of scholarly enquiry. Seemingly unrelated research may some day come together to help explain a significant aspect of international relations. The concern, however, is whether "diversity" amounts to no more than multiple parochialisms— closing off and effectively encapsulating work in separate domains within the field, treating them as if they were mutually exclusive. Scholars at times engage in narrowly focused research programs that ignore alternative conceptual approaches, develop specialized jargon that unintentionally serves to confuse and mystify the uninitiated, and unduly restrict their course syllabi to literature that reinforces their own value and theoretical preferences. For this reason alone, the English School is a useful antidote to such closure.

Notes

1. Barry Buzan, "The English School: An Underexploited Resource in IR," *Review of International Studies,* 27 (2001): 472.
2. See Herbert Butterfield and Martin Wight, eds. *Diplomatic Investigations: Essays in the Theory of International Politics* (Cambridge, MA: Harvard University Press, 1968).
3. Hedley Bull and Adam Watson, eds., *The Expansion of International Society* (Oxford: Clarendon Press, 1984), 1.
4. Martin Wight, *International Theory: Three Traditions,* eds. Gabriele Wight and Brian Porter (Leicester University Press, 1991), 260.
5. See, for example, Andrew Linklater and Hidemi Suganami, *The English School of International Relations* (Cambridge: Cambridge University Press, 2006), especially chapters 5 and 7 on cosmopolitanism, the harm principle as a basis for intervention for humanitarian reasons, the good international citizen, and the transformation of international society.
6. E.H. Carr, *The Twenty Years' Crisis,* 1st ed. (London: Macmillan, 1939), 80 as cited by Tim Dunne, *Inventing International Society: A History of the English School* (New York: Palgrave, 1998), 29.
7. Hedley Bull, "International Theory: The Case for a Classical Approach" in eds. Klaus Knorr and James N. Rosenau, *Contending Approaches to International Politics* (Princeton, NJ: Princeton University Press, 1969), 26. Subsequent quotes are also from this article.
8. This section draws on Tim Dunne, *Inventing International Society: A History of the English School* (London: Macmillan, 1998).
9. *Ibid.,* 161.
10. Hedley Bull, *The Anarchical Society: A Study of Order in World Politics* (London: Macmillan, 1977).
11. Adam Watson, *The Evolution of International Society: A Comparative Historical Analysis* (London: Routledge, 1992). See also Barry Buzan and Richard Little, *International Systems in World History: Remaking the Study of International Relations* (Oxford: Oxford University Press, 2000).
12. Linklater and Suganami, *The English School and International Relations,* 2.
13. Roy Jones, "The English School of International Relations: A Case for Closure?" *Review of International Studies,* 7, 1 (1981): 1–13.
14. Barry Buzan, *From International to World Society? English School Theory and the Social Structure of Globalisation* (Cambridge: Cambridge University Press, 2004).
15. *Ibid.,* 2.
16. Robert H. Jackson, *The Global Covenant: Human Conduct in a World of States* (Oxford: Oxford University Press, 2000); N. J. Wheeler, *Saving Strangers: Humanitarian Intervention in International Society* (Oxford: Oxford University Press, 2000); R. J. Vincent, *Human Rights and International Relations: Issues and Responses* (Cambridge: Cambridge University Press, 1986).
17. Martha Finnemore, "Exporting the English School?" *Review of International Studies,* 27, 3 (2001): 509.
18. Andrew Linklater and Hidemi Suganami, *The English School of International Relations: A Contemporary Reassessment* (Cambridge: Cambridge University Press, 2006), 91.
19. Buzan, *From International to World Society?,* 11.
20. Mathew Paterson, "Global Environmental Governance," in ed., Alex J. Bellamy, *International Society and Its Critics* (Oxford: Oxford University Press, 2005), 162–77.
21. Jacqui True, "Feminism," in Bellamy, 8.

SELECTED READINGS

War, Peace, and the Law of Nations

HUGO GROTIUS

Grotius is known for developing the idea of law among nations, an important element of the English School perspective on international society. The Grotian view of IR is one of the states constrained by mutually agreed-upon rules or laws to govern their interactions with one another in both war and peace. That international relations ought to be governed by law is a classic statement in normative political theory, yet Grotius recognizes the practical and mutually beneficial role that international law can play in interstate relations. Note how Grotius reviews and then refutes the "might makes right" argument, making the case for how the law of nations works to the advantage of the "great society of states." He also undertakes an examination of the role of law with regard to "just war."

The municipal law of Rome and of other states has been treated by many, who have undertaken to elucidate it by means of commentaries or to reduce it to a convenient digest. That body of law, however, which is concerned with the mutual relations among states or rulers of states, whether derived from nature, or established by divine ordinances, or having its origin in custom and tacit agreement, few have touched upon. Up to the present time no one has treated it in a comprehensive and systematic manner; yet the welfare of mankind demands that this task be accomplished.

Cicero justly characterized as of surpassing worth a knowledge of treaties of alliance, conventions, and understandings of peoples, kings and foreign nations—a knowledge, in short, of the whole law of war and peace. And to this knowledge Euripides gives the preference over an understanding of things divine and human, for he represents Theoclymenus as being thus addressed:

> For you, who know the fate of men and gods
> What is, what shall be, shameful world it be
> To know not what is just.

Such a work is all the more necessary because in our day, as in former times, there is no lack of men who view this branch of law with contempt as having no reality outside of an empty name. On the lips of men quite generally is the saying of Euphemus, which Thucydides quotes, that in the case of a king or imperial city nothing is unjust which is expedient. Of like implication is the statement that for those whom fortune favors might makes right, and that the administration of a state cannot be carried on without injustice.

Furthermore, the controversies which arise between peoples or kings generally have Mars as their arbiter. That war is irreconcilable with all law is a view held not alone by the ignorant populace; expressions are often let slip by well-informed and thoughtful men which lend countenance to such a view. Nothing is more common than the assertion of antagonism between law and arms. Thus Ennius says:

> Not on grounds of right is battle joined,
> But rather with the sword do men
> Seek to enforce their claims

Horace, too, describes the savage temper of Achilles in this wise:

> Laws, he declares, were not for him ordained;
> By dint of arms he claims all for himself.

Reprinted by permission of the publisher from "War, Peace, and the Law of Nations" by Hugo Grotius (Washington, D.C.: Carnegie Endowment for International Peace, 1913–25). www.carnegieendowment.org.

Another poet depicts another military leader as commencing war with the words:

Here peace and violated laws I leave behind.

Antigonus when advanced in years ridiculed a man who brought to him a treatise on justice when he was engaged in besieging cities that did not belong to him. Marius declared that the din of arms made it impossible for him to hear the voice of the laws. Even Pompey, whose expression of countenance was so mild dared to say: "When I am in arms, am I to think of laws?"

Among Christian writers a similar thought finds frequent expression. A single quotation from Tertullian may serve in place of many: "Deception, harshness, and injustice are the regular business of battles." They who so think will no doubt wish to confront us with this passage in Comedy:

These things uncertain should you, by
reason's aid,
Try to make certain, no more would you gain
Than if you tried by reason to go mad.

Since our discussion concerning law will have been undertaken in vain if there is no law, in order to open the way for a favorable reception of our work and at the same time to fortify it against attacks, this very serious error must be briefly refuted. In order that we may not be obliged to deal with a crowd of opponents, let us assign to them a pleader. And whom should we choose in preference to Carneades?[1] For he had attained to so perfect a mastery of the peculiar tenet of his Academy that he was able to devote the power of his eloquence to the service of falsehood not less readily than to that of truth.

Carneades, then, having undertaken to hold a brief against justice, in particular against that phase of justice with which we are concerned, was able to muster no argument stronger than this, that, for reasons of expediency, men imposed upon themselves laws, which vary according to customs, and among the same peoples often undergo changes as times change: moreover, that there is no law of nature, because all creatures, men as well as animals, are impelled by nature toward ends advantageous to themselves, that, consequently, there is no justice, or, if such there be, it is supreme folly, since one does violence to his own interests if he consults the advantage of others.

What the philosopher [Horace] here says, and the poet reaffirms in verse,

And just from unjust Nature cannot know,

must not for one moment he admitted. Man is, to be sure, an animal, but an animal of a superior kind, much farther removed from all other animals than the different kinds of animals are from one another; evidence on this point may be found in the many traits peculiar to the human species. But among the traits characteristic of man is an impelling desire for society, that is, for the social life—not of any and every sort, but peaceful, and organized according to the measure of his intelligence, with those who are of his own kind; this social trend the Stoics called "sociableness." Stated as a universal truth, therefore, the assertion that every animal is impelled by nature to seek only its own good cannot be conceded. . . .

This maintenance of the social order, which we have roughly sketched, and which is consonant with human intelligence, is the source of law properly so called. To this sphere of law belong the abstaining from that which is another's, the restoration to another of anything of his which we may have, together with any gain which we may have received from it; the obligation to fulfill promises, the making good of a loss incurred through our fault, and the inflicting of penalties upon men according to their desserts.

From this signification of the word "law" there has flowed another and more extended meaning. Since over other animals man has the advantage of possessing not only a strong bent toward social life, of which we have spoken, but also a power of discrimination which enables him to decide what things are agreeable or harmful (as to both things present and things to come), and what can lead to either alternative, in such things it is meet for the nature of man, within the limitations of human intelligence, to follow the direction of a well-tempered judgment, being neither led astray by fear or the allurement of immediate pleasure, nor carried away by rash impulse. Whatever is clearly at variance with such judgment is understood to be contrary also to the law of nature, that is, to the nature of man. . . .

Herein, then, is another source of law besides the source in nature, that is, the free will of God, to which beyond all cavil our reason tells us we must render obedience. But the law of nature of which we have spoken, comprising alike that which relates to the social life of man and that which is so called in a larger sense, proceeding as it does from the essential traits implanted in man, can nevertheless rightly be attributed to God because of his having willed that such traits exist in us. In this sense, too, Chrysippus and the Stoics used to say that the origin of law should be sought in no other source than Jupiter himself; and from the name Jupiter the Latin word for law (*ius*) was probably derived. . . .

Again, since it is a rule of the law of nature to abide by pacts (for it was necessary that among men there be some method of obligating themselves one to another, and no other natural method can be imagined), out of this source the bodies of municipal law have arisen. For those who had associated themselves with some group, or had subjected themselves to a man or to men, had either expressly promised, or from the nature of the transaction must be understood impliedly to have promised, that they would conform to that which should have been determined, in the one case by the majority, in the other by those upon whom authority had been conferred.

What is said, therefore, in accordance with the view not only of Carneades but also of others, that

Expediency is, as it were, the mother
Of what is just and fair

is not true, if we wish to speak accurately. For the very nature of man, which even if we had no lack of anything would lead us into the mutual relations of society, is the mother of the law of nature. But the mother of municipal law is that obligation which arises from mutual consent; and since this obligation derives its force from the law of nature, nature may be considered, so to say, the great-grandmother of municipal law.

The law of nature nevertheless has the reinforcement of expediency; for the author of nature willed that as individuals we should be weak, and should lack many things needed in order to live properly, to the end that we might be the more constrained to cultivate the social life. But expediency afforded an opportunity also for municipal law, since that kind of association of which we have spoken, and subjection to authority, have their roots in expediency. From this it follows that those who prescribe laws for others in so doing are accustomed to have or ought to have some advantage in view.

But just as the laws of each state have in view the advantage of that state, so by mutual consent it has become possible that certain laws should originate as between all states, or a great many states; and it is apparent that the laws thus originating had in view the advantage, not of particular states, but of the great society of states. And this is what is called the law of nations, whenever we distinguish that term from the law of nature.

This division of law Carneades passed over altogether. For he divided all law into the law of nature and the law of particular countries. Nevertheless if undertaking to treat of the body of law which is maintained between states—for he added a statement in regard to war and things acquired by means of war—he would surely have been obliged to make mention of this law. . . .

But, not to repeat what I have said, that law is not founded on expediency alone, there is no state so powerful that it may not at some time need the help of others outside itself, either for purposes of trade, or even to ward off the forces of many foreign nations united against it. In consequence we see that even the most powerful peoples and sovereigns seek alliances, which are quite devoid of significance according to the point of view of those who confine law within the boundaries of states. Most true is the saying that all things are uncertain the moment men depart from law.

If no association of men can be maintained without law, as Aristotle showed . . . also that association which binds together the human race, or binds many nations together, has need of law; this was perceived by him who said that shameful deeds ought not to be committed even for the sake of one's country. Aristotle takes sharply to task those who, while unwilling to allow anyone to exercise authority over themselves except in accordance with law, yet are quite indifferent as to whether foreigners are treated according to law or not. . . .

Least of all should that be admitted which some people imagine, that in war all laws are in abeyance. On the contrary war ought not to be undertaken except for the enforcement of rights; when once undertaken, it should be carried on only within the bounds of law and good faith. Demosthenes well said that war is directed against those who cannot be held in check by judicial processes. For judgments are efficacious against those who feel that they are too weak to resist; against those who are equally strong, or think that they are, wars are undertaken. But in order that wars may be justified, they must be carried on with not less scrupulousness than judicial processes are wont to be.

Let the laws be silent, then, in the midst of arms, but only the laws of the state, those that the courts are concerned with, that are adapted only to a state of peace; not those other laws, which are of perpetual validity and suited to all times. It was exceedingly well said by Dio of Prusa, that between enemies written laws, that is, laws of particular states, are not in force, but that unwritten laws are in force, that is, those which nature prescribes, or the agreement of nations has established. This is set forth by that ancient formula of the Romans: "I think that those things ought to be sought by means of a war that is blameless and righteous."

The ancient Romans, as Varro noted, were slow in undertaking war, and permitted themselves no license in that matter, because they held the view that a war ought not to be waged except when free from reproach. Camillus said that wars should be carried on justly no less than bravely; Scipio Africanus, that the Roman people commenced and ended wars justly. In another passage you may read: "War has its laws no less than peace." Still another writer admires Fabricius as a great man who maintained his probity in war—a thing most difficult—and believed that even in relation to an enemy there is such a thing as wrongdoing.

The histories in many a passage reveal how great in war is the influence of the consciousness that one has justice on his side; they often attribute victory chiefly to this cause. Hence the proverbs that a soldier's strength is broken or increased by his cause; that he who has taken up arms unjustly rarely comes back in safety; that hope is the comrade of a good cause; and others of the same purport.

No one ought to be disturbed, furthermore, by the successful outcome of unjust enterprises. For it is enough that the fairness of the cause exerts a certain influence, even a strong influence upon actions, although the effect of that influence, as happens in human affairs, is often nullified by the interference of other causes. Even for winning friendships, of which for many reasons nations as well as individuals have need, a reputation for having undertaken war not rashly nor unjustly, and of having waged it in a manner above reproach, is exceedingly efficacious. No one readily allies himself with those in whom he believes that there is only a slight regard for law, for the right, and for good faith.

Fully convinced, by the considerations which I have advanced, that there is a common law among nations, which is valid alike for war and in war,

I have had many and weighty reasons for undertaking to write upon this subject. Throughout the Christian world I observed a lack of restraint in relation to war, such as even barbarous races should be ashamed of; I observed that men rush to arms for slight causes, or no cause at all, and that when arms have once been taken up there is no longer any respect for law, divine or human; it is as if, in accordance with a general decree, frenzy had openly been let loose for the committing of all crimes.

Confronted with such utter ruthlessness, many men who are the very furthest from being bad man, have come to the point of forbidding all use of arms to the Christian, whose rule of conduct above everything else comprises the duty of loving all men. To this opinion sometimes John Ferus and my fellow countryman Erasmus seem to incline, men who have the utmost devotion to peace in both Church and State; but their purpose, as I take it, is, when things have gone in one direction, to force them in the opposite direction, as we are accustomed to do, that they may come back to a true middle ground. But the very effort of pressing too hard in the opposite direction is often so far from being helpful that it does harm, because in such arguments the detection of what is extreme is easy, and results in weakening the influence of other statements which are well within the bounds of truth. For both extremes therefore a remedy must be found, that men may not believe either that nothing is allowable, or that everything is.

At the same time through devotion to study in private life I have wished—as the only course now open to me, undeservedly forced out from my native land, which had been graced by so many of my labors—to contribute somewhat to the philosophy of the law, which previously, in public service, I practiced with the utmost degree of probity of which I was capable. Many heretofore have purposed to give to this subject a well-ordered presentation; no one has succeeded. And in fact such a result cannot be accomplished unless—a point which until now has not been sufficiently kept in view—those elements which come from positive law are properly separated from those which arise from nature. For the principles of the law of nature, since they are always the same, can easily be brought into a systematic form; but the elements of positive law, since they often undergo change and are different in different places, are outside the domain of systematic treatment, just as other notions of particular things are. . . .

In order to prove the existence of this law of nature, I have, furthermore, availed myself to the testimony of philosophers, historians, poets; finally also of orators. Not that confidence is to be reposed in them without discrimination, for they were accustomed to serve the interests of their sect, their subject, or their cause. But when many at different times and in different places affirm the same thing as certain, that ought to be referred to a universal cause; and this cause, in the lines of inquiry which we are following, must be either a correct conclusion drawn from the principles of nature, or common consent. The former points to the law of nature, the latter to the law of nations.

The distinction between these kinds of law is not to be drawn from the testimonies themselves (for writers everywhere confuse the terms law of nature and law of nations), but from the character of the matter. For whatever cannot be deduced from certain principles by a sure process of reasoning, and yet is clearly observed everywhere, must have its origin in the free will of man.

These two kinds of law, therefore, I have always particularly sought to distinguish from each other and from municipal law. . . .

In my work as a whole I have, above all else, aimed at three things: to make the reasons for my conclusions as evident as possible; to set forth in a definite order the matters which needed to be treated; and to distinguish clearly between things which seemed to be the same and were not.

I have refrained from discussing topics which belong to another subject, such as those that teach what may be advantageous in practice. For such topics have their own special field, that of politics, which Aristotle rightly treats by itself, without introducing extraneous matter into it. Bodin, on the contrary, mixed up politics with the body of law with which we are concerned. In some places nevertheless I have made mention of that which is expedient, but only in passing, and in order to distinguish it more clearly from what is lawful.

If anyone thinks that I have had in view any controversies of our own times, either those that have arisen or those which can be foreseen as likely to arise, he will do me an injustice. With all truthfulness I aver that, just as mathematicians treat their figures as abstracted from bodies, so in treating law I have withdrawn my mind from every particular fact. . . .

I beg and adjure all those into whose hands this work shall come, that they assume toward me the same liberty which I have assumed in passing upon the opinions and writings of others. They who shall find me in error will not be more quick to advise me than I to avail myself of their advice.

And now if anything has here been said by me inconsistent with piety, with good morals, with Holy Writ, with the concord of the Christian Church, or with any aspect of truth, let it be as if unsaid.

Note

1. 214(?)–129 B.C., Greek skeptic philosopher and founder of the New or Third Academy in Athens.

Freedom of the Seas

HUGO GROTIUS

In this brief passage from his book The Law of War and Peace *(1608), Grotius observes the growth of trade and other forms of commerce—a very early phase of what we now call globalization. Because Grotius sees trade and commerce as essential to life, he argues that the law must allow such activities not only within a particular country, but also beyond its borders. International trade should be free of restraints, much as it also is supposed to be within a state and its society.*

Most importantly for our purposes here, we see a glimmer in Grotius of what present-day members of the English School characterize as the "society" one finds beyond the boundary of a state: "If it be thought that the small society which we call a state cannot exist without the application of these principles (and certainly it cannot), why will not those same principles be necessary to uphold the social structure of the whole human race and to maintain the harmony thereof?" He mentions in a quote from the Roman poet Virgil "common water" and "common air"—what some present-day writers refer to as the international or global commons.

To the Rulers and to the Free and Independent Nations of Christendom

Now, as there are some things which every man enjoys in common with all other men, and as there are other things which are distinctly his and belong to no one else, just so has nature willed that some of the things which she has created for the use of mankind remain common to all, and that others through the industry and labor of each man become his own. Laws moreover were given to cover both cases so that all men might use common property without prejudice to any one else, and in respect to other things so that each man being content with what he himself owns might refrain from laying his hands on the property of others. . . .

There is not one of you who does not openly proclaim that every man is entitled to manage and dispose of his own property; there is not one of you who does not insist that all citizens have equal and indiscriminate right to use rivers and public places; not one of you who does not defend with all his might the freedom of travel and of trade.

If it be thought that the small society which we call a state cannot exist without the application of these principles (and certainly it cannot), why will not those same principles be necessary to uphold the social structure of the whole human race and to maintain the harmony thereof? If any one rebels against these principles of law and order you are justly indignant, and you even decree punishments in proportion to the magnitude of the offense, for no other reason than that a government cannot be tranquil where trespasses of that sort are allowed. If king act unjustly and violently against king, and nation against nation, such action involves a disturbance of the peace of that universal state, and constitutes a trespass against the supreme Ruler, does it not? . . .

The law by which our case must be decided is not difficult to find, seeing that it is the same among all nations; and it is easy to understand, seeing that it is innate in every individual and implanted in his mind. Moreover the law to which we appeal is one such as no king ought to deny to his subjects, and one no Christian ought to refuse to a non-Christian. For it is a law derived from nature, the common mother of us all, whose bounty falls on all, and whose sway extends over those who rule nations, and which is held most sacred by those who are most scrupulously just. . . .

My intention is to demonstrate briefly and clearly that the Dutch—that is to say, the subjects of the United Netherlands—have the right to sail to the East Indies, as they are now doing, and to engage in trade with the people there. I shall base my argument on the following most specific and unimpeachable axiom of the Law of Nations, called a primary rule or first principle, the spirit of which is self-evident and immutable, to wit: Every nation is free to travel to every other nation, and to trade with it.

God Himself says this speaking through the voice of nature; and inasmuch as it is not His will to have Nature supply every place with all the necessaries of life, He ordains that some nations excel in one art and others in another. Why is this His will, except it be that He wished human friendships to be engendered by mutual needs and resources, lest individuals deeming themselves entirely sufficient unto themselves should for that very reason be rendered unsociable? . . .

Do not the ocean, navigable in every direction with which God has encompassed all the earth, and the regular and the occasional winds which blow now from one quarter and now from another, offer sufficient proof that Nature has given to all peoples a right of access to all other peoples? Seneca thinks this is Nature's greatest service, that by the wind she united the widely scattered peoples, and yet did so distribute all her products over the earth that commercial intercourse was a necessity to mankind. Therefore this right belongs equally to all nations. Indeed the most famous jurists extend its application so far as to deny that any state or any ruler can

---

This passage from Grotius is taken from a 1916 translation of the *The Law of War and Peace* by Ralph Van Deman Magoffin from the original Latin (New York: Oxford University Press, 1916).

debar foreigners from having access to their subjects and trading with them. Hence is derived that law of hospitality which is of the highest sanctity; hence the complaint of the poet Virgil:

> *"What men, what monsters, what inhuman race,*
> *What laws, what barbarous customs of the place,*
> *Shut up a desert shore to drowning men,*
> *And drive us to the cruel seas again."*

And:

> *"To beg what you without your want may*
> *spare—*
> *The common water, and the common air."*

We know that certain wars have arisen over this very matter. . . . Victoria holds that the Spaniards could have shown just reasons for making war upon the Aztecs and the Indians in America, more plausible reasons certainly than were alleged, if they really were prevented from traveling or sojourning among those peoples, and were denied the right to share in those things which by the Law of Nations or by Custom are common to all, and finally if they were debarred from trade.

We read of a similar case in the history of Moses, which we find mentioned also in the writings of Augustine, where the Israelites justly smote with the edge of the sword the Amorites because they had denied the Israelites an innocent passage through their territory, a right which according to the Law of Human Society ought in all justice to have been allowed. . . . Again, as we read in Tacitus, the Germans accused the Romans of 'preventing all intercourse between them and of closing up to them the rivers and roads, and almost the very air of heaven'. When in days gone by the Christians made crusades against the Saracens, no other pretext was so welcome or so plausible as that they were denied by the infidels free access to the Holy Land. It follows therefore that the Portuguese, even if they had been sovereigns in those parts to which the Dutch make voyages, would nevertheless be doing them an injury if they should forbid them access to those places and from trading there.

Is it not then an incalculably greater injury for nations which desire reciprocal commercial relations to be debarred therefrom by the acts of those who are sovereigns neither of the nations interested, nor of the element over which their connecting high road runs? . . .

Inventing International Society

TIM DUNNE

The author provides an important institutional history of the English School that emerged beginning in the 1950s, but that drew on a centuries-long tradition in classical, scholarly thought informed by history, philosophy, and law. Although the English School came into being in part as a reaction to claims to scientific preeminence on the other side of the Atlantic—seen by some in the United Kingdom as hegemonic, it would be wrong to portray the English School only in this light. Indeed, the international-societal focus in the English School has found for IR a rule-oriented or rationalist middle path between the material, power-oriented realists and the ideationally oriented claims of many liberals. Dunne takes the position that the English School has more in common with constructivism than with the positivist-oriented neorealist and neoliberal approaches to IR.

Perhaps the time is ripe for the enunciation of new concepts of universal political organisation which would show how Wales, the United Kingdom and the European Community could each have some world political status while none laid claim to exclusive sovereignty.

Hedley Bull.[1]

From *Inventing International Society* by Tim Dunne, 1998. Reprinted with permission from Palgrave Macmillan.

All histories of ideas are open to contestation. Methodologically, the temptation is to re-write the text, re-interpret the idea, according to current scholarly conventions or prevailing political ideologies. Whilst recognising the twin dangers of presentism and imposing undue coherence upon a particular group of thinkers, the book has shown that there exists a family resemblance linking the work of key thinkers, in British International Relations from E. H. Carr to R. J. Vincent. In a loosely Wittgensteinian sense, a family resemblance denotes the presence of networks of similarities 'overlapping and criss-crossing.'[2] The first part of the conclusion retraces these similarities and in so doing serves as a précis of the 'story' of the English School.

In contemporary academic International Relations, those who belong to the tradition are participating in a much wider-ranging conversation than many of their predecessors. As the paragraphs below suggest, certain elements of the British Committee agenda have fallen by the wayside: few academics who identify with the English School today are interested in the processes of diplomacy or the parallels between Newtonian science and the eighteenth century balance of power. In their place, we find a growing interest in normative questions relating to culture, community and identity. The latter stages of the conclusion consider the relevance of English School thinking to these themes. Although the assessment made below is a broadly favourable one, this is not meant to imply a blanket endorsement of the School. As I have tried to show at a number of points in the text, there are plenty of skeletons in the cupboard; none more chilling than Carr's blindness to Stalin's reign of terror, or more obfuscating than the intrusion of Augustinian dogma into Butterfield's thinking.

In the course of making an assessment of the contribution of the English School, I am aware that the terms of reference of the book are shifting from one where the author tries to be a critical observer, to one where the author becomes an 'advocate' (or what Quentin Skinner once colourfully described as the difference between a 'recording angel' and a 'hanging judge'). By way of a background justification for the advocacy below, I will be deploying what I take to be Andrew Linklater's approach to the history of ideas, which rejects the search for authenticity in favour of seeking out the normative potentiality of a theorist or text. The question, for Linklater, is not whether one interpretation is more faithful than another, but rather, what can we make of it?

I

The development of the English School begins with the work of Carr for the principal reason that he exerted an immense influence over writers like Wight, Butterfield, Bull and Vincent. Carr was the provocateur, whose critique of the degeneration of liberalism into complacent and self-interested statism was regarded as the point of departure for other writers. Apart from broadly agreeing with Carr's view of the breakdown of the inter-war period, Carr's critique of the assumption that there is a latent harmony of international interests enabled post-war theorists to study International Relations from the basis that international society was not a given but had to be created. The conscious attempt by Butterfield and Wight to bring together a group of scholars to engage in a collective enquiry into the morality of states is what marked the English School off from other traditional realist thought of the time.

The need to speak moderation to power was what motivated Butterfield to establish the British Committee as a vehicle for understanding and explaining international relations. The family resemblances shared by Wight and Butterfield, which could be dimly perceived in the 1940s, became institutionalised in the meetings of the Committee. As Michael Howard recalled, it was Martin Wight who provided the intellectual leadership in the first phase of the Committee's proceedings. He prompted his colleagues to ask fundamental questions about the practices of states and the values of civilisations. Wight's own thinking on International Relations had shifted considerably by the late 1950s. It is in his 'international theory' lectures that the evolution in Wight's thinking between the original *Power Politics* and his British Committee work can be discerned. In the lectures, Wight convincingly argued that neither realism nor idealism was able to capture the experience of state practice; instead, he invented a third position, rationalism, which he compiled from the writings and speeches of lawyers, politicians and the handful of philosophers who concerned themselves with interstate relations. Apart from Hedley Bull, it is difficult to know how far other members of the Committee positively endorsed Wight's approach or whether they were powerless to resist, lacking Wight's range and depth in the history of ideas. Nevertheless, there was unanimity in the Committee as to the need to resist the current wave of scientism sweeping all before it in American International Relations.

Whilst it was Wight's approach to 'international theory' which informed the Committee's understanding of the task at hand, it was Hedley Bull who, more than anyone else, brought to the fore the ontological questions about the depth and breadth of international society. The most significant of the early British Committee meetings examining the nature of international society was in October 1961, when Martin Wight presented 'Western Values in International Relations' and Hedley Bull presented 'Society and Anarchy in International Relations'. Herbert Butterfield's painstaking minutes record the consensus which had emerged in the early meetings around the idea that sovereign states constituted a society: 'Wight and Bull in their respective papers were agreed in holding that there is an international society; and no one, in the course of the discussion, questioned this view.'[3] The discussion which followed the papers by Wight and Bull raised a number of fundamental questions about international society. Was a common culture a necessary condition for the element of society to flourish? Or could a rule-governed society be maintained despite the cultural diversity of its participants? Did a society of states require leadership by enlightened great powers acting in accordance with the balance of power? Is a society of states preferable to other kinds of world order, such as empire or hegemony? Recognising that there could not be purely theoretical answers to these questions, from 1964 onwards the British Committee's deliberations shifted from grand theory to a comparative history of earlier states-systems, how they were formed, and the means by which they are sustained or transformed. In these discussions Wight took the lead, excavating new avenues for investigation which others took up in the post-Wightean years of the Committee and after.

II

It would be easy to draw conservative conclusions from this particular episode in the discipline's past. Although a case [has been] made in Chapter 1 for disengaging the English School from its cultural base, a sociological study of the British Committee would no doubt interpret it as an old boys club, imbued with élitist values in a quintessentially English institution, which was sheltered from the prevailing currents of cultural and technological change. This study has suggested we might want to draw a different kind of conclusion. The argument which will be outlined in the final pages of the book is that, during the British Committee era, the English School found themselves on the 'right' side of the key debates of their time. And crucially, even judged by today's standards, their approach to International Relations remains an important voice in the post-positivist dialogue which has, in the last decade, proven to be more resilient than other mainstream theoretical approaches.[4]

One of the reasons for its resilience is due to the distance the English School maintained from policy driven agendas. Even during the *Expansion* project, the most 'applied' phase in the series of meetings which spanned over two decades, the leaders of the group were keenly aware that their comparative advantage was in taking a broad brush to the canvass of colonialism and decolonisation. However, it would be wrong to believe that the principal members of the Committee turned their backs on global politics all together. Butterfield's writings on the Cold War, for example, reveal a deep unease about the crusading 'moralism' advocated by the likes of John Foster Dulles in the 1950s; similarly, Bull was highly critical of the 'belligerence' which accompanied the return of moralism in American foreign policy in the 1980s.[5] In the spirit of 'rationalism', Butterfield, Wight and Bull believed that the Soviet Union had the right to be treated with the same respect as any other great power; failure in the West to advocate co-existence with communism was the cause of insecurity rather than a policy of maintaining security.[6]

Related to the English School's unease about the ideological diplomacy pursued by the U.S. were their misgivings about the replacement of the balance of power with a 'balance of terror'. For Butterfield and Wight in particular, nuclear weapons overturned centuries of accumulated wisdom about the just ends and means of the use of force. Wight detected that weapons of mass destruction had re-activated an interest in doctrines saturated with rationalism such as limited war, although the arms race posed a dialectical dilemma for rationalism: can one side hold on to these principles unless it is confident that its adversary shares them?[7] Alongside these Grotian influences on their thinking about the Cold War, there was an overlay of religious themes (evident in Butterfield's thinking in particular) about how good and evil was a matter for the contest between the city of man and the city of God, not East versus West.

Hedley Bull's approach to nuclear weapons was free from these other-worldly thoughts. In this sense, Bull was more rationalist than Butterfield and Wight on the question of the regulation of the use of force during the Cold War. His pioneering work on arms control in the late 1950s and early 1960s emphasised a middle way between the strategists gunning for superiority and the disarmers who, unwittingly, were jeopardising security. In place of these realist and revolutionist approaches, Bull advocated a policy of limited arms control agreements on the condition that these enhanced national and international security. Throughout Bull's writings on strategic studies, the term 'balance' recurs, as it had done in Butterfield's thinking on structures of governance within the state and in the society of states.

The wind of change sweeping through the international system in the post-war period, as the last phase of decolonisation gathered apace, was never central to the early work of the English School. During the 1960s for example, only Adam Watson wrote a number of papers about the experiences of 'new' states, but these were mostly restricted to discussions about the management of the transition to independence. We should not infer from this any sympathy on their part for the age of empire. From the scattered comments of various members of the English School, it was clear that they opposed colonial control over the non-European world. In a letter to the *New Statesman*, Martin Wight protested against Britain's acquiescence in the annexation of Sarawak by Indonesia, calling the episode the 'most repugnant form of imperialism'[8] This anti-colonial sentiment received more consideration in his essay on 'Western Values' which suggested that intervention was legitimate in order to maintain 'civilised standards', a position which his head of Department at the LSE, Charles Manning, rejected for fear that this would bring white South African rule to an end. On the question of self-government for former colonial territories, as on so many others, Bull aligned himself with Wight. Towards the end of his life. Bull regarded South Africa as the only case where there was a consensus throughout the world on the injustice of a state founded on the principle of white supremacism.

III

The judgements of Wight, Butterfield, and Bull on some of the central questions of their day do not seem out of step when measured against a liberal or social democratic standard. In the closing paragraphs below, I will make the related but more important claim that the English School finds itself on the 'right' side of the main cleavages in the discipline today: first, it operates with a constructivist meta-theory; second, its understanding of theory is normative all the way down; and third, the agenda which has preoccupied the English School from the late 1950s onwards remains relevant to the theory and practice of international relations as the discipline approaches the start of its ninth decade.

In his famous address to the International Studies Association in 1988, Robert Keohane noted that the principal rupture in the field was between 'rationalists' and 'reflectivists'. What is striking about this distinction, and the equally influential distinction by Martin Hollis and Steve Smith between 'explaining' and 'understanding', is that the English School was excluded from both.[9] According to Keohane, the rationalist dimension—the mainstream of International Relations—represented a merger between neorealism and neoliberalism. What holds them together is principally their common interest in the need to 'explain behavioural regularities.'[10] Although Wight believed there were patterns in the history of ideas, these were of a historicist kind. It was this realisation which prompted Keohane to dismiss Wight's work for his neglect of the scientific or behavioural search for laws of action.[11]

A good example of a specific debate in which the English School finds itself in opposition to the 'rationalists' is in terms of its critique of neoliberal understandings of co-operation. In terms of international institutions, there are differences not only in terms of what exactly the institutions are but also the part the institutions play in international society. For English School theorists, institutions are practices embedded in the fabric of international society. As we have seen with Wight and Bull, the institutions of international society have a longer history than the proliferating regimes of the late twentieth century; moreover, English School scholars equate institutions with practices such as sovereignty, balance of power, international law, the diplomatic dialogue, and war. In order to understand the institution of sovereignty, for example, an English School approach would advocate a historical sociology of the term and the meanings given to it by state leaders at particular historical junctures. Such an investigation is not amenable to the 'neo-neo' requirement of framing testable hypotheses across like cases.

The differences between the American and British approaches can also be discerned in terms of their understanding of how co-operation emerges. For neoliberals and (some) neorealists, the specific institutional arrangements (or regimes) emerge as a response to the co-ordination problem where unrestrained individualism leads to sub-optimal outcomes for the players in question. Therefore, the task for neoliberals is to show how compliance with the rules is maintained by the requisite proportion of incentives and sanctions. In short, the crucial contention of the neoliberal model is that co-operation can be understood *without* recourse to common beliefs or shared values.[12] But as Andrew Hurrell has noted, a core assumption of Hedley Bull's is the way in which international co-operation is rooted in the sense of being bound by inter-subjectively created rules.[13]

The discussions within the British Committee on methodology highlighted their opposition to key tenets of positivism. International relations were not amenable to the search for behavioural laws of action, and there was no such thing as value-free enquiry in the social world. In place of positivism, the English School argued for an interpretive understanding of international relations; one which revealed the contingency (and tragedy) of human decision-making, the often irreconcilable meanings that different actors give to the same event, and the way in which cultural values shape diplomatic and political practice. A sense of collective identity and legitimacy in European international society crucially shaped the foreign policy of the great powers towards the Ottoman 'other'. In our own century, the end of the Cold War was brought about in part because the 'enemy,' reinvented itself, and in so doing, shifted the boundaries of Europe eastwards and prompted western European states to re-calculate their interests.

Having suggested reasons why the English School is incompatible with the rationalists, the next move is to consider the location of the School on the 'reflectivist' (or 'constructivist') side of the divide. The number of post-positivist positions is far greater than Keohane alluded to in his category of 'reflectivist'. Most writers now take it to include feminism (in most of its variants), critical theory, post-structuralism, and constructivism. It in this last category that the English School should be situated, although with one crucial qualification. Before outlining the reasons why the English School is constructivist,[14] it is worth re-capping the key elements of constructivism as laid down by Alexander Wendt. He defines the project according to three claims: 'first, states are the principal units of analysis for international political theory; second, the key structures in the state system are inter-subjective rather than material; and third, state identities and interests are an important part of these social structures, rather than given exogenously to the system by human nature or domestic politics.[15]

It should be apparent that there is an affinity between the theoretical core of the English School and these primary colours of constructivism. Writers like Wight, Bull and Vincent, clearly take the state as the central actor (even if the great society of humankind is ultimately the key normative referent). Moreover, the identity of states, given by the term sovereignty, has no meaning outside of the ideas and practices of the society of states where the rules of membership and succession are located. For the English School, sovereignty and nonintervention are constitutive of the society of states, in other words, it is sustained by the reproduction of these practices.

There is also common ground in conjunction with Wendt's second claim in that, for the English School, the notion of a society of states is founded precisely on a belief in the power of inter-subjective structures such as common rules, values and institutions. Here we see how the English School treats practices like war and the balance of power as *ideas*, unlike consistent realists who predominantly regard them as material structures. Moreover, for their effective operation, the 'positive' institutions of international society, such as diplomacy and law, require a highly developed form of what Wight called 'an international social consciousness'. This was in evidence during long periods of European international society, where the needs of the society 'became imprinted on the minds of practising diplomats'.[16] Bull's fear was that the cement which held European international society together might crack under the weight of decolonisation. What is interesting about Bull's thinking on relations between the west and the post-colonial world is the way in which, consistent with the third claim of constructivism, the newly independent states saw it in their interests to play the game of international society. In other words, the act of acquiring a sovereign identity generated common interests in maintaining the diplomatic dialogue and respecting the rights and duties of other states (despite the memory of what they regarded as their own rights as 'peoples' being trampled upon by the colonial powers).

In addition to the consensus on the institutions which sustain international society, there has been some progress in delivering justice in terms of humanitarian principles of universal rights and racial equality. Bull always doubted whether the current structure of sovereign states could deliver both order and justice; he felt the Third World was unlikely to endorse the *status quo* indefinitely, and any attempts to institutionalise just change would (in the absence of consensus) undermine the basis of international order. Bull's thinking on order and justice, which was taken up by Vincent in the late 1980s, makes a significant contribution to constructivist thinking. Not only do these two authors show how norms are generated, and what effect they have on the actors who interpret (and contest) them, the purpose of the English School's theoretical investigations is avowedly normative. Whilst the prevailing North American strand of constructivism has only described norms, the point for Vincent was to change them.

A further question which has attracted the attention of North American constructivists, and which the English School has had a significant impact upon, relates to the impact of globalisation on regional, cultural and local identities. As one influential text put it, 'culture and identity' are making a 'return' to International Relations. But the work of the British Committee, from Wight's paper on 'Western Values' to Bull and Watson's collection, *The Expansion of International Society*, suggests that for the English School, questions of culture and identity never went away. What was driving their interest in culture was the question whether the framework of rules set by states to regulate their practices could cope with cultural diversity. This acceptance of cultural heterogeneity and the attempt to regulate diversity is an aspect of English School thinking which appeals to communitarians. Writers like Terry Nardin in the U.S. endorse the 'egg box' view of international society, in which the purpose of the rules and institutions is to 'separate and cushion' a plurality of states. This is a useful metaphor because it draws our attention to the fragility of political communities, who join together to form a 'practical association' in order to facilitate co-operation whilst preserving their difference. This should not be confused, so the argument runs, with an association which engages in universalist practices such as setting (and policing) civilised standards of conduct.

As a number of theorists have pointed out, there is a point at which the neat distinction between 'practical' and 'purposive' associations breaks down.[17] The society of states since 1945 has engaged in an ever-widening normative agenda which has as its goal some notion of a 'good' which is shared by all states and peoples. In their more solidarist moments, English School theorists put this idea of a world common good at the centre of their enquiries. The idea that the international society tradition can offer critical openings into theorising a universal moral order, has provoked contradictory responses from the International Relations community. For critical theorists like Ken Booth,[18] the society of states cannot be an 'agent' of emancipation, since it is the normative structure of international society which is the permissive cause of human wrongs in the first place. On this reading, the society of states 'is never to be loved, and seldom to be trusted.[19] Nick Wheeler has taken up this challenge, arguing convincingly that the English School is not complacent about the state. The fact that too many states were acting like 'gangsters', resorting to political violence and repression of their own people, rather than 'guardians' as pluralism implied, was the reason why Vincent sought to modify the 'morality of states' model. Pushing international society theory in a cosmopolitan direction, Vincent thought there should be clear limits to what practices of 'diversity' were permitted. In a solidarist world order, the idea of what it means to be a sovereign state would change; membership of international society would become conditional upon satisfying minimum standards of civilised conduct.

Other critical theorists have found the English School more congenial. Andrew Linklater's project of deepening and widening the sense of community in global politics is one which he shares with solidarists. Like many other cosmopolitan thinkers, Linklater is agnostic about the particular institutional form that the community takes, privileging instead the historical and praxeological dynamic of moral inclusion and exclusion. In this critical constellation, individuals, bureaucracies, states, international institutions, NGOs and so on, all have the potential to act in inclusive ways. Not only do states have the potential to act as 'local agents of a world common good', they have considerably more agency than most other actors in world politics. Clearly the question of the contribution that states can make to the transformation of community is one which invites a critical international society approach, combining the insights of Bull's thoughts on alternative forms of community, Carr's understanding of the 'scourges' of economic and social exclusion, Wight's interest in constitutionalism, and Vincent's attempt to modify the principles of international legitimacy in accordance with cosmopolitan values.

The last decade has shown that the ideas and agenda of the English School remain pertinent; in some respects, their search for an understanding of how the institutions of international society can manage the tension between 'the ethic of difference' and the search for 'consensus' on normative issues[20] has never been more urgent. The next stage of the English School needs to build on this normative agenda without losing sight of the traditional pluralist contention that theory should build from the floor up rather than the ceiling down.

Notes

1. Hedley Bull, *The Anarchical Society* (London: Macmillan, 1977), 267.

2. Ludwig Wittgenstein, *Philosophical Investigations*, G.E.M. Anscombe and R. Rhees (Oxford: Blackwell, 1953), 66–67.

3. "The Meaning of "International Society"", British Committee discussion (October 1961), 5–8.

4. Chris Brown, *Understanding International Relations* (London: Macmillan, 1997), 54.

5. See his 'The Classical Approach to Arms Control Twenty Three Years After', in Robert O'Neill and David N. Schwartz (eds), *Hedley Bull on Arms Control* (London: Macmillan, 1987), 126.

6. Carr had quite different reasons for being critical of the West's policy towards the Soviet Union; as far as he was concerned, communism offered the possibility of overcoming the scourges of war and unemployment which had been a feature of late capitalism. Hysteria in the West was not only illfounded (resting on the assumption that 'our' form of governance was democratic and 'their' political system was tyrannical), it was likely to harm the prospects for the Soviet Union to build a new society.

7. Martin Wight, *International Theory: The Three Traditions* (Leicester: Leicester University Press, 1991), 231.

8. I am grateful to Roger Epp for drawing this to my attention. See Epp, 'Martin Wight: International Relations as Realm of Persuasion', in Francis A. Beer and Robert Hariman (eds), *Post-Realism: The Rhetorical Turn in International Relations* (East Lansing: Michigan State University, 1996), 129–131.

9. Hollis and Smith thought that the hegemony of 'explanatory' approaches in International Relations was such that they turned to philosophy to furnish examples for the category of 'understanding'. Martin Hollis and Steve Smith, *Explaining and Understanding International Relations* (Oxford: Clarendon, 1990), see especially Ch.4.

10. Robert Keohane, *International Institutions and State Power* (Boulder, Col.: Westview, 1989), 8. Note that Keohane's use of 'rationalism' is in sharp contrast to Wight's reading of a rationalist tradition in European thinking on international relations. Compare Keohane with Andrew Linklater, 'Rationalism' in Scott Burchill, Andrew Linklater et al., *Theories of International Relations* (London: Macmillan, 1996).

11. Robert Keohane, review of Wight, *International Theory* in *American Political Science Review* 86 (1992), 1112.

12. Keohane expresses this point clearly: 'International Cooperation does not necessarily depend on altruism, idealism, personal honour, common purposes, internalised norms, or a shared belief in a set of values embedded in a culture. At various times and places any of these features of human motivation may indeed play an important role in processes of international cooperation; but cooperation can be understood without reference to any of them.' Keohane, *International Institutions*, 159.

13. Note that this view of the English School and the 'neo-neo's' as opposed to each other has been challenged by Buzan 'From International System to International Society: Structural Realism and Regime Theory meet the English School', *International Organization* 47 (1993), 350. For an interesting meta-theoretical objection to the 'rationalist' / 'reflectivist' synthesis, see Hollis and Smith, *Explaining and Understanding*.

14. This argument is expounded upon in more depth in Timothy Dunne, 'The Social Construction of International Society', *European Journal of International Relations* 1 (1995).

15. Alexander Wendt, 'Collective Identity Formation and the International State'. *American Political Science Review* 88 (1994), 385.

16. Herbert Bufferfield, 'Crowe's Memorandum of January 1, 1970' (July 1960).

17. See, for example, *Understanding International Relations*.

18. Ken Booth, 'Human Wrongs and International Relations', *International Affairs* 71 (1995), 103–26.

19. This, of course, is an adaptation of David Luban's remark about the state.

20. Andrew Hurrell 'Society and Anarchy in the 1990s' in B. A. Roberson (ed.), *The Structure of International Society* (London: Pinter, 1996).

Does Order Exist in World Politics?

HEDLEY BULL

The late Professor Bull identifies three traditions of thought—Hobbesian (or realist), Kantian (or universalist), and Grotian (or internationalist). Bull's own work is a blend of the Hobbesian and Grotian traditions as order in world politics rests, in his view, on both the balance of power and agreed-on rules or norms. Hedley Bull's work and that of his predecessor and mentor, Martin Wight, are core to the present-day English School that focuses not just on the state system, but also on various aspects of international society.

Order in world politics may one day take the form of the maintenance of elementary goals of social life in a single world society or great society of all mankind. . . . It cannot be seriously argued, however, that the society of all mankind is already a going concern. In the present phase we are still accustomed to thinking of order in world politics as consisting of domestic order, or order within states, and international order, or order among them.

No one would deny that there exists within some states a high degree of domestic or municipal order. It is, however, often argued that international order does not exist, except as an aspiration, and that the history of international relations consists simply of disorder or strife. To many people the idea of international order suggests not anything that has occurred in the past, but simply a possible or desirable future state of international relations, about which we might speculate or which we might work to bring about. To those who take this view a study of international order suggests simply a design for a failure world, in the tradition of Sully, Cruce, St. Pierre and other peace theorists.

This present study takes as its starting-point the proposition that, on the contrary, order is part of the historical record of international relations; and in particular, that modern states have formed, and continue to form, not only a system of states but also an international society. To establish this proposition I shall begin by showing first that there has always been present, throughout the history of the modern states system, an idea of international society, proclaimed by philosophers and publicists, and present in the rhetoric of the leaders of states. . . .

The Idea of International Society

Throughout the history of the modern states system there have been three competing traditions of thought: the Hobbesian or realist tradition, which views international politics as a state of war; the Kantian or universalist tradition, which sees at work in international politics a potential community of mankind; and the Grotian or internationalist tradition, which views international politics as taking place within an international society.[1] Here I shall state what is essential to the Grotian or internationalist idea of international society, and what divides it from the Hobbesian or realist tradition on the one hand, and from the Kantian or universalist tradition on the other. Each of these traditional patterns of thought embodies a description of the nature of international politics and a set of prescriptions about international conduct.

The Hobbesian tradition describes international relations as a state of war of all against all, an arena of struggle in which each state is pitted against every other. International relations, on the Hobbesian view, represent pure conflict between states and resemble a game that is wholly distributive or zero-sum: the interests of each state exclude the interests of any other. The particular international activity that, on the Hobbesian view, is most typical of international activity as a whole, or best provides the clue to it, is war itself. Thus peace, on the Hobbesian view, is a period of recuperation from the last war and preparation for the next.

The Hobbesian prescription for international conduct is that the state is free to pursue its goals in relation to other states without moral or legal restrictions of any kind. Ideas of morality and law, on this view, are valid only in the context of a society, but international life is beyond the bounds of any society. If any moral or legal goals are to be pursued in international politics, these can only be the moral or legal goals of the state itself. Either it is held (as by Machiavelli) that the state conducts foreign policy in a kind of moral and legal vacuum, or it is held (as by Hegel and his successors) that moral behaviour for the state in foreign policy lies in its own self-assertion. The only rules or principles which, for those in the Hobbesian tradition, may be said to limit or circumscribe the behaviour of states in their relations with one another are rules of prudence or expediency. Thus agreements may be kept if it is expedient to keep them, but may be broken if it is not.

The Kantian or universalist tradition, at the other extreme, takes the essential nature of international politics to lie not in conflict among states, as on the Hobbesian view, but in the transnational social bonds that link the individual human beings who are the subjects or citizens of states. The dominant theme of international relations, on the Kantian view, is only apparently the relationship among states, and is really the relationship among all men in the community of mankind—which exists potentially, even if it does not exist actually, and which when it comes into being will sweep the system of states into limbo.[2]

Within the community of all mankind, on the universalist view, the interests of all men are one and the same; international politics, considered from this perspective, is not a purely distributive or zero-sum game, as the Hobbesians maintain, but a purely cooperative or non-zero-sum game. Conflicts of interest exist among the ruling cliques of states, but this is only at the superficial or transient level of the existing system of states; properly understood, the interests of all peoples are the same. The particular international activity which, on the Kantian view, most typifies international activity as a whole is the horizontal conflict of ideology that cuts across the boundaries of states and divides human society into two camps—the trustees of the immanent community of mankind and those who stand in its way, those who are of the true faith and the heretics, the liberators and the oppressed.

The Kantian or universalist view of international morality is that, in contrast to the Hobbesian conception, there are moral imperatives in the field of international relations limiting the action of states, but that these imperatives enjoin not coexistence and cooperation among states but rather the overthrow of the system of states and its replacement by a cosmopolitan society. The community of mankind, on the Kantian view, is not only the central reality in international politics, in the sense that the forces able to bring it into being are present; it is also the end or object of the highest moral endeavour. The rules that sustain coexistence and social intercourse among states should be ignored if the imperatives of this higher morality require it. Good faith with heretics has no meaning, except in terms of tactical convenience; between the elect and the damned, the liberation and the oppressed, the question of mutual acceptance of rights to sovereignty or independence does not arise.

What has been called the Grotian or internationalist tradition stands between the realist tradition and the universalist tradition. The Grotian tradition describes international politics in terms of a society of states or international society.[3] As against the Hobbesian tradition, the Grotians contend that states are not engaged in simple struggle, like gladiators in an arena, but are limited in their conflicts with one another by common rules and institutions. But as against the Kantian or universalist perspective the Grotians accept the Hobbesian premise that sovereigns or states are the principal reality in international politics; the immediate members of international society are states rather than individual human beings. International politics, in the Grotian understanding, expresses neither complete conflict of interest between states nor complete identity of interest; it resembles a game that is partly distributive but also partly productive. The particular international activity which, on the Grotian view, best typifies international activity as a whole is neither war between states, nor horizontal conflict cutting across the boundaries of states, but trade—or, more generally, economic and social intercourse between one country and another.

The Grotian prescription for international conduct is that all states, in their dealings with one another, are bound by the rules and institutions of the society they form. As against the view of the Hobbesians, states in the Grotian view are bound not only by rules of prudence or expediency but also by imperatives of morality and law. But, as against the view of the universalists, what these imperatives enjoin is not the overthrow of the system of states and its replacement by a universal community of mankind, but rather acceptance of the requirements of coexistence and cooperation in a society of states.

Each of these traditions embodies a great variety of doctrines about international politics, among which there exists only a loose connection. In different periods each pattern of thought appears in a different idiom and in relation to different issues and preoccupations. This is not the place to explore further the connections and distinctions within each tradition. Here we have only to take account of the fact that the Grotian idea of international society has always been present in thought about the states system. . . .

My contention is that the element of a society has always been present, and remains present, in the modern international system, although only as one of the elements in it, whose survival is sometimes precarious. The modern international system in fact reflects all three of the elements singled out, respectively, by the Hobbesian, the Kantian, and the Grotian traditions; the element of war and struggle for power among states, the element of transnational solidarity and conflict, cutting across the divisions among states, and the element of cooperation and regulated intercourse among states. In different historical phases of the states system, in different geographical theatres of its operation, and in the policies of different states and statesmen, one of these three elements may predominate over the others. . . .

Notes

1. This threefold division derives from Martin Wight. The best published account of it is his "Western Values in International Relations," in *Diplomatic Investigations*, ed. Herbert Butterfield and Martin Wight (London: Allen and Unwin, 1967). The division is further discussed in my "Martin Wight and the Theory of International Relations. The Second Martin Wight Memorial Lecture," *British Journal of International Studies* 2, no. 2 (1976).

2. In Kant's own doctrine there is of course ambivalence as between the universalism of *The Idea of Universal History from a Cosmopolitan Point of View* (1784) and the position taken up in *Perpetual Peace* (1795), in which Kant accepts the substitute goal of a league of 'republican' states.

3. I have myself used the term 'Grotian' in two senses: (i) as here, to describe the broad doctrine that there is a society of states; (ii) to describe the solidarist form of this doctrine, which united Grotius himself and the twentieth-century neo-Grotians, in opposition to the pluralist conception of international society entertained by Vattel and later positivist writers. See "The Grotian Conception of International Society," in *Diplomatic Investigations*.

SUGGESTIONS FOR FURTHER READING

Adler, Emanuel, and Michael Barnett. *Security Communities*. Cambridge, UK: Cambridge University Press, 1998.

Alderson, K., and A. Hurrell, eds. *Hedley Bull on International Society*. London: Macmillan, 2000.

Anderson, Benedict. *Imagined Communities*. London: Verso, 1983.

Armstrong, David. "Law, Justice and the Idea of a World Society," *International Affairs*. 75, 3 (1999): 643–53.

Bellamy, Alex J, ed., *International Society and Its Critics*. Oxford: Oxford University Press, 2005.

Berkhofer, R.F. *Beyond the Great Story: History as Text and Discourse*. Cambridge, MA: Harvard University Press, 1995.

Best, Geoffrey. *War and Law Since 1945*. Oxford: Clarendon Press, 1994.

Booth, Ken. "Human Wrongs and International Relations, *International Affairs*. 71 (1995): 103–26.

Brown, Chris. "International Political Theory and the Idea of World Community." In *International Relations Theory Today*. Eds. Ken Booth and Steve Smith, Cambridge: Cambridge University Press, 1995.

Bull, Hedley. *The Anarchical Society. A Study of Order in World Politics*. London: Macmillan, 1977.

——. "The Grotian Conception of International Society," British Committee paper. April 1962. Later published in *Diplomatic Investigations*. Eds. Herbert Butterfield and Martin Wight, London: Allen and Unwin, 1966.

——. "The Importance of Grotius." In *Hugo Grotius and International Relations*. Eds. Hedley Bull, B. Kingsbury, and Adam Roberts, Oxford, UK: Clarendon Press, 1990.

——. "The Importance of Grotius in the Study of International Relations." In *Hugo Grotius and International Relations*. Eds. Hedley Bull, Benedict Kingsbury, and Adam Roberts. Oxford: Clarendon Press, 1990: 65–93.

——. "International Law and International Order," *International Organization*. 26 (1972): 583–88.

——. "International Theory: The Case for a Classical Approach." In *Contending Approaches to International Politics*. Eds. Klaus Knorr and James N. Rosenau, Princeton, NJ: Princeton University Press, 1969: 20–38. Also published in *World Politics*. 3 (1966): 361–77.

——. "International Theory and International Society: The Viability of the Middle Way," *Review of International Studies*. 21, 2 (1995): 183–96.

——. ed. *Intervention in World Politics*. Oxford, UK: Clarendon Press, 1984.

——. "Introduction: Martin Wight and the Study of International Relations." In *Systems of States*. Ed. M. Wight. Leicester, UK: Leicester University Press, 1977.

——. "Kissinger: The Primacy of Geopolitics," *International Affairs*. 56 (1980): 484–87.

——. "Martin Wight and the Theory of IR," *British Journal of International Studies*. 2, 2 (1976): 101–16.

——. "Society and Anarchy in International Relations," British Committee paper. October 1961. Later published in *Diplomatic Investigations*. Eds. Herbert Butterfield and Martin Wight, London: Allen and Unwin, 1966. (also in Alderson and Hurrell, eds., 2000)

——. "The State's Positive Role in World Affairs," *Dædalus*. 108, 4 (1979): 111–23.

——. "The Twenty Years' Crisis Thirty Years On," *International Journal*. 42 (1969): 626–38.

Bull, Hedley and Adam Watson, eds. *The Expansion of International Society*. Oxford: Oxford University Press, 1984.

Burton, John W. *International Relations: A General Theory*. Cambridge: Cambridge University Press, 1965. [Ususally not considered formally to be part of the English School, his work nevertheless is consistent with both the societal and historical approaches prominent within the English School.]

——. *Systems, States, Diplomacy and Rules*. Cambridge: Cambridge University Press, 1968.

——. *World Society*. Cambridge: Cambridge University Press, 1972.

Butler, Peter F. "The Individual and International Relations." In *The Community of States: A Study in International Political Theory*. Ed. James Mayall, London: George Allen & Unwin, 1982.

Butterfield, Herbert. *Christianity and History*. London: George Bell, 1949.

——. *History and Human Relations*. London: Collins, 1951.

——. "Morality and an International Order." In *The Aberystwyth Papers: International Politics, 1919–1969*. Ed. Brian Porter, London: Oxford University Press, 1972.

——. "The Scientific versus the Moralistic Approach in International Affairs," *International Affairs*. 27 (1951): 411–22.

——. *Statecraft of Machiavelli*. London: Macmillan, 1940.

Butterfield, Herbert, and Martin Wight, eds. *Diplomatic Investigations*. London, Allen and Unwin, 1966; and Cambridge, MA: Harvard University Press, 1968.

Buzan, Barry. "From International System to International Society: Structural Realism and Regime Theory Meet in the English School," *International Organization*. 47 (1993): 327–52.

——. *From International to World Society?: English School Theory and the Social Structure of Globalisation*. Cambridge: Cambridge University Press, 2004.

——. "International Society and International Security." In *International Society After the Cold War*. Eds. Rick Fawn and Jeremy Larkin, London: Macmillan, 1996.

——. "The Timeless Wisdom of Realism?" In *International Theory: Positivism and Beyond*. Eds. Steve Smith, Ken Booth, and M. Zalewski, Cambridge: Cambridge University Press, 1996.

——. *The United States and the Great Powers: World Politics in the Twenty-First Century*. Cambridge, UK: Polity, 2004.

Buzan, Barry, and Richard Little. "The Idea of International System: Theory Meets History," *International Political Science Review*. 15, 3 (1994), 231–56.

———. *International Systems in World History: Remaking the Study of International Relations*, Oxford: Oxford University Press, 2000.

———. "Reconceptualizing Anarchy: Structural Realism Meets World History," *European Journal of International Relations*. 2, 4 (1996): 403–38.

Buzan, Barry, and Ole Waever. *Regions and Powers: The Structure of International Security*. Cambridge, UK: Cambridge University Press, 2003.

Carr, E. H. *Conditions of Peace*. London: Macmillan, 1942.

———. "The Moral Foundations for World Order." In *Foundations for World Order*. Eds. E. L. Woodward et al., Denver CO: University of Denver (Social Science Foundation), 1949.

———. *Nationalism and After*. London: Macmillan, 1945.

———. *The Twenty Years' Crisis, 1919–39*. London: Macmillan, 1939, 1946.

———. *What is History?* 2nd ed. London: Penguin, 1987.

Clark, Ann Marie. "Non-Governmental Organizations and Their Influence on International Society," *Journal of International Affairs*, 48, 2 (1995) 507–25.

Clark, Ian. "Traditions of Thought and Classical Theories of International Relations", In *Classical Theories of International Relations*. Eds. Ian Clark and Iver B. Neumann, London, Macmillan, 1–19.

Cox, Michael, Tim Dunne, and Ken Booth, eds. *Empires, Systems and States: Great Transformations in International Politics*. Cambridge: Cambridge University Press, 2001.

Cronin, Bruce. "The Two Faces of the UN," *Global Governance*. 8, 1 (2002): 53–71.

Cutler, Claire A. "The 'Grotian Tradition' in International Relations," *Review of International Studies*. 17, 1 (1991): 41–65.

Deudney, Daniel. "The Philadelphia System: Sovereignty, Arms Control and Balance of Power in the American State Union 1787–1861," *International Organization*. 49, 2 (1995): 191–228.

Donelan, Michael. "A Community of Mankind." In *The Community of States: A Study in International Political Theory*. Ed. James Mayall London: George Allen & Unwin, 1982.

Donnelly, Jack. "Human Rights: A New Standard of Civilization?" *International Affairs*. 74, 1 (1998): 1–23.

Dunne, Tim. *Inventing International Society: A History of the English School*. London, Macmillan, 1998. See detailed chapters on E.H. Carr, Martin Wight, Herbert Butterfield, Hedley Bull, R.J. Vincent, and the origins of the English School.

Dunne, Tim, and Nicholas Wheeler. "Hedley Bull's Pluralism of the Intellect and Solidarism of the Will," *International Affairs*. 72, 1 (1996): 91–107.

Epp, Roger. "The English School on the Frontiers of International Relations," *Review of International Studies*. 24. Special Issue (1998); and In *The Eighty Years Crisis: International Relations 1919–1999*. Eds. T. Dunne, M. Cox, and K. Booth, Cambridge: Cambridge University Press, 1999.

Finnemore, Martha. "Exporting the English School," *Review of International Studies*. 27, 3 (2001): 509–13.

Hall, Ian. "Challenge and Response: The Lasting Engagement of Arnold J. Toynbee and Martin Wight," *International Relations*. 17, 3 (2003): 389–404.

Halliday, Fred. "International Society as Homogeneity: Burke, Marx, Fukuyama," *Millennium*. 21, 3 (1992): 435–61.

Harris, Ian. "Order and Justice in the Anarchical Society," *International Affairs*. 69, 4 (1993): 725–41.

Hill, Chris. "World Opinion and the Empire of Circumstance," *International Affairs*. 72, 1 (1996): 109–31.

Hobden, Stephen, and John M. Hobson, eds. *Historical Sociology of International Relations*. Cambridge, UK: Cambridge University Press, 2002.

Holsti, K. J. "America Meets the 'English School': State Interests in International Society," *Mershon International Studies Review*. 41 (1997): 275–80.

Hurrell, Andrew. "International Society and the Study of Regimes: A Reflective Approach." In *Regime Theory and International Relations*. Ed. Volker Rittberger, Oxford: Oxford University Press, 1993.

———. "Society and Anarchy in the 1990s." In *International Society and the Development of International Relations Theory*. Ed. B. A. Roberson London, Pinter, 1998.

———. "Keeping History, Law and Political Philosophy Firmly within the English School," *Review of International Studies*. 27, 3 (2001): 489–94.

———. "Order and Justice in International Relations: What Is at Stake?" In *Order and Justice in International Relations*. Eds. Rosemary Foot, John Gaddis, and Andrew Hurrell, Oxford: Oxford University Press, 2003.

Ikenberry, John. "Constitutional Politics in International Relations," *European Journal of International Relations*. 4, 2 (1998): 147–77.

Jackson, Robert H. *The Global Covenant: Human Conduct in a World of States*. Oxford: Oxford University Press, 2000.

———. "Pluralism in International Political Theory," *Review of International Studies*. 18 (1992): 271–81.

———. "The Political Theory of International Society." In *International Relations Theory Today*. Eds. Ken Booth and Steve Smith, Cambridge, UK: Polity Press, 1995.

———. *Quasi-States: Sovereignty, International Relations and the Third World*. Cambridge: Cambridge University Press, 1990.

James, Alan, ed. *The Bases of International Order: Essays in Honour of C.A.W. Manning*. London: Oxford University Press, 1973.

———. "The Equality of States: Contemporary Manifestations of an Ancient Doctrine," *Review of International Studies*. 18, 4 (1992): 377–91.

———. "International Society," *British Journal of International Studies*. 4, 2 (1978): 91–106.

———. *Sovereign Statehood: The Basis of International Society*. London: Allen and Unwin, 1986.

———. "System or Society," *Review of International Studies*. 19, 3 (1993): 269–88.

Keck, Margaret E., and Kathryn Sikkink. *Activists Beyond Borders: Advocacy Networks in International Politics*. Ithaca, NY: Cornell University Press, 1998.

Keene, Edward. *Beyond the Anarchical Society: Grotius, Colonialism and Order in World Politics*. Cambridge, Cambridge University Press, 2002. See chs. 1–2.

Linklater, Andrew. "Citizenship and Sovereignty in the Post-Westphalian State," *European Journal of International Relations*. 2 (1996): 77–103.

———. "Rationalism." In *Theories of International Relations*. 2nd ed. Eds. Scott Burchill *et al.*, NY: Palgrave, 2001: 103–28.

———. *The Transformation of Political Community*. Cambridge, UK: Polity Press, 1998.

———. "What Is a Good International Citizen?" In *Ethics and Foreign Policy*. In *Ethics and Foreign Policy*. Ed. P. Keal, Canberra: Allen & Unwin, 1992.

Linklater, Andrew, and Hidemi Suganami. *The English School of International Relations: A Contemporary Reassessment*. Cambridge: Cambridge University Press, 2006.

Lipschutz, Ronnie D. "Reconstructing World Politics: The Emergence of Global Civil Society." In *International Society After the Cold War*. Eds. Rick Fawn and Jeremy Larkin, *International Society After the Cold War*. Basingstoke, UK: Macmillan, 1996.

Little, Richard. "The English School's Contribution to the Study of International Relations," *European Journal of International Relations* 6, 3 (2000): 395–422.

———. "International System, From International to World Society: A Re-evaluation of the English School." In *International Society and the Development of International Relations Theory*. Ed. B. A. Roberson, London: Pinter, 1998.

———. "Neorealism and the English School: A Methodological, Ontological and Theoretical Reassessment," *European Journal of International Relations*, 1, 1 (1995): 9–34.

Manning, Charles A. W., *The Nature of International Society*. [London School of Economics, 1962] 2nd ed. London: Macmillan, 1975.

Miller, J. D. B., and R. J. Vincent, eds. *Order and Violence: Hedley Bull and International Relations*. Oxford: Clarendon Press, 1990.

Mayall, James. *World Politics: Progress and its Limits*. Cambridge, UK: Polity, 2000.

Neumann, Iver B. "The English School and the Practices of World Society," *Review of International Studies*. 27, 3 (2001): 503–7.

Roberts, Adam. "Humanitarian War: Military Intervention and Human Rights," *International Affairs*. 69, 3 (1993): 429–49.

Suganami, Hidemi. "C.A.W. Manning and the Study of International Relations," *Review of International Studies*. 27,1 (2001): 91–107.

———. "The International Society Perspective on World Politics Reconsidered," *International Relations of the Asia-Pacific*, 2, 1 (2002): 1–28.

Thomas, Scott M. "Taking Religious and Cultural Pluralism Seriously: The Global Resurgence of Religion and the Transformation of International Society," *Millennium*, 29, 3 (2000): 815–41.

Thompson, K. W. "Idealism and Realism: Beyond," *British Journal of International Studies*. 3 (1977): 159–80.

Vincent, R. J. "Edmund Burke and the Theory of International Relations," *Review of International Studies.* 10 (1984): 205–18.

———. "The Factor of Culture in the Global International Order," *Yearbook of World Affairs.* 34 (1980): 252–64.

———. "Hedley Bull and Order in International Politics," *Millennium,* 17, 2 (1988): 195–213.

———. "The Hobbesean Tradition in Twentieth Century International Thought," *Millennium.* 10 (1981): 91–101.

———. *Human Rights and International Relations.* Cambridge: Cambridge University Press, 1986.

———. *Nonintervention and International Order.* Princeton, NJ: Princeton University Press, 1974.

———. "The Place of Theory in the Practice of Human Rights." In *Two Worlds of International Relations.* Eds. Christopher Hill and P. Beshoff, London: Routledge, 1994.

———. "Western Conceptions of a Universal Moral Order," *British Journal of International Studies* 4 (1978): 20–46.

Wæver, Ole. "Europe's Three Empires: A Watsonian Interpretation of Post-Wall European Security." In *International Society After the Cold War.* Eds. Rick Fawn and Jeremy Larkin, London, Macmillan, 1996. See 202–6.

———. "International Society—Theoretical Promises Unfulfilled?" *Cooperation and Conflict.* 27, 1 (1992): 97–128.

Walker, R. B. J. *Inside/Outside: International Relations as Political Theory.* Cambridge, UK: Cambridge University Press, 1993.

Watson, Adam. *The Evolution of International Society.* London: Routledge, 1992.

———. "Foreword: Forum on the English School," *Review of International Studies.* 27, 3 (2001): 467–70.

———. "Hedley Bull, State Systems and International Studies," *Review of International Studies.* 13, 22 (1987):147–53

———. *The Limits of Independence: Relations Between States in the Modern World.* London: Routledge, 1997.

———. "Systems of States," *Review of International Studies.* 16, 2 (1990): 99–109.

Wheeler, Nicholas J. "Pluralist and Solidarist Conceptions of International Society: Bull and Vincent on Humanitarian Intervention," *Millennium: Journal of International Studies.* 21, 3 (1992): 463–89.

———. *Saving Strangers: Humanitarian Intervention in International Society.* Oxford: Oxford University Press, 2000.

Wheeler, Nicholas J. and Tim Dunne. "Good Citizenship: A Third Way for British Foreign Policy," *International Affairs.* 74, 4 (1998): 847–70.

———. "Hedley Bull and the Idea of a Universal Moral Community: Fictional, Primordial or Imagined?" In *International Society and the Development of International Relations Theory.* Ed. B. A. Roberson, London: Pinter, 1998.

———. "Hedley Bull's Pluralism of the Intellect and Solidarism of the Will," *International Affairs.* 72 (1996): 91–108.

Wight, Gabriele, and Brian Porter, eds. *International Theory: The Three Traditions.* London: Leicester University Press, 1991.

Wight, Martin. "An Anatomy of International Thought," *Review of International Studies.* 13 (1987 [1960]): 221–7.

———. *International Theory: The Three Traditions,* Eds. Brian Porter and Gabriele Wight. Leicester: Leicester University Press/Royal Institute of International Affairs, 1991.

———. *Systems of States.* Ed. Hedley Bull, Leicester: Leicester University Press, 1977.

———. "Western Values in International Relations," British Committee paper (October 1961). Later published in *Diplomatic Investigations.* Eds. Herbert Butterfield and Martin Wight, London: Allen and Unwin, 1966.

PART 2

Interpretive Understandings

CHAPTER 6

Constructivist Understandings

In recent years constructivism (or, more precisely, social constructivism) has provided a provocative, intriguing, and fruitful approach to our understanding of international politics. It is fair to say that it ranks among the top three perspectives on international politics, joining realism and liberalism. Constructivism does not claim to offer a global or worldwide vision of IR as do the *images* we have identified in the previous chapters. What it offers instead is an approach to interpretive understanding that already has had enormous impact on theorizing throughout the IR field.

As we will see, constructivism has a number of important intellectual precursors and influences. But its gradual rise in importance in IR was also due to unforeseen events in the 1980s and 1990s. The Cold War (roughly 1946–1991) involving the Soviet Union, the United States, and their respective allies and ideological partners seemed destined to go on forever. Who was a friend and who was an enemy in a world divided between liberal and communist (or socialist) states was particularly clear-cut. IR theorists simply failed to anticipate the peaceful end of the Soviet Union and the collapse of its empire.

Realist power-transition theory might have expected an eventual clash between the superpowers, but not the internal collapse of one of the rivals. Within a few years the traditional enemy of the West was gone. While theory does not aim at making specific point predictions, surely there should have been greater theoretical anticipation of this momentous process. At the same time, there was a noticeable decline in state sovereignty as military intervention and normative justification on humanitarian grounds became evident. Globalization—the intensification of economic, political, social, and cultural relations across borders—also tended to raise doubts about the explanatory power of existing theories and approaches. Economic structuralist theories that relied on Marxist concepts also suffered in academe at a time when liberal democracy and capitalist precepts seemed increasingly to hold sway around the world.

What began in the early 1980s as a constructivist critique of realism and liberalism has dramatically expanded into a robust research program and significant force in empirical research pursued via a diversity of approaches. Yet what they all have in common is an interpretive understanding of observed phenomena, opening us to the subjective dimensions of not only knowing, but also creating the world of which we are so integral a part. At its core, social constructivism, as the term implies, relates to the irreducibly intersubjective dimension of human action to include what we consider to be knowledge and reality, with the assumption that the objects of our knowledge are not independent of our interpretations. Constructivists are particularly interested in the key concepts of norms, rules, and identities and how they affect the conception of ourselves and how we relate to the world.

Constructivism can be seen as a middle ground or bridge between other conceptual approaches to IR discussed in this book. On one end of the spectrum are the positivist, often material-based images in realist and liberal theories that emphasize explanation based on natural science criteria. To explain the actions of actors, it is assumed that rational choices are made among alternatives by evaluating their likely consequences in terms of objectives being sought. Ideas may matter, but in many of these theories they are secondary to (or reflections of) materially oriented interests. Although many constructivists utilize empirical data and some embrace positivist scientific standards for testing hypotheses, their conception of what constitutes explanation very often differs. The English School has the closest affinity to constructivism, which is apparent in the School's emphasis on norms and the importance of history as well as its application of the concept of "society" to international relations.

At the other end of the spectrum are the more radical postmodern, poststructuralist, and some feminist interpretivists whose sociology of knowledge comes close to arguing that only ideas matter, science is merely power disguised as knowledge, and explanation in the realist and liberal sense is an impossibility. Yet, as we will see, one can make the case that they are close cousins of constructivism due to the emphasis on the power of ideas and the importance of interpretive understandings of "the world out there." Given the assertion that there are fundamental differences between causal and intrepretive understandings of the world, however, it makes sense to emphasize constructivism's key ontological and epistemological assumptions.

MAJOR ACTORS AND ASSUMPTIONS

First, constructivism seeks to problematize the identities and interests of states. This is in contrast to neorealists and neoliberals who come close to believing identities and interests are givens. Constructivists are not only interested in the state as agent or actor, but also transnational organizations and international organizations. They emphasize the importance of subjective and intersubjective exchanges and actions taken by human beings as agents of these state and non-state organizational entities.

Second, constructivists view international structure in terms of a social structure infused with ideational factors to include norms, rules, and law. This structure can influence the identities and interests of agents, as well as international outcomes in such areas as humanitarian interventions and taboos on the use of weapons of mass destruction.

Third, constructivism, as the term implies, views the world as a project always under construction, a case of becoming as opposed to being. This is in contrast to the much more restricted view of change on the part of realists and even many liberals and economic structuralists.

Finally, constructivists have done hard thinking on ontological and epistemological issues. Such debate and discussion are a far cry from most causal theorizing where positivist premises lead theorists confidently to seek as objective an explanation of reality as possible, somehow minimizing the subjective part of our understanding. Given the subjectivity of human beings, constructivists underscore the impossibility of pure objectivity.

Constructivists do not deny that explanation in IR is possible. But, as noted in Chapter One, instead of adopting only the causal-explanation approach that tends to be dominated by covering law accounts grounded in theories that presume instrumentally rational behavior on the part of actors, many constructivists also look to models of value-rational behavior. This involves focusing on the ontological orientations and epistemological preferences they bring to their research as well as the normative concerns and principled beliefs of actors or agents. Doing so often results in rich historical and empirical analysis, explaining an event or outcome by detailing the impact of such factors and how they influence the construction and changes of interests and identities over time.

INTELLECTUAL PRECURSORS AND INFLUENCES

The philosophical and sociological foundations of constructivism are deep, consisting of centuries of intellectual development. For our purposes we will limit the discussion to several key scholars who have directly influenced current constructivist works. The importance of these scholars is evident in that other approaches to IR also draw from the wellspring of their insights.

Kant

We discuss in the next chapter intellectual contributions by the German philosopher Immanuel Kant (1724–1804) to the later development of phenomenology—how human consciousness affects our understandings of what we observe or appears to us. The objects we observe are *phenomena,* which Kant distinguishes from what he calls *noumena*—the unknowable essence of objects as things in themselves, quite apart from how we may see them or how they may appear.

His followers, the neo-Kantians of the late-nineteenth and early-twentieth centuries, transferred this perspective from nature to culture and social relations. The net effect was to set the social sciences apart from the natural sciences. Our knowledge—what we think we "know"—flows from our subjectivity, imposing our mental frameworks not just on nature, but also on the social world of which we are so integral a part. It's one thing to observe phenomena in nature around us. It is quite another, as human beings, to be very much a part of—not separate from—the social world we are observing.

Constructivists and others who follow this line of thinking not surprisingly are highly skeptical of the idea that the epistemological and methodological standards of the natural sciences can be directly applied to IR or other social-science inquiry. We take in what appears to us, but then probe to discover what we can about the underlying essence of what we observe. Knowing is indeed a highly subjective endeavor. We also establish shared knowledge or understandings of nature or the world "out there" with others when we engage intersubjectively with them.

Although Kant did not take the argument to these lengths, much less to the social sciences, his original insights on the subjectivity of knowledge—his distinction between the phenomena we observe and the inner essence of these objects—has had a profound impact on phenomenologists and on those who extended his claims to the social sciences—a set of intellectual understandings from which constructivists also draw.

Locke

The English theorist John Locke (1632–1704) has influenced constructivist views on the nature of anarchy. He argued that before society is formed one may be at peace in a state of nature or move from it to a state of war and back again; a state of nature is not necessarily a state of war. It bears repeating—Locke does not see the anarchic state of nature—"want of a common judge," government or central authority—as necessarily warlike. In this Locke clearly opposes the view taken earlier by Thomas Hobbes (1588–1679) who portrays the state of nature as perpetually in a state of war—either actively engaging in fighting or always on guard, preparing for the fight.

Locke posited that a social contract among individuals establishes domestic society. This coming together by contract or agreement and his argument that a state of nature is not necessarily warlike are what capture the interest of some social constructivists. What Locke applied to the domestic level of analysis, Alexander Wendt and other social constructivists have applied to IR. States and the relations established among them are constituted by a Lockean, social-contract or rule-oriented culture—not a Hobbesean, dog-eat-dog, jungle-like one as many realists assume. Hence to constructivists the realist view of anarchy is not the only way to conceptualize a world without legitimate centralized authority; there can be multiple types of anarchy. It is not a state of nature without rules.

The Lockean culture, then, is one of rivalry, not enmity as Hobbists would have it. The concept of sovereignty, for example, involves a shared expectation concerning the rules of the game in the relations among states. These shared expectations are the result of interactions, a socialization and internalization of norms or agreed rules that mitigate the danger of IR becoming nothing more than a Hobbesean "war of all against all." States, therefore, may reach agreements with one another to maintain the peace, whether they remain in a Lockean state of nature or leave it by forming a more peaceful international community as envisioned by Immanuel Kant or those following his lead.

Durkheim

Emile Durkheim (1858–1917) has been cited by neorealists as an inspiration for the idea that structure (in this case the international system) shapes and constrains relations among the units. But Durkheim also engaged in a series of empirical studies to explain how various social outcomes—such as individual feelings of social estrangement and suicide rates—were influenced by different bonds within social orders. He claimed, for example, that the lower incidence of suicide rates in rural areas of France during the Industrial Revolution was due to the strong moral and social bonds of their more traditional communities in the French countryside. The important point in terms of constructivism is that forms of sociality—the nature of relations and interactions among actors—have causal impact. Durkheim believed these relations cannot be reduced just to material factors. Of equal importance, Durkheim stated that like material reality, ideational factors can be studied scientifically. Thus, constructivist scholars are prone to argue that the tenets of positivism are not inherently antithetical to their interpretive approach to understanding IR.

◼ Weber

As noted in Chapter One and discussed in the next chapter as well, the German Max Weber (1864–1920) has influenced both causal and interpretive understanding approaches to IR. Causal models often assume that behavior is instrumentally rational and designed to achieve specific goals that may conflict with other actors' goals. This is a starting point for many realists and liberals interested in developing explanatory theory. But Weber also developed the idea that human actions can be value-driven—a value rationality in which choices follow from beliefs or commitments often rooted in moral, ethical, or religious understandings. This is not any less "rational" than behavior that follows an instrumental approach of maximizing gains or minimizing losses. As Weber argued: "We are *cultural* beings endowed with the capacity and the will to take a deliberate attitude toward the world and to lend it *significance*."[1] This ability of actors to interpret the meaning and significance of their social actions differentiates the social from the natural sciences. Furthermore, Weber argued that ideas also can play a normative role that goes beyond the narrow end of maximizing utility. Both Durkheim and Weber argued that the critical ties that bind individuals to groups are ideational, and such ideas are subject to investigation by social-scientific methods.

We now turn to examining key building blocks or concepts of the constructivist approach to understanding IR. The intellectual debt to foundational work by Kant, Locke, Durkheim, and Weber will become apparent.

INTERSUBJECTIVITY

Central to constructivism is the understanding that international politics is guided by intersubjectively shared and institutionalized norms, rules, ideas, beliefs, and values held by actors (or agents). **Intersubjective** by definition means shared by people—defined by their person-to-person, self-other exchanges—the ideational component of IR not simply being the sum total of the beliefs of individuals. **Institutionalized** means these collective ideas are established or constituted in the social world as **structures** or institutions, practices, and identities. These shared norms and rules set expectations about how the world works and what constitutes legitimate behavior. Although there are differences of opinion among them, all constructivists at a minimum hold that normative or ideational factors or structures are at least as (and likely more) important than **material** structures composed of such elements as population size, weapons systems, manufacturing output, and geographic factors that are themselves subject to interpretation.

To neorealists, economic structuralists, and many liberals, the material constitutes the baseline, and ideas tend to be derivative. Neorealist explanations in particular argue that material objects—power defined as material capabilities—have decisive impact on outcomes unmediated by the ideas people have concerning these objects. Classical realists incorporate international norms or rules in their analyses as do scholars in the English School. Such ideational factors, however, are discounted by neorealists who see them as variables dependent on the preferences of powerful states rather than having an impact independent of the international distribution of power among states. As noted in Chapter Two, for example, neorealists such as Kenneth Waltz and John Mearsheimer see the distribution of material capabilities or power as key to understanding the conduct of states in IR. In Chapter Three, we discussed neoliberalism and its focus on institutions as exemplified in work by Robert Keohane and also Judith Goldstein. While they understand the importance of ideas, material interests remain an important part of explaining outcomes driven by actors who make cost-benefit calculations either within or outside of institutional settings. In sum, constructivists would claim that commitment to materially based understandings found in much realist, liberal, and economic-structuralist theorizing does not grant ideas the important standing they warrant as an independent variable or factor that shapes IR patterns and outcomes.

To make these complex ideas easier to grasp, let's provide three examples to clarify the constructivist emphasis on intersubjectively shared and institutionalized norms and rules. First, we take up the social construction of the concept of **sovereignty,** which consists of a set of rules or standards of behavior providing guidance for states interacting with one another. Specifically, sovereign states came to claim under international law a right to complete jurisdiction over their own territories (the internal or domestic dimension), hence the development of the international norm prescribing noninterference in the internal affairs of other states. Second, states claim a right to be independent or autonomous in the conduct of their foreign relations (the external or international dimension). Sovereignty is therefore not simply a property of individual states, but can be viewed as an intersubjectively shared and socially constructed institution or normative structure among states.

The Peace of Augsburg (1555) and the Peace of Westphalia (1648) marked the emergence of sovereignty among the German and other states as a convenient norm that effectively placed authority in ruling princes, dukes, and kings of the day. Even though practice among them preceded the formalization of sovereignty—respecting the prerogatives of other sovereign states—the new norm in time became globalized in both its domestic and external dimensions. Sovereignty came to be expressed through rules of behavior as exemplified by diplomatic practices. These practices reflected mutual understandings about providing order in the international system, stabilizing actors' expectations, and managing power relations. Similarly, the development of the norm of territorial integrity helped reinforce the norm of sovereignty by acknowledging the socially constructed sanctity of state boundaries.

Of course the internal dimension of sovereignty—non-interference in a state's internal affairs—has been violated many times over the centuries as when one country has invaded another or otherwise intervened in its domestic politics or other matters. But the *claim* to being sovereign in both its internal and external dimensions has remained. In fact, violations of sovereignty when recognized as such do not extinguish the norm, its legitimacy often underscored by the victims of its violation. Estonia, Latvia and Lithuania were incorporated by force within the Soviet Union in 1940, but the *idea* that they were still sovereign states was kept alive. This contributed directly to these Baltic states reemerging at the end of the Cold War.

This intersubjective consensus on the sovereign rights of states, however, has been weakened as another consensus has gradually emerged: growing international support for human rights and a sense that there is a collective responsibility to do something about human rights violations. This idea of universal human rights and attendant responsibilities has encouraged and justified military intervention for humanitarian purposes to include cases in which states violate the human rights of minority groups or even their own citizens. Prohibitions against genocide—the slaughter of people because of their racial, ethnic, or other identity—and the inhumane treatment or torture of captive human beings are vivid examples of widely accepted, intersubjective, socially constructed norms that have also eroded claims to state sovereignty. If states decide that acts of genocide or other inhumane acts demand international diplomatic or armed intervention in the domestic affairs of states, such actions run counter to rights claimed by sovereign states to exercise complete internal jurisdiction over their own territories.

Where the states in question have no particular strategic or economic value to the great powers, it is hard for realists to explain efforts by them to curb human rights violations when no apparent material interests are at stake. But from a constructivist perspective, the normative context has shifted over the decades since 1945 as human rights have gradually been accepted as a widely held norm. Indeed, concern for human rights has had a broad pattern of effect in shaping many states' conceptions of interest. Put another way, commitment to human rights as an idea matters.[2]

A second example is also drawn from human rights. Consider how slavery and the slave trade were once accepted practice in international relations. From the standpoint of the United States and many European countries, slavery was considered an economic imperative—an institution of critical importance to the economic interests of the slave-trading states (and their slave owners) as late as the eighteenth and well into the nineteenth centuries. This intersubjective consensus gradually broke down. Domestic and internationally accepted norms against such exploitation of fellow human beings were slow in development, but by the late-nineteenth century finally became part of the fabric of rules prohibiting such violations of human rights. Various forms of human bondage persist to the present day, but social constructivists note that global and national norms now make such practices not only morally illegitimate, but also illegal. As social constructions, intersubjective norms and the laws or rules associated with them can (and do) change, however slowly.

A third example relates to norms concerning the legitimacy of warfare. Consider that in the first half of the twentieth century European states were engaged in two major world wars, supposedly in defense of their respective national interests. But now at least Western Europe has created what amounts to a zone of peace in which it is hard to imagine that for centuries Germany and France had been bitter rivals resorting to the use of force against each other in major wars. How could a realist explain these developments? From a constructivist perspective, an intersubjective consensus has emerged among elites, citizens, governments, and nongovernmental organizations that force is no longer the appropriate way to resolve differences. Peace as a value and a normative commitment to maintain it multilaterally has an impact on how states define their interests.[3]

The reference to Europe is an appropriate segue to the constructivist recognition that intersubjective understandings can vary across regions and also over time. Hence constructivist research programs often attempt to understand how these shifts in collective meanings occur through detailed empirical research and rich description. How have actors viewed existing normative structures and rules of behavior? How have alternative understandings been devised and propagated through not only state bureaucracies but also international organizations, transnational non-governmental organizations, and advocacy networks?

For example, the post-Cold War decline of communist ideology left intact the current globalized market system and its associated liberal financial institutions, norms and rules by which state and non-state actors operate. The global financial crisis that began in 2008 alerted constructivists to the possible weakening of this intersubjective, capitalist consensus, thus opening the door for states and non-state actors to begin modifying, adapting, or constructing alternatives to the *status quo*. To reiterate, these and other ideas about international relations in global society do not exist somehow in nature. Instead they are of human origin or, in the language of social constructivists, they are constituted or socially constructed.

STRUCTURE, RULES, AND NORMS

Constructivists define *structure* in terms of social relationships and shared meanings, differing on the component elements and their relative importance. These elements may include clusters of rules, norms, principled beliefs, shared knowledge, practices, and even material elements. Material resources, however, acquire meaning for human action only through the structure of shared knowledge in which they are embedded. International politics may be seen as anarchic, but the structure is essentially defined in cultural rather than in realist, essentially material terms. A security dilemma may exist among states, but this dilemma is viewed as itself an ideational social structure composed of intersubjective understandings in which states are prone to make worst-case assumptions about one another's intentions.

Beyond self-help, states may seek allies or coalition partners. The Cold War can be understood as a social structure of intersubjectively shared knowledge and meanings that governed the relations among the United States, the Soviet Union, and their allies. As tentative steps toward reassurance were made by the Soviet Union in the mid-1980s and were reciprocated by the United States, the structure of shared knowledge or meanings began to change. In the immediate aftermath of the Cold War, they stopped acting on the basis of a structure of shared knowledge that emphasized egoistic identities and self-help, shifting for a time from zero-sum (one side's gain, the other's loss) to more positive-sum understandings (seeking mutual gains). Constructivists, therefore, can agree with realists that the world can be a nasty and violent place, but they take issue with the realist explanation and offer an alternative perspective that emphasizes the importance of subjective and intersubjective understandings.

If anarchy is socially constructed and given meaning by actors, IR is not doomed to take place in a Hobbesean world of constant strife. By examining in detail the historical context within which such structures arise, constructivists attempt to explain how and why particular practices become relatively fixed in some cases, but fluid and subject to change or decay in others. Rules and meanings of expected behavior that reflect mutual, intersubjective understandings provide order to international politics, stabilize actors' expectations, and help to manage relations among actors.

Generally accepted diplomatic practices are one example. When such ideational structures persist and become institutionalized or routinized over time, they gain causal and normative force, leading to patterns of behavior that can be empirically analyzed. These structures can either facilitate or serve as obstacles to courses of action states choose to follow. To recognize that structures can and have changed over time, however, is no guarantee that these social constructions necessarily will be changed in the future. Changing structures affecting states, for example, involves altering an existing set of mutually reinforcing expectations.

This conception of structure has come to be applied by constructivists in a number of ways at different levels of analysis from the global to regional or issue-specific international regimes. These ideational structures can impact the behavior of both state and non-state actors at least as much as the materially based power or class structures one finds respectively in realist and economic-structuralist thought.

Rules

Let's delve more deeply into one characterization or component of structure: rules. Constructivists make a distinction between **constitutive** and **regulative rules** and in so doing contrast their approach to IR with that of neorealists and neoliberals. An illustration might be useful. The act of driving cars or other vehicles existed prior to establishing the socially accepted rule in the United States and most other countries that one should drive on the right-hand side of the road and as you enter a traffic circle keep to the right.[4] Or in Britain, Japan, and several other countries, a left-hand rule applies. Such rules, whether right- or left-oriented, were instituted due to increased traffic and the possibility of accidents. As examples of *regulative* rules, they are formulated to regulate an existing activity—driving cars. Other regulative rules are soon added to include issuing licenses, setting speed limits, yielding at intersections, etc.

Contrast this illustration with that of chess. It was not a matter of people pushing bits of wood around the board and bumping into one another that created the need for regulative rules. Rather, the rules of chess create the *very possibility* of playing chess in the first place: "The rules are constitutive of chess in the sense that playing chess is constituted in part by acting according to the rules." Regulative rules are designed to have a causal effect, such as getting people to drive on the right- or left-hand side of the road. "In contrast constitutive rules define the set of practices that make up any particular consciously organized social activity—that is to say, they specify *what counts* as that activity."[5]

These two illustrations make the constructivist point that the epistemology or ways of knowing present in neorealism, for example, lack this concept of constitutive rules. For them, it is a world of antecedent or pre-existing actors and their relations in an anarchic world. The role of theory is basically to explain their conduct or behavior within a system essentially not of their making. Stated another way, constructivists claim that neorealists tend to focus on things as they are or have come to be, thus failing to explain the orgins of states or the system of states that figure so prominently in their analyses.

John Ruggie, for example, has argued that the very concept of the modern state was only possible when a new rule for differentiating the components of the emerging European system replaced the medieval system of overlapping jurisdictions and authorities claimed by popes, kings, fedual lords, and trading associations. He examines not only material but also ideational factors that produced the concept of exclusive territoriality that serves as the constitutive rule defining the modern state system.[6] Constitutive rules are logically prior to what is the focus of most realist and liberal theorists who tend to take as a given the existence of the state and non-state actors engaged in international politics.

Norms

Norms are generally accepted values that define standards of appropriate behavior for agents (actors) with a given identity. Following from the discussion above, in situations where norms operate like rules that define the identity of an actor, they are said to have "constitutive effects" that "specify what actions will cause relevant others to recognize a particular identity." In other situations, norms operate as standards "that specify the proper enactment of an already defined identity. In such instances norms have 'regulative' effects that specify standards of proper behavior." Norms, therefore, either define (constitute) identities or prescribe (regulate) behavior, or they do both.[7]

How norms are developed is an important research interest of constructivists. They can be international or domestic in their origin. When norms take the form of principled beliefs (such as support for decolonization, end of apartheid, human rights, emergence of taboos on certain types of weapons, prohibiting bribery of government officials as the means to secure contracts, etc.), they can lead in certain circumstances to states redefining their interests and even sense of self (identity) as well as influence international outcomes. The impact of these beliefs can be facilitated by transnational networks of non-state actors. Ongoing empirical research also has examined norms governing the conduct of interstate war and humanitarian intervention and the situations under which norms are violated. While repeated violation of international norms on the part of states can erode or eventually invalidate norms, occasional violations usually do not.[8]

AGENTS

The constitutive logic is played out in the important constructivist ontological assumption concerning the relations between structures and **agents.** Constructivists do not privilege any particular agent, actor, or **unit of analysis.** The agents may be states, but also non-state actors to include individuals or groups as well as social movements, corporations, international organizations, non-governmental advocacy groups, or classes.[9] All such non-state agents have the potential to influence the creation of international norms, identities, and the behavior of states, just as states can similarly impact non-state agents.

As noted above, structure (social relations and shared meanings) can have a constitutive—not just a regulative effect—on actors. Structure can encourage actors or agents to redefine their interests and identities in an ongoing socialization process. Thus, unlike neorealism and neoliberalism that tend to hold interest and identities constant in order to isolate the causal factors related respectively to power among states and the dynamics within and between international institutions, constructivism is interested in how ideational structures actually shape the way actors define themselves and relate to other actors.

Of equal importance, these actors or agents have an impact on structures and how they are altered and produced. Hence—and this is the key point—agents (actors) and structures **mutually constitute** one another. Structures are not objects that simply influence actors in a unidirectional manner. As difficult as it may be, agents have the ability to change structures and escape from situations that encourage and replicate, for example, conflictual practices such as war. There is a reciprocal relation between agency and structure. The Hobbesean international system of a perpetual war of all against all or the pessimistic Thucydidean view of interstate war is not necessarily an inevitable state of affairs endlessly replicated through the ages, but rather a socially constructed structure developed over time. Due to the logic of mutual constitution, states may change the rules of the game and escape into a more Lockean (or even Kantian) culture of agreed rules or accepted norms to guide the conduct of international politics. Conversely, a community of peaceful states can degenerate into a more Hobbesean world marked by conflict; change is not necessarily always positive.

IDENTITY

Identities are relatively stable, role-specific understandings and expectations about one's self that are acquired by interacting with or defining the self in relation to a structure composed of social relationships, shared meanings, rules, norms, and practices. Due to this conception of interaction, identity breaks down the realist and liberal dichotomy between the systemic and state levels of analysis and provides a broader perspective on the mutual constitution of state and system or agent and structure, respectively.

At the level of the individual, human consciousness is important—the "self" that interprets (and thus constitutes the "other" outside of oneself), much as the "other" outside of the self gives meaning or identity to the self. For example, the respective identities of professor and student make sense within the context and interaction of a classroom setting; the identities are mutually constituted. But over time these identities can change. For example, the student goes to graduate school and eventually becomes a professor herself and rejoins her *alma mater* as a faculty member. The student-professor identities evolve into one of colleagues.

In terms of IR, the dominant intersubjective understanding and social relationship of the Soviet Union and the United States during the Cold War was that of enemies. Being anti-Soviet and anti-communist was a critical element of how Americans tended to identify themselves and their role in the world. It also provided the framework through which Americans viewed with suspicion and interpreted all Soviet actions. As this social relationship changed in the late 1980s and early 1990s when communist regimes collapsed, the part of American identity associated with anti-communism also began to change. As a result, the U.S. definition of international threats and national interests began to shift as well.

How can one recognize the existence of a particular identity? First, one would look for habitual actions consistent with this identity and interpretations such as U.S. attempts during the Cold War to block the expansion of Soviet influence in the Third World and Western Europe. Such actions are often referred to as **practices.** Second, one would monitor the **discourse** or combination of language and techniques employed to maintain these practices (such as diplomatic language emphasizing constructive engagement, balance of power, the use of force, and deterrence).

Identities can change over time and across contexts. Hence identities are not immutable characteristics of either individuals, groups, states, or whatever agent one is examining. Identities are produced and are not givens, any more than a state's interests are. The empirical-research task for constructivists, therefore, is to explore how interaction and context influence the development of the meaning of self—whether "self" is at the level of individual decisionmaker, decisionmakers as a group, a non-governmental organization, or conceptualized as an aggregate applying to the state, nation or society as a whole. Interactions, such as those during the Cold War, may bolster, undermine, or even change these identities resulting in either positive or negative outcomes.

Influences on identities can stem from any number of sources. Domestic or **endogeneous** sources may include broad cultural aspects of a society or military doctrine resulting from the internal distribution of political power. Identity could also be influenced by race, gender, nationality, religions, or ideologies. External or **exogeneous** sources can include such international norms as **multilateralism** that may contribute to defining a country's identify and the role it assumes in relations with other countries. Principled beliefs such as the moral illegitimacy of slavery and commitment to human rights are additional examples. Empirical studies have examined the development of a collective identity during the Cold War among members of the western North Atlantic Treaty Organization (NATO), which was created in 1949 to counter the perceived Soviet threat. Other studies have examined identity creation and transformation in the case of alliances in the Middle East, and shifts in identity in Japan, Germany, and the Soviet Union.[10]

The construction of identity, therefore, is not limited to perceptions of another actor being friend or foe. Note that the idea of mutual constitution of states and structures goes beyond simply recognizing that there is interaction between them. All images and approaches to IR discuss the impact of interactions. The point is that while the interactions of states contribute to the construction of the norms, shared meanings, and institutions of IR, they in turn also influence the identity and behavior of states (and, of course, human agents who represent them). Through this reciprocal process, both can be redefined.

LOGIC OF APPROPRIATENESS

Identities, rules, and norms come together in the constructivist concept of the **logic of appropriateness.** In the IR literature, a distinction is made between consequence-based and rule-based action. The former sees actions as driven by actors rationally rank-ordering their preferences or interests while being aware that other actors are doing the same. In other words, the actions of actors (individuals, organizations, or states) are driven by the calculation of consequences measured against prior preferences.

What is missing in the logic of consequences is an appreciation of how norms, rules, and identities can also shape actors' behaviors. The logic of appropriateness assumes human actors follow norms and rules that associate particular identities to particular situations. Stated another way, action is associated more with identities informed by norms and rules than just with narrow understandings of self-interest. As noted by March and Olsen: "As a cognitive matter, appropriate action is action that is essential to a particular conception of self. As an ethical matter, appropriate action is action that is virtuous. We 'explain' foreign policy as the application of rules associated with particular identities to particular situations."[11] In terms of IR, the identity perspective sees actors as acting in accordance with rules and norms that are socially constructed. IR is portrayed at least potentially as a community of rule followers tied to one another through intersubjective understandings, sociocultural ties, and a sense of belonging.

If identities are associated with and influenced by current standards of "appropriateness," then how does change in terms of international norms come about? One way is when norm "entrepreneurs" emerge who can create alternative norms or frames of reference. The challenge is that in promoting a new norm, it is done within the current standards of appropriateness defined by existing norms. To overcome the constraint imposed by an existing normative framework, norm entrepreneurs and activists may have to act explicitly *inappropriately*. For example, suffragettes positing alternative norms as to what constituted women's interests chained themselves to fences, engaged in hunger strikes, damaged property, and refused to pay taxes. In the case of IR, norm entrepreneurs such as Greenpeace, Amnesty International, Transparency International, and other transnational advocacy networks as well as those operating within U.N. or other international organizations have made advocacy arguments often with strong moral content concerning the environment, human rights, illicit business practices, and other topical concerns.

INTERESTS

Constructivists claim that the interests of actors (what realists and liberals have tended to take for granted as givens) are constructed and subject to change by the actors themselves as they interact with others. The constructivist take on interests is best understood in contrast to other approaches.

The concept of national interest has long been a central focus in the study of international relations. Particularly for realists, the specific goals of states vary, but all states have an interest in survival, wealth, security, and enough power to secure those interests. The origins of these interests are exogenous (external) to any state as a result of the condition of international anarchy and the security dilemma states face. While a realist may agree that these are indeed *ideas* about basic needs, they are still materially grounded, primary interests that drive state behavior, influenced as well by relative circumstances—the situation a state is in compared to other states.

Constructivists would argue, however, that interests and understandings of opportunities and threats are highly subjective. Consider, for example, a popular constructivist example: How can some 500 nuclear weapons of the United Kingdom be less threatening (or even non-threatening) to the interests of the United States than a small number of North Korean or Iranian nuclear weapons would be? Obviously, North Korean and Iranian words and deeds have led the United States to view North Korea and Iran as hostile and thus threats to its interests. Here is where a constructivist would argue that American leaders are responding to the *social* dimension of relations between the United States and other countries, rather than merely to the material nuclear hardware they may possess or seek to acquire.

These social relations are not fixed in stone for all time, but the American national interest cannot be ascertained without considering them. Yes, the United States has an interest in deterring or containing North Korea and Iran because of perceived hostility (the same holds true for North Korean and Iranian perceptions of the United States). By contrast, the United States has no apparent interest in containing the United Kingdom, given the more positive, non-threatening pattern of relations between the two countries. The importance of this bilateral, essentially social relationship is augmented by international norms and how a state conceives of its identity. All such factors influence a state's definition of its particular national interests.

The historical construction of national interests is a primary research interest of such constructivists as Martha Finnemore and Jutta Weldes.[12] Finnemore has documented successive waves in the diffusion of cultural norms among states. While these states may be very different in terms of their circumstances and role in the international sytsem, they still tend to express identical preferences for national policies and the creation of similar bureaucratic structures. Constructivists also see the concept of security to be historically conditioned by social interaction rather than an objective calculation determined by the distribution of military capabilities. Canada, for example, does not fear invasion or feel its security threatened by the United States despite geographic proximity and the overwhelming superiority of American military capabilities. Subjectivity matters in the understandings Canadians have of their interests and the threats or opportunities facing them.

THE DIVERSITY OF SOCIAL CONSTRUCTIVIST THOUGHT

There is substantial diversity in constructivist thought which has made providing an overview of key concepts and assumptions related to constructivism particularly challenging. Definitions and their application to research questions and case studies can vary from scholar to scholar. Indeed, as we will see, much of the criticism of constructivism comes from within the constructivist camp itself. Although Alexander Wendt's work on constructivism warrants the attention we will be giving to it, we note important (and early) contributions by others who also have pursued this line of inquiry.

In the 1970s well before the constructivist label came into use, Ernst Haas, John Ruggie, and others were working in this vineyard. Although their work then and since has been identified for the most part as being based on the assumptions of the liberal image, Ruggie has observed that "in those days [the 1970s] we were all constructivists, but didn't know it!"[13] Reflecting "on the role of ideas in the heads of actors," Haas came to see not just ideas as such, but ideas grounded in interests as motive forces in international politics: "Ideas have very often acted as the switches and channeled the dynamics of the interests."[14] Indeed, while many scholars brought such interpretive understandings to their work in earlier decades, the language and label of social constructivism have only come into common use in IR since the late 1980s.

▪ Schools of Thought

Influences on the role of ideas drawn from both Durkheim and Weber inform what Ruggie refers to as a "neoclassical" constructivism still within explanatory social science. He personally has subscribed to this perspective along with Nicholas Onuf, Friedrich Kratochwil, Emanuel Adler, Martha Finnemore, Peter Katzenstein, the late Ernst Haas, and feminist scholars like Jean Elshtain. While their theorizing incorporates values, norms, and other ideational factors, they do not reject the canons of science, standards, and methodologies for testing hypotheses or propositions.

Nicholas Onuf's path-breaking *World of Our Making* (1989) in particular set the stage for the important role constructivism has continued to play in international relations theory. Onuf's observation that "people make society and society makes people"[15] is core to constructivist understanding precisely because humans are social beings—we would not be human but for our social relations. Thus, human agency matters and our theories should address the choices agents make. The structure or "social arrangement" of society within which they operate is given by its rules and institutions. Just as these rules and institutions are made by human agency, they also provide the basis and context for agents to act. To Onuf, use of the term *institutions* is not restricted to bricks-and-mortar organizations, but rather may refer to such concepts as balance of power, spheres of influence, treaties, and international regimes. As with domestic societies, international society is itself "a complex institution within which many other related institutions are to be found."

Friedrich Kratochwil and Emanuel Adler also underscore the importance of rules and norms in constructivist understandings. Kratochwil comments: "Norms not only establish certain games and enable the players to pursue their goals within them, they also establish intersubjective meanings that allow the actors to direct their actions towards each other, communicate with each other, appraise the quality of their actions, criticize claims and justify choices."[16] Emphasis is placed on the shared understandings that provide the context for political interactions.

Adler emphasizes "the role of identities, norms and causal understandings in the constitution of national interests." Taking the broad view, he identifies constructivism as "a social theory about the role of knowledge and knowledgeable agents in the constitution of social reality." The goal is advancing understandings of "the role of inter-subjectivity and social context, the co-constitution of agent and structure, and the rule-governed nature of society." Adler comments that "constructivism sees the world as a project under construction, as *becoming* rather than *being* [emphasis added]."[17]

"Postmodern" constructivism is a second category or school of constructivist thought. Ruggie identifies this with the works of David Campbell, James DerDerian, R.B.J. Walker, and such feminist scholars as Spike Peterson. Postmodernist constructivism, in contrast to neoclassical constructivism, rejects the conventional epistemology of social science. It emphasizes instead the linguistic construction of subjects, resulting in "discursive practices" constituting the ontological or foundational units of reality and analysis. (We discuss postmodernism in Chapter 7 as a different category of interpretive understanding, but one which also has had influence within the constructivist camp.)

Finally, Ruggie places Alexander Wendt along with Roy Bhashkar and David Dessler in a "naturalistic" constructivism category between the other two. As with the neoclassical approach, it approaches IR as part of the social sciences, and emphasizes the intersubjective aspects or structures of social life. These ideational structures usually exist independently of human thought and interaction and can, therefore, be treated as non-observables, much like physical non-observables (e.g., subatomic particles) that underlie what we observe in nature. Following Alexander Wendt, we probe deeply in the human psyche to find the ideational core underlying the subjectivity and intersubjectivity that define understanding.

Levels of Analysis

Aside from categorizing constructivism by schools of thought, another way to cut into the literature is by levels of analysis. While committed to the basics of constructivism (agents, structures, identities, norms, etc.), research designs vary in their emphasis. One scholar has characterized these as systemic, unit-level, and holistic constructivisms.[18] The systemic level follows the third image perspective presented by Kenneth Waltz (see the reading appended to Chapter One). The focus is on the interaction of unitary state actors with domestic politics being ignored. It is the interaction and relation of actors to one another that matter. Much of Alexander Wendt's work exemplifies a similar systemic form of constructivism that focuses on the interactions of states and the cultures of rules and norms that have been constructed to guide them.

Unit-level constructivism takes the opposite approach, emphasizing the relation between domestic legal and social norms on the one hand, and the identities and interests of states on the other. Peter Katzenstein's work on the national security policies of Germany and Japan is an example.[19] The puzzle he hopes to solve is why two states that both experienced military defeat in World War II, foreign occupation, economic and democratic development, ended up adopting different domestic and external national security policies. Constitutive national, social, and legal norms are critical to understanding this outcome.

Finally, as the name suggests, holistic constructivists aim to bridge the classic international-domestic divide. Factors at these two levels of analysis are two faces of a single social and political order. The primary concern tends to be on the dynamics of global change such as John Ruggie's work on the rise of sovereign states out of European feudalism and Friedrich Kratochwil's theorizing on the end of the Cold War.

WENDT'S "NATURALIST" CONSTRUCTIVISM

It was in Alexander Wendt's now-classic essay "Anarchy Is What States Make of It" that he made the claim that self-help and power politics are socially constructed under anarchy.[20] Over the years he has continued to elaborate, refine, and defend his arguments. During a period when many IR scholars have attempted to apply constructivist concepts to empirically based case studies, Wendt has exhibited a distinct philosophic turn in his writings.

His most complete statement on social constructivism is to be found in his book *Social Theory of International Politics.* Wendt's interpretive approach to IR is quite clear. For him, the challenge we have as subjective creatures is finding a correct understanding of the world around us in which we are so integral a part. We use science as far as it will take us, fully knowing that we may not get it right. We assume an objective world out there, but are always constrained in our search for reality by our own subjectivities as human beings—a problem identified by Wendt as affected by the ontologies we have and the epistemologies we are prone to adopt. Nevertheless, Wendt is not a pessimist: While we may not have unmediated access to the world, we can still make great strides in understanding how it works, yet be humble about the truth claims we assert.

For Wendt the two basic tenets of constructivism are: "(1) that the structures of human association are determined primarily by shared ideas rather than material forces, and (2) that the identities and interests of purposive actors are constructed by these shared ideas rather than given by nature."[21] His ontology of international relations therefore is *social*—"that it is through ideas that states ultimately relate to one another" and it is "these ideas [that] help define who and what states are."[22] It is not a coincidence that the title of his book parallels that of Kenneth Waltz's *Theory of International Politics.*

Wendt sees the identity of the self as a function of the other, so it is that *agency* and *structure* are mutually constituted—in effect shaping one another. Put another way, states (more precisely, people acting for states) over time have constituted the international or global culture of generally accepted norms and concepts that have legitimacy as part of international relations. This ideational structure, in turn, constitutes and sustains the states in the system or society of states they have constructed. States continue to reinforce or support existing norms, adapt them or constitute new ones that reflect changing circumstances or new points of consensus (such as the norm against slavery). And so this reciprocal process continues.

It should be noted, however, that as opposed to postmodern constructivists, Wendt does not completely reject the materially based structure used in neorealist theorizing (the distribution of capabilities or power among states), but rather incorporates it and redefines it in his conception of social structure. He observes, however, that "the character of international life is determined by the beliefs and expectations that states have about each other, and these are constituted largely by social rather than material structures."

Wendt sees the ideational—a culture of generally accepted norms and other values that have been constructed under anarchy—as the fabric of system structure. It is, however, not that material power and interests are unimportant to Wendt, "but rather that their meaning and effects depend upon the social structure of the system, and specifically on which of the three 'cultures' of anarchy is dominant"—Hobbesean, Lockean, or Kantian.[23] In other words, instead of a single anarchy and a singular logic, there are different understandings of anarchy. Going beyond the Hobbesean anarchy as "state of war" of all against all, for Wendt a Lockean culture is one of rivalry but guided by mutually agreed rules, and a Kantian culture is one of a community of accepted norms. The amount of war and conflict is conditioned by the type of anarchy in existence. All these social structures have three elements: material resources and, more importantly, shared knowledge (ideas), and human practices.

States (and other actors) as agents can shape the world within which they are immersed and not just be prisoners of the *status quo.* Anarchy need not be the dog-eat-dog, jungle-like Hobbesean world as portrayed by many realists in which, drawing from Thucydides, the strong do what they will and the weak do what they must. Wendt sees agreed rules and institutions as giving the systemic culture of international relations today a Lockean character (a perspective drawn from the writings of John Locke, 1632–1704). Although Wendt rejects any claims to inevitability, he is optimistic that the international culture can grow beyond current common understandings of the rules that states and other agents follow in their relations with each other.

Wendt addresses the important interrelations among ideas, material factors, and social interaction. He agonizes over the essence of the mind-body relation and the issue of consciousness. His interest is in how ideational and material factors interact in nature as a whole, human beings and social relationships in particular. Is the material prior to the ideational as realists and other "physicalists" claim? After all, isn't the source of ideas the human brain—a material entity? Wendt objects to contemporary thinking about the mind that is dominated by the materialist worldview of classical physics and the assumption that ultimately reality is purely material.

He raises what he himself terms an heretical thought: Why do we have to assume that contemporary social science and its conceptualization of the relation of mind (ideas) to body (the material world) must be compatible with classical physics? What if consciousness is instead viewed as a quantum mechanical phenomenon, the domain of the subatomic physics of particles and waves? From this perspective, human beings are in effect walking wave particles, not classical material objects.[24] Just as physicists have pondered over the question of whether the character of light is particle (and thus material) or waves of energy (analogous to the ideational in the social sciences), Wendt asks if we can assume there is an ideational-material composite in the social sciences similar to the wave-particle relation posited in the natural sciences. These two interactive factors in physics are encapsulated by the term *quantum.*

Consciousness—to Wendt "the basis of social life"[25]—is the core concept in much theorizing about interpretive understanding. And as noted it is understood by him as "a macroscopic quantum mechanical phenomenon." It is incorrect to view matter as purely material or inanimate; it is both "material and phenomenal, outside and inside." As Wendt summarizes his ontological position: "Matter . . . is an active, 'minded' phenomenon, not the inert, mindless substance of materialism." To him "the mind-body problem is a fundamental problem of *social* science, not just neuroscience."

The material and the ideational, then, are bound together in human consciousness. It is not as if consciousness is external to or separate from human actions, but is integrally a part of them. To rational-choice theorists and others who discount subjective experiences and other aspects of consciousness, "human beings are nothing but sophisticated information-processing machines." He laments this purging of subjectivity from social science, observing that in this "rationalist" position there is "an implicit materialism telling us that consciousness is epiphenomenal"—that it is secondary and thus not causal. Put another way, in physicalist understandings the material determines the ideational, not the other way around.

Wendt explicitly rejects this physicalist understanding that all materialists share—"a belief that in the end it's 'matter all the way down.' "[26] Because human consciousness effectively drops out of this materialist equation, Wendt finds the physicalist approach unacceptable. Indeed, Wendt finds many similarities between the social lives of human beings and the unpredictability or uncertainty one finds in the subatomic or quantum world. He refers to a "quantum consciousness" and a "participatory epistemology" as defining the social context in which human beings act.[27]

We have come a long way from the initial formulations of social constructivism. Wendt does not resolve the dialectic between the ideational and material, any more than physicists have found a new particle-wave synthesis. For Wendt it may be enough merely to posit the material-ideational dualism in the form of a quantum found naturally in human beings. His critics will be quick to note the **reductionism** inherent in Wendt's mind-body formulation—trying to go ever deeper within the human psyche (effectively, they'll say, to brain waves or the synapse between nerve endings) to depict the relation between the ideational and the material.

Some of a positivist bent also object to Wendt's **metaphysics**—his characterization of the ideational metaphorically as a "wave" lacking the materiality of particles, thus coming close to identifying a life force or spirit. In such matters conventional or positivist science is silent, leaving such speculations to theologians. Finally, still others will find fault with Wendt's metaphorical use of *quantum,* borrowed from subatomic physics as if it were analogous to a similar structure in human beings (and presumably other forms of life, although Wendt does not so extend his argument).

Aside from his earlier analysis of the agent-structure issue and the investigation of the relations among mind, body, and consciousness, Wendt also grapples with other dualisms or dialectics that challenge theoretical work in the entire IR field. Is there a synthesis to be found (or should we learn to live with the tensions) between (1) positivism and interpretivism—objective science and human self-understanding; (2) rationalism and constructivism; and (3) idealism and realism—ideas and the material world?

What is interesting is that Wendt does not see a necessary contradiction between science or positivism and interpretive understanding, rejecting the either/or position. In so doing he draws criticism from causal and interpretive theorists alike. Wendt believes one can be informed by (and thus compatible with) the other unless we build them as straw men—constructing them as if they were mutually exclusive. Wendt's positivism is a broad "commitment to *science,* understood as a method for gaining knowledge about the world out there." He therefore sees positivism with a lowercase or "small *p*." What he rejects is certain kind of positivism a (capitalized *P*) when it is treated as "a particular *philosophy* of science" that "privileges Humean causation, law-like generalizations, deductive theory" and the like.[28]

According to Wendt, the "Cartesian world view" one finds in positivism makes several assumptions to include

1. Reality out there is not part of you or me in here, which means we must distinguish between subject and object;
2. We can acquire knowledge of external reality through the scientific method;
3. Success depends on maintaining a distinction between fact and value; and
4. Mind and matter are distinct, irreducible substances.

These assumptions are the foundation of a "classical worldview":

1. The elementary units of reality are physical objects (materialism);
2. Larger objects can be reduced to smaller ones (reductionism);
3. Objects behave in law-like ways (determinism);
4. Causation is mechanical and local (mechanism); and
5. Objects exist independent of the subjects who observe them—(a claim to objectivism).

What this classical worldview lacks is a place for human consciousness—the basis for an interpretivist understanding. What Wendt tries to do, then, is to combine a positivist epistemology with an interpretivist ontology. To him, there is a complementarity between positivism and interpretivism. We need not be forced to choose "between a positivism in which consciousness makes no difference and an interpretivism in which it has no naturalistic basis."[29]

CONSTRUCTIVIST AFFINITIES IN THE BROADER IR FIELD

In sum, constructivism shares at least one characteristic with realism and liberalism: all are rather broad tents within which numerous perspectives and theories can be found. One finds constructivist understandings not only in some critical theory and postmodernist interpretations, but they also are present in feminist scholarship. We also can see constructivist currents in the English School's "Grotian" focus on rules and law in international society to include an emphasis on historical sociology (how these ideational factors emerged over time, which also dovetails nicely with constructivist understandings of how structures come to be).

Constructivism also shares affinities with some liberals who emphasize the role of ideas, learning, and shared expectations in the construction of regime theory. We would even argue that some classical realists have a constructivist flavor in their work when they have a more voluntarist (rather than determinist) take on such matters as the historical development of balance of power. As realist Hans Morgenthau stated: "The confidence in the stability of the modern state system . . . derives . . . not from the balance of power, but [rather] from a number of elements, intellectual and moral in nature, upon which both the balance of power and the stability of the modern state repose." The balance of power in the nineteenth century was embedded in this moral and intellectual climate [read "structure"] which resulted in "temperate and undecisive contests."[30] Yet the realist and liberal emphasis on causal understandings ultimately and decisively separates them from constructivist understandings.

Constructivist interpretations are not as prevalent or as well developed in economic-structuralist work and the associated literature. That said, Antonio Gramsci developed the concept of the historical and ideological *bloc,* an obstacle to social change that maintains a pattern of dominance in society or even on a global scale. We note that such blocs are social constructions that economic structuralists see as serving dominant class interests that go well beyond the boundaries of particular states and their societies.

CONSTRUCTIVISTS AND THEIR CRITICS

Liberal and Realist Critiques

Given the fact that early constructivist work consisted of a critique of the epistemological and ontological assumptions of neorealism and neoliberalism, it is not surprising that there was a response. An initial sympathetic take on interpretive understandings came from Robert Keohane in 1989. In contrasting his own neoliberal institutionalism approach to that of what he terms the "reflective school," he stated that a research program is lacking in the latter. Until that is achieved, and it can be shown via empirical studies that it can "illuminate important issues in world politics, they will remain on the margins of the field, largely invisible to the preponderance of empirical researchers." These reflective approaches (what we call interpretive understandings), he argued, had been adept at pointing out the limitations of rational actor and game-theoretic approaches to international institutions, rather than developing theories of their own.[31]

Five years later, the neorealist John Mearsheimer took on not only constructivism but also other interpretive understandings of IR as they gained in prominence.[32] (Wendt's rebuttal is one of the Selected Readings at the end of this chapter.) Mearsheimer argued it is one thing to criticize hegemonic research programs like realism with its pessimistic view on the possibility of peaceful change. But the problem with social constructivism, critical theory, and postmodernism was that they have little say on the feasibility of the international system evolving into a more peaceful world, the mechanisms as to how this would even occur, little empirical support for their assertions, and even an inability to explain why particular discourses rise and fall. Supposed examples of more communitarian systems such as the feudal era are subject to dispute as are claims that the end of the Cold War illustrated the eroding explanatory power of anarchy and the self-help nature of the international system.

A great deal has changed in recent years on the application of constructivist concepts to IR issues which has reduced the saliency of the Keohane and Mearsheimer critiques. Numerous empirical case studies have been based upon, for example, constructivist concepts while remaining cognizant of the contribution of causal theorizing generally associated with positivism.[33] But the bottom line is that interpretive understandings and realist and liberal approaches to IR still stand in contrast to each other due to basic underlying epistemological and ontological differences. This was particularly evident around 2000 when constructivists pointedly noted the weaknesses of neoliberal and neorealist theorizing on international organizations based upon assumptions of instrumental rationality at odds with subjective or social insights generated by sociological approaches favored by constructivists.[34] Whether or not synthesis occurs between constructivism and any of the four images we identify in this volume, we do see the latter as enriched by the interpretive understanding constructivists bring to their diverse research programs.

■ Debates Within Constructivism and Postmodern Challenges

The most fruitful debates concerning the promise and limitations of constructivism as an approach to IR have really come from within the constructivist camp itself. It is difficult, for example, to get a handle on exactly who is a constructivist and what they have in common beyond the assumptions outlined at the beginning of the chapter. Is constructivism a middle path between causal theory and postmodernism? Or does it also include postmodernism? If so, there is a great difference between an Alexander Wendt who accepts a positivist epistemology (in the broad sense of a commitment to science as a way to gain knowledge of the world out there) and treats states as actors or people with intentions, and a postmodernist such as Andreas Behnke who claims Wendt is not really that far removed from Kenneth Waltz's neorealism.[35]

Such "family" disagreements stem from a number of sources. For example, for analytic purposes should the state as agent be a given? Should scientific methods be used? A positivist epistemology would maintain that a socially constructed international system contains patterns that are subject to generalization and falsifiable hypotheses. Alexander Wendt, Martha Finnemore, and Michael Barnett fall into this camp. A postmodernist, by contrast, might ask if such work is really all that different from the methodological and epistemological conventions of realism and liberalism. What about the role of ethics? Can the "is" be distinguished from the "ought"? Postmodern constructivists are decidedly skeptical about such distinctions. Is anarchy a fundamental organizing principle of the international system? Or does enough authority (or legitimated power) exist in international organizations, international law, and even firms and institutions that it is questionable whether the world is really as anarchic as it is usually portrayed?

The debate on the relation between agency and structure as sources of change in international politics—an ongoing discourse conducted throughout the 1990s that continues to the present—remains unresolved. How important is agency—whether states or non-state actors including human beings acting for them or in their own right? How important is structure—the external or exogenous factors that facilitate or constrain agents? What impact do agents have on these structures that, after all, are of human construction or subject to interpretation by human beings?

The agent-structure debate has moved on from a clash between neorealists and neoliberals on the one hand and constructivists on the other. Others have joined in the fight from postmodern or post-structuralist, critical ranks. As noted by Emanuel Adler, the latter argue that "what matters is neither structures nor agents, but the role of discursive practices." Social "realities" are a function of linguistic construction, our understanding of cultural meanings found in language interactions, and the verbal and non-verbal communications we employ.[36] As a result, Adler doubts whether the agent-structure debate will ever be fully resolved. He states, however, that we are nevertheless left with a much better understanding of how agents and structures relate in the theoretical formulations offered by constructivists.

In sum, constructivism continues to be a leading perspective on IR. It has evolved from a critique of realism and liberalism to a research program that has provided important insights into world politics. In the process, it has caused other perspectives or approaches to take into account constructivist concepts and arguments.

Notes

1. Max Weber, *Methodology of the Social Sciences,* Edward Shils and H. A. Finch, trans. (Glencoe, IL: Free Press, 1949), 81.
2. See the article by Martha Finnemore at the end of this chapter.
3. See Emanuel Adler and Michael Barnett. *Security Communities* (New York: Cambridge University Press, 2002).
4. John Gerard Ruggie, *Constructing the World Polity* (London: Routledge, 1998).
5. *Ibid.,* 22.
6. *Ibid.,* 25–26.
7. Peter Katzenstein, *The Culture of National Security: Norms and Identity in International Politics* (New York: Columbia University Press, 1996), 5.
8. V. P. Shannon, "Norms Are What States Make of Them: The Political Psychology of Norm Violation," *International Studies Quarterly,* 44 (2000): 293–316.
9. For a constructivist argument that international organizations, for example, can be treated as autonomous actors, see Michael N. Barnett and Martha Finnemore, "The Politics, Power and Pathologies of International Organizations," *International Organizations* 53, 4 (Autumn 1999): 699–732.
10. See the articles in Peter J. Katzenstein, ed., *The Culture of National Security: Norms and Identity in World Politics* (New York: Columbia University Press, 1996).
11. James G. March and Johan P. Olsen. "The Institutional Dynamics of International Political Orders. *International Organization* 52, 4 (Autumn 1998): 951.
12. Martha Finnemore, *National Interests in International Society* (Ithaca, NY: Cornell University Press, 1996); Jutta Weldes, *Constructing National Interests: The United States and the Cuban Missile Crisis.* (Minneapolis: University of Minnesota Press, 1999).
13. Annual Meeting, American Political Science Association, Philadelphia, August–September 2003. Cf. Ruggie, *Constructing the World Polity,* 19 and 35.
14. Ernst B. Haas, *Nationalism, Liberalism, and Progress,* vol. 1 (Ithaca, NY: Cornell University Press, 1997), 2–3.
15. This quote and subsequent citations in this paragraph are taken from Nicholas Onuf, "Constructivism: A User's Manual" in Vendulka Kubálková, Nicholas Onuf, and Paul Kowert, eds., *International Relations in a Constructed World* (London and Armonk, NY: M.E. Sharpe, 1998), 58–78.
16. Friedrich Kratochwil, "The Embarrassment of Changes: Neo-realism as the Science of Realpolitik Without Politics," *Review of International Studies,* 19 (1993), 75–76.
17. See Emanuel Adler, "Constructivism and International Relations" in *Handbook of International Relations* eds. Walter Carlsnaes, Thomas Risse, and Beth A. Simmons (London: Routledge, 2002), 95–114.
18. We refer here to insights offered in Christian Reus-Smit, "Constructivism," in *Theories of International Relations,* 3rd ed. Scott Burchill, et al. (New York: Palgrave Macmillan, 2005), 199–201.
19. Peter Katzenstein, *Tamed Power: Germany in Europe* (Ithaca: Cornell University Press, 1999); *Cultural Norms and National Security: Police and Military in Postwar Japan* (Ithaca: Cornell University Press, 1996).
20. Alexander Wendt, "Anarchy Is What States Make of It: The Social Construction of Power Politics" *International Organization,* 46, 2 (Spring 1992) 391–425.
21. Alexander Wendt, *Social Theory of International Politics* (Cambridge, UK: Cambridge University Press, 1999), 1.
22. *Ibid.,* 372
23. *Ibid.,* 20. The three cultures are discussed in detail in Chapter 6 of *Social Theory.*
24. Alexander Wendt, "Social Theory as Cartesian Science" in, eds., Stefano Guzzini and Anna Leander *Constructivism and International Relations: Alexander Wendt and His Critics* (London and New York: Routledge, 2006), 183.
25. *Ibid.,* 184. Subsequent quotes are from, respectively, pages 183, 195, and 185.
26. *Ibid.,* 185.
27. *Ibid.,* 205.
28. *Ibid.,* 214.
29. *Ibid.,* 188, 190, 214.

30. Hans J. Morgenthau, *Politics Among Nations: The Struggle for Power and Peace*, 4th ed. (New York: Alfred Knopf, 1967), 211, 213.

31. Robert O. Keohane, "International Institutions: Two Approaches," *International Institutions and State Power*. (Boulder, CO: Westview Press, 1989). Quotes from p. 173.

32. John J. Mearsheimer, "The False Promise of International Institutions," *International Security*, 19, 3 (Winter 1994/95): 5–49. See also the 2000 article by Dale Copeland, "The Constructivist Challenge to Structural Realism: A Review Essay," in *Constructivism and International Relations*, eds., Stefano Guzzini and Anna Leander (London: Routledge, 2006), 1–20.

33. See, for example, Michael Struett, *The Politics of Constructing the International Criminal Court: NGOs, Discourse, and Agency* (New York: Palgrave Macmillan, 2008); Edward Keene, "A Case Study of the Construction of International Hierarchy: British Treaty-Making Against the Slave Trade in the Early Nineteenth Century," *International Organization*, 61 (Spring 2007): 311–39; Judith Kelley, "Assessing the Complex Evolution of Norms: The Rise of International Election Monitoring," *International Organization*, 62 (Spring 2008): 221–55; Emanuel Adler, "The Spread of Security Communities: Communities of Practice, Self-Restraint, and NATO's Post-Cold War Transformation," *European Journal of International Relations*, 14, 2 (2008): 195–230.

34. Martha Finnemore and Stephen J. Trope, "Alternatives to 'Legalization': Richer Views of Law and Politics," *International Organization*, 55, 3 (Summer 2001): 743–58; Alexander Wendt, "Driving with the Rearview Mirror: On the Rational Science of Institutional Design," *International Organization*, 55, 4 (Autumn 2001): 1019–49; and Michael N. Barnett and Martha Finnemore, "The Politics, Power and Pathologies of International Organizations," *International Organizations* 53, 4 (Autumn 1999): 699–732.

35. Andreas Behnke, "Grand Theory in the Age of Its Impossibility," in Stefano Guzzini and Anna Leander, 49.

36. Emanuel Adler, "Constructivism and International Relations" in eds., *Handbook of International Relations*, Walter Carlsnaes, Thomas Risse, and Beth A. Simmons (London: Routledge, 2002), 104. Adler's references are to Roxanne L. Doty, "Aporia: A Critical Exploration of the Agent-Structure Problematique in International Relations Theory," *European Journal of International Relations*, 3, 3 (1997): 365–92; and to Hidemi Suganimi, "Agents, Structures, Narratives," *European Journal of International Relations* 5, 3 (1999): 365–86.

SELECTED READINGS

Constructing International Politics

ALEXANDER WENDT

In this response to critiques of neoliberal institutionalism and various forms of interpretive understanding by John Mearsheimer, a structural realist, the author uses the occasion to lay out succinctly his own constructivist approach to the IR field. Note that the term critical IR theory *is used to capture postmodernists, constructivists, feminists and neo-Marxists; we use the term in a more limited sense. Also note that Wendt actually shares a number of realist assumptions, a perspective many constructivists would question.*

John J. Mearsheimer's "The False Promise of International Institutions"[1] is welcome particularly in two respects. First, it is the most systematic attempt to date by a neorealist to address critical international relations (IR) theory.[2] Second, it reminds neoliberals and critical theorists, normally locked in their own tug-of-war, that they have a common, non-realist interest in the institutional bases of international life.[3] "False Promise" is likely, therefore, to spur productive discussions on all sides.

Unfortunately, it will be hard for most critical theorists to take seriously a discussion of their research program so full of conflations, half-truths, and misunderstandings. However, to some extent misunderstanding is inevitable when anthropologists from one culture first explore another. A dialogue between these two cultures is overdue, and "False Promise" is a good beginning.

Critical IR "theory," however, is not a single theory. It is a family of theories that includes postmodernists (Ashley, Walker), constructivists (Adler, Kratochwil, Ruggie, and now Katzenstein), neo-Marxists (Cox, Gill), feminists (Peterson, Sylvester), and others. What unites them is a concern with how world politics is "socially constructed,"[4] which involves two basic claims: that the fundamental structures of international politics are social rather than strictly material (a claim that opposes materialism), and that these structures shape actors' identities and interests, rather than just their behavior (a claim that opposes rationalism). However, having these two claims in common no more makes critical theory a single theory than does the fact that neorealism and neoliberalism both use game theory makes them a single theory. Some critical theorists are statists and some are not; some believe in science and some do not; some are optimists and some pessimists; some stress process and some structure.[5] Thus, in my reply I speak only for myself as a "constructivist," hoping that other critical theorists may agree with much of what I say. I address four issues: assumptions, objective knowledge, explaining war and peace, and policymakers' responsibilities.

For their exceptionally detailed and helpful comments I am grateful to Mike Barnett, Mlada Bukovansky, Bud Duvall, Peter Katzenstein, Mark Laffey, David Lumsdaine, Sylvia Maxfield, Nina Tannenwald, Jutta Weldes, and the members of the Yale IR Reading Group.

Assumptions

I share all five of Mearsheimer's "realist" assumptions (p. 10): that international politics is anarchic, and that states have offensive capabilities, cannot be 100 percent certain about others' intentions, wish to survive, and are rational. We even share two more: a commitment to states as units of analysis, and to the importance of systemic or "third image" theorizing.

The last bears emphasis, for in juxtaposing "structure" to "discourse" and in emphasizing the role of individuals in "critical theory" (p. 40), Mearsheimer obscures the fact that constructivists are structuralists. Indeed, one of our main objections to neorealism is that it is not structural enough: that adopting the individualistic metaphors of micro-economics restricts the effects of structures to state behavior, ignoring how they might also constitute state identities and interests.[6] Constructivists think that state interests are in important part constructed by systemic structures, not exogenous to them; this leads to a sociological rather than micro-economic structuralism.

Where neorealist and constructivist structuralisms really differ, however, is in their assumptions about what structure is made of. Neorealists think it is made only of a distribution of material capabilities, whereas constructivists think it is also made of social relationships. Social structures have three elements: shared knowledge, material resources, and practices.[7]

First, social structures are defined, in part, by shared understandings, expectations, or knowledge. These constitute the actors in a situation and the nature of their relationships, whether cooperative or conflictual. A *security dilemma*, for example, is a social structure composed of intersubjective understandings in which states are so distrustful that they make worst-case assumptions about each others' intentions, and as a result define their interests in self-help terms. A *security community* is a different social structure, one composed of shared knowledge in which states trust one another to resolve disputes without war.[8] This dependence of social structure on ideas is the sense in which constructivism has an idealist (or "idea-ist") view of structure. What makes these ideas (and thus structure) "social," however, is their intersubjective quality. In other words, sociality (in contrast to "materiality," in the sense of brute physical capabilities), is about shared knowledge.

Second, social structures include material resources like gold and tanks. In contrast to neorealists' desocialized view of such capabilities, constructivists argue that material resources only acquire meaning for human action through the structure of shared knowledge in which they are embedded.[9] For example, 500 British nuclear weapons are less threatening to the United States than 5 North Korean nuclear weapons, because the British are friends of the United States and the North Koreans are not, and amity or enmity is a function of shared understandings. As students of world politics, neorealists would probably not disagree, but as theorists the example poses a big problem, since it completely eludes their materialist definition of structure. Material capabilities as such explain nothing; their effects presuppose structures of shared knowledge, which vary and which are not reducible to capabilities. Constructivism is therefore compatible with changes in material power affecting social relations (cf. Mearsheimer, p. 43), as long as those effects can be shown to presuppose still deeper social relations.

Third, social structures exist, not in actors' heads nor in material capabilities, but in practices. Social structure exists only in process. The Cold War was a structure of shared knowledge that governed great power relations for forty years, but once they stopped acting on this basis, it was "over."

In sum, social structures are real and objective, not "just talk." But this objectivity depends on shared knowledge, and in that sense social life is "ideas all the way down" (until you get to biology and natural resources). Thus, to ask "when do ideas, as opposed to power and interest, matter?" is to ask the wrong question. Ideas always matter, since power and interest do not have effects apart from the shared knowledge that constitutes them as such.[10] The real question, as Mearsheimer notes (p. 42), is why does one social structure exist, like self-help (in which power and self-interest determine behavior), rather than another, like collective security (in which they do not).

The explanatory as opposed to normative character of this question bears emphasis. Constructivists have a normative interest in promoting social change, but they pursue this by trying to explain how seemingly natural social structures, like self-help or the Cold War, are effects of practice (this is the "critical" side of critical theory). This makes me wonder about Mearsheimer's repeated references (I count fourteen) to critical theorists' "goals," "aims," and "hopes" to make peace and love prevail on Earth. Even if we all had such hopes (which I doubt), and even if these were ethically wrong (though Mearsheimer seems to endorse them; p. 40), they are beside the point in evaluating critical theories of world politics. If critical theories fail, this will be because they do not explain how the world works, not because of their values. Emphasizing the latter recalls the old realist tactic of portraying opponents as utopians more concerned with how the world ought to be than how it is. Critical theorists have normative commitments, just as neorealists do, but we are also simply trying to explain the world.

Objectivity

Mearsheimer suggests that critical theorists do not believe that there is an objective world out there about which we can have knowledge (pp. 41ff). This is not the case. There are two issues here, ontological and epistemological.

The ontological issue is whether social structures have an objective existence, which I addressed above. Social structures are collective phenomena that confront individuals as externally existing social facts. The Cold War was just as real for me as it was for Mearsheimer.

The epistemological issue is whether we can have objective knowledge of these structures. Here Mearsheimer ignores a key distinction between modern and postmodern critical theorists. The latter are indeed skeptical about the possibility of objective knowledge, although in their empirical work even they attend to evidence and inference. Constructivists, however, are modernists who fully endorse the scientific project of falsifying theories against evidence. In an article cited by Mearsheimer, I advocated a scientific-realist approach to social inquiry, which takes a very pro-science line.[11] And despite his claims, there is now a substantial body of constructivist empirical work that embodies a wholly conventional epistemology.[12]

Mearsheimer is right, however, that critical theorists do not think we can make a clean distinction between subject and object. Then again, almost all philosophers of science today reject such a naive epistemology. All observation is theory-*laden* in the sense that what we see is mediated by our existing theories, and to that extent knowledge is inherently problematic. But this does not mean that observation, let alone reality, is theory-*determined*. The world is still out there constraining our beliefs, and may punish us for incorrect ones. Montezuma had a theory that the Spanish were gods, but it was wrong, with disastrous consequences. We do not have unmediated access to the world, but this does not preclude understanding how it works.

Explaining War and Peace

Mearsheimer frames the debate between realists and critical theorists as one between a theory of war and a theory of peace. This is a fundamental mistake. Social construction talk is like game theory talk: analytically neutral between conflict and cooperation.[13] Critical theory does not predict peace.[14] War no more disproves critical theory than peace disproves realism. The confusion stems from conflating description and explanation.

The descriptive issue is the extent to which states engage in practices of *realpolitik* (warfare, balancing, relative-gains seeking) versus accepting the rule of law and institutional constraints on their autonomy. States sometimes do engage in power politics, but this hardly describes all of the past 1300 years, and even less today, when most states follow most international law most of the time,[15] and when war and security dilemmas are the exception rather than the rule, Great Powers no longer tend to conquer small ones, and free trade is expanding rather than contracting.[16] The relative frequency of *realpolitik*, however, has nothing to do with "realism." Realism should be seen as an explanation of *realpolitik*, not a description of it. Conflating the two makes it impossible to tell how well the one explains the other, and leads to the tautology that war makes realism true. Realism does not have a monopoly on the ugly and brutal side of international life. Even if we agree on a *realpolitik* description, we can reject a realist explanation.

The explanatory issue is *why* states engage in war or peace. Mearsheimer's portrayal of constructivist "causal logic" on this issue is about 30 percent right. The logic has two elements, structure and agency. On the one hand, constructivist theorizing tries to show how the social structure of a system makes actions possible by constituting actors with certain identities and interests, and material capabilities with certain meanings. Missing from Mearsheimer's account is the constructivist emphasis on how agency and interaction produce and reproduce structures of shared knowledge over time. Since it is not possible here to discuss the various dynamics through which this process takes place,[17] let me illustrate instead. And since Mearsheimer does not offer a neorealist explanation for inter-state cooperation, conceding that terrain to institutionalists, let me focus on the "hard case" of why states sometimes get into security dilemmas and war, that is, why they sometimes engage in *realpolitik* behavior.

In "Anarchy is What States Make of It" I argued that such behavior is a self-fulfilling prophecy,[18] and that this is due to both agency and social structure. Thus, on the agency side, what states do to each other affects the social structure in which they are embedded, by a logic of reciprocity. If they militarize, others will be threatened and arm themselves, creating security dilemmas in terms of which they will define egoistic identities and interests. But if they engage in policies of reassurance, as the Soviets did in the late 1980s, this will have a different effect on the structure of shared knowledge, moving it toward a security community. The depth of interdependence is a factor here, as is the role of revisionist states, whose actions are likely to be especially threatening. However, on the structural side, the ability of revisionist states to create a war of all against all depends on the structure of shared knowledge into which they enter. If past interactions have created a structure in which status quo states are divided or naive, revisionists will prosper and the system will tend toward a Hobbesian world in which power and self-interest rule. In contrast, if past interactions have created a structure in which status quo states trust and identify with each other, predators are more likely to face collective security responses like the Gulf War.[19] *History matters.* Security dilemmas are not acts of God: they are effects of practice. This does not mean that once created they can necessarily be escaped (they are, after all, "dilemmas"), but it puts the causal locus in the right place.

Contrast this explanation of power politics with the "poverty of neorealism."[20] Mearsheimer thinks it significant that in anarchy, states cannot be 100 percent certain that others will not attack. Yet even in domestic society, I cannot be certain that I will be safe walking to class. There are no guarantees in life, domestic or international, but the fact that in anarchy war is possible does not mean "it may at any moment occur."[21] Indeed, it may be quite unlikely, as it is in most interactions today. Possibility is not

probability. Anarchy as such is not a structural cause of anything. What matters is its social structure, which varies across anarchies. An anarchy of friends differs from one of enemies, one of self-help from one of collective security, and these are all constituted by structures of shared knowledge. Mearsheimer does not provide an argument for why this is wrong; he simply asserts that it is.

Other realist explanations for power politics fare somewhat better. Although neorealists want to eschew arguments from human nature, even they would agree that to the extent human-beings-in-groups are prone to fear and competition, it may predispose them to war.[22] However, this factor faces countervailing dynamics of interdependence and collective identity formation, which sometimes overcome it. The distribution of material capabilities also matters, especially if offense is dominant, and military build-ups will of course concern other states. Again, however, the meaning of power depends on the underlying structure of shared knowledge. A British build-up will be less threatening to the United States than a North Korean one, and build-ups are less likely to occur in a security community than in a security dilemma.

In order to get from anarchy and material forces to power politics and war, therefore, neorealists have been forced to make additional, *ad hoc* assumptions about the social structure of the international system. We see this in Mearsheimer's interest in "hypernationalism," Stephen Walt's emphasis on ideology in the "balance of threat," Randall Schweller's focus on the status quo-revisionist distinction and, as I argued in my "Anarchy" piece, in Waltz's assumption that anarchies are self-help systems.[23] Incorporating these assumptions generates more explanatory power, but how? In these cases the crucial causal work is done by social, not material, factors. This is the core of a constructivist view of structure, not a neorealist one.

The problem becomes even more acute when neorealists try to explain the relative absence of inter-state war in today's world. If anarchy is so determining, why are there not more Bosnias? Why are weak states not getting killed off left and right? It stretches credulity to think that the peace between Norway and Sweden, or the United States and Canada, or Nigeria and Benin are all due to material balancing. Mearsheimer says cooperation is possible when core interests are not threatened (p. 25), and that "some states are especially friendly for historical or ideological reasons" (p. 31). But this totally begs the question of why in an ostensibly "realist" world states do not find their interests continually threatened by others, and the question of how they might become friends. Perhaps Mearsheimer would say that most states today are status quo and sovereign.[24] But again this begs the question. What is sovereignty if not an institution of mutual recognition and non-intervention? And is not being "status quo" related to the internalization of this institution in state interests? David Strang has argued that those states recognized as sovereign have better survival prospects in anarchy than those that are not.[25] Far from challenging this argument, Mearsheimer presupposes it.

Neorealists' growing reliance on social factors to do their explanatory work suggests that if ever there were a candidate for a degenerating research program in IR theory, this is it.[26] The progressive response (in the Lakatosian sense) would be to return to realism's materialist roots by showing that the background understandings that give capabilities meaning are caused by still deeper material conditions, or that capabilities have intrinsic meaning that cannot be ignored. To show that the material base determines international superstructure, in other words, realists should be purging their theory of social content, not adding it as they are doing.[27] And anti-realists, in turn, should be trying to show how the causal powers of material facts presuppose social content, not trying to show that institutions explain additional variance beyond that explained by the distribution of power and interest, as if the latter were a privileged pre-social baseline.

Responsibility

An important virtue of "False Promise" is that it links neorealism and its rivals to the ethical responsibilities of foreign policymakers. These responsibilities depend in part on how much it is possible to change the structure of shared knowledge within anarchy. If such change is impossible, then Mearsheimer is right that it would be irresponsible for those charged with national security to pursue it. On the other hand, if it is possible, then it would be irresponsible to pursue policies that perpetuate destructive old orders, especially if we care about the well-being of future generations.

To say that structures are socially constructed is no guarantee that they can be changed.[28] Sometimes social structures so constrain action that transformative strategies are impossible. This goes back to the collective nature of social structures; structural change depends on changing a system of expectations that may be mutually reinforcing. A key issue in determining policymakers' responsibilities, therefore, is how much "slack" a social structure contains. Neorealists think there is little slack in the system, and thus states that deviate from power politics will get punished or killed by the "logic" of anarchy. Institutionalists think such dangers have been greatly reduced by institutions such as sovereignty and the democratic peace, and that there is therefore more possibility for peaceful change.

The example of Gorbachev is instructive in this respect, since the Cold War was a highly conflictual social structure. I agree with Mearsheimer (p. 46) that Soviet nuclear forces gave Gorbachev a margin of safety for his policies. Yet someone else in his place might have found a more aggressive solution to a decline in power. What is so important about the Gorbachev regime is that it had the courage to see how the Soviets' own practices sustained the Cold War, and to undertake a reassessment of Western intentions. This is exactly what a constructivist would do, but not a neorealist, who would eschew attention to such social factors as naive and as mere superstructure. Indeed, what is so striking about neorealism is its total neglect of the explanatory role of state practice.[29] It does not seem to matter what states do: Brezhnev, Gorbachev, Zhirinovsky, what difference does it make? The logic of anarchy will always bring us back to square one. This is a disturbing attitude if *realpolitik* causes the very conditions to which it is a response; to the extent that realism counsels *realpolitik*, therefore, it is part of the problem. Mearsheimer says critical theorists are "intolerant" of realists for this reason (p. 42). The ironies of this suggestion aside, what matters is getting policymakers to accept responsibility for solving conflicts rather than simply managing or exploiting them. If neorealism can move us in that direction, then it should, but as I see it, neorealist ethics come down to "*sauve qui peut.*"

To analyze the social construction of international politics is to analyze how processes of interaction produce and reproduce the social structures—cooperative or conflictual—that shape actors' identities and interests and the significance of their material contexts. It is opposed to two rivals: the materialist view, of which neorealism is one expression, that material forces *per se* determine international life, and the rational choice–theoretic view that interaction does not change identities and interests. Mearsheimer's essay is an important opening to the comparative evaluation of these hypotheses. But neorealists will contribute nothing further to the debate so long as they think that constructivists are subversive utopians who do not believe in a real world and who expect peace in our time.

Notes

1. John J. Mearsheimer, "The False Promise of International Institutions," *International Security,* 19, 3 (Winter 1994/95). Subsequent references appear in parentheses in the text.

2. Other efforts include Robert Gilpin, "The Richness of the Tradition of Political Realism," *International Organization,* 38, 2 (Spring 1984), 287–304, and Markus Fischer, "Feudal Europe, 800–1300," *International Organization,* 46, 2 (Spring 1992), 427–466.

3. On neoliberalism and critical theory, see Robert Keohane, "International institutions: Two approaches," *International Studies Quarterly,* 32, 4 (December 1988), 379–396, and Wendt, "Collective Identity Formation and the International State," *American Political Science Review,* 88, 2 (June 1994), 384–396. Mearsheimer treats collective security as a third form of institutionalism, but this is unwarranted. Collective security is an approach to international order, arguable on either neoliberal or critical grounds, not a form of institutional analysis.

4. This makes them all "constructivist" in a broad sense, but as the critical literature has evolved, this term has become applied to one particular school.

5. These are far more than differences of "emphasis," as suggested by Mearsheimer's disclaimer, note 127.

6. "Constitute" is an important term in critical theory, with a special meaning that is not captured by related terms like "comprise," "consist of," or "cause." To say that "X [for example, a social structure] constitutes Y [for example, an agent]," is to say that the properties of those agents are made possible by, and would not exist in the absence of, the structure by which they are "constituted." A constitutive relationship establishes a conceptually necessary or logical connection between X and Y, in contrast to the contingent connection between independently existing entities that is established by causal relationships.

The identity-behavior distinction is partly captured by Robert Powell's distinction between preferences over outcomes and preferences over strategies; Robert Powell, "Anarchy in International Relations Theory," *International Organization,* 48, 2 (Spring 1994), 313–344. The main exception to the mainstream neglect of structural effects on state identity is Kenneth Waltz's argument that anarchy produces "like units"; Kenneth Waltz, *Theory of International Politics* (Reading, Mass.: Addison-Wesley, 1979), 74–77. Constructivists think there are more possibilities than this; see Alexander Wendt, "Anarchy Is What States Make of It: The Social Construction of Power Politics," *International Organization,* 46, 2 (Spring 1992), 391–425.

7. What follows could also serve as a rough definition of "discourse."

8. See Karl Deutsch, et al., *Political Community and the North Atlantic Area* (Princeton: Princeton University Press, 1957).

9. For a good general discussion of this point, see Douglas Porpora, "Cultural Rules and Material Relations," *Sociological Theory,* 11, 2 (July 1993), 212–229.

10. On the social content of interests, see Roy D' Andrade and Claudia Strauss, eds., *Human Motives and Cultural Models* (Cambridge: Cambridge University Press, 1992).

11. See Alexander Wendt, "The Agent-Structure Problem in International Relations Theory," *International Organization,* 41, 3 (Summer 1987), 335–370; and, for fuller discussion, Jan Shapiro and Alexander Wendt, "The Difference that Realism Makes," *Politics and Society,* 20, 2 (June 1992), 197–223.

12. See, among others Michael Barnett, "Institutions, Roles, and Disorder," *International Studies Quarterly,* 37, 3 (September 1993), 271–296; David Lumsdaine, *Moral Vision in International Politics* (Princeton: Princeton University Press, 1993); Samuel Barkin and Bruce Cronin, "The State and the Nation," *International Organization,* 48, No. 1 (Winter 1994), 107–130; Rey Koslowski and Friedrich Kratochwil, "Understanding Change in International Politics," *International Organization,* 48, 2 (Spring 1994), 215–248; Thomas Biersteker and Cynthia Weber eds., *State Sovereignty as Social Construct* (Cambridge: Cambridge University Press 1996); and Peter Katzenstein, ed., *The Culture of National Security* (Columbia University Press, 1996).

13. On the social basis of conflict, see Georg Simmel, *Conflict and the Web of Group Affiliations* (Glencoe, Ill.: Free Press, 1955). This is also why I prefer to avoid the term "institutionalism," since it associates sociality with peace and cooperation.

14. Fischer's suggestion that critical theory predicts cooperation in feudal Europe is based on a failure to understand the full implications of this point; see Fischer, "Feudal Europe, 800–1300."

15. See Louis Henkin, *How Nations Behave* (New York: Council on Foreign Relations, 1979), 47.

16. On the inadequacy of "realist" descriptions of international politics, see Paul Schroeder, "Historical Reality vs. Neo-realist Theory," *International Security*, 19, 1 (Summer 1994), 108–148.

17. For a start, see Alexander Wendt, "Collective Identity Formation," and Emanuel Adler, "Cognitive Evolution," in Emanuel Adler and Beverly Crawford, eds., *Progress in Postwar International Relations* (New York: Columbia University Press, 1991), 43–88. The best introduction to processes of social construction remains Peter Berger and Thomas Luckmann, *The Social Construction of Reality* (New York: Anchor Books, 1966).

18. A similar argument is developed in John Vasquez, *The War Puzzle* (Cambridge: Cambridge University Press, 1993).

19. On the role of collective identity in facilitating collective security, see Wendt, "Collective Identity Formation."

20. Richard Ashley, "The Poverty of Neorealism," *International Organization*, 38, 2 (Spring 1984), 225–286.

21. Kenneth Waltz, *Man, the State, and War* (New York: Columbia University Press, 1959), 232.

22. For a good argument to this effect, see Jonathan Mercer, "Anarchy and Identity," *International Organization*, 49, 2 (Spring 1995).

23. John J. Mearsheimer, "Back to the Future," *International Security*, 15, 1 (Summer 1990), 5–56; Stephen Walt, *The Origins of Alliances* (Ithaca: Cornell University Press, 1987); Randall Schweller, "Tripolarity and the Second World War," *International Studies Quarterly*, 37, 1 (March 1993), 73–103; and Wendt, "Anarchy is What States Make of It."

24. Mearsheimer and Waltz both assume sovereignty, without acknowledging its institutional character; see Mearsheimer, "False Promise," 11, and Waltz, *Theory of International Politics*, 95–96.

25. David Strang, "Anomaly and Commonplace in European Political Expansion," *International Organization*, 45, 2 (Spring 1991), 143–162.

26. "Degenerating" problem shifts are adjustments to a theory that are *ad hoc,* while "progressive" shifts are those that have a principled basis in its hard core assumptions. See Imre Lakatos, "Falsification and the Methodology of Scientific Research Programmes," in Lakatos and Alan Musgrave, eds., *Criticism and the Growth of Knowledge* (Cambridge: Cambridge University Press, 1970), 91–196.

27. The significance of Dan Deudney's work lies partly in his appreciation of this point; see Dan Deudney, "Dividing Realism: Structural Realism versus Security Materialism on Nuclear Security and Proliferation," *Security Studies*, 1, 2 and 3 (1993) 7–37.

28. Hence, *contra* Mearsheimer, there is nothing problematic about the fact that critical theorists do not make predictions about the future. What happens in the future depends on what actors do with the structures they have made in the past.

29. This is not true of classical realists; for a sympathetic discussion of the latter from a critical standpoint, see Richard Ashley, "Political Realism and Human Interests," *International Studies Quarterly*, 25, 2 (June 1981), 204–237.

On War and Maintaining the Peace

JOHN LOCKE

John Locke's focus as political theorist is on the social contract that establishes domestic society. It is this coming together by contract or agreement that captures the interest of some present-day international relations theorists, particularly social constructivists. Indeed, Locke does not see the anarchic state of nature—"want of a common judge," government or central authority—as necessarily warlike. In this Locke clearly opposes the view taken earlier by Thomas Hobbes who portrays the state of nature as perpetually in a state of war— either actively engaging in fighting or always on guard, preparing for the fight. To Locke, before society is formed one may remain in a state of nature or move from it to a state of war and back again; the two states of being—nature and war—are not one and the same as they are with Hobbes. We find, then, that in applying Locke's insight to international relations we need not see states as necessarily in a state war with one another. Moreover, states (as if they were persons in a state of nature) may reach agreements with one another to maintain the peace, whether they remain in a state of nature or leave it by forming a community. We have included this extract from Locke's Second Treatise on Government *(1690) as prelude to an article by Alexander Wendt on "The Lockean Culture" taken from his* Social Theory of International Politics. *Chapters where these passages in Locke's Treatise can be found are indicated parenthetically by Roman numerals and sections by Arabic numbers. Italics are added here and there to emphasize what we consider key points in Locke's argument.*

To understand political power right, and derive it from its original, *we must consider, what state all men are naturally in, and that is, a state of perfect freedom* to order their actions, and dispose of their possessions and persons, as they think fit, within the bounds of the law of nature, without asking leave, or depending upon the will of any other man. [It is] *a state also of equality,* wherein all the power and jurisdiction is reciprocal, no one having more than another. (II, 4)

It is often asked as a mighty objection, where are, or ever were there any men in such a state of nature? To which it may suffice as an answer at present, that since *all princes and rulers of independent governments all through the world are in a state of nature,* it is plain the world never was, nor ever will be, without numbers of men in that state. I have named all governors of independent communities, whether they are, or are not, in league with others: for *it is not every compact that puts an end to the state of nature between men, but only this one of agreeing together mutually to enter into one community, and make one body politic; other promises, and compacts, men may make one with another, and yet still be in the state of nature. The promises and bargains between the two men . . . are binding to them, though they are perfectly in a state of nature, in reference to one another: for truth and keeping of faith belongs to men, as men, and not as members of society.* . . . (II, 14)

And here we have the plain difference between the state of nature and the state of war, which however some men have confounded, are as far distant, as a state of peace, good will, mutual assistance and preservation, and a state of enmity, malice, violence and mutual destruction, are one from another. *Men living together according to reason, without a common superior on earth with authority to judge between them, is properly the state of nature. But force, or a declared design of force, upon the person of another, where there is no common superior on earth to appeal to for relief, is the state of war:* and it is the

want of such an appeal gives a man the right of war even against an aggressor, tho' he be in society and a fellow subject. . . . *Want of a common judge with authority, puts all men in a state of nature: force without right, upon a man's person, makes a state of war, both where there is, and is not, a common judge.* . . . (III, 19)

To avoid this state of war (wherein there is no appeal but to heaven, and wherein every the least difference is apt to end, where there is no authority to decide between the contenders) is one great reason of men's putting themselves into society, and quitting the state of nature: for where there is an authority, a power on earth, from which relief can be had by appeal, there the continuance of the state of war is excluded, and the controversy is decided by that power. . . . (III, 21)

Whosoever therefore out of a state of nature unite into a community, must be understood to give up all the power, necessary to the ends for which they unite into society, to the majority of the community, unless they expressly agreed in any number greater than the majority. And this is done by barely agreeing to unite into one political society, which is all the compact that is, or needs be, between the individuals, that enter into, or make up a commonwealth. And thus that, which begins and actually constitutes any political society, is nothing but the consent of any number of freemen capable of a majority to unite and incorporate into such a society. And this is that, and that only, which did, or could give beginning to any lawful government in the world. . . . (III, 99)

Thus, though looking back as far as records give us any account of peopling the world, and the history of nations, we commonly find the government to be in one hand; yet it destroys not that which I affirm, *viz.* that the beginning of politic society depends upon the consent of the individuals, to join into, and make one society; who, when they are thus incorporated, might set up what form of government they thought fit. . . . (III, 106)

The Lockean Culture

ALEXANDER WENDT

Wendt is the prime exponent of the idea that there are mutiple ways to conceptualize anarchy. States and the relations established among them are constituted by a Lockean culture—not a Hobbesean one as many realists assume. It is not a state of nature without rules. The Lockean culture is one of rivalry, not enmity as Hobbists would have it. Consistent with the institution of sovereignty, there is "a shared expectation that states will not try to take away each other's life and liberty." States have constructed the rules that bind them, which are part of an international culture that also constitutes (and regulates) states. Wendt observes that "the Westphalian system is a Lockean culture in which states do tend to comply with these norms and come to each other's aid when in jeopardy. Compliance with these norms is in part a function of the degree of acceptance these norms and rules may have. States effectively internalize the Lockean culture of which they are a part out of "a sense of loyalty and obligation to the group the culture defines."

It is an interesting question how much of international history fits the Hobbesian mold. Judging from the violence and high death rate of states in the past it seems clear that world politics has *often* been Hobbesian, and some Realists might argue that it has always been so. It would make sense for enmity to dominate international history if new states systems are prone to starting out that way, since cultures are self-fulfilling prophecies which are resistant to change. This makes the modern, Westphalian states system all the more surprising, however, since it clearly is not Hobbesian. The death rate of states is almost nil; small states are thriving; interstate war is rare and normally limited; territorial boundaries have "hardened"[1] and so on. Realists tend not to attach much significance to such changes,[2] and focus on continuities instead: wars still happen, power still matters. Yet to my mind the empirical record suggests strongly that in the past few centuries there has been a qualitative structural change in international politics. The kill or be killed logic of the Hobbesian state of nature has been replaced by the live and let live logic of the Lockean anarchical society. . . .[3] Here I focus . . . on how the Lockean ideal type is constituted, and suggest that it is not as much a self-help system as we often assume.

Rivalry

The Lockean culture has a different logic from the Hobbesian because it is based on a different role structure, rivalry rather than enmity. Like enemies, rivals are constituted by representations about Self and Other with respect to violence, but these representations are less threatening: unlike enemies, rivals expect each other to act as if they recognize their sovereignty, their "life and liberty," as a *right*, and therefore not to try to conquer or dominate them. Since state sovereignty is territorial, in turn, this implies recognition of a right to some "property" as well. Unlike friends, however, the recognition among rivals does not extend to the right to be free from violence in disputes. Moreover, some of these disputes may concern boundaries, and so rivalry could involve some territorial revisionism. The right to some property—enough to "live"—is acknowledged, but which property may be disputed, sometimes by force.

Underlying rivalry is a right to sovereignty . . .[4] I [have] argued that sovereignty is an intrinsic property of the states, like being six feet tall, and as such it exists even when there are no other states. This property becomes a "right" only when other states recognize it. Rights are social capacities that are conferred on actors by others' "permission" to do certain things.[5] A powerful state may have the material capability to defend its sovereignty against all comers, but even without that ability a weak state can enjoy its sovereignty if other states recognize it as a right. The reason for this is that a constitutive feature of having a right is self-limitation by the Other, his acceptance of the Self's enjoyment of certain powers. I take this to be implicit in what IR scholars call being "status quo" toward other states. The status quo may be enforced in the last instance by coercion, but as even Hobbes recognized a society based solely on force would not last long. Whether out of self-interest or the perceived legitimacy of its norms, the members of a well-functioning society must also restrain *themselves*. For Hobbes the role of the state was to institutionalize such self-restraint, not be a complete substitute for it.[6] Having a right depends on others' restraint, on being treated by them as an end in yourself rather than as merely an object to be disposed of as they see fit. Absent such restraint rights are nothing more than whatever a person can get away with, which is to say not "rights" at all.

When states recognize each other's sovereignty as a right then we can speak of sovereignty not only as a property of individual states, but as an *institution* shared by many states. The core of this institution is the shared expectation that states will not try to take away each other's life and liberty. In the Westphalian system this belief is formalized in international law, which means that far from being merely an epiphenomenon of material forces, international law is actually a key part of the deep structure of contemporary international politics.[7] Despite the absence of centralized enforcement, almost all states today adhere to this law almost all of the time,[8] and it is increasingly considered binding (and therefore enforceable) even on states that have not agreed to its provisions.[9] Modern inter-state rivalry, in other words, is constrained by the structure of sovereign rights recognized by international law, and to that extent is based on the rule of law. Within that constraint, however, rivalry is compatible with the use of force to settle disputes, and as such the Lockean culture is not a complete rule of law system. What this comes down to in the end is the level of violence that states expect of each other. Rivals expect Others to use violence sometimes to settle disputes, but to do so within "live and let live" limits.

Realists might point out that states can never be "100 percent certain" about each other's intentions because they cannot read each other's minds or be sure they will not change,[10] and from this argue that since in an anarchy the costs of a mistake can be fatal states have no choice but to represent each other as enemies. This reasoning makes sense in a Hobbesian culture, but it is hard to see its force today, when almost all states *know* that almost all other states recognize their sovereignty. This knowledge is not 100 percent certain, but *no* knowledge is that. The question is whether states' knowledge about each other's intentions is sufficiently uncertain to warrant worst-case assumptions, and in most cases today the answer is no. This is precisely what one would expect in a culture based on the institution of sovereignty, which enables states to make reliable inferences about each other's status quoness even without access to their "minds." One could argue that policymakers' complacency is irrational, that because of anarchy they *should* treat each other as enemies, but that actually seems far more irrational than acting on the basis of the vast experience which suggests otherwise. It would be crazy today for Norway and Sweden, Kenya and Tanzania, or almost any other dyad in the international system to represent each other as enemies; rivals perhaps, but not enemies. The exceptions (North and South Korea; Israeli and Palestinian radicals) highlight just how unusual enmity is today. Moreover, despite their Hobbesian inclinations this fact is not lost on most Realists. Waltz's assumption that states seek security rather than power would make little sense if states really did think that others were trying to conquer them. Anarchy may make the achievement of rivalry difficult, but even most Realists seem to think it is possible.

The implications of rivalry for the Self are less clear than they are of enmity because the Other's perceived restraint gives a state a choice. If the Other is an enemy then a state has little choice but to respond in kind. Not so with rivalry. Some states may consider an Other willing to restrain itself a "sucker," and respond by trying to "kill" it, as exemplified perhaps by Hitler's reaction to the Munich agreement. In this case there is an asymmetry in roles (one side sees rivalry, the other enmity), and the result will be a quick descent into a Hobbesian world. The ever-present possibility of such a descent is what motivates Realist "worst-caseism," but this does not happen very often in the modern world because other states' recognition of its sovereignty gives a state space to make another choice—to reciprocate. If it does then states enter the logic of rivalry.

Rivalry has at least four implications for foreign policy. The most important is that whatever conflicts they may have, states must behave in a status quo fashion toward each other's sovereignty. The second implication concerns the nature of rational behavior. Whereas enemies have to make decisions on the basis of high risk-aversion, short time horizons, and relative power, rivalry permits a more relaxed view. The institution of sovereignty makes security less "scarce," so risks are fewer, the future matters more, and absolute gains may override relative losses. If prospect theory defines rational behavior for enemies, then expected-utility theory does for rivals. This does not mean that states no longer worry about security, but their anxiety is less intense because certain pathways on the "game tree"—those involving their own "death"—have been removed. Third, relative military power is still important because rivals know that others might use force to settle disputes, but its meaning is different than it is for enemies because the institution of sovereignty changes the "balance of threat."[11] In the Hobbesian world military power dominates all decision-making, whereas in the Lockean it is less of a priority. Threats are not existential, and allies can be more easily trusted when one's own power is insufficient. Finally, if disputes do go to war, rivals will limit their own violence. In the Westphalian system these limits are expressed in Just War Theory and standards of civilization, which lays down the conditions under and extent to which states may use violence against each other. There is growing empirical evidence that these norms cause states to restrain themselves in modern warfare.[12] Enemies and rivals may be equally prone to violence, but a small difference in roles makes a big difference in its degree.

The Logic of Lockean Anarchy

So far I have talked about rivalry as an inter-psychological relationship, as a conjoining of subjective beliefs about the Self and the Other. If these beliefs change then so does the rivalry. It is important to acknowledge this level in the structure of rivalry because subjective perceptions are a micro-foundation for cultural forms. However, there is another, macro-, level in the organization of rivalry,

in which "rival" is a preexisting position in a stock of shared knowledge that supervenes on the ideas of individual states. This is rivalry as a *collective* representation. Once rivalry acquires this status states will make attributions about each other's "minds" based more on what they know about the structure than what they know about each other, and the system will acquire a logic of its own. Practices of rivalry sustain this logic, such that if their frequency falls below the tipping point it will change, but until then the system will have a macro-structure that can be multiply realized at the micro-level. This structure, Bull's "anarchical society," generates four tendencies.

The first is that warfare is simultaneously accepted and constrained. On the one hand, states reserve and periodically exercise the right to use violence to advance their interests. War is accepted as normal and legitimate,[13] and could be just as common as in the Hobbesian anarchy. On the other hand, wars tend to be limited, not in the sense of not killing a lot of people, but of not killing *states*. Wars of conquest are rare, and when they do occur other states tend to act collectively to restore the status quo (World War II, Korean War, the Gulf War). This suggests that the standard definition of war in IR scholarship as "a conflict producing at least 1000 battle deaths" conflates two different social kinds, what Ruggie calls "constitutive" wars and "configurative" wars.[14] In constitutive wars, which dominate Hobbesian anarchies, the type and existence of units is at stake; in configurative wars, which dominate Lockean anarchies, the units are accepted by the parties, who are fighting over territory and strategic advantage instead. The causes, dynamics, and outcomes of the two kinds of war should vary, and as such they should not be treated as one dependent variable.

Limited warfare underpins a second tendency, which is for the system to have a relatively stable membership or low death rate over time. Membership is key, since this tendency does not apply to states whose sovereignty is not recognized by the system, like the indigenous states of the Americas before the Conquest. Indeed, placing the fate of these unrecognized states next to that of recognized ones provides some of the strongest evidence for a structural difference between Lockean and Hobbesian anarchies. As David Strang[15] shows, since 1415 states recognized as sovereign by European states have a much higher survival rate than those that were not. In the modern era "micro" states like Singapore and

Monaco—much weaker in relative terms than the Aztecs or Incas—are flourishing, and even "failed" states that lack empirical sovereignty manage to persist because international society recognizes their juridical sovereignty.[16] In all of these cases states survived for social not material reasons, because potential predators *let* them live. This indicates a world in which the weak are protected by the restraint of the strong, not a survival of the fittest.

A third tendency is for states to balance power. Waltz sees this as an effect of anarchy as such, but the argument here suggests that balancing is actually more of an effect of the mutual recognition of sovereignty. In the Hobbesian anarchy states balance if they must, but the lack of mutual recognition and resulting pressure to maximize power gives balancing a "knife's edge" quality, enabling a tendency toward concentrating power to dominate. If states think that others recognize their sovereignty, however, then survival is not at stake if their relative power falls, and the pressure to maximize power is much less. The institution of sovereignty in effect "arrests" the Hobbesian tendency toward concentration. In this situation balancing can paradoxically become a relatively stable source of order with respect to the many *non*-existential issues that may remain sources of violent conflict. This is not to deny that balancing also provides insurance against loss of sovereignty, which an unbalanced distribution of power in principle threatens, but in Lockean systems most states most of the time do not in fact need (nor do they have) this insurance because recognition makes it unnecessary.[17] It is precisely because balancing is *not* essential for survival, in other words, that it becomes a basis for order in the first place.

A final tendency is that neutrality or nonalignment becomes a recognized status. If states can resolve their differences then there is no necessity for them to compete militarily at all, since there is no longer a threat of revisionism. It may be difficult to achieve such a condition as long as states are prone to violence and security dilemmas, but assuming that conflicts can be resolved mutual indifference is a stable outcome in a live and let live system.

These tendencies suggest that the anarchy portrayed by Waltz is actually a Lockean rather than Hobbesian system. His analogy to markets, which presuppose institutions that ensure that actors do not kill each other,[18] his emphasis on balancing, his observation that modern states have a low death rate, and his assumption that states are security-rather than power-seeking are all things associated with the relatively self-restrained Lockean culture, not the war of all against all. In one sense this is not surprising, since Waltz's main concern, the Westphalian system, *is* a Lockean culture. Unfortunately, Waltz does not address the possibility that this culture has a different logic than the Hobbesian one with which Realism is often associated, nor the underlying social relations that generate this logic in the first place. This allows Neorealists to trade on the tough, hard-nosed rhetoric of "Realism" while presupposing the kinder, gentler world described by their critics. A Lockean culture, in short, is a condition of possibility for the truth of Neorealism.

Internalization and the Foucault Effect

The institution of sovereignty is the basis of the contemporary international system. There have always been exceptions to its norms, which raise hard questions about the extent to which the system is Lockean,[19] but nevertheless almost all states today obey those norms almost all of the time, which poses even harder questions to any other interpretation of the system. In this section I consider how this widespread compliance should be explained. The three possibilities—coercion, self-interest, and legitimacy—reflect the three degrees to which sovereignty norms can be internalized. Different degrees may apply to different states, but taken in the aggregate they constitute three pathways by which a Lockean culture can be realized, and thus three answers to the question, "what difference does sovereignty make to the international system?" The answer to this question matters for explaining how rivalry works, and for predicting its stability. After briefly reviewing the First and Second Degree arguments I concentrate on the Third, and especially its constitutive aspects, which I suggest can be described together as a "Foucault Effect"[20]—the social constitution of "possessive individuals."

The First Degree, Realist explanation for the Lockean culture holds when states comply with sovereignty norms because they are forced to by the superior power of others. This power might be exercised directly, like the Allied Coalition's roll-back of Iraq's conquest of Kuwait, or indirectly, as in situations where the balance of power, dominance of defensive technology, or other material conditions make the costs of attempting conquest too high.[21] In either case, in order for coercion to explain compliance it must be the case that states neither want to comply of their own accord nor see it as in their self-interest. It must be against their will, which in effect means that they must have revisionist interests toward others' sovereignty. If this were not the case then while it may still be true that some states lack the material power to take away others' sovereignty, this would not explain their status quo behavior, since they do not want to change it in the first place. One cannot be coerced into not doing something one does not want to do.

Sometimes coercion is the explanation for compliance with sovereignty norms. Napoleon, Hitler, and Saddam Hussein would all have revised the life and liberty of other states had they not been prevented by superior power. In cases like these material forces do more explanatory work than shared ideas, since although "shared" in the sense of "commonly known," the institution of sovereignty is not shared in the sense of "accepted" by revisionist states. If this were true of most states in the system then a Lockean culture would quickly degenerate into a Hobbesian. Thus, even though the coercion explanation for compliance with sovereignty norms makes sense in the breach, it is ill-equipped to account for the long term stability of Lockean cultures, which depends on a critical mass of powerful states—enough to prevent the system from tipping into another logic—*not* trying to revise each other's sovereignty. The durability of the modern, Westphalian culture suggests that it has been internalized more deeply than Realism would predict.

The Second Degree, Neoliberal or rationalist, explanation holds when states comply with sovereignty norms because they think it will advance some exogenously given interest, like security or trade. As Barry Weingas[22] shows, sovereignty can be seen as a "focal point" or salient outcome around which expectations naturally converge, which reduces uncertainty in the face of multiple equilibria and enables states to coordinate their actions on mutually beneficial outcomes. In this way the institution of sovereignty exerts a causal or regulative effect on states, which is the usual focus of individualist analyses of institutions. One of the nice features of Weingast's article, however, is that it also reveals constitutive effects, at least on behavior (as opposed to identities and interests), namely the role that shared beliefs about what *counts* as a violation of sovereignty play in enabling the institution to work. In Europe before The Peace of Augsburg in 1555 trying to force another state to be Catholic counted as a legitimate action, and may have been applauded by other states for stamping out heresy. After that the identical physical behavior counted as a violation of a prince's right to determine the religion of his own subjects, and would have been deplored. It is such constitutive effects that make the causal effects of norms possible. Whether causal or constitutive, however, culture matters much more here than in the First Degree case, but still as an intervening variable between power and interest and outcomes.[23]

As with coercion, it is important to define the self-interest explanation narrowly enough that it does not become trivial. On the one hand, to say that states comply with sovereignty for self-interested reasons presupposes that they have enough social space for this to be a choice, so that their respect for others' sovereignty is due in part to a self-restraint which is missing in the coercion case. The institution is now achieving effects on states in part from the inside out, which is what internalization is all about. On the other hand, to count as self-interested the choice must still be made for consequentialist reasons, because the benefits for other interests outweigh the costs, and since these incentives are shaped by how other states are expected to react, to *that* extent the choice is still determined by the external situation. Norm violation remains a live option on the decision tree, and states are engaged in on-going calculations about whether choosing it would be in their interest. The institution of sovereignty is just one more object in the environment that distributes costs and benefits, so that whenever the cost-benefit ratio indicates that breaking its rules will bring a net benefit that is what states will do.[24] What this instrumental attitude rules out is obeying sovereignty norms because they are valued for their own sake. States are status quo toward each other's sovereignty not because they are status quo states, but because this serves some other purpose; status quoness is a strategy, not an interest. Indeed, the self-interest explanation seems to preclude any interest, status quo or revisionist, toward sovereignty itself. Revisionist interests are out because then compliance would be due to coercion, and status quo interests are out because then states would value the norms themselves. Self-interested states are *indifferent* to sovereignty norms, in other words, not in the sense that they do not care if such norms exist (they do, since this helps them advance other interests), but in the sense that they do not care, one way or the other, about the norms as such.

This brings us to the Third Degree or constructivist hypothesis. Instrumentalism may be the attitude when states first settle on sovereignty norms, and continue to be for poorly socialized states down the road. People are the same way. We obey the law initially because we are forced to or calculate that it is in our self-interest. Some people never get beyond that point, but this is not true for most of us, who obey the law because we accept its claims on us as legitimate.[25] Implicit in this legitimacy are identities as law-abiding citizens which lead us to define our interests in terms of the law's "interest." External norms have become a voice in our heads telling us that we *want* to follow them. The distinction between "interest" and "self"-interest is important here: our behavior is still "interested," in the sense that we are motivated to obey the law, but we do not treat the law as merely an object to be used for our own benefit. The costs and benefits of breaking the law do not figure in our choices because we have removed that option from our decision tree. The same thing happens in the fully internalized Lockean culture. Most states comply with its norms because they accept them as legitimate, because they identify with them and want to comply.[26] States are status quo not just at the level of behavior, but of interests as well, and as such are now more fully self-regulating actors.

As an example consider the question of why the US does not conquer the Bahamas. Coercion does not seem to be the answer, since probably no state could prevent the US from taking them, nor is there any evidence that the US has a revisionist desire to do so in the first place. The self-interest argument initially seems to do better: US policymakers might calculate that conquest would not pay because of the damage it would do to the US reputation as a law-abiding citizen, and because the US can achieve most of the benefits of conquest through economic dominance anyway. Both of these assumptions about the cost–benefit ratio are probably true, but there are two reasons to doubt that they explain US inaction. First, it is doubtful that US policymakers are making or even ever did make such calculations. It may be that respecting Bahamian sovereignty is in the self-interest of the US, but if this does not figure in its thinking then in what sense does it "explain" its behavior? Second, the definition of what counts as "paying" is shot through with cultural content. A

state whose main goal was national or religious glory might not care very much about economic benefits or a reputation as law-abiding, and therefore define costs and benefits quite differently. Conquest "paid" for Nazi Germany and Imperial Japan.[27] at least initially, and the US was certainly willing to "pay" to conquer the Native Americans. Why would similar reasoning not apply to the Bahamas? The answer seems to be that the US has a status quo interest toward the Bahamas, but in order for this to be satisfying we also need to ask *why* it has this interest. My proposal is that it stems from having internalized sovereignty norms so deeply that the US defines its interests in terms of the norms, and regulates its own behavior accordingly. The US perceives the norms as legitimate and therefore the Bahamas, as a party to those norms, has a right to life and liberty that the US would not even think of violating.

It seems to me that in the late twentieth century this is why most states follow international law. It also seems that most mainstream IR scholars, Neorealist and Neoliberal alike, must believe it as well, at least implicitly, since their work almost always assumes that the distribution of interests with respect to sovereignty is heavily biased toward the status quo. What the Bahamas Problem suggests, in other words, is that theories purporting to explain contemporary international politics solely by reference to coercion or self-interest in fact presuppose the legitimacy effects of the Lockean culture. That culture has become part of the background knowledge in terms of which modern states define their national interests.

I now want to argue that this tendency to take the culture's deepest effects for granted goes deeper, to the kinds of actors that get to have interests at all. Exogenously given in most rationalist models of international politics are four assumptions about the nature of state "individuals." These assumptions are generally good ones and I shall not dispute them. What I shall argue, rather, is that they are good because they are effects of a Lockean culture so deeply internalized today that we almost forget it is there. What I shall try to do, in other words, is endogenize rationalist assumptions about international politics to their cultural conditions of possibility.

The four constitutive effects I have in mind can be seen as aspects of a "Foucault Effect," the thesis that the self-regulating, possessive individual is an effect of a particular discourse or culture.[28] If the partly essentialist view of identity is correct then this thesis cannot be taken too literally.[29] In the literal sense people are individuals in virtue of self-organizing biological structures that do not presuppose social relations. Although their internal structures are social rather than biological, the same principle applies to states. In both cases self-organization creates pre-social material individuals with intrinsic needs and dispositions. However, the Foucault Effect is not about the constitution of material individuality, but about its meaning, the *terms* of individuality, not individuality per se. It is only in certain cultures that people are treated as intentional agents with identities, interests, and responsibility, the capacities most of us today associate with being an individual or person. The fact that human beings have these capacities naturally does not always mean they have them *socially*, and this matters for their life chances. Slaves, women, and racial "inferiors" were often held to different standards of conduct because they were not considered fully human, and so on. Conversely, the fact that animals do not seem to have such capacities naturally has not always prevented them from having them socially, as evidenced by the fact that in medieval Europe animals were often tried in courts of law and ex-communicated by the Church.[30] The hypothesis of the Foucault Effect, then, is that when moderns conceptualize and treat each other a "individuals," they are drawing on a particular, essentially liberal[31] discourse about what their bodies mean. This discourse makes material into social individuality, creating what we today understand as "rational actors," and, by extension, the possibility of theories that presuppose such creatures.

The Lockean culture individualizes states in a similar manner, although I shall argue that in doing so it paradoxically creates capacities for "other-help"[32] that the conventional, self-help assumption fails to see. The culture affects all four kinds of identities that the "individuals" of international politics can have—corporate, type, collective, and role. . . . In what follows I describe these identity effects using the example of the Westphalian system. This example will affect the specifics of my narrative, but not its general structure.

The first individualizing effect of the Lockean culture is defining the criteria for membership in the system, which determines what kinds of "individuals" have standing and are therefore part of the distribution of interests. As we all know in the Westphalian system it is only states that have such standing; other kinds of individuals, whether biological or corporate, may increasingly be getting it, but this challenges the original constitution of this culture and will continue to be a long, hard fight. The dominance of states in the Westphalian system might be due to inherent competitive advantages in an anarchic world, in which case systemic culture would have little to do with it. However, as Hendrik Spruyt shows, it seems due more importantly to the fact that states recognized each other as the only kind of actor with standing, a fact which they eventually institutionalized by making empirical sovereignty the criterion for entry into international society.[33] Actors that fail this test are not recognized by the international system as "individuals," which makes it much more difficult for their interests to be realized. In this light the institution of sovereignty can be seen as a "structure of closure," exerting structural power that keeps certain kinds of players out of the game of international politics.[34] Interestingly, despite its much less forgiving character the Hobbesian culture is one in which any kind of individual can play, since there are no rules giving certain actors standing and others not. The Lockean culture pays for its relative tranquility with a less open membership policy.

On the surface this seems to be the ultimate self-help policy, since it suggests that the only way for actors to get recognized as members of the system is to *force* their way in, there being no other way to achieve exclusive authority over a territory but to expel other states. But the reality seems more complicated. Many states were only able to "exclude" others because more powerful states did not try to prevent their exclusion. In these cases empirical sovereignty seems to presuppose at least tacit recognition of juridical sovereignty rather than the other way around. This reversal of the official procedure is most obvious for failed states in Africa,[35] but it is true of many other Small Powers as well, who were only able to exclude Great Powers because the latter did not resist. The "self-help" here, in other words, is one that depends on the restraint of the powerful, which amounts to a passive form of "other-help." That might still be self-help in an interesting sense, but not in the ultimate sense of *sauve qui peut*.

This calls attention to the second constitutive effect of the Lockean culture, which is determining what kinds of *type* identities get recognized as individuals. To become a member of the Westphalian system it has never been enough merely to have the corporate identity of a state; within that category it has always been necessary also to conform to type identity criteria which define only certain *forms* of state as legitimate.[36] Historically these criteria were expressed in the "standard of civilization," a set of systemic norms requiring that states' political authority be organized domestically in a certain way, namely like the hierarchical, bureaucratic, and (initially) Christian and monarchical authority of European states.[37] In the eighteenth and nineteenth centuries many non-European polities were empirically sovereign, but because they did not organize their authority in this manner they were not considered civilized—and therefore to have sovereign rights. Norms of what counts as a legitimate type identity have since changed. It is no longer necessary for a state to be Christian or monarchical; now it is being a "nation-" state,[38] having the institutions of a "modern" state[39] refraining from genocide, and, increasingly, being a "capitalist" and "democratic" state. In all these respects being part of Westphalian culture is not just a matter of a state's physical individuality, but of conforming the internal structure of this individuality to external norms about its proper form. As with other type identities, like being "left-handed," this internal structure is rooted in intrinsic features of material actors and as such is constitutionally exogenous to the international system (a state can be democratic all by itself), but its social meaning and consequences are *endogenous*.

The third way in which Lockean culture constitutes states as individuals relates to their collective or social identities. In their interactions within the Lockean culture states tend to be self-interested, but this is not true when it comes to the Lockean culture itself. Part of what it means to fully internalize a culture is that actors identify with it and therefore feel a sense of loyalty and obligation to the group which the culture defines. The peculiar nature of the Lockean culture is such that states are individualized within this group, but because the culture also constitutes their identities relative to non-members—as "civilized" states, for example—they will have a stake or interest in the group which they would not have if its norms were less fully internalized. This social identity matters because it facilitates collective action against outsiders; when the group is threatened, its members will see themselves as a "we" that needs to act collec-

tively, as a team, in its defense. What the fully internalized Lockean culture does, in other words, is give its members an expanded sense of Self that includes the group, and this group consciousness in turn creates a rudimentary capacity for other help, not just in the passive sense of self-restraint but in the active sense of being willing to come to each other's aid. This capacity is only rudimentary, however, because of the limited norms of the Lockean culture. It is only when the actual survival of members is threatened by outsiders, by rogue states, for example, that Lockean states' collective identity will become manifest. For fights within the group states are on their own.

This relates to the final effect of the Lockean culture, which is in a sense to obscure the preceding three effects and constitute states as "possessive" individuals instead. I take this to be an effect on states' role identities, and is a key basis for rivalry. According to C.B. MacPherson, possessive individualism is a distinctive feature of the *liberal* view of the individual.

> Its possessive quality is found in its conception of the individual as essentially the proprietor of his own person or capacities, owing nothing to society for them. The individual was seen neither as a moral whole, nor as a part of a larger social whole, but as an owner of himself. The relation of ownership, having become for more and more men the critical important relation determining their actual freedom and actual prospect of realising their full potentialities, was read back into the nature of the individual.[40]

Liberalism "desocializes" the individual, in other words, drawing a veil over his inherently social qualities and treating them as purely individual possessions instead. A consequence is that it becomes much more difficult to see why people should have any responsibility for each other's welfare, and thus to engage in collective action within the group. If people do not depend on each other for their identities then each is "his own man" and by implication owes nothing to his fellows except perhaps to leave them alone. Self-interest is thereby constituted as the appropriate relationship of Self to Other, which in effect *creates* the collective action problem,[41] but to do so it must forget the Self's dependence on the Other's recognition of his rights and identities. Thus, since that dependence could be threatened by being self-interested all the way down, liberalism arguably contains a deep tension between its legitimation of self-interest and the fact that individuals have an objective interest in the group which makes their individuality possible. This tension may underlie some of the worry today in the West about the erosion of community values in favor of individual self-interest.

As Ruggie has suggested, the Westphalian culture has a similar effect on states.[42] It constitutes states as the individuals with the right to play the game of international politics, but does so in a way that makes each state seem to be the sole proprietor and guardian of that right. Westphalian states are possessive individuals who do not appreciate the ways in which they depend on each other for their identity, being instead "jealous" of their sovereignty and eager to make their own way in the world. An important reason for this individualistic attitude may be the criterion for membership in international society itself, which encourages states to treat juridical sovereignty as an entitlement due them as a result of purely their own efforts to establish empirical sovereignty first. The effect of collective amnesia that juridical sovereignty is dependent on others is to constitute self-interest as the appropriate way to relate to each other, and self-help as its systemic corollary. Self-interest and self-help are not intrinsic attributes of states and anarchy, in other words, but effects of a particular conception of the individual. The role structure of rivalry feeds on this conception. Rivals know that they are members of a group in which individuals do not kill each other, but this collective identity is usually in the background of their interactions, which center instead on jealously protecting and advancing their own interests within that context. As we have seen, these efforts are mitigated by states' self-limiting behavior, as well as by the occasional reminder by threats from outside that they are in fact part of a group, and as such the system is not self-help all the way down. But whether this mutual dependence can in the long run survive an ideology of possessive individualism is not clear.

The suggestion that Westphalian states are afflicted with a possessive individualism stemming from collective amnesia about their social roots raises a concluding question about whether a Lockean culture could be compatible with a more "relational" individualism that acknowledged those roots. In social theory this question has been taken up especially by feminists, who have argued that the atomistic and egoistic view of the individual found in liberalism and its rationalist off-shoots in social science is a gendered view rooted in the male experience.[43] Feminist IR scholars have used these arguments to critique the traditional view of state sovereignty pointing toward the possibility of a relational view in which inter state rivalry would be less intense and collective action more likely.[44]

Whether or not the Westphalian theory of sovereignty is intrinsically gendered is an important and challenging question that I cannot address here. It is clear that feminist critiques can be fruitfully applied to that theory, but less clear whether this is because gender has had a causal impact on Westphalian sovereignty, since there are structurally similar, non-feminist critiques of liberalism that come to many of the same conclusions, but do so via psychological, sociological, or anthropological evidence.[45] Whatever the causal roots of the possessive view of sovereignty might be, in turn, there is also the question of how a relational view would differ from the conception of individuality found in the fully internalized Kantian culture, which I consider in passing below.

The Third Degree Lockean culture is the basis for what we today take to be "common sense" about international politics: that a certain type of state is the main actor in the system, that these actors are self-interested individualists, that the international system is therefore in part a self-help system—but that states also recognize each other's sovereignty and so are rivals rather than enemies, that they have status quo interests which induce them to constrain their own behavior and cooperate when threatened from outside, and that the system is therefore in part an other-help system qualitatively different in its fundamental logic than the Hobbesian world of *sauve qui peut*. This common sense is the starting point for mainstream theorizing in IR, which tends to discount the importance of cultural variables. What I have tried to do is endogenize this starting point, to show that it depends on a particular cultural background which can be taken as given for certain purposes, but without which we cannot make sense of modern international politics. This matters for the larger argument of this book, in turn, because if today's common sense about international politics is a function of historically contingent shared ideas rather than the intrinsic nature of states or anarchy, then the question arises how that common sense might be transformed, and with it the cultural conditions of possibility for mainstream thinking.

Notes

1. Smith (1981).
2. Buzan's (1991) distinction between "immature" and "mature" anarchies is an important exception.
3. Bull (1977). On Locke's view of anarchy see Simmons (1989).
4. On sovereignty as a right see Ruggie (1983a), Fain (1987), Baldwin (1992), Kratochwil (1995), and Reus-Smit (1997).
5. Fain (1987: 134–160).
6. Hanson (1984).
7. Kocs (1994); see also Coplin (1965) and Slaughter (1995).
8. Henkin (1979: 47).
9. Charney (1993).
10. Mearsheimer (1994/1995: 10).
11. Walt (1987).
12. See, for example, Ray (1989), Nadelmann (1990), Price (1995), and Tannenwald (1999).
13. See Jochnick and Normand (1994).
14. Ruggie (1993: 162–163). Ruggie makes a further distinction between configurative and positional wars.
15. Strang (1991).
16. Jackson and Rosberg (1982).
17. On the role of mutual recognition as a basis for social order see Pizzorno (1991).
18. See Nau (1994) for a good discussion of the ways in which the market analogy poses problems for Waltz's account.
19. See especially Krasner (1993, 1995/6). On the significance of exceptions to rules see Edgerton (1985).
20. Burchell, *et al.,* eds. (1991).
21. See Powell (1991), Liberman (1993).
22. Weingast (1995).
23. Krasner (1983a).
24. See Krasner (1993, 1995/6).
25. Tyler (1990); also see Hurd (1999).
26. See Coplin (1965), Franck (1990), Kocs (1994), Koh (1997), and Hurd (1999).
27. Liberman (1993).
28. In various forms this theory of individuation is found throughout holist social theory, back at least to Hegel. I use Foucault's name because his version (see especially 1979) is well known today (see also Pizzorno, 1991); the phrase 'Foucault Effect' is due to Burchell, *et al.,* eds. (1991).
29. See Kitzinger (1992).
30. Evans (1987).
31. Pizzorno (1992).
32. Mercer (1995).
33. Spruyt (1994).
34. Murphy (1984); cf. Guzzini (1993), Onuf and Klink (1989).

35. Jackson and Rosberg (1982).
36. Bukovansky (1999a, b).
37. Gong (1984), Neumann and Welsh (1991).
38. Barkin and Cronin (1994), Hall (1999).
39. McNeely (1995), Meyer, *et al.* (1997).
40. MacPherson (1962: 3), quoted from Shotter (1990: 166).
41. The effect of individualization on collective action is an old theme of Marxist scholarship (see Jessop, 1978; Poulantzas, 1978), and has also featured in more recent work on social movements (Pizzorno, 1991). For an application to the international system see Paros (1999).
42. Ruggie (1983a).
43. See, for example, DiStefano (1983), Scheman (1983), and England and Kilbourne (1990).
44. Keohane (1988b), Tickner (1989), and several contributions to Peterson, ed. (1990).
45. See, for example, Sandel (1982), Sampson (1988), Markus and Kitayama (1991), and Kitzinger (1992).

References

Barkin, Samuel and Bruce Cronin (1994) "The state and the nation: Changing norms and the rules of sovereignty in international relations," *International Organization,* 48, 107–130.

Bukovansky, Mlada (1997) "American identity and neutral rights from independence to the War of 1812," *International Organization,* 51, 209–243.

———— (1999a) "The altered state and the state of nature: The French Revolution in international politics," *Review of International Studies,* 25, 197–216.

———— (1999b) "Ideas and power politics: the American and French Revolutions in international politics," book manuscript, Dartmouth College.

Bull, Hedley (1977) *The Anarchical Society,* New York: Columbia University Press.

Burchell, Graham, Colin Gordon, and Peter Miller, eds. (1991) *The Foucault Effect,* London: Harvester.

Buzan, Barry (1991) *People, States, and Fear,* Boulder: Lynne Rienner, 2nd edn. (1993) "From international system to international society: Structural realism and regime theory meet the English school," *International Organization,* 47, 327–352.

Charney, Jonathon (1993) "Universal international law," *American Journal of International Law,* 87, 529–551.

Coplin, William (1965) "International law and assumptions about the state system," *World Politics,* 17, 615–634.

Distefano, Christine (1983) "Masculinity as ideology in political theory: Hobbesian man considered," *Women's Studies International Forum,* 6, 633–644.

England, Paula and Barbara Stanek Kilbourne (1990) "Feminist critiques of the separative model of self," *Rationality and Society*, 2, 156–171.

Evans, E. (1987) *The Criminal Prosecution and Capital Punishment of Animals*, London: Faber.

Fain, Haskell (1987) *Normative Politics and the Community of Nations*, Philadelphia: Temple University Press.

Franck, Thomas (1990) *The Power of Legitimacy Among Nations*, Oxford: Oxford University Press.

Gong, Gerritt (1984) *The Standard of 'Civilization' in International Society*, Oxford: Clarendon Press.

Goodin, Robert (1992) *Motivating Political Morality*, Oxford: Blackwell.

Guzzini, Stefano (1993) "Structural power: The limits of neorealist analysis," *International Organization*, 47, 443–478.

Hall, Rodney Bruce (1999) *National Collective Identity: Social Constructs and International Systems*, New York: Columbia University Press.

Hanson, Donald (1984) "Thomas Hobbes' 'highway to peace,'" *International Organization*, 38, 329–354.

Henkin, Louis (1979) *How Nations Behave*, 2nd edn, New York: Council on Foreign Relations.

Hurd, Ian (1999) "Legitimacy and authority in international politics," *International Organization*, 53, 379–408.

Jackson, Robert and Carl Rosberg (1982) "Why Africa's weak states persist: The juridical and the empirical in statehood," *World Politics*, 35, 1–24.

Jessop, Bob (1978) "Capitalism and democracy: The best possible political shell?" in G. Littlejohn, *et al.*, eds., *Power and the State*, New York: St. Martins, 10–51.

Jochnick, C. and R. Normand (1994) "The legitimization of violence," *Harvard International Law Journal*, 35, 49–95.

Keohane, Robert (1984) *After Hegemony*, Princeton: Princeton University Press.

_____ (1986a) "Reciprocity in international relations," *International Organization*, 40, 1–27.

_____ (1986b) "Theory of world politics: Structural realism and beyond," in R. Keohane, ed., *Neorealism and its Critics*, New York: Columbia University Press, 158–203.

_____ (1988a) "International institutions: Two approaches," *International Studies Quarterly*, 32, 379–396.

_____ (1988b) "International relations theory: Contributions of a feminist stand-point," *Millennium*, 18, 245–253.

_____ (1990) "International liberalism reconsidered," in J. Dunn, ed., *The Economic Limits to Modern Politics*, Cambridge: Cambridge University Press, 165–194.

Keohane, Robert, ed. (1986) *Neorealism and its Critics*, New York: Columbia University Press.

Keohane, Robert and Lisa Martin (1995) "The promise of institutionalist theory," *International Security*, 20, 39–51.

Keohane, Robert and Joseph Nye (1989) *Power and Interdependence*, 2nd edn, Glenville, IL: Scott Foresman.

Kitzinger, Celia (1992) "The individuated self concept: A critical analysis of social-constructionist writing on individualism," in G. Breakwell, ed., *Social Psychology of Identity and the Self Concept*, Surrey University Press, 251–250.

Kocs, Stephen (1994) "Explaining the strategic behavior of states: International law as system structure," *International Studies Quarterly*, 38, 535–556.

Koh, Harold (1997) "Why do nations obey international law?" *Yale Law Journal*, 106, 2599–2659.

Krasner, Stephen (1978) *Defending the National Interest*, Princeton: Princeton University Press.

_____ (1983a) "Structural causes and regime consequences: Regimes as intervening variables," in S. Krasner, ed., *International Regimes*, Ithaca: Cornell University Press, 1–21.

_____ (1983b) "Regimes and the limits of realism," in Krasner, ed., *International Regimes*, Ithaca: Cornell University Press, 355–368.

_____ (1991) "Global communications and national power: Life on the Pareto frontier," *World Politics*, 43, 336–366.

_____ (1993) "Westphalia and all that," in J. Goldstein and R. Keohane, eds., *Ideas and Foreign Policy*, Ithaca: Cornell University Press, pp. 235–264.

_____ (1995/6) "Compromising Westphalia," *International Security*, 20, 115–151.

Krasner, Stephen, ed. (1983) *International Regimes*, Ithaca: Cornell University Press.

Liberman, Peter (1993) "The spoils of conquest," *International Security*, 18, 125–153.

MacPherson, C. B. (1962) *The Political Theory of Possessive Individualism*, Oxford: Clarendon Press.

Markus, Hazel and Shinobu Kitayama (1991) "Culture and the self: Implications for cognition, emotion, and motivation," *Psychological Review*, 98, 224–253.

McNeely, Connie (1995) *Constructing the Nation-State*, Westport: Greenwood Press.

Mearsheimer, John (1990a) "Back to the future: Instability in Europe after the Cold War," *International Security*, 15, 5–56.

_____ (1990b) "Why we will soon miss the Cold War," *The Atlantic*, 266, 35–50.

_____ (1994/1995) "The false promise of international institutions," *International Security*, 19, 5–49.

Mercer, Jonathan (1995) "Anarchy and identity," *International Organization,* 49, 229–252.

Meyer, John (1977) "The effects of education as an institution," *American Journal of Sociology,* 83, 55–77.

_____ (1980) "The world polity and the authority of the nation-state," in A. Bergesen, ed., *Studies of the Modern World-System,* New York: Academic Press, 109–137.

Meyer, John *et al.* (1997) "World society and the nation-state," *American Journal of Sociology,* 103, 144–181.

Murphy, Raymond (1984) "The structure of closure: A critique and development of the theories of Weber, Collins, and Parkin," *British Journal of Sociology,* 35, 547–567.

_____ (1995) "Sociology as if nature did not matter: An ecological critique," *British Journal of Sociology,* 46, 688–707.

Nadeimann, Ethan (1990) "Global prohibition regimes: The evolution of norms in international society," *International Organization,* 44, 479–526.

Nau, Henry (1993) "Identity and international politics," manuscript, George Washington University.

_____ (1994) "Why markets and international politics differ," manuscript, George Washington University.

Neumann, Iver and Jennifer Welsh (1991) "The Other in European self-definition: An addendum to the literature on international society," *Review of International Studies,* 17, 327–348.

Paros, Laura (1999) "The prison-house of sovereignty," *Alternatives,* forthcoming.

Peterson, V. Spike, ed. (1992) *Gendered States,* Boulder: Lynne Rienner.

Pizzorno, Alessandro (1991) "On the individualistic theory of social order," in P. Bourdieu and J. Coleman, eds., *Social Theory for a Changing Society,* Boulder: Westview, 209–231.

_____ (1992) "Foucault and the liberal view of the individual," in T. Armstrong, ed., *Michel Foucault Philosopher,* Harvester Press, 204–211.

Powell, Robert (1991) "Absolute and relative gains in international relations theory," *American Political Science Review,* 85, 1303–1320.

Price, Richard (1995) "A genealogy of the chemical weapons taboo," *International Organization,* 49, 73–104.

Ray, James Lee (1989) "The abolition of slavery and the end of international war," *International Organization,* 43, 405–441.

Ruggie, John (1983a) "Continuity and transformation in the world polity," *World Politics,* 35, 261–285.

_____ (1983b) "International regimes, transactions, and change: Embedded liberalism in the postwar economic order," in S. Krasner, ed., *International Regimes,* Ithaca: Cornell University Press, 195–232.

_____ (1993) "Territoriality and beyond: Problematizing modernity in international relations," *International Organization,* 47, 139–174.

Ruggie, John, ed. (1993) *Multilateralism Matters,* New York: Columbia University Press.

Sampson, Edward (1988) "The debate on individualism: Indigenous psychologies of the individual and their role in personal and societal functioning," *American Psychologist,* 43, 15–22.

Sandel, Michael (1982) *Liberalism and the Limits of Justice,* Cambridge: Cambridge University Press.

Scheman, Naomi (1983) "Individualism and the objects of psychology," in S.Harding and M. Hintikka, eds., *Discovering Reality,* Dordrecht: Reidel, 225–244.

Shotter, John (1990) "Social individuality versus possessive individualism: The sounds of silence," in I. Parker and J. Shotter, eds., *Deconstructing Social Psychology,* London: RKP, 155–169.

Slaughter, Anne-Marie (1995) "International law in a world of liberal states," *European Journal of International Law,* 6, 503–538.

Smith, Anthony (1981) "States and homelands: The social and geopolitical implications of national territory," *Millennium,* 10, 187–202.

_____ (1989) "The origins of nations," *Ethnic and Racial Studies,* 12, 340–367.

Spruyt, Hendrik (1994) *The Sovereign State and its Competitors,* Princeton: Princeton University Press.

Strang, David (1991) "Anomaly and commonplace in European political expansion: Realist and institutional accounts," *International Organization,* 45, 143–162.

Tannenwald, Nina (1996) "Dogs that don't bark: The United States, the role of norms and the non-use of nuclear weapons since 1945," Ph.D. dissertation, Cornell University.

_____ (1999) "The nuclear taboo: The United States and the normative basis of nuclear non-use," *International Organization,* 53, forthcoming.

Tickner, Ann (1993) *Gender in International Relations,* New York: Columbia University Press.

Tyler, Tom (1990) *Why People Obey the Law,* New Haven: Yale University Press.

Walt, Stephen (1987) *The Origins of Alliances,* Ithaca: Cornell University Press.

_____ (1998) "International relations: One world, many theories," *Foreign Policy,* 110, 29–46.

Weingast, Barry (1995) "A rational choice perspective on the role of ideas: Shared belief systems and state sovereignty in international cooperation," *Politics and Society,* 23, 449–464.

Constructing Norms of Humanitarian Intervention

MARTHA FINNEMORE

Finnemore argues that realist and neoliberal theories have not provided good explanations for the increase in humanitarian interventions since the end of the Cold War by states to protect citizens other than their own. National interest does not seem to be the driving factor. Finnemore argues that one must consider the changing normative context within which such interventions occur.

Since the end of the Cold War, states have increasingly come under pressure to intervene militarily and, in fact, *have* intervened militarily to protect citizens other than their own from humanitarian disasters. Recent efforts to enforce protected areas for Kurds and no-fly zones over Shiites in Iraq, efforts to alleviate starvation and establish some kind of political order in Somalia, the huge UN military effort to disarm parties and rebuild a state in Cambodia, and to some extent even the military actions to bring humanitarian relief in Bosnia are all instances of military action whose primary goal is not territorial or strategic but humanitarian.

Realist and liberal theories do not provide good explanations for this behavior. The interests that these theories impute to states are geostrategic and/or economic, yet many or most of these interventions occur in states of negligible geostrategic or economic importance to the interveners. Thus, no obvious national interest is at stake for the states bearing the burden of the military intervention in most if not all of the these cases. Somalia is perhaps the clearest example of military action undertaken in a state of little or no strategic or economic importance to the principal intervener. Similarly, the states that played central roles in the UN military action in Cambodia were, with the exception of China, not states that had any obvious geostrategic interests there by 1989; China, which did have a geostragetic interest, bore little of the burden of intervening.

Realism and liberalism offer powerful explanations for the Persian Gulf war but have little to say about the extension of that war to Kurdish and Shiite protection through the enforcement of UN Resolution 688. The United States, France, and Britain have been allowing abuse of the Kurds for centuries. Why they should start caring about them now is not clear.

The recent pattern of humanitarian interventions raises the issue of what interests intervening states could possibly be pursuing. In most of these cases, the intervention targets are insignificant by any usual measure of geostrategic or economic interest. Why, then, do states intervene?

This essay argues that the pattern of intervention cannot be understood apart from the changing normative context in which it occurs. Normative context is important because it shapes conceptions of interest. Standard analytic assumptions about states and other actors pursuing their interests tend to leave the sources of interests vague or unspecified. The contention here is that international normative context shapes the interests of international actors and does so in both systematic and systemic ways. Unlike psychological variables that operate at the individual level, norms can be systemic-level variables in both origin and effects.[1] Because they are intersubjective, rather than merely subjective, widely held norms are not idiosyncratic in their effects. Instead, they leave broad patterns of the sort that social science strives to explain.

In this essay I examine the role of humanitarian norms in shaping patterns of humanitarian military intervention over the past 150 years.[2] I show that shifts in intervention behavior correspond with changes in normative standards articulated by states concerning appropriate ends and means of military intervention. Specifically, normative understandings about which human beings merit military protection and about the way in which such protection must be implemented have changed, and state behavior has changed accordingly. This broad correlation establishes the norms explanation as plausible. The failure of alternative explanations to account for changing patterns of intervention behavior increases the credibility of the norms approach. I conclude with a discussion of ways to move beyond this plausibility probe.

The analysis proceeds in five parts. The first shows that realist and liberal approaches to international politics do not explain humanitarian intervention as a practice, much less change in that practice over time, because of their exogenous and static treatment of interests. A constructivist approach that attends to the role of international norms can remedy this by allowing us to problematize interests and their change over time. The next section examines humanitarian action in the nineteenth century. It shows that humanitarian action and even intervention on behalf of Christians being threatened or mistreated by the Ottoman Turks were carried out occasionally throughout the nineteenth century. However, only Christians appear to be deserving targets of humanitarian intervention; mistreatment of other groups does not evoke similar concern.

The third section investigates the expansion of this definition of "humanity" by examining efforts to abolish slavery, the slave trade, and colonization. Protection of nonwhite non-Christians did become a motivation for military action by states, especially Great Britain, in the early nineteenth century, when efforts to stop the slave trade began in earnest. But the scope of this humanitarian action was limited. Britain acted to stop commerce in slaves on the high seas; she did not intervene militarily to protect them inside other states or to abolish slavery as a domestic institution of property rights. It was not until decolonization that this redefinition of "humanity" in more universal terms (not just Christians, not just whites) was consolidated.

The fourth section briefly reviews humanitarian intervention as a state practice since 1945, paying particular attention to the multilateral and institutional requirements that have evolved for humanitarian intervention. Contemporary multilateralism differs qualitatively from previous modes of joint state action and has important implications for the planning and execution of humanitarian interventions. The essay concludes by outlining questions about the role and origins of norms that are not treated here but could be addressed in future research.

Using Norms to Understand International Politics

Humanitarian intervention looks odd from conventional perspectives on international political behavior because it does not conform to the conceptions of interest that they specify. Realists would expect to see some geostrategic or political advantage to be gained by intervening states. Neoliberals might emphasize economic or trade advantages for interveners.

As I discussed in the introduction, it is difficult to identify the advantage for the intervener in most post-1989 cases. The 1989 U.S. action in Somalia is a clear case of intervention without obvious interests. Economically Somalia was insignificant to the United States. Security interests are also hard to find. The U.S. had voluntarily given up its base at Berbera in Somalia because advances in communications and aircraft technology made it obsolete for the communications and refueling purposes it once served. Further, the U.S. intervention in that country was not carried out in a way that would have furthered strategic interests. If the U.S. had truly had designs on Somalia, it should have welcomed the role of disarming the clans. It did not. The U.S. resisted UN pressures to "pacify" the country as part of its mission. In fact, U.S. officials were clearly and consistently interested not in controlling any part of Somalia but in getting out of the country as soon as possible—sooner, indeed, than the UN would have liked. The fact that some administration officials opposed the Somalia intervention on precisely the grounds that no vital U.S. interest was involved underscores the realists' problem.

Intervention to reconstruct Cambodia presents similar anomalies. The country is economically insignificant to the intereveners and, with the end of the Cold War, was strategically significant to none of the five on the UN Security Council except China, which bore very little of the intervention burden. Indeed, U.S. involvement appears to have been motivated by domestic opposition to the return of the Khmers Rouges on moral grounds—another anomaly for these approaches—rather than by geopolitical or economic interests.

Liberals of a more classical and Kantian type might argue that these interventions have been motivated by an interest in promoting democracy and liberal values. After all, the UN's political blueprint for reconstructing these states is a liberal one. But such arguments also run afoul of the evidence. The U.S. consistently refused to take on the state-building and democratization mission in Somalia that liberal arguments would have expected to be at the heart of U.S. efforts. Similarly, the UN stopped short of authorizing an overthrow of Saddam Hussein in Iraq even when it was militarily possible and supported by many in the U.S. armed forces. The UN, and especially the U.S., have emphasized the humanitarian rather than the democratizing nature of these interventions, both rhetorically and in their actions on the ground.

None of these realist or liberal approaches provides an answer to the question, What interests are intervening states pursuing? In part this is a problem of theoretical focus. Realism and most liberals do not investigate interests; they assume them. Interests are givens in these approaches and need to be specified before analysis can begin. In this case, however, the problem is also substantive. The geostrategic and economic interests specified by these approaches appear to be wrong.

Investigating interests requires a different kind of theoretical approach. Attention to international norms and the way they structure interests in coordinated ways across the international system provides such an approach. Further, a norms approach addresses an issue obscured by approaches that treat interests exogenously: it focuses attention on the ways in which interests change. Since norms are socially constructed, they evolve with changes in social interaction. Understanding this normative evolution and the changing interests it creates is a major focus of a constructivist research program and of this analysis.

A constructivist approach does not deny that power and interest are important. They are. Rather, it asks a different and prior set of questions; it asks what interests *are,* and it investigates the ends to

which and the means by which power will be used. The answers to these questions are not simply idiosyncratic and unique to each actor. The social nature of international politics creates normative understandings among actors that, in turn, coordinate values, expectations, and behavior. Because norms make similar behavioral claims on dissimilar actors, they create coordinated patterns of behavior that we can study and about which we can theorize.[3]

Before beginning the analysis, let me clarify the relationship postulated here among norms, interests, and actions. In this essay I understand norms to shape interests and interests to shape action. Neither connection is determinative. Factors other than norms may shape interests, and certainly no single norm or norm set is likely to shape a state's interests on any given issue. In turn, factors other than state interests, most obviously power constraints, shape behavior and outcomes. Thus, the connection assumed here between norms and action is one in which norms create permissive conditions for action but do not determine action. Changing norms may change state interests and create new interests (in this case, interests in protecting non-European non-Christians and in doing so multilaterally through an international organization). But the fact that states are now interested in these issues does not guarantee pursuit of these interests over all others on all occasions. New or changed norms enable new or different behaviors; they do not ensure such behaviors.

I should also offer a rationale for examining justifications for intervention as an indicator of norms and norm change. The conventional wisdom is that justifications are mere fig leaves behind which states hide their less savory and more self-interested reasons for actions. Motivation is what matters; justification is not important.

It is true that justification does not equal motivation. Humanitarian justifications have been used to disguise baser motives in more than one intervention. More frequently, motives for intervention are mixed; humanitarian motives may be genuine but may be only one part of a larger constellation of motivations driving state action.[4] Untangling precise motivations for intervention is difficult and would be impossible in an essay of this length and historical breadth.

The focus here is justification, and for the purposes of this study justification *is* important because it speaks directly to normative context. When states justify their interventions, they are drawing on and articulating shared values and expectations held by other decision makers and other publics in other states. It is literally an attempt to connect one's actions to standards of justice or, perhaps more generically, to standards of appropriate and acceptable behavior. Thus through an examination of justifications we can begin to piece together what those internationally held standards are and how they may change over time.

My aim here is to establish the plausibility and utility of norms as an explanation for international behavior. States may violate international norms and standards of right conduct that they themselves articulate. But they do not always—or even often—do so. Aggregate behavior over long periods shows patterns that correspond to notions of right conduct over time. As shared understandings about who is "human" and about how intervention to protect those people must be carried out change, behavior shifts accordingly in ways not correlated with standard conceptions of interests.

We can investigate these changes by comparing humanitarian intervention practice in the nineteenth century with that of the twentieth century. The analysis is instructive in a number of ways. First, the analysis shows that humanitarian justifications for state action and state use of force are not new.

Second, the analysis shows that while humanitarian justifications for action have been important for centuries, the content and application of those justifications have changed over time. Specifically, states' perceptions of *which* human beings merit intervention has changed. I treat this not as a change of *identity*, but as a change of *identification*. Nonwhite non-Christians always knew they were human. What changed was perceptions of Europeans about them. People in Western states began to identify with non-Western populations during the twentieth century, with profound political consequences, for humanitarian intervention, among other things. Perhaps one could argue that the identity of the Western states changed, but I am not sure how one would characterize or operationalize such a change. Certainly Western states have not taken on an identity of "humanitarian state." Far too many inhumane acts have been committed by these states in this century to make such a characterization credible—nor do Western states themselves proclaim any such identity. Besides, these states were "humanitarian" on their own terms in the nineteenth century. What has

changed is not the fact of the humanitarian behavior but its focus. Identification emphasizes the affective relationships between actors rather than the characteristics of a single actor.[5] Further, identification is an ordinal concept, allowing for degrees of affect as well as changes in the focus of affect. Identification—of Western Europeans with Greeks and of Russians with their fellow Slavs—existed in the nineteenth century. The task is to explain how and why this identification expanded to other groups.

Third, the analysis highlights contestation over these normative justifications and links it to change. Ironically, while norms are inherently consensual (they exist only as convergent expectations or intersubjective understandings), they evolve in part through challenges to that consensus. Some challenges succeed, some fail. The analysis traces the challenges posed by humanitarian claims, noting where they succeed and where they have failed. It also points to instances of continued contestation, even over norms that appear to be gaining wider acceptance. Humanitarian norms have risen in prominence, but their acceptance is still limited and contested; certainly there are many forms of intervention, particularly unilateral intervention, that apparently cannot be justified even by humanitarian norms.

Fourth, the analysis relates evolving humanitarian intervention norms to other normative changes over the past century. When humanitarian intervention is viewed in a broader normative context, it becomes clear that changes in this particular norm are only one manifestation of the changes in a larger set of humanitarian norms that have become more visible and more powerful in the past fifty or one hundred years. Particularly prominent among these changing norms are the norms of decolonization and self-determination, which involved a redefinition and universalization of "humanity" for Europeans that changed the evolution of sovereignty and of humanitarian discourse (both of which are essential components of humanitarian intervention). Thus mutually reinforcing and consistent norms appear to strengthen each other; success in one area (such as decolonization) strengthens and legitimates claims in logically and morally related norms (such as human rights and humanitarian intervention). The relationship identified between decolonization and humanitarian intervention suggests the importance of viewing norms not as individual "things" floating atomistically in some international social space but rather as part of a highly structured social context. It may make more sense to think of a fabric of interlocking and interwoven norms rather than individual norms of this or that—as current scholarship, my own included, has been inclined to do.[6]

Finally, the analysis emphasizes the structuring and organization of the international normative context. Examination of humanitarian norms and intervention suggests that norm institutionalization, by which I mean the way norms become embedded in international organizations and institutions, is critical to patterns of norm evolution. Institutionalization of these norms or norm-bundles in international organizations (such as the UN) further increases the power and elaboration of the normative claims. . . .

Multilateral Intervention in Humanitarian Disasters

To be legitimate, humanitarian intervention must be multilateral. The Cold War made such multilateral efforts politically difficult to orchestrate, but since 1989 several large-scale interventions have been carried out claiming humanitarian justifications as their primary raison d'être. All have been multilateral. Most visible among these have been:

- the U.S., British, and French efforts to protect Kurdish and Shite populations inside Iraq following the Gulf War;
- the UNTAC mission to end civil war and reestablish a democratic political order in Cambodia;
- the large-scale UN effort to end starvation and construct a democratic state in Somalia; and
- current, albeit limited, efforts by UN and NATO troops to protect civilian, especially Muslim, populations from primarily Serbian forces in Bosnia.

While these efforts have attracted varying amounts of criticism concerning their effectiveness, they have received little or no criticism of their legitimacy. Further, and unlike their nineteenth-century counterparts, all have been organized through standing international organizations—most often the United Nations. Indeed, the UN charter has provided the framework in which much of the normative contestation over intervention practices has occurred since 1945. Specifically, the charter enshrines two

principles that at times, and perhaps increasingly, conflict. On the one hand, article 2 enshrines states' sovereign rights as the organizing principle of the international system. The corollary for intervention is a near absolute rule of nonintervention. On the other hand, article 1 of the charter emphasizes promoting respect for human rights and justice as a fundamental mission of the organization, and subsequent UN actions (adoption of the Universal Declaration of Human Rights, among them) have strengthened these claims. Gross humanitarian abuses by states against their own citizens of the kinds discussed in this essay bring these two central principles into conflict.

The humanitarian intervention norms that have evolved within these conflicting principles appear to allow intervention in cases of humanitarian disaster and abuse, but with at least two caveats. First, they are permissive norms only. They do not require intervention, as the cases of Burundi, Sudan, and other states make clear. Second, they place strict requirements on the ways in which intervention, if employed, may be carried out: Humanitarian intervention must be multilateral if states are to accept it as legitimate and genuinely humanitarian. Further, it must be organized under UN auspices or with explicit UN consent. If at all possible, the intervention force should be composed according to UN procedures, meaning that intervening forces must include some number of troops from "disinterested" states, usually midlevel powers outside the region of conflict—another dimension of multilateralism not found in nineteenth-century practice.

Contemporary multilateralism thus differs from the multilateral action of the nineteenth century. The latter was what John Ruggie might call "quantitative" multilateralism and only thinly so.[7] Nineteenth-century multilateralism was strategic. States intervened together to keep an eye on each other and discourage adventurism or exploitation of the situation for nonhumanitarian gains. Multilateralism was driven by shared fears and perceived threats, not by shared norms and principles. States did not even coordinate and collaborate extensively to achieve their goals. Military deployments in the nineteenth century may have been contemporaneous, but they were largely separate; there was virtually no joint planning or coordination of operations. This follows logically from the nature of multilateralism, since strategic surveillance of one's partners is not a shared goal but a private one.

Recent interventions exhibit much more of what Ruggie calls the "qualitative dimension" of multilateralism. They are organized according to and in defense of "generalized principles" of international responsibility and the use of military force, many of which are codified in the United Nations charter, declarations, and standard operating procedures. These emphasize international responsibilities for ensuring human rights and justice and dictate appropriate means of intervening, such as the necessity of obtaining Security Council authorization for action. The difference between contemporary and nineteenth-century multilateralism also appears at the operational level. The Greek intervention was multilateral only in the sense that more than one state had forces in the area at the same time. There was little joint planning and no integration of forces from different states. By contrast, contemporary multilateralism requires extensive joint planning and force integration. UN norms require that intervening forces be composed not just of troops from more than one state but of troops from disinterested states, preferably not great powers—precisely the opposite nineteenth-century multilateral practice.

Contemporary multilateralism is political and normative, not strategic. It is shaped by shared notions about when the use of force is legitimate and appropriate. Contemporary legitimacy criteria for the use of force, in turn, derive from these shared principles, articulated most often through the UN, about consultation and coordination with other states before acting and about multinational composition of forces. U.S. interventions in Somalia and Haiti were not made multilateral because the U.S. needed the involvement of other states for military or strategic reasons. The U.S. was capable of supplying the forces necessary and, in fact, did supply the lion's share of the forces. No other great power was particularly worried about U.S. opportunism in these areas, and so none joined the action for surveillance reasons. These interventions were multilateral for political and normative reasons. For these operations to be legitimate and politically acceptable, the U.S. needed UN authorization and international participation. Whereas Russia, France, and Britain tolerated each other's presence in the operation to save Christians from the infidel Turk, the U.S. had to beg other states to join it for a humanitarian operation in Haiti.

Multilateral norms create political benefits for conformance and costs for nonconforming action.

They create, in part, the structure of incentives facing states. Realists or neoliberal institutionalists might argue that in the contemporary world, multilateral behavior is efficient and unproblematically self-interested because multilateralism helps to generate political support both domestically and internationally for intervention. But this argument only begs the question, *Why* is multilateralism necessary to generate political support? It was not necessary in the nineteenth century. Indeed, multilateralism as currently practiced was inconceivable in the nineteenth century. As was discussed earlier, there is nothing about the logic of multilateralism itself that makes it clearly superior to unilateral action. Each has advantages and costs to states, and the costs of multilateral intervention have become abundantly clear in recent UN operations. One testament to the power of these multilateral norms is that states adhere to them even when they know that doing so compromises the effectiveness of the mission. Criticisms of the UN's ineffectiveness for military operations are widespread. The fact that UN involvement continues to be an essential feature of these operations despite the UN's apparent lack of military competence underscores the power of multilateral norms.

Realist and neoliberal approaches cannot address changing requirements for political legitimacy like those reflected in changing multilateral practice any more than they can explain the "interest" prompting humanitarian intervention and its change over time. A century ago, protecting nonwhite non-Christians was not an "interest" of Western states, certainly not one that could prompt the deployment of troops. Similarly, a century ago states saw no interest in multilateral authorization, coordination, force integration, and use of troops from "disinterested" states. The argument of this essay is that these interests and incentives have been constituted socially through state practice and the evolution of shared norms by which states act. Humanitarian intervention is not new. It has, however, changed over time in some systemic and important ways. First, the definition of who qualifies as human and therefore as deserving of humanitarian protection by foreign governments has changed. Whereas in the nineteenth century European Christians were the sole focus of humanitarian intervention, this focus has been expanded and universalized such that by the late twentieth century all human beings are treated as equally deserving in the international normative discourse. In fact, states are very sensitive to charges that they are "normatively backward" and still privately harbor distinctions. When Boutros Boutros-Ghali, shortly after becoming secretary-general, charged that powerful states were attending to disasters in white, European Bosnia at the expense of nonwhite, African Somalia, the U.S. and other states became defensive, refocused attention, and ultimately launched a full-scale intervention in the latter but not the former.

Second, while humanitarian intervention in the nineteenth century was frequently multilateral, it was not necessarily so. Russia, for example, claimed humanitarian justifications for its intervention in Bulgaria in the 1870s; France was similarly allowed to intervene unilaterally, with no companion force to guard against adventurism. These claims were not contested, much less rejected, by other states, as the claims of India, Tanzania, and Vietnam were (or would have been, had they made such claims) a century later, despite the fact that Russia, at least, had nonhumanitarian motives to intervene. By the twentieth century, not only does multilateralism appear to be necessary to claim humanitarian justifications but sanction by the United Nations or some other formal organization is also required. The U.S., Britain, and France, for example, went out of their way to find authority in UN resolutions for their protection of Kurds in Iraq.

The foregoing account also illustrates that these changes have come about through continual contestation over norms related to humanitarian intervention. The abolition of slavery, of the slave trade, and of colonization were all highly visible, often very violent, international contests about norms. Over time some norms won, others lost. The result was that by the second half of the twentieth century norms about who was "human" had changed, expanding the population deserving of humanitarian protection. At the same time norms about multilateral action had been strengthened, making multilateralism not just attractive but imperative.

Finally, I have argued here that the international normative fabric has become increasingly institutionalized in formal international organizations, particularly the United Nations. As recent action in Iraq suggests, action in concert with others is not enough to confer legitimacy on intervention actions. States also actively seek authorization from the United Nations and restrain their actions to conform to that authorization (as the U.S. did in not going to

Baghdad during the Gulf war).[8] International organizations such as the UN play an important role in both arbitrating normative claims and structuring the normative discourse over colonialism, sovereignty, and humanitarian issues.[9]

Changes in norms create only permissive conditions for changes in international political behavior. One important task of future research will be to define more specifically the conditions under which certain kinds of norms might prevail or fail in influencing action. A related task will be to clarify the mechanisms whereby norms are created, changed, and exercise their influence. I have suggested a few of these here—public opinion, the media, international institutions. More detailed study of individual cases is needed to clarify the role of each of these mechanisms. Finally, the way in which normative claims are related to power capabilities deserves attention. The traditional Gramscian view would argue that these are coterminous; the international normative structure is created by and serves the most powerful. Humanitarian action generally, and humanitarian intervention specifically, do not obviously serve the powerful. The expansion of humanitarian intervention practices since the last century suggests that the relationship between norms and power may not be so simple.

Notes

1. One could have subsystemic normative contexts as well.

2. The term *military intervention* in this essay refers to the deploying of military forces by a foreign power or powers for the purpose of controlling domestic policies or political arrangements in the target state in ways that clearly violate sovereignty. *Humanitarian intervention* is used to mean military intervention with the goal of protecting the lives and welfare of foreign civilians.

3. For a more extended discussion, see Martha Finnemore, *Defining National Interests in International Society* (Ithaca: Cornell University Press, 1996), ch. 1.

4. The U.S. intervention in Grenada is one such case, in which humanitarian justifications were offered (and widely rejected) for action of doubtful humanitarian motivation.

5. Obviously, single-actor characteristics may be defined in relation to or by comparison with those of others, but identification makes affective relationship central in ways that identity does not.

6. The intellectual orientation of the regimes literature probably had much to do with this atomized treatment of norms. Norms were incorporated as a definitional part of

regimes, but regimes were always conceived of as pertaining to individual issue areas. Scholars wrote about norms pertaining to specific issues without addressing either the larger context in which these norms exist or the ways in which they may be related one to another.

7. John G. Ruggie, "Multilateralism: The Anatomy of an Institution," in Ruggie. *Multilateralism Matters* (New York: Columbia University Press, 1993), 6.

8. Inis Claude's classic discussion of this collective legitimation function of the UN is well worth a second reading in the current political environment; see Inis L. Claude Jr., "Collective Legitimization as a Political Function of the United Nations," *International Organization* 20, no. 3 (Summer 1966): 367–79.

9. For more on the role of IOS in creating and disseminating norms, see Martha Finnemore, "International Organizations as Teachers of Norms: The United Nations Educational, Scientific, and Cultural Organization and Science Policy," *International Organization* 47, no. 4 (Autumn 1993): 599–628.

SUGGESTIONS FOR FURTHER READING

Abdelai, Rawi, Yoshiko Herrera, Alastair Johnston, and Rose McDermott. "Identity as a Variable." *Perspectives on Politics* 4, 4 (December 2006): 695–711.

Acharya, Amitav. "How Ideas Spread: Whose Norms Matter? Norm Localization and Institutional Change in Asian Regionalism." *International Organization* 58, 2 (Spring 2004): 239–75.

———. *Constructing a Security Community in Southeast Asia.* London: Routledge, 2001.

Adler, Emanuel. *Communitarian International Relations. The Epistemic Foundations of International Relations.* London: Routledge, 2005.

———. "Constructivism and International Relations." In *Handbook of International Relations,* eds. Walter Carlsnaes and Thomas Risse. London: Sage, 2002.

———. "Seizing the Middle Ground." *European Journal of International Relations* 3, 3 (September 1997): 319–63.

———. "The Spread of Security Communities: Communities of Practice, Self-Restraint, and NATO's Post-Cold War Transformation." *European Journal of International Relations* 14, 2 (June 2008): 195–230.

Adler, Emanuel, and Michael Barnett. *Security Communities.* New York: Cambridge University Press, 2002.

Adler, Emanuel, and Steven Bernstein. "Knowledge in Power: The Epistemic Construction of Global Governance." In *Power and Global Governance,* eds. Michael Barnett and Raymond Duvall. Cambridge: Cambridge University Press, 2005.

Barkin, J. Samuel. "Realist Constructivism and Realist-Constructivisms." *International Studies Review* 6, 2 (June 2004): 348–52.

Barkin, J. Samuel, and Bruce Cronin. "The State and the Nation: Changing Norms and the Rules of Sovereignty in International Relations." *International Organization* 48, 1 (Winter 1994): 107–30.

Barnett, Michael. "Authority, Intervention, and the Outer Limits of International Relations Theory." In *Intervention and Transnationalism in Africa: Global-Local Networks of Power,* eds. Thomas Callaghy, Roland Kassimir, and Robert Latham. Cambridge: Cambridge University Press, 2001.

———. "Social Constructivism." In *The Globalization of World Politics: An Introduction to International Relations,* 3rd ed., eds. John Baylis and Steve Smith. Oxford: Oxford University Press, 2005.

Barnett, Michael N. and Martha Finnemore. "The Politics, Power and Pathologies of International Organizations." *International Organizations* 53, 4 (Autumn 1999): 699–732.

———. *Rules for the World: International Organizations in Global Politics.* New York: Cornell University Press, 2004.

Bially Mattern, Janice. "Power in Realist-Constructivist Research." *International Studies Review* 6, 2 (June 2004): 343–46.

Biersteker, Thomas, and Cynthia Weber. *State Sovereignty as Social Construct.* Cambridge: Cambridge University Press, 1996.

Brglez, Milan. "Reconsidering Wendt's Metatheory: Blending Scientific Realism with Social Constructivism." *Journal of International Relations and Development* 4, 4 (December 2001): 339–62.

Brubaker, Rogers, and Frederick Copper. "Beyond Identity." *Theory and Society* 29, 1 (2000): 1–47.

Burch, Kurt. "Changing the Rules: Reconceiving Change in the Westphalian System." *International Studies Review* 2, 2 (Summer 2000): 181–210.

Caporaso, James, Jeffrey Checkel, and Joseph Jupille. "Integrating Institutions: Rationalism, Constructivism and the Study of the European Union." Special issue of *Comparative Political Studies* 36, 1–2 (February/March 2003): 7–40.

Cardenas, Sonia. "Norm Collision: Explaining the Effects of International Human Rights Pressure on State Behavior." *International Studies Review* 6, 2 (June 2004): 213–32.

Cederman, Lars-Erik. *Emergent Actors in World Politics: How States and Nations Develop and Dissolve.* Princeton, NJ: Princeton University Press, 1997.

_____, and Christopher Daase. "Endogenizing Corporate Identities: The Next Step in Constructivist IR Theory." *European Journal of International Relations* 9, 1 (March 2003): 5–35.

Chayes, Abram, and Antonia Chayes. *The New Sovereignty: Compliance with International Regulatory Agreements.* Cambridge, MA: Harvard University Press, 1995.

Checkel, Jeffrey. "Constructivism and EU Politics." In *Handbook of European Union Politics,* eds. Knud Jorgensen, Mark Pollack, and Ben Rosamond. London: Sage, 2007.

_____. "Going 'Native' in Europe? Theorizing Social Interaction in European Institutions." *Comparative Political Studies* 36, 1–2 (2003): 209–31.

_____. *Ideas and International Political Change: Soviet/Russian Behavior and the End of the Cold War.* New Haven, CT: Yale University Press, 1997.

_____. *International Institutions and Socialization in Europe.* Cambridge: Cambridge University Press, 2007.

_____. "Social Constructivisms in Global and European Politics: A Review Essay." *Review of International Studies* 3, 2 (2004): 229–44.

_____. "Why Comply? Social Learning and European Identity Change." *International Organization* 55, 3 (Summer 2001): 553–88.

Chernoff, Fred. "Attacking the Scientific Approach: Interpretive Constructivism, Poststructuralism and Critical Theory." In *Theory and Metatheory in International Relations,* ed. Fred Chernoff. New York: Palgrave Macmillan, 2007.

Clark, Ian. *Legitimacy in International Society.* Oxford: Oxford University Press, 2005.

Cronin, Bruce. *Cooperation under Anarchy: Transnational Identity and the Evolution of Cooperation.* New York: Columbia University Press, 1999.

Dessler, David. "Constructivism within a Positivist Social Science." *Review of International Studies* 25, 1 (January 1999): 123–37.

Deutsch, Karl, Sydney Burrell, and Robert Kann. *Political Community and the North Atlantic Area: International Organization in the Light of Historical Experience.* Princeton, NJ: Princeton University Press, 1957.

Doty, Roxanne. "Aporia: A Critical Exploration of the Agent-Structure Problematique in International Relations Theory." *European Journal of International Relations* 3, 3 (1997): 365–92.

_____. "Desires All the Way Down." *Review of International Studies* 26, 1 (January 2000): 137–39.

Dunne, Tim. "The Social Construction of International Society." *European Journal of International Relations* 1, 3 (September 1995): 367–89.

Farrell, Theo. "Constructivist Security Studies: Portrait of a Research Program." *International Studies Review* 4, 1 (Spring 2002): 49–72.

Fearon, James, and Alexander Wendt. "Rationalism v. Constructivism: A Skeptical View." In *Handbook of International Relations,* eds. Walter Carlsnaes, Thomas Risse, and Beth Simmons. London: Sage, 2002.

Fearon, James, and David D. Laitin. "Violence and the Social Construction of Ethnic Identity." *International Organization* 54, 4 (Autumn 2000): 845–77.

Fierke, Karin, and Knud Jorgensen, eds. *Constructing International Relations: The Next Generation.* Armonk, NY: M.E. Sharpe, 2001.

Finnemore, Martha. "Constructing Norms of Humanitarian Intervention." In *The Culture of National Security: Norms and Identity in World Politics,* ed. Peter Katzenstein. New York: Columbia University Press, 1996.

_____. *National Interests in International Society.* Ithaca, NY: Cornell University Press, 1996.

_____. "Paradoxes in Humanitarian Intervention." Paper Presented at the Annual Meeting of the American Political Science Association, Philadelphia, August 31, 2006.

_____. *The Purpose of Intervention: Changing Beliefs about the Use of Force.* Ithaca, NY: Cornell University Press, 2003.

_____, and Kathryn Sikkink. "International Norm Dynamics and Political Change." *International Organization* 52, 4 (Autumn 1998): 887–917.

Flockhart, Trine. *Socializing Democratic Norms: The Role of International Organizations for the Construction of Europe.* New York: Palgrave Macmillan, 2005.

Florini, Ann. "The Evolution of International Norms." *International Studies Quarterly* 40, 3 (September1996): 363–89.

Flynn, Gregory, and Henry Farrell. "Piecing Together the Democratic Peace: The CSCE, Norms, and the 'Construction' of Security in Post-Cold War Europe." *International Organization* 53, 3 (Summer 1999): 505–35.

Giddens, Anthony. *The Constitution of Society.* Berkeley: University of California Press, 1984.

Griffiths, Martin, and Terry O'Callaghan. "Constructivism." In *International Relations: The Key Concepts.* New York: Routledge, 2002.

Gurowitz, Amy. "The Diffusion of International Norms: Why Identity Matters." *International Politics* 43, 3 (July 2006): 305–41.

Guzzini, Stefano. "A Reconstruction of Constructivism in International Relations." *European Journal of International Relations* 6, 2 (2000): 147–82.

_____, Anna Leander, eds. *Constructivism and International Relations.* London and New York: Routledge, 2006.

_____. "A Social Theory for International Relations: An Appraisal of Alexander Wendt's Disciplinary and Theoretical Synthesis." *Journal of International Relations and Development,* 4, 4 (2001): 316–38.

Haas, Ernst B. *When Knowledge Is Power: Three Models of Change in International Organizations.* Santa Barbara, CA: University of California Press, 1990.

Hemmer, Christopher, and Peter Katzenstein. "Why Is There No NATO in Asia? Collective Identity, Regionalism, and the Origins of Multilateralism." *International Organization* 56, 3 (Summer, 2002): 575–607.

Hopf, Ted. "The Promise of Constructivism in International Relations." *International Security* 23, 1(1998): 170–200.

_____. *Social Construction of International Politics: Identities and Foreign Policies, Moscow, 1955 and 1999.* Ithaca, NY: Cornell University Press, 2002.

Jörgens, Helge. "Governance by Diffusion—Implementing Global Norms through Cross-National Imitation and Learning." In *Governance for Sustainable Development. The Challenge of Adapting Form to Function,* ed. William Lafferty. Cheltenham: Edward Elgar, 2004.

Kacowicz, Arie Marcelo. *The Impact of Norms in International Society: The Latin American Experience, 1881–2001.* Notre Dame: University of Notre Dame Press, 2005.

Katzenstein, Peter. *The Culture of National Security: Norms and Identity in International Politics.* New York: Columbia University Press, 1996.

_____, and Nobuo Okawara. "Japan's National Security: Structures, Norms, and Policies." *International Security* 17, 4 (Spring 1993): 84–118.

Keohane, Robert. "International Institutions: Two Approaches." *International Studies Quarterly,* 32, 4 (1988): 379–96.

Khagram, Sanjeev, James Riker, and Kathryn Sikkink, eds. *Restructuring World Politics: Transnational Social Movements, Networks, and Norms.* Ann Arbor: University of Minnesota Press, 2002.

Kowert, Paul, and Jeffrey Legro. "Norms, Identity, and Their Limits." In *The Culture of National Security: Norms and Identity in International Politics,* ed. Peter Katzenstein. New York: Columbia University Press, 1996.

Klotz, Audie, and Cecelia Lynch. *Strategies for Research in Constructivist International Relations.* Armonk, NY: M.E. Sharpe, 2007.

Koslowski, Rey. "A Constructivist Approach to Understanding the European Union as a Federal Polity." *Journal of European Public Policy,* 6, 4 (1999): 561–78.

Kratochwil, Friedrich. "The Force of Prescriptions." *International Organization* 38, 4 (Autumn 1984): 685–708.

_____. "Politics, Norms and Peaceful Change: Two Moves to Institutions." In *International Organization and Global Governance: A Reader,* eds. Frederick, Kratochwil and Edward Mansfield. New York: Longman, 2006.

_____. *Rules, Norms, and Decisions.* Cambridge: Cambridge University Press, 1991.

_____, and Edward Mansfield, eds. *International Organization and Global Governance.* New York: Pearson/Longman, 2006.

_____, and John Ruggie. "International Organization: A State of the Art on the Art of the State." *International Organization* 40, 4 (Autumn 1986): 753–76.

Kubálková, Vendulka, Nicholas Onuf, and Paul Kowert, eds. *International Relations in a Constructed World.* Armonk, NY: M.E. Sharpe, 1998.

Lebow, Richard Ned. *The Tragic Vision of Politics.* Cambridge and NY: Cambridge University Press, 2003.

Legro, Jeffrey. "Whence American Internationalism." *International Organization* 54, 2 (Spring 2000): 253–89.

_____. "Which Norms Matter? Revisiting the 'Failure' of Internationalism." *International Organization* 51, 1 (Winter 1997): 31.

March, James G., and Johan P. Olsen. "The Institutional Dynamics of International Political Orders. *International Organization* 52, 4 (Autumn 1998): 943–69.

Mercer, Jonathan. "Anarchy and Identity." *International Organization* 49, 2 (Spring 1995): 229–52.

Meyer, Mary. "Negotiating International Norms: The Inter-American Commission of Women and the Convention on Violence against Women." *Aggressive Behavior* 24, 2 (1998): 135–42.

Modelski, George. "Is World Politics Evolutionary Learning?" *International Organization* 44, 1(Winter 1990): 1–24.

Morgan, Roger. "A European 'Society of States'—but only States of Mind?" *International Affairs* 76, 3 (July 2000): 559–74.

Nadelman, Ethan. "Global Prohibition Regimes: The Evolution of Norms in International Society." *International Organization* 44, 4 (Autumn 1990): 479–526.

Onuf, Nicholas. "Constructivism: A User's Manual." In *International Relations in a Constructed World,* eds. Vendulka Kubálková, Nicholas Onuf, and Paul Kowert, London and Armonk, NY: M.E. Sharpe, 1998: 58–78.

_____. "Institutions, Intentions, and International Relations." *Review of International Studies* 28, 2 (April 2002): 211–28.

_____. *World of Our Making: Rules and Rule in Social Theory and International Relations.* Columbia, SC: University of South Carolina Press, 1989.

Park, Susan. "Norms and International Relations Theorizing Norm Diffusion within International Organizations." *International Politics* 43, 3 (July 2006): 342–61.

Parsons, Craig. "Showing Ideas as Causes: The Origins of the European Union." *International Organization* 56, 1 (Winter 2002): 47–84.

Patrick, Stewart. "Evolution of International Norms: Choice, Learning, Power, and Identity." In *Evolutionary Interpretations of World Politics,* ed. William R. Thompson, New York: Routledge, 2001.

Payne, Rodger, and Nayef Samhat. *Democratizing Global Politics: Discourse Norms, International Regimes, and Political Community.* New York: State University of New York Press, 2004.

Pettman, Ralph. *Commonsense Constructivism, or The Making of World Affairs.* Armonk, NY: M.E. Sharpe, 2000.

Price, Richard, and Christian Reus-Smit. "Dangerous Liaisons? Critical International Theory and Constructivism." *European Journal of International Relations* 4, 3 (1998): 259–94.

Raymond, Gregory A. "Problems and Prospects in the Study of International Norms." *Mershon International Studies Review* 4, 2 (November 1997): 205–45.

Reus-Smit, Christian. "The Constitutional Structure of International Society and the Nature of Fundamental Institutions." *International Organization* 51, 4 (Autumn 1997): 555–89.

_____. "Constructivism." In *Theories of International Relations.* Eds. Scott Burchill and Andrew Linklater, London: Palgrave Macmillan, 1996, 2001.

_____. *The Moral Purpose of the State: Culture, Social Identity, and Institutional Rationality in International Relations.* Princeton, NJ: Princeton University Press, 1999.

Risse, Thomas. "Let's Argue!: Communicative Action in World Politics." *International Organization* 54, 1 (Winter 2000): 1–39.

Ruggie, John G. *Constructing the World Polity: Essays on International Institutionalization.* New York: Routledge, 1998.

_____. "Territoriality and Beyond: Problematizing Modernity in International Relations." *International Organization* 47, 1 (1993): 139–74.

_____. "What Makes the World Hang Together? Neo-Utilitarianism and the Social Constructivist Challenge." *International Organization* 52, 4 (Autumn 1998): 855–85.

Saideman, Stephen. "Conclusion: Thinking Theoretically about Identity and Foreign Policy." In *Identity and Foreign Policy in the Middle East.* eds. Shibley Telhami and Michael Barnett. New York: Cornell University Press, 2002.

Santa-Cruz, Arturo. *International Election Monitoring, Sovereignty, and the Western Hemisphere Idea: The Emergence of an International Norm.* New York: Routledge, 2005.

Shannon, Vaughn. "Norms Are What States Make of Them: The Political Psychology of Norm Violation." *International Studies Quarterly* 44, 2 (June 2000): 293–316.

Sikkink, Kathryn. "Codes of Conduct for Transnational Corporations: The Case of the WHO/UNICEF Code." *International Organization* 40, 4 (Autumn 1986): 815–40.

Simmons, Beth, Frank Dobbin, and Geoffrey Garrett. "Introduction: The International Diffusion of Liberalism." *International Organization* 60, 4 (Fall 2006): 781–810.

Smith, Steve. "Social Constructivisms and European Studies: A Reflectivist Critique." *Journal of European Public Policy.* 6, 4 (1999): 682–91.

_____. "Wendt's World." *Review of International Studies,* 26, 1 (2000): 151–63.

_____. Ken Booth, and Marysia Zalewski, eds. *International Theory: Positivism and Beyond.* Cambridge, UK: Cambridge University Press, 1996.

Snyder, Jack. "Anarchy and Culture: Insights from the Anthropology of War." *International Organization* 56, 1 (Winter 2002): 7–45.

Spruyt, Hendrik. "The End of Empire and the Extension of the Westphalian System: The Normative Basis of the Modern State Order." *International Studies Review* 2, 2 (Summer 2000): 65–92.

Sterling-Folker, Jennifer. "Competing Paradigms or Birds of a Feather? Constructivism and Neoliberal Institutionalism Compared." *International Studies Quarterly* 44, 1 (March 2000): 97–119.

Suganami, Hidemi. "Alexander Wendt and the English School." *Journal of International Relations and Development,* 4, 4 (2001): 403–23.

_____. "On Wendt's Philosophy: A Critique," *Review of International Studies,* 28, 1 (2002): 23–37.

Thomas, Daniel. "Bumerangs and Superpowers: International Norms, Transnational Networks and U.S. Foreign Policy." *Cambridge Review of International Affairs* 15, 1 (April 2002): 25–44.

Thomson, Janice. "State Practices, International Norms, and the Decline of Mercenarism." *International Studies Quarterly* 34, 1 (March 1990): 23–48.

Van Kersbergen, Kees, and Bertjan Verbeek. "The Politics of International Norms: Subsidiarity and the Imperfect Competence Regime of the European Union." *European Journal of International Relations* 13, 1 (2007): 217–38.

Verdirame, Guglielmo. "Testing the Effectiveness of International Norms: UN Humanitarian Assistance and Sexual Apartheid in Afghanistan." *Human Rights Quarterly* 3, 3 (August 2001): 733–68.

Walker, R. B. J. *Inside/Outside: International Relations as Political Theory.* Cambridge, UK: Cambridge University Press, 1993.

Walsh, James. "National Preferences and International Institutions: Evidence from European Monetary Integration." *International Studies Quarterly* 45, 1 (March 2001): 59–80.

Weldes, Jutta. *Constructing National Interests: The United States and the Cuban Missile Crisis.* Minneapolis: University of Minnesota Press, 1999.

Wendt, Alexander. "The Agent-Structure Problem in International Relations Theory." *International Organization* 41, 3:(1987) 335–70.

_____. "Anarchy Is What States Make of It." *International Organization,* 46, 2 (1992): 391–425.

_____. "Collective Identity Formation and the International State." *American Political Science Review,* 88, 2 (1994): 384–96.

_____. "Constructing International Politics." *International Security* 20, 1 (Summer 1995): 71–81.

_____. "Driving with the Rearview Mirror: On the Rational Science of Institutional Design." *International Organization,* 55, 4 (2001): 1019–49.

_____. "Identity and Structural Change in International Politics." In *The Return of Culture and Identity in IR Theory.* eds. Yosef Lapid and Friedrich Kratochwil. Boulder, CO: Lynne Rienner, 1996: 47–64.

_____. "Levels of Analysis vs. Agents and Structures." *Review of International Studies,* 18, 2 (1992): 181–85.

_____. "On Constitution and Causation in International Relations." *Review of International Studies,* 24, 5 (1998): 101–17.

_____. "On the Via Media: A Response to the Critics." *Review of International Studies,* 26, 1 (2000): 165–80.

_____. "Social Theory as Cartesian Science: An Auto-critique from a Quantum Perspective." In *Constructivism and International Relations.* eds. Stefano Guzzini and Anna Leander, London and New York: Routledge: 2006.

_____. *Social Theory of International Politics.* London: Cambridge University Press, 1999.

_____. "The State as Person in International Theory." *Review of International Studies,* 30, 2 (2004): 289–316.

_____. "Why a World State Is Inevitable." *European Journal of International Relations,* 9, 4 (2003): 491–542.

_____, and Daniel Friedheim. "Hierarchy under Anarchy: Informal Empire and the East German State." *International Organization* 49, 4 (Autumn 1995): 689–721.

Wight, Colin. *Agents, Structures and International Relations: Politics as Ontology.* Cambridge, UK: Cambridge University Press, 2006.

_____. "They Shoot Dead Horses Don't They: Locating Agency in the Agent-Structure Problematique." *European Journal of International Relations,* 5, 1 (1999): 109–42.

Winch, Peter. *The Idea of a Social Science.* London: Routledge and Kegan Paul, 1958.

Zaum, Dominique. *The Sovereignty Paradox: The Norms and Politics of International Statebuilding.* New York: Oxford University Press, 2007.

Zehfuss, Maja. *Constructivism in International Relations: The Politics of Reality.* London: Cambridge University Press, 2002.

CHAPTER 7

Positivism, Critical Theory, and Postmodern Understandings

We undertake in this chapter a discussion of the vigorous critiques of mainstream positivist international relations theorizing by **critical theorists** and **postmodernists** (or **poststructuralists**). As in the previous chapter on constructivism, a similar critique that relies on interpretive understanding made by feminists is presented in Chapter Eight. Scholars associated with critical theory and postmodernism have been referred to generically as postpositivists or poststructuralists. Such terminology, however, can be misleading. Although their critiques underscore the subjectivity of human inquiry and reject notions of pure objectivity or value-free science they associate with positivism, many critical theorists (as with constructivists and feminists) have not bolted completely from science *per se* as is evident by their use of empirical evidence in case studies.

For its part, science is open to scholarship that incorporates interpretive understandings along with the canons of logic and evidence that are central to positivism. Furthermore, the line between critical theory and postmodernism is a thin one, some scholars crossing over from one side to the other. Linguistic analysis in postmodern studies, for example, has a clear place in critical theory that scrutinizes "cover stories" and unpacks or deconstructs the language used and roles played by those in positions of power. We represent this boundary, then, as a permeable or dotted line between critical theorists that have not made as radical a departure from the positivist mainstream as most postmodern (or poststructural) scholars have.

What we observe in IR and the other social (as in the natural) sciences is heavily influenced by the interpretive understandings we have of the concepts we employ. Many (though not all) of these critiques or interpretive understandings are informed by **phenomenology**— a subjective or interpretive understanding in human consciousness of what we observe or think we see in the world around us. Before addressing these critiques of mainstream IR scholarship, however, we need first to specify further what we mean by positivist, scientific or "modern" approaches to theory building in IR that go beyond the brief summary in Chapter One. This also entails a summary of intellectual precursors. Without such background, it is difficult to understand the arguments of critical theorists and postmodernists. In essence, these approaches are primarily concerned with critiqueing the mainstream literature discussed in Part One of this book.

POSITIVISM

Positivism involves a commitment to a unified view of science—a belief that it is possible to adapt the epistemologies and methodologies of the natural sciences to explain the social world, which includes international relations. Positivists believe that objective knowledge of the world is possible and, hence, have a faith and commitment to the Enlightenment's rationalist tradition.

We find in the writings of the Frenchman René Descartes (1596–1650) a key contribution to mathematics and the rational bases of modern science. Quarrels between rationalists like Descartes who emphasized the logic to be found in the canons of **deduction** and empiricists who made **inductive** inferences from what they observed ultimately would be resolved in a new rational-empirical synthesis that remains at the core of positivism—a "scientific" approach to knowing.

It was the Scottish writer David Hume (1711–76) who objected to causal inferences being drawn too readily. A skeptic at heart, Hume recognized that causality is itself not directly observable but merely a construct used by human beings to make what they observe around them understandable or even predictable. To Hume, causality is no more than an inference human beings draw from the conjunction of impressions about the things we observe. For example, when we perceive that some factor or event (X) precedes another (Y), our minds may be prone to think that X is the cause of Y.

Consistent with Hume and also influenced by the positivism of the French philosopher Auguste Comte (1798–1857), John Stuart Mill (1806–73) developed formal canons of induction that would allow both natural and social scientists to arrive at causal truth claims by applying systematically one or another of a series of specified tests or methods to observed phenomena.

MILL'S CANONS OF CAUSALITY

John Stuart Mill's (1806–73) understandings of causality underlie the application of the "scientific" method to the testing of hypotheses in the social sciences in general, IR in particular. Using one or another of these canons of induction leads us to infer a causal relation between an independent variable (X) and the dependent variable (Y) it purportedly explains:

Inductive Canon No. 1: the method of agreement—*X is always present whenever Y is also present. Hypothetical example: when in our research we always see an arms race (X) having begun prior to the outbreak of war (Y).*

Inductive Canon No. 2: the method of difference—*X is always absent whenever Y is also absent. Hypothetical example: when in our research we observe no arms races in prolonged periods of peace marked by the absence of war.*

Inductive Canon No. 3: the joint method of agreement and difference—*when X and Y are both present in one set but not in another, as in controlled experiments when X is put in one experiment to see if Y appears, but X is omitted from the other experiment in the expectation that Y will not appear. Hypothetical example: when in two separately controlled experimental simulations, an arms race is introduced in one simulation, but not in the other—the former results in the outbreak of war, but the latter simulation remains without war.*

Inductive Canon No. 4: the method of concomitant variation—*when X and Y both vary in relation to one another either in the same or opposite directions. In other words, a positive or direct relation—as X increases (or decreases), Y also increases (or decreases). Or a negative or inverse relation—as X increases, Y decreases, or as X decreases, Y increases. Hypothetical example: when in our research we assemble all the cases we identify of arms races and all the cases of the outbreak of war, we find a direct* **correlation** *between the two—the* more *arms racing occurs, the* more *wars tend to break out. If, by contrast, we were to find an inverse correlation (rather unlikely in this example), then we would observe that the* more *arms racing occurs, the* lesser *the frequency of war breaking out.*

Inductive Canon No. 5: the method of residues—*as when, in a statistical analysis of the percentage of explained and unexplained variance, a certain independent variable (X) or certain independent variables (X1, X2, etc.) have been identified as accounting for some of the variations in Y, the remaining variation can be accounted for as due to other independent variables present even if they have not been identified as such. Hypothetical example: when in our research arms races account for much, but not all of the cases in which wars break out, we conclude that other factors we may or may not be able to identify account for the rest of the explanation.*

Positivists identify one or another of these causal sequences in the hypotheses or causal models they test empirically. For example, if X is present, then (one tends to find) Y directly or inversely following variations in X. We find different combinations of cause-effect sequences in the often complex causal models constructed by positivist theorists. Some factors that must be present to effect a certain outcome are referred to as *necessary,* but they may not be *sufficient* to have this effect. Theorists wedded to a positivist epistemology try to identify conditions or factors—variables or constants—that are *necessary* or *sufficient* to produce expected effects or outcomes. [Adapted from A. James Gregor, *Metapolitics: A Brief Inquiry into the Conceptual Language of Political Science* (New York: Free Press, 1971), 146–50.]

CAUSE-EFFECT RELATIONS

We also can identify five different patterns of cause-effect relations employed in positivist theorizing:

1. *There can be, as we have discussed, a single causal or independent variable X that can be used to explain or predict an effect on another variable Y that depends causally upon or reacts to variations in X:*

$$X \rightarrow Y.$$

Hypothetical example: When our hypothesis holds that international tensions (X) are causally related to the outbreak of war (Y).

2. *Sometimes an intervening variable Z comes between the independent variable X and the dependent variable Y, moderating or altering the effect X otherwise would have had on Y:* $X \rightarrow Z \rightarrow Y$. *Hypothetical example: When our hypothesis holds that international tensions (X) that can lead to war are exacerbated when policy elites (Z) with a militant orientation come to power or, conversely, reduced when peace-prone policy elites oriented toward conflict resolution take office, the former are more likely to go to*

war (Y) than the latter. The intervening variable—whether war- or peace-oriented policy elites come to power—matters causally.

3. In other cases the independent variable X is itself the result of (or caused by) some third variable Z in what effectively is a "developmental sequence": $Z \rightarrow X \rightarrow Y$. Hypothetical example: In this case, our hypothesis holds that whether war- or peace-oriented elites (Z) come to power has a causal effect on the level of international tensions causally related to the outbreak of war (war-oriented policy elites tending to increase tensions leading to war and peace-oriented elites tending to reduce tensions or create a climate more propitious to peace).

4. Sometimes we see dual or double causes as when X and Z are both causally related to Y, still the dependent variable:

Hypothetical example: In this case our hypothesis holds that international tensions (X) and orientations of policy elites in power (Z) separately are causally related to war (Y)—thus international tensions can cause war or policy elites on their own to choose to go to war quite apart from whether the climate of relations (X) is one of high or reduced tensions. An extension of double cause is the case of multiple causation involving three or more independent variables identified in this case as causally related to the outbreak of war.

5. Looking to the outcome side, dual or double effect occurs when X is causal to both Y and Z:

Hypothetical example: In this case our hypothesis holds that the climate of relations or level of international tensions (X) may produce a greater or lesser likelihood of going to war (Y) and, at the same time, influence whether war-like or peace-oriented policy elites (Z) come to power. As with multiple causation, we also can extend this reasoning to cases of multiple effects involving three or more dependent variables. Dual or multiple effect is also the "spurious correlation" case in which the apparent association or correlation between Y and Z is due only to the fact both are affected causally by the same variable X—variations in Y (likelihood of the outbreak of war) and Z (orientations of policy elites toward war or peace) are each due to variations in X (international tensions). [We draw these cause-effect relations, from Hayward R. Alker, Jr., Mathematics and Politics (New York: Macmillan, 1965) as presented in Ted Robert Gurr, Politimetrics (Englewood Cliffs, NJ: Prentice Hall, 1972), 167.]

Given such causal understandings in models and associated hypotheses, positivists then turn to operationalizing their variables—putting them in measurable form or constructing data-based indicators that allow the researcher to test these cause-effect propositions empirically. Evidentiary tests—whether quantitative or non-quantitative—are used *to confirm hypotheses with some degree of confidence, refute them, or consider the empirical tests inconclusive, thus calling for more data gathering and further tests. This approach to testing truth claims captures the essence of what is commonly referred to as* scientific method.

The epistemological empiricism adopted by scholars in the "Vienna circle" of the 1930s took a somewhat extreme rationalist, scientific form called **logical positivism**—the pursuit of a pure science that would separate fact from value and achieve the precision of mathematics. Among members of the Vienna circle were such luminaries as Moritz Schlick, Otto Neurath, and Rudolf Carnap. They were also influenced by the earlier work of their contemporary, Ludwig Wittgenstein, whose *Tractatus Logico-Philosophicus* (1921) related the thought and ideas we have to the words we use, focusing on the necessary logic and precision of language applied to observations about the world. Following Wittgenstein, the Vienna circle and its followers would seek both logical precision and clarity in scientific language.

In the mid-1930s, Karl Popper addressed empirical tests of **hypotheses** drawn from theories. To "prove" empirically that a certain hypothesis or universal proposition is true is virtually impossible since to do so in an absolute sense would mean submitting it to an infinite number of tests in space and time. Popper argued that to be scientific, claims or propositions have to be stated in falsifiable form. Falsifiability means simply that if a proposition is false, it must be possible empirically to show that it is false. With varying degrees of confidence based on logical consistency and available evidence, one can accept a falsifiable proposition as possibly true at least until, by experiment or other scientific means, one actually shows it to be false.

In the post–World War II period, a broad, somewhat watered-down application of positivist premises to the social sciences—an approach that also included incorporation of statistical methodologies and the use of mathematical equations to specify causal relations among variables—reflected a critical reaction to this "modernist" epistemology. Taking various critiques into account, refinement of positivist epistemology continued during the 1950s and 1960s. Carl Hempel, for example, set forth a deductive-nomological schema for scientific explanation. Hempel applied this formalized deductive approach in the formulation of both universal and probabilistic law-like statements. This covering law approach to theory is still the preferred choice of many scholars working within the positivist framework.

Thomas S. Kuhn's effort in his identification of "scientific revolutions" focused on the natural sciences, but it has perhaps had even greater impact on understanding in the social sciences.[1] Arguing that **paradigms,** or frameworks of understanding, influence the way we observe and make sense of the world around us, Kuhn was criticized for his alleged **relativism**—a direct challenge to the positivist school. To some of his opponents, knowledge was understood to be empirically grounded and not so arbitrary as to be based on such pre-existing or newly discovered frameworks of understanding.

To be fair, Kuhn did not reject empirically based claims as such. He argued only that when theories and component concepts associated with a particular paradigm are challenged empirically or theoretically, holders of this paradigm may be forced through some modification to accommodate the new finding or insight or give way to a new paradigm. Thus, the Ptolomeic idea of the Earth as center of the universe—an understanding also closely tied to and reinforcing certain underlying religious beliefs—was toppled by the Copernican revolution in human understanding of the heavens, a paradigm shift developed further from the empirical observations of Galileo. A highly complex, Earth-centric, Ptolomeic astronomy (still used in celestial navigation) was replaced by a vision that portrayed the Earth as merely one among a number of planets revolving around the Sun—the solar system.

Similarly, it was Einstein's theory of relativity that challenged the Newtonian understanding of gravity and the laws of motion, effectively reducing the Newtonian mechanics paradigm to Earth-based, observable laws. These laws were not as directly applicable either to the macro-universal domain of astrophysics or to the micro-domain concerning motion of subatomic particles in quantum mechanics. Of course, even these new paradigms have remained subject to challenge in an eternally skeptical, scientific approach to knowledge.

There is substantial debate within the social sciences generally, and in particular fields such as international relations, as to whether these fields are developed sufficiently to justify identification of paradigms. Setting this issue aside, the important point in Kuhn's thesis is that knowledge, even in the natural sciences, is grounded in human understanding in the form of paradigms that influence observation and the construction of concepts and theories. At least as much or even more so, such interpretive understanding or agreed meaning would seem to apply to the social sciences that deal with human behavior in all its forms.

Although Kuhn's work received criticism from positivists, by no means did he abandon scientific premises. That's why we represent his argument as coming from within the scientific or positivist community. There is no rejection of science *per se*, but his work on paradigms has influenced or is similar to much of the thinking we place under the interpretive-understanding umbrella.

The same is the case with Stephen Toulmin who argued the lenses or "spectacles" one wears affect science and scientific progress in the continuing quest to make the world around us more intelligible.[2] Accordingly, we need to scrutinize closely and critically the principal images that currently inform much international relations theory. Although Toulmin's critique occurs within the positivist, natural science discourse, he takes a stand against any claim to the idea that work in the sciences can ever be value free. Instead, we need to be more humble in developing our understandings, taking explicitly into account as best we can the subjective dimensions that influence our inquiries. Critical scrutiny of our work by others not wedded to our projects is a safety valve institutionalized in scientific discourse. This discourse helps to keep us from errors to be found in the logic of the arguments we make or the evidence we use to buttress our truth claims.

For his part, Imre Lakatos preferred to see the pursuit of science not as a series of paradigmatic revolutions, but rather in more positive terms as in the spawning of multiple research programs and the ensuing competition among them.[3] Progress in IR from this perspective is facilitated by the development of research programs comparable in durability to those in the natural sciences. Changes in research programs occur only in the fullness of time, often many years after initial challenges to theories within its scope. One falsification is not enough. The bases for such a research-program change do not become established overnight, but rather as part of a progressive process over time.

INTELLECTUAL PRECURSORS: PHENOMENOLOGY AND HERMENEUTICS

Contemporary critiques of mainstream theorizing in IR and the other social sciences reflect to a greater or lesser degree the influence of *phenomenology*. It is, as noted above, a philosophical understanding that leads one to reject claims to knowing any "objective" reality independent of the human consciousness that, after all, gives meaning to the world around us. Interpretation is central to what we see—a reflective, intuitive process by which we gain understanding. We find the influence of phenomenology not just in critical theory and postmodernism, but also in the interpretive understandings of constructivism discussed in Chapter Six and in feminist scholarship we take up in Chapter Eight.

Phenomenology responds to what is really a very old philosophical question. It was, after all, Plato who raised the problem of distinguishing between appearances and underlying realities—the ideal forms, essence, or spirit that lies beyond our senses or world of appearances. In the Platonic understanding "knowledge has for its natural object the real—to know the truth about reality."[4] There is a unity to be found in knowledge between an object we observe and its underlying essence or form. Something may appear to be beautiful, for example, but it is the underlying idea or "essential form of beauty" that makes it appear to us as such. Realizing an underlying form of justice in Plato's ideal republic is an aim or challenge not just within state and domestic society, but also by extension to international relations. This concern for justice continues to resonate today, particularly among critical theorists.

In his *Critique of Pure Reason,* Immanuel Kant (1724–1804) takes up this question or distinction between appearance and reality. Kant calls the objects we observe *phenomena,* which he distinguishes from the abstract *noumena*—the unknowable essence of objects as things in themselves, quite apart from how we may see them or how they may appear.[5] Georg W.F. Hegel (1770–1831) in his *Phenomenology of Spirit* (1807) did accept Kant's claim that we cannot know the "in-itself"—this inner essence of what we observe. Hegel explored the ways and means by which we can unify the objective (the "in-itself or what something actually is") with the subjective (the "for-itself or what we understand it to be") in our consciousness of ourselves and the world around us that we experience. How are we to unify what actually *is* (the objective—the "in-itself") with what we observe or experience in our consciousness (the subjective—the "for-itself")? How can we know "what truth is ... if consciousness [is] still filled and weighed down with . . . so-called natural representations, thoughts, and opinions?" We seek to get beyond these prior perspectives or illusions and focus instead on the phenomena themselves—what Hegel called following the phenomenological path. To him, we try to grasp or understand the essence or "spirit" underlying appearances: "Through an exhaustive experience [in the subjective or conscious] 'of itself'" (the phenomenological path we follow), we can in principle attain "the knowledge of what it [the phenomenon] is in itself."[6]

More easily said than done! As with Kant, phenomenologists following the leads of Edmund Husserl (1859–1938) and his student Martin Heidegger (1889–1976) disputed Hegel's claim that such reality can be uncovered so decisively. Phenomenologists following Husserl have engaged in reflective sudy of phenomena in an effort to approach knowledge of underlying realities in developing what we in this volume, following Weber, prefer to call interpretive understandings. In our reflections about what we observe, we try to identify the meanings or essence of what we experience. For his part, Heidegger focused not only on the objects we experience, but also on the sense of our own being and what we understand to be the essence of things in general—our ontology in relation to the world we experience. Although Heidegger denied being an existentialist, Husserl's influence was reflected in the **existentialism** found particularly in French literary and philosophical circles—Jean-Paul Sartre (1905–80) himself was directly influenced by Husserl.

In sum, phenomenology leads one not to take things as they may at first appear (or have been made to appear). We probe for what underlies or stands behind appearances. We take "a close look at certain phenomena specifically considered in isolation from current or dominant theories of explanation" that may cloud or bias our vision. More to the point, we include "all phenomena of experience" and exclude all "metaphysical and reality judgments."[7]

The language scientists use is a major research concern of postmodernists in particular. **Hermeneutics** directly challenges positivism, arguing that social facts are constituted and given meaning by the structures of language and that consciousness can be studied only as mediated by language. Language is what gives material conditions meaning for humans. Hermeneutic approaches seek to understand or recover the meanings common to actors by interpreting the self-understanding of actors. This is in contrast to the positivist explanation of independent causal processes. Luminaries include Martin Heidegger and Ludwig Wittgenstein in his later work. Indeed, Wittgenstein's *Philosophical Investigations* (1953) paints a picture more prone to coping with ambiguities that come from the context of language use.

We will withhold until later in the chapter discussion of German and French continental European perspectives that have also had an impact on the IR field: (a) Jürgen Habermas and his associates in what is commonly referred to as the Frankfurt school of critical theory and (b) influences on postmodernism such as Friedrich Nietzsche and an updating of his ideas by postmodernist French scholars Michel Foucault, Jacques Derrida, and Jean-François Lyotard.

To summarize the postmodern and critical-theory critique, positivism has been under assault for its attempts to separate facts from values, to define and operationalize value-neutral concepts into precisely and accurately measurable variables, and to test truth claims in the form of hypotheses drawn from or integral to theories. Whether using quantitative or statistical methods or such non-quantitative (or "qualitative") methods as case and comparative-case studies, those who have tried to be scientific have been criticized for ignoring or taking insufficient account of the personal or human dimension of scholarship.

Human consciousness and the inherent subjectivity of human beings matter. As essentially subjective creatures, we are not really able to separate ourselves from the world we are observing. We are part of it. Even if human agency does not impact the "laws" that govern the natural world, what we say and do has effects in the social world. Thus we are hampered by an inability to be completely independent of the phenomena we are observing, however hard we may try to be objective. Our inherent subjectivity just gets in the way.

This happens even in the natural sciences when the concepts we develop and use often have their origins as metaphors drawn from human experiences. Thus physicists speak of "particles" or "waves" of light—references that evoke seashore imagery. That there are "black holes" in outer space is yet another example of the human side grappling with meaning in the natural sciences, describing extraterrestrial phenomena with Earth-bound vocabularies. We leave to others to determine whether such metaphors are apt or whether they mislead us. What interests us here is simply to recognize that positivist science—whether dealing with natural or social phenomena—cannot escape human subjectivity. Put another way, complete value-free science is just not possible.

Of the two, postmodernists are the more skeptical of "scientific" truth claims that are so dependent on the meanings we assign to the concepts we employ. In the extreme, some postmodernists see knowledge in entirely relativist terms. Critical theorists, by contrast, tend not to abandon science, but try merely to expose ideological claims often masquerading as theories with "scientific" bases of support—false pretenses used to legitimate self-serving practices. Indeed, critical theorists search for the ways and means by which the powerful attempt to legitimate their often exploitative positions of dominance—their self-serving manipulation of ideas or meanings in theories others are led to believe have scientific underpinnings.

CRITICAL THEORY: MAJOR ASSUMPTIONS

While IR scholars who are self-proclaimed critical theorists may have their differences, they would agree on the following assumptions. First, the study of IR should be about emancipatory politics. Whatever knowledge critical theory may generate, it is geared toward social and political transformation. To achieve this transformation, the first step is the critical scrutiny of the current understanding of international politics, to understand and explain the existing realities of IR and how they developed over time. To avoid mere idealism—"this is what the world should be"—IR scholars must explain and criticize the current political order in terms of the principles embedded in political institutions and cultural practices. Work done on the comparative historical sociology of states illustrates the use of empirical evidence.[8]

The concept of emancipation is particularly important, and can be traced back to the Enlightenment and particularly the work of Immanuel Kant. Kant, among other things, was interested in how competitive power relations among states could be transformed into a more cosmopolitan order of perpetual peace. Emancipation consists of an essentially negative conception of freedom that emphasizes removing repressive constraints or relations of domination. Simply put, critical theorists are interested in the relation between power and freedom. Influenced intellectually by Karl Marx, many critical theorists draw from his analysis of human inequality and his normative goal of eliminating exploitation.

The theme of emancipation is a primary concern among those who identify with the "Frankfurt School," which is in some respects an outgrowth of the critical work of an earlier generation within this school of thought that included Theodor Adorno, Max Horkheimer, and Herbert Marcuse. The Frankfurt School essentially turned a Marxist critique of political economy into a critique of ideology. The development of critical theory has included rather diverse philosophical influences: escaping from ideological constraints, as in the revolutionary spirit of Rousseau; searching for universal moral principles with the universality of application found in Kant; identifying the oppression of class or other socioeconomic structures observed by Marx; understanding the role of human psychologies in relationships of dominance drawn from the work of Freud; and rejecting determinism in favor of a more Gramsci-style Marxism that adopts a normative, but practical approach to challenging and overthrowing structures of domination.

From the beginning, the Frankfurt School and its current best-known theoretician, Jürgen Habermas, have taken seriously Karl Marx's assertion that heretofore philosophers had only interpreted the world, but the point was to change it. Normative and ethical concerns cannot or should not be separated from our theories of international relations, but should be embedded in them. Instead of using our reason for technical, instrumental means to maintain the stability of society, the larger questions that animated ancient Greek scholars such as Plato need to be seriously addressed: What is the good and just society? Systematic investigation of the existing order includes criticism which, in turn, supports practical political theory that can map routes to societal and political transformation. For critical international relations theorists, the good society is a just and democratic order that should be extended beyond the state to the international domain in the creation of a cosmopolitan community. Simply put, critical theorists are on the voluntarist extreme end of the voluntarism-determinism continuum, seeing great transformative potential residing in those able to see through ideological and other ideational masks that disguise or obscure unjust, exploitative realities.

Andrew Linklater, for example, analyzes what he terms a "triple transformation" required to undermine the relations among sovereignty, territory, and national conceptions of citizenship. These transformations involve widespread recognition (1) that certain moral, political, and legal principles need to be universalized; (2) that material inequality must be reduced; and (3) that there is need for respect for ethnic, cultural, and gender differences.[9]

Second, critical theorists have investigated the relation between knowledge and interest. Knowledge seeking is inherently political. Detached theorizing is an impossibility and a sham. As Robert Cox succinctly stated: "theory is always for someone and for some purpose."[10] With theories being embedded in social and political life, critical theory examines the purposes served by particular theories. Some critical theorists argue that beliefs held by many positivist scholars necessarily bias their truth claims and may well be part of global ideological schemes to legitimate particular world orders. In supporting an alleged agenda of domination, it may be convenient to advance ideologies often masquerading as scientifically based theories. One of the tasks of critical theorists is to unmask such deceptions, probe for deeper understandings or meanings, and expose the class or elite interests these ideologies or alleged theories are designed to serve. As for themselves, critical theorists believe in putting their cards on the table by being "self-reflective."

Third, and following from the above, critical IR theorists have scrutinized the work of realists and liberals in particular. This even applies to the supposed founding fathers of realism. It has been argued, for example, that Thucydides' concern with language and practices (as evident in the numerous dialogues he reconstructs in his *History of the Peloponnesian War*) can be viewed as the beginning of critical theory. Far from being driven by events outside their control (anarchy, distribution of capabilities or balance of power), individuals are the conscious initiators of the events described. Similarly, it has been suggested that Machiavelli is really an interpretive theorist due to his sensitivity to the historical context of political action. At the time he was writing, the modern nation-state was just emerging as a new form of political community in the shadow of Christian universalism. With the political world in flux, Machiavelli did not immediately reject the established Christian temporal understanding for a new form of realist universalism.[11]

According to critical theorists, both realism and liberalism claim to be problem-solving, technical approaches to IR. As a result, there is a built-in bias toward stability and maintaining the *status quo* of international politics. Their work essentially provides answers on how to manage IR and keep the international system within stable bounds and avoid disruption. Transforming IR for the betterment of the vast majority of humanity is supposedly not the goal.

In the IR theories they examine, a major goal of critical theorists is to uncover underlying power and other motives these theories allegedly advance. Not surprisingly, much of their critique about the IR mainstream has been directed toward realists and neorealists whose theories knowingly or unknowingly give legitimacy to states and relations among them. To some critical theorists, these are not really theories. They are instead cover stories—ideologies serving state, class, or elite interests merely masquerading as if they were theories.

One example of criticism applied to a positivist understanding of international relations is Richard Ashley's comment on Kenneth Waltz's system-level structural explanation for the behaviors we observe among states. The influence of Habermas' critical theory is apparent in the following passage. Referring to Waltz and the "poverty of neorealism," Ashley asserts:

> What emerges is a positivist structuralism that treats the given order as the natural order, limits rather than expands political discourse, negates or trivializes the significance of variety across

time and place, subordinates all practice to an interest in control, bows to the ideal of a social power beyond responsibility, and thereby deprives political interaction of those practical capacities which make social learning and creative change possible. What emerges is an ideology that anticipates, legitimizes, and orients a totalitarian project of global proportions: the rationalization of global politics.[12]

Neoliberal institutionalism hardly fares much better, given its emphasis on maintaining international stability at times of international economic unrest. As Robert Cox has noted, neoliberalism is situated between the system of states and the capitalist world economy, providing insight on how the two can coexist. Theory can provide insight on how to resolve crises between them.[13]

Critical theory may be viewed separately from postmodernism since most critical theorists retain strict methodological criteria to guide their work. Theirs is not a complete rejection of science or of positivism. Nevertheless, in terms of intellectual precursors and key assumptions, aspects of critical theory overlap with, or can be understood more broadly, as related to a postmodernist understanding in IR.

POSTMODERNISM: MAJOR ASSUMPTIONS

For postmodernists, what we see, what we choose to see or measure, and the mechanisms or methods we employ are all of human construction that essentially rely on perception and cognitive processes influenced particularly by prior understandings and meanings. Even the language we use reflects an embedded set of values that are an integral part of any culture and found in the narratives or stories people commonly employ to depict understandings of their observations and experiences in the world around them. As means to understand IR, postmodernists engage in linguistic deconstruction of what has been said or written, employing discursive practices that emphasize reasoned argument.

First, as with critical theorists and feminists, postmodernists assume an intimate connection between power and knowledge in the analysis of IR. Following the arguments of Michel Foucault, the production of knowledge is a political process that has a mutually supportive relation to power. This is true not only in IR, but in all aspects of political life where power is exercised. This is not a realist emphasis on the material basis of power, but rather a focus on how actors and commentators, such as during the Cold War or after September 11th, attempt to impose authoritative interpretations on events. Hence reality is structured by language, and the development of linguistic discourses results in a structure or system consisting of knowledge, subjects, and objects. For example, the development of the concept of sovereignty and associated terms and assumptions—state, anarchy, borders, security, and such human identities—is at the heart of much postmodern work in IR.

Second, in terms of methodology, some postmodernists follow Friedrich Nietzsche's lead in tracing over time the genealogy and significance of power-knowledge relations and such dominant discourses in IR as sovereignty and anarchy.[14] Knowledge is always conditioned by a particular time and place. Understanding how particular interpretations of the past continue to guide current thinking and behavior also involves highlighting what has been excluded in historical narratives. Hence, as Foucault argued, history is not about the uncovering of facts and building up a composite picture of the past, but rather exposing "the endlessly repeated play of dominations."[15]

In his studies of sanity, sexuality, and punishment, Foucault explored how concepts we use commonly developed or were socially constructed over time, challenging the generally accepted meanings these concepts purport to convey and the power-based human relations they sustain.

In engaging in this genealogical excavation, many postmodernists follow the approach of Jacques Derrida, who seeks to find the text and subtexts in order to deconstruct—unpack and take apart—the meanings embedded in what we say or write and even in the ways we act. By the term *text* he doesn't simply mean that which is written, but rather it is a metaphor for the need to understand the world as a whole and how different interpretations not only represent but also constitute the world, an ontological position.[16]

Derrida leads us to a poststructural turn, going beyond or not being bound by the accepted symbols or established structures that effectively channel our understandings—a reaction by him and other poststructuralists of similar mind to the universal claims we find in the structuralism of both French philosophical thought and the branch of anthropology called semiotics. Particularly objectionable to them is the attempt to unify the social sciences with a single structuralist methodology based on identifying linguistic or cultural signs and differences. For their part, Françoís Lyotard and his followers reject grand metanarratives employed purportedly to explain all of the world in scientific terms. Scholars arguing in this genre raise similar objections to balance of power and other metanarratives in IR they see masquerading as if they were scientifically based theoretical explanations.

Third, in the process of engaging in genealogical excavations of dominant discourses and power-knowledge relations, postmodernists highlight competing historical perspectives, narratives, or trajectories. Following Nietzsche, not only is there no single historical truth, but rather multiple ones and we have no standard to judge them as no objective standard for truth exists.

This view is different from that of Kuhn and Toulmin's use of paradigms or lenses that influence scientific work. They assume a real, discoverable objective reality out there, but we adopt different lenses that highlight and interpret "facts" in different ways. For postmodernists, these perspectives actually constitute the "real world." A basic ontological assumption, the identification of an historical narrative is not simply the interpretation of a series of actions, but the means by which "reality" is conferred upon events.

Just as postmodernists reject the idea that there is a single truth, so, too, do they reject the idea that the only way to gain knowledge is through a positivist methodology whose application is restricted to conventional approaches favored by realists and liberals. For example, postmodernists have taken the lead not only in textual analysis, but also in the interpretation of art and theater. Christine Sylvester, for example, shows how IR influences the mission of museums and, in turn, how visitors experience and intrepret the art that is displayed.[17]

Finally, many postmodernists have a normative commitment to the idea that the sovereign state is not the only means by which to organize political and social life. The language of IR that emphasizes states in a condition of anarchy reinforces the current exclusionary paradigm that effectively precludes alternative forms of political and social organization. Furthermore, the territorialization of political identity justifies a political discourse and policies that affirm the right of state officials to brutalize their subjects and restrict the possibility of expanding democratic values. Hence postmodernists take issue with the ontological perspective of realists and liberals that privilege the state as the unit of analysis and make it an ontological given for IR theorizing. In some postmodernist understandings, states do not simply use force in an instrumental, means-ends calculation to achieve certain objectives. Rather, the role of violence is important even in the origins and constitution of the state itself.[18]

In sum, postmodernists dive beneath the surface—they deconstruct the words and phrases or text we use—and look for underlying meanings or subtexts in our communications or the narratives we adopt to depict our understandings. As subjective creatures, we human beings are ourselves the source of knowledge we have about the world around us. Even our own identities are formed by the way we come to understand the world around us; the self is defined subjectively by each of us in relation to (an)other.

CRITICAL THEORISTS, POSTMODERNISTS, AND THEIR CRITICS

Mainstream IR has consistently ignored critical theory and postmodernism. When it has addressed these interpretive understandings, there have been two major lines of argument.

First, similar to charges leveled against economic structuralists, critical theorists and postmodernists substitute ideology for explanation and engage in wishful thinking unconstrained by reality. A realist would no doubt suggest this literature belongs in this volume's final chapter on normative theory where the *ought* as opposed to the *is* holds sway. One realist, Randall Schweller, has commented that Andrew Linklater "argues by fiat rather than by the weight of hard evidence, which is in scant supply here." Radical propositions are "supported by nothing more than references to some other critical theorist who shares Linklater's vision or tendency to rely on slippery, undefined, and unmeasured concepts." By Linklater not taking seriously the obstacles to his triple transformation of the international system (increased *moral* and *economic* equality while remaining sensitive to *cultural* differences), Linklater's work "will appear as little more than an intellectual exercise in historical speculation and theoretical wishful thinking."[19]

Second, and following from the above, is the charge that critical theorists and postmodernists simply do not follow the cannons of positivism and causal theorizing. The editors of one of the major IR journals, for example, justified the exclusion of critical theory and postmodernist articles and associated critiques of positivism in the following manner:

> Little of this debate was published in IO, since IO has been committed to an enterprise that postmodernism denies: the use of evidence to adjudicate between truth claims. In contrast to conventional and critical constructivism, postmodernism falls clearly outside the social science enterprise, and in international relations research risks becoming self-referential and disengaged from the world, protests to the contrary notwithstanding.[20]

As one postmodernist responded: "There is a brazen acknowledgment of censorship and suppression in the statement about the publication history of arguably the discipline's most influential journal."

It is true that for many postmodernists, claims made to empirically based, objective truth are necessarily hollow. Our understandings and meanings are, after all, humanly constructed. In the extreme, no knowledge or truth is possible apart from the motivations and purposes people put into their construction. From this extreme perspective (not all postmodernists go so far), truth is entirely relative. It is this highly relative approach to human understanding that leads some postmodernists to deny even the possibility of any empirically based truth claims, thus underscoring their total rejection of positivism.

These are, to say the least, examples of significant challenges to "modernist" science or positivism more generally and to international relations theory in particular. It is difficult, however, to deny or dismiss scientific methodologies that have produced so much accumulated knowledge in so many diverse fields of human inquiry. Defenders of positivism see critical and postmodernist thinkers as misrepresenting the positivist scientific enterprise which, after all, retains an inherently skeptical orientation to truth claims and demands continued and unending empirical tests of such propositions.

On the other hand, postmodern critiques make us skeptical of truth claims made by mainstream journals inducing us to exercise critical scrutiny of the assumptions made about causality, the categories we adopt, the factors we select, how we define these variables or constants, and the way we relate them to each other in the explanatory or predictive theories positivists generate. The cover stories identified by critical theorists and the narratives and particular uses of language that inform postmodernists already have influenced substantially the ways in which concepts are developed and research is conducted across the IR field. Taking the human or subjective into account has encouraged IR theorists—no matter what image or interpretive understanding influences their work—to be more theoretically self-consciousness.

SUMMATION

Positivism—modernist science and the scientific method that combine the logic of rational theorizing with empirical test—has occupied the mainstream of IR theory. In recent decades, however, the Weberian concept of *Verstehen* and phenomenology—a focus on human consciousness as essential to our coming to know the world of which we are a part—are at the root of interpretive understandings in both critical theory and postmodern thought.

If the central question of epistemology is how we know what we think we know, critical theorists and postmodernists set aside many of the abstract universalist claims of logical positivists, focusing instead on the human perception and understandings that give diverse meanings to the concepts and theories we formulate and the behavior we observe. Although some in the extreme entirely reject the scientific or modernist project and the truth claims associated with it, others seek merely to temper blanket claims of objectivity with interpretive understanding—subjectivity and intersubjectivity that necessarily are a part of what human beings observe, think, and do. As such, the scholar or researcher still wedded to science and its canons is at the same time encouraged or cajoled to be humble about truth claims, knowing how much they remain a function of human subjectivity. Just as it historically has accommodated empirical, theoretical, and philosophical critiques by modifying its methods and understandings, science remains open to critical, postmodernist, and other challenges.

Notes

1. Thomas S. Kuhn, *The Structure of Scientific Revolutions,* 2nd ed. (Chicago: University of Chicago Press, 1962, 1970).
2. See Stephen Toulmin, *Foresight and Understanding: An Enquiry into the Aims of Science* (Bloomington: Indiana University Press, 1961), especially 99–102, 108–09, 114–15.
3. Imre Lakatos in *The Methodology of Scientific Research Programmes: Philosophical Papers,* Vol. I, eds. John Worrall and Gregory Currie (Cambridge, UK: Cambridge University Press, 1978), 8–10, 47–52, 70–72, and 85–93.
4. See Plato, *The Republic,* trans. Francis MacDonald Cornford (New York: Oxford University Press, 1941), ch. XIX, v. 477, 185.

5. Immanuel Kant, *Critique of Pure Reason,* Book II, ch. 3.

6. Howard P. Kainz, trans. and ed. *Hegel's Phenomenology of Spirit* (University Park, PA: Pennsylvania State University Press, 1994), 10–11, 9–10, 96–97, 8.

7. Don Ihde, *Experimental Phenomenology* (Albany, NY: State University of New York, 1986), 14–15, and 36.

8. Paul Keal, *European Conquest and the Rights of Indigenous Peoples* (Cambridge: Cambridge University Press, 2003); Heather Rae, *State Identities and the Homogenisation of Peoples* (New York: Cambridge University Press, 2002).

9. See, for example, *The Transformation of Political Community: Ethical Foundations of the Post-Westphalian Era* (Cambridge: Polity Press, 1998).

10. See Robert Cox, "Social Forces, States, and World Orders" in *Neorealism and Its Critics,* ed. Robert O. Keohane (New York: Columbia University Press, 1986), 207.

11. See, for example, Daniel Garst, "Thucydides and Neorealism," *International Studies Quarterly,* 33 (1989): 3–27; R.B.J. Walker, "The Prince and the Pauper: Tradition, Modernity, and Practice in the Theory of International Relations," In *International/Intertextual Relations: Postmodern Readings of World Politics* eds. James Der Derian and Michael J. Shapiro, (Lexington, MA.: Lexington Books, 1989).

12. See Richard K. Ashley, "The Poverty of Neorealism," in *Neorealism and Its Critics,* ed. Robert O. Keohane (New York: Columbia University Press, 1986), 258.

13. Robert Cox, "Multilateralism and World Order," *Review of International Studies,* 18 (1992), 173.

14. Note that the work of Richard Ashley predates Wendt's constructivist critique of anarchy. Ashley, "Untying the Sovereign State: A Double Reading of the Anarchy Problematique," *Millennium: Journal of International Studies,* 17 (1988): 227–62.

15. Michel Foucault, *Discipline and Punish: The Birth of the Prison* (Harmondsworth, England: Penguin, 1977), 228.

16. Jacques Derrida, *Limited Inc.* (Evanston: Northwestern University Press, 1988).

17. See Christine Sylvester, *Art/Museums: International Relations Where You Least Expect It.* (Boulder, CO: Paradigm, 2008).

18. One of the initial analyses remains the best. See R.B.J. Walker, *Inside/Outside: International Relations as Political Theory* (Cambridge: Cambridge University Press, 1993). For an excellent case study of all of these arguments coming into play, see David *Campbell's National Deconstruction: Violence, Identity, and Justice in Bosnia* (Minneapolis: University of Minnesota Press, 1998).

19. Randall L. Schweller, "Fantasy Theory," *Review of International Studies,* 25 (1999), 147, 148.

20. Peter J. Katzenstein, Robert O. Keohane, and Stephen D. Krasner, "*International Organization* and the Study of World Politics," *International Organization,* 52 (1998): 678. The quotation and rebuttal are both in Anthony Burke, "Postmodernism," In *The Oxford Handbook of International Relations* eds. Christian Reus-Smit and Duncan Snidal (Oxford: Oxford University Press, 2008), 370.

SELECTED READINGS

Critical Explorations and the Highway of Critical Security Theory

KEN BOOTH

Booth engages in what is a substantial assault on realism. To him, the realism that informs so much of the discourse in IR is itself the problem—the culprit pretending to offer remedies to the victim. Influenced by the Frankfurt School and the critical-theory tradition with which he identifies, the author seeks emancipation from dangerous ideas that put collective health of human society in jeopardy. Considering all knowledge as part of a social process, Booth departs from traditional theory which he sees as flawed by its reductionism, its grounding in naturalism (as if the state, other institutions, and what they do were part of the natural order of things), and its regressive claims that have dominated politics among nations. The state and other institutions must be "denaturalized" or revealed as essentially human creations that serve powerful interests. This unmasking not only liberates or emancipates us, but also opens us to advancing values central to achieving a more progressive world order that enhances world security. To make this happen, critical theory needs to identify what is real (ontology), how we know it (epistemology), and what can be done about it (praxis).

The Highway of Critical Security Theory

The framework of ideas developed below might be visualized in the Kantian metaphor of a highway. In my adaptation of it, the image to keep in mind is of two major roads, themselves the product of a series of feeder roads, converging and widening into a single highway.[1] The two major roads are the *critical theory tradition in social theory,* and the *radical tradition in international relations theory.* The highway that is produced is *critical security theory.*

The Critical Theory Tradition

The critical theory tradition goes back to Kant.[2] Of most immediate relevance for current purposes, however, is the work of the Frankfurt School, whose origins lay in the establishment of the Institute for Social Research at the University of Frankfurt in 1923. During the Nazi period and World War II, the school was exiled in the United States before being reestablished in Germany in 1950.[3] Key scholars in the school's work over some eighty-plus years have been Max Horkheimer, Theodor Adorno, and Jürgen Habermas.

The most thorough exposition to date bringing together the work of the Frankfurt School and the problematique of security is Richard Wyn Jones's book *Security, Strategy, and Critical Theory.*[4] He describes his approach to thinking about security as developing "in the light" of the Frankfurt School,[5] and I am happy to endorse this formulation. I also share his view that not all critical theories are equally useful when thinking about security and that the use of the word "critical" in the label CSS should signal the special helpfulness of the Frankfurt School. Not all critics of realist-derived security studies would share this view, of course, particularly postmodernists and poststructuralists hostile to metanarratives (other than their own), or those peace researchers committed to positivism.

In addition to the Frankfurt School, there are three other feeder roads into the critical theory tradition:

• The body of ideas identified with Antonio Gramsci, together with those of his interpreters in international studies (the neo-Gramscians). They have contributed with considerable insight to thinking about hegemony, civil society, and the different roles of intellectuals in politics.
• The Marxian tradition offers a deep mine of ideas that are especially useful for thinking about ideology, class, and structural power.
• An embryonic school of critical international relations theory has developed. It has begun to examine cosmopolitan ideas and practices relating to community, democracy, force, and law.[6]

In what follows, seeking to bring together the main themes of the critical theory tradition, I am conscious of synthesizing an enormous amount of sometimes complex theorizing. Purists might squeal, but the risk is worth taking in the interests of shaping a coherent and accessible body of ideas relevant to a critical theory of security. Four core themes emerge.[7]

Theme One: All Knowledge is a Social Process. Knowledge does not simply exist, waiting to be discovered like a glacier. Social and political theories, and the concepts and conceptualizations that derive from them, are the products of social processes. To a greater or lesser degree, theorists both write and are written by the theories of their time and circumstances. In this sense, all knowledge about human society is historical knowledge, emerging as it does from concrete contexts. Social and political theories are not therefore neutral or objective; they contain "nontheoretical interests." They exist in real worlds, not some imagined world of decontextualized theory; their findings, concerns, and implications are not those that might be understood by a disinterested and omniscient god (if she existed), standing apart from earthly context. Theories are, to repeat Robert Cox's famous formulation, "*for* some one or *for* some purpose." One aim of critical theory, then, is to seek to reveal the "interests of knowledge" as a factor in social and political enquiry. Knowledge here includes what is often described as "common sense." From a Gramscian perspective, common sense is equally "*for* some one or *for* some purpose." All political theorizing has some ethical

dimensions, whether it is at the level of sophisticated programmatic planning or down-to-earth common sense. The political realm is necessarily a realm of ethics and morality. If all positions, including the claim to have none, have some nontheoretical (normative) implications, objectivity is a false idol in the study of human society. The most that can be attained is a degree of (subjective) critical distance from the object of enquiry.

Theme Two: Traditional Theory Promotes the Flaws of Naturalism and Reductionism. In a famous essay published in 1937, Max Horkheimer, a key figure in the Frankfurt School, gave the label "traditional theory" to the flawed theorizing that his critical theory would seek to overcome.[8] In particular, he criticized the way traditional theory's commitment to the scientific method had spread uncritically and powerfully into all fields. The fallacy of naturalism is the idea that human beings and societies belong to the same world of nature as everything else and so should be capable of being explained by the same scientific method. In particular, when it comes to explaining human society, the characteristic reductionism of the scientific method is flawed and needs to be replaced by a more holistic perspective. Theorists can therefore be divided between those who see themselves primarily as *scientists* seeking objective truth about society and Frankfurt School critical theorists who accept they are part of a social process (seeking to promote emancipation). The former (falsely) consider that they are working apart from the world they seek to explain, whereas the latter understand they are embedded in society, and that theorizing is a social act. Gramsci made the important distinction, respectively, between *traditional* and *organic* intellectuals.

Theme Three: Critical Theory Offers a Basis for Political and Social Progress. Critical theory stands outside and questions the social and political phenomena it is examining. ... It avoids, as far as possible, the negative consequences of *problem-solving* theories, particularly the legitimizing and replicating of the regressive aspects of prevailing situations. Problem-solving theories such as political realism leave power where it is, whereas critical theory attempts to bring about structural changes in the human interest, that is, re-ordering power in emancipatory ways. Power, in its manifold varieties, cannot be escaped, but it can be reordered in a more benign direction. In the strategic action undertaken to attempt to bring change about, there is no sounder basis than *immanent critique*—the discovery of the latent potentials in situations on which to build political and social progress. This means building with one's feet firmly on the ground, not constructing castles in the air.

Theme Four: The Test of Theory is Emancipation. Human society in global perspective is shaped by ideas that are dangerous to its collective health. The evidence for the latter is widespread. It is revealed in the extent of structural oppression suffered on account of gender, class, or race; it is apparent in the threats to the very environment that sustains all life; it is seen in the risks arising out of the unintended consequences from developments in technology; and, as ever, it is experienced in the regular recourse to violence to settle political differences. A more just society in global perspective would be one that progressively limits the power of regressive structures and processes, steadily squeezing the space for violent behavior in all its direct and indirect manifestations; in this process, new opportunities would open up for the exploration of what it might mean to be human. This exploration, in the spirit of emancipation, begins with critique. A radical rethinking of the theories and practices that have shaped political life is an essential foundation for the reinvention of human society. Such rethinking, to be true to the spirit of emancipation, requires students to embrace a global perspective. The smaller social units of universal human society will not be predictably secure until the whole is systematically secured; this is one reason why what is called political studies (or even science) should be logically regarded as a subfield of the study of world politics or international relations (broadly defined) and not the other way around. Emancipation for critical theorists is both a critical device for judging theory and the continuing goal of practice; its politics seeks to denaturalize and overcome oppressive social divisions in human society at all levels. The only transhistorical and permanent fixture in human society is the individual physical being, and so this must naturally be the ultimate referent in the security problematique. Such reverence for the person—the singular body—should be understood as synonymous with the idea that people exist collectively, in some social context or other. A notion of community remains the best way of expressing how this can be translated into living a good life. The search for multilevel emancipatory communities, locally and globally, is the biggest institutional challenge faced by a critical theory of security. In the pursuit of this objective, *discourse ethics*—wherein communication (the basis for community) rather than traditional politico-military strategizing (the medium of conflict)—must therefore be a priority....

The Radical International Relations Tradition

The critical theory tradition is mainly (though not wholly) important in relation to how we might think about what is reliable knowledge (epistemology), and what should be done (emancipatory praxis). What I am calling the radical international relations tradition relates more to what is real in world politics (ontology), and what values might inform the praxis of global politics in the human interest.[9]

All social and political theories have normative implications, to a lesser or greater extent, either implicitly or explicity. The feeder roads of the radical international theory tradition are explicitly value-laden, and the normative thrust is *progressive*. The latter is a word I use deliberately, fully aware of its problems and reputation. The concept of progress is unfashionable in some circles. To postmodernists, for example, the idea of progress is almost synonymous with all that has gone wrong with the world in the past 200 years; it is part of the modernity that, according to some, led to the Holocaust.[10] Such views underline the need to reconsider the concept of progress. This will become easier as progress ceases to be identified as strongly as it has been with the hubris of nineteenth-century liberalism or twentieth-century totalitarianism (hardly the complete story of the idea of progress), and as the wave of postmodernism and poststructuralism weakens in Western intellectual life. In any case, an idea of progress informs poststructuralist arguments more so than is generally recognized....

Despite all the assaults on the idea of progress, it remains necessary, globally manifested, and (now) is almost universally hard-wired. By "progressive"

I mean simply a belief in the importance of having ideals in society and trying to shape law, politics, and institutions accordingly. The idea of progress derives from the laudable refusal of some people to believe that this is the best of all possible worlds. Without rational ideals to challenge power, it remains where it is, to be countered only by countervailing power or unreason.

Five main schools of thought in the radical international relations tradition are relevant to the development of a critical theory of security:

• The philosophical tradition of social idealism, in which human society is conceived as self-constituted and international politics regarded as just another aspect of human-made reality.

• The Peace Research and Peace Studies School, which since the 1950s has explicitly promoted the value of peace. In the 1960s this project expanded from concentrating on the problem of war into addressing the study of all forms of violence, from direct to structural.

• The World Society or World Order School, which offers inspiration because of the way its proponents developed an explicitly value-framed and progressive approach to the study of global issues.

• Feminist theorizing, whose contribution has been the uncovering of the gender interests served by political and social theories, as well as the exposure of the role(s) played by gender in the workings of world politics in practice.

• Historical sociology, which has a place in this body of ideas because its starting point opens up the state and so challenges the ahistorical biases and inherent conservatism and statism of political realism. Historical sociology therefore interrogates what realism takes as given and so has radical implications for students of international politics.[11]

Together, these feeder roads add the following core themes to those identified earlier:

Theme Five: Human Society is its Own Invention. If this is true in part, it must be so in whole. What we call "international relations," therefore, is one aspect of human-made reality—"facts by human agreement" on a global scale, in other words. The social idealism represented by Philip Allott's writing about the role of law, and of the "self-forged chains" that exist nowhere but in the mind, is of a similar inspiration to that in peace research arguing that political

violence is a learned behavior, not an inevitable feature of human social interaction.[12] Social learning can and does take place, but what has been learned historically has often not been benign. To the contrary, regressive attitudes have been internalized. Central to what Allott calls these "deformed ideas" has been the way humans have internalized conflict as a foundational myth. This has been nowhere stronger than on what he calls the "grandest stage of all," the "tragi-comedy of the state-system." According to this line of thought about the openness of history, human society became what it need not have been. Humans could have chosen different directions and could yet choose a different future. This injunction refers not only to reinventing international politics but also to the need for a new international political economy. This is a dimension of world politics usually ignored or taken for granted by realist security studies. . . .

Theme Six: Regressive Theories have Dominated Politics Among Nations.   Theory constitutes behavior, and some of the key theories that have formed human society on a global scale have not been calculated to produce a more civilized, peaceful, or just system of international relations. Examples of such thinking include ethnocentric and masculinist ideas, as well as the negative images of humanity cultivated by prevailing notions about human nature or the human condition.[13]. . . Ethnocentrism is a particular obstacle to creating a just global society and so must be challenged by more systematic knowledge about the ideas and feelings, and the hopes and fears, of people(s) with different thoughtways. One feature of regressive (noninclusive) theories about humanity is the way they make important sections of society invisible. As a result, gender, race, and class, for example, are frequently downplayed as categorical structures of humanity. The gendered character of how societies and economies work was invisible in the academic study of international relations until feminist theorizing opened the eyes of those who were prepared to see. Above all, the ideology of statism corrupts all it touches. The concept of *human security,* for example, which originally encouraged the idea of a different and more important referent than the sovereign state, has been co-opted and incorporated into statist discourses, reviving old ideas about high and low politics.

Theme Seven: The State and Other Institutions Must be Denaturalized. Human institutions like the state are historical phenomena, not biological necessities. Inquiry into the growth of state formations in different parts of the world will help the process of problematizing all institutional identifiers that divide humanity and that get in the way of recognizing and implementing the view that every person, in principle, has equal moral worth. The temporality of all institutions should lead us to focus on the individual as the ultimate referent for security; the corollary of this is that we should also consider as central to our concerns the ultimate collectivity of individuals, common humanity. Hedley Bull, best known for being one of the leading exponents of the "international society" approach, described "world order" as being "more fundamental and primordial" than international order, because the "ultimate units" of human society are not states or other sociopolitical groupings but individual human beings. The latter are "permanent and indestructible in a sense in which groupings of them of this or that sort are not.". . .[14]

Theme Eight: Progressive World Order Values Should Inform the Means and Ends of an International Politics Committed to Enhancing World Security. In today's circumstances, when the world is not working for the vast majority of its inhabitants, the agenda for progressive change is huge. For students of security, the exploration of conflict resolution and conflict management is a major departure from realism's fatalistic assumption of violence in human affairs and, hence, the belief that force can only be met by force. The neatest and most comprehensive formulation of the ideas that should inform progressive global change grew out of the work of the World Order School, with its advocacy of values such as the delegitimation of violence, the promotion of economic justice, the pursuit of human rights, the spread of humane governance, and the development of environmental sustainability.[15] It is my belief that these normative goals should be pursued in a nondualistic fashion in order to avoid the dangers of *instrumental reason,* that is, the threat of bringing about a perversion of humanity, society, or nature by concentrating entirely on functional processes even in the rational pursuit of a desirable goal.[16] Nuclear strategy is an illustration of the danger of instrumental reason. Its evolution shows how a belief in the absolute priority of national defense, and the subsequent immersion in its processes and goals, perverts intuitions and ideas about humanity, society, and nature and so opens up the possibility of war crimes, environmental disaster, genetic damage, and untold human catastrophe. Instrumental reason is a dimension in what Robert Lifton and E. Markusen have called "the genocidal mentality,[17] the instrumentalist dynamic shows how even good men (and women) can rationalize their activities and become the instruments of profound human wrongs. One counter to the dualistic ends-justify-the-means rationality, as was discussed earlier, is the Gandhian conception of conceiving ends and means as amounting to the same thing: a concrete end might be out of reach, but the means that are its equivalent are not.[18]

The eight core themes just identified point in the direction of the intellectual highway of a critical theory of security. In summary:

- All knowledge is a social process.
- Traditional theory promotes the flaws of naturalism and reductionism.
- Critical theory offers a basis for political and social progress.
- The test of theory is emancipation.
- Human society is its own invention.
- Regressive theories have dominated politics among nations.
- The state and other institutions must be denaturalized.
- Progressive world order values should inform the means and ends of an international politics committed to enhancing world security.

From this sense of direction, I now propose a definition of a distinct theory of security from a Frankfurt School critical theory perspective: *Critical security theory is both a theoretical commitment and a political orientation. As a theoretical commitment it embraces a set of ideas engaging in a critical and permanent exploration of the ontology, epistemology, and praxis of security, community, and emancipation in world politics. As a political orientation it is informed by the aim of enhancing security through emancipatory politics and networks of community at all levels, including the potential community of communities—common humanity.*

This [article] began by distinguishing CSS as a body of knowledge from a *theory* of security with a critical perspective. It then offered a framework and definition of a particular critical theory of security. This particular framework and definition can guide us in our explorations in relation to three fundamental (philosophical-theoretical-political) questions.

• What is real? A critical theory of security seeks to denaturalize and historicize all human-made political referents, recognizing only the primordial entity of the socially embedded individual. The exploration of referents is seen through the lens of emancipatory interests, not predefined ideas about the nature of the political world. Whereas other theories of security narrow the agenda because of their singular, privileged referents, critical theory is open to the exploration of all referents, historical and future-imagined, and therefore must consider the range of different threats associated with them. Imagined referents, the potential of new identities, are particularly significant for critical theory, because herein lies the possibility of the future reality of security, community and emancipation in world politics.

• What is knowledge? Critical security theory questions the reliability of much of what passes for knowledge about world politics. The reliability of this traditional knowledge is under question because of the political and epistemological assumptions of those who have the status of fact makers in contemporary society. In particular, critical theory challenges the ideal of objectivity in traditional theory and instead settles for the more realistic goal of critical distance between theorist and subject. In this way, the presumptions and assumptions of structurally powerful contemporary knowledge are interrogated, while critical theory pursues its own "knowledge-interests" against the test of an inclusive conception of human emancipation. Given the different starting point of critical theory from other theories, the conceptualization of security is different, and this informs what is thought to be relevant and reliable knowledge.

• What might be done? While the spirit of critical theory is forward-looking, guided by emancipatory interests, the understanding of knowledge as a historical process involves rethinking the past as a basis for inventing a better future. History, after all, is not what happened but how it has been interpreted; historiography is partly about discovery, but more about invention. Consequently, what has been done,

and might be done, looks very different depending on how one tells the story of the past. It can be done with regressive assumptions or an emancipatory interest. Similarly, one's conception of practice and problem-solving will vary. On the one side is the traditional theorist who sees practice as separate from theory and conceives problem-solving within a predefined world. On the other side is the Frankfurt School critical theorist who conceives a constitutive relationship between theorizing and practice and who prioritizes solving the (macro) problem of the existing situation rather than the (micro) problems within that situation. For the traditional theorist, what might be done takes place within the parameters of replicating the world; for the Frankfurt School critical theorist what might be done is inspired by the hope of changing the world, not for theory's sake but for improving the lives of real people in real places. . . .

Toward a Critical Theory of Security

The most clearly constructivist school of international relations today is the curiously labeled English School, with its emphasis on norms and rules within a supposed society of states.[19] Although constructivism offers important insights into the dynamics of world politics,[20] it does not in itself constitute a *theory* of international relations, comparable with realism, for example, with its distinctive set of ideas about the centrality of states, the causal significance of the distribution of power, and the logic of balance-of-power policies. Constructivism is a metatheoretical orientation, seeking to offer richer explanations of how the world works[21]; it does not in itself give us a politically relevant ontology or praxiological orientation. It offers little or no guidance as to whether globalization is desirable or whether the U.S.-UK invasion of Iraq in 2003 was sensible. Constructivism is not a theory of security; what it does is act as a counter to those theories claiming that life, including politics among nations, is determined (by biology, for example). It reinforces the idea, to paraphrase Alexander Wendt, that security is what we make it.[22]

While criticizing various contending theories, and outlining the case for a specific critical theory of security, I want to emphasize the desirability of *pluralism*. Any project aimed at rethinking security from the bottom up must not be closed to the ideas and questions raised by different theoretical perspectives. That being said, the drawing of theoretical lines is essential for an effective research strategy, not to mention any political orientation. At the same time, whatever one's theoretical preference, regular engagement with other theoretical perspectives, including political realism, will help keep everybody honest. There should be no synthesis of critical approaches around the lowest common denominator or any misinformed ignoring of the tradition of political realism.

Students of security these days seem to be condemned to a lifetime of theoretical dialectic, but the typical student will not be interested in theory for its own sake but rather for what it can do in helping us to understand what is happening around us ("theory explains the world"), then in engaging with world politics more effectively ("there is nothing more practical than a good theory"). In other words, most of us are interested in theory because we are interested in real people in real places. So, for example, the concept of emancipation should not be allowed to be characterized, as it sometimes is by critics, as abstract or unrelated to real conflicts. . . .

Being directly relevant to real situations—being a set of guidelines for action—has supposed to have been the particular strength of political realism. . . . Unlike most political realists, one of its founding figures, E. H. Carr, questioned what he called "pure realism" or "consistent realism." He argued that sound political thought and sound political life were synonymous with finding a place for both utopianism and realism. Although he struggled to bring together the planes of utopianism and realism, he was sure that it was an "unreal kind of realism" that ignored the element of morality in any world order. He therefore concluded that the "essential ingredients of all effective political thinking" were "a finite goal, an emotional appeal, a right of moral judgement and a ground for action."[23] I believe the framework for a critical theory of security mapped out earlier—albeit in a preliminary way—contains those essential ingredients and in doing so helps to point in the direction of a *utopian realist* theory of security. Carr would have rejected such a possibility (he thought it impossible to bring together the planes of realism and utopianism), but he would have been sympathetic with the attempt. Utopian realism attempts to bring together the theoretical and the empirical, as well as the *where we are* (globally and locally) and the *where we want to go* (a harmonious human community with enhanced world security).[24] It attempts to do so in a nondualistic manner, fusing ends and means in a manner whereby one's ideals are evident in how one acts, not only in what one hopes to achieve.

Old thinking about world politics guarantees old practices; the means recommended by traditional theories will ensure that the end will be the same old world with the same old dangers—and perhaps worse, given the predictable tinderbox of the decades ahead. By this I mean that states with weapons of mass destruction (WMD) will not persuade others to give them up (except by coercion) if those very WMD states themselves continue to develop the weapons and implicitly if not explicitly declare their possession to have political and strategic utility. Likewise, when powerful states use violence, even if it is claimed to be a last resort for humanitarian purposes, they are not acting in a manner calculated to make violence less likely; if they achieve success in their own terms, they do so only by proving to others that strategic violence can have political utility. Consistency requires that those who propose that world politics is run by laws behave lawfully themselves and that those powerful states that proclaim democracy should be willing themselves to live with being outvoted. The strategic challenge for emancipatory politics is to develop ideas for dealing with today's security threats (to whatever referents we are studying) in ways sensitive to the view expressed by Albert Camus that the means one uses today shapes the ends one might perhaps reach tomorrow.[25]

If a critical theory of security is to reverse the "escape from the real" that has characterized so much academic writing about international relations,[26] then it is essential to ask what it means for real people in real places. What, for example, does one's theorizing mean for the people(s) of the Balkans, women in east Africa, the prospects for the poorest classes in some region, the war on terror, the future of the Middle East, the likelihood of resource wars, or the possibility of nuclear weapons being used somewhere? It has only been constraints on space that have prevented more case studies being offered in this volume, to illustrate what critically informed empirical studies might look like. Such an engagement with the real should be the heart of the next stage in the growth of critically informed security studies.[27]

Another central task is that of trying to learn lessons, in the hope of contributing to the prevention of oppressive structures and situations developing in the first place. In this respect, the U.S. led war on Iraq in 2003 will provide fertile ground for lessons. While President George W. Bush and his allies, notably Prime Minister Tony Blair, argued that the war made the world a safer place, critics argue that U.S. and UK leaders and policies over the years contributed significantly to creating the dangerous regional situation in the first place, while their policies in 2002–2004 made the situation less rather than more secure. In light of this record, critics maintain that nobody could have confidence that U.S.-UK policies in Iraq would create postconflict harmony in the region. Critics point out that different attitudes to building up local strongmen, supplying arms to human rights abusers, pursuing nuclear disarmament, strengthening the UN, and the more vigorous (and less partisan) search for a just and lasting peace between Palestine and Israel—to mention only headline items—would have helped create a different relationship between Iraq and the West. The war against Iraq in 2003, according to this argument, has made the world a more dangerous place, not only by exacerbating the situation in the Middle East but also by replicating policies that legitimize violence and that reject multilateral international bodies. Meanwhile, as leaders of many states focus on the war on terror, more important long-term threats to human security and regional order—poverty, disease, environmental decay—remain marginal or ignored. Remembering Camus, we should understand that human society will never achieve tomorrow what its most powerful do not choose to begin to practice today.

There are, however, resources for benevolent change. *Immanent Critique* points to the growing voice of global civil society, for example, though the obstacles to benign change should not be underestimated.[28] Where one stands on these matters is a scholarly responsibility to be considered with utmost seriousness because somewhere, some people, as these very words are being read, are being starved, oppressed, threatened, or killed in the name of some theory of international politics or economics—or security.

The framework of critical security theory outlined above is policy-relevant, concerned with improving the conditions of political possibility in the issue area of security. One familiar difficulty from any critical perspective in this respect is the fact that current crises are the symptoms of particular structural wrongs and so are deeply embedded in the workings of society. In order to deal with such difficulties, as the old saying goes, one would not want to start from here. When one is already embroiled in a crisis, realistic options are massively reduced. The main contribution of critical approaches must therefore be precrisis, to help us think more constructively about ethical commitments, policies, agents, and sites of change, to help humankind, in whole and in part, to move away from the structural wrongs that ensure that crises, like earthquakes, will periodically rent the political landscape.

The critical theory project in security studies—committed to the development of scholarship relating to the in/security of real people in real places—can be translated into the two tasks of critique and reconstruction. Critique entails critical explorations of what is real (ontology), what is reliable knowledge (epistemology), and what can be done (praxis). Reconstruction requires engagement with concrete issues in world politics, with the aim of maximizing the opportunities for enhancing security, community, and emancipation in the human interest. . . .

The one world in which we all live is getting smaller, more overheated, and increasingly overcrowded. Meanwhile, the realities of security are becoming more complex as politico-economic and technocultural globalization interacts with traditional conflicts arising out of international competition and mistrust. Runaway science, irrationalities and extremisms of one sort or another, and growing pressures on resources threaten to add more combustible fuel to the already dangerous global situation. Human society in the decades to come is threatened by a future of complex insecurity. The outcome for world society is as uncertain as it has ever been—perhaps even more so, given current and future destructive capabilities. Confronted by the threat of complex insecurity, human society needs a theory of world security that is ontologically inclusive, epistemologically sophisticated, and praxeologically varied. Old thinking is guaranteed to replicate: Can a critical theory move beyond this and help to emancipate? Security studies will contribute—however remotely or indirectly—to replicating or changing peoples' conditions of existence. As students of security, whether one is new to the subject or has been studying it for decades, we have a choice: we can decide to study in ways that replicate a world politics that does not work for countless millions of our fellow human beings; or we can decide to study in ways that seek to help to lift the strains of life determining insecurity from the bodies and minds of people in real villages and cities, regions and states. The stakes could not be higher.

Notes

1. This elaboration of the metaphor borrows from Hannah Arendt's borrowing. See Young-Bruehl, *Hannah Arendt,* 213.

2. For an accessible summary of the ideas of Kant as applied to international relations, see Williams and Booth, "Kant."

3. Overviews of the work of the Frankfurt School are Held, *Introduction to Critical Theory;* Bernstein, *Recovering Ethical Life;* Stirk, *Critical Theory, Politics, and Society;* and Bottomore, *The Frankfurt School and Its Critics.*

4. Wyn Jones, *Security, Strategy, and Critical Theory.*

5. Ibid., ix.

6. For Gramsci's work see his *Selections from the Prison Notebooks,* and Fiori, *Antonio Gramsci.* For an introduction to Cox's work, see Cox, "Social Forces," and "Gramsci, Hegemony, and International Relations," and Cox and Sinclair, *Approaches to World Order.* For an introduction, with useful references, see Smith, "Marxism and International Relations Theory," in Groom and Light, *Contemporary International Relations,* and Linklater, "Marxism," in Burchill et al., *Theories of International Relations.* Critical international relations theory was launched, in practice if not name, by Linklater: *Men and Citizens in the Theory of International Relations; Beyond Realism and Marxism: Transformation of Political Community;* see also "The Question of the Next Stage in International Relations Theory." On cosmopolitan democracy, see Held, *Democracy and Global Order,* and Held et al., *Global Transformations.* I would add the school of critical realism to this list, although it has not (so far) produced work directly on security. See Patomaki and Wight, "After Postpositivism." A useful collection of essays discussing most of the approaches above is Wyn Jones (ed.), *Critical Theory and World Politics.*

7. Helpful insights for students of security are Wyn Jones, *Security,* and Hofffman, "Critical Theory and the Inter-Paradigm Debate"; and Linklater, "The Achievements of Critical Theory," in Smith et al., *International Theory.* The indispensable starting point is Horkheimer's

seminal essay, "Traditional and Critical Theory," in Horkheimer, *Critical Theory.*

8. Horkheimer, "Traditional and Critical Theory."

9. Note Johansen, *The National Interest and the Human,* and Mel Gurtov, *Global Politics in the Human Interest.*

10. See in particular Bauman, *Modernity and the Holocaust.* A very different perspective on the Enlightenment is captured in Porter, *Enlightenment.*

11. Examples of a key work in each of the schools just mentioned are, respectively: Allott, *Eunomia;* Galtung, *There Are Alternatives;* Falk, *Human Rights Horizons;* Enloe, *Bananas, Beaches, and Bases;* and Tilley, *Coercion, Capital, and European States.*

12. Falk and Kim (eds.), *The War System,* contains an important selection of relevant literature. Also, Allott, "The Future of the Human Past," in Booth (ed.), *Statecraft and Security.*

13. On these notions and human history, see Allott, "The Future of the Human Past."

14. Bull, *The Anarchical Society,* 22.

15. This school of thought has been preeminently represented in the work of Falk. See, inter alia, *A Study of Future Worlds, The Promise of World Order,* and *Human Rights Horizons.*

16. See Horkheimer, *Critique of Instrumental Reason;* and Adorno and Horkheimer, *Dialectic of Enlightenment.*

17. Lifton and Markusen, *The Genocidal Mentality.*

18. This is briefly explained in Richards, *The Philosophy of Gandhi,* 31–32. See also Parekh, *Gandhi's Political Philosophy,* 142–170. I have elaborated the argument in "Two Terrors, One Problem."

19. For a recent set of essays on the English School, see the special issue of *International Relations* 17, 3 (December 2003).

20. Sympathetic overviews of constructivism are: Reus-Smit, "Constructivism," in Burchill et al., *Theories;* and Adler, "Constructivism and International Relations," in Carlsneas et al., *Handbook.*

21. The most prominent, but controversial text, is Wendt, *Social Theory.*

22. The reference is to Wendt's article, "Anarchy Is What States Make of It," 391–425.

23. Carr, *The Twenty Years' Crisis, 1919–1939,* 10, 89.

24. I attempted to challenge the conventional interpretation of Carr as simply a realist in "Security and Anarchy," 527–545.

25. See Hoffmann, *Duties Beyond Borders,* 197.

26. This is elaborated in Booth, "Human Wrongs"; the phrase is Clement Rosset's.

27. See the special issue of *International Relations* 18, 3 (September 2004). A range of articles looks at specific empirical cases through critical lenses.

28. For a selection of perspectives see Lechner and Boli (eds.), *The Globalization Reader,* 2nd ed., pts. 6–10.

Realism and Rhetoric
in International Relations

FRANCIS A. BEER AND ROBERT HARIMAN

Beer and Hariman take on realism as no more than stories or narratives replete with deeply embedded myths advanced in popular discourse as truisms. Labeling themselves as "post-realists," they challenge realism's basic tenets as well as the claim to legitimacy it assumes by wearing the mantle of science. To Beer and Hariman, realism is not really a positivist theory at all. It is instead a very powerful persuasive discourse that dominates the IR field. They unpack what they see as its real meanings and purposes, assessing its impact on conduct in international relations. As critical theorists, the authors do not abandon the canons of science, but do adopt postmodern methods in what they refer to as a linguistic or rhetorical turn in the IR field.

Periodic criticisms of the realist paradigm have not substantially altered either the conventional wisdom of international studies or its considerable influence over foreign affairs. For most political scientists and the many practitioners they school, the analysis, explanation, and evaluation of international relations begins and usually ends with the realist paradigm. Consequently, any reconsideration of international studies has to come to terms with realism: considering how it produces and limits knowledge of foreign affairs, how it describes and structures political practice, how it contains untapped resources and misleading directions, and how it needs to be adapted to changes in world politics and in the conduct of inquiry. Rhetorical scholars have additional interests as well. The realist paradigm is a superb example of persuasive success in twentieth-century modernist culture, and, so long as realist assumptions structure international study, such inquiry will not be hospitable to the rhetorical tradition. By identifying how realism works as a persuasive discourse, one can challenge its hegemony within international studies and demonstrate how a rhetorical sensibility can contribute to more sophisticated and strategic understanding of foreign affairs.

Story Time: Realism's Narrative Structure

The first step in accounting for the rhetoric of realism is to recognize how realist explanation relies on stories about both the world and itself. Recent work in the rhetoric of inquiry has identified how various modes of explanation depend on more or less explicit designs otherwise thought of as "literary," "rhetorical," "imaginative," or "artificial."[1] In particular, compelling accounts of the world often are organized by narrative structures. These narratives can include pervasive myths or powerful formal designs that are dominant in many literatures, or nuanced adaptations of canonical texts in a specific discipline. In any case, the narrative is a source of coherence, meaning, and appeal.[2] Realism is no exception; indeed, its several versions all are grounded firmly in two intertwined stories about the world and about realism's place in it.

Realism's Story of the World

Realism's persuasive power comes partly from its presentation of a taut narrative of world politics. This narrative appears most of the time not in strict story form, but rather in the manner of the *narratio* in a classical oration: that portion of the speech providing a statement of the circumstances of the case.[3] The *narratio* was designed to set the scene for the exposition of arguments, which it preceded. (The predominant usage was in legal argumentation, just as in today's standard format for the legal brief.) The classical handbooks note that narrations can be legendary (involving obviously imaginary characters such as Chiron the centaur), historical (involving actual past characters such as the Peloponnesian War), or "realistic" (involving things that could have happened such as Rousseau's stag hunt). Whatever the type of account, persuasive success usually requires that it be brief, clear, and plausible. The realist's narrative of world politics exemplifies these qualities of persuasive exposition. It sets the scene, and in so doing both structures subsequent argument and defines the natural attitude of the discourse—its most reliable, core knowledge of the world.

Some of the important elements of this narrative are included in the following sketch. In the discourse of realism, nation-states are the primary actors in world politics. Since these states necessarily inhabit a condition of anarchy, they learn to conduct their foreign policies on the basis of national interest defined in terms of power. Consequently, they calculate and compare benefits and costs of alternative policies and rank each other according to their power, which is measured primarily in terms of material and especially military capabilities. Thus, national foreign policy decision makers use whatever means are most appropriate, including direct violence, to achieve the ends of national interest defined in terms of power.

This narrative usually is augmented with several additional claims as well, which establish it as an account of a permanent, ubiquitous, essential condition. These facts of international competition, we are told, are grounded in human nature and confirmed by political history. The key to success in this real world of nation-states competing for survival is to see things as they are rather than as we would want them to be. Alternative accounts are either delusions temporarily afforded by circumstances of relative peace or prosperity, or special pleading by those who lack the capability to defend themselves otherwise. The story of realism continues indefinitely, for it is a story of the fatal limitations of human nature.

The persuasive power of this narrative should not be underestimated. In a few sentences, it produces a coherent account of the international environment that coordinates all the key elements for representing human motivation: an actor (the nation-state) in a scene (the condition of anarchy, a state of nature) uses an agency (calculation) to act (the application of force) for a purpose (national interest).[4] In addition, by articulating this simple but powerful calculus as a universal, even tragic condition, the narrative suggests that it, and it alone, can equip one to survive and explain the natural conditions of state competition.[5] Its full significance, however, becomes more evident in conjunction with realism's other story.

Realism's Story of Itself

Realism complements this story of a world of raw power and rational calculation with a story about itself. In this tale, realism is the primary actor in the world of theory, with power greater than other theories. This story of self-justification develops in three parts. First, realism appears as the natural outgrowth of the dominant development in world politics: the formation of the nation-state. Realism's roots are entwined with the history of the classical and medieval city-states and its branches cover the essential elements of modern foreign policy: state sovereignty and the corresponding monopoly on violence. As it has been developed by those who were key figures in the ascendancy of the state, and by those who were present at crucial periods of global conflict between the great powers of the modern era, realism alone is capable of accounting for decisions for peace and war in a world of states. Realism becomes the only indigenous theory of international relations and foreign policy in the modern world, the only effective way to reason in the domain of world politics. Within this story, realism alone can encompass the Eurocentric world system, the American century, the Pax Americana, and the New World Order. Like the states that it valorizes, realism becomes the privileged form for international order, the hegemonic discourse in modern international relations.

Realism is, secondly, embedded in a history of ideas. The genealogy of realism is a theoretical chronology and a collective biography. It goes from antiquity to modernity, coterminous with our historical records. Realism's ancestors include Mencius, Lao Tzu, and Thucydides. Modern realists include

Machiavelli, Bodin, Hobbes, Richelieu, Ranke, Meinecke, Friedrich von Ghent, Clausewitz, Aron, Carr, Wight, and Bull. Contemporary American realism ranges from the writings of Mahan, Spykman, Mackinder, Lippmann, Kennan, and Morgenthau to the modern neorealist theory of Keohane, Waltz, and their collaborators. This story has a theme as well: It is a story of men with the intellectual courage to admit that humanity is red in tooth and claw, and with the strength to push through the pressures of common opinion and official doctrine to advance rational analysis of the world as it is, not as either the few or the many would like it to be. Realism, while reducing world history to a story of dominant states (and dominant leaders), also reduces the history of ideas to a story of dominant thinkers writing the discourse that will prevail because of its monopoly on reason.

Finally realism presents itself as one version of the most powerful narrative of our time: the story of the development of modern science. What was grounded in world history and identified by a long line of great theorists now has been validated by scientific investigation. In this story, only realism has identified the basic conditions and fundamental laws of international relations. One of the most important tenets of realist theory is the assertion that realism expresses without distortion the permanent essence of politics between nations, the core structures and processes of contemporary world politics. It accounts for phenomena today as well as millennia ago, just as it will be able to account for any future condition. Most important, it escapes the influences of its own historical moment. Thus, realism exemplifies the theoretical norms of scientific positivism. Realist theory is general, simple, and logical. It is parsimonious, buying a great deal with very little. Realism is empirically correct and comprehensible. The hypotheses of realism, Morgenthau tells us, are consistent with "the facts."[6]

Obviously, this summary of realism does not include every nuance or implication. Nor would we claim that it is likely to be untrue because it is so internally coherent. On the other hand, it should be apparent that realism depends on standard means of rhetorical justification: It provides elegant "grand narratives" that make sense of the world while advancing the speaker. Stated otherwise, *realism simultaneously operates as an epistemology, an ontology, and a rhetoric.* First the realist claims to be seeing the world clearly and so presumes that objective knowledge is available to anyone who knows how to acquire it. Second the realist claims that politics is a competition among states pursuing power that can be achieved through rational calculation, and so presumes that attention to other practices or values is a distraction inevitably leading to failure to survive or to understand the consequences of political acts. Finally, the realist acts as a realist in order to obtain persuasive power; the declaration of one's objective understanding of the elements of power invariably operates as an appeal to be granted priority over others who are comparatively benighted. As Hans Blumenberg has observed, "in the modern age anti-rhetoric has become one of the most important expedients of rhetorical art, by means of which to lay claim to the rigor of realism, which alone promises to be a match for the seriousness of man's position (in this case, his position in his 'state of nature')."[7] As these three claims are articulated together in realist discourse, and particularly as they are counterpoised against other discourses labeled utopian, idealistic, moralistic, legalistic, ideological, partisan, emotional, or rhetorical, the persuasive effect is comprehensive. Realism becomes not just an account of world politics, but the predominant context for explanation, evaluation, and action.

Criticism and Change: Post-Realism

Several converging circumstances are inducing a reconsideration of realist discourse. Recent events in Eastern and Central Europe have made it plausible that realists can be unrealistic, unable to even recognize the self-destruction of a major state. The war in the Persian Gulf has demonstrated the continuing violence and self-validating character of realist policies, while also illustrating new dimensions of international complexity ranging from instantaneous worldwide communication to an awareness of long-term environmental damage.

These political changes are matched by intellectual changes. Although realism has been challenged for contradictions and deficiencies on its own terms for the last half century, now other perspectives are raising new epistemological issues and suggesting different approaches to the study of international relations.[8] Moreover, the tenor of the debate has changed. The point now is not to repudiate realism but to understand it as a discursive practice and draw on it selectively while articulating alternative languages for understanding international relations. Instead of proving its interpretive inadequacy, one has to account for its readings (e.g., Thucydides), follow similar patterns of argument (e.g., about a canon for international studies), and reformulate its fundamental concerns (such as the necessity of strategic thinking). In some cases, the critique aims at restoration of an earlier, more complex version of realism; in other cases, the intent is to go well beyond the constraints of realist explanation. In any event, these linguistically oriented critiques have begun the movement from anti-realism to post-realism.

Of course, post-realists do contest many of realism's central claims about itself and about the world. Realists believe that realism is the only story of world politics. Post-realists assert that realism is only one story among many; although it is an important story, it provides neither the only plausible explanation nor the only possible world. Instead of accepting a world of states as a natural world, post-realists note how realist discourse replicates the dynamics of state legitimation. Just as the state defines itself as the sole vehicle for the political process, so does the realist define power politics as an autonomous realm, separated from the obligations of law, religion, custom, and the like. Just as the state defines rational conduct as that which can be measured and maximized by state administration, so does the realist project a persona of autonomous expertise and instrumental rationality. In short, the discourse of realism and the practices of the modern state are mutually reinforcing. Each operates according to a similar skein of relationships that can be interpreted as either linguistic or social practices. Such reciprocal theoretical and political relations between the state and realism are subtle and complex. Post-realist inquiry contends that they need to be explored further before we accept the hegemonic claims of either.

Post-realists challenge realist history, holding that important theorists in the realist canon were not realists as the realists describe them. Thucydides is an important example, as the realist figure to whom the most attention has been paid. Realist political scientists construct Thucydides as the founding father of realism; yet they tend to read him selectively and very simply, featuring a few passages with little attention to the lexical designs in any given passage or to the relationship of the parts of the text to the whole or to the contexts of composition and reception. The realist's Thucydides becomes a simple text with a clear lesson; its use does not require interpretation.

Other readers see Thucydides quite differently: He becomes a master of dialectical argumentation, a dramatist, or an ironist.[9] In these readings, realism is one discourse among many and an object of considerable ambivalence. Thucydides does indeed present realism as a mode of inquiry but also as a cause of the Athenian defeat. He is attempting to trace the dynamics of the war but also is recounting the collapse of cultural understanding brought about by the war. The post-realist does not deny the relevance of Thucydides, or of a Thucydidean realism, but recognizes how the realist appropriation has been used to invent a tradition to legitimate contemporary forms of authority.[10]

Similarly, post-realists note how realism draws from a limited historical base. Most theorists in the realist canon are American or European. Nor are there representatives of different publics, or classes, or religious movements, or cultures of resistance, or technologies, or markets. Moreover, as feminist theorists have taught us, the problem is not merely one of identifying and rectifying specific exclusions, but of recognizing the profound limitations and distortions that occur within a perspective that has been constructed through the negation of crucial areas of human experience.[11] Realist reliance on its canon, and the narrow range of that canon, produces far too selective an account of the actual determinants of political history and of the potential capacity for action within the varied forms of human collectivity. For example, realism provides too simple a story of the rise of the modern state. Post-realism need not deny the state's monopoly of force or its competition with other states, but it should recognize the state's dependencies on legal, economic, and communicative processes and on patterns of cooperation among states and among nations or peoples independently of state policies. Realism sees too few origins, and too many epiphenomena.

Post-realists also offer a range of criticisms of realism's scientific status. We note the following claims: (a) Realism has not produced an irrefutable body of scientific knowledge because it has not been tested adequately or produced sufficiently consistent empirical findings. (b) Realism is not likely to do so, because it is a form of local knowledge, limited by its historical circumstances, and unaware of and disposed to remain unaware of these limitations. (c) Realism could not do so, for it relies on modes of inquiry that are self-validating, or it lacks sufficient conceptual resources, or is limited by too many self-imposed constraints to provide an adequate explanation of international politics. (d) Even if scientifically productive, realism should meet other criteria as well, since it is a mode of action in the world it explains. Consequently, realism must also be evaluated, or developed, as a mode of self-reflection and practical wisdom. In doing so, the realist has to account for all that has been hidden behind the facade of scientism, including involvement with nationalism and imperialism, imposition of an artificial poverty of concepts and information on international studies, and foreclosing debate in the public sphere about foreign policy.

Contemporary realist responses to these criticisms cede a good deal of ground. Realists assert that realism is true, but perhaps not always in standard empirical ways. Realist theory is discontinuously or contingently true. It expresses the essence of world politics, but specific pieces of material evidence at particular times may not directly confirm particular hypotheses. Realist history is not a veridical, word-for-word stenographic record, but a virtual history, presented as if it were real, as it would have happened in accord with the laws of international politics. Realist policy makers act as if they were rational power maximizers, even though they may not be consciously aware that they are doing so. Decision makers "will act as if they solved certain . . . problems, whether or not they actually solve them."[12] The hidden hand writes history through the actors without necessarily requiring their conscious knowledge or cooperation. Realist doctrine is normatively true because decision makers do err. Realism is the doctrine that policy makers should follow if they were rational, even though they may not actually be so.[13]

To summarize these arguments, the post-realist holds the realist accountable for all the criticisms that have accumulated around that body of theory, while adding more as well. These additional criticisms generally are of a particular bent: They begin with the investigation of realism as a language and end with judgments in terms of any of the ideological, ethical, or other considerations that the realist would rule out. Yet post-realism has to recognize that its own story of the collapse of realism should not be a tale of intellectual dishonesty or bad faith.

It will have to invent a tradition as well, and its own formulations can neither invalidate realist claims in every case nor escape entanglement in discursive practices and historical processes beyond its complete apprehension or control. Furthermore, the post-realist accepts the burden of not only criticizing realism but of replacing or refiguring it. To do that, the post-realist needs to suggest how a linguistic turn can be compatible with the conventional aspirations of a social science.

Realism, Rhetoric, and Science

This book accepts the challenge to reconsider the dominant language of international relations in respect to both new international conditions and the intellectual resources available within the context of postmodern theory. The project begins with a shift in perspective: We analyze political realism as a persuasive discourse rather than as a positive theory. We need not deny that realist claims can be veridical representations of an external world, but we also recognize that realist discourse can be believed and have effects independent of its truth value. Realism communicates not only propositions but also attitudes (which are incipient actions); it both represents the world and structures relationships among the speakers, subjects, and audiences of world politics; it describes some events yet also deflects awareness of others. Realism is not only a set of ideas but also a mode of symbolic action.[14]

This approach allows us to recover an intellectual richness in the tradition of realism, a richness lost within the late-modern emphasis on empirical observation and structural explanation.[15] We also open a post-realist space, structured not by a rigid opposition between realism and idealism (or even between authority and dissent) but by a radical inclusiveness. We confront realists with what they have excluded from their calculations, although we do not wholly abandon the calculus of power realists know so well. This critique begins as a revisionary project and then becomes more extroverted. . . .

The return to major realist writers exemplifies a broad rhetorical perspective. We introduce rhetorical studies, the tradition of linguistic analysis most attuned to the political realm, into the linguistic turn already taking place in the study of international relations. Rhetoric, arguably the first political science, offers an analytical program that works well with the common sense and enduring concerns of foreign affairs. The rhetorical tradition includes appreciation of the dynamics of power, valorization of both argument and style, a focus on negotiation, involvement in the dialectic of elites and their publics, a strategic sensibility, and an ambivalent mixture of technical skill and ethical themes.[16]

Within the rhetorical perspective, one takes words seriously but not for their own sake alone. The emphasis is on discourse—with a corresponding wariness of the conventional distinctions between speech and action, language and reality—yet the interest is in the effect the discourse has on conduct. Rhetorical analysis probes the relationship between the content, forms, and functions of discourse and it demonstrates the capacity of speech to affect judgment and action, particularly in respect to political decision making. Thus, realist ideas do not occur transcendentally but rather through the conventions of realist discourse, which also determine how and how well realism functions to produce knowledge, craft policy, secure agreement, or motivate other forms of action.

The rhetorical tradition carries two other assumptions that can contribute directly to international studies: First, it assumes that the appeal and rationality of both political practice and scientific inquiry go beyond their reliance on empirical observation and logical calculation. Instead, rhetorical analysis asks a question of crucial importance for both the political practitioner and the social scientist: What are the appropriate criteria and standards for determining the rationality of any particular discourse?[17] (This question should be familiar to those who have criticized neorealism for its undue reliance on strictly scientific norms of theory construction.) Second, the rhetorical tradition offers itself as a common language for integrating different (disciplinary) accounts of complex phenomena. By serving as a metalanguage for identifying, comparing, and assessing different norms of argument and habits of disciplined conversation, the vocabulary of rhetoric might not fulfill the premodern ideal that "eloquence is one" but it can provide pragmatic service in an academy composed of many, highly specialized vocabularies.[18] In other words, rhetoric as a tradition of erudition has a broader range than the conventional modern conceptions of rhetoric as either the practice of propaganda or the criticism of the formal elements of literary texts.

These limiting conceptions prevailed during the formation of the American academic disciplines in the twentieth century.[19] This process applied a "politics of separation" that divided scientific inquiry from public discourse and gave realism a privileged space in international studies.[20] Such divisions were the means of disciplinary consolidation and the basis for claims to academic status. Consequently, arguments that alter the relationship between scientific inquiry and rhetorical practice are not likely to persuade established realists. In Lakatosian terms, it seems that a shift to a more interpretative inquiry involves only semantic resolution of pertinent problems.[21]

A post-realist perspective, however, has to step outside of this standoff between a narrow conception of science and a derogatory conception of rhetoric. The point is not to abandon the social scientific ideal—though we certainly encourage "enhanced reflexivity" regarding both ideal and actuality—but to recognize that the continued development of the social sciences requires and recommends broadening the definition of scientific inquiry.[22] Indeed, the need for a more expansive conception of the scientific enterprise, independent of one's commitment to a positivist core, has been evident for some time. In international studies, such an expansion is already underway. On the one hand, research programs in artifical intelligence, cognitive science, and political psychology have each required significant adjustment of the narrow conception of positivist inquiry, just as they have offered examples of how a more integrative science might work. On the other hand, obviously self-reflexive and rhetorically sensitive work can make its way between established norms and radical innovations without abandoning or reifying scientific standards. Thus, the many linguistic turns available today might induce vertigo but they need not impel an abandonment of scholarly argument or scientific analysis. Science and language are at odds only within a simplistic conception of each. Positive and interpretive analyses can indeed be compatible if one allows a more complex understanding of both the object and method of the human sciences and admits to the corresponding partiality of any mode of explanation. These are indeed exciting times for international studies, and also demanding times, for now rigor alone is not enough.

Perhaps this shift from a narrow to a broader conception of the social sciences reflects their maturation. Just as the natural sciences have long since moved beyond the simple empiricism that marked their early development, so are the social sciences moving beyond simple oppositions between positive and interpretive theories, data analysis and textual criticism. Social scientific analysis may still rely on proven techniques for controlled observation and inference of objective events. Yet it can also have a richer sense of context that comes from recognizing that scientific explanation must begin and end in conversation with other forms of scholarly investigation, including historical, philosophical, and critical inquiries. The maturing social science presumes a complex field of analytical frameworks and includes a good-faith effort to address questions raised by reflection on one's own conditions of belief. A linguistic turn may be evaluated not as the end but as a means for disciplinary growth.

Notes

1. Herbert W. Simons, ed., *The Rhetorical Turn: Invention and Persuasion in the Conduct of Inquiry* (Chicago: University of Chicago Press, 1990), and Simons, ed., *Rhetoric in the Human Sciences* (London: Sage, 1989); Richard Harvey Brown, *Social Science as Civic Discourse: On the Invention, Legitimations, and Uses of Social Theory* (Chicago: University of Chicago Press, 1989); John S. Nelson, Allan Megill, and Donald N. McCloskey, *The Rhetoric of the Human Sciences: Language and Argument in Scholarship and Public Affairs* (Madison: University of Wisconsin Press, 1987); Donald N. McCloskey, *The Rhetoric of Economics* (Madison: University of Wisconsin Press, 1985); Hayden White, *Metahistory: The Historical Imagination in Nineteenth-Century Europe* (Baltimore: Johns Hopkins University Press, 1973).

2. Richard Harvey Brown, "Narrative in Scientific Knowledge and Civic Discourse," in *Current Perspectives in Social Theory,* ed. John Wilson (Greenwich, Conn.: JAI Press, 1991); Anthony P. Kerby, *Narrative and the Self* (Bloomington: Indiana University Press, 1991): Roger C. Schank, *Tell Me a Story: A New Look at Real and Artificial Memory* (New York: Charles Scribner's Sons, 1990); Paul Ricoeur, *Time and Narrative,* trans. Kathleen Balmey, 3 vols. (Chicago: University of Chicago Press, 1988); W. J. T. Mitchell, *On Narrative* (Chicago: University of Chicago Press, 1981).

3. [Cicero], *Ad Herennium* 1.8.12–1.9.16, trans. Harry Caplan, Loeb Classical Library (Cambridge: Harvard University Press, 1954).

4. Kenneth Burke, *A Grammar of Motives* (Berkeley: University of California Press, 1969).

5. Joel H. Rosenthal, *Righteous Realists: Political Realism, Responsible Power and American Power in the Nuclear Age* (Baton Rouge: Louisiana State University Press, 1991).

6. Hans Morgenthau, *Politics Among Nations: The Struggle for Power and Peace,* 4th ed. (New York: Knopf, 1967), 3.

7. Hans Blumenberg. "An Anthropological Approach to the Contemporary Significance of Rhetoric," in *After Philosophy: End or Transformation?*, eds. Kenneth Baynes, James Bohman, and Thomas McCarthy (Cambridge: MIT Press, 1987), 454.

8. There is a growing contemporary literature that builds on the already extensive library of thought that is critical of realism. Examples of recent work include: Jaap W. Nobel, "Morgenthau's Struggle with Power: The Theory of Power Politics and the Cold War," *Review of International Studies* 21 (1995): 61–86; Steven Forde, "International Realism and the Science of Politics: Thucydides, Machiavelli, and Neorealism," *International Studies Quarterly* 39 (1995): 141–60, Richard Little, "Neorealism and the English School: A Methodological, Ontological and Theoretical Reassessment," *European Journal of International Relations* 1 (1995): 9–34; Brian C. Schmidt, "The Historiography of Academic International Relations." *Review of International Studies* 20 (1994): 349–68; Charles W. Kegley, Jr., "The Neo Idealism Movement in International Studies? Realist Myths and the New International Realities," *International Studies Quarterly* 37 (1993): 131–46; Friedrich Kratochwil, "The Embarrassment of Changes: Neo-Realism as the Science of Realpolitik without Politics," *Review of International Studies* 19 (1993): 63–80; Michael C. Williams, "Neo-realism and the Future of Strategy," *Review of International Studies* 19 (1993): 103–22; Inis H. Claude, Jr., "The Tension between Principle and Pragmatism in International Relations," *Review of International Studies* 19 (1993): 215–26; Ronen P. Palan and Brook M. Blair, "On the Idealist Origins of the Realist Theory of International Relations," *Review of International Studies* 19 (1993): 385–99; K. J. Holsti, "International Relations at the End of the Millennium," *Review of International Studies* 19 (1993): 401–8; Francis A. Beer and B. J. Balleck, "Realist/Idealist Texts: Psychometry and Semantics," *Peace Psychology Review* 1 (1993): 38–44.

9. Michael W. Doyle, "Thucydidean Realism," *Review of International Studies* 16 (1990): 223–38; Daniel Garst, "Thucydides and Neo-Realism," *International Studies Quarterly* 33 (1989): 3–28; Hayward Alker, Jr., "The Dialectical Logic of Thucydides' Melian Dialogue," *American Political Science Review* 82 (1988): 805–20; J. Peter Euben, *Greek Tragedy and Political Theory* (Berkeley: University of California Press, 1986); James Boyd White, *When Words Lose their Meaning: Constitutions and Reconstitutions of Language, Character and Community* (Chicago: University of Chicago Press, 1984); Robert R. Connor, *Thucydides* (Princeton, N.J.: Princeton University Press, 1984); Hunter R. Rawlings III, *The*

Structure of Thucydides' History (Princeton, N.J.: Princeton University Press, 1981); Marc Cogan, *The Human Thing: The Speeches and Principles of Thucydides' History* (Chicago: University of Chicago Press, 1981); Peter R. Pouncey, *The Necessities of War: A Study of Thucydides' Pessimism* (New York: Columbia University Press, 1980).

10. Eric Hobsbawm and Terence Ranger, eds., *The Invention of Tradition* (Cambridge: Cambridge University Press, 1983).

11. Christine Sylvester, *Feminist Theory and International Relations in a Postmodern Era* (Cambridge: Cambridge University Press, 1993); V. Spike Peterson and Anne Sisson Runyan, *Global Gender Issues* (Boulder, Col.: Westview Press, 1993); Cynthia Enloe, *The Morning After: Sexual Politics at the End of the Cold War* (Berkeley: University of California Press, 1993); Betty A. Reardon, *Women and Peace: Feminist Visions of Global Security* (Albany: State University of New York Press, 1993); Ruth H. Howes and Michael R. Stevenson, eds., *Women and the Use of Military Force* (Boulder, Col.: Lynne Rienner, 1993); J. Ann Tickner, *Gender in International Relations: Feminist Perspectives on Achieving Global Security* (New York: Columbia University Press, 1992); V. Spike Peterson, ed., *Gendered States: Feminist (Re)Visions of International Relations Theory* (Boulder, Col.: Lynne Rienner, 1992); Rebecca Grant and Kathleen Newland, eds., *Gender and International Relations* (Bloomington: Indiana University Press, 1991); Jean Bethke Elshtain and Sheila Tobias, eds., *Woman, Militarism, and War: Essays in History, Politics, and Social Theory* (Savage, Md.: Rowman and Littlefield, 1990); *Millennium: Journal of International Studies* 18, no. 2 (1988): Special Issue on Women and International Relations; Jean Bethke Elshtain, *Women and War* (New York: Basic Books, 1987).

12. Christopher Achen and Duncan Snidal, "Rational Deterrence Theory and Comparative Case Studies," *World Politics* 61 (1989): 143–69.

13. Dean R. Gerstein, R. Duncan Luce, Neil J. Smelser, and Sonja Sperlich, eds., *The Behavioral and Social Sciences: Achievements and Opportunities* (Washington, D.C.: National Academy Press, 1988).

14. Kenneth Burke, *A Rhetoric of Motives* (1950; reprint Berkeley: University of California Press, 1969); *A Grammar of Motives.*

15. Richard K. Ashley, "The Poverty of Neorealism," in Keohane, *Neorealism and Its Critics.*

16. Thomas M. Conley, *Rhetoric in the European Tradition* (Chicago: University of Chicago Press, 1993); Stanley Fish, "Rhetoric," in *Critical Terms for Literary Study,* eds. Frank Lentricchia and Thomas McLaughlin (Chicago: University of Chicago Press, 1990); Brian Vickers, *In Defense of Rhetoric* (Oxford: Clarendon Press, 1988); Terry Eagleton, "A Small History of Rhetoric," *Walter Benjamin, or Towards a Revolutionary Criticism* (London: Verso, 1981); Samuel Ijsseling, *Rhetoric and*

Philosophy in Conflict: An Historical Survey (The Hague: Martinus Nijhoff, 1976). Cross-disciplinary initiatives include: R. H. Roberts and J. M. M. Good, *The Recovery of Rhetoric: Persuasive Discourse and Disciplinarity in the Human Sciences* (Charlottesville: University Press of Virginia, 1993); John Bender and David E. Wellerby, eds., *The Ends of Rhetoric: History, Theory, Practice* (Stanford: Stanford University Press, 1990); David Zarefsky, "How Rhetoric and Sociology Rediscovered Each Other," in *The Rhetoric of Social Research: Understood and Believed,* ed., Albert Hunter (New Brunswick: Rutgers University Press, 1990); Gerald B. Wetlaufer, "Rhetoric and Its Denial in Legal Discourse," *Virginia Law Review* 76 (1990): 1545–97.

17. Francis A. Beer, "Words of Reason," *Political Communication* 11 (1994): 185–201; Aristotle, *On Rhetoric,* trans. George A. Kennedy (New York: Oxford University Press, 1991); Aristotle, *Nicomachean Ethics,* trans. Terrence Irwin (Indianapolis: Hackett, 1985); Blumenberg, "An Anthropological Approach"; Martin Hollis and Stephen Lukes. *Rationality and Relativism* (Cambridge: MIT Press, 1983); Richard J. Bernstein, *Beyond Objectivism and Relativism: Science, Hermeneutics, and Praxis* (Philadelphia: University of Pennsylvania Press, 1983); Chaim Perelman and L. Olbrechts-Tyteca, *The New Rhetoric,* trans. John Wilkinson and Purcell Weaver (Notre Dame: University of Notre Dame Press, 1969).

18. Cicero, *De Oratore* 3.5.23, trans. E. W. Sutton and H. Rackham, Loeb Classical Library (Cambridge: Harvard University Press, 1976); Nelson, et al., *Rhetoric of the Human Sciences;* Richard McKeon, "The Uses of Rhetoric in a Technological Age: Architectonic Productive Arts," in *Rhetoric: Essays in Invention and Discovery,* ed. Mark Backman (Woodbridge, Conn.: Ox Bow Press, 1987).

19. Dorothy Ross, *The Origins of American Social Science* (Cambridge: Cambridge University Press, 1991); Peter Novick, *That Noble Dream: The "Objectivity Question" and the American Historical Profession* (Cambridge: Cambridge University Press, 1988); Gerald Graff, *Professing Literature: An Institutional History* (Chicago: University of Chicago Press, 1987); Bruce A. Kimball, *Orators and Philosophers: A History of the Idea of Liberal Education* (New York: Teachers College Press, 1986); David M. Ricci, *The Tragedy of Political Science: Politics, Scholarship and Democracy* (New Haven: Yale University Press, 1984); Alexandra Oleson and John Voss, eds., *The Organization of Knowledge in Modern America, 1860–1920* (Baltimore: Johns Hopkins University Press, 1979); Thomas Haskell, *The Emergence of Professional Social Science: The American Social Science Association and the Nineteenth-Century Crisis of Authority* (Urbana: University of Illinois Press, 1977); Burton J. Bledstein, *The Culture of Professionalism: The Middle Class and the Development of Higher Education in America* (New York: W. W. Norton, 1976); Laurence R. Veysey, *The Emergence*

of the American University (Chicago: University of Chicago Press, 1965).

20. Timothy Engstrom, "Philosophy's Anxiety of Rhetoric: Contemporary Revisions of a Politics of Separation," *Rhetorica* 7 (1989): 209–38; Stanley Hoffmann, "An American Social Science: International Relations," *Daedalus* 106 (1977): 41–60, and *Contemporary International Relations: The Long Road to Theory* (Englewood Cliffs, N.J.: Prentice Hall, 1960).

21. Imre Lakatos, "Falsification and the Methodology of Scientific Research Programmes," in *Criticism and the Growth of Knowledge,* eds., Lakatos and Alan Musgrave (Cambridge: Cambridge University Press, 1970): 118–19.

22. Yosef Lapid, "The Third Debate: On the Prospects of International Theory in a Post-Positivist Era," *International Studies Quarterly* 33 (1989): 215–54.

Writing Security

D A V I D   C A M P B E L L

Campbell blends elements of critical theory and postmodernism drawn from continental European interpretive understandings. The term danger*—a core concept in security studies—is hardly a neutral term. We can unpack or deconstruct the meanings assigned to danger that serve the purposes of states and those in power positions within them. Danger in the form of threats gives the state its identity and justifies its existence. Campbell also takes issue with the "epistemic realism" he observes in security studies as if the world we see is purely material—one composed of objects that are separate somehow from the ideas or beliefs about them and the narratives to which such thinking gives rise.*

Danger is not an objective condition. It is not a thing that exists independently of those to whom it may become a threat. To illustrate this, consider the manner in which the insurance industry assesses risk. In François Ewald's formulation, insurance is a technology of risk the principal function of which is not compensation or reparation, but rather the operation of a schema of rationality distinguished by the calculus of probabilities. In insurance, according to this logic, danger (or, more accurately, risk) is "neither an event nor a general kind of event occurring in reality . . . but a specific mode of treatment of certain events capable of happening to a group of individuals." In other words, for the technology of risk in insurance, "Nothing is a risk in itself; there is no risk in reality. But on the other hand, anything *can* be a risk; it all depends on how one analyzes the danger, considers the event. As Kant might have put it, the category of risk is a category of the understanding; it cannot be given in sensibility or intuition."[1] In these terms, danger is an effect of interpretation. Danger bears no essential, necessary, or unproblematic relation to the action or event from which it is said to derive. Nothing is intrinsically more dangerous for insurance technology than anything else, except when interpreted as such.

This understanding of the necessarily interpretive basis of risk has important implications for international relations. It does not deny that there are "real" dangers in the world: infectious diseases, accidents, and political violence (among others) have consequences that can literally be understood in terms of life and death. But not all risks are equal, and not all risks are interpreted as dangers. Modern society contains a veritable cornucopia of danger; indeed, there is such an abundance of risk that it is

From *Writing Security: United States Foreign Policy and the Politics of Identity,* Revised Edition, by David Campbell, 1998. Reprinted by permission of University of Minnesota Press and Manchester University Press, Manchester, UK.

impossible to objectively know all that threatens us.[2] Those events or factors that we identify as dangerous come to be ascribed as such only through an interpretation of their various dimensions of dangerousness. Moreover, that process of interpretation does not depend on the incidence of "objective" factors for its veracity. For example, HIV infection has been considered by many to be America's major public health issue, yet pneumonia and influenza, diabetes, suicide, and chronic liver disease have all been individually responsible for many more deaths. Equally, an interpretation of danger has licensed a "war on (illegal) drugs" in the United States, despite the fact that the consumption level of (and the number of deaths that result from) licit drugs exceeds by a considerable order of magnitude that associated with illicit drugs. . . .

Furthermore, the role of interpretation in the articulation of danger is not restricted to the process by which some risks come to be considered more serious than others. An important function of interpretation is the way that certain modes of representation crystallize around referents marked as dangers. Given the often tenuous relationship between an interpretation of danger and the "objective" incidence of behaviors and factors thought to constitute it, the capacity for a particular risk to be represented in terms of characteristics reviled in the community said to be threatened can be an important impetus to an interpretation of danger. . . . The ability to represent things as alien, subversive, dirty, or sick has been pivotal to the articulation of danger in the American experience.

In this context, it is also important to note that there need not be an action or event to provide the grounds for an interpretation of danger. The mere existence of an alternative mode of being, the presence of which exemplifies that different identities are possible and thus denaturalizes the claim of a particular identity to be *the* true identity, is sometimes enough to produce the understanding of a threat.[3] In consequence, only in these terms is it possible to understand how some acts of international power politics raise not a whit of concern, while something as seemingly unthreatening as the novels of a South American writer can be considered such a danger to national security that his exclusion from the country is warranted.[4] For both insurance and international relations, therefore, danger results from the calculation of a threat that objectifies

events, disciplines relations, and sequesters an ideal of the identity of the people said to be at risk. . . . The invasion of Kuwait [serves] . . . as a useful touchstone by which to outline some of the assumptions undergirding this study. Consider, for example, this question: How did the Iraqi invasion become the greatest danger to the United States? Two answers to this question seem obvious and were common. Those indebted to a power-politics understanding of world politics, with its emphasis on the behavior of states calculated in rational terms according to the pursuit of power, understood the invasion to be an easily observable instance of naked aggression against an independent, sovereign state. To those indebted to an economistic understanding, in which the underlying forces of capital accumulation are determinative of state behavior, the U.S.-led response, like the Iraqi invasion, was explicable in terms of the power of oil, markets, and the military-industrial complex.

Each of these characterizations is surely a caricature. The range of views in the debate over this crisis was infinitely more complex than is suggested by these two positions; there were many whose analyses differed from those with whom they might normally be associated, and indebtedness to a tradition does not determine one's argument in every instance. But the purpose of overdrawing these positions (which we might call, in equally crude terms, realist and Marxist) is to make the point that although each is usually thought to be the antinomy of the other, they both equally efface the indispensability of interpretation in the articulation of danger. As such, they share a disposition from which this analysis differs. Committed to an *epistemic realism*— whereby the world comprises objects whose existence is independent of ideas or beliefs about them—both of these understandings maintain that there are material causes to which events and actions can be reduced. And occasioned by this epistemic realism, they sanction two other analytic forms: a *narrativizing historiography* in which things have a self-evident quality that allows them to speak for themselves, and a *logic of explanation* in which the purpose of analysis is to identify those self-evident things and material causes so that actors can accommodate themselves to the realm of necessity they engender.[5] Riven with various demands, insistences, and assertions that things "must" be either this or that, this disposition is the most common metatheoretical discourse among practitioners of the discipline of international relations.

But there are alternative ways to think. . . . Contrary to the claims of epistemic realism, I argue that as understanding involves rendering the unfamiliar in the terms of the familiar, there is always an ineluctable debt to interpretation such that there is nothing outside of discourse. Contrary to a narrativizing historiography, I employ a mode of historical representation that self-consciously adopts a perspective. And contrary to the logic of explanation, I embrace a logic of interpretation that acknowledges the improbability of cataloging, calculating, and specifying the "real causes," and concerns itself instead with considering the manifest political consequences of adopting one mode of representation over another.

As such, my argument is part of an emerging dissident literature in international relations that draws sustenance from a series of modern thinkers who have focused on historically specific modes of discourse rather than the supposedly independent realms of subjects and objects.[6] Starting from the position that social and political life comprises a set of practices in which things are constituted in the process of dealing with them, this dissent does not (and does not desire to) constitute a discrete methodological school claiming to magically illuminate the previously dark recesses of global politics. Nor is it the dissent of a self-confident and singular figure claiming to know the error of all previous ways and offering salvation from all theoretical sin. Rather, this form of dissent emerges from a disparate and sometimes divergent series of encounters between the traditions of international relations and theories increasingly prominent in other realms of social and political inquiry. It is a form of dissent that celebrates difference: the proliferation of perspectives, dimensions, and approaches to the very real dilemmas of global life. It is a form of dissent that celebrates the particularity and context-bound nature of judgements and assessments, not because it favors a (so-called) relativist retreat into the incommensurability of alternatives, but because it recognizes the universalist conceits of all attempts to force difference into the strait-jacket of identity.[7] It is a form of dissent skeptical—but not cynical—about the traditions of international relations and their claims of adequacy to reality. It is a form of dissent that is not concerned to seek a better fit between thought and the world,

language and matter, proposition and fact. On the contrary, it is a form of dissent that questions the very way our problems have been posed in these terms and the constraints within which they have been considered, focusing instead on the way the world has been made historically possible.[8]

Consequently, in attempting to understand the ways in which United States foreign policy has interpreted danger and secured the boundaries of the identity in whose name it operates, this analysis adopts neither a purely theoretical nor a purely historical mode. It is perhaps best understood in terms of a history of the present, an interpretative attitude suggested by Michel Foucault.[9] A history of the present does not try to capture *the* meaning of the past, nor does it try to get *a* complete picture of the past as a bounded epoch, with underlying laws and teleology. Neither is a history of the present an instance of presentism—where the present is read back into the past—or an instance of finalism, that mode of analysis whereby the analyst maintains that a kernel of the present located in the past has inexorably progressed such that it now defines our condition. Rather, a history of the present exhibits an unequivocally contemporary orientation. Beginning with an incitement from the present—an acute manifestation of a ritual of power—this mode of analysis seeks to trace how such rituals of power arose, took shape, gained importance, and effected politics.[10] In short, this mode of analysis asks how certain terms and concepts have historically functioned within discourse.

To suggest as much, however, is not to argue in terms of the discursive having priority over the nondiscursive. Of course, this is the criticism most often mounted by opponents to arguments such as this, understandings apparent in formulations like "if discourse is all there is," "if everything is language," or "if there is no reality."[11] In so doing they unquestioningly accept that there are distinct realms of the discursive and the nondiscursive. Yet such a claim, especially after the decades of debates about language, interpretation, and understanding in the natural and social sciences, is no longer innocently sustainable. It can be reiterated as an article of faith to rally the true believers and banish the heretics, but it cannot be put forward as a self-evident truth. As Richard Rorty has acknowledged, projects like philosophy's traditional desire to see "how language relates to the world" result in "the impossible attempts to step outside our skins—the traditions, linguistic and other, within which we do our thinking and self-criticism—and compare ourselves with something absolute."[12] The world exists independently of language, but we can never *know* that (beyond the fact of its assertion), because the existence of the world is literally inconceivable outside of language and our traditions of interpretation.[13] In Foucault's terms, "We must not resolve discourse into a play of pre-existing significations; we must not imagine that the world turns toward us a legible face which we would only have to decipher; the world is not the accomplice of our knowledge; there is no prediscursive providence which disposes the world in our favour."[14]

Therefore, to talk in terms of an analysis that examines how concepts have historically functioned within discourse is to refuse the force of the distinction between discursive and nondiscursive. As Laclau and Mouffe have argued, "The fact that every object is constituted as an object of discourse has *nothing to do* with whether there is a world external to thought, or with the realism/idealism opposition . . . What is denied is not that . . . objects exist externally to thought, but the rather different assertion that they could constitute themselves as objects outside of any discursive condition of emergence."[15] This formulation seeks neither to banish arguments that authorize their positions through reference to "external reality," nor to suggest that any one representation is as powerful as another. On the contrary, if we think in terms of a discursive economy— whereby discourse (the representation and constitution of the "real") is a managed space in which some statements and depictions come to have greater value than others—the idea of "external reality" has a particular currency that is *internal* to discourse. For in a discursive economy, investments have been made in certain interpretations; dividends can be drawn by those parties that have made the investments; representations are taxed when they confront new and ambiguous circumstances; and participation in the discursive economy is through social relations that embody an unequal distribution of power. Most important, the effect of this understanding is to expand the domain of social and political inquiry: "The main consequence of a break with the discursive/extradiscursive dichotomy is the abandonment of the thought/reality opposition, and hence a major enlargement of the field of those categories which can account for social relations.

Synonymy, metonymy, metaphor are not forms of thought that add a second sense to a primary, constitutive literality of social relations; instead, they are part of the primary terrain itself in which the social is constituted."[16] The enlargement of the interpretive imagination along these lines is necessary in order to account for many of the recent developments in world politics, and to understand the texts of postwar United States foreign policy. . . .

Identity is an inescapable dimension of being. No body could be without it. Inescapable as it is, identity—whether personal or collective—is not fixed by nature, given by God, or planned by intentional behavior. Rather, identity is constituted in relation to difference. But neither is difference fixed by nature, given by God, or planned by intentional behavior. Difference is constituted in relation to identity.[17] The problematic of identity/difference contains, therefore, no foundations that are prior to, or outside of, its operation. Whether we are talking of "the body" or "the state," or of particular bodies and states, the identity of each is performatively constituted. Moreover, the constitution of identity is achieved through the inscription of boundaries that serve to demarcate an "inside" from an "outside," a "self" from an "other," a "domestic" from a "foreign."

In the specific case of the body, Judith Butler has argued that its boundary, as well as the border between internal and external, is "tenuously maintained" by the transformation of elements that were originally part of identity into a "defiling otherness."[18] In this formulation, there is no originary or sovereign presence that inhabits a prediscursive domain and gives the body, its sex, or gender a naturalized and unproblematic quality. To be sure, many insist on understanding the body, sex, and gender as naturalized and unproblematic. But for their claim to be persuasive, we would have to overlook (among other issues) the multifarious normalizing codes that abound in our society for the constitution and disciplining of sexuality. In seeking to establish and police understandings of what constitutes the normal, the accepted, and the desirable, such codes effect an admission of their constructed nature and the contingent and problematic nature of the identity of the body.

Understanding the gendered identity of the body as performative means that we regard it as having "no ontological status apart from the various acts that constitute its reality." As such, the idea that gender is an interior essence definitive of the body's identity is a discursively constructed notion that is required for the purposes of disciplining sexuality. In this context, genders are neither "true" or "false," nor "normal" or "abnormal," but "are only produced as the truth effects of a discourse of primary and stable identity." Moreover, gender can be understood as "an identity tenuously constituted in time, instituted in an exterior space through *a stylized repetition of acts*" an identity achieved, "*not* [through] *a founding act, but rather a regulated process of repetition.*"[19]

Choosing the question of gender and the body as an exemplification of the theme of identity is not to suggest that as an "individual" instance of identity the performative constitution of gender and the body is prior to and determinative of instances of collective identity. In other words, I am not claiming that the state is analogous to an individual with a settled identity. To the contrary, I want to suggest that the performative constitution of gender and the body is analogous to the performative constitution of the state. Specifically, I want to suggest that we can understand the state as having "no ontological status apart from the various acts which constitute its reality"; that its status as the sovereign presence in world politics is produced by "a discourse of primary and stable identity" and that the identity of any particular state should be understood as "tenuously constituted in time . . . through *a stylized repetition of acts*," and achieved, "*not* [through] *a founding act, but rather a regulated process of repetition.*"

. . . Much of the conventional literature on the nation and the state implies that the essence of the former precedes the reality of the latter: that the identity of a "people" is the basis for the legitimacy of the state and its subsequent practices. However, much of the recent historical sociology on this topic has argued that the state more often than not precedes the nation: that nationalism is a construct of the state in pursuit of its legitimacy. Benedict Anderson, for example, has argued in compelling fashion that "the nation" should be understood as an "imagined political community" that exists only insofar as it is a cultural artifact that is represented textually.[20] Equally, Charles Tilly has argued that any coordinated, hierarchical, and territorial entity should be only understood as a "nati*on*al state." He stresses that few of these national states have ever become or presently are "nation-states"—national

states whose sovereign territorialization is perfectly aligned with a prior and primary form of identification, such as religion, language, or symbolic sense of self. Even modern-day Great Britain, France, and Germany (and, equally, the United States, Australia, and Canada) cannot be considered nation-states even though they are national states.[21] The importance of these perspectives is that they allow us to understand national states as unavoidably paradoxical entities that do not possess prediscursive, stable identities. As a consequence, all states are marked by an inherent tension between the various domains that need to be aligned for an "imagined political community" to come into being—such as territoriality and the many axes of identity—and the demand that such an alignment is a response to (rather than constitutive of) a prior and stable identity. In other words, states are never finished as entities; the tension between the demands of identity and the practices that constitute it can never be fully resolved, because the performative nature of identity can never be fully revealed. This paradox inherent to their being renders states in permanent need of reproduction: with no ontological status apart from the many and varied practices that constitute their reality, states are (and have to be) always in a process of becoming. For a state to end its practices of representation would be to expose its lack of prediscursive foundations; stasis would be death.[22] Moreover, the drive to fix the state's identity and contain challenges to the state's representation cannot finally or absolutely succeed. Aside from recognizing that there is always an excess of being over appearance that cannot be contained by disciplinary practices implicated in state formation, were it possible to reduce all being to appearance, and were it possible to bring about the absence of movement which in that reduction of being to appearance would characterize pure security, it would be at that moment that the state would wither away.[23] At that point all identities would have congealed, all challenges would have evaporated, and all need for disciplinary authorities and their fields of force would have vanished. Should the state project of security be successful in the terms in which it is articulated, the state would cease to exist. Security as the absence of movement would result in death via stasis. Ironically, then, the inability of the state project of security to succeed is the guarantor of the state's continued success as an impelling identity.

The constant articulation of danger through foreign policy is thus not a threat to a state's identity or existence: it is its condition of possibility. While the objects of concern change over time, the techniques and exclusions by which those objects are constituted as dangers persist. Such an argument, however, is occluded by the traditional representations of international politics through their debts to epistemic realism and its effacement of interpretation. . . .

Border Crossings

Where once . . . objections to the impoverished understanding of "postmodernism" in international relations would have been made in a defensive mode, now they are put forward with an air of resigned exasperation. Where once we were all caught in the headlights of the large North American car of international relations theory, now the continental sportster of critical theories has long since left behind the border guards and toll collectors of the mainstream—who can be observed in the rearview mirror waving their arms wildly still demanding papers and the price of admission—as the occupants go on their way in search of another political problem to explore. Time has moved on for most people, and with it has come a raft of exciting new research in international relations that is indebted, implicitly as well as explicitly, to the Enlightenment ethos articulated by Foucault.

Few things are more problematic and troublesome than the naming of intellectual trends. This has to be constantly borne in mind, because the research being considered here does not constitute a neatly demarcated "school" of thought, it does not often if ever embrace the label of "postmodernism," and many scholars who might be associated with it could easily be identified in other terms. But when considered as the whole it is not, multiple answers abound to the challenge that those who have gained inspiration from the critical themes of continental philosophy should embark on their own research agendas. Of note is work that deals with familiar issues in estranging ways, including research on the performative nature of state identity (particularly its gendered character) in the context of U.S. intervention; studies of the centrality of representation in North-South relations and immigration policies; a deconstructive account of famine and

humanitarian crises; interpretive readings of diplomacy and European security; the radical rethinking of international order and the challenge of the refugee; critical analyses of international law and African sovereignties; a recasting of ecopolitics; the rearticulation of the refugee regime and sovereignty; a problematization of the UN and peacekeeping; a semiotic reading of militarism in Hawaii, and arguments concerning practices of contemporary warfare, strategic identities, and security landscapes in NATO, among many others.

For all the differences, nuances and subtleties, this work incorporates many of the key achievements of "poststructuralism" (meaning the interpretive analytic of "postmodernism"), especially the rethinking of questions of agency, power, and representation in modern political life. . . .

Notes

1. Francois Ewald, 'Insurance and risk,' in *The Foucault Effect: Studies in Governmental Rationality,* edited by Graham Burchell, Colin Gordon and Peter Miller, Hemel Hempstead, 1991, 199.

2. Mary Douglas and Aaron Wildavsky, *Risk and Culture: An Essay on the Selection of Technological and Environmental Dangers,* Berkeley, 1982.

3. 'The threat is posed not merely by *actions* the other might take to injure or defeat the true identity but by the very visibility of its mode of *being* as other.' William E. Connolly, *Identity\Difference: Democratic Negotiations of Political Paradox,* Ithaca, 1991, 66.

4. I am referring here to the policies of the recently curtailed McCarran–Walter Act which excluded from the United States, on ideological grounds, writers like the Nobel Prize winner Gabriel Garcia Marquez.

5. See Hayden White, *The Content of the Form: Narrative Discourse and Historical Representation,* Baltimore, 1987, especially chapter one.

6. See 'Speaking the language of exile: dissidence in international studies,' edited by Richard K. Ashley and R. B. J. Walker, *International Studies Quarterly,* XXXIV, 1990, 259–416.

7. The charge of 'relativism' has become a mantra-like repudiation employed by realists and others seeking to delegitimize an argument such as this. The logic behind this criticism is that any position concerning itself with the constructed nature of reality has to assume (implicitly or explicitly) that all positions are relative to a specific framework, paradigm, or culture, such that we can make no judgments about right and wrong, good or bad, etc. Furthermore, it is often maintained that such an

assumption is contradictory, because the relativist is said to resort to a universal: i.e., that all things are relative. For two reasons, I think such a charge is mistaken and misleading. Firstly, the meaning of relativism is usually ascribed by the objectivist critic, but in a way that refuses to question the terms of the debate. Specifically, the charge of relativism, rests on the dubious assumption that there is indeed some overarching, universal framework to which one is relative. For all the efforts of philosophers and others over the centuries, I am not aware of any agreement on the existance or nature of such an Archimedean point. Indeed, those factors which are sometimes cited as 'universal'—such as tradition or culture—invoke the very intersubjective qualities that the so-called relativist is concerned with. Secondly, the characteristics subsumed under the term relativism by realist critics usually bear the hallmarks of subjectivism rather than relativism. The concern for the lack of standards and truths is usually said to derive from the alleged moral solipsism that results from so-called relativism; the idea that the abandonment of universals leads to an ethical anarchy in which anything goes. But the so-called relativist is concerned with the social and intersubjective nature of paradigms, practices, and standards, and thus rejects the idea that these are the property of individuals. My thinking on these issues has been most influenced by Richard Bernstein, *Beyond Objectivism and Relativism: Science, Hermeneutics and Praxis,* Oxford, 1983.

8. See Jim George and David Campbell, 'Patterns of dissent and the celebration of difference: critical social theory and international relations,' *International Studies Quarterly,* XXXIV, 1990, 269–93.

9. Michel Foucault, *Discipline and Punish: The Birth of the Prison,* trans. by Alan Sheridan, New York, 1979, 31.

10. See Hubert L. Dreyfus and Paul Rabinow, *Michel Foucault: Beyond Structuralism and Hermeneutics,* Brighton, 1983, 118–20.

11. For a good account of these formulations see Judith Butler, 'Contingent foundations: feminism and the question of "postmodernism",' in *Feminists Theorize the Political,* edited by Judith Butler and Joan W. Scott, New York, 1992.

12. Richard Rorty, 'Introduction: pragmatism and philosophy,' in *Consequences of Pragmatism (Essays 1972–1980).* Brighton, 1982, xix.

13. This is different from the claim that there are 'alternative conceptual frameworks' through which we can know the world, for such a position eventually collapses into a Kantian understanding, whereby 'the world' is a thing-in-itself thoroughly independent of our knowledge. See Rorty, 'The world well lost,' in *Consequences of Pragmatism.*

14. Michel Foucault, 'The order of discourse,' in *Language and Politics,* edited by Michael Shapiro, Oxford, 1984, 127.

15. Ernesto Laclau and Chantal Mouffe, *Hegemony and Socialist Strategy: Towards a Radical Democratic Politics,* trans. by Winston Moore and Paul Cammack, London, 1985, 108.

16. Ibid, 110. White has expressed a similar sentiment: 'Tropic is the shadow from which all realistic discourse tries to flee. This flight, however, is futile; for tropics is the process by which all discourse *constitutes* the objects which it pretends only to describe realistically and to analyze objectively.' Hayden White, *Tropics of Discourse: Essays in Cultural Criticism,* Baltimore, 1978. 2.

17. For a general discussion on this theme see Connolly, *Identity\Difference.*

18. Judith Butler, *Gender Trouble: Feminism and the Subversion of Identity,* New York, 1990, 133.

19. Ibid, 136, 140–1, 145 respectively. Emphasis in the original.

20. Benedict Anderson, *Imagined Communities: Reflections on the Origin and Spread of Nationalism,* revised edition, New York, 1991.

21. Charles Tilly, *Capital, Coercion, and European States,* A.D. *990–1990,* New York, 1990.

22. In his account of the importance of speed and temporality to politics, Paul Virilio observed, somewhat grandiosely, that '*Stasis is death* really seems to be *the general law of the World.*' Virilio, *Speed and Politics,* trans. by Mark Polizzotti, New York, 1986, 67.

23. 'In a social configuration whose precarious equilibrium is threatened by an ill-considered initiative, security can henceforth be likened to the absence of movement.' Virilio, *Speed and Politics,* 125.

SUGGESTIONS FOR FURTHER READING

▪ On Positivism

Achinstein, Peter, and Barker, Stephen. *The Legacy of Logical Positivism: Studies in the Philosophy of Science.* Baltimore: Johns Hopkins Press, 1969.

Ayer, Alfred Jules. *Logical Positivism.* Glencoe, IL: Free Press, 1959.

Bergmann, Gustav. *The Metaphysics of Logical Positivism.* New York: Longmans Green, 1954.

Carnap, Rudolph. *An Introduction to the Philosophy of Science.* New York: Basic Books, 1966.

Comte, Auguste. *A General View of Positivism.* Newark, NJ: Irving Publishers Co., 1972.

Deutsch, Karl. "Recent Trends in Research Methods in Political Science." In *A Design for Political Science: Scope, Objectives, and Methods,* ed. Charlesworth, James. Philadelphia: American Academy of Political and Social Science, 1966.

Eckstein, Harry. "Case Study and Theory in Political Science." In *Handbook of Political Science* Vol. 7, eds. Fred Greenstein, and Nelson Polsby. Reading, MA: Addison-Wesley, 1975.

Friedman, Michael. *Reconsidering Logical Positivism.* Cambridge, UK: Cambridge University Press, 1999.

Friedman, Milton. "The Methodology of Positive Economics." In *Essays in Positive Economics,* ed. Milton Friedman. Chicago: University of Chicago Press, 1953.

Giddens, Anthony. *Positivism and Sociology.* London: Henemann, 1974.

Giere, Ronald N., and Alan W. Richardson. *Origins of Logical Empiricism.* Minneapolis: University of Minnesota Press, 1977.

Hanfling, Oswald. *Logical Positivism.* Oxford: B. Blackwell, 1981.

Hartung, Frank. "The Social Function of Positivism." *Philosophy of Science* 12, 2 (1945): 120–33.

Hempel, Karl. *Philosophy of Natural Sciences.* New York: Prentice Hall, 1966.

Jangam, R. T. *Logical Positivism and Politics.* Delhi: Sterling Publishers, 1970.

Kauffman, Felix. *Methodology of Social Sciences.* London: Oxford University Press, 1944.

_____. "Basic Issues in Logical Positivism." In *Philosophic Thought in France and the United States,* ed. Farbin Marver. Albany: State University of New York Press, 1968.

Kockelmans, Joseph. *Philosophy of Science: The Historical Background.* New York: The Free Press, 1968.

Kraft, Victor. *The Vienna Circle: The Origin of Neo-positivism, a Chapter in the History of Recent Philosophy.* New York: Greenwood Press, 1953.

Kuhn, Thomas. *The Structure of Scientific Revolutions.* Chicago: University of Chicago Press, 1962.

Lakatos, Imre. "Falsification and the Methodology of Scientific Research Programmes." In *Criticism and the Growth of Knowledge,* eds. Imre Lakatos and Alan Musgrave. Cambridge: Cambridge University Press, 1970.

Masterman, Margaret. "The Nature of a Paradigm." In *Criticism and the Growth of Knowledge,* eds. Imre Lakatos and Alan Musgrave. Cambridge: Cambridge University Press, 1970.

Mises von, Richard. *Positivism: A Study in Human Understanding.* Cambridge: Harvard University Press, 1951.

Nagel, Ernest. *The Structure of Science.* New York: Harcourt, Brace and World, 1960.

Parrini, Paolo, Wesley C. Salmon, and Merrilee H. Salmon, eds. *Logical Empiricism—Historical and Contemporary Perspectives.* Pittsburgh: University of Pittsburgh Press, 2003.

Popper, Karl. *Conjectures and Refutations. The Growth of Scientific Knowledge.* London: Routledge, 1963.

_____. *The Logic of Scientific Discovery.* New York: Basic Books, 1959.

_____. *Objective Knowledge.* London: Oxford University Press, 1972.

Rescher, Nicholas. *The Heritage of Logical Positivism.* Lanham, MD: University Press of America, 1985.

Sarkar, Sahotra. *The Legacy of the Vienna Circle: Modern Reappraisals.* New York: Garland Pub., 1996.

Scharff, Robert. *Comte After Positivism.* Cambridge: Cambridge University Press, 1995.

Schmidtt, Brian. "Further Ahead or Further Behind? The Debate over Positivism." *Mershon International Studies Review* 41 (1997): 107–12.

Weimer, Walter. *Notes on the Methodology of Scientific Research.* Hillsdale, NJ: Lawrence Erlbaum Assoc., 1979.

Werkmeister, William. "Seven Theses of Logical Positivism Critically Examined." *The Philosophical Review* 46, 3 (May 1937): 276–97.

Wittgenstein, Ludwig. *Tractatus Logico Philosophicus.* London: Routledge, 2001.

On Critical Theory

Ackerly, Brooke, and Jaqui True. "Studying the Struggles and Wishes of the Age: Feminist Theoretical Methodology and Feminist Theoretical Methods." In *Feminist Methodologies for International Relations,* eds. Brooke Ackerly, Maria Stern, and Jaqui True. Cambridge: Cambridge University Press, 2006.

Anievas, Alexander. "Critical Dialogues: Habermasian Social Theory and International Relations." *Politics* 25, 3 (September 2005): 135–43.

Ashley, Richard. "Untying the Sovereign State: A Double Reading of the Anarchy Problematique." *Millennium: Journal of International Studies* 17 (1988): 227–62.

Beiler, Andreas, and Adam Morton. "The Gordian Knot of Agency-Structure in International Relations: A Neo-Gramscian Perspective." *European Journal of International Relations* 7, 1 (2001): 5–35.

Bernstein, Richard. "The Critical Theory of Society." In *The Restructuring of Social and Political Theory.* London: Methuen, 1976.

Booth, Ken. *Theory of World Security.* Cambridge: Cambridge University Press, 2008.

———. *Critical Security Studies and World Politics.* Boulder, CO: Lynne Rienner, 2005.

———, and Daniel Wheeler. *Security Dilemma: Fear, Cooperation and Trust in World Politics.* New York: Palgrave Macmillan, 2007.

Brown, Chris. "Turtles All the Way Down: Anti-Foundationalism, Critical Theory and International Relations." *Millenium: Journal of International Studies* 23, 2 (1994): 227–30.

Cavarero, Adriana. *Horrorism: Naming Contemporary Violence.* New York: Columbia University Press, 2008.

Chandler, David. "The Revival of Carl Schmitt in International Relations: The Last Refuge of Critical Theorists?" *Millenium: Journal of International Studies* 37, 1 (August 2008): 27–48.

Chernoff, Fred. "Reflectivist Opposition to the Scientific Approach: Critical Theory, Poststructuralism, and Interpretive Constructivism." In *Theory and Metatheory in International Relations: Concepts and Contending Accounts.* New York: Palgrave Macmillan, 2007.

Cox, Robert. "Gramsci, Hegemony, and International Relations: An Essay in Method." In *Approaches to World Order,* eds. Robert Cox and Timothy Sinclair. London: Cambridge University Press, 1996.

———. "Social Forces, States and World Orders." In *Approaches to World Order,* eds. Robert Cox and Timothy Sinclair. Cambridge: Cambridge University Press, 1996.

Der Derian, James. *Critical Practices in International Theory: Selected Essays.* London: Routledge, 2009.

———, and Michael Shapiro, eds. *International/Intertextual Relations: Boundaries of Knowledge and Practice in World Politics.* Lexington, MA: Lexington Books, 1998.

Devetak, Richard. "Between Kant and Pufendorf: Humanitarian Intervention, Statist Anti-Cosmopolitanism and Critical International Theory." *Review of International Studies* 33 (2007): 151–74.

———. "Critical Theory." In *Theories of International Relations,* 2nd ed, eds. Scott Burchill, Andrew Linklater, Matthew Paterson, Christian Reus-Smit, and Jaqui True. Houndmills: Palgrave Macmillan, 2001.

Eckersley, Robyn. "The Ethics of Critical Theory." In *The Oxford Handbook of International Relations,* eds. Christian Reus-Smit and Duncan Snidal. Oxford: Oxford University Press, 2008.

Edkins, Jenny. *Poststructuralism & International Relations: Bringing the Political Back In.* Boulder, CO: Lynne Rienner, 1999.

———, and Nick Vaughan-Williams. *Critical Theorists and International Relations.* London: Routledge, 2009.

Eschle, Catherine, and Bice Maiguashca. *Critical Theories, International Relations and 'the Anti-Globalisation Movement': The Politics of Global Resistance.* London: Routledge, 2005.

Fierke, Karin. *Critical Approaches to International Security.* Cambridge, UK: Polity, 2007.

Friedrichs, Jorg. "The Meaning of New Medievalism." *European Journal of International Relations* 7, 4 (2001): 475–501.

George, Jim. "International Relations and the Search for Thinking Space: Another View of the Third Debate." *International Studies Quarterly* 33, 3 (September 1989): 269–79.

———, and David Campbell. "Patterns of Dissent and the Celebration of Difference: Critical Social Theory and International Relations." *International Studies Quarterly* 34, 3 (September 1990): 269–93.

Geuss, Raymond. *The Idea of a Critical Theory: Habermas and the Frankfurt School.* Cambridge: Cambridge University Press, 1981.

Gill, Stephen. *Gramsci, Historical Materialism and International Relations.* New York: Cambridge University Press, 1993.

———. *Power and Resistance in the New World Order,* 2nd ed. New York: Palgrave Macmillan, 2008.

Glazer, Charles. "Structural Realism in a More Complex World." *Review of International Studies* 29 (July 2003): 403–14.

Hoffman, Mark. "Conversations on Critical International Relations Theory." *Millennium:Journal of International Studies* 17, 1 (1988): 91–95.

———. "Restructuring, Reconstruction, Reinscription, Rearticulation: Four Voices in Critical International Theory." *Millenium* 20 (1991): 169–85.

Honneth, Axel. *Disrespect: The Normative Foundations of Critical Theory.* Cambridge: Polity, 2007.

Hutchings, Kimberly. *Time and World Politics: Thinking the Present, Reappraising the Political*. Manchester: Manchester University Press, 2008.

Jabri, Vivienne, and Eleanor O'Gorman. *Women, Culture, and International Relations* (Critical Perspectives on World Politics). Boulder, CO: Lynne Rienner, 1999.

Jackson, Richard, Marie Smith, and Jeroen Gunning. *Critical Terrorism Studies: A New Research Agenda*. London: Routledge, 2009.

Jutila, Matti, Samu Pehkonen, and Tarja Väyrynen. "Resuscitating a Discipline: An Agenda for Critical Peace Research." *Millenium: Journal of International Studies* 36, 3 (May 2008): 623–40.

Keyman, E. Fuat. *Globalization, State, Identity/Difference: Toward a Critical Social Theory of International Relations*. Atlantic Heightlands, NJ: Humanities Press, 1997.

Kissling, Claudia. *Civil Society and Nuclear Non-Proliferation*. Aldershot: Ashgate, 2008.

Krause, Keith. "Critical Theory and Security Studies." *Cooperation and Conflict* 33, 3 (1998): 298–333.

Lapid, Yosef. "The Third Debate: On the Prospects of International Relations in a Post-Positivist Era." *International Studies Quarterly* 33, 3 (September 1989): 235–54.

Leisens, Anthony. *The Critical Theory of Robert W. Cox: Fugitive or Guru*. New York: Palgrave Macmillan, 2008.

Linklater, Andrew. *Critical Theory and World Politics: Citizenship, State and Humanity*. London: Routledge, 2007.

_____. "Marxism." In *Theories of International Relations*, eds. Scott Burchill and Andrew Linklater. London: Palgrave Macmillan, 1996.

_____. "Realism, Marxism and Critical Theory." *Review of International Studies* 12, 4 (1986): 301–12.

_____. "The Changing Contours of Critical International Theory." In *Critical Theory and World Politic*, ed. Richard Wyn Jones. Boulder, CO: Lynne Rienner, 2000.

_____. *Transformation of Political Community: Ethical Foundations of the Post-Westphalian Era*. Cambridge: Polity Press, 1998.

Lynch, Mark. "Critical Theory: Dialogue, Legitimacy, and Justifications for War." In *Making Sense of International Relations Theory*, ed. Jennifer Sterling-Folker. Boulder, CO: Lynne Rienner, 2006.

McCormack, Tara. *Critical Security Theory and Contemporary Power Relations: Emancipation, Critique and the International Order*. New York: Routledge, 2009.

Nizamani, Haider. "Our Region Their Theories: A Case for Critical Security Studies in South Asia." In *International Relations in South Asia*, ed. Navnita Behera. New Delhi: Sage Publications India, 2008.

Odysseos, Louiza. *The Subject of Coexistence: Otherness in International Relations*. Minneapolis, MN: University of Minnesota Press, 2007.

Price, Richard, and Christian Reus-Smit. "Dangerous Liaisons? Critical International Theory and Constructivism." *European Journal of International Relations* 4 (1998): 259–94.

Rengger, Nicholas, and Tristram Thirkell-White. *Critical International Relations Theory after 25 Years*. Cambridge: Cambridge University Press, 2007.

Richmond, Oliver. "Critical Contributions to Peace." In *Peace in International Relations: A New Agenda*. London: Routledge, 2008.

_____. "Reclaiming Peace in International Relations." *Millenium: Journal of International Studies* 36, 3 (May 2008): 439–70.

Roach, Steven. "Critical International Theory and Meta-Dialectics." *Millenium: Journal of International Relations* 35, 2 (March 2007): 321–42.

_____. *Critical Theory and International Relations: A Reader*. New York: Routledge, 2007.

_____. *Critical Theory of International Politics*. New York: Routledge, 2009.

Rush, Fred. *The Cambridge Companion to Critical Theory*. Cambridge: Cambridge University Press, 2004.

Sabia, Daniel, and Jerald Wallulis. *Changing Social Science: Critical Theory and Other Critical Perspectives*. Albany, NY: State University of New York Press, 1983.

Shapcott, Richard. "Critical Theory." In *The Oxford Handbook of International Relations*, eds. Christian Reus-Smit and Duncan Snidal. Oxford: Oxford University Press, 2008.

Sheehan, Michael. *Securing Outer Space: International Relations Theory and the Politics of Space*. New York: Routledge, 2009.

Stephens, Angharad, and Nick Vaughan-Williams. *Terrorism and the Politics of Response*. London: Routledge, 2008.

Stockman, Norman. *Antipositivist Theories of the Sciences: Critical Rationalism, Critical Theory and Scientific Realism.* Dordrecht: D. Reidel, 1983.

Weber, Cynthia. *International Relations Theory. A Critical Introduction,* 2nd ed. New York: Taylor & Francis, 2004.

Weber, Martin. "Constructivism and Critical Theory." In *An Introduction to International Relations: Australian Perspectives,* eds. Richard Devetak, Anthony Burke, and Jim George. Cambridge: Cambridge University Press, 2007.

Win Jones, Richard. *Critical Theory and World Politics.* Boulder, CO: Lynne Rienner, 2000.

_____. "Introduction: Locating Critical International Theory." In *Critical Theory and World Politics,* ed. Richard Wyn Jones. Boulder, CO: Lynne Rienner, 2000.

_____. *Security, Strategy and Critical Theory.* Boulder, CO: Lynne Rienner, 1999.

■ On Postmodernism

Ashley, Richard. "The Achievements of Poststructuralism." In *International Theory: Positivism & Beyond,* eds. Steve Smith, Ken Booth and Marysia Zalewski. Cambridge: Cambridge University Press, 1996.

_____. "The Poverty of Neorealism," *International Organization* 38, 2 (Spring 1984): 225–86.

_____. "The Powers of Anarchy: Theory, Sovereignty, and the Domestication of Global Life." In *International Theory: Critical Investigation,* ed. James Der Derian. London: MacMillan, 1995.

_____, and Robert B. J. Walker. "Speaking the Language of Exile: Dissidence in International Studies." *International Studies Quarterly* 34, 3 (September 1990): 259–68.

Beer, Francis. *Meanings of War and Peace.* College Station, TX Texas A&M University Press, 2001.

Campbell, David. "MetaBosnia: Narratives of the Bosnian War." *Review of International Studies* 24, 3 (1998), 261–81.

_____. *National Deconstruction: Violence, Identity, and Justice in Bosnia.* Minneapolis, MN: University of Minnesota Press, 1998.

_____. "Political Prosaics, Transversal Politics, and the Anarchical World." In *Challenging Boundaries: Global Flows, Territorial Identities,* eds. Michael Shapiro and Hayward Alker. Minneapolis, MN: University of Minnesota Press, 1996

_____. "Security, Order, and Identity in Europe: A Commentary." *Current Research on Peace and Violence* 13, 3 (1990/91): 175–80.

_____. *Writing Security: United States Foreign Policy and the Politics of Identity.* Minneapolis, MN: University of Minnesota Press, 1998.

Dalby, Simon. "American Security Discourse: The Persistence of Geopolitics." *Political Geography Quarterly* 9, 2 (April 1990): 171–88.

Der Derian, James, ed. *International Theory: Critical Investigations,* London: MacMillan, 1995.

_____. "The Terrorist Discourse: Signs, States, and Systems of Global Political Violence." In *World Security: Trends and Challenges at Century's End,* eds. Michael Klare and Daniel Thomas. New York: St. Martin's, 1991.

_____. *On Diplomacy: A Genealogy of Western Estrangement.* Oxford: Basil Blackwell, 1987.

_____, and Michael Shapiro, eds. *International/Inter-Textual Relations. Postmodern Readings of World Politics.* Lanham, MD: Lexington Books, 1989.

Derrida, Jacques. *Limited Inc.* Evanston: Northwestern University Press, 1988.

Devetak, Richard. "Postmodernism." In *Theories of International Relations,* eds. Scott Burchill and Andrew Linklater. London: Palgrave Macmillan, 1996.

_____. "The Project of Modernity and International Relations Theory." *Millennium* 24, 1 (1995): 27–51.

Epstein, Charlotte. *The Power of Words in International Relations.* Cambridge, MA.: MIT Press, 2008.

Foucault, Michel. *Discipline and Punish: The Birth of the Prison.* Harmondsworth, England: Penguin, 1977.

George, Jim. *Discourses of Global Politics: A Critical (Re)Introduction to International Relations.* Boulder, CO: Lynne Rienner, 1994.

Ihde, Don. *Experimental Phenomenology.* Albany, NY: State University of New York, 1986.

Jarvis, Darrill. *International Relations and the Challenge of Postmodernism: Defending the Discipline.* Columbia, SC: University of South Carolina, 2000.

Neufield, Mark. *The Restructuring of International Relations Theory.* Cambridge: Cambridge University Press, 1995.

Shapiro, Michael. "Strategic Discourse/Discursive Strategy: The Representation of Security Policy in the Video Age." *International Studies Quarterly* 34, 3 (1990): 327–40.

_____, and Hayward Alker, eds. *Challenging Boundaries: Global Flows, Territorial Identities,* Minneapolis, MN: University of Minnesota Press, 1996.

Smith, Steve. "Epistemology, Postmodernism and International Relations Theory: A Reply to Østerud." *Journal of Peace Research* 34 (1997): 330–36.

Walker, Robert, ed."Contemporary Militarism and the Discourse of Dissent." *Alternatives* 9, 4 (1983): 303–22.

_____.*Culture, Ideology, and World Order.* Boulder, CO: Westview, 1984.

_____. "Contemporary Militarism and the Discourse of Dissent." *Alternatives* 9, 4 (1983): 303–22.

_____. *Inside/Outside: International Relations as Political Theory.* New York: Cambridge University Press, 1992.

_____. "Realism, Change, and International Political Theory." *International Studies Quarterly* 31, 1 (March 1987): 65–86.

_____. "World Politics and Western Reason: Universalism, Pluralism, Hegemony." *Alternatives* 7, 2 (1981): 195–227.

CHAPTER 8

Feminist Understandings in IR Theory

Feminism as interpretive understanding includes diverse perspectives to include liberal, radical, and postmodern versions as applied to the subject matter of IR. As a result, methodologies may vary. Feminist IR perspectives cannot be divorced from broader historical concerns of the feminist movement whether postcolonial struggles or civil and political rights in the West. Accordingly, we place feminism as a separate critique or interpretive understanding of conventional international relations theory that offers an alternative perspective and starting point for both theory and practice.

Feminist approaches are important for highlighting major blindspots in mainstream IR, providing an alternative lens—**gender**—through which to view world politics, and providing new insights on the often-overlooked political, social, and economic roles that women play in IR. Feminists argue that the IR discipline falls into the trap of believing that the masculine experience is the human experience. Feminism in all its forms has a strong normative commitment to enhancing the prospects of peace and reducing violence and conflict, the latter effects all too often suffered by women.

INTELLECTUAL PRECURSORS AND INFLUENCES

Although feminist approaches to IR began to appear in the 1980s, feminism has deep intellectual and policy-oriented roots. Certainly Plato elevated the role of women alongside men in the idealized republic he constructed even if Aristotle subsequently did not afford women the same equal standing. For his part, the ancient playwright Aristophanes portrayed women in *Lysistrata* not only as more oriented toward peace and less prone to resort to warlike activities than men, but also as powerful, often decisive actors in their own right. In his *Assemblywomen* we see women assuming control of politics and establishing in Athens a society in which communal, egalitarian values become prominent.

This theme—that women matter and can be decisive, trumping the decisions and actions of men—also can be found in the modern political theory of Niccolò Machiavelli. Indeed, Machiavelli portrays *Fortuna* metaphorically as a powerful woman who not only challenges, but also has the capacity to reverse even the most powerful of men.[1] Chances of beating *Fortuna* are at best 50–50.

This is not the place to elaborate in detail the very rich, multicentury social history of modern liberal movements to emancipate women and legitimate feminine understandings. We select here only a few representative samples from an extensive literature and history of feminist movements. For example, we note the ideas advanced by an early feminist writer, Mary Astell (1666–1731), who articulated what has become a "core liberal feminist belief that men and women are equally capable of reason, and that therefore they should be equally educated in its use." Moreover, one even can find in Astell, albeit in embryonic form, some of the core ideas of recent radical feminism: the idea that "man (whether as sexual predator or tyrannous husband) is the natural enemy of woman" as well as "the idea that women must be liberated from the need to please men."[2]

Better known among the early-modern feminist writers but still reflecting Astell's insights, Mary Wallstonecraft (1759–97) in her persuasive *Vindication of the Rights of Women* (1792) refuted the claim "that women were less capable of reason than men" and argued (as Astell had) that since "men and women are equally possessed of reason they must be equally educated in its use."[3] Critical of the lesser place afforded women in French revolutionary thought and actions, Wallstonecraft argued that the education of women would enable them not only to exercise their reason, but also to realize their inner virtues as fellow human beings. Consistent with this logic, women are (and should be treated as) the equals of men in the rights they possess.

One finds similar views expressed in both socialist and liberal writings of the nineteenth and early-twentieth centuries. In his *Subjection of Women* (1861), the utilitarian John Stuart Mill built upon these earlier, foundational writings, railing against the subordinate and often abusive condition women had to endure. The remedy could be found in legislation that equalized the position of women, assuring access to education and employment as well as full protection of the law and political rights as fellow citizens and full participants in society.

Karl Marx did not address feminist issues as directly as his revolutionary and intellectual partner, Friedrich Engels, did in two key works—*The Origin of the Family, Private Property and the State* and *The Condition of the Working Class in England*. Engels referred to "the world historical defeat of the female sex" as "the man took command in the home also; the woman was degraded and reduced to servitude; she became the slave of his lust and a mere instrument for the production of children."[4] Liberation of women will come with the revolution that frees them from the bondage of being treated as private property controlled by men: "The supremacy of the man in marriage is the simple consequence of his economic supremacy, and with the abolition of the latter [economic supremacy based on private property] will [male supremacy over women] disappear of itself." Engels also observed the abuse of women and men in the workplace in early industrial capitalism—"women made unfit for childbearing, children deformed, men enfeebled, limbs crushed, whole generations wrecked, afflicted with disease and infirmity, purely to fill the purses of the bourgeoisie."

Building upon nineteenth-century challenges posed by Maria Stewart (1803–79), a free black woman, and Elizabeth Cady Stanton (1815–1902), Susan B. Anthony (1820–1906) and others, the stage was set for the twentieth-century suffrage movement. American women finally received the right to vote in 1919. Parallel efforts were also underway in Europe and much later in Latin America and elsewhere. It was after the second world war, however, that feminist writings and associated movements put in place the intellectual foundation not just for feminist scholarship in our own times, but also for important efforts to transform the conditions experienced and roles played by women in what has become a truly global project. In the popular literature, feminist writers challenged exclusionary policies toward women, unequal treatment, and other patterns of male dominance.[5] Feminist understandings have had and likely will continue to have substantial impact on a global scale concerning human rights with regard to equal treatment and the empowerment of women, allowing them the same opportunities that traditionally and historically have been reserved in most cultures to men. Some feminists note that empowering women will also give them the means to limit family size voluntarily, thus reducing population growth rates to economically sustainable levels. Women are also seen by many feminists as more prone to approaching issues of peace and conflict resolution from a broader, often social and cultural perspective.

MAJOR ASSUMPTIONS

First, feminist approaches in IR use *gender* as the major category of analysis to highlight women's perspectives on social issues and research. Gender is a set of variable, but socially and culturally constructed characteristics that are stereotypically associated with what it means in any culture to be masculine or feminine. Masculinity is associated with power and forceful activity, a rationality often cold to human concerns, self-empowered autonomy, and assumption of leadership in public roles. Conversely, feminine characteristics supposedly include less assertive or less aggressive behavior, willful dependence on—or interdependence in—nurturing relationships with others, sensitivity to emotional aspects of issues, and a focus on the private realm.

The two gender categories are dependent upon one another for their meaning and permeate all aspects of public and private life. One's gendered identity or self comes to be defined in relation to (an)other—relationships, for example, between mother, father, and child or male and female peers. For its part, society reinforces the idea that to be a "real man" means not to display "feminine" characteristics. Hence the emphasis on gender is not just about women, but men and masculinity as well. In terms of **epistemology,** many feminists, as we will see, pursue empirical research. Yet the positivist dichotomies such as the separation of fact and value are rejected by most feminists who adopt a constructivist approach to their work, emphasizing how knowledge is shaped by culture, history, and context. Gender as a category of analysis tends not to be used by realists of all persuasions nor by the vast majority of liberal theorists.

In sum, feminist scholars claim that as gender permeates social life, it has profound and largely unnoticed effects on the actions of states, international organizations, and transnational actors. Feminist scholarship seeks to develop a research agenda and associated concepts to trace and explain these effects. Feminist approaches to international relations first began to appear frequently in the international relations literature in the 1980s.

Second, from the feminist perspective gender is particularly important as a primary way to signify relationships of power not only in the home, but also in the world of foreign policy and international relations. When we privilege masculinity, women socially but also legally can be cast into a subordinate status. Gender hierarchies perpetuate unequal role expectations, contributing to inequalities between men and women in IR. Feminists emphasize social relations as the key unit of analysis, obviously interested in the causes and consequences of unequal power relationships between men and women. Unequal power relations exist through time, across cultures, and all levels of analysis. This perspective on power is obviously quite different from that of scholars associated with the four images outlined in this book in which power is usually viewed in terms of states, international organizations, multinational corporations, and other nongovernmental organizations, or classes. The realist rational, unitary, power-maximizing state—which many feminists have noted interestingly is associated with male characteristics—leaves no room for gender as an analytical category.

More conventional IR theories are therefore riven with unexamined assumptions about the international system to include the belief that its concepts are gender-neutral. Feminists would take issue with this, and even argue that virtually the entire Western philosophical tradition ignores feminine perspectives or even exalts a masculine bias. This is why, it has been argued, an important task for feminist theory is to make strange what has here-to-fore appeared familiar or natural. The basic assumptions and concepts of IR have been taken as unproblematic by mainstream theorists.[6] Not surprisingly, there are critical theory and postmodern strains of thought within the broader feminist approach to IR.

Third, many contemporary IR theory feminists are dedicated to the emancipatory goal of achieving equality for women via the elimination of unequal gender relations. Rather than basing their analysis on abstract speculation of how anarchy may influence the behavior of rational, unitary states, the emphasis is on how, for example, military conflict among and within states directly affects the lives of the dispossessed, and women in particular. Far from states being viewed as a security provider, they are just as likely to threaten the security of women if one empirically examines not only the system level of analysis but also the state, societal, or local levels. Hence many feminists find highly suspect the view that the **levels of analysis** demarcate a clear division between the international system and state-society, with the former being characterized as one of anarchy and the latter one of community. When gender is introduced as a category of analysis, old assumptions about security as well as new assumptions about who benefits from globalization can be examined in a new light.

STRANDS OF FEMINISM IN IR

Feminist interpretive understandings can be found within a number of the images and approaches discussed in this book.[7] Liberal feminists emphasize the exclusion of women from important public spheres of social, political, and economic life. There are two strands of research. The first seeks to expose the many areas of IR where women are underrepresented and to identify ways to overcome barriers to expanded participation. Such studies look at the underrepresentation of women in security and arms control policymaking circles or international organizations. Liberal feminism of this strand, therefore, tends to accept the position of mainstream IR that the important subject of research is the so-called high politics of military security beloved by realists. As gender stereotyping historically has consigned women to the private sphere, success for women in IR becomes a practical matter of upping their numbers in diplomatic and security policymaking positions.

The second strand of research looks to uncover ways in which women have actually been there, but not reported. If women were not in international organizations or on the battlefield, where were they? The answer is in factories, hospitals, peace campaigns, and even battlefields. One important example of this work is Cynthia Enloe's *Bananas, Beaches, and Bases*[8] in which she finds some women (spouses, mothers, daughters, girlfriends, and the like) "protected," while other categories (non-Americans, racial minorities, prostitutes—so-called camp followers or those cultivated in communities outside military bases at home and abroad) are exploited. Often denigrated as "common whores," camp followers provide necessary support services such as securing supplies, doing laundry, and nursing. Protection (a form of subordination) and exploitation are, then, two manifestations of male dominance associated historically with militaries at home and abroad. Masculinist behaviors associated with militarization of social life thus have adverse effects on women the larger society has tended to ignore. Moreover, such conduct is by no means unique to the American experience. It is indeed a global phenomenon. Other studies look at the role of women on the home front and their role in filling positions in factories vacated by conscripted men. Liberal feminist accounts have also examined the important but usually unreported role of women in Third World economic development.

Some feminists take issue with the liberal feminist approach. The argument is that there is an underlying assumption that including more women in positions previously denied them will eliminate gender inequalities. But feminists approaching the issue from the perspective of class or patriarchy claim that inequalities define the very structures in which women might participate. Participation alone will not alter this fundamental fact.

Some feminists argue that subordination and domination of women by men is the most basic form of oppression. Much of society is structured to reinforce and maintain patriarchy. Masculine pespectives emphasizing conflict dominate the social sciences and IR theorizing, focusing on such key ideas as defining security in terms of aggregating power. A feminist perspective would expand the concept of security to include the empowerment of women, economic development, and concern for the global ecological commons. Some feminists also take the perspective of women as nurturers and hence more likely to be peace-oriented than men. Some say this is the result of genetic code resulting in men who are aggressive and territorial. Others reject biological determinism and point to young men raised in societies that educate them in martial values (e.g. competitive "contact" or combative sports) and devalue by comparison the work of women to include their running households and raising children.

One of the contributions of feminists is to reject the idea that IR is limited to "high politics," a position logically following from the rejection of the distinction between public and private realms. The danger, say some, is that the supposedly more peace-loving and nurturing female also plays to stereotypes of those who would prefer to confine them to subordinate status and caution against the role of women in national security policymaking positions.

Finally, postmodern feminism aims to displace realist and liberal positivist discourse and epistemology with a commitment to skepticism concerning truth claims about IR. The emergence of postmodern theory—assessing the historical legacy of colonial and imperial experiences Third World societies and cultures still have to confront—also has an important feminist component relating in particular to these development and human rights challenges. Much of this work has focused on Third World countries and the roles women have played and continue to play in tribal and other settings. Postmodernists are therefore allied with postcolonial critics of liberal and radical feminism by rejecting the implicit assumption that women are essentially a homogeneous group unaffected by race, class, culture, sexuality, and history. What connects all of them is a concern for the nature of power relationships up and down the levels of analysis.

Postmodernists tend to reject the idea that there is some ultimate core or essential identity to women that would have the effect of constraining them. The category of "women" is a socially constructed fiction and postmodernists engage in the task of deconstructing that fiction composed as it is of particular social or cultural understandings. Feminist critics of postmodernism, however, are concerned that if the category of "women" is essentially indeterminate, then how can an alternative world order with a different role for women be suggested? If critical discourse has the subversive effect of undermining concepts and creating conceptual disarray, what will be the replacement? Despite differences and often pointed criticisms of the respective feminist approaches to IR, however, all perspectives have contributed to identifying the absence of women from mainstream IR theory and utilize the concept of gender to highlight the inequality of power relations between men and women.

GENDER, WAR, AND SECURITY STUDIES

Scholars with a feminist perspective have been critical of "masculinist" approaches to conflict that tend to emphasize power and balance-of-power politics, coercive diplomacy, unilateralism, and the use of force. From this perspective, conduct in international relations seems similar to schoolyard conflicts, particularly among boys in which the strong do what they will and the weak do what they must. As such, arms races and the use of force in warfare are masculinist constructs. It is not surprising that with some exceptions the perpetrators of guerrilla, terrorist, and other examples of politically motivated violence in IR tend to be men or boys, rarely women or girls. Women are not usually found on the battlefront but rather consigned to the homefront. Those engaged in supporting the war effort through work such as in munition factories are expected to relinquish these roles once the male heroes return from the war.

One of the first feminist works to examine war from conventional and unconventional perspectives was Jean Bethke Elshtain's *Women and War* (1987). She was not interested in contemporary IR research on war but cast her net much more broadly. Her starting point is Georg Hegel's Just Warriors/Beautiful Souls dichotomy—Western men are seen fit to plan, conduct, and narrate wars, while women are viewed as too soft and motherly to do much more than be the receivers of warrior tales. Her personal testimony is followed by historical perspectives on war, peace, and armed civic virtue dating back to ancient Greece. Women are absent from historical accounts, and part of her mission is to show how women have made sense of war and have not merely stood by to suffer it or stand by their warrior man out of duty.[9]

A major effort to summarize empirical studies ranging up and down all levels of analysis is Joshua Goldstein's *War and Gender*.[10] The puzzle he is interested in is the fact that despite political, economic, and cultural differences, gender roles in war are consistent across all known human societies (although this is changing). Historically, when faced with the prospect of war, the response has been in a gender-based way to assemble fighters who were usually exclusively male. War is a diverse, multifaceted enterprise, just as gender norms outside war show similar diversity. Yet such diversity vanishes when it comes to the connection between war and gender. Goldstein applies the three strands of feminist thought outlined above to provide possible answers to this puzzle.

Perhaps reflecting a masculinist orientation that historically or traditionally warfare is essentially a male enterprise, only in more recent decades are women allowed to assume combat roles in U.S. military units. Even now, women are not integrated in ground-combat units that remain a male preserve, even though women frequently find themselves in the line of fire performing their "non-combat" duties. Women are allowed to serve in combat-related tasks at sea and as fighter, bomber, and helicopter pilots. On sexual orientation, homophobic prejudices drawn from the larger society become particularly acute in the all-male military setting, given an institutional culture emphasizing the masculine and discounting the feminine.

The concept of *security* itself has come under scrutiny and become a contested concept. The question asked by feminists is "Security for whom?" Does it make sense to continue to view the patriarchal state as the mainstay of security? Is the security of individuals or groups adequately understood in terms of being members of a given national community? Is achieving security to be found in the traditional realist conception? An even more basic question is "What is meant by security?" Is it limited to deterring or preventing an outside power from attacking the state of which one is a citizen? Perhaps the denial of basic human rights, widespread poverty, environmental degradation, and gender inequality could also be viewed as security issues that are applicable to men, women, and children. Challenging the entire discourse of "security" is in line with the concerns of critical therorists and postmodernists and an expansive notion of security attune to many liberal conceptions.[11] This struggle over meaning—what is meant by security and peace in relation to masculinity or femininity —is a constant concern of feminists.

GENDER AND INTERNATIONAL ORGANIZATIONS

Feminist critiques are not limited to the state, mainstream theories of IR, and conceptions of security. International organizations and non-governmental organizations, so often seemingly beloved by liberal scholars, have also come under scrutiny. The purpose of such work is to ask questions that have gone unasked, and view such organizations from the perspective of gender.

One of the best known IR feminist scholars working on these topics for many years is Sandra Whitworth. A recurrent theme of her work is how international organizations are part of a complex political and social processes that aid in the construction of assumptions about the proper roles of women and men in the workforce. Early case studies involved the International Planned Parenthood Federation (IPPF) and the International Labour Organisation (ILO).[12] The case studies examine the ways in which such organizations over time understood and organized their programs around shifting views of gender. How these understandings came to exist and how activists managed to influence their construction and redefinition is the main theme of the book. The underlying assumption is that such institutions are a reflection of the interests, norms, and ideas of hegemonic groups.

Whitworth's *Men, Militarism, and UN Peacekeeping*[13] brings gendered understanding to national participation in international organizations. As a professor at a Canadian university, she was all too well aware of the positive global image of UN peacekeepers in general and Canadian forces in particular. Widespread faith and a belief in the necessity of peacekeeping were reinforced with the end of the Cold War and the dramatic expansion in the number of peacekeeping missions. Not only did the number increase, but the scope of the missions did as well. Mandates went beyond military and peacekeeping responsibilities to include also monitoring human rights, conducting elections, delivering aid, helping to repatriate refugees, and rebuilding state bureaucracies.

At a 1993 peacekeeping workshop sponsored by Canada's Department of National Defence, Whitworth was given three minutes to comment on the workshop proceedings. Her remarks were not about what had been discussed, but what had been ignored: Who benefits from peacekeeping operations? Who is excluded? What is the effect of peacekeeping operations on the local people? Audience reaction was silence. Problematizing the impact of peacekeeping operations on those most affected from Whitworth's feminist perspective was encouraged by disturbing press reporting that challenged blanket assertions that UN peacekeepers were in all cases selfless, benign soldiers. It is one thing to point to the actions of men in combat, but rather a unique approach to examine militarized masculinity from the perspective of peacekeeping missions. For soldiers involved in the latter operations, there is the seeming contradiction between what is generally regarded as appropriate masculine behavior inculcated from basic training onward to the demands of restricted weapons use and the ability to engage skillfully in community relations.

As Whitworth notes, in some cases states and even the UN have had a tendency to dismiss any information that contradicts the image of UN peacekeepers as altruistic and benign, preferring to view negative reports as merely isolated examples of "a few bad apples." But over time the United Nations and national governments have confronted the charges of sexual exploitation and physical violence against those who are supposed to be protected. Whitworth, however, argues that while attention to gender has made such concerns more visible within the UN, such critiques have had minimal impact on the actual UN way of doing business. In other words, by incorporating the language of gender into official UN policy, it ironically has had the effect of silencing criticism by ensuring that broader issues such as militarized masculinity do not end up on formal UN agendas.

Whitworth and other feminist scholars have addressed the empirical neglect of women and gender relations. In no small way they have contributed to the growth of transnational women's networks that have worked with sympathetic actors in states and international organization bureaucracies to effect policy changes. Amnesty International in 1990, for example, added gender to its list of forms of political persecution. As a result of media coverage of the Yugoslavian civil war in the 1990s and political pressure, rape is now considered a war crime under the Geneva Conventions Against War Crimes and hence can be prosecuted by the International Criminal Court.

GENDERED UNDERSTANDINGS AND IR THEORY

Feminists utilize gender as an interpretive lens through which to view international relations in general and IR theory in particular. With such a perspective, we become more aware of inequality and patterns of dominance, making us more sensitive to the discourse and concepts used to analyze international relations. As such, feminist scholarship offers a counterweight to masculinist understandings that are more prevalent in IR theories that emphasize power, balance of power, and instrumental rationality in the conduct of state and non-state institutions and their agents.

It is not as if men are incapable of producing gendered analysis such as that done by Whitworth and her feminist colleagues any more than women cannot be hard-headed realists. Perhaps in order to be taken seriously in a still male-dominated world that extends as well to academic communities, it may be that many women seeking positions in public or university life have been forced to adopt what some feminist theorists have labeled "masculinist" understandings.

Our principal focus here, however, is on the interpretive understandings associated with gender. Gendered understandings lead us to be critical of theoretical work in IR that masks the masculine or overlooks the feminine. Such a task can be done from a diverse series of perspectives although feminists tend to be more associated with liberal, postcolonial, constructivist, postmodern, or critical theory than with other approaches to IR. Many liberal feminist theorists are also likely to see themselves comfortably within the positivist or scientific camp, merely introducing gender as an important albeit frequently overlooked or neglected explanatory factor in IR or other social-scientific work.

FEMINISTS AND THEIR CRITICS

What Critics?

Given the vigorous feminist critique of mainstream IR theorizing over the past several decades, one would expect a robust response. This has not been the case. Silence, not spirited rebuttal, more often has been the result. Perhaps the best way to interpret this lack of response is to note the lack of feminist work in the leading IR journals. One exception has been the British publication, *Review of International Studies*. Approaches compatible with feminism such as constructivism and even critical theory and postmodernism have received critiques, but feminist perspectives on IR are usually an afterthought in such reviews. It is always possible that mainstream scholars often find feminist IR understandings, at least in terms of their own work, to be irrelevant, interesting but tangential, or dangerous to address for fear of being cast as an ignorant male "who just doesn't get it."

Research Program and Cumulative Knowledge

One early sympathetic observer of the feminist literature is Robert Keohane who called for dialogue across paradigms.[14] He claimed that aspects of feminist understanding could fit comfortably under the neoliberal institutionalism research program. Indeed, what was missing was a feminist research program that could produce cumulative knowledge about IR.

In what still stands today as the best rejoinder not only to Keohane, but also to mainstream theorists in general, is J. Ann Tickner's "You Just Don't Understand: Troubled Engagements between Feminist and IR Theorists."[15] It is all the more interesting as it was published in one of the major IR journals, *International Studies Quarterly*. Tickner noted that very often IR-trained feminists frequently encounter awkward silences when presenting academic papers at conferences. She raised the key question of whether the difficulty in cross-cultural conversations was essentially due to the very different realities, epistemologies, and research interests of feminists and mainstream IR scholars. Furthermore, she argued that these differences themselves are gendered, making communication all the more difficult.

In particular, conventional IR scholars (realists, neorealists, neoliberals, peace researchers, behavioralists, and empiricists committed to data-driven methods) misunderstand the feminist meaning of gender that emphasizes the socially constructed nature of gender and the fact it embodies relationships of power inequality. Second, feminists and non-feminists ontologically see different realities when they look at international politics. Feminists look at unequal social-power relations across the levels of analysis as opposed to a realist ontology in which supposedly rational, unified states are the most important players. Finally, there is an epistemological divide for those feminists questioning the positivist approach to knowledge. Although committed to epistemological pluralism, many feminists are skeptical of methodologies that claim facts are neutral and prefer more historically based, interpretive understandings that raise the question of the extent to which gender roles and patriarchy are variable across time and space. The problem-solving framework of mainstream IR implicitly accepts the given order in IR, and feminists join with constructivists, critical theorists, and postmodernists to question this assumption.

Notes

1. Hannah Pitkin, *Fortune Is a Woman* (Chicago: University of Chicago, 1984, 1999).
2. For eighteenth and nineteenth century thought, we draw on Valerie Bryson, *Feminist Political Theory*, 2nd ed. (New York: Palgrave MacMillan, 1992, 2003), 9–10.
3. *Ibid.*, 16.
4. Friedrich Engels, *The Origin of the Family, Private Property and the State* (Peking: Foreign Languages Press, 1978), 65 as cited by Bryson, 59. Subsequent quotes same page.
5. For example, see Betty Friedan's now classic *Feminine Mystique* (New York: Dell, 1964).
6. Sandra Harding, *Whose Science? Whose Knowledge? Thinking from Women's Lives* (Ithaca, NY: Cornell University Press, 1991), 123.
7. This section draws on Sandra Whitworth, *Feminism and International Relations* (New York: St. Martin's Press, 1994), 12–25.
8. Cynthia Enloe, *Bananas, Beaches, and Bases: Making Feminist Sense of International Politics* (London: Pandora, 1989).
9. Christine Sylvester, *Feminist International Relations: An Unfinished Journey* (Cambridge: Cambridge University Press, 2002), 8–14. In Chapter Two the author provides excellent overviews of the life and work of not only Elshtain, but also Cynthia Enloe and J. Ann Tickner.
10. Joshua Goldstein, *War and Gender: How Gender Shapes the War System and Vice Versa* (Cambridge: Cambridge University Press, 2001).
11. For examples of feminist thought on security, see Jill Steans, *Gender and International Relations* (Cambridge: Polity Press, 1998), Chapter 5.
12. Sandra Whitworth, *Feminism and International Relations: Towards a Political Economy of Gender in Interstate and Non-Governmental Institutions* (New York: St. Martin's Press, 1994).
13. Sandra Whitworth, *Men, Militarism and UN Peacekeeping: A Gendered Analysis* (Boulder: Lynne Rienner, 2004).
14. Robert O. Keohane, "International Relations Theory: Contributions of a Feminist Standpoint." *Millennium* 18 (1989): 245–53.
15. J. Ann Tickner, *International Studies Quarterly,* 41 (1997) 611–32.

SELECTED READINGS

The Logic of Masculinist Protection: Reflections on the Current Security State

IRIS MARION YOUNG

Gender matters in understanding the construction of the security state, which directly reflects masculinist understandings. Young observes how the protection role assumed by males—frequently characterized as "loving self-sacrifice"—effectively subordinates those in the protected position. So it is with the security state that assumes the male-protective role and uses this responsibility to impose its will on the citizenry, particularly when faced by threats or dangers. The security state has two faces—"one facing outward to defend against enemies and the other facing inward to keep those under protection under necessary control."

Much writing about gender and war aims to explain bellicosity or its absence by considering attributes of men and women (Goldstein 2001). Theories adopting this approach attempt to argue that behavioral propensities of men link them to violence and those of women make them more peaceful and that these differences help account for the structure of states and international relations. Such attempts to connect violence structures with attributes or behavioral propensities that men or women supposedly share, however, rely on unsupportable generalizations about men and women and often leap too quickly from an account of the traits of persons to institutional structures and collective action. Here I take a different approach. I take gender not as an element of explanation but rather one of interpretation, a tool of what might be called ideology critique (Cohn 1993). Viewing issues of war and security through a gender lens, I suggest, means seeing how a certain logic of gendered meanings and images helps organize the way people interpret events and circumstances, along with the positions and possibilities for action within them, and sometimes provides some rationale for action.

I argue that an exposition of the gendered logic of the masculine role of protector in relation to women and children illuminates the meaning and effective appeal of a security state that wages war abroad and expects obedience and loyalty at home. In this patriarchal logic, the role of the masculine protector puts those protected, paradigmatically women and children, in a subordinate position of dependence and obedience. To the extent that citizens of a democratic state allow their leaders to adopt a stance of protectors toward them, these citizens come to occupy a subordinate status like that of women in the patriarchal household. We are to accept a more authoritarian and paternalistic state power, which gets its support partly from the unity a threat produces and our gratitude for protection. At the same time that it legitimates authoritarian power over citizens internally, the logic of masculinist protection justifies aggressive war outside. I interpret Thomas Hobbes as a theorist of authoritarian government grounded in fear of threat and the apparent desire for protection such fear generates.

Although some feminist theorists of peace and security have noticed the appeal to protection as justification for war making (Stiehm 1982; Tickner 1992, 2001), they have not elaborated the gendered logic of protection to the extent that I try to do here. These accounts concentrate on international relations,

From "The Logic of Masculinist Protection: Reflections on the Current Security State" by Iris Marion Young in *Signs: Journal of Women in Culture and Society*, 29, 1, 2003. Reprinted by permission of The University of Chicago Press.

moreover, and do less to carry the analysis to an understanding of the relation of states to citizens internally. My interest in this essay is in this dual face of security forms, those that wage war outside a country and conduct surveillance and detention inside. I notice that democratic values of due process, separation of powers, free assembly, and holding powerful actors accountable come into danger when leaders mobilize fear and present themselves as protectors....

Masculinism as Protection

Several theorists of gender argue that masculinity and femininity should not be conceptualized with a single logic but rather that ideas and values of masculinity and femininity, and their relation to one another, take several different and sometimes overlapping forms (Brod and Kaufman 1994; Hooper 2001). In this spirit, I propose to single out a particular logic of masculinism that I believe has not received very much attention in recent feminist theory, that associated with the position of male head of household as a protector of the family, and, by extension, with masculine leaders and risk takers as protectors of a population. Twenty years ago Judith Stiehm called attention to the relevance of a logic of masculinist protection to analysis of war and security issues, and I will draw on some of her ideas (Stiehm 1982). Her analysis more presupposes than it defines the meaning of a masculine role as protector, so this is where I will begin.

The logic of masculinist protection contrasts with a model of masculinity assumed by much feminist theory, of masculinity as self-consciously dominative. On the male domination model, masculine men wish to master women sexually for the sake of their own gratification and to have the pleasures of domination. They bond with other men in comradely male settings that give them specific benefits from which they exclude women, and they harass women in order to enforce this exclusion and maintain their superiority (MacKinnon 1987; May 1998, chaps. 4–6).

This image of the selfish, aggressive, dominative man who desires sexual capture of women corresponds to much about male-dominated institutions and the behavior of many men within them. For my purposes in this essay, however, it is important to recall another apparently more benign image of masculinity, one more associated with ideas of chivalry. In this latter image, real men are neither selfish nor

do they seek to enslave or overpower others for the sake of enhancing themselves. Instead, the gallantly masculine man is loving and self-sacrificing, especially in relation to women. He faces the world's difficulties and dangers in order to shield women from harm and allow them to pursue elevating and decorative arts. The role of this courageous, responsible, and virtuous man is that of a protector.

The "good" man is one who keeps vigilant watch over the safety of his family and readily risks himself in the face of threats from the outside in order to protect the subordinate members of his household. The logic of masculinist protection, then, includes the image of the selfish aggressor who wishes to invade the lord's property and sexually conquer his women. These are the bad men. Good men can only appear in their goodness if we assume that lurking outside the warm familial walls are aggressors who wish to attack them. The dominative masculinity in this way constitutes protective masculinity as its other. The world out there is heartless and uncivilized, and the movements and motives of the men in it are unpredictable and difficult to discern. The protector must therefore take all precautions against these threats, remain watchful and suspicious, and be ready to fight and sacrifice for the sake of his loved ones (Elshtain 1987, 1992). Masculine protection is needed to make a home a haven.

Central to the logic of masculinist protection is the subordinate relation of those in the protected position. In return for male protection, the woman concedes critical distance from decision-making autonomy. When the household lives under a threat, there cannot be divided wills and arguments about who will do what, or what is the best course of action. The head of the household should decide what measures are necessary for the security of the people and property, and he gives the orders that they must follow if they and their relations are to remain safe. As Stiehm puts it: "The protector cannot achieve status simply through his accomplishment, then. Because he has dependents he is as socially connected as one who is dependent. He is expected to provide for others. Often a protector tries to get help from and also control the lives of those he protects—in order to 'better protect' them" (1982, 372).

Feminine subordination, in this logic, does not constitute submission to a violent and overbearing bully. The feminine woman, rather, on this construction, adores her protector and happily defers to his judgment in return for the promise of security that he offers. She looks up to him with gratitude for his manliness and admiration for his willingness to face the dangers of the world for her sake. That he finds her worthy of such risks gives substance to her self. It is only fitting that she should minister to his needs and obey his dictates.

Hobbes is the great theorist of political power founded on a need and desire for protection. He depicts a state of nature in which people live in small families where all believe some of the others envy them and desire to enlarge themselves by stealing from or conquering them. As a consequence, everyone in this state of nature must live in a state of fear and insecurity, even when not immediately under attack. Households must live with the knowledge that outsiders might wish to attack them, especially if they appear weak and vulnerable, so each must construct defensive fortresses and be on watch. It is only sensible, moreover, to conduct preemptive strikes against those who might wish to attack and to try to weaken them. But each knows that the others are likely to make defensive raids, which only adds to fear and insecurity. In Hobbes's state of nature some people may be motivated by simple greed and desire for conquest and domination. In this state of nature everyone has reason to feel insecure, however, not because all have these dominative motives but because he or she is uncertain about who does and each person understands his or her own vulnerability.

In her contemporary classic, *The Sexual Contract*, Carole Pateman interprets Hobbes along the lines of contemporary feminist accounts of men as selfish aggressors and sexual predators. In the state of nature, roving men take advantage of women encumbered by children and force them to submit to sexual domination. Sometimes they keep the women around as sexual servants; thus arises marriage. These strong and aggressive men force other men to labor for them at the point of a sword. On Pateman's account, this is how the patriarchal household forms, through overpowering force (1988, chap. 3).

One can just as well read Hobbes's ideas through the lens of the apparently more benign masculinity of protection. Here we can imagine that men and women get together out of attraction and feel love for the children they beget. On this construction, families have their origin in a desire for companionship and caring. In the state of nature, however, each unit has reason to fear the strangers who might rob or kill its members; each then finds it prudent at times to engage in preemptive strikes and to adopt a threatening stance toward the outsiders. On this alternative account, then, patriarchal right emerges from male specialization in security. The patriarch's will rules because the patriarch faces the dangers outside and needs to organize defenses. Female subordination, on this account, derives from this position of being protected. As I will discuss in the next section, however, Hobbes does not think that it is a good idea to leave this armed power in the hands of individual male heads of household. Instead, the sovereign takes over this function.

Both Pateman's story of male domination and the one I have reconstructed depict patriarchal gender relations as upholding unequal power. It is important to attend to the difference, however, I think, because in one relation the hierarchial power is obvious and in the other it is more masked by virtue and love. Michel Foucault (1988, 1994) argues that power conceived and enacted as repressive power, the desire and ability of an agent to force the other to obey his commands, has receded in importance in modern institutions. Other forms of power that enlist the desire of those over whom it is exercised better describe many power relations both historically and today. One such form of power Foucault calls pastoral power. This is the kind of power that the priest exercises over his parish and, by extension, that many experts in the care of individuals exercise over those cared for. This power often appears gentle and benevolent both to its wielders and to those under its sway, but it is no less powerful for that reason. Masculinist protection is more like pastoral power than dominative power that exploits those it rules for its own aggrandizement.

The State as Protector and Subordinate Citizenship

The gendered logic of masculinist protection has some relevance to individual family life even in modern urban America. Every time a father warns his daughter of the dangerous men he fears will exploit her and forbids her from "running around" the city, he inhabits the role of the male protector. Nevertheless, in everyday family life and other sites of interaction between men and women, the legitimation of female inequality and subordination by appeal to a need for protection has dwindled. My purpose in articulating a logic of masculinist protection is not to argue that it describes private life today but rather to argue that we learn something about public life, specifically about the relation of a state to its citizens, when state officials successfully mobilize fear. States often justify their expectations of obedience and loyalty, as well as their establishment of surveillance, police, intimidation, detention, and the repression of criticism and dissent, by appeal to their role as protectors of citizens. I find in Hobbes a clever account of authoritarian rule grounded in the assumption of threat and fear as basic to the human condition, and thus a need for protection as the highest good.

Hobbes tells a story about why individuals and families find it necessary to constitute a sovereign, a single power to rule them all. In response to the constant fear under which they live, families may join confederations or protection associations. Such protection associations, however, no matter how large and powerful, do not reduce the reasons for fear and insecurity. As long as the possibility exists that others will form larger and stronger protective associations, the nasty state of war persists. As long as there is a potential for competition among units, and those units hold the means to try to force their desires on one another, they must live in fear. Without submission to a common power to which they yield their separate forces, moreover, members of a protective association are liable to turn on one another during times when they need to rely on one another for protection from others (Hobbes [1668] 1994, chap. 17, 3, 4; cf. Nozick 1974, chap. 2). So Hobbes argues that only a Leviathan can assure safety and quell the fear and uncertainty that generate a spiral of danger. All the petty protectors in the state of nature give up their powers of aggression and defense, which they turn over to the sovereign. They make a covenant with one another to live in peace and constitute civil society under the common rule of an absolute authority who makes, interprets, and enforces the laws of the commonwealth for the sake of peace and security of subjects.

Readers of Hobbes sometimes find in the image of Leviathan a mean and selfish tyrant who sucks up the wealth and loyalty of subjects for his own aggrandizement. Democratic values and freedoms would be much easier to assert and preserve in modern politics if the face of authoritarianism were so ugly and easy to recognize. Like the benevolent patriarch, however, Leviathan often wears another aspect, that of the selfless and wise protector whose actions aim to foster and maintain security. What I call a security state is one whose rulers subordinate citizens to ad hoc surveillance, search, or detention and repress criticism of such arbitrary power, justifying such measures as within the prerogative of those authorities whose primary duty is to maintain security and protect the people.

The security state has an external and an internal aspect. It constitutes itself in relation to an enemy outside, an unpredictable aggressor against which the state needs vigilant defense. It organizes political and economic capacities around the accumulation of weapons and the mobilization of a military to respond to this outsider threat. The state's identity is militaristic, and it engages in military action but with the point of view of the defendant rather than the aggressor. Even when the security regime makes a first strike, it justifies its move as necessary to preempt the threatening aggressor outside. Security states do not justify their wars by appealing to sentiments of greed or desire for conquest; they appeal to their role as protectors.

Internally, the security state must root out the enemy within. There is always the danger that among us are agents who have an interest in disturbing our peace, violating our persons and property, and allowing outsiders to invade our communities and institutions. To protect the state and its citizens, officials must therefore keep a careful watch on the people within its borders and observe and search them to make sure they do not intend evil actions and do not have the means to perform them. The security state overhears conversations in order to try to discover conspiracies of disaster and disruption, and it prevents people from forming crowds or walking the streets after dark. In a security state there cannot be separation of power or critical accountability of official action to a public. Nor can a security state allow expression of dissent.

Once again, Hobbes explains why not. It is necessary that the sovereign be one. The commonwealth can secure peace only if it unites the plurality of its members into one will. Even if the sovereign consists of an assembly of officials and not only one ruler, it must be united in will and purpose. It is the mutual covenant that each man makes to all the others to give over his right of governing his own affairs to the sovereign, on condition that all others do the same, that gives the sovereign both its power and unity of will (Hobbes [1668] 1994, chap. 17, 13). Sovereign authority, then, must be absolute, and it cannot be divided. The sovereign decides what is necessary to protect the commonwealth and its members. The sovereign decides what actions or opinions constitute a danger to peace and properly suppresses them. "The condition of man in this life shall never be without inconveniences; but there happeneth in no commonwealth any greater inconvenience, but what proceeds from the subject's disobedience and breach of these covenants from which the commonwealth hath its being, and whosoever, thinking sovereign power too great, will seek to make it less, must subject himself to the power that can limit it, that is to say, to a greater" (Hobbes [1668] 1994, chap. 20, li, 135).

Through the logic of protection the state demotes members of a democracy to dependents. State officials adopt the stance of masculine protector, telling us to entrust our lives to them, not to question their decisions about what will keep us safe. Their protector position puts the citizens and residents who depend on state officials' strength and vigilance in the position of women and children under the charge of the male protector (cf. Berlant 1997). Most regimes that suspend certain rights and legal procedures declare a state of emergency. They claim that special measures of unity and obedience are required in order to ensure protection from unusual danger. Because they take the risks and organize the agency of the state, it is their prerogative to determine the objectives of protective action and their means. In a security state there is no room for separate and shared powers, nor for questioning and criticizing the protector's decisions and orders. Good citizenship in a security regime consists of cooperative obedience for the sake of the safety of all.

The authoritarian security paradigm, I have argued, takes a form analogous to that of the masculine protector toward his wife and the other members of his patriarchal household. In this structure, I have suggested, masculine superiority flows not from acts of repressive domination but from the willingness to risk and sacrifice for the sake of the others (Elshtain 1987, 1992). For her part, the subordinate female in this structure neither resents nor resists the man's dominance, but rather she admires it and is grateful for its promise of protection.

Patriotism has an analogous emotive function in the constitution of the security state. Under threat from outside, all of us, authorities and citizens, imagine ourselves a single body enclosed on and loving itself. We affirm our oneness with our fellow citizens and together affirm our single will behind the will of the leaders who have vowed to protect us. It is not merely that dissent is dangerous; worse yet, it is ungrateful. Subordinate citizenship does not merely acquiesce to limitations on freedom in exchange for a promise of security; the consent is active, as solidarity with the others uniting behind and in grateful love of country....

Is It a Good Deal?

I discussed earlier how the logic of masculinist protection constitutes the "good" men who protect their women and children by relation to other "bad" men liable to attack. In this logic, virtuous masculinity depends on its constitutive relation to the presumption of evil others. Feminists have much analyzed a correlate dichotomy between the "good" woman and the "bad" woman. Simply put, a "good" woman stands under the male protection of a father or husband, submits to his judgment about what is necessary for her protection, and remains loyal to him. A "bad" woman is one who is unlucky enough not to have a man willing to protect her, or who refuses such protection by claiming the right to run her own life. In either case, the woman without a male protector is fair game for any man to dominate. There is a bargain implicit in the masculinity protector role: either submit to my governance or all the bad men out there are liable to approach you, and I will not try to stop them.

I have argued so far that the position of citizens and residents under a security state entails a similar bargain. There are bad people out there who might want to attack us. The state pledges to protect us but tells us that we should submit to its rule and decisions without questioning, criticizing, or demanding independent review of the decisions. Some of the measures in place to protect us entail limitation on our freedom and especially limitation of the freedom of particular classes of people. The deal is this: you must trade some liberty and autonomy for the sake of the protection we offer. Is it a good deal?

Some years ago, Susan Rae Peterson likened the state's relation to women under a system of male domination to a protection racket. The gangland crowd offers protection from other gangs to individuals, their families, and businesses, for a fee. If some people decline their services, the gangsters teach them a brutal lesson and by example teach a lesson to others who might wish to go their own way. Thus those who wish to break free of the racketeer's protection discover that they are most in danger from him. Insofar as state laws and policies assume or reinforce the view that a "good" woman should move under the guidance of a man, Peterson argued, the state functions as a protection racket. It threatens or allows men to threaten those women who wish to be independent of the individualized protection of husbands or boyfriends. Not only do the protectors withhold protection from the women who claim autonomy, but they may become attackers (Peterson 1977; cf. Card 1996).

The security state functions as a similar protection racket for those who live under it. As long as we accept the state's protection and pay the price it exacts not only in taxpayer dollars but also in reduction of our freedom and submission to possible surveillance, we are relatively safe. If we try to decline these services and seek freedom from the position of dependence and obedience in which they put us, we become suspect and thereby threatened by the very organization that claims to protect us....

The logic of masculinist protection positions leaders, along with some other officials such as soldiers and firefighters, as protectors and the rest of us in the subordinate position of dependent protected people. Justifications for the suspension of due process or partial abrogation of privacy rights and civil liberties, as well as condemnation of dissent, rest on an implicit deal: that these are necessary trade-offs for effective protection. The legitimacy of this deal is questionable, however, not only because it may not be effective in protecting us but also because it cheapens and endangers democracy. Subordinate citizenship is not compatible with democracy. The relation of leaders to citizens under democratic norms ought to be one of equality, not in the sense of equal power but in the sense that citizens have an equal right and responsibility with leaders to make policy judgments, and thus that leaders entrusted with special powers should be held accountable to citizens. Institutions of due process, public procedure and record, organized opposition and criticism, and public review both enact and recognize such equal citizenship. Trading them for protection puts us at the mercy of the protectors.

War and Feminism

The logic of masculinist protection, I have argued, helps account for the rationale leaders give for deepening a security state and its acceptance by those living under their rule. There are two faces to the security state, one facing outward to defend against enemies and the other facing inward to keep those under protection under necessary control....

The stance of the male protector, I have argued, is one of loving self-sacrifice, with those in the feminine position as the objects of love and guardianship. Chivalrous forms of masculinism express and enact concern for the well-being of women, but they do so within a structure of superiority and subordination. The male protector confronts evil aggressors in the name of the right and the good, while those under his protection submit to his order and serve as handmaids to his efforts. Colonialist ideologies have often expressed a similar logic. The knights of civilization aim to bring enlightened understanding to the further regions of the world still living in cruel and irrational traditions that keep them from developing the economic and political structures that will bring them a good life. The suppression of women in these societies is a symptom of such backwardness. Troops will be needed to bring order and guard fledgling institutions, and foreign aid workers to feed, cure, and educate, but all this is only a period of tutelage that will end when the subject people demonstrate their ability to gain their own livelihood and run their own affairs. Many people living in Asian, African, and Latin American societies believe that not only U.S. military hegemony but also international trade and financial institutions, as well as many Western-based nongovernmental development agencies, position them in this way as feminized or infantilized women and children under the protection and guidance of the wise and active father.

In its rhetoric and practice, according to some scholars, the British feminist movement of the late nineteenth and early twentieth centuries aligned itself with the universal humanitarian civilizing mission invoked as the justification for the British Empire. Feminists endorsed male imperial leaders' assessment of the status of women in other nations as a measure of their level of moral development. Such interest in the status of women was useful to feminists in pointing out the hypocrisy of denying women's rights in the center as one fought for them in the periphery. Providing services for Indian women and other oppressed women in the empire also offered opportunities for the employment of middle-class professional women (Burton 1994).

Some contemporary feminists have worried that Western feminists today have had some tendency to express and act in similar ways in relation to non-Western women. In a well-known essay, Chandra Mohanty, for example, claims that Western feminists too often use an objectified general category of third-world women, who are represented as passive and victimized by their unenlightened cultures and political regimes (1991). Uma Narayan claims that much feminist discussion of the situation of women in Asian and African societies, or women in Asian and African societies, or women in Asian immigrant communities in Western societies, "replicates problematic aspects of Western representations of Third World nations and communities, aspects that have their roots in the history of colonization" (1997, 43).

Assuming that these criticisms of some of the discourse, attitudes, and actions of Western feminists have some validity, the stance they identify helps account for the ease with which feminist rhetoric can be taken up by today's imperialist power and used for its own ends. It also helps account for the support of some feminists for the war against Afghanistan. Sometimes feminists may identify with the stance of the masculine protector in relation to vulnerable and victimized women. The protector-protected relation is no more egalitarian, however, when between women than between men and women....

Democratic citizenship should first involve admitting that no state can make any of us completely safe and that leaders who promise that are themselves suspect. The world is full of risks. Prudence dictates that we assess risks, get information about their sources, and try to minimize them, and we rightly expect our government to do much of this for us. In a democracy citizens should not have to trade this public responsibility for submission to surveillance, arbitrary decisions, and the stifling of criticism.

In making this claim I am extending recent feminist arguments against a model of citizenship that requires each citizen to be independent and self-sufficient in order to be equal and fully autonomous. Feminist theorists of care and welfare have argued that the rights and dignity of individuals should not

be diminished just because they need help and support in order to carry out their chosen projects (Tronto 1994; Kittay 1999). Persons who need care or other forms of social support ought not to be forced into a position of subordination and obedience in relation to those who provide care and support; not only should they retain the rights of full citizens to choose their own way of life and hold authorities accountable but also they ought to be able to criticize the way in which support comes to them (Sevenhuijsen 1998; Hirschmann 2002, chap. 5; Young 2003). This feminist argument rejects the assumption behind a notion of self-sufficient citizenship that a need for social support or care is more exceptional than normal. On the contrary, the well-being of all persons can be enhanced by the care and support of others, and in modern societies some of this generalized care and support ought to be organized and guaranteed through state institutions. The organization of reasonable measures to protect people from harm and to make people confident that they can move and act relatively safely is another form of social support. Citizens should not have to trade their liberty of movement or right to protest and hold leaders accountable in return for such security.

Democratic citizenship thus means ultimately rejecting the hierarchy of protector and protected. In the article I cited above, Stiehm argues that rejection of this hierarchy implies installing a position of defender in place of both that of the protector and the protected. A society of defenders is "a society composed of citizens equally liable to experience violence and equally responsible for exercising society's violence" (1982, 374). Modern democracies, including U.S. democracy, are founded partly on the principle that citizens should be able to defend themselves if they are also to defend the republic from tyranny. In the twenty-first century, in a world of organized and less organized military institutions and weapons capable of unimaginable destruction, it is hard to know what it might mean for world citizens to exercise collective self-defense. It certainly does not mean that every individual should amass his or her own weapons cache. Nor does it mean whole groups and nations engaging in arms races. The distinction between defender and protector invokes an ideal of equality in the work of defense, and today this may have at least as much to do with political processes that limit weapons and their use as with wielding arms.

The United States claims to use its arms to do this, much as a policeman does in domestic life. In a democratic relationship, however, the policeman-protector comes under the collective authority of the people whose neighborhood he patrols. Democratic citizenship at a global level, then, would constitute a relationship of respect and political equality among the world's peoples where none of us think that we stand in the position of the paternal authority who knows what is good for the still-developing others. To the extent that global law enforcement is necessary, it is only legitimate if the world's peoples together have formulated the rules and actions of such enforcement (cf. Archibugi and Young 2002).

References

Archibugi, Daniele, and Iris Marion Young. 2002. "Envisioning a Global Rule of Law." *Dissent* 49 (Spring): 27–37.

Berlant, Lauren. 1997. "The Theory of Infantile Citizenship." In her *The Queen of America Goes to Washington City: Essays on Sex and Citizenship*, 25–54. Durham, N.C.: Duke University Press.

Brod, Harry, and Michael Kaufman, eds. 1994. *Theorizing Masculinities*. London: Sage.

Burton, Antoinette. 1994. *Burdens of History: British Feminists, Indian Women, and Imperial Culture, 1865–1915*. Chapel Hill: University of North Carolina Press.

Card, Claudia. 1996. "Rape Terrorism." In her *The Unnatural Lottery: Character and Moral Luck*, 97–117. Philadelphia: Temple University Press.

Cohn, Carol. 1993. "Wars, Wimps, and Women: Talking Gender and Thinking War." In *Gendering War Talk*, ed. Miriam Cooke and Angela Woollacott, 227–48. Princeton, N.J.: Princeton University Press.

Elshtain, Jean Bethke. 1987. *Women and War*. Chicago: University of Chicago Press.

———. 1992. "Sovereignty, Identity, Sacrifice." In *Gendered States: Feminist (Re)visions of International Relations Theory*, ed. V. Spike Peterson, 141–54. Boulder, Colo.: Lynne Rienner.

Firestone, David. 2002. "Are You Safer Today than a Year Ago?" *New York Times*, Sunday, November 17, sec. 4, 1.

Foucault, Michel. 1988. "Technologies of the Self." In *Technologies of the Self: A Seminar with Michel Foucault*, ed. Luther Martin, Huck Guttman, and Patricia Hutton, 19–49. Amherst: University of Massachusetts Press.

———. 1994. "*Omnes et Singulatim:* Toward a Critique of Political Reason." In *The Essential Works of Foucault*, vol. 3, *Power*, ed. James D. Faubion, 298–325. New York: New Press.

Goldstein, Joshua S. 2001. *War and Gender: How Gender Shapes the War System and Vice Versa*. Cambridge: Cambridge University Press.

Hirschmann, Nancy J. 2002. *The Subject of Liberty: Toward a Feminist Theory of Freedom*. Princeton, N.J.: Princeton University Press.

Hobbes, Thomas. (1668) 1994. *Leviathan*. Indianapolis: Hackett.

Hooper, Charlotte. 2001. *Manly States: Masculinities, International Relations, and Gender Politics*. New York: Columbia University Press.

Kittay, Eva Feder. 1999. *Love's Labor: Essays on Women, Equality, and Dependency*. New York: Routledge.

MacKinnon, Catharine. 1987. *Feminism Unmodified: Discourses on Life and Law*. Cambridge, Mass.: Harvard University Press.

May, Larry. 1998. *Masculinity and Morality*. Ithaca, N.Y.: Cornell University Press.

Mobanty, Chandra Talpade. 1991. "Under Western Eyes: Feminist Scholarship and Colonial Discourse." In *Third World Women and the Politics of Feminism*, ed. Chandra Talpade Mohanty, Ann Russo, and Lourdes Torres, 51–80. Bloomington: Indiana University Press.

Narayan, Uma. 1997. "Restoring History and the Politics of 'Third World Traditions': Contesting the Colonialist Stance and Contemporary Contradictions of Sati." In her *Dislocating Cultures: Identities, Traditions, and Third World Feminism*, 41–80. New York: Routledge.

Nozick, Robert. 1974. *Anarchy, State, and Utopia*. New York: Basic Books.

O'Connor, Karen. 2002. "For Better or for Worse? Women and Women's Rights in the Post 9/11 Climate." In *American Government in a Changed World: The Effects of September 11, 2001*, ed. Dennis L. Dresang et al., 171–91. New York: Longman.

Pateman, Carole. 1988. *The Sexual Contract*. Stanford, Calif.: Stanford University Press.

Peterson, Susan Rae. 1977. "Coercion and Rape: The State as a Male Protection Racket." In *Feminism and Philosophy*, ed. Mary Vetterling-Braggin, Frederick A. Elliston, and Jane English, 360–71. Totowa, N.J.: Littlefield Adams.

Sevenhuijsen, Selma. 1998. *Citizenship and the Ethics of Care: Feminist Considerations on Justice, Morality, and Politics*. New York: Routledge.

Stiehm, Judith. 1982. "The Protected, the Protector, the Defender." *Women's Studies International Forum* 5(3/4): 367–76.

Tickner, J. Ann. 1992. *Gender in International Relations: Feminist Perspectives on Achieving Global Security*. New York: Columbia University Press.

———. 2001. *Gendering World Politics: Issues and Approaches in the Post–Cold War Era.* New York: Columbia University Press.

———. 2002. "Feminist Perspectives on 9/11." *International Studies Perspectives* 3(4): 333–50.

Tronto, Joan. 1994. *Moral Boundaries: A Political Argument for an Ethic of Care.* New York: Routledge.

Young, Iris Marion. 2003. "Autonomy, Welfare Reform, and Meaningful Work." In *The Subject of Care: Feminist Perspectives on Dependency,* ed. Eva Feder Kittay and Ellen K. Feder, 40–60. Lantham, Md.: Rowman & Littlefield.

Why Women Can't Rule the World: International Politics According to Francis Fukuyama

J. ANN TICKNER

A prominent feminist scholar and former president of the International Studies Association, the author takes on what she sees as Francis Fukuyama's misrepresentations about feminism and the feminist standpoint. In the process she provides feminist understandings about how and why gender matters not only to theorizing about IR, but also about the challenges women face globally. IR feminists want to rid the field of "idealistic associations of women with peace, idealism, and impracticality," particularly since such characterizations effectively "disempower women and keep them in their place, which is out of the 'real world' of international politics." What feminists want is for "women and men [to] participate in reducing damaging and unequal hierarchical structures, such as gender and race."

Feminist perspectives on international relations have proliferated in the last ten years, yet they remain marginal to the discipline as a whole, and there has been little engagement between feminists and international relations (IR) scholars. As I have suggested elsewhere, I believe this is largely due to misunderstandings about feminist IR scholarship that are reflected in questions that feminists frequently are asked when presenting their work to IR audiences.[1] Many of these misunderstandings reflect considerable ontological and epistemological differences, which are particularly acute with respect to mainstream IR approaches. In other words, feminists and IR scholars frequently talk about different worlds and use different methodologies to understand them.[2]

A different kind of misunderstanding, also prevalent, arises from the fact that talking about gender involves issues of personal identity that can be very threatening, even in academic discourse. Feminists are frequently challenged by their critics for seeming to imply (even if it is not their intention) that women are somehow "better" than men. In IR, this often comes down to accusations that feminists are implying that women are more peaceful than men or that a world run by women would be less violent and morally superior. Critics will support their challenges by reference to female policymakers, such as Margaret Thatcher, Golda Meir, or Indira Gandhi, who, they claim, behaved exactly like men.[3]

Most IR feminists would deny the assertion that women are morally superior to men. Indeed, many of them have claimed that the association of women with peace and moral superiority has a long history of keeping women out of power, going back to the debates about the merits of female suffrage in the early part of the century. The association of women with peace can play into unfortunate gender stereotypes that characterize men as active, women as passive; men as agents, women as victims; men as rational, women as emotional. Not only are these stereotypes damaging to women, particularly to their credibility as actors in matters of international politics and national security, but they are also damaging to peace.

As a concept, peace will remain a "soft" issue, utopian and unrealistic, as long as it is associated with femininity and passivity.[4] This entire debate about aggressive men and peaceful women frequently comes up when issues about women and world politics are on the table. Moreover, it detracts from what feminists consider to be more pressing agendas, such as striving to uncover and understand the disadvantaged socioeconomic position of many of the world's women and why women are so poorly represented among the world's policymakers.

A current version using the claim that women are more peaceful than men to women's disadvantage, and the types of agenda-deflecting debates it may engender, can be found in Francis Fukuyama's recent article, "Women and the Evolution of World Politics," in *Foreign Affairs,* as well as in the commentaries on it in the subsequent issue.[5] Unlike the type of criticism mentioned above that, often mistakenly, accuses feminists of claiming the morally superior high ground for women, Fukuyama boldly asserts that indeed women *are* more peaceful than men. But, as has so often been the case, Fukuyama deploys his argument to mount a strong defense for keeping men in charge. Not only does this type of reasoning feed into more strident forms of backlash against women in international politics, but it also moves our attention further away from more important issues. Hypothesizing about the merits or disadvantages of women in charge, or debating the relative aggressiveness of men and women, does little to address the realities of a variety of oppressions faced by women worldwide. Fukuyama's views not only deflect from important feminist agendas, but they also support some disturbing trends in IR more generally, which are reinforcing polarized views of the world in terms of civilization clashes and zones of peace versus zones of turmoil.[6]

Foreign Affairs chose to publish Fukuyama's article under the cover title (in red) "What If Women Ran the World?" This title was surely designed to provoke (and perhaps frighten) its readers, most of whom are probably unfamiliar with IR feminist scholarship. More problematically, it is likely that this will be the only article that mentions feminist IR scholarship to which readers of *Foreign Affairs* will be exposed.[7] Responses in the subsequent issue of *Foreign Affairs* were, for the most part, quite hostile to Fukuyama's position, and asked what was wrong with his argument. Katha Pollitt asserts, "just about everything."[8] Nevertheless, by focusing on the need to rebut Fukuyama's sociobiological and over-generalized portrayal of warlike men and peaceful women, these responses, like the article itself, refocus conversations in unproductive ways that do little to clarify many of the issues with which IR feminists are concerned.

Fukuyama's article is not overtly antifeminist. Indeed, he cites what he calls "a vigorous feminist subdiscipline within the field of international relations" (p. 32) quite favorably, albeit chastising postmodernism for its commitment to social constructionism and radical feminism for its misguided utopianism (p. 40).[9] Curiously, in light of his misgivings about utopianism, Fukuyama offers a seemingly optimistic, even radical vision of a different, relatively peaceful, "feminized" world (in the West at least), where men's aggressive animal instincts have been tamed and channeled into productive activities associated with liberal democracy and capitalism. Fukuyama supports his central claim—that men have "naturally" aggressive instincts—by comparing their behavior to the aggressive and even Machiavellian behavior of male chimpanzees in Gombe National Park in Tanzania. This type of aggression, which, Fukuyama argues, is atypical of most intraspecies behavior, is as true of male humans as it is of their nearest evolutionary relatives, male chimpanzees.

Fukuyama notes that, as with chimps, violence in all types of human societies has been perpetrated largely by men. He develops this claim by documenting recent discoveries in the life sciences and evolutionary psychology that find profound differences between the sexes, especially in areas of violence and aggression. Whereas he is careful to say that culture also shapes human behavior, Fukuyama believes that this line of thinking will replace social constructionist views of gender differences that came about as a reaction to the misuse of Darwinism to reinforce racial superiority and class stratification. In other words, these findings have profound implications for all the social sciences.

Fukuyama also notes that feminists prefer to see such behavior as a product of patriarchal culture rather than rooted in human biology because biologically rooted behavior is harder to change; therefore, they will not be happy with his claims. Fukuyama goes on to hypothesize about a feminized world that would follow different rules. He sees the realization of such a world as a distinct possibility, at least in the West, as women gain more political power. What he calls the "feminization" of world politics has been taking place gradually as women have won the right to vote. The right to vote, along with a relative increase in numbers of elderly women, has resulted in a gender gap with respect to voting on issues of foreign policy and national security, with women being less supportive of national defense spending and involvement in war than men. In spite of these trends, Fukuyama predicts that men will continue to play an important role, particularly in international politics where toughness and aggression are still required.

Given the difficulties of changing genetically programmed behavior and presuming that this new world would have to include socially constructed feminized men, this hypothetical picture seems like a considerable leap from reality. Even though Fukuyama's portrait of this feminized world is seemingly sympathetic, I believe that his message is, in fact, deeply conservative—offering one more iteration of the well-established argument that a "realistic" view of international politics demands that "real" men remain in charge. Accepting its premises actually silences, rather than promotes, feminist agendas and women's equality. Although many of his claims can be successfully challenged on empirical grounds, as his critics demonstrated by their rebuttals in *Foreign Affairs*, his views feed into a conservative agenda that serves not to put women in control, but to keep them out of positions of power.

Why is this the case? Because Fukuyama tells us that no matter how attractive it may seem, we should not move further toward this feminized world; instead, we must keep things the way they are—with strong men at the helm. He argues that women are not able to deal with today's threats that come from violent leaders, such as Slobodan Milosevic, Saddam Hussein, and Mobutu Sese Seko. On the horizon are threats from states in the Middle East, Africa, and South Asia, led by aggressive younger men unsocialized in the ways of mature democracies. Fukuyama claims that people in agricultural societies, presumably outside the zone of peace, with their surpluses of young, hotheaded men, are less concerned with military casualties and therefore more prone to pick fights (p. 38), an assertion that appears to have disturbingly racist overtones.

Closer to home, citing the necessity for combat readiness in the face of these dangers, Fukuyama, by advocating separation of men and women in single-sex military units, effectively advises against women in combat positions. Although he does not deny that women could do as well in combat as men (which was indeed demonstrated in the Gulf War), he claims that their presence destroys combat units' cohesion, which he believes is built on male bonding (p. 37). This "false necessity," together with the need to channel what he calls the biologically rooted male desire to dominate into successful competition in universities, corporations, and political arenas, seems to imply fewer rather than more opportunities for women in both military and civilian life.[10]

And what of men's biological or naturally aggressive tendencies?[11] As feminists have pointed out, one of the main reasons why today's military is recruiting women is because not enough "aggressive" men are joining up. Much of basic training involves overcoming men's reluctance to kill. Advances in military technology have depersonalized warfare so that the problems associated with the long-standing reluctance of men in combat to fire their weapons have been lessened.[12] Violence inside states, which is more prevalent in the United States than in many states outside the western democratic "zone of peace," about which Fukuyama speaks so favorably, stems at least as much from lack of economic opportunities as it does from innate male aggression.[13] Tenure in universities and corporate success are not just about satisfying the need for social recognition of alpha males; they are much-needed guarantees of income and job security, important to both men *and* women.

If we were to accept that men do have aggressive tendencies, the leap from aggressive men to aggressive states is problematic, as many international relations scholars have pointed out.[14] Do men's aggressive tendencies really get channeled into international war, thus leading to the possibility of domestic peace between wars? The high homicide rate in the United States makes one skeptical of this possibility, whereas Switzerland, a country with one of the lowest homicide rates in the world, is rarely an international aggressor. If most men, particularly young men, have violent tendencies, as Fukuyama claims, why is it that some states are so much more peaceful than others? Statesmen do not choose war lightly. Nor is war generally decided at the ballot box where, according to Fukuyama, significant numbers of women are voting for peace. It has often been older men who send young men off to war to fight for what they see as legitimate national interests. Would American policymakers in the 1960s or today's Vietnam veterans be satisfied with the explanation that America fought in Vietnam as an outlet for the aggressive tendencies of its young men?

Now to turn to some of the real feminist agendas for international politics—agendas that are completely silenced by Fukuyama's article. I know of no international relations feminists who hypothesize about or advocate women running the world, as the cover title of Fukuyama's article and the turn-of-the-century illustration depicting a woman in boxing gloves "flooring her beau" (p. 29) suggest. Although Fukuyama includes socially feminized men (who must have overcome their aggressive genes) in the ruling coalitions of his feminized world, such a world is unappealing and sure to threaten, or perhaps amuse, those presently in charge, as well as reinforce culturally defined gender stereotypes about international politics and women.

What IR feminists *have* argued for is getting rid of idealistic associations of women with peace. Associations of women with peace, idealism, and impracticality have long served to disempower women and keep them in their place, which is out of the "real world" of international politics.

When Fukuyama claims that sociobiology was misused at the turn of the century, with respect to race and ethnicity, he, too, is misusing it. He does this under the guise of evidence about profound genetically rooted differences between the sexes by inferring that these differences predetermine men's and women's different (and unequal) roles with respect to contemporary international politics.[15] Of course, feminists want women to participate more fully in global politics and contribute to making the world a less dangerous place. But, rather than killing each other, haven't many men been working toward this goal also?

Wherever men's genes may have pointed, they founded the discipline of international relations by trying to understand why states go to war and trying to devise institutions to diminish its likelihood in the future. Preferred futures are not feminized, but ones in which women *and* men participate in reducing damaging and unequal hierarchical social structures, such as gender and race.

Many feminists would agree that biology may indeed be a contributing factor to certain aggressive behaviors. Yet understanding and working to lessen various insecurities that women face can only be achieved if we acknowledge a need for diminishing socially constructed gender hierarchies that result in the devaluation of women's lives and their economic and social contributions to society. In spite of Fukuyama's assertion that social constructionism is being effectively challenged by new findings in evolutionary biology, the fact that the majority of subsistence farmers in Africa are women, while men are more frequently found in the more prosperous cash crop sector, can hardly be explained by biology alone. Culturally assigned roles, which have little to do with biology, diminish women's socioeconomic position in most societies. Speculating about women in charge, whether their boxing gloves are on or off, seems far removed from the lived reality of the vast majority of the world's women. Katha Pollitt states that even in the United States, where Fukuyama claims that women are fast gaining political power, women constitute only 12 percent of Congress and, after eighty years of female suffrage, have not even won the right to paid maternity leave or affordable day care.[16] Running foreign policy, she concludes, seems like a fantasy.[17] Nevertheless, by focusing on these unlikely futures, Fukuyama effectively silences more pressing agendas and deflects investigations away from trying to understand why the world's women are so often disempowered and even oppressed.

Of course, IR feminists are concerned with issues of war and peace. But rather than debating whether men are aggressive and women peaceful, they are asking new questions about conflict, as well as trying to expand conventional agendas. Feminist agendas include human rights issues such as rape in war, military prostitution, refugees (the majority of whom are women and children), and more generally issues about civilian casualties.[18] Even though civilians now account for well over 80 percent of wartime casualties, understanding the reasons for and consequences of these disturbing trends has not been at the center of international relations investigations. Feminists have also joined the debate about whether security should be defined more broadly to include issues of structural and ecological violence. With this question in mind, feminists are investigating the often negative effects of structural adjustment and economic globalization on women, as well as problems associated with the degradation of the environment.[19] All of these issues seem closer to women's lived realities than debates about their likelihood of running the world.

By asserting that developed democracies tend to be more feminized than authoritarian states, and by linking this to the popular claim about the relative peacefulness of democracies, Fukuyama obscures deeper truths and hides more progressive practical possibilities.

Kal Holsti has suggested that a better explanation for "zones of peace," which actually extend well beyond Western democracies, is the diminished likelihood of war between strong states with governments seen as legitimate by their populations.[20] There are very few states where women have reached a critical mass in political decisionmaking, which makes any link between the democratic peace and the political participation of women tenuous at best. A more fruitful line of investigation is one that is illustrated by a study outlining the results of survey data collected in several Middle Eastern countries, democratic and otherwise. The data show that in the case of the Arab-Israeli dispute, women are not less militaristic than men, but both women and men who are more supportive of gender equality are also more favorably disposed to compromise.[21] A cluster of such attitudes could be the building blocks not for a more feminized world, whatever that may mean, but for a more just and peaceful world in which gender and other social hierarchies of domination, which have resulted in the subordination of women, are diminished.

The debate surrounding Fukuyama's article appears to have stimulated a race to demonstrate who can be more aggressive than whom. Marshaling evidence of women's participation in wars, with pictures of female soldiers on parade and documenting women's violence in matters of abuse of children and servants, Ehrenreich and Pollitt assure us that women can be every bit as aggressive as men.[22]

Are these the debates we should be having? Surely they deflect from the real issues with which international relations scholars are struggling— namely to try to understand the roots of war and what can be done to prevent it. Investigating the enormous variations in levels of conflict across history and societies is surely a more promising place to begin than in deterministic, biologically rooted theories about the aggressive nature of men. International relations feminists have added a new and important dimension to these investigations.

Rather than joining debates about aggressive men and peaceful women, IR feminists are striving to better understand unequal social hierarchies, including gender hierarchies, which contribute to conflict, inequality, and oppression. Evidence suggests that war is more likely in societies with greater gender inequality. Intentionally or not, Fukuyama's musings about women running the world deflect attention away from this more pressing agenda of working toward a world with increased gender equality. Such a world could, I believe, be a less conflictual one for both women and men. Let us turn our attention to more productive conversations between feminist and international relations scholars about the evolution of world politics, conversations that strive to better understand how such a world could be realized.

Notes

1. J. Ann Tickner, "You Just Don't Understand: Troubled Engagements Between Feminists and IR Theorists," *International Studies Quarterly* 41, 4 (1997), 611–632.

2. The symposium in *International Studies Quarterly* 42, 1 (1998), 193–209 is an exception to the lack of engagement. It also demonstrates some of the conversational difficulties to which I refer.

3. Tickner, "You Just Don't Understand," 613.

4. For elaboration on this claim, see Jean B. Elshtain, "The Problem with Peace," in Jean Elshtain and Sheila Tobias, eds., *Women, Militarism and War* (Savage, Md.: Rowman and Littlefield, 1990), 255–266; and Christine Sylvester, "Some Dangers in Merging Feminist and Peace Projects," *Alternatives* 12, No. 4 (1987), 493–509.

5. Francis Fukuyama, "Women and the Evolution of World Politics," *Foreign Affairs* 77, 5 (1998), 24–40; and Barbara Ehrenreich, Katha Pollitt, et al., "Fukuyama's Follies: So What If Women Ran the World?" *Foreign Affairs* 78, 1 (1999), 118–129.

6. See, for example, Samuel Huntington, *The Clash of Civilizations and the Remaking of World Order* (New York: Simon and Schuster, 1996); and Max Singer and Aaron Wildavsky, *The Real World Order: Zones of Peace,*

Zones of Turmoil (Chatham, N.J.: Chatham House Publishers, 1993). Fukuyama also draws on the democratic peace argument to support his global polarization view. For further discussion of this point, see Miriam Fendius Elman, "The Never-Ending Story: Democracy and Peace," in this issue of *International Studies Review.*

7. Indeed, Fukuyama's article has received much worldwide attention in the press, as well as in the foreign policy community. See, for example, Katie Grant, "Why We Need Men in Our New Feminine World," *Glasgow Herald,* January 11, 1999, 13.

8. Katha Pollitt, "Father Knows Best," *Foreign Affairs* 78, 1 (1999), 123.

9. Since *Foreign Affairs* does not allow footnotes, it is often difficult to know to which specific literature Fukuyama refers when making such criticism.

10. This type of argument has shown up in more virulent forms. See, for example, Harvey Mansfield, "Why a Woman Can't Be More Like a Man," *Wall Street Journal,* November 3, 1997, A22. Mansfield accuses feminists of "feminizing America." He argues that women are not cut out for war and that men must be allowed to fulfill their traditional role as protectors, a role that is being undermined as women gain equal access to jobs outside the home. Fukuyama also addresses some of these issues in his new book *The Great Disruption: Human Nature and the Reconstitution of Social Order* (New York: Free Press, 1999).

11. R. Brian Ferguson, "Perilous Positions," *Foreign Affairs* 78, 1 (1999), 125 claims that chimpanzees' naturally aggressive tendencies are also questionable. He contends that the Gombe chimps became aggressive only after human-induced changes in their feeding patterns.

12. While there has been evidence documenting soldiers' reluctance to kill, I realize this is a controversial argument. For further discussion of this issue, including positions that refute this hypothesis, see Joanna Bourke, *An Intimate History of Killing: Face to Face Killing in Twentieth Century Warfare* (London: Granta Books, 1999).

13. The recent dramatic drop in the crime rate in the United States seems to support this position.

14. For examples, see Kenneth Waltz, *Theory of International Politics* (Reading, Mass.: Addison Wesley, 1979),
Chap. 2; and Jane Jaquette, "States Make War," *Foreign Affairs* 78, 1 (1999), 128–129.

15. The popularity of sociobiological arguments about sex differences is evidenced by a cover story in *Time,* March 8, 1999, 57, by Barbara Ehrenreich entitled "The Real Truth about the Female." Ehrenreich's position is much more sympathetic to women—she cites feminist scholars who are doing serious work in this area—but it is indicative of a trend toward emphasizing the sociobiological roots of human behavior and its appeal to wider audiences. Many feminists would probably argue that biology and culture are mutually constitutive of each other.

16. Pollitt, "Father Knows Best," 125.

17. Katie Grant points out that if, as Fukuyama claims, men can become feminized, we do not necessarily need women to run things, even in this new gentler world. Grant, "Why We Need Men."

18. Ruth Seifert, "The Second Front: The Logic of Sexual Violence in Wars," *Women's Studies International Forum* 19, 1–2 (1996), 35–43; Cynthia Enloe, *Bananas, Beaches, and Bases: Making Feminist Sense of International Politics* (Berkeley: University of California Press, 1990); Katharine Moon, *Sex Among Allies: Military Prostitution in US-Korean Relations* (New York: Columbia University Press, 1997); and Susan Forbes Martin, *Refugee Women* (London: Zed Books, 1992).

19. Eleonore Kofman and Gillian Youngs, eds., *Globalization: Theory and Practice* (London: Pinter, 1996); Maria Mies and Vandana Shiva, *Ecofeminism* (London: Zed Books, 1993); and Rosi Braidotti et al., *Women, the Environment and Sustainable Development: Towards a Theoretical Synthesis* (London: Zed Books, 1994).

20. Kalevi Holsti, *The State, War, and the State of War* (Cambridge, U.K.: Cambridge University Press, 1996).

21. Mark Tessler and Ina Warriner, "Gender, Feminism, and Attitudes Toward International Conflict: Exploring Relationships with Survey Data from the Middle East," *World Politics* 49, 2 (1997), 250–281.

22. Barbara Ehrenreich, "Men Hate War Too," *Foreign Affairs* 78, 1 (1999), 120–121; and Katha Pollitt, "Father Knows Best," 123.

SUGGESTIONS FOR FURTHER READING

Ackerly Brooke, Maria Stern, and Jacqui True, eds. *Feminist Methodologies for International Relations.* New York: Cambridge University Press, 2006.

Agathangelou, Anna. *Global Political Economy of Sex: Desire, Violence, and Insecurity in Mediterranean Nation-States.* London: Palgrave, 2005.

Agathangelou, Anna and L. H. M. Ling. "The House of IR: From Family Power Politics to the Poisies of Worldism," *International Studies Review* 6 (2004): 21–49.

———. "Power, Borders, Security, Wealth: Lessons of Violence and Desire from September 11th," *International Studies Quarterly* 48 (2004): 517–38.

Alexander, M. Jacqui. "Redrafting Morality: The Postcolonial State and the Sexual Offenses Bill of Trinidad and Tobago." In *Third World Women and the Politics of Feminism*. eds. Chandra Talpade Mohanty, Ann Russo, and Lourdes Torres, Bloomington: Indiana University Press, 1991: 133–52.

Arrendondo, Gabriela F. *et al.*, eds. *Chicano Feminisms: A Critical Reader*. Durham, NC: Duke University Press, 2003.

Beckman, Peter R., and Francine D'Amico. *Women, Gender, and World Politics: Perspectives, Policies, and Prospects*. Westport, CT: Bergin & Garvey Publishers, 1994.

Bryson, Valerie. *Feminist Political Theory*. 2nd ed. New York: Palgrave MacMillan, 1992, 2003.

Butler, Judith. *Gender Trouble: Feminism and the Subversion of Identity*. New York: Routledge, 1990.

Carpenter, R. Charlie. "Gender Theory in World Politics: Contributions of a Nonfeminist Standpoint?" *International Studies Review*. 4, 3 (2002): 153–65.

———. "Women, Children and Other Vulnerable Groups: Gender, Strategic Frames and the Protection of Civilians as a Transnational Issue," *International Studies Quarterly*. 49 (2005): 295–334.

Carver, Terrell, ed. "The Forum: Gender and International Relations," *International Studies Review*. 5 (2003): 287–302.

Chowdhry, Geeta, and Sheila Nair, eds. *Power, Postcolonialism and International Relations: Reading Race, Gender, Class*. London: Routledge, 2002.

Cohn, Carol. "Sex and Death in the Rational World of Defense Intellectuals." *Signs: Journal of Women in Culture and Society* 12, 4 (Summer 1987): 687–718.

Collins, Patricia Hill. *Black Feminist Thought: Knowledge, Consciousness, and the Politics of Empowerment*. 2nd ed. New York: Routledge, 2000.

Crenshaw, Kimberle, Neil Gotanda, Gary Peller, and Kendall Thomas, eds. *Critical Race Theory: The Key Writings That Formed the Movement*. New York: New Press, 1996.

Davis, Angela. *Women, Race, and Class*. New York: Vintage Books, 1981.

Eisenstein, Zillah. *Against Empire: Feminisms, Racism, and the West*. London: Zed Book, 2004.

Elshtain, Jean. "Feminist Inquiry and International Relations." In *New Thinking in International Relations Theory*, eds. Michael Doyle, and John Ikenberry, Boulder, CO: Westview Press, 1997.

———. *Women and War*. New York: Basic Books, 1987.

Enke, Anne. "Smuggling Sex through the Gates: Race, Sexuality, and the Politics of Space in Second Wave Feminism," *American Quarterly*. 55, 4 (2003): 635–67.

Enloe, Cynthia. *Bananas, Beaches, and Bases: Making Feminist Sense of International Politics*. Berkeley: The University of California Press, 1990.

———. *The Curious Feminist: Searching for Women in a New Age of Empire*. Berkeley: University of California Press, 2004.

———. *Does Khaki Become You?: The Militarization of Women's Lives*. London: Pandora, 1983.

———. "Margins, Silences, and Bottom Rungs: How to Overcome the Underestimation of Power in International Relations." In *International Theory: Positivism and Beyond*, eds. Steve Smith, Ken Booth, and Marysia Zalewski, New York: Cambridge University Press, 1996.

———. *The Morning After: Sexual Politics at the End of the Cold War*. Berkeley: University of California Press, 1993.

Goldstein, Joshua. *War and Gender: How Gender Shapes the War System and Vice Versa*. Cambridge: Cambridge University Press, 2001.

Grant, R and K. Newland, eds. *Gender and International Relations*. Bloomington: Indiana University Press, 1991.

Harding, Sandra *Whose Science? Whose Knowledge? Thinking from Women's Lives*. Ithaca, NY: Cornell University Press, 1991.

Hartspock, N. *The Feminist Standpoint Revisited and Other Essays*. Boulder, CO: Westview, 1998.

Hekman, Susan. "Truth and Method: Feminist Standpoint Theory Revisited." *Signs: Journal of Women in Culture and Society* 22, 2 (Winter 1997): 341–65.

hooks, bell [sic]. *Feminist Theory: From Margin to Center*. 2nd ed. Cambridge, MA: South End Press, 2000.

Hooper, Charlotte. *Manly States*. New York: Columbia University Press, 2000.

———. "Masculinist Practices and Gender Politics: The Operation of Multiple Masculinities in International Relations." In *The Man Question in International Relations*, eds. M. Zalewski and J. Parpart, Boulder, CO: Westview Press, 1998.

———. "Masculinities in Transition: The Case of Globalization." In *Gender and Global Restructuring: Sightings, Sites and Resistances,* eds. M. Marchand and A. S. Runyan. London: Routledge, 2000.

Howes, Ruth, and Michael Stevenson, eds. *Women and the Use of Military Force.* Boulder, CO: Lynne Rienner, 1993.

Imam, Ayesha, Amina Marna, and Fatou Sow, eds. *Engendering African Social Sciences:* Chippenham, UK: Antony Rowe, 1997.

Jabri, Vivienne, and Eleanor O'Gorman, eds. *Women, Culture, and International Relations.* Boulder, CO: Lynne Rienner, 1999.

James, Stanlie, and Abena Busia, eds. *Theorizing Black Feminisms: The Visionary Pragmatism of Black Women.* New York: Routledge, 1993.

Kalu, Anthonia. "Women and the Social Construction of Gender in African Development," *Africa Today.* 43, 3 (Summer, 1996): 269–88.

Kaplan, Caren *et al.,* eds. *Between Woman and Nation: Nationalisms, Transnational Feminisms and the State.* Durham, NC: Duke University Press, 1999.

Kelly, Rita Mae *et al.* eds, *Gender, Globalization, and Democratization.* Lanham, MD: Rowman and Littlefield, 2001.

Keohane, Robert. "Beyond Dichotomy: Conversations between International Relations and Feminist Theory." *International Studies Quarterly* 42, 1 (March 1998): 193–97.

Lippa, Richard A. *Gender, Nature, and Nurture,* 2nd ed. New York: Taylor & Francis—Lawrence Erlbaum Associates, 2005.

Locher, Birgit, and Elisabeth Prügl. "Feminism and Constructivism: Worlds Apart or Sharing the Middle Ground?" *International Studies Quarterly* 45, 1 (March 2001): 111–29.

Mbire-Barungi, Barbara. "Ugandan Feminism: Political Rhetoric or Reality?" *Women's Studies International Forum.* 22, 4 (1999): 435–39.

McClintock, Anne. *Imperial Leather: Race, Gender, and Sexuality in the Colonial Contest.* London: Routledge, 1995.

Meyer, M., and Elisabeth Prügl. *Gender Politics in Global Governance.* Lanham, MD: Rowman and Littlefield, 1999.

Midgley, Clare, ed. *Gender and Imperialism.* Manchester: Manchester University Press, 1998.

Mikell, Gwendolyn. "African Feminism: Towards a New Politics of Representation," *Feminist Studies.* 21, 2 (Summer, 1995): 405–24.

Mohanty, Chandra Talpade. *Feminism without Borders: Decolonizing Theory, Practicing Solidarity.* Durham, NC: Duke University Press, 2003.

———, Ann Russo, and Lourdes Torres, eds. *Third World Women and the Politics of Feminism.* Bloomington: Indiana University Press, 1991.

Moraga, Cherrie, and Gloria Anzaldúa, eds., *This Bridge Called My Back: Writings By Radical Women of Color.* Berkeley, CA: Third Woman Press, 1981, 2002.

Murphy, Craig. "Seeing Women, Recognizing Gender, Recasting International Relations." *International Organization* 50, 3 (Summer 1996): 513–38.

Naples, Nancy, ed. *Community Activism and Feminist Politics: Organizing across Race, Class, and Gender.* London: Routledge, 1998.

Niva, S. "Tough and Tender: New World Order Masculinity and the Gulf War." In *The "Man" Question in International Relations,* eds. M. Zalewski, and J. Parpart, Boulder, CO: Westview Press, 1998.

Nnaemeka, Obioma. "Nego-Feminism: Theorizing, Practicing, and Purging Africa's Way," *Signs: Journal of Women in Culture and Society.* 29, 2 (2004): 357–85.

Nussbaum, Martha. *Sex and Social Justice.* Oxford, UK: Oxford University Press, 1999.

Okeke, Philomina. "Postmodern Feminism and Knowledge Production; The African Context," *Africa Today.* 43, 3 (Summer, 1996): 223–34.

Oyewùmi, Oyèrónké, ed. *African Women and Feminism: Reflecting on the Politics of Sisterhood.* Hawrenceville, NJ: Africa World Press, 2003.

Pateman, Carole. *The Sexual Contract.* Stanford, CA: Stanford University Press, 1988.

Peterson, V. Spike. *Gendered States: Feminist (Re)visions of International Theory.* Boulder, CO: Lynne Rienner, 1992.

———, and S. Runyan. *Global Gender Issues.* Boulder, CO: Westview Press, 1993.

Pettman, J. *Worlding Women: A Feminist International Politics.* London: Routledge, 1996.

Pierson, Jan Nederveen. *Empire and Emancipation: Power and Liberation on a World Scale.* London: Pluto Press, 1990.

Rosen, Ruth. *The World Split Open: How the Modern Women's Movement Changed America.* New York: Viking, 2000.

Rai, Shirin, ed. *Women and the State: International Perspectives.* Bristol, PA: Taylor and Francis, 1996.

Smith, Barbara, ed. *Home Girls: A Black Feminist Anthology.* New York: Kitchen Table/Women of Color Press, 1983.

Spelman, Elizabeth. *Inessential Women: Problems of Exclusion in Feminist Thought.* Boston: Beacon Press, 1988.

Steans, Jill. *Gender and International Relations: An Introduction.* New Brunswick: Rutgers University Press, 1998.

Stienstra, D. *Women's Movements and International Organizations.* New York: St. Martin's Press, 1994.

Sylvester, Christine. "The Contributions of Feminist Theory to International Relations." In *International Theory: Positivism and Beyond,* eds. Steve Smith, Ken Booth, and Marysia Zalewski. New York: Cambridge University Press, 1996.

———. "The Emperors' Theories and Transformations: Looking at the Field through Feminist Lenses." In *Transformations in the Global Political Economy,* eds. D. Pirages, and C. Sylvester, London: Macmillan, 1992.

———. *Feminist International Relations: An Unfinished Journey.* New York: Cambridge University Press, 2002.

———. *Feminist Theory and International Relations in a Postmodern Era.* Cambridge: Cambridge University Press, 1994.

———. "'Masculinity,' 'Femininity,' and 'International Relations': Or Who Goes to the 'Moon' with Bonaparte and the Adder?" In *The 'Man' Question in International Relations,* eds. J. Parpart, and M. Zalewski, Boulder, CO: Westview, 1998.

Tickner, J. Ann. *Gender in International Relations: Feminist Perspectives on Achieving Global Security.* New York: Columbia University Press, 1992.

———. *Gendering World Politics.* New York: Columbia University Press, 2001.

———. "Hans Morgenthau's Principles of Political Realism: A Feminist Reformulation." *Millennium: Journal of International Studies* 17, 3 (1998): 429–40.

———. "You Just Don't Understand: Troubled Engagements between Feminists and IR Theorists." *International Studies Quarterly* 41 (1998): 611–32.

True, Jacqui. "Feminism." In *Theories of International Relations,* eds. Scott Burchill, and Andrew Linklater, London: Palgrave Macmillan, 1996.

———, and Michael Mintrom. "Transnational Networks and Policy Diffusion: The Case of Gender Mainstreaming." *International Studies Quarterly* 45, 1 (March 2001): 27–57.

Weber, C. *Faking It: US Hegemony in a "Post-Phallic" Era.* Minneapolis: University of Minnesota Press, 1999.

Whitworth, S. *Feminism and International Relations: Towards a Political Economy of Gender in Interstate and Non Governmental Institutions.* London: Macmillan, 1994.

Whitworth, Sandra. *Men, Militarism and UN Peacekeeping: A Gendered Analysis.* Boulder: Lynne Rienner, 2004.

Zalewski, Marysia. "Well, What Is the Feminist Perspective on Bosnia?" *International Affairs* 71, 2 (April 1995): 339–56.

PART 3

Normative Considerations

9

Normative IR Theory: Ethics and Morality

In this final chapter we discuss the role of normative theory in IR, important contributors to this literature, and the challenge of applying normative concerns to actual foreign policy choices by the use of contemporary examples. Until recent years, textbooks on international relations were conspicuous for the absence of much discussion of normative theory. This was a rather strange turn of events in that the intellectual traditions underlying the images discussed in this book are a blend of normative (what *should* be the case?) and empirical questions (what *is* the case?). For writers as divergent as Machiavelli, Grotius, Kant, Carr, or Marx, it was inconceivable to discuss politics without at least some attention to the relation between facts and values. The two were thought by them to be inseparable, although they differed on the relative importance of each. Constructivists, critical theorists, postmodernists, and feminists necessarily incorporate normative considerations within the subjectivities and intersubjectivities that define their interpretive understandings. The examination of socially constructed norms or rules that have guided actual conduct in international relations, for example, often rests on or is buttressed by normative theories that contribute to their legitimacy or acceptance over time. The law of war, intervention, norms on distributive justice, human rights, and humanitarian law all relate to the domain of normative theory.

NORMS, ETHICS, AND MORALITY

Philosophers differ on what is meant by norms, morality, and ethics.[1] For our puposes in the context of IR theory, what they have in common is that they all prescribe what the world *should* be and what *ought* to be right conduct. Explicit in this conception is the idea that norms might require people, states, or international and transnational actors to act in ways that do not promote the actor's self-interest.

In this chapter we raise some of the issues central to an understanding of normative international relations theory. When, if ever, is war just, and what is just conduct in war? Are there universally understood human rights? On what grounds are armed or other forms of intervention legitimate? On what moral bases should statesmen make foreign policy choices?

It is not our intention here to delve deeply into such complex questions, an enterprise well beyond the scope of this effort. Over the centuries, many international relations theorists have grappled with normative questions, and we want here only to alert the readers to some of the most critical of these.

Second, we also want to recognize normative international relations theory building as a legitimate enterprise worthy of more scholarly efforts. As discussed in Chapter One, normative theory differs fundamentally from empirical theory. Propositions in normative theory that deal with what *ought* to be are not subject to the formal empirical tests of hypotheses about what *is,* which is the realm of empirical theory. An explicit expression of this position is to be found in the article by James Rosenau in Chapter One.

Nevertheless, value orientations are present even among empirical theorists in all four international relations images we identify. *What* is studied and *how* it is studied are preferences that vary from theorist to theorist across all four images. Although empirical theorists as positivists try to minimize the effect of individual value bias through objective testing of hypotheses, personal values cannot be filtered out completely. Values are less problematic in social constructivism, critical theory, postmodernism, and feminism as they are central to interpretive understandings.

Third, normative IR theory is important if not inescapable in the realm of foreign policy. Policymaking is all about making choices. Choices among competing alternatives made by policymakers are informed not just by knowledge of what *is* or could be the possible outcome of a decision, but also by a rationale for what *ought* to be. Developing the bases for such choices is the domain of normative theory.

NORMATIVE THEORY: ALTERNATIVE PERSPECTIVES

■ The Levels of Analysis

There are differing perspectives on how to approach a discussion of normative theory and IR. One way of looking at this is in terms of the levels of analysis—the individual, the community, and the world. In terms of the individual, the simple yet important question is do we have duties beyond borders? Particularly in an era of globalization, how might we live in a world threatened by not only weapons of mass destruction but also global climate change?[2]

The national or community position on norms holds that obligations to fellow citizens take priority over those of strangers living in other nations, states, or cultures. The attempt to develop and justify normative universal criteria is questionable from this perspective. This does not mean, however, that states are unable to come to common agreement in certain areas. In fact international law provides bases for states to respect one another's autonomy.[3] Furthermore, the idea that there is a pluralism of values among societies or groups does not mean there is no basis for criticizing, for example, the abuse of human rights.

A third perspective—and our major focus in this chapter—concerns universal or cosmopolitian normative theorizing. This dates back to the Stoics and natural law thinking, Kantian moral imperatives, utilitarian principles, and social contract bases for moral choice.

Moral Relativism

Universal or cosmopolitan perspectives are in direct conflict with the idea of moral relativism, which holds that no universal standard exists by which to assess an ethical proposition's truth. If we really believe, however, in a strict moral relativism—that values and rights can have no independent standing of their own—then we are saying in effect that there is no such thing as morality or ethics.

One significant problem with moral relativism is that it gives us no universal basis for condemning atrocities and such human tragedies as the Holocaust. Just because eliminating the Jews as a people may have been considered legitimate within a Nazi political subculture, this belief did not make it right. Even if we have difficulty agreeing on many other values, genocide is so offensive to the human spirit that it is condemned as mass murder on universal, not just on particular cultural grounds. Any rational human being, regardless of cultural origin, should understand the immorality of such atrocities.

What about a religious basis for universal human rights? Islam, Christianity, Judaism, Hinduism, Buddhism, and other religions do not just limit themselves to their followers but frequently also make universally applicable moral claims. As a practical matter, rejection of religion by some and the absence of theological consensus even among the followers of various religious groups prevent us from using particular religions as the solitary bases for common, worldwide acceptance of human rights and other moral claims. Instead, many writers have tried to identify secular or non-religious bases for their universalist positions to which we now turn.

Secular Bases for Moral or Ethical Choice

Stoics. As discussed in Chapter Three, the Stoics argued that we are all part of a larger community of humankind, regardless of our different political communities and cultures. The ability to reason is a quality shared by all humans, and this makes it possible for us to determine the laws of nature that are applicable to all regardless of the community in which one lives. Stoic ideas were very influential in republican and imperial Rome. For example, the Roman orator Cicero (106–43 B.C.) states that "true law is right reason in agreement with nature; it is of universal application, unchanging and everlasting." He asserts: "Justice is one; it binds all society, and is based on one law." Indeed, he observes: "Justice does not exist at all if it does not exist in Nature."[4]

This universalism was the basis for the idea of law common to the nations of the Roman empire—a law of the peoples or, in Latin, a *jus gentium*. That values transcend a single community or state was also central to the thought of Augustine, Aquinas, and other religious writers of the Middle Ages. As discussed in previous chapters, Grotius and others would contribute to a secular basis for international law—whether based on general principles consistent with reasoned understanding of natural law, customary international practice, the writings of jurists (as in decisions rendered by judges or justices), or commitments in treaties or conventions voluntarily undertaken by states—the four generally accepted sources of international law. Similarly, natural law thinking played an important role in the social-contract theories of Hobbes and Locke.

Kant. Immanuel Kant (1724–1804), whose work has already been mentioned in other chapters, has us use our rational faculty to look inward. The moral element is captured by the oft-quoted phrase of one standing alone at night in awe looking upward reflectively at "the starry sky above me and the moral law within me." This vision of the universal transcends space and time and yet can be discovered within oneself.

In this regard Kant is best known for his writings on reason with direct application to discovering universal maxims or ethical imperatives we are duty-bound to follow not just in our private lives, but also in the positions we hold in our public lives. For Kant, a fundamental principle is to act always so that you respect every human being as a rational, thinking agent capable of choice. According to Kant, the individual has free will to choose the correct moral course, clearly a voluntarist position. Individual behavior is not predetermined, but the individual is obligated, nevertheless, to follow the moral law that is discoverable through the proper exercise of reason.

According to Kant, one should exercise free will and act according to the "categorical imperative"—independent of contingencies—whereby one acts "according to the maxim which you can at the same time will to be a universal law." Moreover, one should "treat humanity, in your own person, and in the person of everyone else as an end as well as a means, never merely as a means." Put another way, we are to treat other human beings as ends worthy in themselves, not just as means. Finally, the correct prescription for a moral conduct is knowable by the individual and amounts to those precepts that have universally binding character.[5]

It is this universal dimension in Kantian ethics that is also the basis for his thinking on international relations. Kant addressed war and peace in international society, looking toward an improvement in state behaviors among liberal republics that would make them decidedly less prone to use force against other states—in effect a democratic peace (see the discussion in Chapter Three). The Kantian ideal was indeed a future, cosmopolitan international society of individuals, states, or other actors following ethical principles and aiming toward perfection. In other words, "right reason" is to be used to discern obligations stemming from universal law that transcends the laws made by individual states. This was to be the path toward "perpetual peace"—a world free of war. A federation of peaceful states could (but would not necessarily) come to be established as a response to the very real security needs of states.

Utilitarians. In contrast to Kantian ethics, the writings of Jeremy Bentham (1748–1832), John Stuart Mill (1806–1873), and others focus on attaining the greatest good for the greatest number as the principal criterion of utilitarian thought. We should be concerned with assessing outcomes or the consequences of our actions. A "society is rightly ordered," according to utilitarians, if "its major institutions are arranged so as to achieve the greatest net balance of satisfaction."[6] Utilitarians take this abstract principle and apply it to a wide range of human circumstances, including a defense of liberty and other human rights as representing the greatest good for the greatest number. The main application of utilitarian principles was to be within domestic societies. In principle, however, utilitarian and Kantian criteria provide a philosophical basis for international law because the application of these criteria transcends the boundaries of any given state or society. In practice, of course, we face enormous obstacles trying to apply either Kantian or utilitarian ethics as the basis for constructing some radically new and just world order, given the present division of the world into separate, sovereign states with very different perspectives on global issues.

Social Contract Theorists.   The question of the scope of justice is an issue dating back to the beginning of philosophy. Should conceptions of justice have boundaries, limiting it to particular societies or cultures? Or is justice by nature universal and cosmopolitan? Social contract theorists are of interest to normative IR theory as they begin with the domestic question of justice and have provided insight on the expansion of such normative concerns to international politics.

The social contract approach as a guide to right behavior assumes that individuals may voluntarily agree to bind or obligate themselves to some set of principles. The challenge is explaining how this might come about. In Rousseau's stag hunt analogy discussed in Chapters Two and Three, the hunters in a state of nature can be understood as maximizing individual, short-term self-interest by going for the hare. In a world of no sovereign authority to compel collaboration or to force the honoring of contracts, no other outcome can be expected. For Thomas Hobbes, escaping the state of nature could only be achieved by the people elevating a sovereign—whether a monarch or legislature—to provide the order and security that comes from governance.

Although Hobbes finds a way out of a figurative state of nature for domestic politics, he sees no such social-contract remedy to resolve the problems of cooperation among states exisiting in an anarchic international system. As noted by English School theorists and some constructivists, however, different assumptions about the state of nature result in different prospects for international collaboration. The seventeenth-century English writer John Locke reasoned that human beings have certain **natural rights** to life, liberty, and property, which they surrender only as part of a social contract. The notion among social-contract theorists that, quite apart from cultural context, human beings have rights as part of their nature obviously provides another secular ground for making universalistic moral claims. To Locke (and to Thomas Jefferson, who followed Locke's lead), human rights are thus part of human nature. The citizenry or people who empower governments in the first place must therefore strictly limit the authority of governments to abridge them. In fact, governments are created in part to guarantee certain civil rights, which are those rights that individuals have as members of the societies to which they belong. This conception can be applied to the domestic as well as the international levels of analysis.

Building on this social-contract approach as a means to finding justice within a society, John Rawls asks what would be considered fair if individuals were in a state of nature and none knew in advance what one's place in society, class position, wealth, or social status would be. Behind this common "veil of ignorance" about outcomes, what principles of distributive justice would these hypothetically free agents choose?

One principle taken from Rawls' analysis is that "all social values—liberty and opportunity, income and wealth, and the bases of self-respect—are to be distributed equally unless an unequal distribution of any, or all, of these values is to everyone's advantage." Beyond that, socioeconomic inequality is admissible only if it benefits everyone in society and if there is an equal opportunity for everyone to acquire those positions associated with unequal rewards.

Whether one extends such propositions as the basis for global justice for individuals or for states as if they were individuals was not altogether clear in Rawls' now classic *A Theory of Justice*. In that volume he formulates a "conception of justice for the basic structure of society," observing that "the conditions for the law of nations may require different principles arrived at in a somewhat different way."[7]

In his later work, however, Rawls takes up this challenge by exploring the ways and means of extending a "law of peoples" that transcends the borders of states and their respective societies. The idea of constructing an international or global society logically calls for the application of universal norms. Similar to the intended universal applicability of the Roman law of peoples (or, in Latin, the *jus gentium*), he finds that behind a veil of ignorance "a well ordered nonliberal society" or authoritarian regime in our times "will accept the same law of peoples that well ordered liberal societies accept."[8] Not surprisingly, he finds the fabric of this law in the liberal understandings of human rights, freedom, independence, and non-intervention.

If one allows social contract theory to be applied to states as if they were individual persons, it becomes a basis for a **positivist** (in the legal, not epistemological sense) interpretation of international law. Among positivists, international law and the obligation to follow other international rules or norms stem not from natural law or natural rights, but rather from affirmative actions taken by states. Kantian, utilitarian, or other principles may be part of the calculus of deciding which rules are to be made binding, but it is the voluntary contract, or choice, made by states in the form of a treaty, convention, or customary practice (so routine in performance as to amount to an implicit contract) that creates the obligation.

Norms, morality, and ethics, therefore, are not new to the study of international relations. They may be addressed in terms of "right reason" to discern obligations stemming from some aspect of natural law or provide the greatest good for the greatest number under utilitarian reasoning. Alternatively, they may conform more closely to a positivist approach to constructing international law—that treaties, for example, are binding and that such obligations ought to be kept. The Kantian perspective in particular contrasts sharply with the views of Machiavelli and Hobbes described in Chapter Two. Although concerns for moral choices certainly are present in classical realism, power and the balance of power have clearly been the more important considerations in this tradition. It is, however, incorrect to view power and values as if they were mutually exclusive approaches to international politics. As E. H. Carr, an intellectual precursor in the realist tradition and of the English School, has observed:

> The utopian who dreams that it is possible to eliminate self-assertion from politics and to base a political system on morality alone is just as wide of the mark as the realist who believes that altruism is an illusion and that all political action is self-seeking.[9]

In short, international politics involves a blend of values and power, utopianism and realism. Such a perspective can be found in virtually all the intellectual precursors discussed in this book. There is disagreement, however, as to the relative importance of values and power, and which values should be pursued.

JUSTICE AND WAR

One fairly well developed area that stands as an exception to our general observation of the paucity of normative international relations theory is that dealing with the morality of war itself (*jus ad bellum*) and the ethical or moral constraints within any given war (*jus in bello*). Scholars of all perspectives have examined this issue, and it is therefore an appropriate place to start our overview of normative theory and the challenges of its application.

Informed speculation on this subject builds on a tradition in Western thought extending back to the ancient Greeks. Contrary to the absolute pacifism of many early Christians, the writings of St. Augustine (354–430 A.D.) drew from the work of Cicero (and Plato before him), addressing war as something that was to be avoided but that was sometimes necessary: "It is the wrong-doing of the opposing party which compels the wise man to wage wars."[10] The corpus of just war theory grew with additions made by Aquinas, Suarez, Vitoria, and other religious and political philosophers of the medieval period.

That we can develop a theory of just war through the exercise of right reason and right conduct are philosophical assumptions underlying normative theory on armed conflict. Perhaps not surprisingly, given their preoccupation with national security issues, much contemporary thinking on just war has occurred primarily among realists, particularly classical realists. The subject has also been of substantial interest in the English School, steeped as it is in the history of international relations and the Grotian and other philosophical understandings that go with it. Not all realists would accept the Machiavellian characterization of war as something useful for acquiring or maintaining rule and that, if postponed, might work only to the advantage of the enemy. A Machiavellian principle underscored by Clausewitz, as noted in Chapter Two, is that war is decidedly not a legitimate end in itself, but is merely a means used to achieve essentially political purposes. That war should not be waged without "legitimate" purpose—that it should at least be subordinate to the political objective or serve some national interest—can be understood as a limited but nevertheless moral statement in itself.

Defense against provoked aggression is generally conceded (except by absolute pacifists) to be a legitimate political objective justifying war. Nevertheless, in just-war thinking, war is a last resort to be undertaken only if there appears to be some chance of success. The death and destruction wrought by war are to be minimized, consistent with achieving legitimate military purposes. Indeed, there can be no positive moral content in war unless legitimate political objectives and military purposes are served. Following conventional military logic found in Clausewitz, the purpose in any war is to destroy or substantially weaken an enemy's war-making capability. Military necessity, so defined, however, does not justify the use of means disproportionate to the ends sought or the use of weapons that are indiscriminate or that cause needless human suffering. Moreover, the lives of non-combatants are to be spared.

Just-war theory does not confine itself merely to whether one has a right to use armed force or resort to war in international relations. It goes beyond the *jus ad bellum* to raise questions of right conduct in war once armed conflict breaks out—the *jus in bello*. Very real limits are set in an effort to confine the death and destruction of warfare to what is militarily necessary, thus reducing war's barbarity. These principles that specify the bases for moral legitimacy of going to war and the conduct or use of force *in* war are summarized in Table 9.1. As with any set of moral or ethical principles, their application depends upon right intention, which critics observe cannot always be assumed when it comes to the conduct of states still sovereign in an anarchic world lacking in viable enforcement authority.

Scholars in the English School, liberals, and classical realists of Grotian persuasion identify rules or laws that constrain states, statesmen, and soldiers in the exercise of their war powers. Treaties or conventions based largely on earlier just-war thinking have come into force beginning with the Hague Conventions in the late nineteenth and early twentieth centuries. These were followed by the twentieth-century Geneva Conventions and other agreements which collectively provide the basis for the contemporary law of war. Defining aggression and dealing with insurgencies in which the very legitimacy of the parties is in question remain on the agenda of important moral and legal challenges.

TABLE 9.1   Just-War Principles

Jus Ad Bellum	Jus In Bello
1. Just cause	1. Military necessity
2. Legitimate authority	2. Spare non-combatants and other defenseless persons
3. Proportionality of war	
4. Chance of success	3. Proportional means
5. War as last resort; exhaust peaceful means to resolve dispute	4. Means not immoral *per se:* not indiscriminate or causing needless suffering

Note: Application of all principles assumes right intention.

Applying Just-War Theory in the Twenty-First Century

Quite apart from such concerns, however, the focus on limits in just-war theory and international law could be seen as impractical in an age dominated by weapons of mass destruction (WMD). Furthermore, can just-war theory be used to legitimate deterrence doctrines arguing that in order to maintain peace one must threaten devastation even on a global scale?[11] The continuing proliferation of nuclear weapons capabilities has made countries in some regions—the Middle East and South Asia—particularly vulnerable. Nevertheless, just-war theory, imperfect as it may be, ought not be set aside. Indeed, in a time of increasing global insecurity, the effort in just-war theory to put practical limits on the use of force and thus to reduce, if not completely eliminate, the barbarity of warfare remains salient in what is at best a still emergent, global civil society.

Just-war theory did not prevent obliteration bombing of cities or other population centers in World War II. At the time, many defenders of this strategy saw these raids as undermining societal morale in enemy countries, thus weakening an enemy's will to resist. But postwar evaluation of strategic bombing and other uses of air power raised a serious challenge to this rationale. Rage among survivors contributed in many cases to an increased will to resist rather than to submit. If so, then obliteration bombing proved to be counterproductive or dysfunctional, even militarily speaking. With the benefit of hindsight, obliteration bombing of population centers has been discredited both militarily and morally in the years since World War II. Put another way, there can be no moral justification under just-war doctrine for such mass death and destruction, particularly because these military actions did not serve legitimate military purposes. Just because military purposes are served, of course, is not enough to justify *any* conduct in war. Additional conditions need to be met to satisfy *jus in bello* obligations.

Although the principle of military necessity can be construed so broadly in the interest of national security as to allow almost any conduct in war, we expect political authorities or military commanders to approach the use of force with a spirit consistent with the human-cost reduction purpose of just-war theory. Indeed, it is a narrow construction of military necessity that is prescribed by just-war theory. Destroying an enemy's war-making capability focuses destructive efforts on an adversary's armed forces and *only* those parts of the society's infrastructure that directly contribute to its war-making effort. It is not a call to destroy an entire society, its population, or anything else of material or cultural value. People will still be killed and property destroyed, but probably far less damage will be sustained when the principle of military necessity is narrowly interpreted to limit the destructiveness of war to what is absolutely necessary for military purposes.

A distinction is therefore often drawn between **counterforce** and **countervalue** targets. Counterforce targets include military headquarters, troop or tank formations, combat aircraft, ships, maintenance facilities, and other military installations the destruction of which would directly weaken an enemy's war-making capability. Countervalue targets are factories, rail junctions, civilian airports, and power plants in or near cities that contribute to an enemy's war-making capability or overall war effort. Even if people are not the intended victims, the bombing of countervalue targets usually produces more civilian, non-combatant casualties than counterforce targeting.

Moreover, compatible with the *jus in bello,* the means used to accomplish military purposes need to be proportional to the goal. If a 300-pound bomb can be used to destroy a particular military target, a 10,000-pound bomb ought not to be used, particularly if doing so increases the **collateral destruction** of lives and property. In the same spirit, navy warships may choose to avoid sinking an enemy merchant ship by disabling the propeller. If feasible, they can then board and search the cargo. Again, just-war theory aims to reduce unnecessary death or other damage.

One possible way to achieve this is to invoke the **dual** or **double-effect principle** in dealing with the moral problem of killing non-combatants and producing collateral damage in warfare. Any action may have two or more effects or consequences. If the intent is to destroy a legitimate target that contributes to an enemy's war-making capability or overall war effort, then every reasonable effort must be made to avoid unnecessary casualties or other destruction. The "good effect" is destroying the legitimate military target. Dropping bombs, sending missiles, landing artillery shells, or firing on such a target may also have unintended human and material consequences—the "bad effect."

Following double-effect logic and assuming proportionality—that the target is worth destroying in light of its military value when weighed against the expected consequences—just-war theory would seem to support the idea that killing non-combatants or destroying civilian property may be morally justifiable when both effects occur simultaneously or the good effect precedes the bad. For example, in targeting an armaments factory at night when most workers were expected to be at home, it is accepted that a few workers may still be killed when the factory is destroyed. Or a bomb may go astray and kill some people in a residential area next to the factory, even though efforts were made to avoid this unfortunate outcome. That is the misfortune of war. Bad things happen in war, which is why just-war theory puts so much emphasis on avoiding war in the first place.

If warriors *intend* the bad effect or if it precedes the good, such conduct does not satisfy the principle of double effect and is understood, therefore, to be morally wrong. Bombing workers at their homes next to the armaments factory (the bad effect) will likely reduce or eliminate the production capacity of the factory (the good effect, militarily speaking). The problem is that this good effect depends upon achieving the bad effect first. However good one's objectives or purposes may be, just-war theorists argue that good ends cannot justify evil means: the ends do not justify the means. It would be morally wrong to bomb the village. If factory production must be halted, then the factory itself should be targeted, preferably at a time when as many workers as possible can be spared.

■ Morality and Weaponry

Any weapon can be used immorally, but some could not be used morally even if one intended to do so. Immoral weapons are those that are indiscriminate or cause needless suffering. A rifle is not immoral in itself; if used properly, it can be used with discrimination, sparing noncombatants. If used improperly to murder non-combatants, for example, it is the action and not the weapon that is immoral.

The same is true for most conventional bombs delivered accurately by airplanes or missiles. They can be used morally or immorally, depending for the most part on the target selected and how it is to be destroyed. The more accurate, the better is true from both a military and a moral position. Indeed, destruction of a legitimate military target is more likely, and collateral or unnecessary death and destruction, if not eliminated, can at least be minimized if accurate weapons are employed.

By contrast, wildly inaccurate weapons—including chemical or biological agents as in gas or germ warfare—by their very nature eliminate the distinction between combatant and non-combatant. Such weapons usually are not useful militarily, as winds disperse chemical agents indiscriminately, and diseases can spread to both sides of the battlefield and more generally across societies. Such weapons are immoral in themselves and have been declared illegal. Treaties prohibit the use of chemical and biological weapons.

The international consensus that led to these chemical and biological conventions rests on this moral argument. Not only are these weapons indiscriminate, but also they fail another moral test by causing needless suffering. Rifle bullets or other antipersonnel weapons designed to prolong or otherwise increase agony also fail this moral test. Killing in war is supposed to be as humane as possible. Most categories of weapons that are intended to enhance rather than reduce human suffering have also been defined in treaties as illegal. In 1997, for example, 122 governments signed a treaty banning antipersonnel landmines that cause the death and disfigurement of thousands of civilians every year.

Nuclear weapons are a more controversial case. The two atomic bombs that the United States dropped on the Japanese cities of Hiroshima and Nagasaki in 1945 were justified at the time by many on the utilitarian grounds that the bombings would shorten the war. Those who made this argument saw the loss of life at Hiroshima and Nagasaki as precluding an even greater loss of life that would have resulted from an Allied invasion of the Japanese home islands. The Japanese had fought tenaciously to defend islands in the Pacific such as Iwo Jima and Guam; it was believed they would fight with even greater determination to defend their homeland. Others questioned the morality of bombing people even for this purpose, suggesting that if the bombs were to be used at all, they should have been directed toward strictly military targets, not population centers interspersed with military targets. Decisionmakers responded that the Japanese leaders should take the blame, as they made the decision to locate military-related plants where they did.[12]

Each of the weapons dropped on Japan was less than 20 kilotons (20,000 tons) in yield. Many nuclear weapons today have a much larger multi-megaton (multi-million tons) yield, with such heat, blast, and radiation effects that they cannot be used with discrimination, so these weapons fail on human-suffering grounds as well. On the other hand, some have argued that lower-yield, tactical nuclear weapons (perhaps as small as one kiloton or less, with reduced-radiation effects) can be used with discrimination and need not cause unnecessary suffering. Critics are skeptical of any such claim. They also counter that using any nuclear weapons at all "opens Pandora's box," legitimating this category of weaponry and increasing the likelihood that even larger nuclear weapons will be employed by one or another of the parties. Indicative of the lack of consensus on these issues, and unlike chemical and biological agents, nuclear weapons have not yet been declared illegal, however ill advised or immoral their use might be.

JUSTICE AND HUMAN RIGHTS

The quest for universal understanding of socioeconomic, political, and legal rights belonging to individuals, groups, classes, societies, and humanity as a whole has proven to be an evolutionary and still ongoing process.[13] Particularly challenging is unequal, adverse treatment human beings suffer based on such factors as race or ethnicity, national origin, social or economic class, age, gender, and sexual identity or orientation. Gross violations of labor, safety and health standards for adults as well as children, illegal trafficking of persons for prostitution or slave labor, torture, and genocide are among the more extreme forms of human exploitation on the global human-rights agenda.

■ The Enlightenment

Although the concept of rights in Western thought has roots in ancient Greek, Roman, and religious writings, it was the Enlightenment and the social contract theorists that collectively provided stronger philosophical ground for specifying human aspirations for liberty and equality, coupled with communitarian concerns and human obligations in society. The liberal spirit of the Enlightenment would, of course, be developed further in the nineteenth-century work of the utilitarians and Kantians.

Hobbes, Locke, Rousseau, and other classic social-contract theorists differed on the relative emphasis or importance each placed on liberty, equality, community, and order, but a common theme was that human beings—the people—are the ultimate source of legitimate political authority in society. This democratic understanding is explicit in Locke and Rousseau. Even for Hobbes, the monarch (or "assembly" acting as legislature) rested legitimately not on divine right but rather on the people who vested the sovereign with authority and power to maintain societal order in the interest of their own security.

The thirteenth-century English *Magna Carta* and the late eighteenth-century U.S. Bill of Rights and French Declaration of the Rights of Man are documentary statements of aspirations to rights taking a political or legal form. Content analysis of these documents, however, reveals greater focus on *individual* political and legal rights in the English and American documents. The French declaration, by contrast, extends itself to the socioeconomic realm with applications not just to individuals, but also to larger aggregations at both communal and societal levels. In short, a people may have rights as a class, group, or society as a whole.

In the present-day global society, these differences in understandings across societies and cultures remain. Culture obviously matters in how we interpret or understand rights in different social contexts. There are differences in relative importance, for example, of liberty, equality, and order and whether rights or obligations are to be applied primarily at the individual level of analysis or at larger human aggregations. Thus, the United States tends to focus on human rights as individual political and legal rights and liberties, whereas many other states and societies accept these civil rights and liberties as part of a much larger package that also puts a higher premium on socioeconomic rights and communitarian understandings.

Current Application

Notwithstanding different cultural understandings or interpretations of how human rights should be defined and implemented, human-rights advocates adopt a universalist rather than a relativist view. Whether using a methodology of social contract, utilitarian, Kantian, Aristotelian virtue-based or of religious origin, advocates search for universal, underlying values that inform our understandings of human rights in practice. Thus, respect for life, human dignity, and justice or fairness are broadly understood and accepted even as there is disagreement on how these values are to be applied in particular human-rights contexts. Even so, because there is an understanding of such underlying, universal values as respect for life and human dignity, there is at least a basis for discourse aimed in the interest of justice and fairness at resolving differences in how these values are applied across societies.

Although politics clearly plays a role in these determinations, giving a relatively louder voice to the preferences of some states over others, at a more fundamental level is the continuing discourse that develops consensus across cultures and societies on the realization of these values in common practice. Thus, the Universal Declaration of Human Rights adopted by the U.N. General Assembly in 1948 emphasizes the political and legal, individual preferences of its sponsors. Nevertheless, six of the thirty articles—20% of the declaration—do address socioeconomic and cultural rights, albeit in individual, rather than collective terms. Importantly, this 20% would serve as a foundation for later expansion in U.N. treaties or agreements not just on civil and political rights, but also on such matters as economic, social, and cultural rights; elimination of racial discrimination; elimination of discrimination against women; and providing for a children's bill of rights.

Humanitarian Treatment and the Sovereign State

Human rights claims and demands for humanitarian treatment grounded in treaty commitments often collide with the prerogatives of a sovereign state. States claim a *right* under international law to exclusive jurisdiction over all persons within its territory. Many human-rights advocates, however, see both moral and legal bases for action (to include armed intervention in such severe cases as genocide) when decisions or policies of governments violate human rights. This is particularly so when states have legally bound themselves in treaties specifying commitment to these same rights. When national security considerations conflict with these obligations, compliance by states cannot be taken for granted.

There are difficulties, of course, beyond the question of when armed intervention in the domestic affairs of a sovereign state legally can be legitimate, which we discuss below. For example, the jurisdiction of the International Court of Justice (ICJ) as a legal remedy or alternative to using force is limited to ruling on disputes or cases states voluntarily bring to the court for judicial decision. Even when the court has rendered a decision, compliance still depends on the will of states to carry out their obligations specified in these rulings. Beyond states as parties to legal disputes on human rights or other matters, an International Criminal Court (ICC) has been established to hold individuals accountable for genocide, crimes against humanity, war crimes, and the crime of aggression. The kinds of cases the ICC may take are important, but remain limited, its jurisdiction also severely constrained by the fact not all states have yet authorized this tribunal. The United States has been among the most prominent non-subscribers to the Rome Statute of the International Criminal Court (agreed in 1998, entering into force in 2002).

The Convention on the Prevention and Punishment of the Crime of Genocide (1948, entering into force in 1951) defined genocide as "any of the following acts committed with intent to destroy, in whole or in part, a national, ethnical [sic], racial or religious group": "(a) killing members of the group; (b) causing serious bodily or mental harm to members of the group; (c) deliberately inflicting on the group conditions of life calculated to bring about its physical destruction in whole or in part; (d) imposing measures intended to prevent births within the group; [and] (e) forcibly transferring children of the group to another group." Although the convention does not provide armed intervention as an explicit remedy to stop genocide, when such severe human rights violations threaten international peace and security, there is a legal basis for humanitarian intervention under U.N. auspices (namely under Articles 34, 41, and 42). Beyond using threats to international peace and security to legitimate armed intervention, some see emerging in customary international law the occurrence of genocide as a legitimate basis in itself for armed intervention. By contrast, opponents of this view (particularly governments complicit in genocidal actions) politically oppose what they see as an expansion of the U.N. agenda. They claim such efforts are meddling in the internal affairs of sovereign states which amounts to a violation of international law.

In just-war theory and the law of war discussed below, an effort must be made to spare non-combatants and other defenseless persons. Guilty or not, non-combatants—civilian populations—are not the proper object of warfare. Even captured enemy soldiers are now defenseless persons who may be taken prisoner but may not be executed just because they are prisoners. Prisoners of war (sometimes called PWs or POWs) have rights, and under the Geneva Conventions these guarantees of humanitarian treatment have been made part of international law.

This is why the establishment by the United States of the prison at Guantánamo Bay, Cuba, has been so controversial. The prison was established following the overthrow of the Taliban régime in Afghanistan in the fall of 2001 to hold suspected terrorists (as were prisons also established at Bagram Air Base in Afghanistan and at other locations, some secret). The U.S. government, relying on law dating back to the Civil War and World War II, declared that these individuals were not prisoners of war, but rather "enemy combatants" held as "detainees." As a result, they allegedly could not invoke the international legal rights associated with prisoners of war—a perspective hotly disputed by critics of American prison policies in Cuba and elsewhere.

For its part, the U.S. Supreme Court in *Hamdan v. Rumsfeld* (2006) ruled that Common Article 3 of the Geneva Conventions that provides safeguards to those held in such prisons does apply. In this regard, the article holds that they are to be treated "humanely" with the following prohibitions: "(a) violence to life and person, in particular murder of all kinds, mutilation, cruel treatment and torture; (b) taking of hostages; (c) outrages upon personal dignity, in particular, humiliating and degrading treatment; and (d) the passing of sentences and the carrying out of executions without previous judgment pronounced by a regularly constituted court affording all the judicial guarantees which are recognized as indispensable by civilized peoples." Moreover, those who are "wounded and sick shall be collected and cared for."

Practical concern for finding information deemed vital to national security frequently conflicts with the moral and legal obligations to afford humane treatment in the interrogations of those taken captive. The Convention against Torture and Other Cruel, Inhuman or Degrading Treatment or Punishment (1984, entering into force in 1987) defines torture as "any act by which severe pain or suffering, whether physical or mental, is intentionally inflicted on a person for such purposes as obtaining from him or a third person information or a confession, punishing him for an act he or a third person has committed or is suspected of having committed, or intimidating or coercing him or a third person, or for any reason based on discrimination of any kind, when such pain or suffering is inflicted by or at the instigation of or with the consent or acquiescence of a public official or other person acting in an official capacity. It does not include pain or suffering arising only from, inherent in or incidental to lawful sanctions." Those who argue that torture is legitimate—or who stretch the operational definitions of what constitutes torture—are in effect saying that the *end* (national security) *justifies the means* to that end.

ARMED INTERVENTION AND STATE SOVEREIGNTY

The issue of armed intervention is a good example of where traditional concerns with the laws of war blend with concerns over human rights. The 1928 Pact of Paris (or Kellogg-Briand Pact) was an unsuccessful attempt to eliminate the use of force in international relations. It was supposed to help outlaw "recourse to war for the solution of international controversies." Hope was placed in world peace through law in a system of **collective security** under the League of Nations. As such, collective security is different from **collective defense**—alliances or coalitions that rely ultimately on armed defense or military power rather than law.

The League of Nations tried to substitute law-abiding behavior for individual and collective-*defense* relations based on power, balance of power, and military might. Law-abiding states under collective-*security* arrangements enforce international law against law-breaking states. But the League of Nations seemed powerless to counter such aggressive actions as French intervention in Germany and the Italian capture of the Mediterranean island of Corfu (1923), the outbreak of the China-Japan war (1931), the Bolivia–Paraguay Chaco war (1932–1935), Italy's invasion of Ethiopia (1935), Germany's annexation of Austria and part of Czechoslovakia (1938), and finally the outbreak of World War II in 1939.

In an attempt to put the lessons of the interwar period to practical effect, the United Nations Charter (1945) does specify conditions under which force may legally be used: (1) unilaterally in self-defense; (2) multilaterally when authorized by the U.N. Security Council "to maintain or restore international peace and security"; and (3) in multilateral, often regional, collective-defense action as, for example, in the North Atlantic Treaty Organization (NATO).

Armed interventions still occur frequently enough, sometimes justified by the participants as serving humanitarian purposes or as a measure to maintain or restore international peace and security—a broad grant of legal authority for U.N.–sponsored actions. In a world of sovereign states, diplomatic and other forms of intervention in the domestic affairs of another state, especially armed intervention, are normally prohibited under international law. Article 2 of the U.N. Charter establishes the United Nations "on the principle of sovereign equality of all its Members." Members pledge themselves to "settle their international disputes by peaceful means" and to "refrain in their international relations from the threat or use of force against the territorial integrity or political independence of any state."

States that have suffered violation of their legal rights may choose arbitration, mediation, or a judicial remedy as offered by the International Court of Justice or an appropriate regional or national court. As noted above, a critical weakness is that these tribunals do not have enforcement powers. As a practical matter, then, states often resort to self help to include the use of force, which remains very much a part of international relations. As we have observed, in an anarchic world that lacks a central government or other governing authority with the power to enforce international law, sovereign states do not always comply with such legal authorizations and restrictions. States sometimes choose to violate or ignore their obligations under international law. At other times, political leaders and diplomats have proven to be quite capable of interpreting or manipulating legal principles to justify what they already have done or plan to do in any event.

Intervention and Civil Wars

If applying international law is difficult in the case of interstate wars, it is even more complicated when the conflict is internal to a particular state and society—a civil war. Given the crises of authority faced by so many states today, it is not surprising that internal wars, not interstate wars, are the most likely threat to international peace and security. It is often difficult to contain civil wars within the borders of the affected state. Quite apart from outside interference, civil wars can spill beyond their borders and become interstate wars.

Even when motives are legitimate and not contrived, interventions in the domestic affairs of sovereign states conflict with a long-established principle of international law that prohibits them. Consider the American Civil War (1861–1865) and the debate in Great Britain as to whether or not Britain should support the South. The southern states claimed sovereignty as the Confederate States of America and sought outside assistance in their struggle against the United States of America, from which they claimed to be separate.

The Lincoln administration in Washington denied the South's claim, arguing that the southern states had no right to secede from the Union in the first place. Thus, to Lincoln it was not a war between sovereign states, but rather a civil war fought between loyal U.S. armed forces and those loyal to the rebellious states. Through careful diplomacy, Washington made its interpretation of events clear to the British, stressing that outside intervention was illegal. Whether they accepted the Lincoln administration's rationale or not, London chose not to intervene either diplomatically or militarily even as it continued to trade with the South.

Determining the difference between an interstate war and a civil war is often difficult. American armed intervention in Vietnam, for example, was justified by the United States as coming to the defense of South Vietnam (the Republic of Vietnam) against aggression from North Vietnam (the Democratic Republic of Vietnam). If this were factually correct, then going to the aid of a victim of aggression was legitimate under international law. On the other hand, if the situation in Vietnam were understood as a civil war, with a single state torn between two rival governments and an insurgent movement tied to one of the parties, then outside intervention in such an internal matter would not have been legitimate under international law.

The war in Vietnam was fought not only by the regular forces of North and South Vietnam, the United States, the Republic of Korea, and Australia; it also involved guerrilla warfare supported by North Vietnam. This capitalized on North Vietnam's ties with the people in the countryside. By using antigovernment and ideological appeals, knowledge of the terrain, and the protective cover of the jungle canopy, these non-uniformed irregulars (or guerrillas) conducted a very successful campaign against the South Vietnamese government and its allies. This guerrilla warfare included terrorism, ambushes, rocket attacks, and sometimes even fire-fights with regular forces. These guerrillas were part of an antigovernment insurgent move-ment that, coupled with the efforts of North Vietnamese regulars, eventually succeeded in winning the war and wresting control of the South Vietnamese government.

The former Yugoslavia provides another example of the important distinction between *civil* war and *interstate* war. Serbs opposed both the secession of "breakaway republics" and their recognition in the early 1990s by outside states as independent, sovereign states. From the Ser-bian perspective, the ensuing war among competing parties was really a civil war precluding any legal right to intervention by outside parties. Having been recognized as separate, independent, and sovereign states by U.N. members, however, Croatia, Slovenia, and Bosnia-Herzegovina were seen by other observers as engaging in a war among states against Serbia. As an interstate war, then, outside intervention by the U.N., NATO, or other legitimate authorities acting in compliance with the U.N. Charter was presented as legitimate.

Criteria for Humanitarian Intervention

In the absence of an invitation from the legitimate government of a state, even humanitarian intervention—using force to stop the fighting among competing groups, provide the necessary security to feed starving people, halt genocide or ethnic cleansing, or for similar humanitarian purposes—legally conflicts with the principle of non-intervention in the domestic affairs of a state. As noted above, a basis under customary international law may be emerging to give legal legitimacy to intervention intended to stop genocide. For its part, the U.N. Charter does not give the Security Council authority to use force for humanitarian purposes *per se*. Armed intervention under U.N. auspices in the internal affairs of a state, however justifiable the humanitarian purpose might seem, is legitimate in this strict interpretation only if the problem cannot likely be contained, thus posing a threat to international peace and security.

The case of Kosovo in 1999 illustrates this point. No one denied that Kosovo was a province of Yugoslavia. The Serbs stated that whatever actions they took in the province were, therefore, an internal matter, and outside intervention was a violation of Yugoslavian sovereignty. The Serbian policy of systematic ethnic "cleansing" (forcing the ethnic separation, movement or murdering of peoples), however, led to NATO military action on the grounds of humanitarian in-tervention and the claim that Serbian actions were a threat to regional peace and security.

Humanitarian motives may genuinely accompany actions taken primarily for national-interest reasons. In other cases, however, humanitarian motives are presented as a pretext used by political leaders and diplomats in an effort to justify armed interventions done exclusively (or almost entirely) for national-interest reasons. Propagandists like to present humanitarian purposes for armed intervention to make the behavior seem less self-serving.

Events in 1989 brought an end to the Cold War, but not to armed intervention. Subse-quent years have been marked by a continuation of armed interventions by outside states and multilateral coalitions of states as in responses to Iraq's armed intervention and takeover of Kuwait, civil strife in Somalia and Haiti, and genocide in the Balkan states and central Africa. Following terrorist attacks on the United States engineered by *al-Qaeda*, regimes were over-turned by interventions under NATO auspices in Afghanistan in 2001 and in Iraq in 2003 by the United States, United Kingdom, and a coalition of other states. The latter invasion was justified, among other reasons, on the presumption that Iraq possessed (and likely would use) weapons of mass destruction.

Policymakers face decisions about whether or not to intervene with armed force to respond to aggression, prevent or stop genocide, restore order, or maintain the peace. Both economic and military capabilities as well as domestic political support (or opposition) typically are part of the decision-making calculus. We can also identify at least five additional and often competing criteria or factors typically weighed by policymakers considering armed intervention. Moreover political support for (or opposition to) armed intervention is often expressed in terms of one or more of the several criteria we now take up in turn:

1. *Sovereignty.* Under international law, states are normally prohibited from intervention in the domestic affairs of other sovereign states unless requested by the legitimate government of the state subject to such intervention. However, as noted above, use of force (including armed intervention) is allowed under the U.N. Charter for collective security as when the Security Council authorizes using force in response to a contingency endangering international peace and security (Chapter VII, particularly Article 42). Similarly, self-defense or collective defense by alliances or coalitions of states is justified in responding to aggression against a sovereign state (Chapter VII, Article 51).

2. *National Interest.* Armed intervention is an option often weighed against considerations of national interest and related national security objectives. Some argue that armed intervention should be pursued only if there is a *vital* national interest to be served. Even if one considers this criterion to be decisive, as many realists do, there is no escaping the practical difficulty in trying to define precisely what the national interest (much less *vital* national interest) might be in a particular case. The national interest is subject to multiple interpretations, but even with this ambiguity, it remains part of the decision-making calculus. Thus, when states act in self-defense or come to the aid of other states to repel aggression, they claim legal legitimacy for acting in the national interest. Indeed the U.N. Charter in Article 51 recognizes "the inherent right of individual or collective self-defense." Of course, not all interventions taken to advance national interest meet this self-defense criterion and amount instead to acts of aggression.

3. *Human Rights.* A consensus has been forming, mainly in the last half of the twentieth century that continues to the present, that holds that human beings have rights that may supersede those claimed by sovereign states. The groundwork was laid by the Universal Declaration of Human Rights, passed by the UN General Assembly in 1948. This human rights consensus rests on increasing understanding and acceptance of respect for life, human dignity, and justice or fairness as universal ethical or moral principles that have global application to individuals, groups, and other categories or classes of human beings.[14] Both unilateral and multilateral voluntary assistance for relief in natural disasters are manifestations of these principles in action. The enormous human and material cost suffered by the victims of mass destruction and atrocities throughout the twentieth century resulted in substantial growth in international law which has come to (1) define certain civil or political, social, and economic rights and (2) prohibit certain acts defined as war crimes, genocide, and other crimes against peace and humanity. When such human rights

violations are also understood to endanger international peace and security, there is clearer legal ground for humanitarian, armed intervention under U.N. Security Council auspices. This follows Chapter VII of the U.N. Charter or is based on an emerging consensus in customary international law of a human rights rationale for intervention at least in such extreme cases as stopping genocide.

4. *Expected Net Effect on the Human Condition.* Armed intervention has very real costs not just to people and property in states and societies subject to intervention, but also to the armed forces conducting such interventions. The extent of these costs usually cannot be known with certainty, but policymakers nevertheless try to estimate what they are likely to be. It is extraordinarily difficult, if not impossible, to quantify with precision the net effect (benefits minus costs) on the human condition even after an armed intervention has occurred. Deaths and other casualties can be counted and property losses estimated, but some human costs (for example, psychological damage) may not be known for many years, if then. The problem is compounded when one tries to estimate what these costs might be in advance of an armed intervention. Nevertheless, this criterion typically plays on the minds of policymakers who contemplate whether armed intervention will better or worsen the human condition. At the very least, expected net effect on the human condition can influence how an armed intervention is implemented. Using this criterion, policymakers may select options expected to minimize or reduce adverse consequences to both armed forces and the peoples subject to their actions.

5. *Degree of Multilateralism.* As unilateral armed intervention, regardless of motivation or justification, has come increasingly into disfavor, policymakers have been more prone to look for multilateral support and cooperation in conducting armed interventions. U.N. Security Council mandates, for example, provide political and legal ground for proceeding. In the absence of such Security Council action, proceeding multilaterally under Article 51 as a collective-defense response is still viewed by most policymakers as politically preferable to unilateral action. This helps explain why the George W. Bush administration, despite a generally dismissive attitude toward the United Nations, sought a U.N. Security Council resolution in the fall of 2002 requiring Iraq to readmit weapons inspectors. This effort ultimately included an elaborate oral and visual presentation by Colin Powell, then secretary of state, to the U.N. Security Council on alleged Iraqi weapons of mass destruction.

These five criteria often compete with each other, and choices concerning how much weight to give to one over the other have to be made sooner or later. That said, we are left with an analytical framework that specifies factors that typically are part of decisions to engage in armed intervention. Because states usually intervene to serve their interests does not mean that they always do so for only self-serving purposes. They may wish to intervene quite genuinely for humanitarian reasons or, consistent with their broad interests, to contribute to restoration of international peace and security. This seems to be the case in NATO's intervention in Kosovo. In such cases states may weigh the costs and benefits of armed intervention or in terms of how well they serve the human condition.

In some cases the use of force for humanitarian purposes may cause even more bloodshed than if no intervention had taken place. In other cases the reverse is true: armed intervention at relatively low cost may succeed in providing greater security and meeting human needs.

The difficulty, of course, is that expected net costs or benefits to human beings are not always easy to estimate accurately.

ALTERNATIVE IMAGES AND FOREIGN POLICY CHOICE

The relative emphasis placed on order, justice, freedom, and change—values that are part of foreign policymaking and that have a direct bearing on international politics—varies widely among realists, liberals, economic structuralists, and adherents to the English School. Realist concern with power and the balance of power is closely related to value commitments of statesmen who see order as essential to national security. If they are committed further to the avoidance of war, they may see their tasks as one of managing conflict and seeking to maximize accomplishment of state objectives, however constrained by states comprising the balance. Following Machiavelli, the realist sees national security or the national interest—at a minimum, survival in an anarchic world—as the *raison d'état* justifying state policy. The first generation of English School scholars such as Hedley Bull also placed emphasis on the importance of international order. Bull's major question was in fact where order comes from in an *Anarchical Society.*

To some extent, the value bias among liberals is also conservative, if not to the same degree. To liberals and more recent work in the English School, change should be (and usually is) evolutionary and incremental. If change is to be willed, then reformist, not revolutionary, measures typically are the appropriate ones. Liberal theories, given the fragmentation of states and proliferation of actors that are their starting point, focus on the formation of coalitions and countercoalitions, whether within a state or across national borders. This is hardly the environment for radical changes that would require greater societal unity or at least a strong and unitary leadership. Faction against faction, governmental department against governmental department—the Madisonian formula underlying the American Constitution—is not the means to sweeping change. There are simply too many obstacles (or potential obstacles in the form of opposing groups or factions) to make change easy to come by.

Many liberals, however, place greater emphasis on democratic notions of human rights and justice for individuals, groups, and societies than they do on order within and among states. Richard Falk, for example, identifies four values to be maximized as part of his World Order Models Project: minimization of collective violence; maximization of economic well-being; maximization of social and political justice; and maximization of ecological quality. To minimize collective violence, order remains important to Falk, but his focus quickly shifts to social and welfare issues that need to be addressed as part of the world order. The liberalism in Falk's approach is evident in his characterization of it as "a transnational social movement dedicated to global reform."[15]

Justice, especially distributive justice, is a central concern not only to a number of liberals but also to many economic structuralists. As noted, John Rawls presents a non-Marxist formulation that supports the normative preferences of both liberals like Falk and those economic structuralists who focus on patterns of human exploitation and inequalities in the distribution of wealth between the industrial countries of the North and the less-developed countries of the South. Economic structuralists of Marxist persuasion and many postcolonial theorists and historians do not need Rawls, of course, given their own long-standing moral concern with exploitative class relations and associated prescriptions for overturning what they see as the existing, unjust world order.

To many economic structuralists, reformism and incremental change are merely prescriptions for maintaining the status quo. If justice is to be served, what may be needed is revolutionary change that sweeps out an unjust world order and replaces it with one that allows for an equitable distribution of wealth and resources. Whether understood as exploitation of peasants and workers by an international *bourgeoisie* or as domination by highly industrial core states and societies over poor, industrially underdeveloped peripheral states, the answer is always the same: justice requires change. Order, peace, and individual freedom will only be established after fundamental (or revolutionary) change of the existing order has been effected.

RATIONALITY AND FOREIGN POLICY CHOICE

Foreign policy choice is the domain in which moral and ethical values apply directly. On the basis of some set of criteria, decisionmakers ultimately choose authoritatively among competing alternatives. Can the rational choice model allow us to avoid or side-step normative issues?

The rational model, often a critical element in realist thinking, amounts to policymakers' ordering of alternatives, making decisions, and taking actions to achieve the most efficient outcome in terms of ends sought. This process is, however, not value free. First, determining the objective or ends to be sought obviously involves value choices. Second, the idea that the means chosen to achieve these goals should be the most efficient, the best, or even just "good enough" is itself a value underlying the decision-making calculus. Finally, even if statesmen can reach a consensus on what general values should be pursued internationally, there may be honest disagreement as to how these values are to be defined and implemented. A good example of this problem involves human rights, which we already have mentioned above.

Notwithstanding a Universal Declaration of Human Rights in 1948 and a number of human rights conventions since then, it often has been difficult to forge a consensus among governments on which criteria should apply in approaching questions of human rights: Which rights are to be protected, the relative importance or weight of different values when they conflict, and whose rights—individuals, groups, classes, states—take precedence.

In sum, contrary to what one might first presume, the rational model of foreign policy decision making is by no means a value-free approach, particularly given the wide range of values pursued by statesmen and different views as to how a particular value should be defined and implemented. As has been discussed in Chapter Three, some liberals challenge whether foreign policy decision making can ever conform to a rational model when the actors involved are various organizations and small groups of individuals and when decisions are typically the outcome of bargaining, compromising, "end-running," or related tactics. Each separate actor may act rationally to achieve its own goals and values, but this is not the same thing as assuming that statesmen act rationally to achieve the goals or interests of the entire state and society. Similarly, some economic structuralists may question the rationality of a decision-making or foreign-policy process that, from their point of view, is dominated by narrow class interests. Whatever may be the rationality of individuals, institutions, or classes in maximizing or serving their own values or interests, the outcome for the whole may be suboptimal or less than the best.

VALUES, CHOICES, AND THEORY

The case for normative theory is not subject to debate for critical theorists, postmodernists, and feminists. Normative theory also has a place in many English School and classical realist formulations. The same is probably true for most constructivists. The idea of divorcing norms from inquiry is at a minimum difficult to achieve if not impossible. The traditional debate has been over the role of normative theory in the four images. For realists and liberals of positivist bent, explanatory theory and normative theory occupy separate realms.

We conclude, however, that normative theory is indeed relevant to each of the images and associated theories we discuss in this book to the extent that one finds allowance for the exercise of human will. How much can political leaders, heads of international organizations, or directors of transnational organizations affect the course of events? If those statesmen are driven internally, consistent with some psychological theories, or if they are severely constrained by their external environment, then normative theory plays a reduced, if any, role in their decision making. On the other hand, if human beings do have some degree of control over their affairs, including international relations, and if causal theories take this effect of the will into account and exclude determinist inevitabilities, then why has the normative part often been neglected in international relations theory?

A central argument made in this book is that the image, set of assumptions, and interpretive understandings one holds concerning international relations do affect the sense one makes of "facts" and the types of explanations or predictions one offers. Although it is important to come to an understanding of biases or perspectives associated with any particular image or interpretive understanding of international relations and world politics, we are by no means making the argument that such knowledge is a function only of prior assumptions, preferences, or values. When what we see as facts contradicts the image or understanding we hold, then it is the image or understanding that should be altered or even overturned to accommodate new information. Our knowledge of international relations is imperfect and various biases color our vision, but the world has a way of breaking down our preconceptions when these preconceptions are fallacious. Scientific skepticism about claims to truth forces testing of various propositions or hypotheses with historical, interpretive, or other empirical data. Whether in the natural or social realms, scientific progress that enhances our knowledge of the world is painfully slow, but it is persistent.

Notes

1. Morality is sometimes viewed narrowly as the religious principles of a particular tradition, group, or individual, e.g., Christian morality. Ethics can be viewed as either the philosophical study of morality, or the same as morality (e.g., Christian ethics). One could also draw a distinction between normative and value considerations, perhaps seeing value as just one part of normative theory. Indeed, one can see that some normative considerations are non-moral ones, as when an artist uses the terms *ought* and *right* in an esthetic context that does not have the moral content usually associated with these words. For our purposes, however, we use the terms *normative, moral, ethics,* and *value* interchangeably.

2. For example, Mary Midgley, "Individualism and the Concept of Gaia," *Review of International Studies,* 26 (2000): 29–44; Stanley Hoffmann, *Duties beyond Borders: On the Limits and Possibilities of Ethical International Politics* (Syracuse, NY: Syracuse University Press, 1981).

3. A prime example of this perspective is Terry Nardin, *Law, Morality and the Relations of States* (Princeton, NJ: Princeton University Press, 1983). Nardin refers to "communitarian" norms.

4. See, for example, Cicero, "'The Republic' and 'The Laws'" in William Ebenstein, *Great Political Thinkers,* 4th ed. (New York: Holt, Rinehart and Winston, 1969), pp. 136–38.

5. Immanuel Kant, *Foundations of the Metaphysics of Morals,* trans. by Lewis White Beck (Indianapolis: Bobbs-Merrill, 1959), 66–67. The literature on Kant is vast, and no attempt is made to summarize it here. We are particularly drawn, however, to the late Hannah Arendt's *Lectures on Kant's Political Philosophy* (Chicago: University of Chicago Press, 1982).

6. See John Rawls, *A Theory of Justice* (Cambridge, MA: Harvard University Press, 1971), 22.

7. *Ibid.,* 62 and 8, respectively.

8. See John Rawls' lecture on "The Law of Peoples" in Stephen Shute and Susan Hurley, eds. *On Human Rights* (New York: Basic Books, 1993), 41–82. The quote is on p. 43. Cf. his later *The Law of Peoples* (Cambridge, MA: Harvard University Press, 2001). See also his *Justice as Fairness: A Restatement* (Cambridge, MA: Belknap Press of Harvard University Press, 2001).

9. E. H. Carr, *The Twenty Years' Crisis, 1919–1939* (New York: Harper & Row, 1964), 97.

10. St. Augustine, "The City of God" in Ebenstein, *Great Political Thinkers,* 181–84.

11. See, for example, Louis René Beres, *Mimicking Sisyphus: America's Countervailing Nuclear Strategy* (Lexington, MA: Lexington Books, 1983).

12. See, for example, Ward Wilson, "The Winning Weapon: Rethinking Nuclear Weapons in Light of Hiroshima," *International Security* 31, 4 (Spring 2007); 162–79.

13. For an overview, see Jack Donnelly, *International Human Rights* (Boulder, CO: Westview Press, 2006).

14. Other covenants address Racial Discrimination (1966), Discrimination against Women (1979), Torture and Other Cruel, Inhuman or Degrading Treatment or Punishment (1984), and the Rights of a Child (1989).

15. See Richard A. Falk, *A Study of Future Worlds* (New York: Free Press, 1975), 11–30, and Falk, *The End of World Order: Essays on Normative International Relations* (New York: Holmes and Meier, 1983), 53.

SELECTED READINGS

Morality, Politics, and Perpetual Peace

IMMANUEL KANT

In this essay, Kant presents an argument for politics compatible with moral principle within a state and among states. He rejects classic notions that in politics might makes right or that one must compromise ethics for prudential reasons. Moral principle—not expediency—guides us in the ideal politics he prescribes. He tells us that we "cannot compromise here and seek the middle course of a pragmatic conditional law between the morally right and the expedient." Consistent with this idealism, he concludes that "all politics must bend its knee before the right" in a progressive effort "to reach the stage where it will shine with an immortal glory."

Taken objectively, morality is in itself practical, being the totality of unconditionally mandatory laws according to which we ought to act. It would obviously be absurd, after granting authority to the concept of duty, to pretend that we cannot do our duty, for in that case this concept would itself drop out of morality (*ultra posse nemo obligatur*). Consequently, there can be no conflict of politics, as a practical doctrine of right, with ethics, as a theoretical doctrine of right. That is to say, there is no conflict of practice with theory, unless by ethics we mean a general doctrine of prudence, which would be the same as a theory of the maxims for choosing the most fitting means to accomplish the purposes of self-interest. But to give this meaning to ethics is equivalent to denying that there is any such thing at all.

Politics say, "Be ye wise as serpents"; morality adds, as a limiting condition, "and guileless as doves." If these two injunctions are incompatible in a single command, then politics and morality are really in conflict; but if these two qualities ought always to be united, the thought of contrariety is absurd, and the question as to how the conflict between morals and politics is to be resolved cannot even be posed as a problem. Although the propositions, "Honesty is the best policy," implies a theory which practice unfortunately often refutes, the equally theoretical "Honesty is better than any policy" is beyond refutation and is indeed the indispensable condition of policy.

The tutelary divinity of morality yields not to Jupiter, for this tutelary divinity of force still is subject to destiny. That is, reason is not yet sufficiently enlightened to survey the entire series of predetermining causes, and such vision would be necessary for one to be able to foresee with certainty the happy or unhappy effects which follow human actions by the mechanism of nature (though we know enough to have hope that they will accord with our wishes). But what we have to do in order to remain in the path of duty (according to rules of wisdom) reason instructs us by her rules, and her teaching suffices for attaining the ultimate end.

Now the practical man, to whom morality is mere theory even though he concedes that it can and should be followed, ruthlessly renounces our fond hope [that it will be followed]. He does so because he pretends to have seen in advance that man, by his nature, will never will what is required for realizing the goal of perpetual peace. Certainly the will of each individual to live under a juridical constitution according to principles of freedom (i.e., the distributive unity of the will of all) is not sufficient to this end. That all together should will this condition (i.e., the collective unity of the united will)—the solution

---

to this troublous problem—is also required. Thus a whole of civil society is formed. But since a uniting cause must supervene upon the variety of particular volitions in order to produce a common will from them, establishing this whole is something no one individual in the group can perform; hence in the practical execution of this idea we can count on nothing but force to establish the juridical condition, on the compulsion of which public law will later be established. We can scarcely hope to find in the legislator a moral intention sufficient to induce him to commit to the general will the establishment of a legal constitution after he has formed the nation from a horde of savages; therefore, we cannot but expect (in practice) to find in execution wide deviations from this idea (in theory).

It will then be said that he who once has power in his hands will not allow the people to prescribe laws for him; a state which once is able to stand under no external laws will not submit to the decision of other states how it should seek its rights against them; and one continent, which feels itself superior to another, even though the other does not interfere with it, will not neglect to increase its power by robbery or even conquest. Thus all theoretical plans of civil and international laws and laws of world citizenship vanish into empty and impractical ideas, while practice based on empirical principles of human nature, not blushing to draw its maxims from the usages of the world, can alone hope to find a sure ground for its political edifice.

If there is no freedom and no morality based on freedom, and everything which occurs or can occur happens by the mere mechanism of nature, certainly politics (which is the art of using this mechanism for ruling men) is the whole of practical wisdom, and the concept of right is an empty thought. But if we find it necessary to connect the latter with politics, and even to raise it to a limiting condition thereon, the possibility of their being united must be conceded. I can easily conceive of a moral politician, i.e., one who so chooses political principles that they are consistent with those of morality; but I cannot conceive of a political moralist, one who forges a morality in such a way that it conforms to the statesman's advantage.

When a remediable defect is found in the constitution of the state or in its relations to others, the principle of the moral politician will be that it is a duty, especially of the rulers of the state, to inquire how it can be remedied as soon as possible in a way

conforming to natural law as a model presented by reason; this he will do even if it costs self-sacrifice. But it would be absurd to demand that every defect be immediately and impetuously changed, since the disruption of the bonds of a civil society or a union of world citizens before a better constitution is ready to take its place is against all politics agreeing with morality. But it can be demanded that at least the maxim of the necessity of such a change should be taken to heart by those in power, so that they may continuously approach the goal of the constitution that is best under laws of right. A state may exercise a republican rule, even though by its present constitution it has a despotic sovereignty, until gradually the people become susceptible to the influence simply of the idea of the authority of law (as if it possessed physical power) and thus is found fit to be its own legislator (as its own legislation is originally established on law). If a violent revolution, engendered by a bad constitution, introduces by illegal means a more legal constitution, to lead the people back to the earlier constitution would not be permitted; but, while the revolution lasted, each person who openly or covertly shared in it would have justly incurred the punishment due to those who rebel. As to the external relations of states, a state cannot be expected to renounce its constitution even though it is a despotic one (which has the advantage of being stronger in relation to foreign enemies) so long as it is exposed to the danger of being swallowed up by other states. Thus even in the case of the intention to improve the constitution, postponement to a more propitious time may be permitted.[1]

It may be that despotizing moralists, in practice blundering, often violate rules of political prudence through measures they adopt or propose too precipitately; but experience will gradually retrieve them from their infringement of nature and lead them on to a better course. But the moralizing politician, by glossing over principles of politics which are opposed to the right with the pretext that human nature is not capable of the good as reason prescribes it, only makes reform impossible and perpetuates the violation of law.

Instead of possessing the *practical science* they boast of, these politicians have only *practices;* they flatter the power which is then ruling so as not to be remiss in their private advantage, and they sacrifice the nation and, possibly, the whole world. This is the way of all professional lawyers (not legislators) when they go into politics. Their task is not to reason too nicely about the legislation but to execute the momentary commands on the statute books; consequently, the legal constitution in force at any time is to them the best, but when it is amended from above, this amendment always seems best, too. Thus everything is preserved in its accustomed mechanical order. Their adroitness in fitting into all circumstances gives them the illusion of being able to judge constitutional principles according to concepts of right (not empirically, but a priori). They make a great show of understanding *men* (which is certainly something to be expected of them, since they have to deal with so many) without understanding *man* and what can be made of him, for they lack the higher point of view of anthropological observation which is needed for this. If with these ideas they go into civil and international law, as reason prescribes it, they take this step in a spirit of chicanery, for they still follow their accustomed mechanical routine of despotically imposed coercive laws in a field where only concepts of reason can establish a legal compulsion according to the principles of freedom, under which alone a just and durable constitution is possible. In this field the pretended practical man thinks he can solve the problem of establishing such a constitution without the rational idea but solely from the experience he has had with what was previously the most lasting constitution—a constitution which in many cases was opposed to the right.

The maxims which he makes use of (though he does not divulge them) are, roughly speaking, the following sophisms:

1. *Fac et excusa.* Seize every favourable opportunity for usurping the right of the state over its own people or over a neighboring people; the justification will be easier and more elegant *ex post facto,* and the power can be more easily glossed over, especially when the supreme power in the state is also the legislative authority which must be obeyed without argument. It is much more difficult to do the violence when one has first to wait upon the consideration of convincing arguments and to meet them with counterarguments. Boldness itself gives the appearance of inner conviction of the legitimacy of the deed, and the god of success is afterward the best advocate.

2. *Si fecisti, nega.* What you have committed, deny that it was your fault—for instance, that you have brought your people to despair and hence to rebellion. Rather assert that it was due to the obstinacy of your subjects; or, if you have conquered a neighboring nation, say that the fault lies in the nature of man, who, if not met by force, can be counted on to make use of it to conquer you.

3. *Divide et impera.* That is, if there are certain privileged persons in your nation who have chosen you as their chief (*primus inter pares*), set them at variance with one another and embroil them with the people. Show the latter visions of greater freedom, and all will soon depend on your untrammeled will. Or if it is foreign states that concern you, it is a pretty safe means to sow discord among them so that, by seeming to protect the weaker, you can conquer them one after another.

Certainly no one is now the dupe of these political maxims, for they are already universally known. Nor are they blushed at, as if their injustice were too glaring, for great powers blush only at the judgment of other great powers but not at that of the common masses. It is not that they are ashamed of revealing such principles (for all of them are in the same boat with respect to the morality of their maxims); they are ashamed only when these maxims fail, for they still have political honor which cannot be disputed—and this honor is the aggrandizement of their power by whatever means.[2]

All these twistings and turnings of an immoral doctrine of prudence in leading men from their natural state of war to a state of peace prove at least that men in both their private and their public relationships cannot reject the concept of right or trust themselves openly to establish politics merely on the artifices of prudence. Thus they do not refuse obedience to the concept of public law, which is especially manifest in international law; on the contrary, they give all due honor to it, even when they are inventing a hundred pretenses and subterfuges to escape from it in practice, imputing its authority as the source and union of all laws, to crafty force.

Let us put an end to this sophism, if not to the injustice it protects, and force the false representatives of power to confess that they do not plead in favor of the right but in favor of might. This is revealed in the imperious tone they assume as if they themselves could command the right. Let us remove the delusion by which they and others are duped, and discover the supreme principle from which the intention to perpetual peace stems. Let us show that everything evil which stands in its way derives from the fact that the political moralist begins where the moral politician would correctly leave off, and that, since he thus subordinates principles to the end (putting the cart before the horse), he vitiates his own purpose of bringing politics into agreement with morality.

To make practical philosophy self-consistent, it is necessary, first, to decide the question: In problems of practical reason, must we begin from its material principles, i.e., the end as the object of choice? Or should we begin from the formal principles of pure reason, i.e., from the principle which is concerned solely with freedom in outer relations and which reads, "So act that you can will that your maxim could become a universal law regardless of the end"?

Without doubt it is the latter which has precedence, for as a principle of law it has unconditional necessity. On the other hand, the former is obligatory only if we presuppose the empirical conditions of the proposed end, i.e., its practicability. Thus if this end (in this case, perpetual peace) is a duty, it must be derived from the formal principle of the maxims of external actions. The first principle, that of the political moralist, pertaining to civil and international law and the law of world citizenship, is merely a problem of technique (*problema technicum*); the second, as the problem of the moral politician to whom it is an ethical problem (*problema morale*), is far removed from the other in its method of leading toward perpetual peace, which is wished not merely as a material good but also as a condition issuing from an acknowledgment of duty.

For the solution of the former, the problem of political prudence, much knowledge of nature is required so that its mechanism may be employed toward the desired end; yet all this is uncertain in its results for perpetual peace, with whatever sphere of public law we are concerned. It is uncertain, for example, whether the people are better kept in obedience and maintained in prosperity by severity or by the charm of distinctions which flatter their vanity, by the power of one or the union of various chiefs, or perhaps merely by a serving nobility or by the power of the people. History furnishes us with contradictory examples from all governments (with the exception of the truly republican, which can alone appeal to the mind of a moral politician). Still more uncertain is an international law allegedly erected on the statutes of ministries. It is, in fact, a word

without meaning, resting as it does on compacts which, in the very act of being concluded, contain secret reservations for their violation.

On the other hand, the solution of the second problem, that of political wisdom, presses itself upon us, as it were; it is clear to everyone and puts to shame all affectation. It leads directly to the end, but, remembering discretion, it does not precipitately hasten to do so by force; rather, it continuously approaches it under the conditions offered by favorable circumstances.

Then it may be said, "Seek ye first the kingdom of pure practical reason and its righteousness, and your end (the blessing of perpetual peace) will necessarily follow." For it is the peculiarity of morals, especially with respect to its principles of public law and hence in relation to a politics known a priori, that the less it makes conduct depend on the proposed end, i.e., the intended material or moral advantage, the more it agrees with it in general. This is because it is the universal will given a priori (in a nation or in the relations among different nations) which determines the law among men, and if practicing consistently follows it, this will can also, by the mechanism of nature, cause the desired result and make the concept of law effective. So, for instance, it is a principle of moral politics that a people should unite into a state according to juridical concepts of freedom and equality, and this principle is based not on prudence but on duty. Political moralists may argue as much as they wish about the natural mechanism of a mass of men forming a society, assuming a mechanism which would weaken those principles and vitiate their end; or they may seek to prove their assertions by examples of poorly organized constitutions of ancient and modern times (for instance, of democracies without representative systems). They deserve no hearing, particularly as such a pernicious theory may itself occasion the evil which it prophesies, throwing human beings into one class with all other living machines, differing from them only in their consciousness that they are not free, which makes them, in their own judgment, the most miserable of all beings in the world.

The true but somewhat boastful sentence which has become proverbial, *Fiat iustitia, pereat mundus* ("Let justice reign even if all the rascals in the world should perish from it"), is a stout principle of right which cuts asunder the whole tissue of artifice or force. But it should not be misunderstood as a permission to use one's own right with extreme rigor (which would conflict with ethical duty); it should be understood as the obligation of those in power not to limit or to extend anyone's right through sympathy or disfavor. This requires, first, an internal constitution of the state erected on pure principles of right, and, second, a convention of the state with other near or distant states (analogous to a universal state) for the legal settlement of their differences. This implies only that political maxims must not be derived from the welfare or happiness which a single state expects from obedience to them, and thus not from the end which one of them proposes for itself. That is, they must not be deduced from volition as the supreme yet empirical principle of political wisdom, but rather from the pure concept of the duty of right, from the *ought* whose principle is given a priori by pure reason, regardless of what the physical consequences may be. The world will by no means perish by a diminution in the number of evil men. Moral evil has the . . . property of being opposed to and destructive of its own purposes (especially in the relationships between evil men); thus it gives place to the moral principle of the good, though only through a slow progress.

Thus objectively, or in theory, there is no conflict between morals and politics. Subjectively, however, in the selfish propensity of men (which should not be called "practice," as this would imply that it rested on rational maxims), this conflict will always remain. Indeed, it should remain, because it serves as a whetstone of virtue, whose true courage (by the principle, *tu ne cede malis, sed contra audentior ito*)[3] in the present case does not so much consist in defying with strong resolve evils and sacrifices which must be undertaken along with the conflict, but rather in detecting and conquering the crafty and far more dangerously deceitful and treasonable principle of evil in ourselves, which puts forward the weakness of human nature as justification for every transgression.

In fact, the political moralist may say: The ruler and people, or nation and nation, do each other no injustice when by violence or fraud they make war on each other, although they do commit injustice in general in that they refuse to respect the concept of right, which alone could establish perpetual peace. For since the one does transgress his duty against the other, who is likewise lawlessly disposed toward him, each gets what he deserves when they destroy each other. But enough of the race still remains to let this game continue into the remotest ages in order that

posterity, some day, might take these perpetrators as a warning example. Hence providence is justified in the history of the world, for the moral principle in man is never extinguished, while with advancing civilization reason grows pragmatically in its capacity to realize ideas of law. But at the same time the culpability for the transgressions also grows. If we assume that humanity never will or can be improved, the only thing which a theodicy seems unable to justify is creation itself, the fact that a race of such corrupt beings ever was on earth. But the point of view necessary for such an assumption is far too high for us, and we cannot theoretically support our philosophical concepts of the supreme power which is inscrutable to us.

To such dubious consequences we are inevitably driven if we do not assume that pure principles of right have objective reality, i.e., that they may be applied, and that the people in a state and, further, states themselves in their mutual relations should act according to them, whatever objections empirical politics may raise. Thus true politics can never take a step without rendering homage to morality. Though politics by itself is a difficult art, its union with morality is no art at all, for this union cuts the knot which politics could not untie when they were in conflict. The rights of men must be held sacred, however much sacrifice it may cost the ruling power. One cannot compromise here and seek the middle course of a pragmatic conditional law between the morally right and the expedient. All politics must bend its knee before the right. But by this it can hope slowly to reach the stage where it will shine with an immortal glory.

Notes

1. These are permissive laws of reason. Public law laden with injustice must be allowed to stand, either until everything is of itself ripe for complete reform or until this maturity has been brought about by peaceable means; for a legal constitution, even though it be right to only a low degree, is better than none at all, the anarchic condition which would result from precipitate reform. Political wisdom, therefore, will make it a duty to introduce reforms which accord with the ideal of public law. But even when nature herself produces revolutions, political wisdom will not employ them to legitimize still greater oppression. On the contrary, it will use them as a call of nature for fundamental reforms to produce a lawful constitution founded upon principles of freedom, for only such a constitution is durable.

2. Even if we doubt a certain wickedness in the nature of men who live together in a state, and instead plausibly cite lack of civilization, which is not yet sufficiently advanced, i.e., regard barbarism as the cause of those anti-lawful manifestations of their character, this viciousness is clearly and incontestably shown in the foreign relations of states. Within each state it is veiled by the compulsion of civil laws, because the inclination to violence between the citizens is fettered by the stronger power of the government. This relationship not only gives a moral veneer (*causae non causae*) to the whole but actually facilitates the development of the moral disposition to a direct respect for the law by placing a barrier against the outbreak of unlawful inclinations. Each person believes that he himself would hold the concept of law sacred and faithfully follow it provided he were sure that he could expect the same from others, and the government does in part assure him of this. Thereby a great step (though not yet a moral step) is taken toward morality, which is attachment to this concept of duty for its own sake and without regard to hope of a similar response from others. But since each one with his own good opinion of himself presupposes a malicious disposition on the part of all the others, they all pronounce the judgment that they in fact are all worth very little. We shall not discuss how this comes about, though it cannot be blamed on the nature of man as a free being. But since even respect for the concept of right (which man cannot absolutely refuse to respect) solemnly sanctions the theory that he has the capacity of conforming to it, everyone sees that he, for his part, must act according to it, however others may act.

3. "Yield not to evils, but go against the stronger" (*Aeneid* VI. 95).

The Nature of Politics

E.H. CARR

The English writer, E. H. Carr, has influenced realists, liberals, and the English School. He argues that the practice and study of politics require an appreciation of realism as well as utopianism, power as well as morality. Here he explores the tension between realism and utopian thought.

Man has always lived in groups. The smallest kind of human group, the family, has clearly been necessary for the maintenance of the species. But so far as is known, men have always from the most primitive times formed semi-permanent groups larger than the single family; and one of the functions of such a group has been to regulate relations between its members. Politics deals with the behavior of men in such organised permanent or semi-permanent groups. All attempts to deduce the nature of society from the supposed behavior of man in isolation are purely theoretical, since there is no reason to assume that such a man ever existed. Aristotle laid the foundation of all sound thinking about politics when he declared that man was by nature a political animal.

Man in society reacts to his fellow men in two opposite ways. Sometimes he displays egoism, or the will to assert himself at the expense of others. At other times he displays sociability, or the desire to cooperate with others, to enter into reciprocal relations of good-will and friendship with them, and even to subordinate himself to them. In every society these two qualities can be seen at work. No society can exist unless a substantial proportion of its members exhibits in some degree the desire for cooperation and mutual good-will. But in every society some sanction is required to produce the measure of solidarity requisite for its maintenance; and this sanction is applied by a controlling group or individual acting in the name of the society.

"The Nature of Politics" from *The Twenty Years' Crisis, 1919–1939*, by E. H. Carr and Professor Michael Cox, published 1960. Reprinted with permission of Palgrave Macmillan.

Membership of most societies is voluntary, and the only ultimate sanction which can be applied is expulsion. But the peculiarity of political society, which in the modern world takes the form of the state, is that membership is compulsory. The state, like other societies, must be based on some sense of common interests and obligations among its members. But coercion is regularly exercised by a governing group to enforce loyalty and obedience; and this coercion inevitably means that the governors control the governed and "exploit" them for their own purposes.[1]

The dual character of political society is therefore strongly marked. Professor Laski tells us that "every state is built upon the consciences of men."[2] On the other hand, anthropology, as well as much recent history, teaches that "war seems to be the main agency in producing the state"; and Professor Laski himself, in another passage, declares that "our civilisation is held together by fear rather than by good-will."[3] There is no contradiction between these apparently opposite views. When Tom Paine, in the *Rights of Man,* tries to confront Burke with the dilemma that "governments arise either *out* of the people or *over* the people," the answer is that they do both. Coercion and conscience, enmity and good-will, self-assertion and self-subordination, are present in every political society. The state is built up out of these two conflicting aspects of human nature. Utopia and reality, the ideal and the institution, morality and power, are from the outset inextricably blended in it. In the making of the United States, as a modern American writer has said, "Hamilton stood for strength, wealth, and power, Jefferson, for the American dream"; and both the power and the dream were necessary ingredients.[4]

If this be correct, we can draw one important conclusion. The utopian who dreams that it is possible to eliminate self-assertion from politics and to base a political system on morality alone is just as wide of the mark as the realist who believes that altruism is an illusion and that all political action is based on self-seeking. These errors have both left their mark on popular terminology. The phrase "power politics" is often used in an invidious sense, as if the element of power or self-assertion in politics were something abnormal and susceptible of elimination from a healthy political life. Conversely, there is a disposition, even among some writers who are not strictly speaking

realists, to treat politics as the science of power and self-assertion and exclude from it by definition actions inspired by the moral consciousness. Professor Catlin describes the *homo politicus* as one who "seeks to bring into conformity with his own will the wills of others, so that he may the better attain his own ends."[5] Such terminological implications are misleading. Politics cannot be divorced from power. But the *homo politicus* who pursues nothing but power is as unreal a myth as the *homo economicus* who pursues nothing but gain. Political action must be based on a coordination of morality and power.

This truth is of practical as well as theoretical importance. It is as fatal in politics to ignore power as it is to ignore morality. The fate of China in the nineteenth century is an illustration of what happens to a country which is content to believe in the moral superiority of its own civilisation and to despise the ways of power. The Liberal Government of Great Britain nearly came to grief in the spring of 1914 because it sought to pursue an Irish policy based on moral authority unsupported (or rather, directly opposed) by effective military power. In Germany, the Frankfort Assembly of 1848 is the classic example of the impotence of ideas divorced from power; and the Weimar Republic broke down because many of the policies it pursued—in fact, nearly all of them except its opposition to the communists—were unsupported, or actively opposed, by effective military power.[6] The utopian, who believes that democracy is not based on force, refuses to look these unwelcome facts in the face.

On the other hand, the realist, who believes that, if you look after the power, the moral authority will look after itself, is equally in error. The most recent form of this doctrine is embodied in the much-quoted phrase: "The function of force is to give moral ideas time to take root." Internationally, this argument was used in 1919 by those who, unable to defend the Versailles Treaty on moral grounds, maintained that this initial act of power would pave the way for subsequent moral appeasement. Experience has done little to confirm this comfortable belief. The same fallacy is implicit in the once popular view that the aim of British policy should be "to rebuild the League of Nations, to make it capable of holding a political aggressor in restraint by armed power, and thereafter to labour faithfully for the mitigation of just and real grievances."[7] Once the enemy has been crushed or the "aggressor" restrained by force, the "thereafter" fails to arrive. The illusion that priority can be given to power and that morality will follow, is just as dangerous as the illusion that priority can be given to moral authority and that power will follow.

Before proceeding, however, to consider the respective roles of power and morality in politics, we must take some note of the views of those who, though far from being realists, identify politics with power and believe that moral concepts must be altogether excluded from its scope. There is, according to this view, an essential antinomy between politics and morality; and the moral man as such will therefore have nothing to do with politics. This thesis has many attractions, and reappears at different periods of history and in different contexts. It takes at least three forms.

1. Its simplest form is the doctrine of non-resistance. The moral man recognises the existence of political power as an evil, but regards the use of power to resist power as a still greater evil. This is the basis of such doctrines of non-resistance as those of Jesus or of Gandhi, or of modern pacifism. It amounts, in brief, to a boycott of politics.

2. The second form of the antithesis between politics and morality is anarchism. The state, as the principal organ of political power, is "the most flagrant, most cynical and most complete negation of humanity."[8] The anarchist will use power to overthrow the state. This revolutionary power is, however, not thought of as political power, but as the spontaneous revolt of the outraged individual conscience. It does not seek to create a new political society to take the place of the old one, but a moral society from which power, and consequently politics, are completely eliminated. "The principles of the Sermon on the Mount," an English divine recently remarked, would mean "sudden death to civilised society."[9] The anarchist sets out to destroy "civilised society" in the name of the Sermon on the Mount.

3. A third school of thought starts from the same premise of the essential antithesis between morality and politics, but arrives at a totally different conclusion. The injunction of Jesus to "render unto Caesar the things that are Caesar's, and unto God the things that are God's," implies the coexistence of two separate spheres: the political and the moral. But the moral man is under an obligation to assist—or at any rate not to obstruct—the politician in the discharge of his non-moral functions. "Let every soul be subject to the higher powers. The powers that be are ordained of God." We thus recognise politics as necessary but non-moral. This tradition, which remained dormant throughout the Middle Ages, when the ecclesiastical and the secular authority was theoretically one, was revived by Luther in order to effect his compromise between reformed church and state. Luther "turned on the peasants of his day in holy horror when they attempted to transmute the 'spiritual' kingdom into an 'earthly' one by suggesting that the principles of the gospel had social significance."[10] The division of functions between Caesar and God is implicit in the very conception of an "established" church. But the tradition has been more persistent and more effective in Lutheran Germany than anywhere else. "We do not consult Jesus," wrote a German liberal nineteenth-century pastor, "when we are concerned with things which belong to the domain of the construction of the state and political economy"[11] and Bernhardi declared that "Christian morality is personal and social, and in its nature cannot be political."[12] The same attitude is inherent in the modern theology of Karl Barth, which insists that political and social evils are the necessary product of man's sinful nature and that human effort to eradicate them is therefore futile; and the doctrine that Christian morality has nothing to do with politics is vigorously upheld by the Nazi régime. This view is basically different from that of the realist who makes morality a function of politics. But in the field of politics it tends to become indistinguishable from realism.

The theory of the divorce between the spheres of politics and morality is superficially attractive, if only because it evades the insoluble problem of finding a moral justification for the use of force.[13] But it is not ultimately satisfying. Both non-resistance and anarchism are counsels of despair, which appear to find widespread acceptance only where men feel hopeless of achieving anything by political action; and the attempt to keep God and Caesar in watertight compartments runs too much athwart the deepseated desire of the human mind to reduce its view of the world to some kind of moral order. We are not in the long run satisfied to believe that what is politically good is morally bad; and since we can neither moralise power nor expel power from politics, we are faced with a dilemma which cannot be completely resolved.[14] The planes of utopia and of reality never coincide. The ideal cannot be institutionalised, nor the institution idealised. "Politics," writes Dr. Niebuhr, "will, to the end of history, be an area where conscience and power meet, where the ethical and coercive factors of human life will interpenetrate and work out their tentative and uneasy compromises."[15] The compromises, like solutions of other human problems, will remain uneasy and tentative. But it is an essential part of any compromise that both factors shall be taken into account.

We have now therefore to analyse the part played in international politics by these two cardinal factors: power and morality.

Notes

1.   "Everywhere do I perceive a certain conspiracy of the rich men seeking their own advantage under the name and pretext of the commonwealth" (More, *Utopia*). "The exploitation of one part of society by another is common to all past centuries." (*Communist Manifesto*).

2.   *A Defence of Liberty against Tyrants* (*Vindiciae contra Tyrannos*), ed. Laski, Introd. 55.

3.   Linton, *The Study of Man*, 240; Laski, *A Grammar of Politics*, 20.

4.   J. Truslow Adams, *The Epic of America*, 112. The idea that the state has a moral foundation in the consent of its citizens as well as a power foundation was propounded by Locke and Rousseau and popularised by the American and French revolutions. Two recent expressions of the idea may be quoted. The Czecho-Slovak declaration of independence of October 18, 1918, described Austria-Hungary as "a state which has no justification for its existence, and which, since it refuses to accept the fundamental basis of modern world-organisation [i.e. self-determination], is only an artificial and unmoral construction." In February

1938, Hitler told Schuschnigg, the then Austrian Chancellor, that "a régime lacking every kind of legality and which in reality ruled only by force, must in the long run come into continually increasing conflict with public opinion" (speech in the Reichstag of March 17, 1938). Hitler maintained that the two pillars of the state are "force" and "popularity." (*Mein Kampf,* 579).

5.   Catlin, *The Science and Method of Politics,* 309.

6.   It is significant that the world *Realpolitik* was coined in the once famous treatise of von Rochau, *Grundsätze der Realpolitik* published in 1853, which was largely inspired by the lessons of Frankfort. The inspiration which Hitler's *Realpolitik* has derived from the lessons of the Weimar Republic is obvious.

7.   Winston Churchill, *Arms and the Covenant,* 368. The argument that power is a necessary motive force for the remedy of "just" grievances is further developed on 209–216.

8.   Bakunin, (*Œuvres,* i. p. 150; cf. vi. 17: "If there is a devil in all human history, it is this principle of command and authority."

9.   The Dean of St. Paul's, quoted in a leading article in *The Times,* August 2, 1937.

10.   R. Niebuhr, *Moral Men and Immoral Society,* 77.

11.   Quoted in W. F. Bruck, *Social and Economic History of Germany,* 65.

12.   Bernhardi, *Germany and the Next War* (Engl. transl.), 29.

13.   "Force in the right place," as Mr. Maxton once said in the House of Commons, is a meaningless conception, "because the right place for me is exactly where I want to use it, and for him also, and for everyone else." (House of Commons, November 7, 1933: *Official Record,* col. 130). Force in politics is always the instrument of some kind of group interest.

14.   Acton was fond of saying that "great men are almost always bad men," and quotes Walpole's dictum that "no great country was ever saved by good men" (*History of Freedom,* 219). Rosebery showed more acuteness when he remarked that "there is one question which English people ask about great men: Was he 'a good man'?" (*Napoleon: The Last Phase,* 364)

15.   R. Niebuhr, *Moral Man and Immoral Society,* 4.

Jus Post Bellum: Just War Theory and the Principles of Just Peace

ROBERT E. WILLIAMS, JR. AND DAN CALDWELL

The article combines normative concerns about human rights with the question of justice and war, particularly in the peace that follows the end of hostilities. When fighting has stopped, how is justice to be served, correcting for the damages wrought by war to people and property? Put another way, what are the bases of a just peace—a jus post bellum —what Michael Walzer calls "the least developed part of just war theory." There is debate about just how far post-war responsibilities go. Beyond the punishment of those judged responsible for human rights abuses as well as the imposition of reasonable measures to prevent future abuses, to what extent is the victor responsible to restore order and attend to both reconstruction of the vanquished and restoration of state sovereignty, or self-determination? Apart from the salience of the post-war responsibilities raised by the authors, we include this article because it is an example of the marriage of human rights and security—subjects too often rendered in our two separate domains of inquiry. Indeed, can human rights exist in the absence of security—indeed, isn't security itself a human right?—and, conversely, what can being secure mean in the absence of respect for human rights?

The just war tradition is based on the paradox that killing may be necessary to save lives, that the devastation of war may be required to prevent the destruction of deeply held values. Pacifists think the paradox is in reality a contradiction. Their position is understandable when we think of the consequences of modern warfare. How could the deaths of millions—some estimates put the number of people killed in the wars of the twentieth century alone at 90 million—possibly be justified in the name of saving lives? In fact, there are enormous numbers of war-related deaths that cannot be justified even in terms of the just war idea of waging war in order to save lives. There have been, after all, unjust wars and, within those wars that were just, unjustifiable killings. But the principle, and the paradox it engenders, is well illustrated by those cases in which a military response almost certainly did save lives (as in Kosovo) or would have if it had been forthcoming (as in Rwanda).

Over time, philosophers have divided just war thinking into two parts, *jus ad bellum* and *jus in bello*—the before and after considerations separated by the point of entry into war. The first has to do with the moral reasoning that justifies the resort to war—proper authority, just cause, last resort, right intention, and perhaps other concerns—while the second has to do with the legitimacy of the means used to wage war. These considerations relate to why and how a war is fought. But this conventional division sometimes obscures the fundamental inseparability of motive and means. If war can only be justified by a concern for the lives and dignity—in essence, the human rights—of those we seek to defend (whether our own citizens or the victims of attack or oppression elsewhere), then how we wage that war will matter a great deal. It is inconsistent to go to war for the defense of human rights if such a war is likely to result in the deaths of extraordinary numbers of the civilians we seek to save or, on balance, increase their misery. Likewise, it is inconsistent to claim to be waging a war for the defense of lives from future terrorist attacks if such a war is likely to increase those attacks or result, on balance, in less security. Of course, such consequentialist judgments are difficult to make, but a concern for justice requires that we make them to the best of our ability. More to the point, however, is the under-standing that how a war is fought is integrally re-lated to its rationale. Reconciling means and ends is, indeed, a matter of integrity.

A just war is one that seeks to right a wrong, and, not incidentally, at a cost that will not leave us won-dering whether or not the wrong that has been righted might have been preferable to the wrongs we have left behind. War is never a good thing, but we consider it justified if a persuasive case has been made that it is the lesser of two (or ten or a hundred) evils. It must be expected to produce less evil than a reliance on diplo-macy, less evil than economic sanctions, less evil than passive resistance, less evil than doing nothing—less evil, that is, than anything we can plausibly offer as an alternative. Thus we must, to be moral, concern our-selves with the evils that war produces and that raises questions about how we fight and what we do after we have fought. Likewise, it means that how we *intend* to fight and what we *intend* to do after we have fought must be part of the moral calculus in determining whether or not we may justly go to war.

We begin to see, then, why retrospection is so important to moral judgment in the sense of evalua-tion and why intention is so important to moral judg-ment in the sense of discernment. World War II is called "the good war" not just because of the defeat of fascism and the liberation of captive peoples. Perhaps it was "the good war" not even primarily for these rea-sons. After all, the liberation brought by Allied armies came too late for many, including two-thirds of Europe's pre-war Jewish population. World War II is judged favorably by so many in large measure because of the postwar order it established. Notwithstanding the Cold War and scores of civil wars and ethnic con-flicts that followed, World War II led, in many parts of the world, to decolonization, democratization, and development. It produced, in other words, significant improvements in human rights.

Of course, here we must recognize that the postwar order may have been judged quite differ-ently by, for example, the Poles and the French. It may be only a slight exaggeration to say that World War II was fully justified only when the United States began to reconstruct Western Europe and to rehabil-itate and reform Germany and Japan. Would it even be controversial to suggest that the Soviets' war of self-defense against German aggression was morally tainted by Stalin's postwar policy of carting off to Russia economic assets from the parts of Europe occupied by the Red Army or to claim that the Soviet Union fought a just war up to the point at which the Nazis were expelled from Soviet territory, but that its "liberation" of Eastern Europe proved to be unjust because it merely replaced one alien dictatorship with another?

What happens after the shooting stops and the surrender is signed is important to the moral justifi-cation of warfare, just as the means employed is. And yet there has always been inadequate attention paid to considerations of *jus post bellum* in the just war tradition.

The Need for *Jus Post Bellum* Criteria

Since the late medieval period when questions con-cerning the morality of warfare came to be divided into the *jus ad bellum* and the *jus in bello,* theolo-gians, philosophers, and lawyers have separated the principles by which entry into war is judged from those used to judge the conduct of war. Michael Walzer (2000:21) has stated the distinction particu-larly well:

> The moral reality of war is divided into two parts. War is always judged twice, first with ref-erence to the reasons states have for fighting, secondly with reference to the means they adopt. The first kind of judgment is adjectival in character: we say that a particular war is just or unjust. The second is adverbial: we say that the war is being fought justly or unjustly.[1]

Jus ad bellum considerations offer moral guidance up to the point at which the fighting begins; the princi-ples associated with *jus in bello* apply as long as the fighting continues. But what happens after the fight-ing stops? As the example of World War II suggests, replete as it is with postwar occupations, regime changes, boundary shifts, war crimes trials, repatria-tions, reconstruction efforts, and many other activi-ties, the aftermath of war inevitably raises deep and difficult questions of justice. Where are the princi-ples that can guide policy makers, as well as individ-ual soldiers, through the postwar moral thicket?

Recently, a few scholars have attempted to ad-dress this question,[2] but it remains the case that *jus post bellum* is "the least developed part of just war the-ory," as Walzer (2004:161) notes. In spite of the many studies that have appeared concerning war crimes tribunals, truth commissions, and other strategies for achieving justice in the aftermath of conflict, general principles of justice such as those embodied in the just war tradition are absent. As political scientists Charles Kegley and Gregory Raymond (1999:243) have stated, "While scholars have argued for centuries about the conditions under which it is just to wage war, far less thought has gone into how to craft a just peace."

To be fair, the classical sources of the just war tradition always demonstrated some concern for the aftermath of war, especially insofar as those sources related the end of war to the *ends* of war. It has been widely acknowledged that only some just purpose could give meaning to the death and destruction caused by war. Grotius (1949:375) approvingly quoted Aristotle's view that "the purpose of war is to remove the things that disturb peace." Augustine (1958:452) believed that peace "is the purpose of waging war. . . . What, then, men want in war is that it should end in peace." This view of the ends of war is also held by more recent commentators. Even the one whom we remember for his declaration that "war is hell," William Tecumseh Sherman, in a speech delivered in St. Louis in 1865, said, "The legitimate object of war is a more perfect peace" (quoted in Shelton 1999). Echoing this tradition, the British military strategist B. H. Liddell-Hart (1974:339) wrote, "The object in war is a better state of peace." Clearly there has been a consistent acknowledgment of the importance of securing in war "a more perfect peace."

Before we attempt to determine what a set of *jus post bellum* principles might look like, it is important to consider the argument that no such effort is necessary since the other parts of the just war tradition—especially the right intention principle as it relates to both *jus ad bellum* and *jus in bello*—imply the existence of norms applicable to the end, and the aftermath, of war. James Turner Johnson (1999:208) has pointed out that "the way a war is fought and the purpose at which it aims, including the peace that is sought for the end of the conflict, are not unrelated, whether in practical or in moral terms." To the medieval just war theorists, the view that war is justified only by the peace it seeks to restore served as a restraint on both the resort to war and the means employed in waging war. It is also possible, however, to invert the relationship and argue that the restraint of war—that is, the traditional just war stance itself—implies something about the "end of peace." The fundamental problem with this position is that just war theorists rarely discuss the "end of peace" and what such an objective implies. We can concede that there is an important link between why and how a war is fought and how it concludes, but this no more eliminates the need for principles to insure a just peace than the existence of *jus ad bellum* principles eliminates the need for principles to insure that war is fought justly.

Aquinas (1916:II:2, Q. 40, Art. 1) maintained that a just war is one that is waged with proper authority, just cause, and right intention. While an assessment of whether proper authority and just cause exist must be based on circumstances prevailing at the time the decision is made to go to war, right intention involves a state of mind related to future conditions. Those who fight in a just war must "intend the advancement of good, or the avoidance of evil" so that the justification derived from legitimate authority and just cause is not undone by "a wicked intention." It is not enough, in other words, to have justifiable reasons for going to war if, having entered the war, the justified side intends to fight in violation of *jus in bello* norms or to pursue unjust ends.

The right intention principle prohibits the pursuit of unjust ends. Therefore, it may be argued, *jus ad bellum* considerations look to the end of the war and tacitly, if not explicitly, establish certain general requirements for postwar justice. Augustine, Aquinas, and their successors (at least among the ethicists if not also among the lawyers) failed to develop *jus post bellum* principles, according to this argument, because their assumptions about the just war subsumed the major postwar concerns.

This argument, although appealing for the way it seeks to preserve the simplicity of the just war theory, fails on several counts. First, right intention is subject to diverse interpretations, none of which has ever assumed a clearly preeminent position among theorists and policy makers. Consequently, an argument that the right intention component of *jus ad bellum* obviates the need to define *jus post bellum* principles runs immediately into a thicket of tangled interpretations. James F. Childress (1982:77, 78) has suggested that "for the war as a whole, right intention is shaped by the pursuit of a just cause, but it also encompasses motives." Having impure motives (such as hatred for the enemy) would not, however, vitiate the justification of a war in which the other *jus ad bellum* requirements were met. Furthermore, to the extent that improper motives might lead combatants to act dishonorably in the war, *jus in bello* principles are available to address the wrongs.[3]

Childress (1982:78, 79) notes that an alternative understanding of right intention links the concept to the pursuit of peace that all just wars must embrace. To go to war with right intention, therefore, is to fight for a just peace. This, in turn, requires eschewing methods of warfare (assassination, torture, and acts of treachery, for example) that would make it difficult to establish a just peace at the end of the war. Again, it is difficult to see what is gained from this understanding of right intention that is not already available via the *jus in bello* principles.

In our view, the principle of right intention has a limited, although not inconsequential, purpose. It seeks to insure that the stated reasons for the resort to war, reasons that must provide a just cause, are in fact the actual reasons. In other words, ulterior motives are excluded. The state must have a legitimate reason for going to war and it must confine itself to the pursuit of ends linked to that reason. Just cause cannot be transformed into license for unjust pursuits.

A second objection to the argument that *jus post bellum* concerns are adequately addressed by *jus ad bellum* principles relates to the potential for changes in the moral landscape in the course of a war. *Jus ad bellum* principles require those who make the decision to go to war to deal first and foremost with matters of fact, with the "situation on the ground," as it were. Has an act of aggression occurred? Is an attack imminent? Is the use of force necessary to save innocent lives? These are the kinds of questions just war theory asks decision makers to answer. Only with respect to the question of whether fighting offers a reasonable chance of success does the just war theory ask leaders to peer into the future.

What Clausewitz called the "fog of war" obscures events not only for the individual soldier but for those who make policy as well. Neither the course of a war nor its outcome is entirely predictable. It seems reasonable, therefore, to look to a different set of principles to guide policy in the aftermath of a war than those that were employed to determine whether to go to war in the first place. The articulation of *jus post bellum* principles simply acknowledges the fact that we know different things and are confronted with different challenges before, during, and after a war. As Douglas Lackey (1989:43) puts it in opening his discussion of just peace, "There is room [in just

war theory] for one further rule, a rule that takes into consideration facts available to moral judges after the war ends."

Human Rights as the Foundation of *Jus Post Bellum* Principles

The effort to develop *jus post bellum* principles is necessary precisely because the theologians, philosophers, and lawyers who developed and refined the just war tradition gave insufficient attention to the aftermath of war. Consequently, the needed principles are not to be found merely by digging more deeply into the work of Augustine, Aquinas, Suarez, or Grotius. Even Paul Ramsey, Michael Walzer, James Turner Johnson, and other modern expositors of just war theory have only touched upon *jus post bellum* principles.

It is important, because there is so little prior guidance, to begin with this question: What ought to be the foundations of *jus post bellum* principles? Because our intent is to build on existing just war theory rather than to begin anew, *jus post bellum* principles must have the same foundations as those principles underlying *jus ad bellum* and *jus in bello*. Our first task, then, is to provide a reasonable account of the basis for existing just war theory.

Unfortunately, this is not a simple matter. Just war theory is commonly regarded as an artifact of Christian ethics—with good reason—but to leave the argument there is to ignore major differences between Augustine and Grotius, to name but two. It is also to smooth over profound differences in the medieval world and the modern world. Furthermore, it overlooks both the differences among Christian thinkers and the contributions to the theory from non-Christian (or at least less explicitly Christian) sources, as, for example, with the role that chivalric codes played in the elaboration of the *jus in bello* principles that are now so important to the just war tradition (Johnson 1975:64–75).

An appeal to Scripture, while fundamental to many of the most important contributors of just war theory, has historically failed to settle the issue of how war is to be regarded. Hebrew Scripture, particularly in its texts recounting the history of the Israelites' conquest of Canaan, seems to sanction holy wars waged without restraint. Christian Scripture, on the other hand, points in a pacifist direction and, indeed, the available historical evidence suggests that the Christian community uniformly adopted a pacifist stance until the conversion of Constantine. Those appealing to Scripture have, consequently, been divided. Of course, others in the world are entirely unmoved—in any direction—by appeals to Scripture.

Natural law was to have offered a broader foundation for just war theory, one that would appeal both to Christians and to astute non-Christians. Francisco de Vitoria famously employed natural law to argue for the rights of the native peoples encountered by Spanish conquistadors in the New World.[4] There are now, however, only a few philosophers who continue to base just war theories on some concept of natural law (see, e.g., Finnis 1996 and Boyle 1996).

The just war tradition, it seems, has flourished for centuries as a slowly evolving but always recognizable set of principles resting on various theoretical foundations. Today, the concept of human rights offers the broadest possible base for the just war tradition, thanks in part to Walzer's *Just and Unjust Wars*.

As anyone who has read the opening pages of *Just and Unjust Wars* is aware, Walzer's revision of the just war theory attempts to steer clear of the endless debates over the foundations of morality. In a well-known metaphor, Walzer (2000:xxi) promises a "tour of the rooms" and a "discussion of architectural principles" of the ethical superstructure in which we live while leaving others to examine the controversial "substructure of the ethical world." Nevertheless, as Walzer is quick to point out, a "doctrine of human rights" is central to his understanding of just war theory. Without attempting to ground the theory of human rights in natural law or utilitarianism or various accounts of human qualities, Walzer (2000:xxi–xxii) asserts that "the arguments we make about war are most fully understood . . . as efforts to recognize and respect the rights of individual and associated men and women."

The human rights doctrine underlying Walzer's view of just war is only sporadically brought into full view in *Just and Unjust Wars,* but it informs almost every case and every conclusion. And, at times, Walzer is explicit about his human rights substructure as he conducts his "tour of the rooms." For example, in an early discussion of the legalist paradigm, which Walzer (2000:72) takes as his starting point, he states, "The defense of rights is a reason for fighting. I want now to stress again, and finally, that it is the only reason." In justifying limited grounds for intervention, he argues that his

exceptions to the general rule of non-intervention are based on standards that "reflect deep and valuable, though in their applications difficult and problematic, commitments to human rights" (2000:108).

The commitment to a human rights doctrine is even more apparent when Walzer takes up *jus in bello* considerations. The case of the rape of Italian women by Moroccan soldiers during World War II is the occasion for a more extensive discussion of how just war theory conforms to the requirements of human rights (2000:133–137). Later, in his discussion of war crimes, Walzer (2000:304) asserts that "it is the doctrine of rights that makes the most effective limit on military activity." Human rights is at the heart of *Just and Unjust Wars,* and the case Walzer makes has influenced other scholars to treat just war theory in the same way (see, e.g., Luban 1980).

In spite of the centrality of human rights in Walzer's account of the war convention, his just war theory, like traditional accounts, is fundamentally centered on the state (Smith 1997:8). His concern, to put it differently, is more with the ethics of national security than with the ethics of what has more recently come to be called human security. However, as Walzer acknowledged in the preface to the third edition of *Just and Unjust Wars,* states are often the violators rather than the defenders of the human rights of their citizens. "It isn't too much of an exaggeration," Walzer (2000:xi) writes, "to say that the greatest danger most people face in the world today comes from their own states." Far from undermining Walzer's work, this observation suggests the significance of the steps he took to ground just war theory in a doctrine of human rights. Given the ability of states to both protect and threaten security,[5] a modern account of just war theory, including one that proposes *jus post bellum* principles, would do well to proceed from a foundation of human rights.

Jus Post Bellum Principles

Every war is different. This fact—or truism—is worth noting as we seek to develop *jus post bellum* principles. Some wars end with a surrender, some with an armistice. Some wars end with the victors occupying the territory of the vanquished, some without a foreign occupation. Some wars end with regime change, some without. Some wars are followed by continued resistance or unconventional war, some are followed by a complete cessation of violence. Some wars end with the commitment of international organizations to build peace, some end without international interest.[6] Each of these conditions bears on the question of how justice is to be done in the aftermath of war.

Of course, it is not only the situation that exists after the war that affects the quest for a just peace. Much that happened during the war will be significant. Were noncombatants generally spared or not? Were economic assets—farms, factories, and infrastructure—generally destroyed or preserved? Were populations displaced? Were atrocities committed? Were limits—the laws of armed conflict—observed?

Finally, as we work backward from the aftermath of the war to its origins, we must acknowledge that *jus ad bellum* considerations will inevitably affect the prospects for a just peace. When the winner is perceived to have waged an unjust war, a host of considerations may make postwar justice more difficult to obtain. International organizations may be less likely to support postwar stabilization efforts. Insurgencies may be more likely. Allies may be less willing to assist in peacekeeping and reconstruction efforts. After major combat operations in the Iraq War ended, many of America's European allies cited what Secretary of State Colin Powell called the "Pottery Barn rule": "You break it, you own it" (Woodward 2004:150).

The variability of war may be a problem for those seeking to build descriptive theory, but normative theorists seem quite capable of developing—and applying—principles that work regardless of the particular characteristics of a war. The just war tradition, after all, is a set of standards for moral reasoning concerning means and ends in the use of force. It is not a checklist or a decision tree capable of producing definitive conclusions. Principles merely assist us in doing the difficult work of moral reasoning; they do not absolve us of responsibility for that work.

In addition to looking at the way the differences among wars affect our views of postwar justice, it is important to consider which aspects of the moral situation change and which do not when wars end. There are, after all, many aspects of what Walzer calls the "war convention" that remain unchanged. The principle of command responsibility, for example, persists as long as there are soldiers present to command. That soldiers' primary responsibility may have shifted from fighting battles to patrolling the streets or guarding prisoners does not alter the commander's ultimate responsibility for their actions. Likewise, the inadmissibility of superior orders as a defense against charges of violations of the rules of war, a principle established definitively at Nuremberg, is unaffected by the transition from war to peace.

But some elements of the war convention *are* affected by a surrender or an armistice. When the fighting is over, no more exceptions based on military necessity are possible since the concept pertains specifically to actions taken in war.[7] To stop fighting is to be done with military objectives and morally dubious means of attaining them.[8]

The concept of noncombatant immunity is also profoundly affected by the termination of war. When hostilities end, all become noncombatants and have (or ought to have) their peace-time right to life restored. As a result, those who continue to kill are murderers, even if their victims are soldiers. This is because the status of soldiers changes with the onset of peace. Soldiers become, for as long as their presence is necessary, the moral (and sometimes the functional) equivalents of policemen. The rules concerning peacekeeping, consequently, must be based on *jus post bellum* principles rather than the other aspects of the just war tradition.

Proportionality is a principle associated with both *jus ad bellum* and *jus in bello* that appears applicable to the aftermath of war, although perhaps in ways that are different from its wartime applications. In assessing postwar efforts to promote justice—particularly retributive justice—a sense of proportionality seems essential. If punishment for crimes against peace or war crimes is appropriate at all, the punishment must fit the crime.

To provide a sound basis for a set of *jus post bellum* principles, we must return to the linkage between just war theory and human rights. A just war is one fought in defense of human rights when those rights—at least the fundamental rights to life and liberty—cannot be secured in any other way. Likewise, a war is fought justly if it is fought with respect for the human rights of noncombatants, including the rights of soldiers who have become noncombatants by virtue of surrender or capture. A war is concluded justly—that is, a just peace exists—when the human rights of those involved in the war—both winners and losers—are more secure than they were before the war. In other words, a successful war (and a just peace) is characterized first and foremost by the vindication of the rights for which the war was fought. While such a principle does not preclude punishment (indeed, punishment for the violation of human rights may be essential if those rights are to be vindicated), it does require that a state, having waged war and made peace to vindicate human rights, respect in the aftermath of war the rights even of those who were most responsible for the war. Victors may punish crimes, but they must neither abuse criminals nor punish those who are guilty of no crime.

A focus on the human rights foundation of just war theory suggests, too, that a just peace may well be impossible if the war is won by those who initiated it in violation of the human rights of others. When people's lives, liberty, property, and security are taken away through an act of aggression, only the defeat of the aggressor can vindicate those rights. When a humanitarian catastrophe necessitates intervention, only the defeat of those whose human rights abuses caused the catastrophe can secure justice. To put it simply, an unjust war cannot produce a just peace.

Here it may be useful to clarify what it means to say that a war—or a peace—is just. A just war, that is, one that conforms to the *jus ad bellum* principles, is one that is justifiable. Since the time of Aquinas, who held that a just war was one waged in response to a fault, it has generally been thought that only one side in a war can be justified (with the possibility that neither side might be).[9] This means that, with respect to a particular party's involvement in a war, we can pronounce it just or unjust (i.e., justifiable or unjustifiable). The evaluation of *jus in bello,* however, is not so simple. When we ask whether a war is being fought justly or unjustly, we must evaluate many different aspects of the conduct of the war. One military operation may have been conducted with exemplary respect for the lives of noncombatants while another may have involved enormous "collateral damage." Justice (or injustice) in war is, depending on one's purpose in making the judgment, either a vast cumulative judgment about how the war was fought or a series of judgments about individual acts in the war. Either way, an all-or-nothing judgment must be considered a gross oversimplification.

Jus post bellum is more complicated still. In some respects, postwar justice must be evaluated in a manner akin to the way we evaluated the *jus ad bellum:* either the just purposes for which the war was fought are achieved (in which case the peace is just)

or they are not. In other respects, however, postwar justice is like justice in war: some actions taken after the war will be just and some will be unjust. Both the transcendent policies, planned and implemented by the state, and the individual acts of decency or depravity committed by soldiers and civilians in the occupied territory must be taken into account in assessments of *jus post bellum.* Consequently, rather than being able to conclude that a particular postwar situation is just or unjust, we may have to acknowledge that there are only degrees of justice and injustice in the aftermath of war.[10]

It should be obvious that winning a just war does not guarantee a just peace. Taking advantage of a victory to subjugate a people and to violate human rights is a grave injustice no matter which side, aggressor or defender, is responsible. The aftermath of World War II provides a dramatic case in point. The Soviets removed roughly a third of the industrial capacity located in their zone of occupation in Europe. Russian troops in the eastern part of Germany raped as many as two million women (Gaddis 1997:45). And in most states occupied by the Red Army at the end of the war, the right of self-determination was effectively denied for a generation.

Are there any *jus post bellum* principles that emerge from these observations? There is, arguably, one fundamental principle supported by a series of more specific prescriptions. The basic principle is this: A just peace is one that vindicates the human rights of all parties to the conflict.[11] *Jus post bellum,* in other words, requires in the case of a war against aggression the restoration of the *status quo ante bellum* with respect to the rights of the victims of aggression. It requires, in the case of humanitarian intervention, the securing of the rights of those whom the intervention was intended to assist. It requires respect for the rights of those in the aggressor state. It permits, subject to limitations imposed by a fundamental respect for human rights and the concept of proportionality, both the punishment of those adjudged responsible for human rights abuses (including crimes against peace, war crimes, and crimes against humanity) and the imposition of reasonable measures intended to prevent future human rights abuses. Finally, it points in the direction of several specific policies.

The victor must, in the first place, restore order. Without order, a society can descend into a Hobbesian state of nature in which even the right to life may be impossible to secure. The need to establish order is often cited as an excuse for denying rights, and this is an authoritarian temptation that must be resisted, but the fact remains that public order is an essential foundation for the restoration of human rights. The widespread violence that has plagued Iraq since the end of U.S. combat operations in May 2003 has jeopardized the ability of both the occupation forces and the Iraqi government to secure the human rights of Iraq's people. Postwar chaos consequently represents a significant U.S. failure with respect to *jus post bellum.*

The second necessity derived from the principle of the vindication of human rights is economic reconstruction. Without the rehabilitation in some small measure of war-torn economies, it may be difficult to secure the most basic of human rights, the right to basic subsistence. How much responsibility a state that has been the victim of aggression must bear for the economic reconstruction of its enemy is a difficult question. What seems clear is that winning a war and administering a state as an occupying power confers a certain responsibility for the welfare of the people of that state. Not even those who were responsible for the war should be allowed to starve to death.

A third requirement derived from the *jus post bellum* principle mandating the vindication of human rights is the restoration of sovereignty, or self-determination. Surrender and occupation suspend sovereignty, but only temporarily if the surrender leads to a just peace. Self-determination is a fundamental human right articulated in both the International Covenant on Civil and Political Rights and the International Covenant on Economic, Social, and Cultural Rights. Its restoration must be an urgent objective of the occupying power.

Finally, *jus post bellum* permits (and some would argue that it requires) the punishment of human rights violations related to the war and its origins. This postwar prescription is supported by the practices instituted by the Allies in the Nuremberg and Tokyo war crimes trials after World War II and, more recently, by the examples of the United Nations tribunals established to address human rights violations in the former Yugoslavia and in Rwanda. Much has been written about war crimes trials and transitional justice that need not be recapitulated here (see, e.g., the works by Howard Ball 1999, Gary Jonathan Bass 2000, and Martha Minow 1998). What is important for our purposes is that the vindication of human rights requires a commitment to

equal justice, not a show of what Hermann Goering at Nuremberg dismissed as "victors' justice." To put the point in contemporarily relevant terms, human rights can be vindicated in Iraq and Afghanistan only if American violations of the laws of war are prosecuted along with our enemies' crimes.

Conclusion

James Turner Johnson (1999:191) has suggested that "perhaps the most difficult problem posed by contemporary warfare, all in all, is the difficulty of achieving a stable, secure ending to it." The difficulty is both strategic and moral, a matter of what can be done and what ought to be done to conclude a war successfully. On the strategic side, the possibilities for postwar settlement have evolved rapidly along with the international system itself. Since the beginning of the twentieth century the world has seen, at the conclusion of wars, plebiscites and partitions, disarmament and de-Nazification, peacekeeping and peace enforcement, reparations and regime change, nation-building and neutralization, to name just a few of the means employed to secure peace. While these strategies have often been rooted in moral principles (such as the Wilsonian commitment to self-determination), modern theorists have not done an adequate job of articulating the fundamental principles underlying what ought to be done in the aftermath of war, nor have we received adequate guidance from the ancients.

The great philosophers of the just war tradition did recognize an important point that modern leaders sometimes forget (or, more accurately, hope their democratic polities will forget): Waging a just war involves facing ethical challenges before, during, and after—sometimes long after—the war itself. Before the war, justice requires that all reasonable means to resolve the conflict or protect the lives and dignity of those being oppressed be tried and found wanting. It also requires that a just cause be articulated (and not a range of potentially just causes from which a credulous public may choose). During the war, justice requires respect for the human rights of noncombatants, even to the point of imposing limits on the conduct of warfare that may be inconvenient or worse. After the war, justice requires the vindication of human rights—vindication in the sense of defense, restoration, and, at times, punishment of past violations. Only when the ethical obligations attending each phase of a war are met is it possible to argue that the war was just.

Writing in the sixteenth century, the Lord de la Noue offered a vigorous defense of *jus in bello* principles, arguing that just wars must be fought with restraint (Johnson 1975: 106–107). To make the point, he described a peasant who confronted a soldier with an account of the current war's devastation and a question: "Who will believe that your cause is just when your behaviors are so unjust?" This question reminds us that judgments concerning the justice of the ends are inextricably linked to the justice of the means. A similar point can be made regarding consequences. Because what happens once the fighting stops is also critical to the moral evaluation of war, a concept of *jus post bellum* is important to inform both our postwar policies and the final judgments we make concerning wars.

Notes

1. The addition of *jus post bellum* principles would mean, of course, that war is always judged *three times*. In fact, this is what happens. We invariably evaluate, in both political and moral terms, war's *outcome*.

2. See, among others, Orend (2000, 2002), Alford (2002), Kellogg (2002), Iasiello (2004), and Allan and Keller (2006).

3. Notwithstanding these points, Childress (1982:78) believes "this criterion of right intention, understood not merely as pursuit of a just cause but also as proper motives, remains significant in part because war is conducted between public, not private, enemies. Furthermore, an attitude of regret, if not remorse, is appropriate when a prima facie obligation is overridden."

4. Paul Gordon Lauren (2003:29) places Vitoria within the broader context of the development of human rights.

5. This ambivalence is addressed in Caldwell and Williams (2006:118–20).

6. The literature on war termination is rich and varied. In addition to Kegley and Raymond (1999), see Kecskemeti (1958), Iklé (1971), Taylor (1985), and Pillar (1988).

7. Military necessity is a problematic moral concept in any case as Walzer makes clear. See Walzer (2000:144–147, 239–242, 251–268, 323–325).

Authors' note: The authors would like to thank Martin Cook, James Turner Johnson, Joel Rosenthal, Michael Walzer, and three anonymous reviewers for their comments and suggestions.

8. This self-evident proposition was challenged by lawyers advising the Department of Defense concerning torture and interrogation. In a classified memorandum leaked to the *Wall Street Journal,* an argument was advanced that "necessity" might be used as a defense against an allegation of a violation of the U.S. Torture Act (18 U.S.C. §2340). See "Working Group Report on Detainee Interrogations in the Global War on Terrorism: Assessment of Legal, Historical, Policy, and Operational Considerations," March 6, 2003, in Greenberg and Dratel (2005:260–261). It should be noted, of course, that a war without end, such as the "war on terrorism," might be construed as making exceptions based on military necessity available indefinitely. However, the clear language of the Convention Against Torture and Other Cruel, Inhuman or Other Degrading Treatment or Punishment (Art. 2, Sec. 2: "No exceptional circumstances whatsoever, whether a state of war or a threat or war, internal political instability or any other public emergency, may be invoked as a justification of torture.") rules out a necessity defense where torture is concerned *even in the context of war.*

9. Johnson (1975:185–195) discusses the views of Vitoria and Suarez on this issue along with the possibility of "simultaneous ostensible justice."

10. Michael Walzer (2004:162–168), examining the situation in Iraq roughly eight months after the United States' invasion in March 2003, argued for the possibility of a just settlement of an unjust war. If one accepts, as Walzer does, that the invasion was unjust, however, it would be more accurate to suggest that the settlement can only be more or less unjust. To claim that a just peace can come from an unjust war is, from a theoretical perspective, to concede more to consequentialism than a rights-based just war theory ought to concede. From a practical perspective, it is almost certain to under-value the costs imposed by the side initiating the unjust war.

11. In stating the principle in this form, we endorse the primary assertion of Orend (2002:46), who suggests that "the proper aim of a just war is the vindication of those rights whose violation grounded the resort to war in the first place." Where we differ from Orend's analysis is in the articulation of the prescriptions that are derived from this basic principle.

References

Alford, Roger P. (2002) On War as Hell. *Chicago Journal of International Law* 3:207–218.

Allan, Pierre, and Alexis Keller, eds. (2006) *What Is a Just Peace?* New York: Oxford University Press.

Aquinas, Thomas. (1916) *The Summa Theologica of St. Thomas Aquinas.* Translated by the Fathers of the

English Dominican Province. London: Burns Oates & Washbourne, Ltd.

Augustine. (1958) *The City of God.* Translated by Gerald G. Walsh, Demetrius B. Zema, Grace Monahan, and Daniel J. Honan. Garden City: Image Books.

Ball, Howard. (1999) *Prosecuting War Crimes and Genocide: The Twentieth-Century Experience.* Lawrence: University Press of Kansas.

Bass, Gary Jonathan. (2000) *Stay the Hand of Vengeance: The Politics of War Crimes Tribunals.* Princeton: Princeton University Press.

Boyle, Joseph. (1996) Just War Thinking in Catholic Natural Law. In *The Ethics of War: Religious and Secular Perspectives,* edited by Terry Nardin. Princeton: Princeton University Press.

Caldwell, Dan, and Robert E. Williams Jr. (2006) *Seeking Security in an Insecure World.* Lanham: Rowman & Littlefield.

Childress, James F. (1982) *Moral Responsibility in Conflict: Essays on Nonviolence, War and Conscience.* Baton Rouge: Louisiana State University Press.

Finnis, John. (1996) The Ethics of War and Peace in the Catholic Natural Law Tradition. In *The Ethics of War: Religious and Secular Perspectives,* edited by Terry Nardin. Princeton: Princeton University Press.

Gaddis, John Lewis. (1997) *We Now Know: Rethinking Cold War History.* Oxford: Clarendon Press.

Greenberg, Karen J., and Joshua J. Dratel., eds. (2005) *The Torture Papers: The Road to Abu Ghraib.* New York: Cambridge University Press.

Grotius, Hugo. (1949) *The Law of War and Peace (De Jure Belli ac Pacis).* Translated by Louise R. Loomis. Roslyn: Walter J. Black, Inc.

Iasiello, Louis V. (2004) *Jus Post Bellum.* The Moral Responsibilities of Victors in War. *Naval War College Review* 57:33–52.

Iklé, Fred Charles. (1971) *Every War Must End.* New York: Columbia University Press.

Johnson, James Turner. (1975) *Ideology, Reason, and the Limitation of War: Religious and Secular Concepts, 1200–1740.* Princeton: Princeton University Press.

Johnson, James Turner. (1999) *Morality and Contemporary Warfare.* New Haven: Yale University Press.

Kecskemeti, Paul. (1958) *Strategic Surrender: The Politics of Victory and Defeat.* Palo Alto: Stanford University Press.

Kegley, Charles W., Jr., and Gregory A. Raymond. (1999) *How Nations Make Peace.* New York: St. Martin's/ Worth.

Kellogg, Davida E. (2002) Jus Post Bellum: The Importance of War Crimes Trials. *Parameters* 32:87–99.

Lackey, Douglas P. (1989) *The Ethics of War and Peace.* Englewood Cliffs: Prentice Hall.

Lauren, Paul Gordon. (2003) *The Evolution of International Human Rights.* 2nd edition. Philadelphia: University of Pennsylvania Press.

Liddell-Hart, B. H. (1974) *Strategy.* 2nd edition. New York: Praeger Publishers.

Luban, David. (1980) Just War and Human Rights. *Philosophy and Public Affairs* 9:160–181.

Minow, Martha. (1998) *Between Vengeance and Forgiveness: Facing History after Genocide and Mass Violence.* Boston: Beacon Press.

Orend, Brian. (2000) *War and International Justice: A Kantian Perspective.* Blasdell: Wilfrid Laurier University Press.

Orend, Brian. (2002) Justice After War. *Ethics and International Affairs* 16:43–56.

Pillar, Paul R. (1988) *Negotiating Peace: War Termination as a Bargaining Process.* Princeton: Princeton University Press.

Shelton, Gen., Henry H. (1999) Shaping a Better World: Military Engagement in Peacetime. U.S. Foreign Policy Agenda. Department of State, International Information Programs. Available at http://usinfo.state.gov/journals/itps/1299/ijpe/shelton.htm (Accessed May 16, 2006).

Smith, Michael Joseph. (1997) Growing Up with Just and Unjust Wars: An Appreciation. *Ethics and International Affairs* 11:3–18.

Taylor, A. J. P. (1985) *How Wars End.* London: H. Hamilton.

Walzer, Michael. (2000) *Just and Unjust Wars: A Moral Argument with Historical Illustrations.* 3rd edition. New York: Basic Books.

Walzer, Michael. (2004) *Arguing About War.* New Haven: Yale University Press.

Woodward, Bob. (2004) *Plan of Attack.* New York: Simon and Schuster.

SUGGESTIONS FOR FURTHER READING

In addition to normative theory understood as philosophical and moral argument, we also include in this list more recent writings about how and why norms, values, or ideas matter in international relations and world politics. We have arranged these selections categorically—a broad, general category followed by human rights, war and peace, and humanitarian intervention.

On Idealism and Realism—An Old Debate

Carr, E. H. *The Twenty Years' Crisis, 1919–1939.* New York: Harper & Row, 1964.

Herz, John H. *The Nation-State and the Crisis of World Politics.* New York: David McKay, 1976.

_____. *Political Realism and Political Idealism.* Chicago: University of Chicago Press, 1951.

_____. "Political Realism Revisited." *International Studies Quarterly* 25, 2 (June 1981): 182–97.

Kegley, Charles W. "Neo-Idealism: A Practical Matter." *Ethics and International Affairs* 2 (1988): 173–97.

Kennan, George F. "Morality and Foreign Policy." *Foreign Affairs* 64, 2 (Winter 1985–86): 205–18.

Morgenthau, Hans J. *In Defense of the National Interest.* New York: Alfred A. Knopf, 1960.

_____. *Politics among Nations,* 5th ed. New York: Knopf, 1978.

_____. *Truth and Power.* New York: Praeger, 1970.

Niebuhr, Reinhold. *Christian Realism and Political Problems.* New York, Scribners, 1953.

Osgood, Robert E. *Ideals and Self-Interest in American Foreign Relations.* Chicago: University of Chicago Press, 1953.

Wolfers, Arnold. "Statesmanship and Moral Choice." *World Politics* (1949): 175–95.

General

Adler, Emanuel, and Beverly Crawford, eds. *Progress in Postwar International Relations.* New York: Columbia University Press, 1991.

Arendt, Hannah. *Lectures on Kant's Political Philosophy,* ed. Ronald Beiner. Chicago: University of Chicago Press, 1982.

Beck, Robert J., Anthony Clark Arend, and Robert D. Vander Lugt, eds. *International Rules.* New York: Oxford University Press, 1996.

Beitz, Charles R. *Political Theory and International Relations.* Princeton, NJ: Princeton University Press, 1979.

Björkdahl, Annika. "Norms in International Relations: Some Conceptual and Methodological Reflections." *Cambridge Review of International Affairs* 15, 1 (April 2002): 9–23.

Brysk, Alison. *Globalization and Human Rights.* Berkeley: University of California Press, 2002.

_____. *Human Rights and Private Wrongs: Constructing Global Civil Society.* New York: Routledge, 2005.

Booth, Ken, Tim Dunne, and Michael Cox. "Special Issue: How Might We Live? Global Ethics in a New Century." *Review of International Politics.* 26, 5 (December 2000): 1–234.

Brandt, Richard B. *Ethical Theory: The Problems of Normative and Critical Ethics.* Englewood Cliffs, NJ: Prentice-Hall, 1959.

Cochran, Molly. *Normative Theory in International Relations: A Pragmatic Approach.* Cambridge: Cambridge University Press, 1999.

Diehl, Paul F., Charlotte Ku, and Daniel Zamora. "The Dynamics of International Law: The Interaction of Normative and Operating Systems." *International Organization* 57, 1 (Winter 2003): 43–75.

Donelan, Michael. *Elements of International Political Theory.* New York: Oxford University Press, 1990.

Falk, Richard. *Explorations at the Edge of Time: The Prospects for World Order.* Philadelphia: Temple University Press, 1992.

_____. *On Humane Governance: Toward a New Global Politics.* University Park: Pennsylvania State University Press, 1995.

_____. "Perspectives on Global Justice: Norms, Structures, Processes and Context." In *Between Cosmopolitan Ideals and State Sovereignty: Studies in Global Justice,* eds. Ronald Tinnevelt, and Gert Verschraegen. New York: Palgrave Macmillan, 2006.

Franck, Thomas M. *Fairness in International Law and Institutions.* New York: Oxford University Press, 1995.

Frost, Mervyn. *Ethics in International Relations: A Constitutive Theory.* Cambridge, England: Cambridge University Press, 1996.

_____. *Towards a Normative Theory of International Relations.* Cambridge, England: Cambridge University Press, 1986.

Gilbert, Alan. *Democratic Individuality.* Cambridge, England: Cambridge University Press, 1990.

Hirsch, Moshe. "Compliance with International Norms in the Age of Globalization: Two Theoretical Perspectives." In *The Impact of International Law on International Cooperation: Theoretical Perspectives.* eds. Eyal Benvenisti and Moshe Hirsch. New York: Cambridge University Press, 2004.

Hoffmann, Stanley. *Duties beyond Borders: On the Limits and Possibilities of Ethical International Politics.* Syracuse, NY: Syracuse University Press, 1981.

Nardin, Terry. *Law, Morality and the Relations of States.* Princeton, NJ: Princeton University Press, 1983.

Nelson, Daniel, and Laura Neack, eds. *Global Society in Transition: An International Politics Reader.* New York: Kluwer Law International, 2002, Chapter 3.

Nolan, Cathal J., ed. *Ethics and Statecraft: The Moral Dimension of International Affairs.* Westport, CT: Praeger, 1995.

Onuf, Nicholas. *World of Our Making: Rules and Rule in Social Theory and International Relations.* Columbia: University of South Carolina Press, 1989.

Rosenthal, Joel H., ed. *Ethics and International Affairs.* Washington, DC: Georgetown University Press, 1995.

Singer, Peter. *How Are We to Live? Ethics in an Age of Self-Interest.* Oxford: Oxford University Press, 1997.

Thompson, Jana. *Justice and World Order: A Philosophical Inquiry.* New York: Routledge, Chapman & Hall, 1992.

Thompson, Kenneth W., ed. *Ethics and International Relations.* New Brunswick, NJ: Transaction Books, 1985.

_____. *Traditions and Values in Politics and Diplomacy.* Baton Rouge, LA: State University Press, 1992.

Walzer, Michael. *Thick and Thin: Moral Argument at Home and Abroad.* Notre Dame, IN: University of Notre Dame Press, 1994.

Wapner, Paul, and Lester Edwin J. Ruiz. *Principled World Politics: The Challenge of Normative International Relations.* Lanham, MD: Rowman and Littlefield, 2000.

◾ On Human Rights

Alston, Philip, Ryan Goodman, and Henry J. Steiner. *International Human Rights in Context: Law, Politics, Morals.* New York: Oxford University Press, 2007.

Apodaca, Clair. *Understanding U.S. Human Rights Policy: A Paradoxical Legacy.* London: Routledge, 2006.

Barry, Brian, and Robert E. Goodin, eds. *Free Movement: Ethical Issues in the Transnational Migration of People and Money.* University Park: Pennsylvania State University Press, 1992.

Donnelly, Jack. *International Human Rights.* Boulder, CO: Westview Press, 1993, 2006.

_____. *Universal Human Rights.* New Delhi, India: Manas Publications, 2005.

_____. *Universal Human Rights in Theory and Practice.* Ithaca, NY: Cornell University Press, 2002.

Finnemore, Martha. "Constructing Norms of Humanitarian Intervention." In *The Culture of National Security: Norms and Identity in International Politics,* ed. Peter Katzenstein. New York: Columbia University Press, 1996.

Forsythe, David P. *Human Rights in International Relations.* 2nd ed. Cambridge, England: Cambridge University Press; 2006.

Greenberg, Karen J., and Joshua J. Dratel, eds. *The Torture Papers: The Road to Auy Ghraib.* New York: Cambridge University Press, 2005.

Haas, Ernst B. *Global Evangelism Rides Again: How to Protect Human Rights without Really Trying.* Berkeley: University of California Institute of International Studies, 1978.

_____. *Human Rights and International Action: The Case of Freedom of Association.* Stanford, CA: Stanford University Press, 1970.

Hunt, Lynn. *Inventing Human Rights: A History.* New York: W.W. Norton, 2007.

Ignatieff, Michael, Kwame Anthony Appiah, David A. Hollinger, and Thomas W. Laqueur. *Human Rights as Politics and Idolatry.* Princeton, NJ: Princeton University Press, 2003.

Ishay, Micheline R. *The History of Human Rights: From Ancient Times to the Globalization Era.* Berkeley, CA: University of California Press, 2004.

_____, ed. *The Human Rights Reader.* New York: Routledge, 1997, 2007.

Klotz, Audie. *Norms in International Relations: The Struggle against Apartheid.* Ithaca, NY: Cornell University Press, 1999.

Lauren, Paul Gordon. *The Evolution of International Human Rights: Visions Seen,* 2nd ed. Phildelphia: University of Pennsylvania Press, 2003.

Pogge, Thomas W. *World Poverty and Human Rights: Cosmopolitan Responsibilities and Reforms.* Cambridge, UK: Polity, 2002.

Shute, Stephen, and Susan Hurley, eds. *On Human Rights: The Oxford Amnesty Lectures, 1993.* New York: Basic Books, 1993.

■ On War and Peace

Alford, Roger P. "On War Is Hell," *Chicago Journal of International Law.* 3 (2002): 207–18.

Allan, Pierre, and Alexis Keller, eds. *What Is a Just Peace?* New York: Oxford University Press, 2006.

Arendt, Hannah. *On Violence.* New York: Harcourt, Brace and World, 1970.

Bass, Gary Jonathan. *Stay the Hand of Vengeance: The Politics of War Crimes Tribunals.* Princeton, NJ: Princeton University Press, 2000.

Best, Geoffrey. *War and Law Since 1945.* New York: Oxford University Press, 1994.

Booth, Ken. *Law, Force and Diplomacy.* London: Allen & Unwin, 1985.

Bull, Hedley. "Recapturing the Just War for Political Theory." *World Politics* 31, 4 (July 1979): 588–99. [A review of Walzer, *Just and Unjust Wars.*]

Childress, James F. *Moral Responsibility in Conflict: Essays on Nonviolence, War and Conscience.* Baton Rouge, LA: Louisiana State University Press, 1982.

Doyle, Michael W. *Ways of War and Peace.* New York: W. W. Norton, 1997. [Part Four addresses conscience and power.]

Elshtain, Jean. *Just War against Terror: The Burden of American Power in a Violent World.* New York: Basic Books, 2003.

_____. *Women and War.* New York: Basic Books, 1987.

Garcia, Denise. *Small Arms and Security: New Emerging International Norms.* London: Routledge, 2006.

Hoffmann, Stanley. *On War and Morality.* Princeton: Princeton University Press, 1989.

Howard, Michael, et al., eds. *The Laws of War: Constraints on Warfare in the Western World.* New Haven, CT: Yale University Press, 1994.

Johnson, James Turner. *Can Modern War Be Just?* New Haven, CT: Yale University Press, 1984.

_____. *Ideology, Reason, and the Limitation of War: Religious and Secular Concepts, 1200–1740.* Princeton, NJ: Princeton University Press, 1975.

_____. *Just War Tradition and the Restraint of War.* Princeton, NJ: Princeton University Press, 1981.

_____. *Morality and Contemporary Warfare.* New Haven, CT: Yale University Press, 1999.

Kegley Jr., Charles, and Raymond Gregory. "Normative Constraints on the Use of Force Short of War." *Journal of Peace Research* 23, 3 (September 1986): 213–27.

Lackey, Douglas P. *The Ethics of War and Peace.* Englewood Cliffs [now Upper Saddle River], NJ: Prentice Hall, 1989.

Nardin, Terry, ed. *The Ethics of War: Religious and Secular Perspectives.* Princeton, NJ: Princeton University Press, 1996.

O'Brien, William V. *The Conduct of Just and Limited War.* New York: Praeger, 1981.

Orend, Brian. "Justice after War," *Ethics and International Affairs.* 16 (2002): 43–56.

_____. *War and International Justice: A Kantian Perspective.* Blasdell: Wilfrid Laurier University Press, 2000.

Price, Richard. "Emerging Customary Norms and Anti-Personnel Landmines." In *The Politics of International Law,* ed. Christian Reus-Smit. New York: Cambridge University Press, 2004.

Ramsey, Paul. *The Just War: Force and Political Responsibility.* New York: University Press of America, 1968, 1983.

Rapoport, Anatol. *The Origins of Violence.* New Brunswick, NJ: Transaction Publishers, 1989, 1995.

_____. *Peace: An Idea Whose Time Has Come.* Ann Arbor: University of Michigan Press, 1992.

_____. *Strategy and Conscience.* New York: Schocken Books, 1969.

Raymond, Gregory. "International Norms: Normative Orders and Peace." In *What Do We Know about War,* ed. John A. Vasquez. Lanham, MD: Rowman and Littlefield, 2000.

Reisman, W. Michael, and Christ T. Antonious, eds. *The Laws of War: A Comprehensive Collection of Primary Documents on International Law Governing Armed Conflict.* New York: Vintage, 1994.

Walzer, Michael. *Just and Unjust Wars.* New York: Basic Books, 1977.

Welch, David A. *Justice and the Genesis of War.* New York: Cambridge University Press, 1993.

On Humanitarian Intervention

Campbell, Kenneth J. *Genocide and the Global Village.* 2nd rev. ed. New York: Palgrave Macmillan, 2001.

Frye, Alton. *Humanitarian Intervention: Crafting a Workable Doctrine.* New York: Council on Foreign Relations Press, 2000.

Haass, Richard N. *Intervention: The Use of American Military Force in the Post-Cold War World.* Washington, D.C.: Carnegie Endowment for International Peace, 1999.

Hoffmann, Stanley. *The Ethics and Politics of Humanitarian Intervention.* South Bend, IN: University of Notre Dame Press, 1997.

Holzgrefe, J.L. and Robert O. Keohane, eds. *Humanitarian Intervention: Ethical, Legal and Political Dilemmas.* Cambridge, UK: Cambridge University Press, 2003.

Janzekovic, John. *The Use of Force in Humanitarian Intervention: Morality and Practicalities.* Aldershot, Hampshire (UK): Ashgate, 2006.

Kuperman, Alan J. *The Limits of Humanitarian Intervention: Genocide in Rwanda.* Washington, D.C.: Brookings Institution Press, 2001.

Kusano, Hiroki. "Humanitarian Intervention: The Interplay of Norms and Politics." In *International Intervention in the Post-Cold War World: Moral Responsibility and Power Politics,* eds. Michael C. Davis, Wolfgang Dietrich, Bettina Scholdan, and Dieter Sepp. Armonk, NY: M.E. Sharp, 2004.

Minow, Martha. *Between Vengeance and Forgiveness: Facing History after Genocide and Mass Violence.* Boston: Beacon Press, 1998.

Orford, Anne. *Reading Humanitarian Intervention: Human Rights and the Use of Force in International Law.* Cambridge, England: Cambridge University Press, 2003.

The Responsibility to Protect: The Report of the International Commission on Intervention and State Sovereignty. Ottawa: IDRC Books, 2002.

Weiss, T. *Humanitarian Intervention: Ideas in Action.* Cambridge, England: Polity, 2007.

Welsh, Jennifer M., ed. *Humanitarian Intervention and International Relations.* New York: Oxford University Press, 2006.

Wheeler, Nicholas J. *Saving Strangers: Humanitarian Intervention in International Society.* New York: Oxford University Press, 2002.

GLOSSARY

absolute gains   See **relative gains.**

abstraction   A general idea, principle, or concept without physical or tangible quality. International relations theorists sometimes write of systems, interdependence, the balance of power, and equilibrium— examples of abstractions that may be useful to the theorist who wishes to explain or account for political or other phenomena.

action   A movement or physical act, as when the state or its decisionmakers take some concrete step in a given situation. An action is the practical expression of policy. See also **policy, interaction.**

actor   A participant or player. The state is considered by realists to be the principal actor in international relations; non-state actors include transnational actors such as multinational corporations and banks. See also **rational, unitary, transnational, transgovernmental.**

agency, agent   A voluntarist, non-determinist focus on the role played by human beings and human institutions in effecting outcomes; human beings matter and what they think and do matter. The concept is particularly associated with liberals and social constructivists.

agent-structure   An ontological question raised by social constructivists in particular. As stated by *Emanuel Adler:* "The agent-structure debate focuses on the nature of international reality; more precisely, whether what exists in IR, and the explanation for it, should revolve around actors, structures, or both." To what extent can states (and other actors) as agents shape the world within which they are immersed and not just be prisoners of the structure of the international system? How much of structure is a given, and how much is created by human agency?

aggregation   The bringing together of parts into a single whole, as when the state is understood to be a *unitary* actor. Liberals tend to see the state not as a single, unitary whole but as many parts, thus disaggregating or breaking the state apart into its component institutions, groups, and individual persons.

amoral   Morally neutral; without moral content. See also **moral.**

anarchic   See **anarchy.**

anarchy   The absence of legitimate political authority. International politics or the international system is said to be anarchic in that there is no central or superordinate authority over states.

anthropology   The scientific study of humankind, including its physical, social, and cultural origins and development.

appeasement   The policy of allowing another state to have what it wants—an attempt to avoid aggression by that state; for an example (Munich), see **learning.**

assumption   A premise or statement taken to be true without empirical or factual proof. The theorist typically makes assumptions as the starting point in developing a given theory. For example, some balance-of-power theorists make assumptions about the state as principal, unitary, and rational actor.

asymmetry, asymmetric   Not symmetrical; lacking precise correspondence or relation between or among components. An interdependent relation is said to be asymmetric if Party *A* is more dependent on Party *B* than Party *B* is on Party *A.*

autarky   An independent posture of self-sufficiency without dependence on other actors. Autarky occurs when a state attempts as a matter of policy to exist in economic isolation from other states.

authority   A legitimate right to direct or command and to make, decide, and enforce rules. The term *authority* has a moral or legal quality and, as such, can be distinguished from control by brute force or by coercion. See also **power.**

autonomous development   See **development.**

balance of payments   Accounting concept by which the international economic transactions (inflows and outflows) of states and their corporate and private elements are tracked. Balance of payments includes export and import of goods and services (balance of trade), capital investment and other "invisible" or financial flows, and gold or other financial reserve transactions. "Balance" is achieved when gold or other financial reserves flow in or out to cover differences in the other accounts as when a country exporting more than it imports receives foreign currency that it can hold as a financial reserve.

balance of power   A key concept among realists that refers to a condition of equilibrium among states. Realists differ on whether the equilibrium or balance among states is (a) created by statesmen or (b) occurs quite apart from the will of statesmen as an inherent characteristic of international politics. Balance-of-power considerations may be used by decisionmakers as justification for a given foreign policy. Some critics have noted that the multiple definitions or meanings of balance of power diminish its utility as a concept in international relations theory.

behavior   The actions and interactions among units; the behavior of policymakers or of states. *Behavioralism* refers to a way to study politics or other social phenomena that focuses on the actions and interactions among units by using scientific methods of observation to include quantification of variables whenever possible. A practitioner of *behavioralism* is often referred to as a *behavioralist.* *Behaviorism* refers to the ideas held by those behavioral scientists who consider only observed behavior as relevant to the scientific enterprise and who reject what they consider to be metaphysical notions of "mind" or "consciousness."

behavioralism   See **behavior.**

bipolar, bipolarity   The condition of having two poles as when the distribution of power or capabilities in international politics is said to be *bipolar.* Some theorists consider the Cold War international political system to have had a bipolar *structure*—the United States and the former Soviet Union. Others consider it today to be unipolar, multipolar, or to conform to some other characterization. See also **structure.**

bourgeoisie   The capitalist (and, at the time of its emergence, the "middle") class. The class defined in Marxian terms by its relation to the means of production—its ownership of capital, including factories and other machinery of production in a capitalist economic mode as well as means of finance. A member of this class is sometimes referred to as a *bourgeois.*

bureaucracy   The administrative arm of government staffed primarily by appointed, non-elected officials. A given governmental agency may be referred to as a bureaucracy, whereas the generic category of such agencies may be referred to as the bureaucracy. An individual member of a bureaucracy or administrator is sometimes referred to as a *bureaucrat. Bureaucracy, bureaucrat,* and *bureaucratic* are words sometimes used to convey negative connotations about government, but most academic usage is merely descriptive of the governmental administrative function.

bureaucratic politics   The formulation of policy is a function of the competition among opposing individuals who represent diverse governmental institutions. Coalitions and counter-coalitions typically form as a part of the process of bureaucratic politics. See also **organizational process.**

capitalism   An economic system or mode of production that emphasizes private ownership of the means of production and a free market. One who owns the means of production is a capitalist, or *bourgeois.* See also **bourgeoisie.**

capitalist world-system   An economic-structuralist approach to international relations that emphasizes the impact of the worldwide spread of capitalism; a focus on class and economic relations and the division of the world into a core, periphery, and semi-periphery. See also **core, periphery, semi-periphery, class, economic structuralism.**

categorical imperative   Concept associated with the work of Immanuel Kant—that one ought to act "according to the maxim that you can at the same time will [such conduct] to be a universal law" and that one should treat others "as an end as well as a means, never merely as a means."

causality   *B* occurs on account of *A,* which precedes it in time. *A* produces or is responsible for the subsequent occurrence of *B.* In this sequence, *A* is the *cause* and *B* is the *effect.* Some causes have multiple effects, as when *A* causes *B, C,* and *D.* Some effects have multiple causes, as when effect *T* is caused by *Q, R,* and *S.* Some causes may be *necessary,* but not *sufficient* to produce a given effect, as when *A* is necessary to cause *D* but will not do so unless *B* or *C* is also present (thus, *A* and *B* or *A* and *C* are *necessary and sufficient* causes of *D*). Some causes are sufficient in themselves to produce a given effect, as when the presence of *A* always produces *B.* An *efficient* cause is the factor immediately responsible for a given effect, whereas a *permissive* cause may refer to an underlying condition that allows a certain effect to be produced (Kenneth Waltz, for example, argues that international anarchy is the permissive cause of—the absence of any obstacle to—war, whereas other factors proximate to a particular situation, such as misperception in a crisis, are among the efficient causes of a given war). Some theorists reject causality as an abstract or metaphysical notion: One can observe *B* as coming after or following *A* in terms of time, but that does not prove that *A* is a "cause" of *B.*

causal modeling   The depiction, such as by a computer simulation or diagram, of sequential relations among two or more variables and how they result in a particular event, action, or outcome, including the relative importance or "weight" of each variable in producing a particular outcome. Causal models depict cause—effect relations, as in a model of an arms race that hypothesizes a causal connection between the decision of country A to increase the level of its military expenditure and an increase in the later military expenditure of country B in an action–reaction sequence or arms race spiral.

center   The term used especially by many dependency theorists to refer to First World or the industrialized countries in the global political economy—Japan and the countries in Europe and North America with advanced industrial or postindustrial economies. Also sometimes used to refer to the elites or dominant classes. See also **core** and **periphery, economic structuralism.**

city-state   A political entity composed of a city and its surrounding territory as in the city-states of ancient Greece (Sparta, Athens, Corinth, etc.) or Renaissance Italy (Florence, Venice, Padua, etc.).

civil society   Term associated with the rule of law and includes networks of relationships among people and the groups or organizations to which they belong. See also **international civil society.**

civil war   See **war.**

class   An analytical component of society with an identifiable characteristic or set of characteristics that differentiate it from other components. In Marxian usage, the term is defined by relations to the means of production. Under capitalism the *bourgeoisie* is defined by its ownership of capital (not only money but, significantly, the factories and machinery that are the means of production), and the *proletariat,* or working class, is defined by its labor. Under feudalism, the *aristocracy* is defined by its ownership of land, and the *serfs,* or peasants, by their labor. As such, *class* is different from a *stratum* of society defined, for example, as a socioeconomic category based on income, wealth, or level of living. See also **economic structuralism.**

class conflict   A concept associated with Marxism that emphasizes the inevitable clash of interests between strata, or classes, defined in terms of their relations to the means of production (i.e., how goods are produced). Marx, for example, analyzed the conflict between the *bourgeoisie* (owners of capital, especially factories and machinery of production) and the *proletariat,* or workers, who were being exploited by the bourgeoisie. Marx argued that eventually exploitation would reach the point at which a proletarian revolution would occur and the power of the bourgeoisie would be broken. See also **proletarian revolution, Marxism, economic structuralism.**

classical realists   These scholars include such twentieth-century figures as E. H. Carr, Hans Morgenthau, and Arnold Wolfers. While appreciating the importance of conceptualization, they were skeptical of quantitative approaches to understanding international relations. Heavily influenced by reading history and the works by the likes of Thucydides, Machiavelli, and Hobbes, they also differ from modern-day neorealists by putting emphasis on norms or values that also play a part in international politics, not just balance of power as an abstract structure. Furthermore, the role of values has to be considered.

coalition   A combination or alliance of individuals, factions, or states, including both temporary and more enduring groupings of actors, around a common interest or purpose.

coercive diplomacy   Term developed by Alexander George and his associates to describe how threats of force are used successfully or unsuccessfully as part of diplomacy to achieve national objectives. Both positive and negative measures (carrots and stick) are part of the coercive-diplomacy kit. See also **compellance (compellence), deterrence, dissuasion.**

cognition   The process by which human beings come to know or acquire knowledge through perception, reasoning, and (some would say) intuition. The term *cognitive* refers to this process.

cognitive dissonance   A concept developed by Leon Festinger wherein human beings tend not to perceive what is contrary to their preconceived or previously held perspectives. To avoid cognitive dissonance, individuals either (a) unconsciously screen out information or evidence that contradicts what they already believe to be true, or (b) interpret such discordant information in such a way as to support their preconceptions.

collateral destruction   Damage to human beings and property coincident to or following the intentional destruction of military targets; the damage is not confined to the intended targets, but spills over to harm other victims and property.

collective conscience, collective consciousness   Concept associated with Emile Durkheim referring to shared meanings or commonly held moral understandings in a society.

collective defense   A function performed by alliances that pool power or capabilities of state members to balance or countervail against the power of other states, alliances, or other coalitions. The right to individual and collective defense is legally recognized by Article 51 of the UN Charter. See also **collective security.**

collective goods theory   Relates to the allocation of, and payment for, goods that, once provided, cannot easily be denied to others and whose use does not deny their use to others. Providing national security or international security through alliances has been described by some theorists as collective goods. Collective goods are referred to by some as public goods. See also **public choice theory.**

collective security   The term is used commonly as if it were synonymous with *collective defense;* however, such usage overlooks the important distinction that, in principle, collective security is based on international law-enforcement obligations, whereas collective defense is merely a form of balance-of-power politics. Under collective security, states agree to enforce international law by confronting any aggressor with the preponderant power that comes from pooling their collective efforts. A variety of diplomatic, economic, and other measures including the use of force may be employed. Unlike *collective defense* or *balance of power* policies, collective security is understood as a law-enforcement or police activity. Unlike an *alliance* that is directed against adversaries, the goal in collective security is to encourage international law-abiding behavior by states, dissuading them from committing aggression or other illegal actions taken against other states. See also **collective defense.**

colonialism   See **imperialism.**

communism   A mode of production in Marxist thought that is to be achieved after the passing of capitalism and a socialist transition period. Communism is a classless society in which each person produces according to his or her ability and receives or consumes according to need. In Marxist thought, given the absence of classes, the state as an instrument of class domination ceases to exist. See also **economic structuralism, modes of production.**

communist   An individual committed to the eventual attainment of communism, particularly through revolutionary means that would lead to the overthrow of capitalism. See also **economic structuralism, modes of production.**

comparative advantage   The concept holds that countries specialize in the production of those goods and services which they produce more efficiently. In a free trade environment there would be, according to theory, a global specialization or division of labor with aggregate productivity maximized. As critics point out, however, free trade theory does not address such matters as equity in the distribution of wealth. Some dependency theorists see free trade theory as the vehicle by which Third World countries are kept in a status of dependency and precluded from development.

compellence   Word created by game theorist Thomas Schelling to refer to using threats of force by one state to force or compel another state to change its course of action or to do something the compelling state wants. It is referred to by Alexander George as a kind of *coercive diplomacy* as, for example, when the United States threatened the Soviet Union in an effort to force withdrawal of missiles from Cuba in 1962. This is in contrast to *deterrence* in which one state threatens another to keep it from doing something the deterring state does not want to see happen as when states with nuclear weapons arsenals use them to deter others from attacking by threatening retaliation. See also **coercive diplomacy, deterrence.**

complex interdependence   A term developed by Robert Keohane and Joseph Nye that refers to the multiple transnational channels that connect societies, including interstate, transgovernmental, and transnational relations. The resulting relations are extremely complex, with economic interests assuming far greater importance than in classical realism. See also **interdependence, globalization.**

comprador class   A term referring originally to those in the business stratum who served as local agents for foreign, colonial business interests. In contemporary usage, it refers to the aggregate of business elites in a Third World country or countries who maintain close links with their counterparts in the industrial countries of the First World. Particularly in Marxist usage, the term is used to explain relations of exploitation by the bourgeoisie of Third World workers and peasants. See also **economic structuralism.**

concept   An idea of a general or abstract nature; sometimes referred to as a *construct*. Such concepts as *power, interdependence, order, justice,* and *peace* are used in the construction of international relations theories.

condition   A set of circumstances or state of being. An underlying condition of international politics, for example, is the absence of a single or central source of authority. When a given population has established a sense of community, this can be described as a condition.

conflict   Disagreement; the opposition or clash of units. Conflicts may be non-violent or at varying degrees or levels of violence. Some theorists see the management of conflicts that cannot be resolved as being central to maintaining peace. Conflict of interest among states or other actors is a widely used concept.

consciousness   Refers to one's inner self, being, or awareness.

constant   A factor that does not vary. See also **variable.**

constitutionalism   The liberal idea that individual freedom is served by constraining the power or authority of government and setting formal limits, whether written or unwritten.

constitutive   From the constructivist perspective, defines the set of practices or means by which any particular consciously organized social activity or institution comes to be. See also **regulative rules.**

construct   Used synonymously with *concept*. A construct can be understood as an abstraction created or put together often out of simpler elements. See also **concept.**

constructivism   See **social constructivism.**

core   A term sometimes used synonymously with *center,* a reference to the industrialized countries in the global political economy. The term is also sometimes used to refer to the elites or dominant classes. See also **center** and **periphery.**

correlation   An association between two, or among more than two, variables, of such a nature that a change in one seems to be tied or related to a change in another. A correlation among variables, however, does not necessarily mean that they are causally linked. See also **causality, variable.**

cost   A loss as opposed to a benefit; something paid as opposed to something received. The concept is central to rational choice or game theory, including coalition and alliance formation. Costs may be distributed asymmetrically or unevenly among the actors in interdependence relations.

counterforce   See **targeting.**

counterintuitive   Against, or contrary to, what is thought to be true. See also **intuition, intuitive.**

countervalue   See **targeting.**

covering laws   See **deductive-nomological.**

crisis   A situation characterized by surprise, high threat to values or interests, and short decision time.

critical theory   Associated with Jürgen Habermas and others in the "Frankfurt School" in Germany that offers a theory of social reality based on the dialectic of knowledge and power, arguing that theory must be connected to practice. This also entails a critique of positivist–empiricist approaches to knowledge, critical theorists claiming all knowledge is historical and political in nature. Current "dissidents" in the field of international relations have also drawn, among others, from Antonio Gramsci's own version of critical theory, Ludwig Wittgenstein's work on linguistics and hermeneutics, and the poststructuralist perspective of such writers as Michel Foucault. Critical theory challenges the stated and unstated assumptions and alleged objectivity of mainstream social science. Ideologies that represent particular interests, while masquerading as "theories," are especially suspect. Such theories are depicted deceptively as if they were objective portrayals of sociopolitical time and space. Critical theorists reject the pretense to objective knowledge—the logical positivism of the "Vienna Circle" advanced in the interwar period and followed by many social scientists in subsequent decades. The rigid division between normative and empirical theory is illusory. Moreover, what we think we know really is a function of language and sociopolitical context. Critical theory calls for interpretive understanding of time and space, an insight drawn originally from Max Weber's work in social science methodology. See also **interpretive understanding, postmodernism, poststructuralism.**

customary international law   Established practice by states over time gives a customary base for international law. For example, centuries of practice had established immunities and other diplomatic rights long before they were codified formally in a treaty.

decision   Making a choice among often-competing alternatives or options; making a judgment or drawing a conclusion. A *rational* decision-making process is one in which alternative means to achieve certain objectives are evaluated and the option or options best (or at least satisfactorily) leading to the attainment of these objectives are selected. See also **policy,** which can be understood as being composed of both *decisions* and *actions.*

decision making   See **decision.**

deconstruct   See **postmodernism.**

deduction   Conclusions drawn logically and necessarily from specified premises; reasoning from general rules to particular cases See also **induction.**

deductive-nomological   Formal approach to scientific explanation often associated with work by Carl Hempel and others who focus on *covering laws* that relate the *explanans* (explanatory sentences) to the *explanandum* (what is to be explained). See also **deduction, nomology, nomothetic.**

democratic peace   That democracy or republican forms of governance are propitious to peace are central to Kantian thought. This hypothesis has generated a great deal of research. The Wilsonian idea of making the world safe for democracy as the principal remedy for ending warfare is often referred to by critics of democratic-peace theory (viz., President Woodrow Wilson's representation of World War I as the "war to end all wars" and thus "make the world safe for democracy" to flourish). For his part, Michael Doyle's claim is not that democracies are inherently less prone to war, but rather that they tend not to go to war with other democracies. See also **Kantian.**

dependency   A situation in which the economies of Third World countries are conditioned by and subordinate to the economic development, expansion, and contraction of the economies of advanced capitalist states. It is a situation of exploitation and is examined in an historical context. Domestic constraints and structures (such as land tenure patterns) are also critical in inhibiting balanced economic development. See also **economic structuralism.**

dependent variable   The thing that is to be explained or accounted for. Some theorists have tried to explain, or find the causes of, war, which is their dependent variable. See also **variable, independent variable, intervening variable.**

description   A verbal statement that provides an understanding or meaning. Description is often differentiated from *explanation* or *prediction,* which are understood to be *theoretical* tasks. Thus, *theory* is considered to be different from mere *description.* From this perspective, description is a necessary but pre-theoretical task.

détente   An easing or relaxation of tensions as when the relations between major powers are said to be less tense. The Cold War, for example, was said to have given way in the late 1960s and 1970s to a period of détente.

determinism, deterministic   A philosophical view that what we observe inevitably occurs as the consequence of factors over which human beings have no volition or control. Most social theorists who accept the characterization or who can be labeled as *determinists* do not reject totally the role of human will, as the strict definition of determinism would imply, but they do allow much less freedom of action for individuals to affect outcomes than those theorists labeled as *voluntarists.* The determinism–voluntarism issue among social science theorists has its analog in theological disputes over determinism or predestination on the one hand and free will on the other. Critics consider *structural realists* and *Marxist class analysts* and other *economic structuralists* to be overly deterministic, but this claim is often rejected by these theorists. See also **voluntarism, economic structuralism.**

deterrence   Psychological effect on an opponent that results in a decision not to take some act such as attacking or starting a war. Deterrence is thought to be achieved either through fear of retaliatory punishment or through rational calculation that taking this action will not succeed in achieving intended objectives or that the costs of doing so will be too high. See **compellence, coercive diplomacy, dissuasion.**

development   The process associated with the industrialization of societies. *Modernization* is a term sometimes used synonymously with *development,* but some theorists differentiate between the two. For some, *modernization* refers to societal values and processes that undergo major changes from pre-industrial traditional society, including the effects of industrialization, whereas *development* refers to the building of societal or governmental administrative infrastructure more capable of coping with increasing demands brought on by the modernization process. *Autonomous* development occurs in isolation, or independent of what is going on outside of a given country, a circumstance more difficult to achieve in the contemporary period than may have been true in the nineteenth century. *Reflexive* development, when and if it occurs, is responsive to external economic conditions and may well be dependent on them.

diachronic   Refers to a study over a period of time; sometimes referred to as a *longitudinal* study, as in a study of the causes of war between 1815 and 1945. See also **synchronic.**

dialectic, dialectical materialism   A form of reasoning or argument that juxtaposes contradictory ideas with the goal of resolving the contradiction and thus moving closer to the truth. The term is associated with the ancient Greek philosophers, the German philosopher Hegel, and Karl Marx. Marx substituted materially based class conflict and the contradictions between relations and modes of production for the clash of ideas—dialectical materialism. Whereas Hegel argued that the dialectical clash of ideas moved history forward, Marx focused on the importance of material forces. See also **class conflict, proletarian revolution, Marxism, relations of production, modes of production.**

diffuse   Dispersed widely; not concentrated or narrowly focused. When a state is said to be a functionally diffuse actor, it performs a multitude of functions. The opposite of functionally diffuse is to be functionally specific or more narrowly focused.

diplomacy   The process or art of communication among states and their statesmen in international relations, negotiation, including positive inducements or persuasive tactics, compromise, threats, or other measures understood to be part (or tools) of diplomacy. Diplomacy is the state's political or policy element in the conduct of its foreign relations. The terms *diplomat* and *diplomatic* have a positive connotation, referring in common parlance to peaceful, non-warlike approaches. As a technical term, *diplomacy* includes the threat or imposition of punishment or sanctions as tactics that may be employed by the diplomat in addition to (or in place of) more positive inducements.

disaggregation   See **aggregation**.

discourses   See **social constructivism**.

dissuade, dissuasion   From a position of strength to persuade other states not to do something they might otherwise do; dissuasion is usually seen as using both positive and negative measures to persuade. See also **coercive diplomacy, deterrence**.

distributive justice   The question of the rightness of (or moral criteria associated with) the allocation of scarce resources, particularly material or economic resources. The rightness of a particular distribution of wealth or profit could be subject to normative standards of distributive justice. See also **justice, normative, social contract**.

dual or double-effect principle   See **just war**.

dyad, dyadic   As between two units. See also **interdependence**.

East   During the Cold War years, *East* referred to the Soviet Union and other Marxist-Leninist countries, mainly those in Eastern Europe. A more traditional meaning is the Orient or countries of Asia. Variants are the Far East (the countries of East Asia, including China, Japan, and the Koreas), the Middle East (originally referring to such south Asian countries as India and Pakistan, but now more commonly used to refer to Egypt, Israel, Jordan, Syria, Saudia Arabia, and neighboring countries), and the Near East (originally referring to countries in North Africa and Arabia; now more commonly referred to as the Middle East). See also **East–West**.

East—West   During the Cold War years, *East–West* referred to conflict between capitalist, industrial democracies of the First World or West (including West Europe, North America, and paradoxically even Japan) and the Marxist-Leninist countries of the Second World, or East (including the former USSR and other Marxist-Leninist countries, mainly those in Eastern Europe, but sometimes including China, particularly in the Maoist years). The more traditional meaning of East–West refers to Europe and the Americas as "West" and Asia as "East"—the meaning in Kipling's observation that East is East and West is West and never the twain shall meet. See also **East** and **West**.

econometrics   Quantitative techniques used in economic analysis.

economic development   The sustained expansion of production in an economy such that the standard or level of living is raised for the citizenry. See also **development**.

economic structuralism, structuralist   As used in this volume, *economic structuralism* refers to an image of politics. To understand the overall economic or class structure in world captalism, one must examine more than the distribution of power among states (realism), chart the movements of transnational actors and the internal political processes of states that cross national borders (liberals), or a combination of the two (English School). Economic structuralism focuses on the importance of economy, especially capitalist relations of dominance or exploitation, to understanding world politics. The economic-structuralist image is influenced by Marxist analyses of exploitative relations, although not all economic structuralists are Marxists. Dependency theory, whether understood in Marxist or non-Marxist terms, is categorized here as part of the economic-structuralist image. Also included is the view that international relations are best understood if one sees them as occurring within a capitalist world-system. See also **postcolonialism, image, dependency**.

efficient cause   See **causality**.

elite   The upper stratum or strata of a society.

empirical, empirically   Factual or known through observation. Propositions or hypotheses may be subject to empirical or factual tests to determine whether observed "facts" are consistent with what is predicted.

empiricism, empiricist   The epistemological position that the only grounds for making truth claims is through direct observation of the world using our senses. Consistent with the philosophical view that knowledge is rooted in experience, empiricists adopt a scientific focus on observation of facts and hypothesis testing as the virtually exclusive source of knowledge.

endogenous factor   See **system.**

English School   Scholars influenced by the earlier work of Herbert Butterfield, Martin Wight, Hedley Bull, and others. The school focuses on the societal aspects of international relations rather than seeing politics in purely abstract, systemic terms. Power, law or rules based on enlightened self-interest, and emergent global norms are all part of an anarchical international society. In this volume we represent English School as an image that combines aspects of realism and liberalism in the context of international society. English School understandings have also been seen as a middle way between realism and idealism and between realism and liberalism as images. See also **image.**

epistemic community   Term used by Peter Haas, Emanuel Adler, and others to refer to expert elites that operate transnationally or globally often affecting policy outcomes on issues in which their particular knowledge makes them relevant. Scientists and other technical elites (though not referred to as *epistemic communities*) were also the subject of earlier policy-related studies by the late Ernst Haas. See also **functionalism** and the reference there to *neofunctionalism.*

epistemology   The study of how one knows or how one acquires knowledge.

equilibrium   When various elements of a system are in balance. When disturbed, some systems are said to have an inherent tendency to restore this balance or equilibrium. For example, when a state or group of states upsets the balance of power, other states respond in opposition, restoring the balance.

ethnocentrism   An inward-looking tendency or favorable disposition toward the people or nation with which one identifies, particularly when it is seen as superior to others.

European Union (EU)   A collaborative association of European states previously known as the European Communities (EC)—the European Coal and Steel Community (ECSC), European Economic Community (EEC), and European Atomic Energy Community (EURATOM). Since agreeing at a summit meeting in December 1991 in the city of Maastricht in the Netherlands to move beyond a customs union and common market toward a full economic and monetary union, the association of states is now referred to as the European Union.

existentialism   An approach that believes philosophical thinking begins with the human subject; much of academic philosophy, in both style and content, is viewed as too abstract, superficial, and remote from actual human experience.

exogenous factor   See **system.**

expected utility, expected utility theory (model)   Rational-choice concept in which actors compare the relative attractiveness of options and choose the alternative that maximizes expected gains or minimizes expected losses. Concept used by Bruce Bueno de Mesquita and others concerning conflict situations that may lead to war. The expected utility model also addresses how policy positions emerge in the presence of competing interests, leading to predictions and strategic opportunities for altering them. See also **rational choice theory.**

explanandum   See **deductive-nomological.**

explanans   See **deductive-nomological.**

explanation   See **theory.**

externality   When an international actor takes an action that has an intended or unintended impact (positive or negative) on another actor.

factor analysis   A quantitative technique by which the analyst tries to identify underlying and related elements or factors (usually as part of a causal explanation of some observed phenomenon or phenomena).

falsifiability   Associated with Karl Popper's thought, to be "scientific" propositions or hypotheses have to be stated in a form that, if they are false, they can be shown to be false through empirical tests. When empirical tests fail to show a proposition or hypothesis is false, we gain greater confidence that it may be true.

federalism   See **world federalism.**

feedback   A concept in systems theory and communication theory (or cybernetics) by which responses to decisions or actions taken are returned by affected elements to the sender or taker of these decisions or actions, thus allowing for corrective actions.

feminism, feminist   An interpretive, "gendered" understanding or approach to theory that takes into account the constructive and collaborative potential of human beings, often rejecting such cold, abstract analysis as found in neorealist and other structural explanations; the focus is more on human dimensions of international relations, also multilateral relations rather than unilateral or hegemonic dominance. In the policy realm, feminism also seeks the empowerment of women, putting women on an equal plain with men.

feudal, feudalism   A system of political, social, and economic organization that existed in Europe from approximately the ninth to approximately the fifteenth centuries. Reciprocal rights and duties were expected between the lord and his vassals—for example, protection of the vassal by the lord in return for the vassal's giving up a percentage of his crops. Feudalism is viewed in Marxist usage as a mode of production dominant in the Middle Ages and that preceded capitalism. See also **modes of production.**

First World   See **Third World.**

force   Usually refers to efforts undertaken by states in an attempt to compel others to take a certain course of action or to cease an action. The term usually means the use of armed or military force.

foreign policy   Refers to external affairs, particularly to decisions and actions taken by states in their dealings with other states or such "external" actors as international organizations, multinational corporations, and other transnational or non-state actors.

functionalism, functionalist   A focus on purposes or tasks, particularly those performed by organizations. Some theorists have explained the growth of organizations, particularly international organizations, as a response to an increase in the number of purposes or tasks demanding attention. *Neofunctionalism* as a theory of regional integration emphasizes the political calculation and payoff by or to elites who agree to collaborate in the performance of certain tasks. See also **integration, spillover.**

functionally diffuse   See **diffuse.**

fungibility   The condition that exists when one element or unit has no unique identity and can easily be exchanged or replaced by another of like nature. Money is said to be fungible (for example, funds in a national budget can easily be shifted from one account to another when cuts are made in one area of the budget to fund increases in another). Whether the power of states, like money, is fungible and can readily be transferred from one issue area to another is a point of some dispute among international relations theorists.

game theory   A decision-making approach based on the assumption of actor rationality. Each actor tries to maximize gains or minimize losses often under conditions of uncertainty and incomplete information, which requires each actor to rank order preferences, estimate probabilities, and try to discern what the other actor is going to do. In a competitive, two-person *zero-sum* game, what one actor wins the other loses; if *A* wins 5, *B* loses 5, and the sum is zero. In a two-person, *non-zero-sum* or *variable sum* game, gains and losses are not necessarily equal; it is possible that both sides may gain. This is sometimes referred to as a *positive-sum* game in which the parties effectively cooperate. In some games, both parties can lose, and by different amounts or to a different degree. So-called *n-person* games include more than two actors or sides. Game theory has contributed to the development of models of deterrence and arms race spirals, but it is also the basis for work concerning the question of how collaboration among competitive states in an anarchic world can be achieved: The central problem is that the rational decision for an individual actor such as a state may be to "defect" and go it alone as opposed to taking a chance on collaboration with another state actor. Dealing with this problem is a central concern of much of the literature on international regimes, regional integration, and conflict resolution. See also **anarchy, rational, rational choice theory, theory.**

gender   Refers to masculine, feminine, or transgendered identities people have. As such, gender can be differentiated from sex as a biological category and sexual preference or orientation as another form of identity. Gender is the core factor contributing to feminist interpretive understandings.

general theory   See **theory.**

global civil society   See **international (global) civil society.**

globalization   The continued increase in transnational and worldwide economic, social, and cultural interactions that transcend the boundaries of states, aided by advances in technology.

governance   As defined by Robert Keohane, governance involves the processes and institutions, both formal and informal, that guide and restrain the collective activities of groups. Globally, the question of governance (or "partial global governance") is one of how the various institutions and processes of global society could be meshed more effectively in a way that would be regarded as legitimate by attentive publics controlling access to key resources.

government   The lawmaking, judicial, administrative, and enforcement apparatus of a state.

Grotian   Refers to the influence of Hugo Grotius, seventeenth-century Dutch scholar usually identified as the father of international law. The Grotian view is that international relations, although lacking central authority, can be subject to rules or norms, some of which have the binding character of law, that are expressly or tacitly agreed to by states.

groupthink   According to Irving Janis: a "mode of thinking that people engage in when they are deeply involved in a cohesive in-group, when the members' strivings for unanimity override their motivation to realistically appraise alternative courses of action." Indicators of groupthink include social pressure to enforce conformity, limiting discussion to a few alternatives, failing to re-examine initial decisions, and making little attempt to seek information from outside experts who may challenge a preferred policy.

guerrilla warfare   See **war.**

hard power   See **power.**

hegemonic stability   The view that stability in international relations stems from the presence of hegemony or dominance. The absence of hegemony or hegemons would imply a lack of order in the relations among states whether in commercial activities (trade, the exchange of money, and investment), social issues, or security concerns. See also **hegemony.**

hegemony, hegemon   Relations of dominance as when a major power exercises hegemony over countries within its sphere of influence. A state exercising hegemony is sometimes referred to as a *hegemon*. An alternative characterization reflecting preeminent position for a state, but not necessarily implying dominance, is to refer to it as a leader exercising leadership of other states within its sphere. The difference between hegemony and leadership is often a subtle distinction and perhaps more a matter of nuance or connotation intended by the user of the terms. See also **hegemonic stability.**

hermeneutics   Subordinates explanation and description to interpretation and understanding of meaning. As a field of study it owes much to Ludwig Wittgenstein's work on how human beings interpret or draw meanings as is reflected in the language they construct and use. Social facts are constituted by the structures of language.

heuristic   Refers to the illustrative value of some device or schematic presentation. Such a presentation is not intended as an actual or precise, empirically verified representation of relations among variables in a model, but it is useful for gaining a better understanding of some concept or set of concepts under investigation.

high politics   Refers to matters of security, particularly the strategic interests of states. Realists have tended traditionally to draw a distinction between such high political concerns and those dealing with socioeconomic or welfare issues supposedly of lesser interest to goverment leaders or diplomats—the so-called *low politics.*

historical materialism   Economically oriented methodological approach to the study of society and history which was first articulated by Karl Marx (1818–1883). Historical materialism looks for the causes of developments and changes in the means by which people in societies live and are organized. The starting point is the economic base, with everything else (social classes, political structures, ideologies) influenced by this material base.

historical sociology   Study of a society's past (particularly its social structure and culture) usually intended to shed light on how what we observe now developed over time, oftentimes centuries.

Hobbesian (or Hobbist)   Deriving from the influence of Thomas Hobbes, seventeenth-century English philosopher, who characterized anarchic politics—the absence of a sovereign or central authority—as producing grave threat to individual security. The absence of central authority in international relations in this Hobbesian view poses a security threat to all states to which they may respond internally by strengthening their power positions, or externally by forming alliances. International security in the Hobbesian view rests, therefore, more on power and the balance of power than on law and other rules or norms.

human rights   Regardless of culture, national, state, or other identity, human beings possess certain rights by virtue of being human. Many of these rights have been codified in treaties and conventions. Intellectual foundations of human rights may be found in normative theories associated with Kantian, utilitarian, and social contract as well as Aristotelian virtue-based modes of thought. See also **natural rights, Kantian, utilitarian, social contract, virtue-based ethics.**

hypothesis, hypotheses (plural)   A proposition usually relating two or more variables (such as "Arms races cause wars") but subject to empirical or factual tests. In one view, hypotheses may be verified or confirmed to the extent that tests do not show the hypotheses to be false. Repeated tests, including *replication* of earlier work, increase confidence in the correctness of the original hypothesis, although it is always subject to being shown to be false in subsequent tests and thus can never be confirmed with 100% certainty. A *null* hypothesis, the starting point, is a proposition in which no relation between or among variables is specified (as in "there is no relation between arms races and the onset of war") in contrast to a *working* hypothesis in which such a relation is specified. If one's empirical tests show no relation, then the null hypothesis is retained and the working hypothesis is rejected.

idealist, idealism   One who sees such values or human preferences as justice or a desire for world peace as potentially decisive and capable of overcoming obstacles to their realization. Referred to by critics as utopian in that the idealist does not understand the political or other realities that constrain human choice. An idealist considers ideas alone as having important causal effects as opposed to others who see power or material factors as being the determinants of political outcomes. A classic debate within international relations pits idealism against realism.

ideal (pure) type   A concept developed by the German sociologist Max Weber to describe an extreme, or pure, case that is not found in this form anywhere but that serves as an analytical benchmark useful in comparing real-world cases. Strictly defined, ideal types for democracy or modern and traditional societies are constructed by theorists even though the actual cases they examine are, at best, only approximations of the conditions they specify.

identity   See **social constructivism.**

ideology   A belief system or set of ideas or values usually held as a matter of conviction. Ideological views are usually not subjected to the same standards of empirical test as are theories and associated hypotheses. Marxism–Leninism as ideology offers not only explanation and prediction of world politics but also a means for interpreting social relations. Liberalism as ideology leads some to advocate free or open trade and commerce.

idiographic   A detailed study of a particular case or event. See also **nomothetic.**

IGO (or IO)   An abbreviation used to designate international, governmental organizations in which membership is composed of states—for example, the United Nations and its affiliated agencies. See also **INGO, NGO.**

image   As used in this book, an image refers to a general perspective of international relations and world politics that consists of certain assumptions about actors and processes. See also **realism, liberalism, English School, economic structuralism.**

imperialism   In its classic meaning, a position or policy of preeminence or dominance with respect to foreign elements, as in the Roman, Ottoman, or British empires. Imperialism in earlier centuries involved the establishment of colonies, which led to so-called *colonialism.* Although most of these colonies have become formally independent states, the relations of economic, social, cultural, and even political dominance by the former colonial power remain—so-called *neocolonialism.* Some theorists also contend that contemporary imperialism involves economic and other forms of exploitation or dominance by multinational corporations in less developed countries. Marxist theories of imperialism tend to emphasize the economic dynamics of capitalism and associated class relations.

incrementalism   A step-by-step rather than a comprehensive, all-encompassing, sweeping approach. In an incremental decision-making process, decisions are often deferred until information on which to base a choice has been maximized (or until not making a decision would foreclose certain options and thus, in effect, be a decision in itself).

independent variable   A factor used to explain some outcome. See also **variable, dependent variable, intervening variable.**

indeterminacy   The degree to which an outcome cannot be predicted with a reasonable degree of confidence or is subject to seemingly random influences. There may be a great deal of indeterminacy in voluntarist theories that maximize the effect of human choice or volition. See also **determinism, voluntarism.**

indeterminate solution   Refers to problems in which the outcome cannot be predicted with much, if any, confidence, as when the influence of variables appears to have random effect. See also **indeterminacy.**

individualism   Associated with *liberalism,* individuals have particular value in themselves and for what they can do—that people as individuals have more importance than the groups, tribes, communities, or societies to which they may belong. See also **liberalism.**

induction, inductive   Logical and inferential process by which we posit general statements based on observation of only a part or sample of a class of facts; the general statement is an answer to the question posed in this text by James Rosenau: "Of what is this an instance?" Induction lacks the logical certainty of deduction. See also **deduction.**

INGO   An abbreviation sometimes used to designate international, non-governmental organizations, those in which membership is composed of private individuals and groups, but usually *not* states or their governments. Examples are the International Red Cross and the World Council of Churches. See also **IGO, NGO.**

institution, institutionalism   See **neoliberal institutionalism.**

institutionalized   As used by constructivists, collective ideas are expressed in actual social orders (termed structures or institutions) and in established practices and identities.

insurgency   See **war.**

integration   The coming together of separate states or other political units under a common authority. Integration may occur as an international or regional phenomenon with varying degrees of authority given to institutions established to deal with common issues or problems facing member states. Integration can be viewed either as *process* or as *outcome* that reflects and encourages cooperation among states operating under conditions of international anarchy (i.e., lack of common government). Research on integration has tended to focus on the assignment of economic and social tasks to regional or international authorities. Earlier theories of regional integration saw political union as a possible outcome of collaboration in economic or social issues. See also **functionalism, ramification, spillover.**

interaction   An exchange between two, or among more than two, units as in the *interactions* of states, groups, classes, or individuals. By contrast, *actions* do not refer to the back-and-forth of an exchange but to steps or measures taken by a state, group, class, individual, or other unit. See also **action.**

interdependence, interdependent   A relation or relations between two (a *dyadic* relation) or among more than two units in which one is *sensitive* or *vulnerable* to the decisions or actions of the other or others. The flow of capital or money to or from one country may respond to (or be *sensitive* to) changes in the interest rates in other countries—so-called *sensitivity interdependence.* To the extent that one unit may be adversely affected by decisions or actions of another, it is said to be *vulnerable* to the other unit or units, as when State *A* depends on State *B* as the principal source of its oil supply and thus is vulnerable or would be adversely affected by its cutoff. To many theorists, such *vulnerability interdependence* is to be minimized or avoided altogether. Interdependence may be *symmetric* (affecting both or all sides equally), but it is more likely to be *asymmetric* (with effects varying from actor to actor). State *A* may be more or less dependent on a supply of oil from State *B* than State *B* is on the security of its investments in State *A*. See also **complex interdependence, balance of power.**

interest   That which is of importance to a unit (state, class, group, or individual), usually including, as a minimum, its survival. *National* interest refers to matters of importance to a state. Some theorists have found the concept of national interest to be too vague; they prefer to substitute the notion that states do formulate certain objectives that can be identified more easily. Others view the national interest as little more than what leaders say it is. What realists and liberals have tended to take for granted as given, constructivists see as actually quite malleable—constructed and subject to change by the actors themselves as they interact with others.

interest group liberalism   An approach to politics that emphasizes competing groups or institutions. Not only is interest group liberalism thought to be an accurate description of democratic politics, particularly in the United States, but it is also thought by many to be the way politics *should* be conducted. See also **liberalism.**

international   Specifically, relations between or among states. More loosely, it is a reference to matters outside a state, which has led to the synonymous usage by many persons of the terms *international politics* and *world politics.*

international (global) civil society   Just as the rule of law is central to domestic understandings of civil society, so it is with international law in what some see as an increasingly global, civil society beyond the borders of particular states. This society includes networks of relationships among people around the world that are not necessarily associated with the state *per se* as well as organizations that aggregate individual interests below the level of the state, but operate across the border of any single state. Nongovernmental organizations (NGOs) are an example. The role of institutions and norms are associated with the English School and liberal images of international relations. For the English School, the concept of *international society* is heavily associated with Hugo Grotius. See also **civil society.**

International Court of Justice   Located in the Hague; a principal organ of the United Nations. See also **international law.**

international governmental or intergovernmental organizations (IGOs)   See **international organization.**

international law   A body of rules considered to be binding on states and other actors even though there is no central enforcement authority to assure compliance. Sources of international law include treaties or covenants made by states, customary practice, generally accepted principles, and the writings of jurists. International courts such as the International Court of Justice interpret international law and apply it to individual cases brought by states. National courts and enforcement systems (those of individual states) are the primary mechanisms for dealing with international law. International law (particularly that based on treaty commitments) may have precedence over domestic laws that conflict with such international obligations.

international law of war, international law of armed conflicts International law governing warfare and the use of force in international relations requires legitimate reasons for using force and places specific limitations on the actual use of force. See also **just war.**

international organization An institution composed of states as members (for example, the United Nations [UN], European Union [EU], and the North Atlantic Treaty Organization [NATO]). More broadly, the term refers to patterns of behavior or structures and actors that cross or go beyond national frontiers.

international politics The *political* focus is on choices made by actors with authority to do so on issues external to states or that cross the frontiers or boundaries of state jurisdiction. *International politics* is often used synonymously with *world politics* or *international relations,* although these terms do have separate, more precise meanings. See also **international relations, world (or global) politics.**

international regimes See **regime.**

international relations The total of political, social, economic, cultural, and other interactions among states (and even non-state) actors. *International politics* can be understood to be a part (or subset) of international relations, although the terms *international relations, world politics,* and *international politics* are often used synonymously. See also **international politics, world (or global) politics.**

international security In its narrowest construction, the term refers to defense matters among states and their respective societies. In the broadest sense, it encompasses a very wide range of issues that affect the welfare of human beings—not just defense, but also economics, health, environment, human rights, and other social or "human security" questions that cross national boundaries. Critics of broad definitions argue that if *security* as a concept can be construed to mean so many things, then as a practical matter does it really mean anything? Their preference is to retain the more traditional distinction that sees *security* and related defense issues as separate from *welfare* issues.

international society Term used within the English School that sees relations among states and other actors subject to rules or law, a perspective that owes much to insights drawn from Dutch legal writer Hugo Grotius. This Grotian position is sometimes referred to as "rationalist"—seeing order and justice in international politics as a function of rules that both facilitate and constrain decisions and actions. See also **rationality, society, world society, international civil society.**

international system An aggregation of similar or diverse entities united by regular interaction that sets them apart from other systems; e.g., the *interstate* or *international* system of states or *world politics* understood as a system composed of both state and non-state actors. See also **system.**

interpretive understanding An approach to knowledge that assumes that what we know is based on an interpretation of what we think we see, alerting us to the subjective character of all human beings, the institutions or units they construct, and the processes in which they engage. Try as we might to reduce bias, we remain subjective creatures. Pursuit of objectivity and value-free scholarship is therefore an elusive goal. That concepts are constructs defined by the meanings we give them is a view that owes much to the thinking of Max Weber. In this volume we identify interpretive understandings associated with feminism, social constructivism, critical theory, and post-modernism. Elements of interpretive understanding can also be found among some scholars associated with liberalism, the English School, and postcolonial theorists. See also **feminism, social constructivism, critical theory, postmodernism.**

intersubjective, intersubjectivity Interpretations or understandings one derives from reflecting on exchanges or interactions with others. The idea that shared knowledge results from the exchange of ideas, depicting the social world in terms of collectively meaningful understandings or identical structures—itself an ontological assumption. See also **subjective, subjectivity, objective, objectivity.**

intervening variable Variable that may come between the cause(s) or independent variable(s) and the effect or dependent variable, thus affecting the outcome. See also **variable, dependent variable, independent variable.**

intervention   Interference in the domestic affairs of another state by diplomatic, economic, military, or other means.

intuition, intuitive   That which is held, assumed, or seems to be true *a priori* (beforehand). The term refers to a view that usually has not been subject to formal or empirical tests but merely seems to make sense. See also **counterintuitive.**

jus ad bellum   See **just war.**

jus gentium   The law of nations—the idea that laws are applicable to all of humanity, nations, and individuals, which is a core concept in international law. Associated with the Roman Empire but its basis is also to be found in the universalism in Greco-Roman Stoic thought. See also **Stoicism, international law.**

jus in bello   See **just war.**

justice   In common usage, that which is right, fair, or equitable for (or pertaining to relations among) individuals, groups, classes, states, or other units. See also **distributive justice, just war.**

just war   Normative theory referring to conditions under which (1) states rightfully go to war (*jus ad bellum*) with just cause, as in self-defense in response to aggression, when the decision to go to war is made by legitimate authority in the state, as a last resort after exhausting peaceful remedies, *and* with some reasonable hope of achieving legitimate objectives; (2) states exercise right conduct in war (*jus in bello*) when the means employed are proportional to the ends sought, when non-combatants are spared, when weapons or other means that are immoral in themselves are not used (typically those that are indiscriminate or cause needless suffering), *and* when actions are taken with a *right intention* to accomplish legitimate military objectives and to minimize collateral death and destruction. Sometimes the same actions in warfare can have both positive, morally legitimate effects (as in destroying a military target without any unnecessary loss of life or property) and morally negative or evil effects, as when there is also *collateral damage*—loss of life or destruction of property. According to the *principle of dual or double-effect* such actions are legitimate only if the positive or legitimate purpose is intended, efforts have been taken to minimize collateral damage, the collateral damage caused is not disproportionate, and it occurs at the same time or after the positive effect (a provision to assure that positive or morally legitimate ends do not rely on evil means, but that evil consequences are merely another effect). Many of these principles of just war are part of the body of international law and thus are legally binding on states and their agents.

Kantian   Deriving from the influence of Immanuel Kant, eighteenth-century East Prussian philosopher whose ethical writings emphasized certain *categorical imperatives* as being universal, morally binding norms such as the obligation to treat other human beings as ends important in themselves and not merely as means. In normative international relations theory, the Kantian preference was for a cosmopolitan world society, perhaps a world federation based on universal values in which perpetual peace would be maintained. Kantian thought is foundational to much democratic-peace theory. See also **categorical imperative, democratic peace.**

laissez faire   The classical liberal idea that governments ought not intervene in markets—that they should be left alone because competitive markets are understood to be self-regulating.

law   In domestic and international politics, the term refers to authoritative rules that are binding on those subordinate to them. In the natural sciences, the term refers to a general statement that specifies some regularity, as in Newton's second law of motion that force is equal to the time derivative of momentum: $F = d(mv)/dt = m(dv/dt) = ma$. Such specificity of relations among variables and constants has been elusive in the social sciences, and theorists have had to be content with identifying tendencies and generating what are at best "lawlike" statements.

LDC   Abbreviation for *less*-developed country. In some usages, LDC refers to *lesser*-developed country. See also **Third World, South.**

learning   Inferences or lessons drawn from the experiences of states (and statesmen) that guide future policy choices. For example, correctly or incorrectly (the inference is disputed by some), statesmen "learned" that appeasement of aggressors does not make such states less aggressive but may actually whet their appetites for more aggressive behavior (the case usually cited is appeasement of Hitler's Germany in 1938 when diplomats, meeting in Munich and wishing to avoid war, allowed the Germans to annex that portion of western Czechoslovakia inhabited primarily by Germanic peoples). Statesmen may "learn" the benefits of international collaboration as opposed to going it alone, an inference that might lead them to create new and expand existing international organizations.

legitimacy   The implication of the existence of *right*, as when a government is said to have, or to have been granted, a right to govern based on such criteria as its popular acceptance, the legal or constitutional processes that brought it to or maintains it in a position of authority, traditional grounds as in the divine right of kings, or the charismatic quality of its leadership that commands a following and thus contributes to its popular acceptance. See also **authority.**

less-developed country, lesser-developed country (LDC)   A country in Latin America, Africa, Asia, or the Pacific that is in the early stages of industrialization or that has not yet industrialized to the extent that Japan and most of the countries in Europe and North America have. See also **North–South.**

levels of analysis   Individuals, groups, state and society, international system or society as separate points of focus. Such levels help scholars to be systematic in their approach to understanding international relations. In explaining a phenomenon such as war, for example, the theorist may identify possible causes as being some characteristic or characteristics of the international system, states and their societies, groups or individuals. In accounting for or explaining such a phenomenon, one may look both within a unit such as a state, as well as how the unit relates to its external environment, which are different levels of analysis. In current usage, "unit level" factors such as state, society, interest groups, bureaucracies, and individuals are contrasted to structural factors operating at the system level. See also **structure, system.**

Leviathan   The biblical beast of gargantuan proportions used as a metaphor by Thomas Hobbes to refer to the state—the supreme authority that provides order and security to individuals living under its sway; also the title of Hobbes's classic work. See also **Hobbesian.**

liberal institutionalism   See **neoliberal institutionalism.**

liberalism, neoliberalism (liberals and neoliberals)   Political philosophy (sometimes referred to as an ideology) with origins in the seventeenth and eighteenth centuries that emphasizes individual liberty to be achieved through a minimal state. A *laissez-faire* government, one that provides for law and order (sometimes referred to as a "night watchman" state) but otherwise constrained or not granted authority to infringe on the rights of individuals, is said to be a liberal government. In both domestic and international economy, this classic liberalism implies commitment to free market principles without government intervention, including free trade policies and unconstrained commercial activities both at home and abroad. In contemporary American political usage, influenced by President Franklin Roosevelt and those who have followed him, *social liberalism* usually means enhancing individual rights and well-being through government action or government programs—a substantial departure from the *laissez-faire* of classic liberalism. In this volume we use the term *liberalism* to describe an image of international relations that includes both state and non-state actors as principal players in a wide diversity of issues. In earlier editions of this volume, we used the term *pluralism* to capture this more complex or even fragmented image of multiple kinds of actors operating in multiple channels on diverse issues. Some of the original formulations of the liberal image put emphasis on non-state actors, discounting the relative importance of the state. By contrast, *neoliberals* brought the state back in as principal actor, adding a focus on institutions, hence the term *neoliberal institutionalism.* See also **interest group liberalism, ideology, image, neoliberal institutionalism, pluralism.**

linkage   Coupling among units or issues as in ties that cross state boundaries and thus link internationally or transnationally the domestic elements (corporations, groups, individuals, etc.) of various states. In another sense, various policies may be tied to one another in such a way that international trade policy is affected by changes in international monetary policy (linkages sometimes referred to as "policy interdependence"). The term *linkage* has also been used to describe foreign policy connections, as when a government ties negotiations with another government in one field (such as progress in arms control) to behavior by that government in another field (such as demonstration that it will not intervene in the affairs of some third state).

Lockean   Constructivists such as Alexander Wendt use this term as a shorthand to refer to John Locke's understanding of people in society coming together by contract or agreement. Unlike Hobbes, Locke does not see the anarchic state of nature—"want of a common judge," government or central authority—as necessarily warlike. In applying Locke's insight to international relations we need not see states as necessarily in a state of war with one another. Moreover, states (as if they were persons in a state of nature) may reach agreements with one another to maintain the peace, whether they remain in a state of nature or leave it by forming a community.

logical positivism   Pursuit of a pure science that would separate fact from value and achieve the precision of mathematics, a perspective identified with scholars in the "Vienna circle" of the 1930s.

logic of appropriateness   A concept associated with social constructivism in which it is assumed human actors follow norms and rules with which they identify, not just narrow understandings of self-interest.

longitudinal   See **diachronic.**

low politics   See **high politics.**

Machiavellian, Machiavellianism, Machiavellism   Deriving from an interpretation of Niccolò Machiavelli, the sixteenth-century Florentine political philosopher. In its pejorative meaning, the term refers to unprincipled behavior by statesmen or other state agents who aim to achieve certain objectives deemed to be in the state's interest. In this view, the ends of the state (its survival and its continuing security) may justify means or actions taken for these purposes, even though the same means might otherwise be considered immoral or illegal.

macrotheory   See **theory.**

Madisonian   Deriving from the influence of James Madison, often referred to as the "father of the U.S. Constitution." Madison's ideas (along with those of such other Federalists as Alexander Hamilton and John Jay) on the separation of powers among various branches of government and the division of powers between central and state governments were central to framing the U.S. Constitution.

Marxism   A body of thought inspired by the German Karl Marx. It emphasizes the *dialectical* unfolding of historical periods—changes in modes and relations of production over time. It stresses the importance of economic and material forces and *class analysis.* It predicts that contradictions inherent in each historical epoch eventually lead to the rise of a new dominant class. The era of capitalism, according to Marx, is dominated by the *bourgeoisie* and will give way to a *proletarian,* or working class, revolution and an era of *socialism* in which the workers own the *means of production* and move toward a classless, *communist* society in which the state, historically a tool of the dominant class, will wither away. A number of contemporary theorists have drawn on Marxian insights and categories of analysis—an influence most evident in work on *dependency* and the *capitalist world-system.* See also **dialectic, means of production, proletarian revolution, class, capitalist world-system, bourgeoisie, socialism, economic structuralism.**

materialism   In many realist and liberal accounts, explanation of IR phenomena is grounded in terms of material objects (such as money and the economy as a whole, weapons systems and warfare-oriented organizational structures, and both demographic and geographic factors) as having decisive impact on outcomes unmediated by the ideas people have concerning these objects.

means of production   A concept particularly associated with Marxist analyses that refers to factors essential to the production of goods—combinations of land, labor, and capital. Classes are defined in Marxian terms as relations to the means of production: The feudal aristocracy owned land, the bourgeoisie owns capital (including factories and machines), and the proletariat is defined by its labor. See also **class, modes of production, relations of production, Marxism.**

mercantilism, mercantile   A theory in early capitalism that saw the wealth of a nation as a function of the amount of gold and other treasure that could be accumulated. Accordingly, running trade surpluses (exports more than imports), while finding new gold in mines or accepting it in payment for goods or services sold became national economic policy. In his *Wealth of Nations* (1776) Adam Smith challenged this view, arguing that the true wealth of a nation was to be found in its productive capacity, not its treasure.

Present-day *neomercantilist* policies pursued by some states try to maximize trade surplus, accumulating large monetary-reserve balances.

metaphysics   The study of the fundamental nature of reality and being which is outside objective experience.

methodology   The approach one takes to an academic study; modes of research and analysis, as in the use of historical case and comparative case studies, or the use of statistics as in formal hypothesis testing or causal modeling of variables. See also **causal modeling.**

microtheory   See **theory.**

minimum winning coalition   The smallest number of actors needed to agree to a policy or course of action in order to put it into effect. See also **game theory.**

MNC   See **multinational corporation.**

modernism, modernist   See **postmodernism.**

modernization   See **development.**

modes of production   The organization of the economy for the production of goods, as in such historical epochs identified by Marx as slavery, feudalism, and capitalism. According to Marx, as technology has advanced, the mode of production has also changed—feudalism being a more productive mode than slavery and capitalism being more productive than feudalism.

monopoly   Occurs when a firm has solitary or complete control of a market. Marx noted an increasing concentration of capital or a tendency toward monopoly in advanced capitalism.

moral   Principles of right and wrong in one's behavior.

multilateralism   Refers to an effort to cooperate or collaborate with other states rather than trying to go it alone. See also **unilateralism.**

multinational corporation (MNC)   A firm usually with headquarters in one country but with production facilities in more than one country. Because they operate across national borders, MNCs are among those units referred to as transnational actors. See also **transnational.**

multipolar, multipolarity   A distribution of power in the international system with more than two centers or "poles," such as a world in which there are five principal or major powers.

mutual constitution   For constructivists, there is a reciprocal relation between agency (actors) and structure. Structures are not objects that simply influence actors in a unidirectional manner. Rather, agents have the ability to change structures and escape from situations that encourage and replicate, for example, conflictual practices such as war.

nation   A group of people with a common identity. A nation coterminous with state boundaries is referred to as a *nation-state,* although in common language the terms *nation, state,* and *nation-state* are often used synonymously. It is possible for there to be a nation without a single state—for example, a *non-state nation* such as the Palestinian and Kurdish peoples in the Middle East. Some states such as India contain more than one nation and are sometimes referred to as *multinational* states.

nation-state   See **nation.**

national interest   See **interest.**

national security   Issues dealing with the survival, welfare, and protection of a state.

national self-determination   The view that a people with a common identity have the right to be independent from outside control, as in establishing a state for such a national group. National self-determination has been an important rallying cry for Third World countries that demanded an end to colonial rule.

nationalism   Promoting national identity usually to the exclusion of other, competing identities and legitimizing actions of a state taken for national purposes. Nations without states often solidify movements to establish a nation-state around nationalist themes.

NATO   The North Atlantic Treaty Organization; a mutual defense organization founded in 1949 by the United States, Canada, and Western European countries. There are currently twenty-six members.

natural law, universal law   A philosophical view dating back at least to the time of the ancient Greeks and developed further by the Romans that posits there are laws inherent in nature that transcend any laws made by mere mortals. All leaders and all forms of government, it is argued, are bound by these laws, and they should not be violated. Some scholars have dealt with natural law as a means to develop a body of international law to govern the relations among states.

natural rights   Reference is to a theory that finds human rights in nature that can be discovered through reason. Social-contract theorists such as Locke and Rousseau saw rights in this naturalist understanding; however, utilitarians such as Bentham and Mill argued that human rights rested on other grounds also discoverable through reason—the greatest good or happiness for the greatest number. See also **human rights, utilitarian.**

neoclassical realists   These scholars, while appreciating the insights of neorealism and the importance of systemic structure, have attempted to incorporate international institutions and explanatory factors at the state-society level of analysis to explain war. They tend to take their cue from classical realists.

neocolonialism   See **imperialism.**

neofunctionalism   See **functionalism, spillover.**

neoliberal institutionalism   Like realism, neoliberal institutionalism is utilitarian and rational in orientation—states are treated as rational egoists and interstate cooperation occurs when states have significant interests in common. The goal is to discover how, and under what conditions, institutions matter. As such, neoliberal institutionalism addresses both security and non-security or welfare issues. In this regard, institutions provide information, reduce transaction costs, make commitments more credible, establish focal points for coordination, and aid in the operation of reciprocity and multilateralism among states. The term *institution* may also refer not just to organizations, but also to such accepted patterns of recurrent or institutionalized relations as *multilateralism*—a meaning advanced by John Ruggie and others. The concept is particularly associated with Robert Keohane, although he rejects the "neoliberal" adjective.

neoliberalism, neoliberal   Critical of liberal theories that discount the relative importance of states, the neoliberal position is that states also matter alongside a wide array of non-state actors. See also **neoliberal institutionalism.**

neorealism   A label applied to *structural realists* or those realists who are interested in explaining state behavior under conditions of anarchy and who emphasize the importance of the structure of the international system and how this influences and constrains state behavior. The term may also have negative connotations in the eyes of some critics who claim that the neorealists have neglected the importance of values and norms as stressed by earlier realists such as Hans Morgenthau and E. H. Carr. Neorealists deny the validity of such charges, and some even reject the neorealist label. See also **structure, structural determinist, structural realist.**

neostructuralism   Associated with economic structuralism, neostructuralism is interested in understanding how global processes interact with other processes of state and social transformation occurring at multiple levels of the world-system. The study of international relations, therefore, is not limited to foreign policy or patterns of distributions of capabilities, nor confined to reducing international relations to economic variables. Influences include Fernand Braudel, Karl Polanyi, and Antonio Gramsci.

neutrality, neutral   States that announce they do not take sides in an international dispute or war nor join an alliance. Some, like Switzerland, claim *permanent* neutrality. Others choose to be neutral, perhaps more accurately, *non-aligned* as a tactical choice that serves their interests at a particular time.

newly industrializing country (NIC)   Countries such as Taiwan, Singapore, South Korea, or Malaysia whose rapid economic growth over recent decades made the label *Third World* inappropriate. All such countries exhibited strong *market* orientations, developed industrially, and heavily emphasized exports.

NIC   Newly industrializing country.

nomology   Study relating to discoverable scientific laws that contribute to human understanding. See also **deductive-nomological.**

nomothetic   Related to finding general or universal laws that cover numerous, different cases over time. See also **idiographic.**

non-governmental organization (NGO)   Transnational organizations that have a standing independent of governments, often with diversified members that work to fulfill specific political, social, or economic objectives that may benefit or have some positive or negative impact on a wide-range of persons. Examples include human rights organizations; multinational corporations and banks; labor unions; privately owned telecommunications, newspaper, and other print media firms; churches and other religious organizations; etc. See also **international organization.**

non-state actors   International actors other than governments, such as international organizations, multinational corporations, international banks, terrorist groups, and the Red Cross. Liberals with a transnationalist perspective on international relations emphasize the importance of such non-state actors. See also **transnational.**

non-zero-sum   See **game theory.**

normative, norm   A principle of right action; a standard to guide behavior, as in norms or obligations governing the conduct of war, transit on the high seas, diplomacy, trade and commerce. Normative judgments are often equated to value judgments and the idea of what *ought* to be; some norms may have the binding character of international law. For constructivists and many liberals, norms define standards of appropriate behavior. For constructivists they are part of international structure.

normative theory   Value-oriented or philosophical theory that focuses on what ought to be. As such it is usually differentiated from *empirical* theories that try to explain the way things are or predict what they will be.

North   See **North–South.**

North–South   Terms meant to distinguish between the advanced industrialized states of the northern hemisphere and the poorer states of the southern hemisphere. The South is also referred to as the Third World. Debate and discussion revolve around the question of how the North–South economic gap can be bridged and what, if any, obligation the North has toward the South.

n-person game   See **game theory.**

objective, objectivity   Aim in positivism is to test propositions empirically and reduce bias as much as possible. The idea that there is a truth "out there" that we are equipped to find even though we are essentially subjective persons. See **subjective, intersubjective, intersubjectivity.**

oligopoly   An economic market in which a few firms control the production (or distribution) of certain goods or services. Marx and Lenin argued that capitalism tended to move toward greater concentration of capital, resulting in oligopolies or monopolies. See **monopoly.**

ontology   Consists of our assumptions (often unstated) of what the world ultimately consists of—how we see or understand the essence of things around us. A philosophical term referring to the study of existence or being or, in Kant's terms, "the more general properties of things." Are there, for example, actual "structures" out there that influence the behavior of actors? If so, are they essentially material-based (a view associated with structural realism) or ideationally based (a view associated with constructivism). Dialectical materialism as universal law or set of laws with historical implications for humanity is an example of a materialist ontology central to Marxist thought.

operationalize, operationalization   See **variable.**

optimal   In the context of decision making, the best possible outcome.

order   From the perspective of the English School, order results not simply from power and the balance of power, but also from the acceptance of rules and institutional arrangements that are in the enlightened, rational self-interest of states and other actors. This allows English School theorists to speak of an "international society" rather than a "system of states" which is associated with the realist perspective on IR.

organizational process   A model developed by Graham Allison to distinguish *bureaucratic politics* from organizational process—the institutional perspectives, routines, standard procedures, and processes of particular bureaucracies.

pacta sunt servanda   Latin for "treaties are binding"; the idea that treaties or formal covenants are legally binding even in the absence of a central authority to enforce adherence to them.

paradigm   A pattern, model, or perspective that helps one organize and guide research. A paradigm may include key assumptions about the world and the best way to go about understanding it. The concept was central in Thomas Kuhn's influential *The Structure of Scientific Revolutions* (1962) and has since been applied to the social sciences. According to Kuhn, a scientific era is characterized by a dominant paradigm that represents "normal science"; the majority of scholars work within this paradigm, often accepting the assumptions of the paradigm in an unquestioning manner. These assumptions have an impact on how research is conducted and the resultant scholarly work. See also **research program.**

parsimonious theory   A theory that contains only a few elements yet can explain or predict a wide variety of phenomena. See also **theory, hypothesis.**

partial theory   See **theory.**

peace   A wide variety of definitions exist, including the absence of war; a situation of security, order, or stability; harmonious relations among states. For some theorists, it means worldwide collaboration to solve common global problems.

Peace of Westphalia   Two peace treaties signed in 1648 that ended both the Thirty Years' War in Germany and the Eighty Years' War between Spain and the Netherlands. The Peace initiated a new order in central Europe based on the concept of state sovereignty.

perception, perceptual   Awareness of the world through the medium of the senses. In international relations, the literature on deterrence and crisis situations, for example, often deals with the importance of perception and misperception.

periphery   The less-developed countries or areas of Asia, Latin America, and Africa. In the dependency literature, the periphery is dominated by the *center,* which consists of the economically and politically dominant countries of the world (usually viewed as those in North America, Europe, and Japan). The literature on the capitalist world-system has applied the concept of periphery back to the origins of capitalism in Europe. The periphery plays a subordinate but important role in a worldwide capitalist division of labor by providing raw materials and cheap labor. As capitalism expanded, countries that at one time were part of the center slipped into peripheral or semiperipheral status. See also **semi-periphery, core, center.**

permissive cause   See **causality.**

phenomenology   A philosophical term referring to a subjective or interpretive understanding in human consciousness of what we observe or think we see—*phenomena* in the world around us. Classification and description of phenomena, including identifying their formal structures, have been part of an attempt to establish their scientific foundations. Following Edmund Husserl and others, the focus is on carefully describing the phenomena we experience—an interpretive approach to human understanding and the categories of understanding we construct. For our purposes in this volume, we see phenomenology contributing to constructivism, critical theory, postmodernism, and other interpretive understandings.

phenomenon, phenomena (plural)   An observed or observable occurrence.

pluralism, pluralist   As used in earlier editions of this book, pluralism referred to an image of international relations that assumes that non-state actors are important entities in international relations. In this edition we have adopted the more commonly used term *liberalism* and refer to a *liberal image* of international relations. The state is not necessarily a rational and unitary actor but is composed of a multitude of competing bureaucracies, individuals, and groups. The agenda of world politics is extensive and goes well beyond security concerns. Much of the work on decision making and transnationalism falls within this liberal image that captures the pluralism we find in a multiplicity of factors and actors. In the English School, *pluralism* is a term used to describe a condition in which states have little in common other than the calculations of interest that drive the behavior of states—a "thin morality" with cooperation among states based almost entirely on calculations of mutual advantage. *Pluralism* in English School usage stands in contrast to the *solidarism* one finds in international society. See also **image, liberalism, solidarism.**

policy   A decision or a course of action chosen from alternatives.

political culture   Those norms, values, and orientations of a society's culture that are politically relevant; e.g., many societies have a tradition of deferring to political authorities in the making of domestic and foreign policies. Other, more participant political cultures reflect a public interest in political matters and attempt to influence political decisions.

political economy   There are at least two major ways in which this term is used in international relations research: (1) the view that politics and economies are inextricably linked, leading one to study the interrelations of political and economic variables, and (2) the use of economic models of rationality to explain political actions. For example, some theorists use economic models of rationality in order to determine under what conditions international collaboration can be achieved among states.

politics, political   Numerous definitions have been offered including the processes that determine who gets what, when, and how (Harold Lasswell), the authoritative allocation of values (David Easton), or simply authoritative choice.

polity   In common usage, a political system such as the American polity or the Canadian polity. In the original Aristotelian usage, the term referred to an ideal form of government.

positive-sum game   See **game theory.**

positivism   A view of scientific inquiry that assumes (1) the unity of the natural and social sciences—we can study society as we study the natural world; (2) we can draw a distinction between facts and values; (3) regularities exist in the social as well as the natural world and they can be identified; (4) empirical validation or falsification is the hallmark of "real" inquiry. Hence knowledge comes from empirical testing of propositions or hypotheses against evidence or facts. In terms of *international law,* the view that laws stem only from the actions of those having the political authority to make them rather than being the derivation of divine or natural law.

postcolonialism   An interdisciplinary perspective that encompasses economic, political, social, and cultural aspects of decolonization and afterward, highlighting the importance of race, gender, and ethnicity in understanding anticolonial struggles. Postcolonialism would include the literature on dependency and the capitalist world-system.

postmodernism, postmodernist   A rejection of scientific or "modernist" epistemology, postmodernism *deconstructs* or takes apart the meanings embedded in what we say and write, looking for underlying meanings or *subtexts*; in the extreme, some postmodernists adopt a purely relativist position—that no knowledge or truth is possible apart from the motivations and purposes people put into their construction. See also **critical theory, hermeneutics.**

poststructuralism, poststructuralist   A deconstruction of the dominant readings of reality. Going beyond or not being bound by the accepted symbols or established structures that effectively channel our understandings, it is a reaction to the universal claims we find in the structuralism of both French philosophical thought and the branch of anthropology called semiotics. Particularly objectionable to poststructuralists is the attempt to unify the social sciences with a single structuralist methodology based on identifying linguistic or cultural signs and differences. For their part, Francois Lyotard and his followers reject grand meta-narratives employed purportedly to explain all of the world in scientific terms. Poststructuralists raise similar objections to balance of power and other meta-narratives in IR they see masquerading as scientifically based theoretical explanations. Poststructuralists can be understood as a category within postmodernist thought, although the terms *postmodernism* and *poststructuralism* are sometimes used synonymously.

power   Capabilities, or the relative capabilities, of actors such as states. The ability to control or influence outcomes or the actions of others. Central to realist works on international relations. Joseph Nye introduces the distinction between hard and soft power, the former referring to military and economic capabilities, the latter to values and culture that define a country, the image it projects, and the expectations it generates abroad "Smart" power is the optimal combination of hard and soft components. For more detailed discussion of power, see discussion in the text, particularly Chapter Two on realism.

practices   See **social constructivism.**

prediction   See **theory.**

progressive theory   A theory is considered progressive if it leads researchers to ask new and interesting questions.

proletarian   See **proletarian revolution, proletariat.**

proletarian revolution   A Marxist concept referring to the rising up of the working class, or proletariat, and the overthrow of the capitalist system dominated by the bourgeoisie who own capital—the factories, industries, and banks. The revolution is, theoretically, the result of contradictions internal to the nature of capitalism.

proletariat   A Marxist concept referring to a particular class or stratum of people, in this case the working class. The proletariat is usually viewed as being in opposition to the bourgeois class, which owns the means of production. See also **Marxism, means of production.**

prophecy   See **self-fulfilling prophecy.**

proposition   In theory, a statement that affirms or denies something. Example: "Arms races cause conflict."

public choice theory   The use of economic methods to analyze what are essentially political problems (issues involving choices or decisions by political authorities). See also **collective goods theory, rational choice theory.**

pure type   See **ideal type.**

ramification   A concept developed by David Mitrany in his work on functionalist integration: Successful collaboration by states in one particular technical area would encourage the expansion of collaboration into other areas. Mitrany hypothesized that if states became increasingly integrated in a number of technical or functional areas, the cost of breaking these ties (such as by going to war) would be high enough to prevent such actions from occurring in the first place. See also **functionalism, spillover.**

rational, rationalist   To act rationally requires a rank ordering of preferred goals, consideration of all feasible alternatives to attain those goals in the light of existing capabilities, and consideration of the costs and benefits associated with using particular methods to attain particular goals. This is *instrumental* rationality or what Max Weber in German called *Zweckrationalität*. The assumption is often made in international relations research that actors do indeed act rationally in this way. The assumption is made in order to develop hypotheses and to produce insights on world politics. On the other hand, one can as Weber did refer in German to *Wertrationalität* or value rationality—subscription to values like duty, loyalty or commitment, courage or bravery, trust and the like. Thus, following value rationality, risks are taken and losses suffered that would not have been willfully taken were instrumental rationality the driving criterion. Institutional or bureaucratic rationality is yet another form of rational action identified by Weber in the procedures and routines that enhance organizational or bureaucratic efficiency in the way decisions are made, recurrent tasks are pursued, and follow-up actions are taken. Finally, we take note of rationalism or the *rationalist* position in the English School that refers to rules or law that are mechanisms for providing order and justice in international society. See also **decision, action, policy, rational choice theory, English School, international society.**

rational choice theory   Theory that assumes actor rationality in economics and politics, focusing on the instrumentally rational dimension—maximizing interest or utility—in the development of explanatory and predictive theories. See also **collective goods theory, decision, expected utility, game theory, rational.**

rationality See **rational.**

realism, realist A perspective on international relations that focuses on the state as unitary and rational actor and on the actions and interactions of states. Realists attempt to understand patterns of conflict and collaboration under conditions of anarchy or lack of common government. Security issues are usually the most important for realists. *National interest* or objectives, *power,* and *balance of power* are key concepts for most realists. *Classical realists* see power and power relations as important, but also put greater emphasis on values or norms than *structural realists* who see the distribution of power or material capabilities as having primacy. See also **image, neorealism (structural realism), classical realists, neoclassical realists.**

Realpolitik A German term referring to power politics. It emphasizes policies based more on practical power considerations and less on moral or ethical considerations. The attainment and maintenance of state security in a hostile world through power or balance-of-power politics is viewed as the primary goal of leaders.

reductionism An analytic approach leading to oversimplification and incompleteness of explanation. In some usages, the term refers to explanations that look only within a unit, such as state or individual, ignoring the environment within which the unit is immersed and the interaction of that unit with elements in its environment. Reducing the explanation of some phenomenon such as war among states to something deep within the human psyche (as being, for example, at the level of synapses between nerve endings) is an extreme example of *reductio ad absurdum*—explanation reduced to an absurd degree of oversimplification and incompleteness—as if one could explain the recurrence of war among states purely in neurological terms. Similarly, theorists who have tried to explain revolution solely in social or social-psychological terms, ignoring economic, political, and other factors, have been criticized for reductionism.

reflectivism, reflectivist As opposed to a purely rationalist view as in abstract cost-benefit calculations, reflectivists take into account the ideas, understandings, or consciousness in relation to interests that influence the decisions we make and the actions we take. See also **cognition.**

reformism The idea that revolution or the violent overthrow of an existing capitalist political-economic order is not necessary, but that change can occur incrementally and non-violently. The possibility of evolving toward socialism by peaceful means such as parliamentary methods or the creation of trade unions is a tenet of reformism. The issue of reformism is one reason the socialist movement split in the late nineteenth and early twentieth centuries. V. I. Lenin and Rosa Luxemburg argued that the reformist policies of Karl Kautsky, Eduard Bernstein, and others were wrong. Lenin believed that capitalism could not be reformed to benefit the working class, that a revolution was required. See also **proletarian revolution.**

regime, international regime In its domestic context, an existing governmental or constitutional order defined in terms of sets of rules and institutions established to govern relations among individuals, groups, or classes within a state. In its international context, the term is defined as voluntarily agreed-upon sets of principles, norms, rules, and procedures around which actor expectations converge in a given area of international relations. The literature on international regimes blossomed in the 1970s. Scholars argued that international collaboration was obviously not restricted to formal international organizations such as the United Nations—cooperation was necessary in monetary and trade areas, telecommunications, maritime and air traffic control, and a whole host of areas of greater and lesser importance.

regulative rules For constructivists, formal or informal practices that influence behavior. See **constitutive.**

reified, reification Giving a concrete reality to what is in fact an abstract concept of analysis. For example, some critics claim that realists have reified the state, attributing to it human characteristics such as rationality, or treating the state as if it operated in the international arena like an actual human being. The concept of system, used by some realist, liberal, English School rationalist and economic structuralist theorists, has also been criticized on similar grounds.

relations of production   In Marxist usage the term refers to classes and the roles they play in economic or productive activities—for example, the bourgeoisie or owners of capital in the dominant position over the working classes in a capitalist *mode of production.* See also **class, mode of production.**

relative and absolute gains   This distinction is important as it can be viewed as a key assumption underlying much of IR theorizing. If, for example, one believes the international system is composed of states that are satisfied as long as everyone receives some positive pay-off (absolute gains), then stability or peace seems more likely. If, however, states are driven by relative gains and both gain but one more than the other (thus changing their overall positions relative to each other) then conflict may be more likely.

relativism   Humans can understand and evaluate beliefs and behaviors only in terms of their historical or cultural context; truth is always relative to some particular frame of reference.

relativist, relativism   A view that what is true varies from individual to individual, group to group, and context to context. See **natural law.**

research program   A term developed by Imre Lakatos to identify work within a particular school of thought or understanding.

satisficing   A less-than-optimal choice that does not completely maximize the values or goals one is pursuing but is good enough; work on decision making shows that people often choose the first viable option that is minimally acceptable.

scientific method   An approach to explaining and understanding the natural and social world. To accept the scientific method is to adopt positivist assumptions that assume (1) the unity of the natural and social sciences—we can study society as we study the natural world; (2) we can draw a distinction between facts and values; (3) regularities exist in the social as well as the natural world and they can be identified; (4) empirical validation or falsification is the hallmark of "real" inquiry. Hence knowledge comes from empirical testing of propositions or hypotheses against evidence or facts.

scientific proposition   See **falsifiability.**

Second World   See **Third World.**

security   For realists, the basic survival and protection of the state. Liberals have a more expansive definition, also applying the concept to individuals and groups of people. In fact, from this perspective the state may not even be a provider of security, but rather a threat to the security of many people.

security dilemma   A term coined by John Herz: In an anarchic international system, State A may sincerely increase its level of defense spending only for defensive purposes and self-preservation, but it is rational for other states to assume the worst and impute aggressive intentions to State A. They therefore also increase their level of arms, leading State A to feel insecure and contemplate a further increase in military spending. Hence, by initially trying to enhance its own security, State A sets in motion a process that results ironically in its feeling less secure. In another usage, the term merely refers to the security problem faced by all states in a world without central authority or lack of common government among states. See also **anarchy, self-help.**

self-fulfilling prophecy   To predict a particular outcome and then choose policies or actions that help to bring about the predicted outcome even though this is not the intended effect. For example, predicting that State B will increase support for a war of national liberation against an ally of State A, State A provides its ally with more military assistance to combat rebels, resulting in State B's feeling it is necessary to increase its support for the guerrillas. State A's prophecy that State B will increase support for the guerrillas hence becomes self-fulfilling.

self-help   In the international arena, there is no superordinate authority, world government, or "Leviathan" to ensure order or to see that all parties to an agreement keep their end of a bargain. Each state must look after its own security and not assume the help of other states. See also **anarchy.**

semiotics   The signs and symbols people use in communications with each other, which have been particularly important in anthropological studies of culture.

semi-periphery   As used by capitalist world-system theorists (see Chapter Four), term refers to those countries or regions that occupy an intermediate position between core and peripheral areas. The semi-pheriphery is engaged in a mix of activities, some associated with the core and some with the periphery. It serves as an outlet for investment when wages, and thus the cost of production, in core areas become too high. The semi-periphery may at one time have been a core or peripheral area, or it may be moving into either status. See also **bourgeoisie, class conflict.**

sensitivity interdependence   See **interdependence.**

social constructivism   Social theories that attempt to explain the formation and transformation of identities and interests, in particular those of states. The fundamental structures of international politics are social rather than strictly material or capabilities as neorealists would have it. These social structures shape actors' (agents') identities and interests, not just their behavior. According to Alexander Wendt, social structures are made up of collective meanings, shared knowledge and material resources and practices. What makes ideas (and thus structure) "social" is their intersubjective quality. Material resources only acquire meaning for human action through the structure of shared knowledge. Habitual actions that result from these interpretations are often referred to as *practices*. The combination of language and techniques employed to maintain these practices is referred to as *discourses*. *Identities* are relatively stable, role-specific understandings and expectations about one's self that are acquired by interacting with a structure composed of social relationships, collective meanings, beliefs, and rules.

social contract   A philosophical idea used by theorists such as Thomas Hobbes, John Locke, and Jean-Jacques Rousseau to justify their preference for a particular type of political order. Living in an imaginary "state of nature"—a condition without any social or political structure—individuals contract with one another to create a political community or society governed by certain rules. For Hobbes, the social contract resulted in the establishment of a sovereign or central authority that is given the task of maintaining order. In international relations, however, no such sovereign exists. The late-twentieth-century writings of John Rawls on the bases of a just society apply social contract theory to the question of how decisions on society's rules and how it is organized likely would be made by individuals making these choices behind a *veil of ignorance*—not knowing how they would individually be affected by outcomes from these decisions. See also **self-help, security dilemma.**

socialism   Ownership of the means of production and distribution of goods by the society or the people as a whole (the public) rather than by private individuals. In a more limited form of socialism, only major industries and utilities are publicly owned. In some usages, socialism refers not only to public ownership of the means of production; it also includes public welfare programs and government acts in the name of the people in carrying out these programs. In Marxist thought, socialism is a stage or mode of production between capitalism and communism.

social structure   Typically refers to the arrangement or relative position within a particular society of such units as classes, elites and masses, patrons and clients, tribes, and extended families or clans. As adapted to the international context, it has both social and material meanings. Can include class or material-based understandings as well as networks of individuals and organizations.

society   Term in domestic usage referring to the people, typically within a state but sometimes across two or more states. Analytically we can understand *society* as including state or political régime, economy, social structure, and culture. The concept is used in the English School to describe international or world society. See also **international society, world society, international civil society.**

society of states   The view that at certain times in history states have agreed upon basic rules, norms, and international laws to govern their relations. The nineteenth-century Concert of Europe is one example. See also **English School.**

sociology   The study of society, particularly social groups and classes and relations among them.

soft power   See **power.**

solidarism   Term used in the English School to describe a cosmopolitan "thick morality" among states in international society that goes well beyond ephemeral calculations of mutual advantage in a pluralist world. Shared norms, rules and institutions among states define this solidarist understanding of international society. See also **pluralism.**

South See **North–South.**

sovereign, sovereignty The supreme, independent, and final authority. The attribute of a state that refers "internally" to its right to exercise complete jurisdiction over its own territory. In international relations, states as sovereign units have a right "externally" to be independent or autonomous with respect to other states. States may differ in their power, but as sovereign entities all are legal equals.

spillover In the regional integration literature, a concept referring to a process whereby successful collaboration by states in one technical area leads to the realization by state authorities that it is in their rational self-interest to expand collaboration into related fields. Thus, progress in reducing barriers to trade may depend on, and lead to, further progress in rules facilitating the exchange of money among states.

stability, destabilizing An attribute of a system. Some theorists compare unipolar, bipolar, and multipolar international systems in terms of which is more or less stable. Stable deterrence relations are said to depend on maintaining second-strike capabilities that would allow either party to absorb a first strike prior to choosing whether and how to retaliate. By contrast, when one party fears it has lost (or will lose) its second-strike capability, this may be *destabilizing* because it may be prone in a crisis to launch first or to launch on warning of an attack even before it has confirmed that an attack has actually taken place. See also **system, equilibrium, deterrence.**

state A legal entity composed of territory, a population, and an administration or government. It possesses sovereignty and recognition by other states. See also **government, sovereignty.**

state of nature A philosophical construct referring to a time prior to the creation of civil society—a world without governmental authority. An analogy to the *anarchic* structure of the international system. An important concept, particularly for realists who follow the thinking of Hobbes, as it raises the issue of how order and stability can be achieved in an international system of states competing for power and prestige.

Stoicism An ancient Greco-Roman philosophy that saw humankind in universal, unifying terms. Our similarities, particularly our common ability to reason, outweigh any differences among us. Stoicism also counseled acceptance of things not easily changed and promoted inner discipline or self-control, the fortitude one displays especially when in difficult circumstances. Among the Stoics are Seneca, Emperor Marcus Aurelius, and Paul of Tarsus (St. Paul). Early Christian universalism was also influenced by Stoic thought; beyond the common human ability to reason was added the idea of a soul or spirit—another aspect seen as shared by human beings wherever they might be, whatever language they spoke, or however different their appearance. Liberalism as philosophy or ideology also has Stoic roots.

structural See **structure.**

structural determinist One who believes that the structure of the international system largely determines the behavior of individual states and that there is very little effective choice for leaders of states. The term is usually used in a negative or critical sense against realists, neorealists, and some Marxists. Few, if any, theorists would admit to complete structural determinism in their theories, but some do assign greater weight to structure as a determinant of the behavior of states and other actors. See also **system, structure, neorealism, realism, Marxism, structural realism, neoclassical realists.**

structural realism, structural realist A term preferred by Kenneth Waltz and other neorealists because in their view it more accurately describes neorealism's focus on structure (the distribution of power) as a principal determinant of the behavior of states, the principal units in the international system. See also **neorealism.**

structural transformation As used by economic structuralists, the historical and geographical expansion of the capitalist world-system, incorporating new areas of the globe and non-integrated sectors of the world economy.

structure   The arrangement of parts of a whole, as in the structure of the international system being defined by realists in terms of the distribution of capabilities or power among states. The international system structure, following this usage, may be bipolar, multipolar, or unipolar. Some theorists look for underlying structure associated with the anarchy of the system—the lack of central authority. For others, structure refers to observed patterns of behavior as among states, although still others contend that such a definition confuses underlying *structure* with *behavior,* or the interactions of states—concepts that are, and should be, kept analytically separate. Some theorists of dependency and the capitalist world-system use the term *structure* to describe relations or mechanisms of dominance, dependence, and exploitation. From the perspective of the English School, structure is defined in terms of rules, laws, and institutional arrangements states have established to provide some degree of order to an anarchic international society. For social constructivists, structure is made up of shared meanings, practices, rules, and norms. Structures thus may be ideational or cultural, not just material. Finally, structure may be defined as exogenous or external to agents, whether these agents be units like states or individuals. See also **social structure, system, behavior, bipolar, multipolar, structural determinist, structural realism.**

subjective, subjectivity   Term(s) refer to the human dimension—that people or subjects are conscious and thinking, forming their views based on their own interpretations and understandings. See also **intersubjective, intersubjectivity, objective, objectivity.**

suboptimal   Less than the best choice or outcome, although it may be deemed good enough. See also **optimal.**

subsidiarity   The principle of leaving authority or tasks to be performed at lower, often more local levels rather than centralizing them. In the European Union (EU), for example, not all tasks are directed centrally by the Commission or other institutions in Brussels. Many tasks are left to lesser EU institutions within the European region, member states, and their local institutions.

subtext   See **postmodernism.**

supranational   Beyond or above the state. For example, a world government would be a supranational authority that governs the relations among states.

surplus value   In Marxist usage, the value of goods and services produced comes from the labor put into their production. After paying wages (which tend toward subsistence or minimum levels) and other costs, the remainder is *surplus* that can be pocketed or invested by the owners of land or capital.

synchronic   Refers to a study of phenomena at a given point in time as opposed to over a period of time. See also **diachronic.**

synthesis   Putting together parts, analysis having broken the whole into parts. Alternatively, the outcome of conflict or tension between thesis and antithesis. See also **dialectic.**

system   A set of interrelated parts or an arrangement of units connected in such a way as to form a unity or whole; an abstract concept used by many theorists to bring order to their work. The use of the term varies. For example, some theorists see the *international* system as being composed of states and other actors, whereas some authors see world capitalism as a system composed of classes with conflicting interests. Some systems are said to be *open* to external influences, whereas others are *closed* systems. Factors external to a system that may affect it are *exogenous,* whereas those internal to the system are often referred to as *endogenous* factors. Some systems are said to have certain inherent qualities or attributes, such as a tendency toward balance or equilibrium, although not all systems theorists assign such automaticity to systems. Some theorists use systems merely as taxonomies, or frameworks, for organizing research and analysis.

systemic   See **system.**

taxonomy, taxonomies   A classification as in a categorization of states as democratic, socialist, or fascist.

teleology, teleological   That phenomena are to be explained by the purposes they serve. In systems theory, for example, it is teleological to argue that the need for a system to return to some natural state of equilibrium causes units within the system to behave the way they do. It may be that unit interactions within a system have a tendency to produce equilibrium, but it is teleological in effect to reverse the causal flow and argue that this systemic purpose (equilibrium) somehow causes the behavior of actors within the system to occur so as to achieve this result. Similarly, some functionalist theories have been criticized to the extent that they are also teleological.

terms of trade   The ratio of a country's average export prices to its average import prices, especially regarding merchandise trade. When import prices rise faster than export prices, the terms of trade worsen. This is said to be the case for most less-developed countries since the 1950s; the prices of raw materials have generally lagged behind the prices of imported manufactured goods from developed countries.

terrorism, terror   Rational or purposive, intentional use of the "irrational" or intimidating effects of violence, usually for political purposes. For its use as an insurgent tactics, See also **war.**

theory   For positivists and those who seek causal theories such as neorealists and neoliberals, theory is an intellectual construct composed of a set of interrelated propositions that helps one to identify or select facts and interpret them, thus facilitating explanation and prediction concerning the regularities and recurrences or repetitions of observed phenomena with the goal of making the world more intelligible. *Explanation* involves accounting for, or understanding causes of, such phenomena as war, arms races, and regional integration. In a loose sense, *prediction* amounts merely to forecasting, but in a strict sense it implies explanation sufficient to anticipate outcomes, given the presence of certain variables or conditions (for example, theories that would predict war as the outcome of arms races). *General* theories attempt a comprehensive or complete explanation of some phenomenon, whereas *partial* theories are often understood as initial steps or attempts to explain narrower aspects of the phenomenon under investigation. There are considerable differences about the use of the terms *microtheory* and *macrotheory*. Most theorists use the term *microtheory* to refer to partial theories and *macrotheory* to refer to grand theory that would, for example, explain all of international relations. Strutural realists draw from microtheory in economics and refer to relations among component units—instead of firms in a market, states in an international system. For English School scholars, theory may mean nothing more than developing a set of interrelated concepts and categories to guide research and help structure questions. Positivist-influenced causal theories are contrasted in this book with interpretive understanding approaches to knowledge. For a more extensive discussion, see the Chapters in Part II. Normative theory deals with norms or values—what *ought* to be done. See also **parsimonious theory, hypothesis.**

Third World   A term developed in the 1960s referring to the economically less-developed (or underdeveloped) states of Asia, Africa, and Latin America. The *First World* includes the more industrially developed states in North America, Europe, Japan, Australia, and New Zealand; the *Second World* consists of the few remaining Marxist-Leninist countries. Some theorists have identified the poorest of the less-developed countries as constituting a *Fourth World*. See also **North–South, East, West,** and **East–West.**

traditionalism   A mode of thinking about international relations that emphasizes the studying of such disciplines as diplomatic history, international law, and philosophy in an attempt to develop better insights. Traditionalists tend to be skeptical of behavioralist approaches that are confined to strict scientific standards that include formal hypothesis testing and, usually, the use of statistical analysis. See also **behavior, methodology.**

transformation, system transformation   A *fundamental* change in the system, as in a shift from a multipolar to a bipolar world or vice versa. The creation of a world government to replace an anarchic system of sovereign states would be such a system transformation. In a domestic context, the overthrow of the bourgeoisie by the proletariat would be considered a transformation of the political, social, and economic order.

transgovernmental   Relations involving links, ties, or even coalitions among bureaucratic or other official actors of different states. To the extent that these are effective, they may be a means for bypassing central government authorities in each state, although some theorists consider such circumvention of authority more an exception to the usual pattern in which the state remains unitary and speaks with one voice. See also **transnational.**

transnational, transnationalism   Interactions and coalitions across state boundaries that involve such diverse non-governmental actors as multinational corporations and banks, church groups, and terrorist networks. In some usages, transnationalism includes both non-governmental as well as *transgovernmental* links. The term *transnational* is used both to label the actor (for example, a transnational actor) or a pattern of behavior (for example, an international organization that acts *transnationally*—operates across state borders). Theorists focusing on transnationalism often deemphasize the state as primary and unitary actor. See also **transgovernmental.**

transnational civil society   See **international civil society.**

uneven development   A concept used by Marxists and other theorists that emphasizes capitalism's unequal spread of global economic benefits. In Lenin's *Imperalism*, for example, he argued that the increasing concentration of capital in advanced capitalist states led to monopolies and cartels that sought foreign investments once national markets were exhausted. This spread of capitalism inevitably resulted in the exploitation of colonies. In the present period, uneven development continues to characterize not only individual national economies but the capitalist world as a whole. Both domestically and internationally, benefits accrue to the few.

unilateralism   Refers to a propensity for a state to go it alone rather than cooperate or collaborate with other states.

unipolar, unipolarity   See **structure.**

unitary   Undivided, whole. In many realist analyses, states are viewed as unitary actors that speak ultimately with one voice.

unit of analysis   That which is being studied, such as a state.

universalism   A Kantian, cosmopolitan view consistent with Greco-Roman Stoicism portraying a world in which principles or values have applicability everywhere—a perspective that also has influence among Liberal and English School scholars in particular.

utilitarian, utilitarianism   An ethical doctrine developed in the nineteenth century that postulated that the greatest happiness or greatest good for the greatest number should be the aim of all action. The term can also mean a belief that the value of anything is determined solely by its utility. Utilitarian thinking as applied to theory building tends to emphasize rational decision-making process in which actors seek to maximize benefit or minimize cost.

utopian   See **idealist.**

values   Refers to the way things *ought* to be quite apart from the way things *are*. Political values would include preferences with respect to liberty, equality, order, and so on. A value is an estimate made of the worth or goodness of a goal or action. Also refers to measures as in numerical values. See also **normative.**

variable   A characteristic of an object or class of objects that may take on different values. The variable may be quantitative (such as height) or qualitative (such as marital status). In international relations research, for example, the class of objects may be states and the variable military power. Researchers wish to *operationalize* a variable, which means finding a way to measure the variable. Military power may be operationalized, for example, by using such indicators as number of nuclear weapons, amount of the gross national product devoted to military expenditures, or number of persons under arms. A *dependent variable* is simply what one is trying to explain, such as the frequency and intensity of war since 1800. *Independent variables* are factors that may help to explain or predict the dependent variable. See also **independent variable, dependent variable, intervening variable.**

variable sum game   See **game theory.**

veil of ignorance   See **social contract.**

Verstehen   See **interpretive understanding.**

virtue-based ethics   Associated with Aristotelian thought that good attributes—often the mean between extremes—are the bases of good conduct. Thus, rather than be either wasteful or stingy, one is generous; rather than profligacy or withdrawal from life's pleasures, one opts for temperance; rather than either cowardice or recklessness when facing danger, one is courageous; etc. Reason and judgment are central to this moral or ethical understanding. If one wishes to be good, one approach is to emulate virtuous persons as role models.

voluntarism, voluntarist A philosophical position that reality is created by human will; that humans can affect, if not control, their destinies. In international relations, it generally means that decisionmakers have effective choice and are able to influence outcomes. As used in this volume, voluntarism is in opposition to the philosophical idea of determinism. *Social constructivism,* for example, is a voluntarist formulation, One also finds theories premised on voluntarism among most liberals and English-School rationalists and many classical realists. See also **determinism, social constructivism, realism, liberalism.**

vulnerability interdependence See **interdependence.**

war To engage in hostilities and military operations, usually for some political purpose. War among states is *interstate* war; war between opposing parties within a state is *civil* war or *insurgency.* War involving irregulars and unconventional, hit-and-run tactics is *guerrilla* warfare to which insurgents may resort. Insurgents may also use terror or other tactics. The explanation of war is traditionally the primary concern of many realist scholars of international relations.

welfare issues Socioeconomic and other issues associated with improving the living conditions and standards of people.

West Generally, the countries of North America and Europe (and, paradoxically, Japan because of its level of industrial development and its links to other advanced capitalist states). See **East–West.**

world federalism The goal of individuals favoring a world government that would have authority in certain areas over constituent states.

world (or global) politics The term favored by those who emphasize the multidimensional or pluralist nature of international relations today, which includes not simply states, but also a wide diversity of international and non-governmental, transnational organizations, other groups, and individuals; not simply the physical security of the state, but also environmental, human rights, and demographic issues. See also **international politics, international relations.**

world society In ordinary usage the term suggests *global* or *worldwide,* but in the English School it refers to a Kantian world in which agreed norms or principles are the source of order and justice. See also **society, international society.**

zero-sum game See **game theory.**

INDEX